Theory of Functions and Applications

Theory of Functions and Applications

Editor

Inna Kalchuk

Basel • Beijing • Wuhan • Barcelona • Belgrade • Novi Sad • Cluj • Manchester

Editor
Inna Kalchuk
Lesya Ukrainka Volyn
National University
Lutsk
Ukraine

Editorial Office
MDPI
St. Alban-Anlage 66
4052 Basel, Switzerland

This is a reprint of articles from the Special Issue published online in the open access journal *Axioms* (ISSN 2075-1680) (available at: https://www.mdpi.com/journal/axioms/special_issues/theory_of_functions_and_applications).

For citation purposes, cite each article independently as indicated on the article page online and as indicated below:

Lastname, A.A.; Lastname, B.B. Article Title. *Journal Name* **Year**, *Volume Number*, Page Range.

ISBN 978-3-7258-0989-9 (Hbk)
ISBN 978-3-7258-0990-5 (PDF)
doi.org/10.3390/books978-3-7258-0990-5

© 2024 by the authors. Articles in this book are Open Access and distributed under the Creative Commons Attribution (CC BY) license. The book as a whole is distributed by MDPI under the terms and conditions of the Creative Commons Attribution-NonCommercial-NoDerivs (CC BY-NC-ND) license.

Contents

About the Editor vii

Preface ix

Inna Kal'chuk
Theory of Functions and Applications
Reprinted from: *Axioms* 2024, 13, 168, doi:10.3390/axioms13030168 1

Dmytro Bushev and Inna Kal'chuk
On the Realization of Exact Upper Bounds of the Best Approximations on the Classes $H^{1,1}$ by Favard Sums
Reprinted from: *Axioms* 2023, 12, 763, doi:10.3390/axioms12080763 4

Roma Kačinskaitė, Antanas Laurinčikas and Brigita Žemaitienė
Joint Discrete Universality in the Selberg–Steuding Class
Reprinted from: *Axioms* 2023, 12, 674, doi:10.3390/axioms12070674 21

Zouaoui Chikr Elmezouar, Fatimah Alshahrani, Ibrahim M. Almanjahie, Zoulikha Kaid, Ali Laksaci and Mustapha Rachdi
Scalar-on-Function Relative Error Regression for Weak Dependent Case
Reprinted from: *Axioms* 2023, 12, 613, doi:10.3390/axioms12070613 35

Cheng-shi Huang and Zhi-jie Jiang
On a Sum of More Complex Product-Type Operators from Bloch-Type Spaces to the Weighted-Type Spaces
Reprinted from: *Axioms* 2023, 12, 566, doi:10.3390/axioms12060566 52

Shuang Li, Jinming Cai and Kun Li
Matrix Representations for a Class of Eigenparameter Dependent Sturm–Liouville Problems with Discontinuity
Reprinted from: *Axioms* 2023, 12, 479, doi:10.3390/axioms12050479 78

Tareq Hamadneh, Ibraheem Abu Falahah, Yazan Alaya Al-Khassawneh, Abdallah Al-Husban, Abbas Kareem Wanas and Teodor Bulboacă
Initial Coefficients Upper Bounds for Certain Subclasses of Bi-Prestarlike Functions
Reprinted from: *Axioms* 2023, 12, 453, doi:10.3390/axioms12050453 92

Ibtisam Aldawish, Mohamed Jleli and Bessem Samet
On Hermite–Hadamard-Type Inequalities for Functions Satisfying Second-Order Differential Inequalities
Reprinted from: *Axioms* 2023, 12, 443, doi:10.3390/axioms12050443 103

Roger Arnau, José M. Calabuig and Enrique A. Sánchez Pérez
Measure-Based Extension of Continuous Functions and p-Average-Slope-Minimizing Regression
Reprinted from: *Axioms* 2023, 12, 359, doi:10.3390/axioms12040359 114

Lenka Mihoković
Coinciding Mean of the Two Symmetries on the Set of Mean Functions
Reprinted from: *Axioms* 2023, 12, 238, doi:10.3390/axioms12030238 134

Mircea Merca
From Symmetric Functions to Partition Identities
Reprinted from: *Axioms* 2023, 12, 126, doi:10.3390/axioms12020126 149

Waleed Mohamed Abd-Elhameed and Amr Kamel Amin
New Formulas and Connections Involving Euler Polynomials
Reprinted from: *Axioms* **2022**, *11*, 743, doi:10.3390/axioms11120743 . . . . **162**

Mohammad Izadi and Hari M. Srivastava
Fractional Clique Collocation Technique for Numerical Simulations of Fractional-Order Brusselator Chemical Model
Reprinted from: *Axioms* **2022**, *11*, 654, doi:10.3390/axioms11110654 . . . . **184**

Amany Nabih, Clemente Cesarano, Osama Moaaz, Mona Anis and Elmetwally M. Elabbasy
Non-Canonical Functional Differential Equation of Fourth-Order: New Monotonic Properties and Their Applications in Oscillation Theory
Reprinted from: *Axioms* **2022**, *11*, 636, doi:10.3390/axioms11110636 . . . . **204**

Mohammad Abu-Ghuwaleh, Rania Saadeh and Ahmad Qazza
A Novel Approach in Solving Improper Integrals
Reprinted from: *Axioms* **2022**, *11*, 572, doi:10.3390/axioms11100572 . . . . **221**

Nicola Fabiano, Milanka Gardašević-Filipović, Nikola Mirkov, Vesna Todorčević and Stojan Radenović
On the Distribution of Kurepa's Function
Reprinted from: *Axioms* **2022**, *11*, 388, doi:10.3390/axioms11080388 . . . . **240**

About the Editor

Inna Kalchuk

Inna Kalchuk graduated from the Faculty of Mathematics of Lesya Ukrainka Volyn State University in 2003. In 2008, she received a PhD in mathematics and physics. She now works as an Associate Professor at the Department of Function Theory and Methods of Teaching Mathematics, Lesya Ukrainka Volyn National University (Lutsk, Ukraine). She has published more than eighty scientific articles and conference proceedings and two monographs. Her research areas include function approximation and its applications.

Preface

This publication is devoted to current issues and methods of modern theory of functions of real and complex variables, as well as their applied aspects. The main idea of this Special Issue is to invite researchers specializing in this topic to present their scientific results, which will make a significant contribution to the further development of function theory and demonstrate its importance in the field of practical application. The publication includes 16 articles, which were selected from 30 manuscripts that were submitted to the Special Issue "Theory of Functions and Applications" of the MDPI journal Axioms. The publication contains the results of current research by scientists from around the world: Italy, Spain, France, Lithuania, China, Canada, Ukraine, Serbia, Croatia, Romania, the Republic of Korea, Azerbaijan, Taiwan, Jordan, Egypt, Saudi Arabia, Iran, and Iraq. All the articles issue are new and original and will be valuable and interesting to readers.

I would like to take this opportunity to thank everyone who contributed to the success of this Special Issue, namely, the authors of the articles for their qualitative contributions, the reviewers for their valuable comments aimed at improving the presented work, and the MDPI editorial staff. I would especially like to thank the Section Managing Editor, Ms. Lizzy Zhou, for her continuous help, patience, attention, and support during the work on this Special Issue.

Inna Kalchuk
Editor

Editorial

Theory of Functions and Applications

Inna Kal'chuk

Faculty of Information Technologies and Mathematics, Lesya Ukrainka Volyn National University, 43025 Lutsk, Ukraine; k.inna.80@gmail.com

1. Introduction

In this editorial, we present "Theory of Functions and Applications", a Special Issue of *Axioms*. This Special Issue comprises 15 articles devoted to exploring current problems in both the theory of functions and in real and complex variables, as well as the applied applications of both. Though the featured articles are concerned with a variety of topics, issues related to the following fields take particular precedence in this Special Issue: function approximation, functional analysis, complex analysis, differential equations, numerical methods, and mathematical modeling. The main aim of this Special Issue is to share scholars' theories and methods relating to function theory, their significant, topical, and novel findings in this area, and applications and solutions for applied problems in related scientific fields.

2. Overview of the Published Papers

In contribution 1, focusing on oscillations for delay differential equations, investigated the asymptotic properties of solutions for the fourth-order delay differential equation with a non-canonical operator. They studied novel properties that contribute to achieving more effective terms in the oscillation of differential equations, established criteria that guarantee the exclusion of decreasing solutions and that ensure the oscillation of the studied equation, and also demonstrated the theoretical aspect of their work through the use of examples.

In contribution 2, extremal problems relating to the approximation theory were considered; for instance, the approximative properties of Favard sums on the Hölder classes of functions of one and two variables were studied. In this paper, it is proven that the value of the approximation of the class $H^{1,1}$ using the Favard method is greater than the value of the best approximation of this class using trigonometric polynomials. Moreover, the authors constructed classes for which these approximative characteristics are equal.

The problems considered in contribution 3 concern shifts in the wide class $\tilde{S}$ of L functions and the approximations of analytical functions relating to these. Using the continuous universality theorem, the authors proved that each set of the analytic non-vanishing functions in a strip can be approximated simultaneously by discrete shifts, which are defined by the Dirichlet series from the Selberg–Steuding class and the linearly independent multiset over the field of rational numbers. The probabilistic approach based on the weak convergence of probability measures in the space of analytic functions was also used in their research.

The contribution 4 focuses on nonparametric prediction in Hilbertian statistics; specifically, the authors discuss the Hilbert RE-regression for weak functional time series data. In addition to conducting an empirical study investigating the behavior of RE-regression estimation, they also obtained a new kernel estimation for RE-regression that improved the robustness of the classical regression in its minimizing of the effect of the largest variables.

In contribution 5, the authors studied the boundedness and compactness of the sum operator, as defined by the complex products of composition, multiplication, and the m-th-iterated radial derivative operators of Bloch-type spaces to weighted-type spaces on the unit ball. They also characterized the boundedness and compactness of all products of composition, multiplication, and m-th-iterated radial derivative operators.

In contribution 6 studied matrix representations of Sturm–Liouville problems with boundary- and interface-contained eigenparameters. In particular, they constructed a class of Sturm–Liouville problems based on a given matrix eigenvalue problem relating to a certain type and condition, depending on the eigenparameter. The authors proved that each Sturm–Liouville problem is equivalent to the original matrix's eigenvalue problem, using the method of characteristic-function factorization.

In contribution 7, the authors investigated two classes of normalized holomorphic and bi-univalent functions, which include bi-prestarlike functions. They found upper bounds for the first two coefficients $|a_2|$ and $|a_3|$ of the Taylor–Maclaurin series for the functions of each of these classes, and their findings can be used in the geometric theory of functions.

The authors of contribution 8 devoted their study to the class of twice-continuously differentiable functions (including the class of convex functions), and its characteristics, satisfying second-order differential inequalities; they and obtained new Hermite–Hadamard-type inequalities for the indicated functions.

The work in contribution 9 focuses on the issue of extending continuous functions, defined by subsets of metric spaces, to the entire space, so that the extended function preserves the basic properties of the original function. The authors proposed a new method that optimizes the integral p-mean instead of its maximum value. They also considered the more general theoretical approach based on measure-valued representations of metric spaces and the duality formula. In addition to this, they also discovered some explicit formulas relating to specific extensions that satisfy Lipschitz-type inequalities.

In contribution 10, the author compared two symmetries of different origins on the set of average functions and found the asymptotic series expansion for both of them in terms of a recursive algorithm for their coefficients, enabling them to perform a coefficient comparison. As a result, the author obtained the class of the means, which allowed for interpolating between those harmonic, geometric, and arithmetic.

In contribution 11 the author proved that some results of q-analyses and the partition theory can be obtained as specializations of fundamental relations between complete and elementary symmetric functions; specifically, he showed that Rothe's q-binomial theorem is a specialization of the generating function of elementary symmetric functions. He also obtained the Uchimura identity, which provides connections between partitions and divisors. All results are accompanied by combinatorial interpretations involving well-known functions in the partition theory.

In contribution 12, the authors found new expressions for the high-order derivatives of different symmetric and non-symmetric polynomials in terms of Euler polynomials, as well as obtaining connection formulas between different polynomials and Euler polynomials. They also proved some new definite integral formulas of the products of different symmetric and non-symmetric polynomials with the Euler polynomials.

Contribution 13 is devoted to the study of the fractional analogue of the Brusselator model. The authors proposed an effective hybrid method, which is based on a combination of the quasi-linearization approach and the matrix-collocation method for the approximate processing of fractional Brusselator equations; these methods were used to model the problem of an autocatalytic chemical reaction. The authors analyzed the convergence and error of this method and also presented some numerical models to test its accuracy.

In contribution 14, the authors proved new theorems that simplify the calculation of improper integrals. Their results allow us to establish many examples of improper integral formulas and solve them directly, without complex calculations or the use of computer software. They presented some applications related to finding Green's function, one-dimensional vibrating-string problems, wave motion in elastic solids, and computing Fourier.

In contribution 15, the authors studied the hypothesis of Kurepa's function distribution and performed the analysis using PARI/GP software (version 2.13.4).

Conflicts of Interest: The author declares no conflicts of interest.

List of Contributions:

1. Nabih, A.; Cesarano, C.; Moaaz, O.; Anis, M.; Elabbasy, E.M. Non-Canonical Functional Differential Equation of Fourth-Order: New Monotonic Properties and Their Applications in Oscillation Theory. *Axioms* **2022**, *11*, 636.
2. Bushev, D.; Kal'chuk, I. On the Realization of Exact Upper Bounds of the Best Approximations on the Classes $H^{1,1}$ by Favard Sums. *Axioms* **2023**, *12*, 763.
3. Kačinskaitė, R.; Laurinčikas, A.; Žemaitienė, B. Joint Discrete Universality in the Selberg–Steuding Class. *Axioms* **2023**, *12*, 674.
4. Chikr Elmezouar, Z.; Alshahrani, F.; Almanjahie, I.M.; Kaid, Z.; Laksaci, A.; Rachdi, M. Scalar-on-Function Relative Error Regression for Weak Dependent Case. *Axioms* **2023**, *12*, 613.
5. Huang, C.-S.; Jiang, Z.-J. On a Sum of More Complex Product-Type Operators from Bloch-Type Spaces to the Weighted-Type Spaces. *Axioms* **2023**, *12*, 566.
6. Li, S.; Cai, J.; Li, K. Matrix Representations for a Class of Eigenparameter Dependent Sturm–Liouville Problems with Discontinuity. *Axioms* **2023**, *12*, 479.
7. Hamadneh, T.; Abu Falahah, I.; AL-Khassawneh, Y.A.; Al-Husban, A.; Wanas, A.K.; Bulboacă, T. Initial Coefficients Upper Bounds for Certain Subclasses of Bi-Prestarlike Functions. *Axioms* **2023**, *12*, 453.
8. Aldawish, I.; Jleli, M.; Samet, B. On Hermite–Hadamard-Type Inequalities for Functions Satisfying Second-Order Differential Inequalities. *Axioms* **2023**, *12*, 443.
9. Arnau, R.; Calabuig, J.M.; Sánchez Pérez, E.A. Measure-Based Extension of Continuous Functions and p-Average-Slope-Minimizing Regression. *Axioms* **2023**, *12*, 359.
10. Mihoković, L. Coinciding Mean of the Two Symmetries on the Set of Mean Functions. *Axioms* **2023**, *12*, 238.
11. Merca, M. From Symmetric Functions to Partition Identities. *Axioms* **2023**, *12*, 126.
12. Abd-Elhameed, W.M.; Amin, A.K. New Formulas and Connections Involving Euler Polynomials. *Axioms* **2022**, *11*, 743.
13. Izadi, M.; Srivastava, H.M. Fractional Clique Collocation Technique for Numerical Simulations of Fractional-Order Brusselator Chemical Model. *Axioms* **2022**, *11*, 654.
14. Abu-Ghuwaleh, M.; Saadeh, R.; Qazza, A. A Novel Approach in Solving Improper Integrals. *Axioms* **2022**, *11*, 572.
15. Fabiano, N.; Gardašević-Filipović, M.; Mirkov, N.; Todorčević, V.; Radenović, S. On the Distribution of Kurepa's Function. *Axioms* **2022**, *11*, 388.

Disclaimer/Publisher's Note: The statements, opinions and data contained in all publications are solely those of the individual author(s) and contributor(s) and not of MDPI and/or the editor(s). MDPI and/or the editor(s) disclaim responsibility for any injury to people or property resulting from any ideas, methods, instructions or products referred to in the content.

Article

On the Realization of Exact Upper Bounds of the Best Approximations on the Classes $H^{1,1}$ by Favard Sums

Dmytro Bushev and Inna Kal'chuk *

Faculty of Information Technologies and Mathematics, Lesya Ukrainka Volyn National University, 43025 Lutsk, Ukraine; bushev-d@ukr.net
* Correspondence: k.inna.80@gmail.com

Abstract: In this paper, we find the sets of all extremal functions for approximations of the Hölder classes of H^1 2π-periodic functions of one variable by the Favard sums, which coincide with the set of all extremal functions realizing the exact upper bounds of the best approximations of this class by trigonometric polynomials. In addition, we obtain the sets of all of extremal functions for approximations of the class H^1 by linear methods of summation of Fourier series. Furthermore, we receive the set of all extremal functions for the class H^1 in the Korneichuk–Stechkin lemma and its analogue, the Stepanets lemma, for the Hölder class $H^{1,1}$ functions of two variables being 2π-periodic in each variable.

Keywords: Favard sums; best approximation; exact upper bounds; extremal functions; uniform metric

MSC: 41A52; 42A10

1. Introduction

The exact values of approximation characteristics are especially valued in the theory of function approximation. Finding the exact values of approximation characteristics even for functions and classes of functions of one variable is a rare phenomenon. The exact values of approximation characteristics in the theory of approximation of functions and classes of functions of many variables being 2π-periodic in each variable, except the result of the work [1], are unknown.

In the theory of function approximation, as in other branches of mathematics, it is difficult to formulate the problem and attract the attention of specialists to it. The problem of finding the exact values of approximation characteristics for functions and classes of functions of many variables remains relevant. The exact values of approximation characteristics even for the simplest classes of functions of many variables have not been found. Forty years ago, the famous Ukrainian mathematician Oleksandr Stepanets called its solution the problem of the twenty-first century.

Let H^1, $H^{1,1}$ be the classes of functions $f(x)$ and $f(x,y)$ that are 2π-periodic in the variable x and the variables x, y, for which the following conditions hold, respectively:

$$|f(x) - f(x')| \leq |x - x'|, \quad |f(x,y) - f(x',y')| \leq |x - x'| + |y - y'|. \tag{1}$$

Let

$$E_n(f) = \inf_{T_{n-1}} \|f(x) - T_{n-1}(x)\|_C$$

be the best approximation of the function $f(x)$ by the trigonometric polynomials $T_{n-1}(x)$ of the degree $(n-1)$, where C is the space of 2π-periodic continuous functions with the uniform norm $\|f\|_C = \max_t |f(t)|$.

Let
$$E_{n,m}(f) := \inf_{T_{n-1,m-1}} \|f(x,y) - T_{n-1,m-1}(x,y)\|_C$$
be the best approximation of the function $f(x,y)$ by the trigonometric polynomials $T_{n-1,m-1}(x,y)$ of the degree $(n-1)$ in the variable x and the degree $(m-1)$ in the variable y in the uniform metric.

Let
$$F_n(u) = \frac{1}{2} + \sum_{k=1}^{n-1} \frac{k\pi}{2n} \cot \frac{k\pi}{2n} \cos ku$$
be the Favard kernel, and
$$F_n(f,x) = \frac{1}{\pi} \int_{-\pi}^{\pi} f(t) F_n(t-x) dt,$$
$$F_{n,m}(f,x,y) = \frac{1}{\pi^2} \int_{-\pi}^{\pi} \int_{-\pi}^{\pi} f(t,z) F_n(t-x) F_m(z-y) dt dz$$
be Favard sums of the degree $(n-1)$ and double rectangular Favard sums of the degree $(n-1)$ in the variable x and the degree $(m-1)$ in the variable y, respectively.

Favard proved in 1936 that
$$\mathcal{E}_n = \sup_{f \in H^1} \|f(x) - F_n(f,x)\|_C = \frac{\pi}{2n} = E_n(H^1) := \sup_{f \in H^1} E_n(f),$$
i.e., the Favard method implements the exact upper bound of the best approximations on the class H^1. In the work [1], the exact value of approximations of classes $H^{1,1}$ by Favard sums was found, namely, for $n, m \geq 2$
$$\mathcal{E}_{n,m} := \sup_{f \in H^{1,1}} \|f(x,y) - F_{n,m}(f,x,y)\|_C$$
$$= \frac{\pi}{2n} + \frac{\pi}{2m} + \frac{8}{\pi^2} \int_0^{\frac{\pi}{n}} \Phi_n(x) \Phi_m(x) dx, \qquad (2)$$
where $\Phi_k(x) = \sum_{i=1}^{k-1} \overline{\Phi}_i^k(x)$ is the sum of permutations in descending order of the functions $\Phi_i^k = \left| \int_{i\pi/k}^x F_k(t) dt \right|$ (for definition of the permutation, see, e.g., [2] (p. 130)).

2. Main Result

Theorem 1. *For any natural numbers n and m, $n, m \geq 2$, it is asserted that*
$$\mathcal{E}_{n,m} > E_{n,m}\left(H^{1,1}\right) := \sup_{f \in H^{1,1}} E_{n,m}(f).$$

Theorem 1 was formulated without proof in [3]. We should note that the exact value of $E_{n,m}\left(H^{1,1}\right)$, as well as the best linear approximation method reflecting the class $H^{1,1}$ into the space of all trigonometric polynomials $T_{n-1,m-1}(x,y)$ of the degree at most $(n-1)$ in the variable x and $(m-1)$ in the variable y are unknown. However, it was found that $E_{n,m}\left(H^{1,1}\right) \geq \frac{\pi}{2n} + \frac{\pi}{2m}$. According to the result of J. Mairhuber [4], the polynomial of the best approximation $T_{n-1,m-1}(x,y)$ for the function $f(x,y)$ is not unique, which makes it difficult to find this polynomial.

Let us denote by $W_{[a,b]}^1$ and $W_p^{1,1}$ the classes of functions $f(x)$ and $f(x,y)$ defined on the segment $[a,b]$ and the rectangle $P = [a,b] \times [a_1, b_1]$ satisfying conditions (1). The summable function $\psi(x) \in V_{a,b}^c$ if almost everywhere on (a,c) $(a < c < b)$ $\psi(x) > 0$ $(\psi(x) < 0)$, almost everywhere on (c,b) $\psi(x) < 0$ $(\psi(x) > 0)$ and $\int_a^b \psi(t) dt = 0$.

Let $\psi(x) \in V_{a,b}^c$, $\varphi(y) \in V_{a_1,b_1}^{c_1}$ and $t = \rho(x)$, $z = \delta(y)$ be the functions defined by the equalities

$$\int_a^x \psi(t)dt = \int_a^{\rho(x)} \psi(t)dt, \quad x \in [a,c], \, \rho(x) \in [c,b],$$

$$\int_{a_1}^y \varphi(z)dz = \int_{a_1}^{\delta(y)} \varphi(z)dz, \quad y \in [a_1, c_1], \, \delta(y) \in [c_1, b_1],$$

and $\rho^{-1}(x)$ and $\delta^{-1}(x)$ be the inverse functions to $\rho(x)$ and $\delta(x)$.

M.P. Korneichuk [2] (pp. 190–198) for the class $W_{[a,b]}^1$ and O.I. Stepanets [5] (p. 52) for the class $W_p^{1,1}$ proved the following statements.

Lemma K [2]. *The following equalities hold*

$$\sup_{f \in W_{[a,b]}^1} \left| \int_a^b f(x)\psi(x)dx \right| = \int_a^c |\psi(t)|(\rho(t) - t)dt = \int_c^b |\psi(t)|(t - \rho^{-1}(t))dt$$

$$= \left| \int_a^b f^*(x)\psi(x)dx \right|. \tag{3}$$

In this case, the upper bound in (3) *is implemented by functions from the class* $W_{[a,b]}^1$ *of the form* $f^*(x) = K \pm x$, *where* K *is arbitrary constant.*

Lemma S [5]. *The following equalities hold*

$$\sup_{f \in W_p^{1,1}} \left| \int_a^b \int_{a_1}^{b_1} f(x,y)\psi(x)\varphi(y)dxdy \right|$$

$$= 2 \int_a^c \int_{a_1}^{c_1} |\psi(t)\varphi(z)| \min\{\rho(t) - t, \delta(z) - z\} dt \, dz = \left| \int_a^b \int_{a_1}^{b_1} f^*(x,y)\psi(x)\varphi(y)dx \, dy \right|, \tag{4}$$

and the exact upper bound in (4) *is realized by the function* $f^*(x,y)$ *specified in this lemma* (*see* [5] (*pp. 52–54*)).

Let us denote by $\gamma_{nm}^*(x,y)$, $f^*(x)$, $f^*(x,y)$ the arbitrary extremal functions from the classes $H^{1,1}$, $W_{[a,b]}^1$, $W_p^{1,1}$ implementing exact upper bounds in (2)–(4), respectively, i.e., such that

$$\mathcal{E}_{n,m} = \|\gamma_{nm}^*(x,y) - F_{n,m}(\gamma_{nm}^*, x, y)\|_C,$$

$$\sup_{f \in W_{[a,b]}^1} \left| \int_a^b f(x)\psi(x)dx \right| = \left| \int_a^b f^*(x)\psi(x)dx \right|,$$

$$\sup_{f \in W_p^{1,1}} \left| \int_a^b \int_{a_1}^{b_1} f(x,y)\psi(x)\varphi(y)dxdy \right| = \int_a^b \int_{a_1}^{b_1} f^*(x,y)\psi(x)\varphi(y)dxdy.$$

Let us prove that all extremal functions $\gamma_{nm}^*(x,y)$ realizing the exact upper bound in (2) have the same oscillations equal to $\pi/n + \pi/m$. To do this, we have to establish that if two arbitrary extremal functions realizing the exact upper bound in (4) coincide on one of the larger sides of P, then they coincide on the entire rectangle and have the same oscillations. The proof of the last statement is based on the description of the set of all extremal functions that realize the exact upper bound in (3).

Lemma 1. *The set of all extremal functions* $f^*(x)$ *realizing the exact upper bound in* (3) *is the set of functions of the form* $f^*(x) = K \pm x$, *where* K *is an arbitrary constant.*

Proof. If for the arbitrary extremal function almost everywhere on $[a,b]$ $f^{*\prime}(x) = \pm 1$, then due to the absolute continuity of all functions of the class $W^1_{[a,b]}$ (see [5] (pp. 15–16)), $f^*(x) = \pm x + K$.

Let us prove that almost everywhere on $[a,b]$ $f^{*\prime}(x) = \pm 1$. To do this, we have to establish that any extremal function $f^*(x)$ satisfies the equalities

$$f^*(x) - f^*(\rho(x)) = \rho(x) - x, \tag{5}$$

or

$$f^*(x) - f^*(\rho(x)) = -(\rho(x) - x) \tag{6}$$

for $x \in [a,c]$ and almost everywhere on $[a,c]$

$$f^{*\prime}(x) = f^{*\prime}(\rho(x)). \tag{7}$$

Since $f^*(x)$ is absolutely continuous on $[a,b]$, and therefore, differentiable almost everywhere on $[a,b]$ (see [6] (p. 229)), $\rho(x)$ is absolutely continuous on $[a,c]$ (see [5] (p. 19)) and $c \leq \rho(x) \leq b$, then $f^*(\rho(x))$ is differentiable almost everywhere on $[a,c]$. From (5) and (6) we then get that almost everywhere on $[a,c]$

$$f^{*\prime}(x) - f^{*\prime}(\rho(x))\rho'(x) = \rho'(x) - 1, \tag{8}$$

or

$$f^{*\prime}(x) - f^{*\prime}(\rho(x))\rho'(x) = -\rho'(x) + 1. \tag{9}$$

Using (7)–(9), we have almost everywhere on $[a,c]$ $f^{*\prime}(x) = -1$ or $f^{*\prime}(x) = 1$. Let us prove that $f^*(x)$ satisfies equalities (5) and (6). If $f^*(x)$ is an extremal function, then, performing transformations such as in the proof of Theorem 3.1 (see [5] (p. 20)), we obtain

$$\left| \int_a^b f^*(x)\psi(x)dx \right| = \left| \int_a^c (f^*(t) - f^*(\rho(t)))\psi(t)dt \right|$$

$$= \int_a^c (\rho(t) - t)|\psi(t)|dt. \tag{10}$$

Without loss of generality, we may assume that $\psi(x) > 0$ almost everywhere on $[a,c]$. It then follows from (10) that

$$\int_a^c \psi(t)((\rho(t) - t) + f^*(t) - f^*(\rho(t)))dt = 0$$

or

$$\int_a^c \psi(t)((\rho(t) - t) - (f^*(t) - f^*(\rho(t))))dt = 0. \tag{11}$$

Since $c \leq \rho(t) \leq b$ and $f^* \in W^1_{[a,b]}$ for $t \in [a,c]$, then $\rho(t) - t \geq |f^*(t) - f^*(\rho(t))|$, whence $\rho(t) - t \pm (f^*(t) - f^*(\rho(t))) \geq 0$ for $t \in [a,c]$. From (11), due to the non-negativity and summability of functions $\psi(t)((\rho(t) - t) \pm (f^*(t) - f^*(\rho(t)))$ (see [6] (Theorem 6, p. 131)), it follows that equalities (5) and (6) are valid almost everywhere on $[a,c]$. Since these functions are continuous, equalities (5) and (6) are valid for $x \in [a,c]$.

Let us prove that $f^*(x)$ satisfies the relation (7). Since $f^* \in W^1_{[a,b]}$, then for $x, x + \Delta x, \rho(x), (\rho(x) + \Delta x) \in [a,b]$, using (5) and (6), we have

$$|f^*(x + \Delta) - f^*(\rho(x) + \Delta x)| \leq \rho(x) - x = |f^*(x) - f^*(\rho(x))|. \tag{12}$$

As a result of the continuity of $f^*(x)$, for $\Delta x \to 0$ the sign of $(f^*(x) - f^*(\rho(x)))$ coincides with the sign of $(f^*(x + \Delta x) - f^*(\rho(x) + \Delta x))$. Therefore, from (12) it follows

$$f^*(x + \Delta x) - f^*(x) \leq f^*(\rho(x) + \Delta x) - f^*(\rho(x)), \tag{13}$$

or
$$f^*(x + \Delta x) - f^*(x) \geq f^*(\rho(x) + \Delta x) - f^*(\rho(x)). \tag{14}$$

Using (13) and (14) we have
$$f^{*\prime}(x+0) \leq f^{*\prime}(\rho(x)+0) \quad \text{and} \quad f^{*\prime}(x-0) \geq f^{*\prime}(\rho(x)-0),$$

or
$$f^{*\prime}(x+0) \geq f^{*\prime}(\rho(x)+0) \quad \text{and} \quad f^{*\prime}(x-0) \leq f^{*\prime}(\rho(x)-0).$$

Therefore, due to the differentiability of the function $f^*(x)$, we obtain that $f^{*\prime}(x) = f^{*\prime}(\rho(x))$ almost everywhere on $[a, c]$. In a similar way, we prove that $f^{*\prime}(x) = \pm 1$ almost everywhere on $[c, b]$. Lemma 1 has been proved. □

Corollary 1. *Let $\varphi(y)$ be the function that is summable and sign-preserving almost everywhere on $[a_1, b_1]$. Then*
$$\sup_{f \in W_p^{1,1}} \left| \int_a^b \int_{a_1}^{b_1} \psi(x)\varphi(y) f(x,y) dx dy \right|$$
$$= \left| \int_{a_1}^{b_1} \varphi(y) \int_a^c \psi(t)(\rho(t) - t) dt dy \right|, \tag{15}$$

where $\psi(x), \rho(x)$ are the same functions as in Lemma K. Moreover, the set of all extremal functions $f^*(x,y) \in W_p^{1,1}$ realizing the exact upper bound in (15) has the set of functions of the form
$$f^*(x,y) = \pm x + g(y),$$
where $g(y)$ is the arbitrary function from the class $W_{[a_1,b_1]}^1$.

Proof. The relation (15) was proved in [5] (Lemma 5.1, p. 54). Just as it was done in the proof of Lemma 5.1, using Lemma 1 and the fact that $\int_a^b \psi(x) g(y) dx = 0$ for the arbitrary function $g(y)$, we get that
$$f^*(x,y) = \pm x + g(y),$$
where $g(y) \in W_{[a_1,b_1]}^1$. The corollary has been proved. □

Let
$$\mathfrak{E}^* = \left\{ f_n^*(x) \in H^1 : \sup_{f \in H^1} \|f(x) - F_n(f, x)\|_C = \frac{\pi}{2n} \right.$$
$$= \|f_n^*(x) - F_n(f_n^*, x)\|_C \bigg\}$$

be the set of all extremal functions for the Favard method on the class H^1. The following statement is then true.

Theorem 2. *The set $\mathfrak{E}^*$ is the set of functions of the form*
$$f_n^*(x) = \pm \varphi_n(x - x_0) + C,$$
where $\varphi_n(t)$ is the $2\pi/n$-periodic even function, $\varphi_n(t) = t$ for $t \in [0, \pi/n]$, x_0 and C are arbitrary constants.

Proof. We can prove that
$$\sup_{f \in H^1} \|f(x) - F_n(f,x)\|_C = \frac{2}{\pi} \sup_{f \in H} \left| \int_0^\pi f(t) F_n(t) dt \right|,$$

where H is the subset of even functions $f(x)$ from the class H^1 such that

$$\|f(x) - F_n(f, x)\|_C = |f(0) - F_n(f, 0)| = |F_n(f, 0)|.$$

Moreover, the arbitrary extremal function $f_n^*(x)$ can be obtained from the arbitrary extremal function

$$\varphi_n(t) \in H : \frac{2}{\pi} \sup_{f \in H} \left| \int_0^\pi f(t) F_n(t) dt \right| = \frac{2}{\pi} \left| \int_0^\pi \varphi_n(t) F_n(t) dt \right|$$

by shifting its graph parallel to the OX- and OY-axes, i.e.,

$$f_n^*(x) = \varphi_n(x - x_0) + C.$$

Let us prove that the extremal function $\varphi_n(t) \in H$ is unique up to a sign. It is clear that

$$\sup_{f \in H} \frac{2}{\pi} \left| \int_0^\pi f(t) F_n(t) dt \right|$$

$$\leq \frac{2}{\pi} \left(\sup_{f \in H} \left| \int_0^{\pi/n} f(t) F_n(t) dt \right| + \sum_{k=1}^{n-1} \sup_{f \in H} \left| \int_{k\pi/n}^{(k+1)\pi/n} f(t) F_n(t) dt \right| \right). \quad (16)$$

Since $F_n(t) > 0$ on $[0, \frac{\pi}{n}]$ and $f(t) \in H$, then

$$\sup_{f \in H} \left| \int_0^{\pi/n} f(t) F_n(t) dt \right| = \int_0^{\pi/n} t F_n(t) dt. \quad (17)$$

Since (see [7]) $\int_{k\pi/n}^{(k+1)\pi/n} F_n(t) dt = 0$ then applying Lemma K for each segment $[k\pi/n, (k+1)\pi/n]$ we get

$$\sup_{f \in H} \left| \int_{k\pi/n}^{(k+1)\pi/n} f(t) F_n(t) dt \right| = \int_{k\pi/n}^{(k+1)\pi/n} ((-1)^k t + C_k) F_n(t) dt. \quad (18)$$

From (16)–(18), due to the continuity of the extremal function $\varphi_n(t)$, it follows that $\varphi_n(t)$ is $2\pi/n$-periodic even function, $\varphi_n(t) = t$ for $t \in [0, \pi/n]$ and

$$\sup_{f \in H} \frac{2}{\pi} \left| \int_0^\pi f(t) F_n(t) dt \right| = \frac{2}{\pi} \int_0^\pi \varphi_n(t) F_n(t) dt. \quad (19)$$

We assume that there is another extremal function $\overline{\varphi}_n(t) \in H$. Then

$$0 = \frac{2}{\pi} \int_0^\pi \varphi_n(t) F_n(t) dt - \frac{2}{\pi} \int_0^\pi \overline{\varphi}_n(t) F_n(t) dt$$

$$= \frac{2}{\pi} \left(\int_0^{\pi/n} \varphi_n(t) F_n(t) dt - \int_0^{\pi/n} \overline{\varphi}_n(t) F_n(t) dt \right) \quad (20)$$

$$+ \sum_{k=1}^{n-1} \left(\int_{k\pi/n}^{(k+1)\pi/n} \varphi_n(t) F_n(t) dt - \int_{k\pi/n}^{(k+1)\pi/n} \overline{\varphi}_n(t) F_n(t) dt \right).$$

From (16)–(19) it follows

$$\int_0^{\pi/n} \varphi_n(t) F_n(t) dt - \int_0^{\pi/n} \overline{\varphi}_n(t) F_n(t) dt \geq 0, \quad (21)$$

$$\int_{k\pi/n}^{(k+1)\pi/n} \varphi_n(t) F_n(t) dt - \int_{k\pi/n}^{(k+1)\pi/n} \overline{\varphi}_n(t) F_n(t) dt \geq 0, \, k = \overline{1, n-1}. \quad (22)$$

In the inequality (21), the equal sign is possible only if $\overline{\varphi}_n(t) = \varphi_n(t) = t$ for $t \in [0, \pi/n]$.

Since $\varphi_n(t)$ is the extremal function of Lemma K on each segment $[k\pi/n, (k+1)\pi/n]$, then by Lemma 1 the equal sign in (22) is possible only if $\overline{\varphi}_n(t) = \varphi_n(t) + C_k$ for $t \in [k\pi/n, (k+1)\pi/n]$. In order to justify the equal sign present in (20), it must take place in (21) and (22). Therefore, due to the continuity of functions $\overline{\varphi}_n(t)$ and $\varphi_n(t)$, the equality $\overline{\varphi}_n(t) = \varphi_n(t)$ holds on $[0, \pi/n]$ and $[k\pi/n, (k+1)\pi/n]$. As a result of the parity and 2π-periodicity of these functions, the equality $\overline{\varphi}_n(t) = \varphi_n(t)$ holds on the entire real axis.

Therefore, $\varphi_n(t)$ is the unique extremal function from the class H up to a sign. The theorem has been proved. □

In a similar way, we can describe the set of all extremal functions for the arbitrary linear approximation method

$$U_n(\Lambda, f, x) = \frac{1}{\pi} \int_{-\pi}^{\pi} f(t) U_n(\Lambda, t - x) dt,$$

where $U_n(\lambda, t) = \frac{1}{2} + \sum_{k=1}^{n-1} \lambda_k^{(n)} \cos kt$ is the kernel of the method (approximation properties of linear methods studied, for example, in [8–11]). Since any trigonometric polynomial of the order $(n-1)$ has at most $2n-2$ roots on $[-\pi, \pi)$ (see, e.g., [12] (p. 214)), then the function $\Phi(x) = \int_x^\pi U_n(\lambda, t) dt$ can have at most n roots on $[0, \pi]$. Let $\Phi(x) = \int_x^\pi U_n(\lambda, t) dt$ have exactly m roots x_k ($k = \overline{1, m}$) on $[0, \pi]$, $0 \le m \le n$, and the function $f_{u_n}^*(x) \in H^1$ is such that

$$\sup_{f \in H^1} \|f(x) - U_n(\Lambda, f, x)\|_C = \|f_{u_n}^*(x) - U_n(\Lambda, f_{u_n}^*, x)\|_C,$$

i.e., it is the arbitrary extremal function for the $U_n(\Lambda, f, x)$ on the class H^1. Then, analogously to the proof of Theorem 2, we can prove the following statement.

Theorem 3. *The set of all extremal functions $f_{u_n}^*(x)$ for the method $U_n(\Lambda, f, x)$ on the class H^1 is the set of functions of the form*

$$f_{u_n}^*(x) = \pm \varphi_{u_n}(x - x_0) + K,$$

where x_0 and K are arbitrary constants and $\varphi_{u_n}(t)$ is the even 2π-periodic continuous function such that $\varphi_{u_n}'(t) = 1$ for $t \in [0, x_1]$ and $\varphi_{u_n}'(t) = (-1)^k$ for $t \in (x_k, x_{k+1})$, i.e.,

$$\varphi_{u_n}(t) = \begin{cases} t, & t \in [0, x_1], \\ (-1)^k t + 2\sum_{i=1}^k (-1)^{i+1} x_i, & t \in (x_k, x_{k+1}), \end{cases}$$

$$k = \overline{1, m}, \ 0 \le m \le n.$$

Let $\widehat{\mathfrak{E}} = \left\{ \widehat{f}_n(x) \in H^1 : E_n(H^1)_C = \frac{\pi}{2n} = E_n(\widehat{f}_n)_C \right\}$ be the set of all extremal functions realizing the exact upper bound of the best approximations on the class H^1.

Theorem 4. *The set $\widehat{\mathfrak{E}} = \mathfrak{E}^*$ and for each function from these sets the best approximation polynomials are constants.*

Proof. According to Theorem 2 and the Chebyshev criterion (see, e.g., [2] (p. 46)), for any function $f_n^*(x) \in \mathfrak{E}^*$ it follows that

$$E_n(f_n^*) = E_n(\pm \varphi_n(x - x_0) + C) = E_n(\varphi_n) = \|\varphi_n\|_C = \frac{\pi}{2n} = E_n(H^1).$$

These relations imply that for any function $f_n^*(x) \in \mathfrak{E}^*$ the polynomials of the best approximation are constants and $\mathfrak{E}^* \subseteq \widehat{\mathfrak{E}}$. For any function $\widehat{f}_n(x) \in \widehat{\mathfrak{E}}$, it follows that

$$E_n(\widehat{f}_n) = \frac{\pi}{2n} = \left\|\widehat{f}_n(x) - T_{n-1}^*(\widehat{f}_n, x)\right\|_C$$

$$\leq \left\|\widehat{f}_n(x) - F_n(\widehat{f}_n, x)\right\|_C \leq \sup_{f \in H^1} \|f(x) - F_n(f, x)\|_C = \frac{\pi}{2n},$$

where $T_{n-1}^*(\widehat{f}_n, x)$ is the best approximation polynomial of the degree $(n-1)$ of the function $\widehat{f}_n(x)$. This means that $\left\|\widehat{f}_n(x) - F_n(\widehat{f}_n, x)\right\|_C = \frac{\pi}{2n}$, i.e., $\widehat{f}_n(x) \in \mathfrak{E}^*$. So $\mathfrak{E}^* \supseteq \widehat{\mathfrak{E}}$. Taking into account that $\mathfrak{E}^* \subseteq \widehat{\mathfrak{E}}$, the theorem has been proved. □

Corollary 2. *If $n - 1 > 0$ and $T_{n-1}^*(f, x)$ is the polynomial of the best approximation of the function $f(x) \in H^1$ then $E_n(f)_C < \pi/2n$.*

Proof. For each function $f(x) \in H^1$ the inequality $E_n(f)_C \leq \pi/2n$ is true. If $E_n(f) = \pi/2n$, then using Theorem 4 we get $\deg T_{n-1}^*(f, x) = 0$ that contradicts the condition of the Corollary 2. The corollary has been proved. □

Corollary 3. *If the approximation method is different from the Favard method, i.e., $U_n(\Lambda, f, x) \neq F_n(f, x)$, then*

$$\sup_{f \in H^1} \|f(x) - U_n(\Lambda, f, x)\|_C > \sup_{f \in H^1} \|f(x) - F_n(f, x)\|_C = \frac{\pi}{2n}. \quad (23)$$

Moreover, the set of all extremal functions $f_{u_n}^*(x)$ for the method $U_n(\Lambda, f, x)$ on the class H^1 does not intersect with the set of extremal functions $f_n^*(x)$ for the Favard method on this class.

Proof. If $f(x) \in H^1$, then

$$f(x) - U_n(\Lambda, f, x) = \frac{1}{\pi} \int_{-\pi}^{\pi} \left(D_1(t) - \sum_{k=1}^{n-1} \frac{\lambda_k^{(n)}}{k} \sin kt\right) f'(x - t) dt,$$

where $D_1(u) = \sum_{k=1}^{\infty} \frac{\sin ku}{k}$ is the 2π-periodic Bernoulli function (see, e.g., [2] (pp. 109–111)). Since the function $f(x)$ belongs to the class H^1 and the Bernoulli kernel $D_1(u)$ has a unique polynomial of the best approximation in the metric L (see, for example, [2] (p. 59–69)), we prove that the Favard method presents the unique best approximation method on the class H^1. Therefore, the relations (23) hold.

Let the extremal function $f_{u_n}^*(x)$ for the method $U_n(\Lambda, f, x)$ belong to the set $\mathfrak{E}^*$. So, according to Theorem 2 we have

$$f_{u_n}^*(x) = \pm \varphi_n(x - x_0) + C$$

and as a result of the $2\pi/n$-periodicity of the function $\varphi_n(t)$ (see, e.g., [2] (p. 61)) we get

$$U_n(\Lambda, f_{u_n}^*, x) = \frac{1}{\pi} \int_{-\pi}^{\pi} \frac{1}{2}(\varphi_n(t) + C) dt = \frac{\pi}{2n} + C.$$

Then

$$\|f_{u_n}^*(x) - U_n(\Lambda, f_{u_n}^*, x)\|_C = \frac{\pi}{2n}$$

that contradicts the fact proved above. The corollary has been proved. □

Lemma 2. Let $f^*(x,y) \in W_p^{1,1}$ be an arbitrary extremal function of Lemma S, K_{f^*} be the oscillation of the function $f^*(x,y)$ on P, $b - a \leq b_1 - a_1$ and $y_0 \in [a_1, c_1]$ such that $\delta(y_0) - y_0 = b - a$. Then

$$b - a \leq K_{f^*} = \max\{\max_{a_1 \leq y \leq y_0} f^*(a,y), \max_{\delta(y_0) \leq y \leq b_1} f^*(b,y)\}$$

$$- \min\{\min_{\delta(y_0) \leq y \leq b_1} f^*(a,y), \min_{a_1 \leq y \leq y_0} f^*(b,y)\} \leq b_1 - a_1.$$

Moreover, if two arbitrary extremal functions coincide on one of the larger sides of the rectangle P, then they coincide over the entire rectangle.

Proof. Without loss of generality, we may assume that $\psi(x) > 0$ almost everywhere on $[a, c]$ and $\psi(x) < 0$, almost everywhere on $[c, b]$, $\varphi(y) > 0$ almost everywhere on $[a_1, c_1]$ and $\varphi(y) < 0$ almost everywhere on $[c_1, b_1]$. Let us break P into sets E_i ($i = \overline{1,8}$):

$$E_1 = \{(x,y) \in [a,c] \times [a_1,c_1] : \rho(x) - x \leq \delta(y) - y\},$$
$$E_2 = \{(x,y) \in [c,b] \times [a_1,c_1] : x - \rho^{-1}(x) \leq \delta(y) - y\},$$
$$E_3 = \{(x,y) \in [c,b] \times [a_1,c_1] : \delta(y) - y \leq x - \rho^{-1}(x)\},$$
$$E_4 = \{(x,y) \in [c,b] \times [c_1,b_1] : y - \delta^{-1}(y) \leq x - \rho^{-1}(x)\},$$
$$E_5 = \{(x,y) \in [c,b] \times [c_1,b_1] : x - \rho^{-1}(x) \leq y - \delta^{-1}(y)\},$$
$$E_6 = \{(x,y) \in [a,c] \times [c_1,b_1] : \rho(x) - x \leq y - \delta^{-1}(y)\},$$
$$E_7 = \{(x,y) \in [a,c] \times [c_1,b_1] : y - \delta^{-1}(y) \leq \rho(x) - x\},$$
$$E_8 = \{(x,y) \in [a,c] \times [a_1,c_1] : \delta(y) - y \leq \rho(x) - x\}.$$

Let us prove that the arbitrary extremal function $f^*(x,y)$ satisfies the relations:

$$f^*(x,y) = -x + K_1(y), \qquad (x,y) \in E_1 \cup E_2, \tag{24}$$

$$f^*(x,y) = x + K_2(y), \qquad (x,y) \in E_6 \cup E_5, \tag{25}$$

$$f^*(x,y) = -y + v_1(x), \qquad (x,y) \in E_8 \cup E_7, \tag{26}$$

$$f^*(x,y) = y + v_2(x), \qquad (x,y) \in E_3 \cup E_4. \tag{27}$$

Here, $K_1(y) \in W^1_{[a_1,c_1]}$ if $(x,y) \in E_1 \cup E_2$ for each fixed x, $K_2(y) \in W^1_{[c_1,b_1]}$ if $(x,y) \in E_6 \cup E_5$ for each fixed x, $v_1(x) \in W^1_{[a,c]}$ if $(x,y) \in E_8 \cup E_7$ for each fixed y and $v_2(x) \in W^1_{[c,b]}$ if $(x,y) \in E_3 \cup E_4$ for each fixed y. Applying the same transformations as in the proof of Lemma S and Lemma 1, we establish that the arbitrary extremal function $f^*(x,y)$ on $[a,c] \times [a_1,c_1]$ satisfies the equality

$$f^*(x,y) - f^*(\rho(x),y) - f^*(x,\delta(y)) + f^*(\rho(x),\delta(y))$$
$$= 2\min\{\rho(x) - x, \delta(y) - y\}.$$

This equality is equivalent to equalities:

$$f^*(x,y) - f^*(\rho(x),y) = \rho(x) - x, \qquad (x,y) \in E_1, \tag{28}$$

$$f^*(x,\delta(y)) - f^*(\rho(x),\delta(y)) = -(\rho(x) - x), \qquad (x,y) \in E_1, \tag{29}$$

$$f^*(x,y) - f^*(x,\delta(y)) = \delta(y) - y, \qquad (x,y) \in E_8, \tag{30}$$

$$f^*(\rho(x),y) - f^*(\rho(x),\delta(y)) = -(\delta(y) - y), \qquad (x,y) \in E_8. \tag{31}$$

Substituting $x = \rho^{-1}(t)$ and $t = x$ in (28), we get $f^*(x,y) - f^*(\rho^{-1}(x),y) = \rho^{-1}(x) - x$, if $(x,y) \in E_2$ because E_1 maps to E_2 after the replacement. Therefore, on $E_1 \cup E_2$ the extremal function $f^*(x,y)$ for each fixed $y(a_1 \leq y \leq c_1)$ satisfies the equalities $f^*(x,y) - f^*(\rho(x),y) = \rho(x) - x$ if $(x,y) \in E_1$, $f^*(x,y) - f^*(\rho^{-1}(x),y) = \rho^{-1}(x) - x$ if $(x,y) \in E_2$.

Thinking in the same way as in the proof of Lemma 1 and Corollary 1, we conclude that the arbitrary extremal function $f^*(x,y)$ on $E_1 \cup E_2$ satisfies relation (24). Similarly, using (29)–(31), we prove that equalities (25)–(27) hold, respectively. Taking into account the definiteness of the extremal function on each of the sets E_i and its continuity, we write it on the sides of the rectangle:

$$f^*(a,y) = \begin{cases} -y + v_1(a), & y_0 \leq y \leq \delta(y_0), \\ u_1(y), & a_1 \leq y \leq y_0, \\ u_2(y), & \delta(y_0) \leq y \leq b_1, \end{cases}$$

$$f^*(b,y) = \begin{cases} y + v_2(b), & y_0 \leq y \leq \delta(y_0), \\ u_1(y) - (b-a), & a_1 \leq y \leq y_0, \\ u_2(y) + (b-a), & \delta(y_0) \leq y \leq b_1, \end{cases} \tag{32}$$

where

$$u_1(y) = -a + K_1(y), u_2(y) = a + K_2(y),$$

$$u_1(y_0) = -y_0 + v_1(a), u_2(\delta(y_0)) = -\delta(y_0) + v_1(a),$$

$$f^*(x,a_1) = -x + K_1(a_1), f^*(x,b_1) = x + K_2(b_1).$$

Let us prove that

$$K_{f^*} = \max_{a_1 \leq y \leq b_1} \{f^*(a,y), f^*(b,y)\} - \min_{a_1 \leq y \leq b_1} \{f^*(a,y), f^*(b,y)\}.$$

We have to prove that

$$\forall (\alpha, \beta) \in P \min_{a_1 \leq y \leq b_1} \{f^*(a,y), f^*(b,y)\} \leq f^*(\alpha, \beta)$$

$$\leq \max_{a_1 \leq y \leq b_1} \{f^*(a,y), f^*(b,y)\}. \tag{33}$$

Let $y_0 \leq \beta \leq \delta(y_0)$. Let us prove that

$$f^*(b,y_0) = f^*(a,\delta(y_0)) \leq f^*(x,\beta) \leq f^*(a,y_0) = f^*(b,\delta(y_0))$$

for $x \in [a,b]$.

Since $f^*(a,y_0) = u_1(y_0) = -y_0 + v_1(a)$ and $f^*(b,\delta(y_0)) = u_2(\delta(y_0)) + (b-a) = -\delta(y_0) + v_1(a) + (b-a)$ then, taking into account that $b - a = \delta(y_0) - y_0$, we get

$$f^*(a,y_0) = f^*(b,\delta(y_0)). \tag{34}$$

Similarly, we can prove that

$$f^*(b,y_0) = f^*(a,\delta(y_0)). \tag{35}$$

If $x - a \leq \beta - y_0$, then $f^*(x,\beta) \leq f^*(a,y_0)$. Indeed,

$$f^*(a,y_0) - f^*(x,\beta) = f^*(a,y_0) - f^*(a,\beta) + f^*(a,\beta) - f^*(x,\beta).$$

Taking into account relation (32) for the function $f^*(a,y)$, we get

$$f^*(a,y_0) - f^*(a,\beta) = \beta - y_0.$$

Since the function $f^*(x,\beta)$ belongs to the class $W^1_{[a,b]}$, we then get

$$f^*(a,\beta) - f^*(x,\beta) \geq -(x-a),$$

hence
$$f^*(x,\beta) \leq f^*(a,y_0). \tag{36}$$

If $x - a \geq \beta - y_0$ then, taking into account definition (32) of the extremal function $f^*(b,y)$ and the fact that $f^*(x,\beta)$ belongs to the class $W^1_{[a,b]}$, we get

$$f^*(b, \delta(y_0)) - f^*(x,\beta)$$

$$= f^*(b, \delta(y_0)) - f^*(b,\beta) + f^*(b,\beta) - f^*(x,\beta)$$

$$= \delta(y_0) - \beta + f^*(b,\beta) - f^*(x,\beta)$$

$$= \delta(y_0) - y_0 - (\beta - y_0) + f^*(b,\beta) - f^*(x,\beta)$$

$$\geq b - a - (\beta - y_0) - (b - x) = (x - a) - (\beta - y_0) \geq 0. \tag{37}$$

From relations (34), (36) and (37), it follows that

$$f^*(x,\beta) \leq f^*(a,y_0) = f^*(b, \delta(y_0)). \tag{38}$$

If $x - a \leq \delta(y_0) - \beta$ then similarly we prove that

$$f^*(x,\beta) \geq f^*(a, \delta(y_0)) = f^*(b,y_0). \tag{39}$$

If $x - a \geq \delta(y_0) - \beta$ then we prove that

$$f^*(x,\beta) \geq f^*(b,y_0) = f^*(a, \delta(y_0)). \tag{40}$$

Let $a_1 \leq \beta \leq y_0$. Then, according to the definitions of the function $\delta(y)$ and the sets E_1, E_2, we get $\delta(\beta) - \beta \geq \delta(y_0) - y_0 = b - a$, $(x,\beta) \in E_1 \cup E_2$ and $f^*(x,\beta) = -x + K_1(\beta)$. According to (32) $K_1(\beta) = u_1(\beta) + a$. This is why

$$f^*(x,\beta) = (-x + a) + u_1(\beta) \leq u_1(\beta) = f^*(a,\beta) \leq \max_{a_1 \leq y \leq y_0} f^*(a,y)$$

$$\leq \max_{a_1 \leq y \leq b_1} f^*(a,y) \leq \max_{a_1 \leq y \leq b_1} \{f^*(a,y), f^*(b,y)\}. \tag{41}$$

Similarly, we prove that

$$f^*(x,\beta) \geq \min_{a_1 \leq y \leq y_0} \{f^*(b,y)\} \geq \min_{a_1 \leq y \leq b_1} \{f^*(a,y), f^*(b,y)\}. \tag{42}$$

Let $\delta(y_0) \leq \beta \leq b_1$. So, $(x,\beta) \in E_6 \cup E_5$ and $f^*(x,\beta) = x + K_2(\beta)$. Therefore, we prove that

$$\min_{a_1 \leq y \leq b_1} \{f^*(a,y), f^*(b,y)\} \leq \min_{\delta(y_0) \leq y \leq b_1} \{f^*(a,y)\} \leq f^*(x,\beta)$$

$$\leq \max_{\delta(y_0) \leq y \leq b_1} \{f^*(b,y)\} \leq \max_{a_1 \leq y \leq b_1} \{f^*(a,y), f^*(b,y)\}. \tag{43}$$

Relations (38)–(43) imply equality (33). Taking into account the definition (32) of functions $f^*(a,y)$ and $f^*(b,y)$, from (33), we obtain

$$K_{f^*} = \max\left\{\max_{a_1 \leq y \leq y_0} f^*(a,y), \max_{\delta(y_0) \leq y \leq b_1} f^*(b,y)\right\}$$

$$- \min\left\{\min_{\delta(y_0) \leq y \leq b_1} f^*(a,y), \min_{a_1 \leq y \leq y_0} f^*(b,y)\right\}.$$

The points where the extreme values of the function $f^*(x,y)$ (extreme points) are reached, lie on one of the larger sides of the rectangle or on both sides. If the extremal points lie on one of the larger sides of the rectangle, then, given the definition of the extremal function on the larger sides and the fact that functions $f^*(a,y)$ and $f^*(b,y)$ belong to the class $W^1_{[a_1,b_1]}$, we conclude that

$$b - a \leq K_{f^*} \leq b_1 - a_1. \tag{44}$$

If the extreme points lie on both larger sides, then (32) implies that

$$K_{f^*} = \max_{a_1 \leq y \leq y_0} u_1(y) - \min_{a_1 \leq y \leq y_0} (u_1(y) - (b-a)),$$

or

$$K_{f^*} = \max_{\delta(y_0)) \leq y \leq b_1} (u_2(y) + (b-a)) - \min_{\delta(y_0) \leq y \leq b_1} u_2(y).$$

So,

$$b - a \leq K_{f^*} \leq b - a + y_0 - a_1 < b_1 - a_1,$$

or

$$b - a \leq K_{f^*} \leq b - a + b_1 - \delta(y_0) < b_1 - a_1. \tag{45}$$

From (44) and (45), it follows that $b - a \leq K_{f^*} \leq b_1 - a_1$.

Let $f_1^*(x,y)$ and $f_2^*(x,y)$ be arbitrary extremal functions coinciding on one of the larger sides of the rectangle P, i.e., $f_1^*(a,y) \equiv f_2^*(a,y)$, or $f_1^*(b,y) \equiv f_2^*(b,y)$. Then

$$f_1^*(a,y) = \begin{cases} -y + v_1^1(a), & y_0 \leq y \leq \delta(y_0), \\ u_1^1(y), & a_1 \leq y \leq y_0, \\ u_2^1(y), & \delta(y_0) \leq y \leq b_1, \end{cases}$$

$$f_2^*(a,y) = \begin{cases} -y + v_2^1(a), & y_0 \leq y \leq \delta(y_0), \\ u_1^2(y), & a_1 \leq y \leq y_0, \\ u_2^2(y), & \delta(y_0) \leq y \leq b_1, \end{cases}$$

where $u_1^1(y) = -a + K_1^1(y)$, $u_2^1(y) = a + K_2^1(y)$ and $u_1^2(y) = -a + K_1^2(y)$, $u_2^2(y) = a + K_2^2(y)$, $u_1^1(y) = u_1^2(y)$, $u_2^1(y) = u_2^2(y)$.

Taking into account the definition of the extremal function $f^*(x,y)$ on $E_1 \cup E_2$ and on $E_6 \cup E_5$ and the fact that $f_1^*(a,y) = f_2^*(a,y)$, we get $f_1^*(x,y) = f_2^*(x,y)$ on $E_1 \cup E_2$ and $E_6 \cup E_5$. On the set $E_8 \cup E_7$ $f_1^*(x,y) = -y + v_1^1(x)$, and $f_2^*(x,y) = -y + v_1^2(x)$. Let $y = l_1(x)$ be the line separating the sets E_1 and E_8, i.e., $\rho(x) - x = \delta(l_1(x)) - l_1(x)$ for $x \in [a,c]$. Since $f^*(x,y)$ is continuous on $y = l_1(x)$, then, taking into account the definition of the extremal function on E_1 and E_8, we get: $-x + K_1^1(l_1(x)) = -l_1(x) + v_1^1(x)$ and $-x + K_1^2(l_1(x)) = -l_1(x) + v_1^2(x)$. Since $K_1^1(l_1(x)) = K_1^2(l_1(x))$, then $v_1^1(x) = v_1^2(x)$ and $f_1^*(x,y) = f_2^*(x,y)$ by $E_8 \cup E_7$. We prove, similarly, that $f_1^*(x,y) = f_2^*(x,y)$ on $E_3 \cup E_4$. So, $f_1^*(x,y) = f_2^*(x,y)$ on the entire rectangle P. The lemma has been proved. □

Lemma 3. *The set of all extremal functions for the Favard method on the class $H^{1,1}$ is the set of functions given by relations*

$$\gamma^*_{nm}(x,y) = \pm f^*_{nm}(x - x_0, y - y_0) + K,$$

where $f^*_{nm}(x,y)$ is the extremal function constructed in [1], x_0, y_0, K are arbitrary constants.

Proof. From [1] it follows that

$$f^*_{nm}(x,y) = \begin{cases} x+y, (x+y) \in [0, \frac{\pi}{n}] \times [0, \frac{\pi}{m}], \\ x + \varphi(y), (x,y) \in [0, \frac{\pi}{n}] \times [0, \pi], \\ y + \psi(x), (x,y) \in [0, \pi] \times [0, \frac{\pi}{m}], \\ (-1)^{(k+1)(i+1)} F_{k,i}(x,y) + C_{k,i} + r(y), (x,y) \in \\ \in [\frac{k\pi}{n}, \frac{(k+1)\pi}{n}] \times [\frac{i\pi}{m}, \frac{(i+1)\pi}{m}], k = \overline{1, n-1}, i = \overline{1, m-1}. \end{cases}$$

Here $\varphi(y)$ is the $2\pi/m$-periodic even function, $\varphi(y) = y$ for $y \in [0, \pi/m]$, $\psi(x)$ is the even, $2\pi/n$-periodic function, $\psi(x) = x$ for $x \in [0, \pi/n]$, and $F_{k,i}(x,y) \in W^{1,1}_{P_{k,i}}$ such that

$$\sup_{f \in W^{1,1}_{P_{k,i}}} \left| \int_{k\frac{\pi}{n}}^{(k+1)\frac{\pi}{n}} \int_{i\frac{\pi}{m}}^{(i+1)\frac{\pi}{m}} f(x,y) F_n(x) F_m(y) dxdy \right|$$

$$= \int_{k\frac{\pi}{n}}^{(k+1)\frac{\pi}{n}} \int_{i\frac{\pi}{m}}^{(i+1)\frac{\pi}{m}} (-1)^{(k+1)(i+1)} F_{k,i}(x,y) F_n(x) F_m(y) dxdy,$$

i.e., $F_{k,i}(x,y)$ are the extremal functions of Lemma S for the class $W^{1,1}_{P_{k,i}}$ on the rectangles $P_{k,i} = [k\frac{\pi}{n}, (k+1)\frac{\pi}{n}] \times [i\frac{\pi}{m}, (i+1)\frac{\pi}{m}]$, $C_{k,i}$ are constants, which are chosen so that $f^*_{nm}(x,y)$ is continuous on $[\frac{\pi}{n}, \pi] \times [\frac{\pi}{m}, \pi]$, $r(y) = f^*(\frac{\pi}{n}, y) - (F_{1,i}(\frac{\pi}{n}, y) + C_{1,i})$ is the function that guarantees the continuity of $f^*_{nm}(x,y)$ on the line $x = \pi/n$ if $n \geq m$. We can prove that

$$\sup_{f \in H^{1,1}} \| f(x,y) - F_{nm}(f, x, y) \|_C$$

$$= \frac{4}{\pi^2} \sup_{f \in H_0} \left| \int_0^{\pi} \int_0^{\pi} f(t,z) F_n(t) F_m(z) dtdz \right|,$$

where H_0 is the subset of functions from the class $H^{1,1}$ that are even in each of the variables, such that

$$\| f(x,y) - F_{nm}(f,x,y) \|_C = |f(0,0) - F_{nm}(f,0,0)| = |F_{nm}(f,0,0)|.$$

Moreover, if $\varphi^*_{nm}(x,y) \in H_0$ is such that

$$\frac{4}{\pi^2} \sup_{f \in H_0} \left| \int_0^{\pi} \int_0^{\pi} f(x,y) F_n(x) F_m(y) dxdy \right|$$

$$= \frac{4}{\pi^2} \int_0^{\pi} \int_0^{\pi} \varphi^*_{nm}(x,y) F_n(x) F_m(y) dxdy,$$

i.e., the arbitrary extremal function from the class H_0, then

$$\gamma^*_{nm}(x,y) = \pm \varphi^*_{nm}(x - x_0, y - y_0) + K.$$

Let us prove that the extremal function $\varphi_{nm}^*(x,y) \in H_0$ is unique and coincides with $f_{nm}^*(x,y) \in H_0$. We suppose that there exists another extremal function $\overline{f}_{nm}^*(x,y) \in H_0$, different from $f_{nm}^*(x,y)$. Then

$$0 = \frac{4}{\pi^2}\left(\int_0^\pi \int_0^\pi f_{nm}^*(t,z)F_n(t)F_m(z)dtdz\right.$$

$$\left. - \int_0^\pi \int_0^\pi \overline{f}_{nm}^*(t,z)F_n(t)F_m(z)dtdz\right)$$

$$= \frac{4}{\pi^2}\left(\left(\int_0^{\frac{\pi}{n}} \int_0^{\frac{\pi}{m}} f_{nm}^*(t,z)F_n(t)F_m(z)dtdz\right.\right.$$

$$\left.- \int_0^{\frac{\pi}{n}} \int_0^{\frac{\pi}{m}} \overline{f}_{nm}^*(t,z)F_n(t)F_m(z)dtdz\right)$$

$$+ \left(\sum_{i=1}^{m-1}\left(\int_0^{\pi/n} \int_{i\pi/n}^{(i+1)\pi/m} f_{nm}^*(t,z)F_n(t)F_m(z)dtdz\right.\right. \tag{46}$$

$$\left. - \int_0^{\pi/n} \int_{i\pi/n}^{(i+1)\pi/m} \overline{f}_{nm}^*(t,z)F_n(t)F_m(z)dtdz\right)$$

$$+ \sum_{k=1}^{n-1}\left(\int_{k\pi/n}^{(k+1)\pi/n} \int_0^{\pi/m} f_{nm}^*(t,z)F_n(t)F_m(z)dtdz\right.$$

$$\left. - \int_{k\pi/n}^{(k+1)\pi/n} \int_0^{\pi/m} \overline{f}_{nm}^*(t,z)F_n(t)F_m(z)dtdz\right)$$

$$+ \sum_{k=1}^{n-1}\sum_{i=1}^{m-1}\left(\int_{k\pi/n}^{(k+1)\pi/n} \int_{i\pi/m}^{(i+1)\pi/m} f_{nm}^*(t,z)F_n(t)F_m(z)dtdz\right.$$

$$\left. - \int_{k\pi/n}^{(k+1)\pi/n} \int_{i\pi/m}^{(i+1)\pi/m} \overline{f}_{nm}^*(t,z)F_n(t)F_m(z)dtdz\right).$$

Taking into account that $f_{nm}^*(x,y)$ belongs to the class H_0 and its construction, similarly as it was done in Theorem 2, we get:

$$\int_0^{\pi/n}\int_0^{\pi/m} f_{nm}^*(t,z)F_n(t)F_m(z)dtdz$$

$$- \int_0^{\pi/n}\int_0^{\pi/m} \overline{f}_{nm}^*(t,z)F_n(t)F_m(z)dtdz \geq 0, \tag{47}$$

$$\int_0^{\pi/n}\int_{i\pi/m}^{(i+1)\pi/m} f_{nm}^*(t,z)F_n(t)F_m(z)dtdz$$

$$- \int_0^{\pi/n}\int_{i\pi/m}^{(i+1)\pi/m} \overline{f}_{nm}^*(t,z)F_n(t)F_m(z)dtdz \geq 0, \tag{48}$$

$$\int_{k\pi/n}^{(k+1)\pi/n}\int_0^{\pi/m} f_{nm}^*(t,z)F_n(t)F_m(z)dtdz$$

$$- \int_{k\pi/n}^{(k+1)\pi/n}\int_0^{\pi/m} \overline{f}_{nm}^*(t,z)F_n(t)F_m(z)dtdz \geq 0, \tag{49}$$

$$\int_{k\pi/n}^{(k+1)\pi/n}\int_{i\pi/m}^{(i+1)\pi/m} f_{nm}^*(t,z)F_n(t)F_m(z)dtdz$$

$$- \int_{k\pi/n}^{(k+1)\pi/n}\int_{i\pi/m}^{(i+1)\pi/m} \overline{f}_{nm}^*(t,z)F_n(t)F_m(z)dtdz \geq 0. \tag{50}$$

It follows from (46) that inequalities (47)–(50) must contain the equal sign. In (47) there is the equal sign only if
$$\overline{f}^*_{nm}(t,z) = f^*_{nm}(t,z)$$
on $[0, \pi/n] \times [0, \pi/m]$. The equal sign in (48), according to Corollary 1, is possible if and only if
$$\overline{f}^*_{nm}(t,z) = \varphi(z) + f_i(t)$$
on $[0, \pi/n] \times [i\pi/m, (i+1)\pi/m]$. Similarly, in (49) the equal sign is possible if and only if
$$\overline{f}^*_{nm}(t,z) = \psi(t) + g_k(z)$$
on $[k\pi/n, (k+1)\pi/n] \times [0, \pi/m]$. The equal sign in (50) is possible if and only if $\overline{f}^*_{nm}(t,z)$ is the extremal function of Lemma S for the class $W^{1,1}_{P_{k,i}}$ on each rectangle $P_{k,i}$. For $0 \le t \le \frac{\pi}{n}$
$$\overline{f}^*_{nm}(t, \frac{\pi}{m}) = f^*_{nm}(t, \frac{\pi}{m}) = \frac{\pi}{m} + t,$$
but, on the other hand, $\overline{f}^*_{nm}(t, \frac{\pi}{m}) = \frac{\pi}{m} + f_1(t)$, because $\overline{f}^*_{nm}(t,z) = \varphi(z) + f_1(t)$ on $[0, \pi/n] \times [\pi/m, 2\pi/m]$. As a result of the continuity of the function $\overline{f}^*_{nm}(t,z)$ we have $f_1(t) = t$.

We prove similarly that $f_i(t) = t, ß = \overline{2, m-1}$. Therefore, on $[0, \pi/n] \times [0, \pi]$ we obtain
$$\overline{f}^*_{nm}(t,z) = f^*_{nm}(t,z). \tag{51}$$
We prove similarly that on $[0, \pi] \times [0, \pi/m]$
$$\overline{f}^*_{nm}(t,z) = f^*_{nm}(t,z). \tag{52}$$

Since $f^*_{nm}(t,z)$ and $\overline{f}^*_{nm}(t,z)$ are the extremal functions of Lemma S for the class $W^{1,1}_{P_{1,i}}$ on each rectangle $P_{1,i}$ and coincide on the larger side $\{(\frac{\pi}{n}, z) : i\frac{\pi}{m} \le z \le (i+1)\frac{\pi}{m}\}$ of the rectangle, then according to Lemma 2 they coincide on all rectangles $P_{1,i}$. We prove similarly that
$$\overline{f}^*_{nm}(t,z) = f^*_{nm}(t,z)$$
on $P_{2,i}, P_{3,i}, \ldots, P_{k,i}, \ldots, P_{n-1,i}$. So, on $[\pi/n, \pi] \times [\pi/m, \pi]$ we have
$$\overline{f}^*_{nm}(t,z) = f^*_{nm}(t,z). \tag{53}$$

From (51)–(53), taking into account the parity and 2π-periodicity in both variables of functions $f^*_{nm}(x,y)$ and $\overline{f}^*_{nm}(x,y)$ we get that $\overline{f}^*_{nm}(x,y) = f^*_{nm}(x,y)$ on the whole plane XOY. Thus, our assumption is wrong. Therefore, $f^*_{nm}(x,y)$ is the unique extremal function from the class H_0. Since any extremal function $\gamma^*_{nm}(x,y)$ has the form $\gamma^*_{nm}(x,y) = \pm \varphi^*_{nm}(x - x_0, y - y_0) + K$, and $\varphi^*_{nm}(x,y) = f^*_{nm}(x,y)$, then
$$\gamma^*_{nm}(x,y) = \pm f^*_{nm}(x - x_0, y - y_0 + K).$$

The lemma has been proved. □

Proof of Theorem 1. Let us prove that there exists the function $\widehat{f}_{nm}(x,y) \in H^{1,1}$, realizing the exact upper bound of the best approximation on the class $H^{1,1}$, i.e., $E_{n,m}(\widehat{f}_{nm}) = E_{n,m}(H^{1,1})$. Since $E_{n,m}(f) = E_{n,m}(f - f(0,0))$, then $E_{n,m}(H^{1,1}) = E_{n,m}(H^{1,1}_0)$, where $H^{1,1}_0$ is the subset of functions from the class $H^{1,1}$ that are equal to 0 at the origin. Let us prove that $H^{1,1}_0$ is the compact set in the metric space of 2π-periodic functions in each of the variables. If $f(x,y) \in H^{1,1}_0$ then $|f(x,y) - f(0,0)| = |f(x,y)| \le |x| + |y| \le 2\pi$. This implies that the set $H^{1,1}_0$ is bounded and (see, for example, [13] (pp. 123–125)) compact. The best approximation functional $E_{n,m}(f)$ is known to be continuous (see, for example, [2]

(p. 17)). Since $E_{n,m}(f)$ is the continuous functional and the set $H_0^{1,1}$ is compact, then there exists the function $\widehat{f}(x,y) \in H_0^{1,1}$ on which the functional $E_{n,m}(f)$ reaches its exact upper bound, i.e., $E_{n,m}(H^{1,1}) = E_{n,m}(H_0^{1,1}) = E_{n,m}(\widehat{f}_{nm})$. Let us assume that $E_{n,m}(H^{1,1}) = \mathcal{E}_{n,m}$. Since

$$\mathcal{E}_{n,m} = E_{n,m}(H^{1,1}) = E_{n,m}(\widehat{f}_{nm}) = \left\| \widehat{f}_{nm}(x,y) - T^*_{n-1,m-1}(\widehat{f},x,y) \right\|_C$$

$$\leq \left\| \widehat{f}_{nm}(x,y) - F_{n,m}(\widehat{f}_{nm},x,y) \right\|_C \leq \mathcal{E}_{n,m},$$

then

$$\left\| \widehat{f}_{nm}(x,y) - F_{n,m}(\widehat{f}_{nm},x,y) \right\|_C = \mathcal{E}_{n,m}. \tag{54}$$

Here, $T^*_{n-1,m-1}(\widehat{f},x,y)$ is the polynomial of the best approximation of the function $\widehat{f}_{nm}(x,y)$ of the degree $(n-1)$ in the variable x and the degree $(m-1)$ in the variable y in the uniform metric. It follows from relation (54) that the function $\widehat{f}_{nm}(x,y)$ belongs to the set of extremal functions for the Favard method on the class $H^{1,1}$, i.e.,

$$\widehat{f}_{nm}(x,y) = \pm f^*_{n,m}(x - x_0, y - y_0) + K. \tag{55}$$

Since $K_{f^*_{nm}} = \pi/n + \pi/m$, from relation (55) we get $K_{\widehat{f}_{nm}} = pi/n + \pi/m$. Since $E_{n,m}(\widehat{f}_{nm}) \leq K_{\widehat{f}_{nm}}/2 = \pi/2n + \pi/2m$, and as a result (2) $\mathcal{E}_{n,m} > \pi/2n + \pi/2m$, then our assumption is wrong. Hence, the statement of Theorem 1 is true. □

Let us denote by $H^{1,1}_{u+v} := \{f(x,y) \in H^{1,1} : f(x,y) = u(x) + v(y)\}$ as the subset of the functions from the class $H^{1,1}$ that can be represented as a sum of two functions, each of which depends on only one variable. It follows from the definition of the class $H^{1,1}$ that

$$u(x) \in H^1, \quad v(x) \in H^1. \tag{56}$$

Theorem 1 (see, for example, [14]) implies the following statement.

Lemma 4. *If the functions $u(x)$ and $v(y)$ are continuous 2π-periodic in the variables x and y, and $T^*_{n-1}(u,x)$, $T^*_{m-1}(v,y)$ are the polynomials of the best approximation of these functions, then $E_{n,m}(u+v) = E_n(u) + E_m(v)$, and $T^*_{n-1}(u,x) + T^*_{m-1}(v,y)$ is the unique polynomial of the best approximation for the function $f(x,y) = u(x) + v(y) \in H^1$.*

Using Lemmas 4 and (56), we prove the relation

$$E_{n,m}(H^{1,1}_{u+v}) = E_n(H^1) + E_m(H^1) = \frac{\pi}{2n} + \frac{\pi}{2m}.$$

From the last relation and the equality

$$\sup_{f \in H^{1,1}_{u+v}} \|f(x,y) - F_{n,m}(f,x,y)\|_C = \sup_{u \in H^1} \|u(x) - F_n(u,x)\|_C$$

$$+ \sup_{v \in H^1} \|v(y) - F_m(v,y)\|_C = \frac{\pi}{2n} + \frac{\pi}{2m}$$

the following statement follows.

Theorem 5. *For any natural numbers n and m*

$$\sup_{f \in H^{1,1}_{u+v}} \|f(x,y) - F_{n,m}(f,x,y)\|_C = \frac{\pi}{2n} + \frac{\pi}{2m} = E_{n,m}(H^{1,1}_{u+v}),$$

that is, the Favard method implements the exact upper bound of the best approximations on the class $H^{1,1}_{u+v}$.

3. Conclusions

In this paper, we proved that the approximation of the class $H^{1,1}$ by Favard method is greater than the value of the best approximation of this class by trigonometric polynomials, the exact value of which being unknown. We have also managed to build classes for which these values are equal.

The question of Theorem 1 validity for Hölder classes of functions of $n \geq 3$ variables being 2π-periodic in each variable, still remains open. To solve it, we have to establish analogues of equality (1) and Lemmas 2 and 3 for these classes of functions.

Author Contributions: Conceptualization, D.B. and I.K.; methodology, D.B. and I.K.; formal analysis, D.B. and I.K.; writing—original draft preparation, D.B. and I.K.; writing—review and editing, D.B. and I.K. All authors have read and agreed to the published version of the manuscript.

Funding: This research received no external funding.

Institutional Review Board Statement: Not applicable.

Informed Consent Statement: Not applicable.

Data Availability Statement: Not applicable.

Conflicts of Interest: The authors declare no conflicts of interest.

References

1. Stepanets, A.I. A sharp estimate of the deviations of Favard sums over the classes $H^{1,1}_{A,B}$. Studies in the theory of approximation of functions and their applications *Akad. Nauk Ukrain SSR Inst. Mat. Kiev.* **1978**, *195*, 174–181. (In Russian)
2. Korneichuk, N.P. *Extremal Problems in Approximation Theory*; Nauka: Moscow, Russia, 1976. (In Russian)
3. Bushev, D.N. Inequalities of the type of Bernstein inequalities and their application to the investigation of the differential properties of the solutions of differential equations of higher order. *Dokl. Akad. Nauk USSR* **1984**, *2*, 3–4. (In Russian)
4. Mairhuber, J. On Haar's theorem concerning Chebysheff approximation problems heving unique solutions. *Proc. Am. Math. Soc.* **1971**, *7*, 609–615.
5. Stepanets, A.I. *Uniform Approximations by Trigonometric Polynomials*; Naukova Dumka: Kiev, Ukraine, 1981. (In Russian); English translation: VSP: Leiden, The Netherland, 2001.
6. Natanson, I.P. *Theory of Functions of a Real Variable*; Nauka: Moscow, Russia, 1974. (In Russian); English translation by Leo F. Boron: Dover Publications: New York, NY, USA, 2016.
7. Stechkin, S.B. The approximation of continuous periodic functions by Favard sums. *Trudy Mat. Inst. Steklov* **1971**, *109*, 26–34. (In Russian)
8. Kal'chuk, I.; Kharkevych, Y. Approximation Properties of the Generalized Abel-Poisson Integrals on the Weyl-Nagy Classes. *Axioms* **2022**, *11*, 161. [CrossRef]
9. Kal'chuk, I.V.; Kharkevych, Y.I. Approximation of the Classes $W^r_{\beta,\infty}$ by Generalized Abel–Poisson Integrals. *Ukr. Math. J.* **2022**, *74*, 575–585. [CrossRef]
10. Zhyhallo, T.; Kharkevych, Y. On Approximation of functions from the Class $L^{\psi}_{\beta,1}$ by the Abel-Poisson integrals in the integral metric. *Carpathian Math. Publ.* **2022**, *14*, 223–229. [CrossRef]
11. Kharkevych, Y.I. On Some Asymptotic Properties of Solutions to Biharmonic Equations. *Cybern. Syst. Anal.* **2022**, *58*, 251–258. [CrossRef]
12. Dzyadyk, V.K. *Introduction to the Theory of Uniform Approximation of Functions by Polynomials*; Nauka: Moskow, Russia, 1977. (In Russian)
13. Timan, A.F. *Theory of Approximation of Functions of a Real Variable*; Fizmatgiz: Moscow, Russia, 1960. (In Russian); English translation by J. Berry: International Series of Monographs on Pure and Applied Mathematics 34; Pergamon Press and MacMillan: Oxford, UK, 1963.
14. Newman, D.; Shapiro, H. Some theorems on Cebysev approximation. *Duke Math. J.* **1963**, *30*, 673–681. [CrossRef]

Disclaimer/Publisher's Note: The statements, opinions and data contained in all publications are solely those of the individual author(s) and contributor(s) and not of MDPI and/or the editor(s). MDPI and/or the editor(s) disclaim responsibility for any injury to people or property resulting from any ideas, methods, instructions or products referred to in the content.

Article

Joint Discrete Universality in the Selberg–Steuding Class

Roma Kačinskaitė [1,2,*,†], Antanas Laurinčikas [1,†] and Brigita Žemaitienė [1,†]

[1] Institute of Mathematics, Faculty of Mathematics and Informatics, Vilnius University, Naugarduko Str. 24, LT-03225 Vilnius, Lithuania; antanas.laurincikas@mif.vu.lt (A.L.); brigita.zemaitiene@mif.vu.lt (B.Ž.)

[2] Department of Mathematics and Statistics, Faculty of Informatics, Vytautas Magnus University, Universiteto Str. 10, Akademija, LT-53361 Kaunas District, Lithuania

* Correspondence: roma.kacinskaite@mif.vu.lt

† These authors contributed equally to this work.

Abstract: In the paper, we consider the approximation of analytic functions by shifts from the wide class $\widetilde{S}$ of L-functions. This class was introduced by A. Selberg, supplemented by J. Steuding, and is defined axiomatically. We prove the so-called joint discrete universality theorem for the function $L(s) \in \widetilde{S}$. Using the linear independence over $\mathbb{Q}$ of the multiset $\{(h_j \log p : p \in \mathbb{P}), j = 1, \ldots, r; 2\pi\}$ for positive h_j, we obtain that there are many infinite shifts $(L(s + ikh_1), \ldots, L(s + ikh_r))$, $k = 0, 1, \ldots$, approximating every collection $(f_1(s), \ldots, f_r(s))$ of analytic non-vanishing functions defined in the strip $\{s \in \mathbb{C} : \sigma_L < \sigma < 1\}$, where σ_L is a degree of the function $L(s)$. For the proof, the probabilistic approach based on weak convergence of probability measures in the space of analytic functions is applied.

Keywords: analytic functions; discrete shifts; limit theorem; simultaneous approximation; Selberg–Steuding class; weak convergence

MSC: 11M06; 11M41; 11M36

1. Introduction

One of the most important branches of the function theory is the approximation of analytic functions, and is widely used not only in mathematics but also in other natural sciences. In the 1980s, it was discovered that there exist analytic objects that approximate large classes of analytic functions. S.M. Voronin found [1] that the first such object as the Riemann zeta-function $\zeta(s)$, $s = \sigma + it$, given by

$$\zeta(s) = \sum_{m=1}^{\infty} \frac{1}{m^s} = \prod_{p \in \mathbb{P}} \left(1 - \frac{1}{p^s}\right)^{-1}, \quad \sigma > 1,$$

where $\mathbb{P}$ is the set of all prime numbers. As is well-known, $\zeta(s)$ has the meromorphic continuation of the whole complex plane with $\text{Res}_{s=1} \zeta(s) = 1$. Voronin proved [1] (see also [2]) that if $0 < c < \frac{1}{4}$, the function $f(s)$ is continuous and non-vanishing on the disc $|s| \leq c$, and analytic in the interior of that disc, then there exists a real number $\tau = \tau(\epsilon, f)$ such that

$$\max_{|s| \leq c} \left| \zeta\left(s + \frac{3}{4} + i\tau\right) - f(s) \right| < \epsilon$$

for any $\epsilon > 0$.

Thus, Voronin reported that all non-vanishing analytic functions on the strip $D = \{s \in \mathbb{C} : \frac{1}{2} < \sigma < 1\}$, and uniformly on discs can be approximated by shifts $\zeta(s + i\tau)$ of one and the same function $\zeta(s)$. The Bohr–Courant theorem [3] claims that the set

$$\{\zeta(\sigma + it) : t \in \mathbb{R}\}$$

Citation: Kačinskaitė, R.; Laurinčikas, A.; Žemaitienė, B. Joint Discrete Universality in the Selberg–Steuding Class. *Axioms* **2023**, *12*, 674. https://doi.org/10.3390/axioms12070674

Academic Editor: Inna Kalchuk

Received: 8 May 2023
Revised: 26 June 2023
Accepted: 5 July 2023
Published: 8 July 2023

Copyright: © 2023 by the authors. Licensee MDPI, Basel, Switzerland. This article is an open access article distributed under the terms and conditions of the Creative Commons Attribution (CC BY) license (https://creativecommons.org/licenses/by/4.0/).

is dense everywhere on a complex plane for every fixed $\frac{1}{2} < \sigma \leq 1$. From here, it follows that the set of values of the function $\zeta(s)$ is very rich. Thus, in terms of approximation, the function $\zeta(s)$ is universal, and this might be natural in view of the remark above.

We denote by $\mathcal{H}(D)$ the space of the analytic on D functions equipped with the topology of uniform convergence on the compacta. Since the space $\mathcal{H}(D)$ has an infinite-dimension, the Voronin theorem is a infinite-dimensional extension of the Bohr–Courant denseness theorem.

The above-mentioned Voronin universality theorem has a more general statement which follows the Mergelyan theorem on the approximation of analytic functions by polynomials [4]. We denote by $\mathcal{K}(D)$ the set of compact subsets of the strip D with connected complements, and by $\mathcal{H}_0(K, D)$ the class of continuous non-vanishing functions on $K \in \mathcal{K}(D)$ that are analytic in the interior of K. Moreover, we let mes$A$ stand for the Lebesgue measure of a measurable set $A \subset \mathbb{R}$. Then the following statement on the $\zeta(s)$'s universality is known, see, for example, [5–9].

Theorem 1. *Suppose that $K \in \mathcal{K}(D)$ and $f(s) \in \mathcal{H}_0(K, D)$. Then, for every $\epsilon > 0$,*

$$\liminf_{T \to \infty} \frac{1}{T} \text{mes} \left\{ \tau \in [0, T] : \sup_{s \in K} |f(s) - \zeta(s + i\tau)| < \epsilon \right\} > 0.$$

The inequality of the theorem shows the infinitude of shifts of $\zeta(s + i\tau)$ approximating a given function $f(s) \in H_0(K, D)$.

The statement of Theorem 1 was influenced by a probabilistic method proposed in [6]. The initial Voronin method based on the Riemann-type rearrangement theorem in the Hilbert space was developed in [7,8].

Since τ in the shifts $\zeta(s + i\tau)$ of Theorem 1 is an arbitrary real number, Theorem 1 is called a continuous universality theorem. Parallel to continuous universality theorems for zeta-functions, there are discrete universality theorems when τ takes values from a certain discrete set. These were proposed by A. Reich [10] for Dedekind zeta-functions of algebraic number fields $\mathbb{K}$. If $\mathbb{K} = \mathbb{Q}$, we deal with a discrete universality for the Riemann zeta-function. As an example, we now state a classical result in the following (see [6]).

Theorem 2. *Suppose that $K \in \mathcal{K}(D)$, $f(s) \in \mathcal{H}_0(K, D)$ and $h > 0$. Then, for every $\epsilon > 0$,*

$$\liminf_{N \to \infty} \frac{1}{N+1} \# \left\{ 0 \leq k \leq N : \sup_{s \in K} |f(s) - \zeta(s + ikh)| < \epsilon \right\} > 0.$$

Here $\#A$ denotes the number of elements of the set $A \subset \mathbb{R}$, and N runs over the set $\mathbb{N}_0 = \mathbb{N} \cup \{0\}$.

Note that discrete universality theorems were also investigated in [6–8].

Some other functions given by a Dirichlet series also fulfil the property of universality in the Voronin sense. For example, Dirichlet L-functions $L(s, \chi)$ with arbitrary Dirichlet character χ,

$$L(s, \chi) = \sum_{m=1}^{\infty} \frac{\chi(m)}{m^s}, \quad \sigma > 1,$$

are universal, as was mentioned by Voronin in [2]. Let $\mathfrak{A} = \{a_m : m \in \mathbb{N}\} \subset \mathbb{C}$ be a periodic sequence. Then the periodic zeta-function

$$\zeta(s; \mathfrak{A}) = \sum_{m=1}^{\infty} \frac{a_m}{m^s}, \quad \sigma > 1,$$

also has the universal approximation property [11]. For values of the parameters α and λ, the Hurwitz zeta-function $\zeta(s, \alpha)$ and Lerch zeta-function $L(\lambda, \alpha, s)$, for $\sigma > 1$, respectively given by

$$\zeta(s,\alpha) = \sum_{m=0}^{\infty} \frac{1}{(m+\alpha)^s} \quad \text{and} \quad L(\lambda,\alpha,s) = \sum_{m=0}^{\infty} \frac{e^{2\pi i \lambda m}}{(m+\alpha)^s},$$

are universal (see [12]). In other words, they approximate analytic functions from the class $\mathcal{H}(K,D)$ considered continuous on K and analytic in the interior of K functions. This observation leads to certain conjectures. For example, by the Linnik–Ibragimov conjecture (or programme), see [8], all functions in a certain half-plane defined by a Dirichlet series, with analytic continuation left of the absolute convergence abscissa and satisfying some natural growth hypotheses are universal in the Voronin sense. However, currently there are Dirichlet series which their universality is not known, for example, the function $L(\lambda,\alpha,s)$ with an algebraic irrational parameter. Results in this direction for the Hurwitz zeta-function $\zeta(s,\alpha)$, as in [13], are presented.

To obtain more general results, the universality of separate functions and some classes of functions are considered. One such class was introduced by A. Selberg (see [14,15]), known as the Selberg class $\mathcal{S}$. The structure of the class $\mathcal{S}$ was studied by various authors, see [8,16–20], but until now its structure was not completely known. However, the class includes all main zeta- and L-functions, for example, $\zeta(s)$, $L(s,\chi)$, the zeta-functions of certain cusp forms, etc. The Selberg class $\mathcal{S}$ is defined axiomatically, with its functions

$$L(s) = \sum_{m=1}^{\infty} \frac{a(m)}{m^s}, \quad a(m) \in \mathbb{C},$$

satisfying four axioms. Recall that the notation $a \ll_\theta b$, $b > 0$, means that there is a positive constant $c = c(\theta)$ such that $|a| \leq cb$, and that $\Gamma(s)$ denotes the Euler gamma-function. The axioms of the class $\mathcal{S}$ have the names:

(1) (Ramanujan conjecture). The estimate $a(m) \ll_\epsilon m^\epsilon$ is valid with any $\epsilon > 0$.
(2) (Analytic continuation). For some $l \in \mathbb{N}_0$, $(s-1)^l L(s)$ in an entire function of finite order.
(3) (Functional equation). Let

$$\Lambda_L(s) = L(s) q^s \prod_{j=1}^{j_0} \Gamma(\lambda_j s + \alpha_j),$$

where $q, \lambda_j \in \mathbb{R}^+$, and $\alpha_j \in \mathbb{C}$ such that $\Re \alpha_j \geq 0$. Then the functional equation of the form

$$\Lambda_L(s) = w \Lambda_L(1 - \bar{s})$$

is valid. Here, $|w| = 1$, and, as usual, by $\bar{s}$ we denote the conjugate of s.
(4) (Euler product). Let

$$\log L_p(s) = \sum_{l=1}^{\infty} \frac{b(p^l)}{p^s}$$

with coefficients $b(p^l)$ such that $b(p^l) \ll p^{\alpha l}$, $\alpha < \frac{1}{2}$. Then the representation

$$L(s) = \prod_{p \in \mathbb{P}} L_p(s)$$

holds.

Axioms (1)–(4) of the class $\mathcal{S}$ are insufficient to prove universality as they do not include the analogue of the prime number theorem. Therefore, J. Steuding, who was first to study the class $\mathcal{S}$ with an emphasis on universality [8], introduced the following axioms.
(5) There exists $\kappa > 0$ such that

$$\lim_{x \to \infty} \frac{1}{\pi(x)} \sum_{p \leq x} |a(p)|^2 = \kappa,$$

where function $\pi(x)$ counts the number of primes up to x. Moreover, in [8] the Euler product of the type

$$L(s) = \prod_{p \in \mathbb{P}} \prod_{j=1}^{l} \left(1 - \frac{\alpha_j(p)}{p^s}\right)^{-1} \quad (6)$$

was required with some complex $\alpha_j(p)$.

For the universality for the above functions, we need one important ingredient of the class $\mathcal{S}$. For $L \in \mathcal{S}$, the quantity

$$d_L = 2 \sum_{j=1}^{j_0} \lambda_j$$

is called the degree of the function L. The degree is an deep characteristic of the class $\mathcal{S}$. If $d_L = 1$, then $L(s)$ coincides with $\zeta(s)$ or $L(s + ia, \chi)$ with some $a \in \mathbb{R}$. For $L \in \mathcal{S}$, let

$$\sigma_L = \max\left(\frac{1}{2}, 1 - \frac{1}{d_L}\right).$$

We denote by $D_{\sigma_L} = \{s \in \mathbb{C} : \sigma_L < \sigma < 1\}$, $K(D_{\sigma_L})$ the class of compact subsets of the strip D_{σ_L} with connected complements, and $\mathcal{H}_0(K, D_{\sigma_L})$ the class of continuous non-vanishing functions on K that are analytic in the interior of K. Then, in [8], the following universality theorem has been proved.

Theorem 3. *Suppose that $L(s)$ satisfies Axioms (2), (3), (5) and (6). Let $K \in K(D_{\sigma_L})$ and $f(s) \in \mathcal{H}_0(K, D_{\sigma_L})$. Then, for every $\epsilon > 0$, the inequality*

$$\liminf_{T \to \infty} \frac{1}{T} \mathrm{mes}\left\{\tau \in [0, T] : \sup_{s \in K} |f(s) - L(s + i\tau)| < \epsilon\right\} > 0$$

holds.

In [21], Axiom (6) was removed. Thus, Theorem 3 holds for the so-called Selberg–Steuding class $\widetilde{\mathcal{S}}$; more precisely, for the functions belonging to the Selberg class and satisfying Axiom (5).

The discrete version of Theorem 3 has been obtained in [22].

Theorem 4. *Suppose that $L(s)$, K and $f(s)$ are the same as in Theorem 3. Then, for every $h > 0$ and $\epsilon > 0$,*

$$\liminf_{N \to \infty} \frac{1}{N+1} \#\left\{0 \leq k \leq N : \sup_{s \in K} |f(s) - L(s + ikh)| < \epsilon\right\} > 0.$$

We can consider a simultaneous approximation of a tuple of analytic functions by a tuple of shifts of zeta- or L-functions. This type of universality is called joint universality. This phenomenon of a Dirichlet series was also introduced by Voronin. In [23], he studied the joint functional independence of Dirichlet L-functions using the joint universality. Of course, the joint universality is more complicated, but, on the other hand, it is more interesting. Obviously, in the case of joint universality, the approximating shifts require some independence conditions. For example, Voronin used Dirichlet L-functions with pairwise non-equivalent Dirichlet characters. Later, the joint universality theorems were proven for zeta-functions defined by a Dirichlet series with periodic coefficients, Matsumoto zeta-functions, and automorphic L-functions. For these proofs, see the very informative paper [9].

This paper deals with the discrete joint universality property for L-functions for the class $\widetilde{\mathcal{S}}$. Let

$$L(s) = \sum_{m=1}^{\infty} \frac{a(m)}{m^s},$$

$h_1, ..., h_r$ be fixed positive numbers, and $\underline{h} = (h_1, \ldots, h_r)$. We define the multiset

$$A(\mathbb{P}, \underline{h}, 2\pi) = \{(h_j \log p : p \in \mathbb{P}), j = 1, \ldots, r; \, 2\pi\},$$

and then we prove the following theorem.

Theorem 5. *Suppose that $L(s) \in \widetilde{S}$, and the set $A(\mathbb{P}, \underline{h}, 2\pi)$ is linearly independent over the field of rational numbers $\mathbb{Q}$. For $j = 1, \ldots, r$, let $K_j \in \mathcal{K}(D_L)$ and $f_j(s) \in \mathcal{H}_0(K_j, D_L)$. Then, for every $\underline{h} \in (\mathbb{R}^+)^r$ and $\epsilon > 0$,*

$$\liminf_{N \to \infty} \frac{1}{N+1} \# \left\{ 0 \le k \le N : \sup_{1 \le j \le r} \sup_{s \in K_j} |f_j(s) - L(s + ikh_j)| < \epsilon \right\} > 0.$$

Moreover, for all but at most countably many $\epsilon > 0$, the limit

$$\lim_{N \to \infty} \frac{1}{N+1} \# \left\{ 0 \le k \le N : \sup_{1 \le j \le r} \sup_{s \in K_j} |f_j(s) - L(s + ikh_j)| < \epsilon \right\}$$

exists and is positive.

In [24], a joint continuous universality theorem for a function $L(s) \in \widetilde{S}$ on the approximation of analytic functions by shifts $\left(L(s + ia_1\tau), \ldots, L(s + ia_r\tau)\right)$ with linear independence over $\mathbb{Q}$ real algebraic numbers $a_1, \ldots, a_r$ was obtained.

For example, for $r = 3$, we can take $h_1 = 1$, $h_2 = \sqrt{2}$, and $h_3 = \sqrt{3}$ in Theorem 5.

We denote by $\mathcal{B}(\mathcal{X})$ the Borel σ-field of the space $\mathcal{X}$, and let P and P_n, where $n \in \mathbb{N}$, be probability measures on $(\mathcal{X}, \mathcal{B}(\mathcal{X}))$. We report that P_n converges weakly to P as $n \to \infty$, and write $P \xrightarrow[n \to \infty]{w} P$, if, for all bounded continuous functions $g(x)$ on $\mathcal{X}$,

$$\lim_{n \to \infty} \int_{\mathcal{X}} g(x) dP_n = \int_{\mathcal{X}} g(x) dP.$$

We derive Theorem 5 from a probabilistic joint discrete limit theorem on weakly convergent probability measures in the space of analytic functions. For proof of the latter theorem, we consider the weak convergence of probability measures on the infinite-dimensional torus, and in the space of analytic functions for certain absolutely convergent Dirichlet series. After this, we show a comparison in the mean between the initial L-function and functions defined by an absolutely convergent Dirichlet series. This will give the desired joint discrete limit theorem for the tuple of functions we are interested in.

2. Case of the Torus

We define the infinite-dimensional torus as

$$\mathbb{T} = \prod_{p \in \mathbb{P}} \{s \in \mathbb{C} : |s| = 1\},$$

where $\mathbb{T}$ is the infinite Cartesian product over prime numbers of unit circles. Since each circle is a compact set, by the Tikhonov theorem, $\mathbb{T}$ with the product topology and operation of pairwise multiplication is a compact topological abelian group. Now, we construct the set

$$\mathbb{T}^r = \mathbb{T}_1 \times \ldots \times \mathbb{T}_r,$$

where $\mathbb{T}_j = \mathbb{T}$, $j = 1, \ldots, r$. Then, the Tikhonov theorem again shows that $\mathbb{T}^r$ is a compact topological group. We denote by $\mathbf{t} = (\mathbf{t}_1, .., \mathbf{t}_r)$, $\mathbf{t}_j \in \mathbb{T}_j$, $\mathbf{t}_j = (\mathbf{t}_j(p) : p \in \mathbb{P})$, $j = 1, \ldots, r$, the elements of $\mathbb{T}^r$.

For $A \in \mathcal{B}(\mathbb{T}^r)$, we set

$$Q_{N,\mathbb{T}^r,\underline{h}}(A) = \frac{1}{N+1}\#\left\{0 \leq k \leq N : \left((p^{-ikh_1} : p \in \mathbb{P}), \ldots, (p^{-ikh_r} : p \in \mathbb{P})\right) \in A\right\}.$$

In this section, we consider the weak convergence for $Q_{N,\mathbb{T}^r,\underline{h}}$ as $N \to \infty$.

Proposition 1. *Suppose that the set $A(\mathbb{P},\underline{h},2\pi)$ is linearly independent over $\mathbb{Q}$. Then, $Q_{N,\mathbb{T}^r,\underline{h}} \xrightarrow[n\to\infty]{w} m^H$, where m^H is the probability Haar measure on $(\mathbb{T}^r, \mathcal{B}(\mathbb{T}^r))$.*

Proof. The characters of the $\mathbb{T}^r$ are of the form

$$\prod_{j=1}^{r}\prod_{p\in\mathbb{P}}{}^{*}\mathbf{t}_j^{l_{jp}}(p)$$

with integers l_{jp}, where the star indicates that only a finite number of l_{jp} are not zeroes. Therefore, the Fourier transform $\mathcal{F}_{N,\mathbb{T}^r,\underline{h}}(\underline{l}_1,..,\underline{l}_r)$, $\underline{l}_j = (l_{jp} : l_{jp} \in \mathbb{Z}, p \in \mathbb{P})$, $j = 1,\ldots,r$, can be represented by

$$\begin{aligned}
\mathcal{F}_{N,\mathbb{T}^r,\underline{h}}(\underline{l}_1,..,\underline{l}_r) &= \int_{\mathbb{T}^r}\prod_{j=1}^{r}\prod_{p\in\mathbb{P}}{}^{*}\mathbf{t}_j^{l_{jp}}(p)\,dQ_{N,\mathbb{T}^r,\underline{h}} \\
&= \frac{1}{N+1}\sum_{k=0}^{N}\prod_{j=1}^{r}\prod_{p\in\mathbb{P}}{}^{*}p^{-ikl_{jp}h_j} \\
&= \frac{1}{N+1}\sum_{k=0}^{N}\exp\left\{-ik\sum_{j=1}^{r}h_j\sum_{p\in\mathbb{P}}{}^{*}l_{jp}\log p\right\}.
\end{aligned} \quad (1)$$

By a continuity theorem on the compact groups, for the proof of Proposition 1, it is sufficient to show that the Fourier transform $\mathcal{F}_{N,\mathbb{T}^r,\underline{h}}(\underline{l}_1,..,\underline{l}_r)$ converges, as $N \to \infty$, to the Fourier transform

$$\mathcal{F}_{m^H}(\underline{l}_1,\ldots,\underline{l}_r) = \begin{cases} 1 & \text{if } (\underline{l}_1,\ldots,\underline{l}_r) = (\underline{0},\ldots,\underline{0}), \\ 0 & \text{otherwise} \end{cases}$$

of the Haar measure m^H. Here, $\underline{0} = (0,0,\ldots)$.

Equality (1), obviously, gives

$$\mathcal{F}_{N,\mathbb{T}^r,\underline{h}}(\underline{0},\ldots,\underline{0}) = 1. \quad (2)$$

Thus, it remains to consider only the case $(\underline{l}_1,\ldots,\underline{l}_r) \neq (\underline{0},\ldots,\underline{0})$. Since the set $A(\mathbb{P},\underline{h},2\pi)$ is linearly independent over $\mathbb{Q}$, we have, in this case,

$$\exp\left\{-i\sum_{j=1}^{r}h_j\sum_{p\in\mathbb{P}}{}^{*}l_{jp}\log p\right\} \neq 1. \quad (3)$$

Actually, if (3) is false, then

$$\sum_{j=1}^{r}h_j\sum_{p\in\mathbb{P}}{}^{*}l_{jp}\log p = 2\pi m$$

for some $m \in \mathbb{Z}$ and the integers $l_{jp} \neq 0$. However, this contradicts the assumption that the set $A(\mathbb{P},\underline{h},2\pi)$ is linearly independent. Now, using (3) and the formula for the sum of geometric progressions, we deduce from (1) that, for $(\underline{l}_1,\ldots,\underline{l}_r) \neq (\underline{0},\ldots,\underline{0})$,

$$\mathcal{F}_{N,\mathbb{T}^r,\underline{h}}(\underline{l}_1,\ldots,\underline{l}_r) = \frac{1 - \exp\left\{-i(N+1)\sum_{j=1}^{r}h_j\sum_{p\in\mathbb{P}}^{*}l_{jp}\log p\right\}}{(N+1)\left(1 - \exp\left\{-i\sum_{j=1}^{r}h_j\sum_{p\in\mathbb{P}}^{*}l_{jp}\log p\right\}\right)}.$$

Hence,
$$\lim_{N\to\infty} \mathcal{F}_{N,\mathbb{T}^r,\underline{h}}(\underline{l}_1,\dots,\underline{l}_r) = 0$$
for $(\underline{l}_1,\dots,\underline{l}_r) \neq (\underline{0},\dots,\underline{0})$. This, together with (2), shows that
$$\lim_{N\to\infty} \mathcal{F}_{N,\mathbb{T}^r,\underline{h}}(\underline{l}_1,\dots,\underline{l}_r) = \mathcal{F}_{m^H}(\underline{l}_1,\dots,\underline{l}_r),$$
thus proving the Proposition 1.
□

We apply Proposition 1 for the proof of weak convergence for the measures defined by means of certain absolutely convergent Dirichlet series connected to the function $L(s)$. We fix a number $\beta > \frac{1}{2}$, and
$$v_n(m;\beta) = \exp\left\{-\left(\frac{m}{n}\right)^\beta\right\}, \quad m,n \in \mathbb{N}.$$

We define the functions
$$L_n(s) = \sum_{m=1}^{\infty} \frac{a(m)v_n(m;\beta)}{m^s}$$
and
$$L_n(s,\mathbf{t}_j) = \sum_{m=1}^{\infty} \frac{a(m)\mathbf{t}_j(m)v_n(m;\beta)}{m^s}, \quad j = 1,\dots,r,$$
where, for $m \in \mathbb{N}$,
$$\mathbf{t}_j(m) = \prod_{p^l \| m} \mathbf{t}_j^l(p).$$

If $L(s) \in \widetilde{S}$, then $a(m) \ll m_\epsilon^\epsilon$ with arbitrary $\epsilon > 0$. Obviously, $v_n(m;\beta)$ decreases exponentially with respect to m. Therefore, the series for $L_n(s)$ and $L_n(s,\mathbf{t}_j)$ are absolutely convergent for $\sigma > \sigma_a$ with arbitrary finite σ_a and fixed $n \in \mathbb{N}$. Let
$$\underline{L}_n(s + ik\underline{h}) = \bigl(L_n(s + ikh_1),\dots,L_n(s + ikh_r)\bigr)$$
and
$$\underline{L}_n(s,\mathbf{t}) = \bigl(L_n(s,\mathbf{t}_1),\dots,L_n(s,\mathbf{t}_r)\bigr).$$

Moreover, let $\mathcal{H}(D_L)$ stand for the space of analytic on D_L functions endowed with the topology of uniform convergence on compact sets, and let
$$\mathcal{H}^r(D_L) = \prod_{j=1}^{r} \mathcal{H}(D_L).$$

For $A \in \mathcal{B}(\mathcal{H}^r(D_L))$, we set
$$P_{N,n,\underline{h}}(A) = \frac{1}{N+1}\#\{0 \leq k \leq N : \underline{L}_n(s + ik\underline{h}) \in A\}.$$

Proposition 2. On $(\mathcal{H}^r(D_L), \mathcal{B}(\mathcal{H}^r(D_L)))$, a probability measure P_n exists such that $P_{N,n,\underline{h}} \xrightarrow[N\to\infty]{w} P_n$.

Proof. Let the mapping $u_n : \mathbb{T}^r \to \mathcal{H}^r(D_L)$ be given by $u_n(\mathbf{t}) = \underline{L}_n(s,\mathbf{t})$. The absolute convergence of the series for $L_n(s,\mathbf{t}_j), j = 1,\dots,r$, implies the continuity of u_n. Hence, u_n is

$(\mathbb{T}^r, \mathcal{H}^r(D_L))$-measurable. Therefore, every probability measure P on $(\mathbb{T}^r, \mathcal{B}(\mathbb{T}^r))$ induces the unique probability measure $P u_n^{-1}$ on $(\mathcal{H}^r(D_L), \mathcal{B}(\mathcal{H}^r(D_L)))$ given by

$$P u_n^{-1}(A) = P(u_n^{-1} A), \quad A \in \mathcal{B}(\mathcal{H}^r(D_L)).$$

Let $Q_{N,\mathbb{T}^r,\underline{h}}$ be from Proposition 1. Then, for every $A \in \mathcal{B}(\mathcal{H}^r(D_L))$,

$$\begin{aligned} P_{N,n,\underline{h}}(A) &= \frac{1}{N+1} \#\left\{ 0 \le k \le N : ((p^{-ikh_j} : p \in \mathbb{P}), j = 1, \ldots, r) \in u_n^{-1} A \right\} \\ &= Q_{N,\mathbb{T}^r,\underline{h}}(u_n^{-1} A) = Q_{N,\mathbb{T}^r,\underline{h}} u_n^{-1}(A). \end{aligned}$$

Hence, we have $P_{N,n,\underline{h}} = Q_{N,\mathbb{T}^r,\underline{h}} u_n^{-1}$. Therefore, Proposition 1, the continuity of u_n and Theorem 5.1 in [25] show that $P_{N,n,\underline{h}} \xrightarrow[N\to\infty]{w} P_n$, where $P_n = m^H u_n^{-1}$. □

We see that the measure P_n is independent of $\underline{h}$. This allows us to obtain the weak convergence of P_n as $n \to \infty$, and identify the limit measure. Let

$$L(s, \mathbf{t}_j) = \sum_{m=1}^{\infty} \frac{a(m) \mathbf{t}_j(m)}{m^s}, \quad j = 1, \ldots, r.$$

It is known [8] that the Dirichlet series for $L(s, \mathbf{t}_j)$, for almost all $\mathbf{t}_j$, is uniformly convergent on compact subsets of the strip D_L. Thus, $L(s, \mathbf{t}_j)$, for $j = 1, \ldots, r$, is a $\mathcal{H}(D_L)$-valued random element. The probability Haar measure m^H on $(\mathbb{T}, \mathcal{B}(\mathbb{T}))$ is the product of the Haar measure m_j^H on $(\mathbb{T}_j, \mathcal{B}(\mathbb{T}_j))$, i.e., for $A = A_1 \times \ldots \times A_r \in \mathcal{B}(\mathbb{T}^r)$,

$$m^H(A) = m_1^H(A_1) \cdot \ldots \cdot m_r^H(A_r).$$

The above remarks show that

$$\underline{L}(s, \mathbf{t}) = (L(s, \mathbf{t}_1), \ldots, L(s, \mathbf{t}_r))$$

is a $\mathcal{H}^r(D_L)$-valued random element defined on the probability space $(\mathbb{T}^r, \mathcal{B}(\mathbb{T}^r))$. We denote by $P_{\underline{L}}$ the distribution of $\underline{L}(s, \mathbf{t})$.

The measure P_n coincides with that studied in the continuous case in [24]. Therefore, we have the following proposition.

Lemma 1. *The relation* $P_n \xrightarrow[n\to\infty]{w} P_{\underline{L}}$ *holds. Moreover, the support of the measure $P_{\underline{L}}$ is set as*

$$\left(\{ g \in \mathcal{H}(D_L) : \text{either } g(s) \ne 0 \text{ or } g(s) \equiv 0 \} \right)^r.$$

Proof. The first assertion of the lemma is contained in Lemma 7 in [24], while the second one is in Lemma 9 in [24]. □

3. Limit Theorem

We start this section with a mean value estimate for the collection of L-functions we are interested in.

Let

$$\underline{L}(s + ik\underline{h}) = (L(s + ikh_1), \ldots, L(s + ikh_r)).$$

In this section, we estimate the distance between $\underline{L}(s + ik\underline{h})$ and $L_n(s + ik\underline{h})$ in the mean. Let $\underline{d}$ be the metric on the space $\mathcal{H}^r(D_L)$, i.e., for $\underline{g}_l = (g_{l1}, \ldots, g_{lr})$, $l = 1, 2$,

$$\underline{d}(\underline{g}_1, \underline{g}_2) = \max_{1 \le m \le r} d(g_{1m}, g_{2m}),$$

and d is the metric in $\mathcal{H}(D_L)$ which induces its uniform convergence topology on compact sets.

Lemma 2. *For arbitrary positive fixed numbers $h_1, \ldots, h_r$,*

$$\lim_{n \to \infty} \limsup_{N \to \infty} \frac{1}{N+1} \sum_{k=0}^{N} d\big(\underline{L}(s+ik\underline{h}), \underline{L}_n(s+ik\underline{h})\big) = 0.$$

Proof. Since

$$d(g_1, g_2) = \sum_{j=1}^{\infty} 2^{-j} \frac{\sup_{s \in K_j} |g_1(s) - g_2(s)|}{1 + \sup_{s \in K_j} |g_1(s) - g_2(s)|}, \quad g_1, g_2 \in \mathcal{H}(D_L),$$

where $\{K_j : j \in \mathbb{N}\} \subset D_L$ is a certain sequence of compact sets, it suffices to show that, for every compact set $K \subset D_L$,

$$\lim_{n \to \infty} \limsup_{N \to \infty} \frac{1}{N+1} \sum_{k=0}^{N} \sup_{s \in K} |L(s+ikh_j) - L_n(s+ikh_j)| = 0, \quad j = 1, \ldots, r. \tag{4}$$

We fix a compact set K, a positive number h, and $L(s) \in \widetilde{S}$. We use the integral representation [24]

$$L_n(s) = \frac{1}{2\pi i} \int_{\beta - i\infty}^{\beta + i\infty} L(s+z) l_n(z; \beta) dz, \tag{5}$$

where

$$l_n(s; \beta) = \frac{1}{\beta} \Gamma\left(\frac{s}{\beta}\right) n^s,$$

and the fixed number $\beta > \frac{1}{2}$ is the same as in the definition of $v_n(m; \beta)$. There exists $\delta = \delta(K)$ such that $\sigma_L + 2\delta \leq \sigma \leq 1 - \delta$ for $\sigma + it \in K$. Thus, $\beta_1 \stackrel{def}{=} \sigma - \sigma_L - \delta > 0$. Let $\beta = \sigma_L + \delta$. The integrand in (5) has a simple pole at the point $z = 0$, and a possible simple pole at the point $z = 1 - s$. Therefore, by the residue theorem and (1),

$$L_n(s) - L(s) = \frac{1}{2\pi i} \int_{-\beta_1 - i\infty}^{-\beta_1 + i\infty} L(s+z) l_n(z; \beta) dz + r(s),$$

where

$$r(s) = \operatorname*{Res}_{z=1-s} L(s+z) l_n(z; \beta) = \gamma l_n(1-s; \beta),$$

and $\gamma = \operatorname{Res}_{s=1} L(s)$. If $\alpha = 0$ in Axiom (2), then $r(s) = 0$. Hence, for $s = \sigma + it \in K$,

$$L(s+ikh) - L_n(s+ikh)$$
$$= \frac{1}{2\pi i} \int_{-\infty}^{\infty} L(s+ikh+\sigma_L - \sigma + \delta + i\tau) l_n(\sigma_L - \sigma + \delta + i\tau; \beta) d\tau + r(s+ikh)$$
$$= \frac{1}{2\pi i} \int_{-\infty}^{\infty} L(\sigma_L + \delta + ikh + i\tau) l_n(\sigma_L + \delta - s + i\tau) d\tau + r(s+ikh)$$
$$\ll \int_{-\infty}^{\infty} |L(\sigma_L + \delta + ikh + i\tau)| \sup_{s \in K} |l_n(\sigma_L + \delta - s + i\tau)| d\tau + \sup_{s \in K} |r(s+ikh)|.$$

From this, we have

$$\frac{1}{N+1} \sum_{k=2}^{N} \sup_{s \in K} |L(s+ikh) - L_n(s+ikh)|$$

$$\ll \int_{-\infty}^{\infty} \left(\frac{1}{N+1} \sum_{k=2}^{N} |L(\sigma_L + \delta + ikh + i\tau)| \right) \sup_{s \in K} |l_n(\sigma_L + \delta - s + i\tau)| d\tau$$

$$+ \frac{1}{N+1} \sum_{k=2}^{N} \sup_{s \in K} |r(s+ikh)|. \tag{6}$$

By the Cauchy–Schwarz inequality,

$$\frac{1}{N+1}\sum_{k=2}^{N}|L(\sigma_L+\delta+ikh+i\tau)| \ll \left(\frac{1}{N}\sum_{k=2}^{N}|L(\sigma_L+\delta+ikh+i\tau)|^2\right)^{\frac{1}{2}}. \qquad (7)$$

To estimate the last mean square, we apply the Gallagher lemma, see Lemma 1.4 in [26], and the known estimate [8]

$$\int_{-T}^{T}|L(\sigma+it)|^2 dt \ll_\sigma T \qquad (8)$$

which is valid for fixed σ, $\sigma_L < \sigma < 1$. Application of the Gallagher lemma gives

$$\sum_{k=2}^{N}|L(\sigma_L+\delta+ikh+i\tau)|^2$$

$$\ll_h \int_{\frac{3}{2}h}^{Nh}|L(\sigma_L+\delta+iv+i\tau)|^2 dv +$$

$$+ \left(\int_{\frac{3}{2}h}^{Nh}|L(\sigma_L+\delta+iv+i\tau)|^2 dv \int_{\frac{3}{2}h}^{Nh}|L'(\sigma_L+\delta+iv+i\tau)|^2 dv\right)^{\frac{1}{2}}. \qquad (9)$$

The Cauchy integral formula together with (8) gives, for $\sigma_L < \sigma < 1$, the bound

$$\int_{-T}^{T}|L'(\sigma+it)|^2 dt \ll_\sigma T.$$

This, and (8) and (9) lead to the estimate

$$\sum_{k=2}^{N}|L(\sigma_L+\delta+ikh+i\tau)|^2 \ll_{h,\delta} N(1+|\tau|). \qquad (10)$$

To estimate $l_n(\sigma_L+\delta-s+i\tau)$ for $s \in K$, we use the well-known estimate

$$\Gamma(\sigma+it) \ll e^{-c|t|}, \quad c > 0,$$

which is valid for large $|t|$ uniformly in any fixed strip. Thus, for $s \in K$, we find

$$l_n(\sigma_L+\delta-s+i\tau) \ll_\beta n^{\sigma_L+\delta-\sigma}e^{-\frac{c}{\beta}|\tau-t|} \ll_{\beta,K} n^{-\delta}c^{-c_1|\tau|}$$

with $c_1 > 0$. Now, the latter estimate, and (7) and (10) show that

$$\int_{-\infty}^{\infty}\left(\frac{1}{N+1}\sum_{k=2}^{N}|L(\sigma_L+\delta+ikh+i\tau)|\right)\sup_{s \in K}|l_n(\sigma_L+\delta-s+i\tau)|d\tau$$

$$\ll_{\beta,K,h,\delta} n^{-\delta}\int_{-\infty}^{\infty}e^{-c_1|\tau|}(1+|\tau|)^{\frac{1}{2}}d\tau \ll_{\beta,K,h,\delta} n^{-\delta}. \qquad (11)$$

Similarly, the definition of $r(s)$ yields that, for $s \in K$,

$$r(s+ikh) \ll_\beta n^{1-\sigma}e^{-\frac{c}{\beta}|kh+t|} \ll_{\beta,K} n^{1-\sigma_L-2\delta}e^{-c_2 kh}$$

with $c_2 > 0$. Hence,

$$\frac{1}{N+1}\sum_{k=2}^{N}\sup_{s\in K}|r(s+ikh)| \ll_{\beta,K} n^{1-\sigma_L-2\delta}\frac{1}{N}\sum_{k=2}^{N}e^{-c_2 kh}$$

$$\ll_{\beta,K,h} n^{1-\sigma_L-2\delta}\left(\frac{\log N}{N}+\frac{1}{N}\sum_{k\geq \log N}^{\infty}e^{-c_2 kh}\right)$$

$$\ll_{\beta,K,h} n^{1-\sigma_L-2\delta}\frac{\log N}{N}.$$

This, and (6) and (11) lead to the estimate

$$\frac{1}{N+1}\sum_{k=2}^{N}\sup_{s\in K}|L(s+ikh)-L_n(s+ikh)| \ll_{\beta,K,h,\delta} \left(n^{-\delta}+n^{1-\sigma_L-2\delta}\frac{\log N}{N}\right).$$

Therefore, taking $N\to\infty$ and then $n\to\infty$, we obtain

$$\lim_{n\to\infty}\liminf_{N\to\infty}\frac{1}{N+1}\sum_{k=2}^{N}\sup_{s\in K}|L(s+ikh)-L_n(s+ikh)|=0.$$

Since, obviously,

$$\lim_{N\to\infty}\frac{1}{N+1}\sum_{k=0}^{1}\sup_{s\in K}|L(s+ikh)-L_n(s+ikh)|=0,$$

thus proving (4). □

Now we are ready to prove the desired joint discrete limit theorem for the collection of L-functions belonging to the class $\widetilde{S}$. For $A\in\mathcal{B}(\mathcal{H}^r(D_L))$, we set

$$P_{N,\underline{h}}(A)=\frac{1}{N+1}\#\{0\le k\le N:\underline{L}(s+ik\underline{h})\in A\}.$$

Let P_n and $P_{\underline{L}}$ be the same as in Lemma 1.

Theorem 6. Suppose that $\underline{L}(s)\in\widetilde{S}$, and the set $A(\mathbb{P},\underline{h},2\pi)$ is linearly independent over $\mathbb{Q}$. Then $P_{N,\underline{h}}\xrightarrow[N\to\infty]{w}P_{\underline{L}}$.

Proof. In view of Lemma 1, it suffices to show that P_n and $P_{N,\underline{h}}$ have the same limit measure as $n\to\infty$ and $N\to\infty$, respectively. We denote by $\xrightarrow{\mathcal{D}}$ the convergence in distribution. On some probability space $(\Omega,\mathcal{A},P)$, we define the random variable $\tilde{\zeta}_N$ by

$$P\{\tilde{\zeta}_N=k\}=\frac{1}{N+1},\quad k=0,1,\ldots,N.$$

Let the $\mathcal{H}^r(D_L)$-valued random elements $X_{N,n,\underline{h}}$ and $X_{N,\underline{h}}$ be defined by

$$X_{N,n,\underline{h}}=X_{N,n,\underline{h}}(s)=\underline{L}_n(s+i\underline{h}\tilde{\zeta}_N)$$

and

$$X_{N,\underline{h}}=X_{N,\underline{h}}(s)=\underline{L}(s+i\underline{h}\tilde{\zeta}_N).$$

Then the assertion of Proposition 2 can be written in the form

$$X_{N,n,\underline{h}}\xrightarrow[N\to\infty]{\mathcal{D}}P_n. \tag{12}$$

Moreover, by Lemma 1,

$$X_n\xrightarrow[n\to\infty]{\mathcal{D}}P_{\underline{L}}, \tag{13}$$

where X_n is the $\mathcal{H}^r(D_L)$-valued random element with distribution P_n. Application of Lemma 2 and defining the above random elements show that, for $\epsilon>0$,

$$\lim_{n\to\infty}\limsup_{N\to\infty}P\{\underline{d}(X_{N,\underline{h}},X_{N,n,\underline{h}})\ge\epsilon\}$$

$$=\lim_{n\to\infty}\limsup_{N\to\infty}\frac{1}{N+1}\#\left\{0\le k\le N:\underline{d}\bigl(\underline{L}(s+ik\underline{h}),\underline{L}_n(s+ik\underline{h})\bigr)\ge\epsilon\right\}$$

$$\le\frac{1}{\epsilon(N+1)}\sum_{k=0}^{N}\underline{d}\bigl(\underline{L}(s+ik\underline{h}),\underline{L}_n(s+ik\underline{h})\bigr)=0.$$

Taking into account the separability of the space $(\mathcal{H}^r(D_L), \underline{d})$, the latter equality, and (12) and (13), we deduce that the hypotheses of Theorem 4.2 in [25] are satisfied. Therefore, we have

$$X_{N,\underline{h}} \xrightarrow[N\to\infty]{\mathcal{D}} P_{\underline{L}}.$$

From last relation we obtain the assertion of the theorem. □

4. Proof of Theorem 5

The proof of Theorem 5 we derive from Theorem 6, Lemma 1 and the Mergelyan theorem mentioned in Section 1 (see [4]).

Proof of Theorem 5. Since $f_j(s) \neq 0$ on K_j, application of the Megelyan theorem for $\log f_j(s)$ implies the existence of polynomials $q_1(s), \ldots, q_r(s)$ such that

$$\sup_{1\leq j\leq r}\sup_{s\in K_j}\left|f_j(s) - e^{q_j(s)}\right| < \frac{\epsilon}{2}. \tag{14}$$

In view of the second part of Lemma 1, the tuple $\left(e^{q_1(s)}, \ldots, e^{q_r(s)}\right)$ is an element of the support of the measure $P_{\underline{L}}$. Therefore, the set

$$\mathcal{G}(\epsilon) = \left\{(g_1, \ldots, g_r) \in \mathcal{H}^r(D_L) : \sup_{1\leq j\leq r}\sup_{s\in K_j}|g_j(s) - e^{q_j(s)}| < \frac{\epsilon}{2}\right\}$$

is an open neighbourhood of the support element, and thus by a property of supports,

$$P_{\underline{L}}(\mathcal{G}(\epsilon)) > 0. \tag{15}$$

Now, Theorem 6 and Theorem 2.1 in [25] give

$$\liminf_{N\to\infty} P_{N,n,\underline{h}}(\mathcal{G}(\epsilon)) \geq P_{\underline{L}}(\mathcal{G}(\epsilon)) > 0. \tag{16}$$

Inequality (14) shows the inclusion of $\mathcal{G}(\epsilon) \subset \mathcal{G}_1(\epsilon)$, where

$$\mathcal{G}_1(\epsilon) = \left\{(g_1, \ldots, g_r) \in \mathcal{H}^r(D_L) : \sup_{1\leq j\leq r}\sup_{s\in K_j}|g_j(s) - f_j(s)| < \epsilon\right\}.$$

Therefore, by (16),

$$\liminf_{N\to\infty} P_{N,n,\underline{h}}(\mathcal{G}_1(\epsilon)) > 0,$$

and we have the first assertion of the theorem.

For the proof of second inequality of the theorem, we observe that, for different values of ϵ, the boundaries of $\mathcal{G}_1(\epsilon)$ do not intersect. This remark implies that the set $\mathcal{G}_1(\epsilon)$ is a continuity set of the measure $P_{\underline{L}}$ for all but at most countably many $\epsilon > 0$. This result, Theorem 6 and Theorem 2.1 in [25], in virtue of (15), imply

$$\liminf_{N\to\infty} P_{N,n,\underline{h}}(\mathcal{G}_1(\epsilon)) = P_{\underline{L}}(\mathcal{G}_1(\epsilon)) \geq P_{\underline{L}}(\mathcal{G}(\epsilon)) > 0$$

for all but at most countably many $\epsilon > 0$.

Theorem 5 is therefore proven. □

5. Concluding Remarks

In this paper we have obtained that every tuple $(f_1(s), \ldots, f_r(s))$ of analytic non-vanishing functions in the strip D_L can be approximated simultaneously by discrete shifts $(L(s + ikh_1), \ldots, L(s + ikh_r))$, where $L(s)$ is a Dirichlet series from the Selberg–Steuding class, and the multiset $\{(h_j \log p : p \in \mathbb{P}), j = 1, \ldots, r; 2\pi\}$ with positive $h_1, \ldots, h_r$ is linearly independent over a field of rational numbers. For proof of the above theorem, results of a continuous universality theorem from [24] were applied.

We conjecture that Theorem 5 can be extended to include approximations by shifts $(L_1(s+ikh_1),\dots,L_r(s+ikh_r))$, where $L_1(s),\dots,L_r(s)$ are functions from the Selberg–Steuding class. For this, a modification to Lemma 1 is needed.

Author Contributions: Conceptualization, R.K., A.L. and B.Ž.; methodology, R.K., A.L. and B.Ž.; investigation, R.K., A.L. and B.Ž.; writing—original draft preparation, R.K., A.L. and B.Ž.; writing—review and editing, R.K., A.L. and B.Ž. All authors have read and agreed to the published version of the manuscript.

Funding: This research received no external funding.

Institutional Review Board Statement: Not applicable.

Informed Consent Statement: Not applicable.

Data Availability Statement: Not applicable.

Acknowledgments: The authors thank the referees for their useful remarks and comments.

Conflicts of Interest: The authors declare no conflict of interest.

References

1. Voronin, S.M. Theorem on the "universality" of the Riemann zeta-function. *Math. USSR-Izv.* **1975**, *9*, 443–453. [CrossRef]
2. Karatsuba, A.A.; Voronin, S.M. *The Riemann Zeta-Function*; De Gruyter Expositions in Mathematics 5; W. de Gruyter: Berlin, Germany, 1992.
3. Bohr, H.; Courant, R. Neue Anwendungen der Theorie der diophantischen Approximationen auf die Riemannsche Zetafunktion. *J. Math.* **1914**, *144*, 249–274. [CrossRef]
4. Mergelyan, S.N. Uniform approximations to functions of a complex variable. *Am. Math. Soc. Transl.* **1952**, *101*, 99.
5. Laurinčikas, A. *Limit Theorems for the Riemann Zeta-Function*; Kluwer Academic Publishers: Dordrecht, The Netherlands; Boston, MA, USA; London, UK, 1996.
6. Bagchi, B. The Statistical Behaviour and Universality Properties of the Riemann Zeta-Function and Other Allied Dirichlet Series. Ph.D. Thesis, Indian Statistical Institute, Calcutta, India, 1981.
7. Gonek, S.M. Analytic Properties of Zeta and *L*-Functions. Ph.D. Thesis, University of Michigan, Ann Arbor, MI, USA, 1979.
8. Steuding, J. *Value Distribution of L-Functions*; Lecture Notes Math 1877; Springer: Berlin/Heidelberg, Germany; New York, NY, USA, 2007.
9. Matsumoto, K. A survey on the theory of universality for zeta and *L*-functions. In *Number Theory. Plowing and Starring through High Wave Forms, Proceedings of 7th China-Japan Seminar, Fukuoka, Japan, 28 October–1 November 2013*; Kaneko, M., Kanemitsu, S., Liu, J., Eds.; Series on Number Theory and Its Applications 11; World Scientific: Hackensack, NJ, USA, 2015; pp. 95–144.
10. Reich, A. Werteverteilung von Zetafunktionen. *Arch. Math.* **1980**, *34*, 440–451. [CrossRef]
11. Laurinčikas, A.; Šiaučiūnas, D. Remarks on the universality of the periodic zeta function. *Math. Notes* **2006**, *80*, 532–538. [CrossRef]
12. Laurinčikas, A.; Garunkštis, R. *The Lerch Zeta-Function*; Kluwer Academic Publishers: Dordrecht, The Netherlands; Boston, MA, USA; London, UK, 2002.
13. Sourmelidis, A.; Steuding, J. On the value-distribution of Hurwitz zeta-functions with algebraic parameter. *Constr. Approx.* **2022**, *55*, 829–860. [CrossRef]
14. Selberg, A. Old and new conjectures and results about a class of Dirichlet series. In Proceedings of the Amalfi Conference on Analytic Number Theory, Maiori, Amalfi, Italy, 25–29 September 1989; Bombieri, E., Ed.; Universitá di Salerno: Salerno, Italy, 1992; pp. 367–385.
15. Selberg, A. *Collected Papers. Volume I. Reprint of the 1989 Original*; Springer Collected Works in Mathematics; Springer: Berlin/Heidelberg, Germany, 2014.
16. Kaczorowski, J.; Perelli, A. On the structure of the Selberg class. II. Invariants and conjectures. *J. Reine Angew. Math.* **2000**, *524*, 73–96. [CrossRef]
17. Kaczorowski, J.; Perelli, A. On the structure of the Selberg class. IV. Basic invariants. *Acta Arith.* **2002**, *104*, 97–116. [CrossRef]
18. Kaczorowski, J.; Perelli, A. On the prime number theorem for the Selberg class. *Arch. Math.* **2003**, *80*, 255–263.
19. Perelli, A. Non-linear twists of *L*-functions: A survey. *Milan J. Math.* **2010**, *78*, 117–134. [CrossRef]
20. Kaczorowski, J.; Perelli, A. Structural invariants of *L*-functions and applications: A survey. *Riv. Mat. Univ. Parma (N.S.)* **2022**, *13*, 137–159.
21. Nagoshi, H.; Steuding, J. Universality for *L*-functions in the Selberg class. *Lith. Math. J.* **2010**, *50*, 293–311. [CrossRef]
22. Laurinčikas, A.; Macaitienė, R. Discrete universality in the Selberg class. *Proc. Steklov Inst. Math.* **2017**, *299*, 143–156. [CrossRef]
23. Voronin, S.M. On the functional independence of Dirichlet *L*-functions. *Acta Arith.* **1975**, *27*, 493–503. (In Russian)

24. Kačinskaitė, R.; Laurinčikas, A.; Žemaitienė, B. On joint universality in the Selberg–Steuding class. *Mathematics* **2023**, *11*, 737. [CrossRef]
25. Billingsley, P. *Convergence of Probability Measures*, 2nd ed.; Willey: Chichester, UK, 1999.
26. Montgomery, H.L. *Topics in Multiplicative Number Theory*; Lecture Notes in Mathematics 227; Springer: Berlin/Heidelberg, Germany, 1971.

Disclaimer/Publisher's Note: The statements, opinions and data contained in all publications are solely those of the individual author(s) and contributor(s) and not of MDPI and/or the editor(s). MDPI and/or the editor(s) disclaim responsibility for any injury to people or property resulting from any ideas, methods, instructions or products referred to in the content.

Article

Scalar-on-Function Relative Error Regression for Weak Dependent Case

Zouaoui Chikr Elmezouar [1], Fatimah Alshahrani [2], Ibrahim M. Almanjahie [1], Zoulikha Kaid [1], Ali Laksaci [1] and Mustapha Rachdi [3,*]

[1] Department of Mathematics, College of Science, King Khalid University, Abha 62223, Saudi Arabia; zchikrelmezouar@kku.edu.sa (Z.C.E.); imalmanjahi@kku.edu.sa (I.M.A.); zqayd@kku.edu.sa (Z.K.); alikfa@kku.edu.sa (A.L.)
[2] Department of Mathematical Sciences, College of Science, Princess Nourah bint Abdulrahman University, Riyadh 11671, Saudi Arabia; fmalshahrani@pnu.edu.sa
[3] Laboratory AGEIS, University of Grenoble Alpes, UFR SHS, BP. 47, Cedex 09, F38040 Grenoble, France
* Correspondence: mustapha.rachdi@univ-grenoble-alpes.fr; Tel.: +33-4-76-82-58-53

Abstract: Analyzing the co-variability between the Hilbert regressor and the scalar output variable is crucial in functional statistics. In this contribution, the kernel smoothing of the Relative Error Regression (RE-regression) is used to resolve this problem. Precisely, we use the relative square error to establish an estimator of the Hilbertian regression. As asymptotic results, the Hilbertian observations are assumed to be quasi-associated, and we demonstrate the almost complete consistency of the constructed estimator. The feasibility of this Hilbertian model as a predictor in functional time series data is discussed. Moreover, we give some practical ideas for selecting the smoothing parameter based on the bootstrap procedure. Finally, an empirical investigation is performed to examine the behavior of the RE-regression estimation and its superiority in practice.

Keywords: complete convergence (a.co.); relative error regression; nonparametric prediction; kernel method; bandwidth parameter; functional data; financial time series; quasi-associated process

MSC: 62R20; 62G05; 62G08

1. Introduction

This paper focuses on nonparametric prediction in Hilbertian statistics, which is an intriguing area of research within nonparametric Hilbertian statistics. Various approaches exist for modeling the relationship between the input Hilbertian variable and the output real variable. Typically, this relationship is modeled through a regression model, where the regression operators are estimated using the least square error. However, this rule is not relevant for some practical cases. Instead, we consider in this paper the relative square error. The primary advantage of this regression is the possibility of reducing the effect of the outliers. This kind of relative error is used as a performance measure in many practical situations, namely in time series forecasting. The literature on the subject of nonparametric analysis is limited. Most existing works consider a parametric approach. In particular, Narula and Wellington [1] were the first to investigate the use of the relative square error in the estimation method. For practical purposes, relative regression has been applied in areas such as medicine by Chatfield [2] and financial data by Chen et al. [3]. Yang and Ye [4] considered the estimation by RE-regression in multiplicative regression models. Jones et al. [5] also focused on the use of this model but with the nonparametric estimation method and stated the convergence of the local linear estimator obtained by the relative error as a loss function. The RE-regression estimation has been deeply studied for time series data in the last few years, specifically by Mechab and Laksaci [6] for the quasi-associated time series, and Attouch et al. [7] for the spatial process. The nonparametric

Hilbertian RE-regression was first developed by Demongeot et al. [8], who focused on strong consistency and gave the asymptotic law of the RE-regression. To summarize, functional statistics is an attractive subject in mathematical statistics; the reader may refer to some survey papers, such as [9–15], for recent advances and trends in functional data analysis and/or functional time series analysis.

In this article, we focus on the Hilbertian RE-regression for weak functional time series data. In particular, the correlation of our observations is modeled by using the quasi-association assumption. This correlation includes many important Hilbertian time series cases, such as the linear and Gaussian processes, as well as positive and negative associated processes. Our ambition in this contribution is to build a new Hilbertian predictor in the Hilbertian time series. This predictor is defined as the ratio of the first and the second inverted conditional moments. We use this explicit expression to construct two estimators based on the kernel smoothing and/or k-Neighbors Number (kNN). We prove a strong consistency of the constructed estimator, which provides good mathematical support for its use in practice. Thus, treating the functional RE-regression by the kNN method under quasi-associated assumption is a great theoretical development which requires nonstandard mathematical tools and techniques. On the one hand, it is well known that the establishment of the asymptotic property in the kNN method is more difficult than the classical kernel estimation due to the random feature of the bandwidth parameter. On the other hand, our weak structure of the functional time series data requires additional techniques and mathematical tools alternative to those used in the mixing case. Clearly, this theoretical development is very useful in practice because the kNN estimator is more accurate than the kernel method and the quasi-association structure is sufficiently weak to cover a large class of functional time series data. Furthermore, the applicability of this estimator is highlighted by giving some selection procedures to determine the parameters involved in the estimator. Then, real data are used to emphasize the superiority and impact of this contribution in practice.

This paper is organized as follows. We introduce the estimation algorithms in Section 2. The required conditions, as well as the main asymptotic results, are demonstrated in Section 3. We discuss some selectors for the smoothing parameter in Section 4. The constructed estimator's performance over the artificial data is evaluated in Section 5. Finally, we state our conclusion in Section 6 and demonstrate proofs of the technical results in the Appendix A.

2. The Re-Regression Model and Its Estimation

As discussed in the introduction, we aim to evaluate the relationship between an exogenous Hilbertian variable X and a real endogenous variable Y. Specifically, the variables (X, Y) belong in $\mathcal{H} \times \mathbb{R}$. The set $\mathcal{H}$ constitutes a separable Hilbert space. We assume that the norm $\|\cdot\|$ in $\mathcal{H}$ is associated with the inner product $\langle \cdot, \cdot \rangle$. Furthermore, we define on $\mathcal{H}$ a complete orthonormal basis $(e_k)_{k \geq 1}$. In addition, we suppose that Y is strictly positive, and we suppose that the Hilbertian operators $\mathbb{E}[Y^{-1}|X]$ and $\mathbb{E}[Y^{-2}|X]$ exist and are, almost surely, finite. The RE-regression is defined by

$$R(x) = \arg\min_{\theta} \mathbb{E}\left(\left(\frac{Y - \theta}{Y} \right)^2 \bigg| X = x \right). \tag{1}$$

By differentiating with respect to θ, we prove that

$$R(x) = \frac{\mathbb{E}[Y^{-1}|X = x]}{\mathbb{E}[Y^{-2}|X = x]}. \tag{2}$$

Clearly, the RE-regression $R(\cdot)$ is a good alternative to the traditional regression, in the sense that, the traditional regression, based on the least square error, treats all variables with equal weight. This is inadequate when the observations contain some outliers. Thus, the traditional regression can lead to irrelevant results in the presence of outliers. Thus, the main advantage of the RE-regression $R(\cdot)$ compared to the traditional regression is the possibility to reduce the effect of the outliers (see Equation (1)). So, we can say that the robustness feature is one of the main advantages of the RE-regression. Additionally, unlike the classical robust regression (the M-egression), the RE-regression is very easy to implement in practice. It has an explicit definition based on the ratio of the first and the second inverted conditional moments (see Equation (2)).

Now, consider $(X_i, Y_i)_{i=1,\ldots,n}$ strictly stationary observations, as copies of a couple (X, Y). The Hilbertian time series framework of the present contribution is carried out using the quasi-association setting (see Douge [16] for the definition of the Hilbert space). We use the kernel estimators of the inverse moments $\mathbb{E}[Y^{-1}|X]$ and $\mathbb{E}[Y^{-2}|X]$ as conditional expectations of $Y^{-\gamma}$ ($\gamma = 1, 2$), given $X = x$, to estimate $R(x)$ by

$$\widetilde{R}(x) = \frac{\sum_{i=1}^{n} Y_i^{-1} K\left(\frac{\|x - X_i\|}{h_n}\right)}{\sum_{i=1}^{n} Y_i^{-2} K\left(\frac{\|x - X_i\|}{h_n}\right)}, \tag{3}$$

where h_n is a positive sequence of real numbers, and K is a real-function so-called kernel. The choice of h_n is the determining issue of the applicability of the estimator $\widetilde{R}$. A common solution is to utilize kernel smoothing with the kNN estimation, for which

$$\widehat{R}(x) = \frac{\sum_{i=1}^{n} Y_i^{-1} K\left(\frac{\|x - X_i\|}{A_n^k}\right)}{\sum_{i=1}^{n} Y_i^{-2} K\left(\frac{\|x - X_i\|}{A_n^k}\right)}, \tag{4}$$

where

$$A_n^k(x) = \min\left\{a_n > 0; \ \sum_{i=1}^{n} \mathbb{1}_{B(x, a_n)}(X_i) = k\right\},$$

where $B(x, a_n)$ is an open ball of radius $a_n > 0$ centered x. In $\widehat{R}$, the smoothing parameter is the number k. Once again, the selection of k is crucial.

3. The Consistency of the Kernel Estimator

We demonstrate the almost complete convergence of $\widetilde{R}(\cdot)$ to $R(\cdot)$ at the fixed point x in $\mathcal{H}$. Hereafter, N_x is the given neighborhood of x, and $C_1, C_2, C, \ldots$ are strictly positive constants. In the sequel, we put $K_i(x) = K(h_n^{-1}\|x - X_i\|)$, $i = 1, \ldots, n$, $R_\gamma(u) = \mathbb{E}[Y^{-\gamma}|X = u]$, and $\gamma = 1, 2$, and we denote this by

$$\lambda_k := \sup_{s \geq k} \sum_{|i-j| \geq s} \sum_{k=1}^{\infty} \sum_{l=1}^{\infty} |Cov(X_j^k, X_i^k)| + \sum_{k=1}^{\infty} |Cov(Y_j, X_i^k)| + \sum_{l=1}^{\infty} |Cov(X_j^l, Y_i)| + |Cov(Y_j, Y_i)|,$$

where $X_i^k := \langle X_i, e_k \rangle$. Moreover, we assume the following conditions:

(D1) For all $d > 0$ $\phi_x(d) := \mathbb{P}(X \in B(x, d)) > 0$, and $\lim_{d \to 0} \phi_x(d) = 0$.

(D2) For all $(x_1, x_2) \in \mathcal{N}_x^2$,

$$|R_\gamma(x_2) - R_\gamma(x_1)| \leq C \, d^{k_\gamma}(x_2, x_1) \ \text{for } k_1, k_2 > 0.$$

(D3) The covariance coefficient is $(\lambda_k)_{k \in \mathbb{N}}$, such that $\lambda_k \leq C e^{-ak}$, $a > 0$, $C > 0$.

(D4) K is the Lipschitzian kernel function, which has $(0, 1)$ as support and satisfies the following:

$$0 < C_2 \leq K(\cdot) \leq C_3 < \infty.$$

(D5) The endogenous variable Y gives:

$$\mathbb{E}[\exp(|Y|^{-\gamma_1})] < C \text{ and } \forall i \neq j \mathbb{E}\left(|Y_i^{-\gamma_2} Y_j^{-\gamma_3}| \, | \, X_i, X_j\right) \leq C' < \infty, \quad (\gamma_i)_{i=1,2,3} = 1, 2.$$

(D6) For all $i \neq j$,

$$0 < \sup_{i \neq j} \mathbb{P}\big[(X_j, X_i) \in B(x,d) \times B(x,d)\big] =\leq C(\phi_x^{\frac{a+1}{a}}(d)).$$

(D7) There exist $\xi \in (0,1)$ and $\xi_1 \in (0, 1-\xi)$, $xi_2 \in (0, a-1)$, such that

$$\frac{\log n^5}{n^{1-\xi-\xi_1}} \leq \phi_x(h_n) \leq \frac{1}{\log n^{1+\xi_2}}.$$

Brief comment on the conditions: Note that the required conditions stated above are standard in the context of Hilbertian time series analysis. Such conditions explore the fundamental axes of this contribution. The functional path of the data is explored through the condition (D1), the nonparametric nature of the model is characterized by (D2), and the correlation degree of the Hilbertian time series is explored by conditions (D3) and (D6). The principal parameters used in the estimator, namely the kernel and the bandwidth parameter, are explored through the conditions, (D4), (D5), and (D6). Such conditions are of a technical nature. They allow for retaining the usual convergence rate in nonparametric Hilbertian time series analysis.

Theorem 1. *Based on the conditions (D1)–(D7), we get*

$$|\widetilde{R}(x) - R(x)| = O(h_n^{k_0}) + O_{a.co.}\left(\sqrt{\frac{\log n}{n^{1-\xi}\phi_x(h_n)}}\right), \tag{5}$$

where $k_0 = \min(k_1, k_2)$.

Proof of Theorem 1. Firstly, we write

$$\widetilde{R}(x) = \frac{\widetilde{R_N}(x)}{\widetilde{R_D}(x)},$$

where

$$\widetilde{R_N}(x) = \frac{1}{n\mathbb{E}[K(h_n^{-1}\|x - X_1\|)]} \sum_{i=1}^n Y_i^{-1} K(h_n^{-1}\|x - X_i\|),$$

and

$$\widetilde{R_D}(x) = \frac{1}{n\mathbb{E}[K(h_n^{-1}\|x - X_1\|)]} \sum_{i=1}^n Y_i^{-2} K(h_n^{-1}\|x - X_i\|).$$

We use a basic decomposition (see Demongeot et al. [8] to deduce that Theorem 1 is a consequence result of the below lemmas). □

Lemma 1. *Using the conditions (D1) and (D3)–(D7), we get*

$$|\widetilde{R_N}(x) - \mathbb{E}\widetilde{R_N}(x)| = O_{a.co.}\left(\sqrt{\frac{\log n}{n^{1-\xi}\phi_x(h_n)}}\right),$$

and

$$|\widetilde{R_D}(x) - \mathbb{E}\widetilde{R_D}(x)| = O_{a.co.}\left(\sqrt{\frac{\log n}{n^{1-\xi}\phi_x(h_n)}}\right).$$

Lemma 2. *Under conditions (D1),(D2), (D4), and (D7), we get*

$$\left|\mathbb{E}\widetilde{R_N}(x) - R_1(x)\right| = O(h_n^{k_1}),$$

and
$$\left|\mathbb{E}\widetilde{R_D}(x) - R_2(x)\right| = O(h_n^{k_2}).$$

Corollary 1. *Using the conditions of Theorem 1, we obtain*
$$\sum_{n=1}^{\infty} P\left(\widetilde{R_D}(x) < \frac{R_2(x)}{2}\right) < \infty.$$

Next, to prove the consistency of $\widehat{R}(x)$, we adopt the following postulates:
(K1) $K(\cdot)$ has a bounded derivative on $[0,1]$;
(K2) The function $\phi_x(\cdot)$, such that

$$\phi_x(a) = \phi(a)L(x) + O(a^\alpha \phi(a)) \quad \text{and} \quad \lim_{a \to 0} \frac{\phi(ua)}{\phi(a)} = \zeta(u),$$

where $L(\cdot)$, ζ are positive and bounded functions, and ϕ is an invertible function;
(K3) There exist $\xi \in (0,1)$ and $\xi_1, \xi_2 > 0$, such that

$$n^{\xi+\xi_1} \log n^5 \leq k \leq n \log n^{-1-\xi_2}.$$

Theorem 2. *Under conditions (D1)–(D6) and (K1)–(K3), we have*

$$|\widehat{R}(x) - R(x)| = O\left(\left(\phi^{-1}\left(\frac{k}{n}\right)\right)^{k_0}\right) + O_{a.co.}\left(\sqrt{\frac{n^\xi \log(n)}{k}}\right). \quad (6)$$

Proof of Theorem 2. Similarly to Theorem 1, write

$$\widehat{R}(x) = \frac{\widehat{R_N}(x)}{\widehat{R_D}(x)},$$

where
$$\widehat{R_N}(x) = \frac{1}{n\mathbb{E}[K(A_n^{k-1}\|x - X_1\|)]} \sum_{i=1}^{n} Y_i^{-1} K(A_n^{k-1}\|x - X_i\|),$$

and $\widehat{R_D}(x) = \frac{1}{n\mathbb{E}[K(A_n^{k-1}\|x - X_1\|)]} \sum_{i=1}^{n} Y_i^{-2} K(A_n^{k-1}\|x - X_i\|),$

and we define, for a sequence $\beta_n \in (0,1)$, such that $\beta_n - 1 = O\left(\left(\phi^{-1}\left(\frac{k}{n}\right)\right)^{k_0} + \sqrt{\frac{n^\xi \log(n)}{k}}\right)$, $h_n^- = \phi^{-1}\left(\frac{\sqrt{\beta_n}k}{n}\right)$, and $h_n^+ = \phi^{-1}\left(\frac{k}{n\sqrt{\beta_n}}\right)$. Using standard evidence (see Bouzebda et al. [17]), we deduce that Theorem 2 is the outcome of Theorem 1 and the two lemmas below. □

Lemma 3. *Under the conditions of Theorem 2, we have*

$$\left|\frac{\sum_{i=1}^{n} K(h_n^{-1}\|x - X_i\|)}{\sum_{i=1}^{n} K(h_n^{+-1}\|x - X_i\|)} - \beta_n\right| = O\left(\left(\phi^{-1}\left(\frac{k}{n}\right)\right)^{k_0}\right) + O_{a.co.}\left(\sqrt{\frac{n^\xi \log(n)}{k}}\right).$$

Lemma 4. *Based on the conditions of Theorem 2, we obtain*

$$\mathbf{1}_{h_n^- \leq \phi^{-1}\left(\frac{k}{n} \leq h_n^+\right)} \to 1, \quad a.co..$$

Corollary 2. *Using the conditions of Theorem 2, we get*

$$|\widehat{R_N}(x) - R_1(x)| = O\left(\left(\phi^{-1}\left(\frac{k}{n}\right)\right)^{k_0}\right) + O_{a.co.}\left(\sqrt{\frac{n^{\xi}\log(n)}{k}}\right),$$

and

$$|\widehat{R_D}(x) - R_2(x)| = O\left(\left(\phi^{-1}\left(\frac{k}{n}\right)\right)^{k_0}\right) + O_{a.co.}\left(\sqrt{\frac{n^{\xi}\log(n)}{k}}\right).$$

4. Smoothing Parameter Selection

The applicability of the estimator is related to the selection of the parameters used for the construction of the estimator $\widehat{R}$. In particular, the bandwidth parameter h_n has a decisive effect on the implementation of this regression in practice. In the literature on nonparametric regression analysis, there are several ways to achieve this issue. In this paper, we adopt two approaches common in classical regression to the relative one. The two selections are the cross-validation rule and the bootstrap algorithm.

4.1. Leave-One-Out Cross-Validation Principle

In classical regression, the leave-one-out cross-validation rule is obtained using the mean square error. This criterion has been employed for predicting Hilbertian time series by several authors in the past (see Feraty and View [18] for some references). The leave-one-out cross-validation rule is easy to execute and has shown good behavior in practice. However, it is a relatively time-consuming rule. We overcome this inconvenience by reducing the cardinal of the optimization set of the rule. Thus, we adopt this rule for this kind of regression analysis. Specifically, we consider some subset of smoothing parameters (resp. number of the neighborhood) H_n (resp. K_n), and we select the best bandwidth parameter as follows.

$$h_n^{opt} = \arg\min_{h_n \in H_n} \sum_{i=1}^{n} \left(\frac{(Y_i - \widetilde{R}^{-i}(X_i))^2}{Y_i^2}\right) \qquad (7)$$

or

$$k^{opt} = \arg\min_{k \in K_n} \sum_{i=1}^{n} \left(\frac{(Y_i - \widehat{R}^{-i}(X_i))^2}{Y_i^2}\right),$$

where $\widetilde{R}^{-i}(X_i)$ (resp. $\widehat{R}^{-i}(X_i)$) is the leave-out-one estimator of $\widetilde{R}$ (resp. $\widehat{R}$). The latter is calculated without the observation (X_i, Y_i). It is worth noting that the efficiency of this estimator is also linked to the determination of the subset H_n, where the rule (7) is optimized. Often, we distinguish two cases, the local case and the global case. In the local one, the subset H_n is defined with respect to the number of neighborhoods near the location point. For the global case, the subset H_n is the quantile of the vector distance between the Hilbertian regressors. The choice of K_n is easier, and it suffices to take K_n as a subset of a positive integer. This selection procedure has shown good behavior in practice, but there is no theoretical result concerning its asymptotic optimality. This will be a significant prospect for the future.

4.2. Bootstrap Approach

In addition to the leave-one-out cross-validation rule, the bootstrap method constitutes another important selection method. The principle of the latter is based on the plug-in estimation of the quadratic error. In the rest of this subsection, we describe the principal steps of this selection procedure.

Step 1. We choose an arbitrary bandwidth h_0 (resp. k_0), and we calculate $\widetilde{R}_{h_0}(x)$ (resp. $\widehat{R}_{k_0}(x)$).

Step 2. We estimate $\widetilde{\epsilon} = Y - \widetilde{R}_{h_0}(x)$ (resp. $\widehat{\epsilon} = Y - \widehat{R}_{k_0}(x)$).

Step 3. We create a sample of residual ϵ^* (resp. ϵ^{**}) from the distribution

$$G^* = ((\sqrt{5}+1)/2\sqrt{5})\delta_{\hat{\epsilon}(1-\sqrt{5})/2} - ((1-\sqrt{5})/2\sqrt{5})\delta_{\hat{\epsilon}(\sqrt{5}+1)/2},$$

(resp. $G^* = ((\sqrt{5}+1)/2\sqrt{5})\delta_{\hat{\epsilon}(1-\sqrt{5})/2} - ((1-\sqrt{5})/2\sqrt{5})\delta_{\hat{\epsilon}(\sqrt{5}+1)/2}$),

where δ is the Dirac measure (see Hardle and Marron [19] for more details).

Step 4. We reconstruct the sample $(Y_i^*, X_i^*)_i = (\epsilon^* - \widetilde{R}_{h_0}(X_i), X_i)$, (resp. $(Y_i^{**}, X_i^{**})_i = (\epsilon^{**} - \widehat{R}_{k_0}(X_i), X_i)$,

Step 5. We use the sample $(Y_i^*, X_i^*)_i$ to calculate $\widetilde{R}_{h_0}(X_i)$ and $(Y_i^{**}, X_i^{**})_i$ to calculate $\widehat{R}_{k_0}(X_i)$.

Step 6. We repeat the previous steps N_B times and put $\widetilde{R}_{h_0}^r(X_i)$ (resp. $\widehat{R}_{k_0}^r(X_i)$), the estimators, at the replication r.

Step 7. We select h (resp. k) according to the criteria

$$h_{optBoo} = \arg\min_{h \in H_n} \sum_{r=1}^{N_B} \sum_{i=1}^{n} (\widetilde{R}_h^r(X_i) - \widetilde{R}_{h_0}^r(X_i))^2, \tag{8}$$

and

$$k_{optBoo} = \arg\min_{k \in K_n} \sum_{r=1}^{N_B} \sum_{i=1}^{n} (\widehat{R}_k^r(X_i) - \widetilde{R}_{k_0}^r(X_i))^2.$$

Once again, the choice of the subset H_n (resp. K_n) and the pilot bandwidth h_0 (resp. k_0) have a significant impact on the performance of the estimator. It will be very interesting to combine both approaches in order to benefit from the advantage of both selections. However, the time cost of this idea is very important.

5. Computational Study

5.1. Empirical Analysis

As a theoretical contribution, we wish in this empirical analysis to inspect the easy implementation of the built estimator $\widetilde{R}$ in practice. As the determination of h_n is the principal challenge of the computation ability of $\widetilde{R}$, we compared in this computational study the two selections discussed in the previous section. For this purpose, we conducted an empirical analysis based on artificial data generated through the following nonparametric regression

$$Y_i = \tau(X_i) + \epsilon_i, \qquad i = 1, \ldots, n \tag{9}$$

where $\tau()$ is known regression operator r and (ϵ_i) sequence of independent random variable generated from a Gaussian distribution $\mathcal{N}(0, 0.5)$. The model, in (9), shows the relationship between an endogenous and exogenous variable.

On the other hand, in order to prospect the dependency of the data, we generated the Hilbertian regressor by using the Hilbertian GARCH process through *dgp.fgarch* from the R-package *rockchalk*. We plotted, in Figure 1, a sample of the exogenous curves $X(t)$.

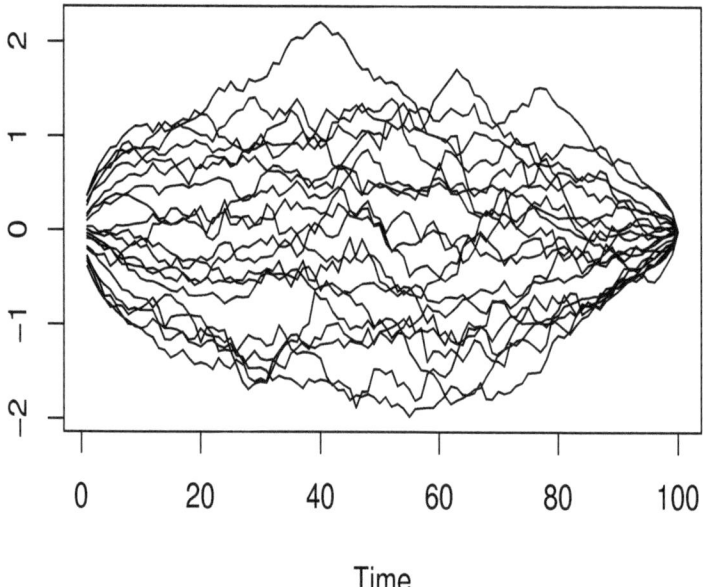

Figure 1. Displayed is a sample of the functional curves.

The endogenous variable Y was generated by

$$\tau(x) = 4 \int_0^\pi \frac{x^2(t)}{1+x^2(t)} dt.$$

For this empirical analysis, we compared the two selectors (7) and (8) with the mixed one obtained by using the optimal h of the rule (7) as the pilot bandwidth in the bootstrap procedure (8). For a fair comparison between the three algorithms, we optimized over the same subset H_n. We selected the optimal h for the three selectors, and the subset H_n of the quantiles of the vector distance between the Hilbertian curves observations of X_i (the order of the quantiles was $\in \{1/5, 1/10, 1/15, 0.5\}$. Finally, based on a quadratic kernel on $(0,1)$, the estimator was computed, and we utilized the L^2 metric associated with the PCA definition based on the $m = 3$ first eigenfunctions of the empirical covariance operator associated with the $m = 3$ greatest eigenvalues (see Ferraty and Vieu [18]).

The efficiency of the estimation method was evaluated by plotting the true response value $(Y_i)_i$ versus the predicted values $\widehat{R}(X_i)$. In addition, we used the relative error defined by

$$RSE = \sum_{i=1}^{n} \left(\frac{(Y_i - \widetilde{R}^{-i}(X_i))^2}{Y_i^2} \right)$$

to evaluate the performance of this simulation study, which performed over 150 replications. The prediction results are depicted in Figure 2.

It shows clearly that the $\widetilde{R}$ of the relative regression was very easy to implement in practice, and both selection algorithms had satisfactory behaviors. Typically the mixed approach performed better compared to the two separate approaches. It had an $RSE = 0.35$. On the other hand, the cross-validation rule had a small superiority ($RSE = 0.52$) over the bootstrap approach $RSE = 0.65$) in this case. Of course, this small superiority was justified by the fact that the efficiency of the bootstrap approach was based on the pilot bandwidth parameter h_0, whereas the cross-validation rule was strongly linked to the relative error loss function.

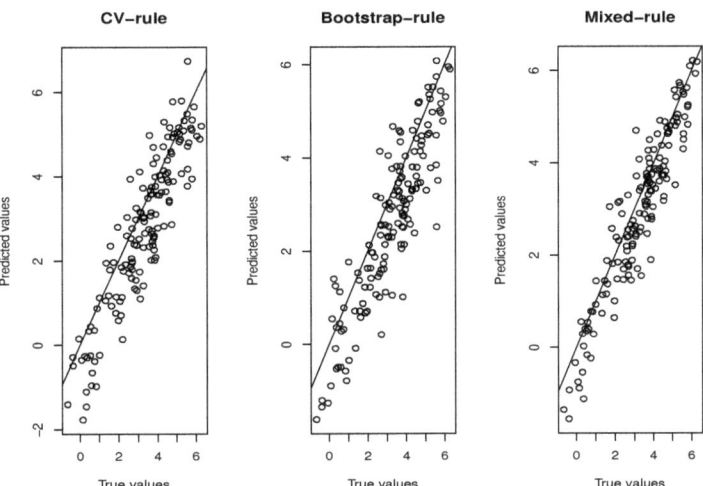

Figure 2. Prediction results.

5.2. A Real Data Application

We devote this paragraph to the real application of the RE-regression as a predictor. Our ambition is to emphasize the robustness of this new regression. To do this, we compared it to the classical regression defined by the conditional expectation. For this purpose, we considered physics data corresponding to the monthly number of sunspots in the years 1749–2021. These data were available at the website of WDC-SILSO, Royal Observatory of Belgium, Brussels, http://www.sidc.be (accessed on 1 April 2023). The prediction of sunspots is very useful in real life. It can be used to forecast the space weather, assess the state of the ionosphere, and define the appropriate conditions of radio shortwave propagation or satellite communications. It is worth noting that these kinds of data can be viewed as a continuous time process, which is the principal source of a Hilbertian time series by cutting the continuous trajectory into small intervals with fixed larger intervals. To fix these ideas, we plotted the initial data in Figure 3.

To predict the value of a sunspot in the future, given its past observations in a continuous path, we use $(Z_t)_{t\in[0,b)}$ the whole data set, as a real-valued process in continuous time. We then constructed, from Z_t, n Hilbertian variables $(X_i)_{i=1,\ldots,n}$, where

$$\forall t \in [0,b), \quad X_i(t) = Z_{n^{-1}((i-1)b+t)}, \quad Y_i = X_i(b).$$

Thus, our objective was to predict Y_n, knowing $(X_i, Y_i)_{i=1,\ldots,n-1}$ and X_n. At this stage, $\widetilde{R}(X_n)$ was the predictor of Y_n. In this computational study, we aimed to forecast the sunspot number one year ahead, given the observation of the past years. Thus, we fixed on month j in $1,\ldots,12$, and computed the estimator $\widetilde{R}$ by the sample $(Y_i^j, X_i)_{i=1\ldots272}$, with Y_i^j as the sunspot number of jth months in the $(i+1)$th year, and we repeated this estimation procedure for all $j = 1,\ldots,12$.

As the main feature of the RE-regression is its insensitivity to the outliers, we examined this property by detecting the number of outliers in each prediction step j. To do this, we used a MAD-Median rule (see Wilcox and Rand [20]). Specifically, the MAD-Median rule considers an observation Y_i as an outlier if

$$\frac{|Y_i - M|}{\text{MAD} * 0.6745} > C,$$

where M and MAD are the medians of $(Y_i)_i$, and $(Y_i - M)_i$ respectively, and $C = \sqrt{\chi^2_{0.975}}$ (with one degree of freedom). Table 1 summarizes the number of outliers for each step j.

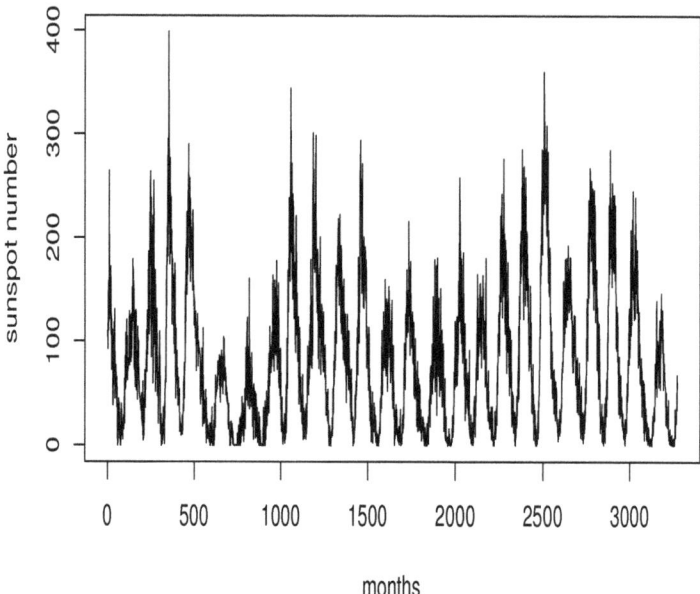

Figure 3. Initial data.

Table 1. Number of outliers with respect to j.

Months	1	2	3	4	5	6	7	8	9	10	11	12
Outliers	15	26	13	5	24	25	7	9	11	8	9	15

Both estimators $\widetilde{R}$ and

$$\widehat{R}(x) = \frac{\sum_{i=1}^{n} Y_i K(h_n^{-1} \|x - X_i\|)}{\sum_{i=1}^{n} K(h_n^{-1} \|x - X_i\|)}$$

were simulated using the quadratic kernel $K(x)$, where

$$K(x) = \frac{3}{2}(1 - x^2) \mathbb{1}_{[0,1]},$$

and norm L^2 was associated with the PCA-metric with $m = 3$. The cross-validation rule (7) is used to choose the smoothing parameter h. Figure 4 shows the prediction results, where we drew two curves showing the predicted values (the dashed curve for the relative regression and the point curve for the classical regression) and the observed values (solid curve).

Figure 4 shows that $\widetilde{R}$ performed better in terms of the prediction results compared to $\widehat{R}$. Even though both predictors had good behavior, the ASE of the relative regression (2.09) was smaller than the classical regression, which was equal to 2.87.

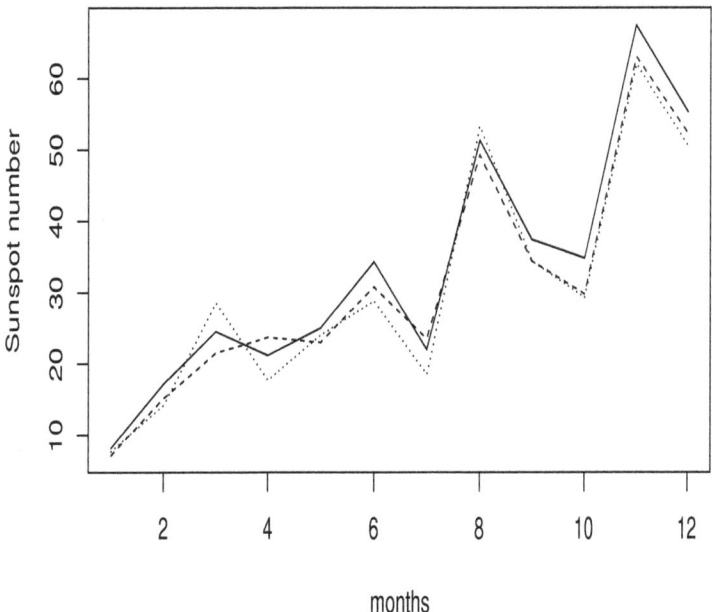

Figure 4. Comparison of the prediction result.

6. Conclusions

In the current contribution, we focused on the kernel estimation of the RE-regression when the observations exhibited quasi-associated autocorrelation. It constituted a new predictor in the Hilbertian time series, an alternative to classical regression based on conditional expectation. Clearly, this new estimator increased the robustness of the classical regression because it reduced the effect of the largest variables. Therefore, it made this Hilbertian model insensitive to the outlier observations; this is the main feature of this kind of regression. We provided in this contribution two rules to select the bandwidth parameter. The first was based on adapting the cross-validation rule to the relative error loss function. The second was obtained by the adaptation of the wild bootstrap algorithm. The simulation experiment highlighted the applicability of both selectors in practice. In addition to these features, the present work opened an important number of questions for the future. First, establishing the asymptotic distribution of the present estimator allows extending the applicability of this model to other applied issues in statistics. The second natural prospect focuses on the treatment of some alternative Hilbertian time series, including the ergodic case, the spatial case, and the β-mixing case, among others. It will also be very interesting to study another type of data (missing, censored, ...) or another estimation method, such as the kNN, local linear method, ..., etc.

Author Contributions: The authors contributed approximately equally to this work. Formal analysis, F.A.; Validation, Z.C.E. and Z.K.; Writing—review & editing, I.M.A., A.L. and M.R. All authors have read and agreed to the published version of the manuscript.

Funding: This research project was funded by the Deanship of Scientific Research, Princess Nourah bint Abdulrahman University, through the Program of Research Project Funding after Publication, grant No. (43-PRFA-P-25).

Data Availability Statement: The data used in this study are available through the link http://www.sidc.be (accessed on 1 April 2023).

Acknowledgments: The authors would like to thank the Associate Editor and the referees for their very valuable comments and suggestions which led to a considerable improvement of the manuscript. The authors also thank and extend their appreciation to the Deanship of Scientific Research, Princess Nourah bint Abdulrahman University for funding this work.

Conflicts of Interest: The authors declare no conflict of interest.

Appendix A

In this appendix, we briefly give the proof of preliminary results; the proofs of Lemmas 3 and 4 are omitted, as they can be obtained straightforwardly through the adaptation of the proof of Bouzebda et al. [17].

Proof of Lemma 1. Clearly, the proof of both terms is very similar. So, we will focus only in the first one. In fact, the difficulty in this kind of proof comes from the fact that the quantity Y_i^{-1} is not bounded. So, to deal with this problem, the truncation method is used to define

$$\widetilde{R}_N^*(x) = \frac{1}{n\,\mathbb{E}[K_1(x)]} \sum_{i=1}^n K\left(h_n^{-1}\|x - X_i\|\right) Y_i^{-1} \mathbb{1}_{|Y_i| > \mu_n} \text{ with } \mu_n = n^{-\xi/6}.$$

Then, the desired result is a consequence of

$$\left|\mathbb{E}[\widetilde{R}_N^*(x)] - \mathbb{E}[\widetilde{R}_N(x)]\right| = O\left(\sqrt{\frac{\log n}{n^{1-\xi}\phi_x(h_n)}}\right), \tag{A1}$$

$$\left|\widetilde{R}_N^*(x) - \widetilde{R}_N(x)\right| = O_{a.co.}\left(\sqrt{\frac{\log n}{n^{1-\xi}\phi_x(h_n)}}\right), \tag{A2}$$

and

$$\left|\widetilde{R}_N^*(x) - \mathbb{E}[\widetilde{R}_N^*(x)]\right| = O_{a.co.}\left(\sqrt{\frac{\log n}{n^{1-\xi}\phi_x(h_n)}}\right). \tag{A3}$$

We start by proving (A3). For this, we write

$$\widetilde{R}_N^*(x) - \mathbb{E}\left[\widetilde{R}_N^*(x)\right] = \sum_{i=1}^n Y_i \quad \text{where} \quad Y_i = \frac{1}{n\,\mathbb{E}[K_1(x)]} \chi(X_i, Y_i),$$

with

$$\chi(z, w) = w^{-1} K(h_n^{-1}\|x - z\|)) \mathbb{1}_{|w| > \mu_n} - \mathbb{E}\left[K_1(x) Y^{-1} \mathbb{1}_{|Y_1| > \mu_n}\right], z \in \mathcal{H}, w \in \mathbb{R}.$$

Observe that,

$$\|\chi\|_\infty \leq C\mu_n^{-1}\|K\|_\infty \text{ and } \mathrm{Lip}(\chi) \leq\leq C\mu_n^{-1}h_n^{-1}\mathrm{Lip}(K).$$

The key tool for proving (A3) is the application of Kallabis and Newmann's inequality (see [21], p. 2). We apply this inequality on Y_i. It requires evaluating asymptotically two quantities: $Var(\sum_{i=1}^n Y_i)$ and $Cov(Y_{s_1} \ldots Y_{s_u}, Y_{t_1} \ldots Y_{t_v})$, for all $(s_1, \ldots, s_u) \in \mathbb{N}^u$ and $(t_1, \ldots, t_v) \in \mathbb{N}^v$.

Concerning the variance term, we write

$$Var\left(\sum_{i=1}^n Y_i\right) = \sum_{i=1}^n \sum_{j=1}^n Cov(Y_i, Y_j) = nVar(Y_1) + \sum_{i=1}^n \sum_{\substack{j=1 \\ j \neq i}}^n Cov(Y_i, Y_j).$$

Note that the above formula has two terms. For the $Var(Y_1)$ and under (D5), we obtain

$$\mathbb{E}\left[Y^{-2}\mathbb{1}_{|Y_1|>\mu_n}K_1^2(x)\right] \leq \mathbb{E}\left[K_1^2(x)\mathbb{E}\left[Y_1^{-2}|X_1\right]\right]$$
$$\leq C\mathbb{E}[K_1^2].$$

Then, we use

$$\mathbb{E}\left[K_1^j(x)\right] = O(\phi_x(h_n))$$

to deduce that

$$Var(Y_1) = O\left(\frac{1}{n\phi_x(h_n)}\right). \tag{A4}$$

Now, we need to examine the covariance term. To do that, we use the techniques of Massry to obtain the decomposition:

$$\sum_{i=1}^{n}\sum_{\substack{j=1\\j\neq i}}^{n}Cov(Y_i,Y_j) = \sum_{i=1}^{n}\sum_{\substack{j=1\\0<|i-j|\leq m_n}}^{n}Cov(Y_i,Y_j)$$
$$+ \sum_{i=1}^{n}\sum_{\substack{j=1\\|i-j|>m_n}}^{n}Cov(Y_i,Y_j)$$
$$=: T_I + T_{II}.$$

Note that (m_n) is a positive sequence of real number integers, which tends to infinity as $n \to \infty$.

We use the second part of (D5) to obtain

$$|Cov(Y_i,Y_j)| \leq C\left|\mathbb{E}[K_i(x)K_j(x)]\right| + \left|\mathbb{E}[K_i(x)]\mathbb{E}[K_j(x)]\right|$$
$$\leq C\left(\phi_x^{(a+1)/a}(h_n) + \phi_x^2(h_n)\right).$$

Therefore,

$$T_I \leq Cnm_n\phi_x^{(a+1)/a}(h_n). \tag{A5}$$

Since the observations are quasi-associated, and the kernel K is bounded, based on the Lipschitz, we obtain

$$T_{II} \leq \left(h_n^{-1}\text{Lip}(K)\right)^2\sum_{i=1}^{n}\sum_{\substack{j=1\\|i-j|>m_n}}^{n}Y_{i,j}$$
$$\leq C\left((\mu_nh)^{-1}\text{Lip}(K)\right)^2\sum_{i=1}^{n}\sum_{\substack{j=1\\|i-j|>m_n}}^{n}Y_{i,j}$$
$$\leq C\left((\mu_nh)^{-1}\text{Lip}(K)\right)^2\sum_{i=1}^{n}\sum_{\substack{j=1\\|i-j|>m_n}}^{n}Y_{i,j}$$
$$\leq Cn\left((\mu_nh)^{-1}\text{Lip}(K)\right)^2Y_{m_n}$$
$$\leq Cn\left((\mu_nh)^{-1}\text{Lip}(K)\right)^2e^{-am_n}. \tag{A6}$$

Then, by (A5) and (A6), we obtain

$$\sum_{i=1}^{n}\sum_{\substack{j=1\\j\neq i}}^{n} Cov(Y_i, Y_j) \leq C\left(nm_n\phi_x^{(a+1)/a}(h_n) + n\left((\mu_n h)^{-1}\mathrm{Lip}(K)\right)^2 e^{-am_n}\right).$$

Putting $m_n = \log\left(\frac{((\mu_n h)^{-1}\mathrm{Lip}(K))^2}{a\phi_x^{(a+1)/a}(h_n)}\right)$, we obtain

$$\frac{1}{n\phi_x(h_n)}\sum_{i=1}^{n}\sum_{\substack{j=1\\j\neq i}}^{n} Cov(Y_i, Y_j) \to 0, \text{ as } n \to \infty. \tag{A7}$$

Combining together results (A4) and (A7), we show that

$$Var\left(\sum_{i=1}^{n} Y_i\right) = O\left(\frac{1}{n\phi_x(h_n)}\right). \tag{A8}$$

We evaluate the covariance term

$$Cov(Y_{s_1}\ldots Y_{s_u}, Y_{t_1}\ldots Y_{t_v}), \quad (s_1,\ldots,s_u,t_1,\ldots,t_v)) \in \mathbb{N}^{u+v}.$$

To do that, we treat the following cases:

- The first case is $t_1 > s_u$; based on the definition of quasi-association, we obtain

$$\begin{aligned}
|Cov(Y_{s_1}\ldots Y_{s_u}, Y_{t_1}\ldots Y_{t_v})| &\leq \left(\left((\mu_n h)^{-1}\mathrm{Lip}(K)\right)^2 (n\mathbb{E}[K_1(x)])^{-1}\right)^2\\
&\qquad \left(\frac{C}{n\mu_n\mathbb{E}[K_1(x)]}\right)^{u+v-2}\sum_{i=1}^{u}\sum_{j=1}^{v} Y_{s_i,t_j}\\
&\leq \left(h_n^{-1}\mathrm{Lip}(K)\right)^2 \left(\frac{C}{n\mu_n\mathbb{E}[K_1(x)]}\right)^{u+v} vY_{t_1-s_u}\\
&\leq \left(h_n^{-1}\mathrm{Lip}(K)\right)^2 \left(\frac{C}{n\mu_n\phi_x(h_n)}\right)^{u+v} ve^{-a(t_1-s_u)}. \tag{A9}
\end{aligned}$$

On the other hand, we have

$$\begin{aligned}
|Cov(Y_{s_1}\ldots Y_{s_u}, Y_{t_1}\ldots Y_{t_v})| &\leq \left(\frac{C\|K\|_\infty}{n\mu_n\mathbb{E}[K_1(x)]}\right)^{u+v-2} \times\\
&\qquad (|\mathbb{E}[Y_{s_u}Y_{t_1}]| + \mathbb{E}|Y_{s_u}|\mathbb{E}|Y_{t_1}|)\\
&\leq \left(\frac{C\|K\|_\infty}{n\mu_n\mathbb{E}[K_1(x)]}\right)^{u+v-2}\left(\frac{C}{n\mu_n\mathbb{E}[K_1(x)]}\right)^2 \times\\
&\qquad \left(\phi_x^{(a+1)/a}(h_n) + \phi_x^2(h_n)\right)\\
&\leq \left(\frac{C}{n\mu_n\phi_x(h_n)}\right)^{u+v}\phi_x^{(a+1)/a}(h_n). \tag{A10}
\end{aligned}$$

Furthermore, taking a $\frac{1}{2(a+1)}$-power of (A9) and a $\left(\frac{2a+1}{a+1}\right)$-power of (A10), we get for $1 \leq s_1 \leq \ldots \leq s_u \leq t_1 \leq \ldots \leq t_v \leq n$:

$$|Cov(Y_{s_1}\ldots Y_{s_u}, Y_{t_1}\ldots Y_{t_v})| \leq \phi_x(h_n)\left(\frac{C}{n\phi_x(h_n)}\right)^{u+v} ve^{-a(t_1-s_u)/(2(a+1))}.$$

Article

On a Sum of More Complex Product-Type Operators from Bloch-Type Spaces to the Weighted-Type Spaces

Cheng-Shi Huang [1] and Zhi-Jie Jiang [1,2,*]

[1] School of Mathematics and Statistics, Sichuan University of Science and Engineering, Zigong 643000, China; 320070108101@stu.suse.edu.cn
[2] South Sichuan Center for Applied Mathematics, Sichuan University of Science and Engineering, Zigong 643000, China
* Correspondence: jiangzhijie@suse.edu.cn

Abstract: The aim of the present paper is to completely characterize the boundedness and compactness of a sum operator defined by some more complex products of composition, multiplication, and mth iterated radial derivative operators from Bloch-type spaces to weighted-type spaces on the unit ball. In some applications, the boundedness and compactness of all products of composition, multiplication, and mth iterated radial derivative operators from Bloch-type spaces to weighted-type spaces on the unit ball are also characterized.

Keywords: mth iterated radial derivative operator; Bloch-type space; weighted-type space; boundedness; compactness

MSC: 47B38; 47B33; 47B37; 30H05

1. Introduction

In this section, we provide a detailed introduction to the operators involved and the motivation of the paper.

Let $\mathbb{N}$ be the natural number set, $\mathbb{N}_0 = \mathbb{N} \cup \{0\}$, $B(a,r) = \{z \in \mathbb{C}^n : |z-a| < r\}$ the open ball in the complex vector space $\mathbb{C}^n$ centered at a with radius r and $\mathbb{B} = B(0,1)$. Let $z = (z_1, z_2, \ldots, z_n)$ and $w = (w_1, w_2, \ldots, w_n)$ be two points in $\mathbb{C}^n$. Define $\langle z, w \rangle = z_1 \overline{w}_1 + z_2 \overline{w}_2 + \cdots + z_n \overline{w}_n$ and $|z|^2 = \langle z, z \rangle$.

1.1. Operators Involved in the Paper

Let Ω be a domain in $\mathbb{C}^n$, $H(\Omega)$ the set of all holomorphic functions on Ω and $S(\Omega)$ the set of all holomorphic self-maps of Ω. Let $\varphi \in S(\Omega)$. Associated with φ is the composition operator C_φ, which is defined by $C_\varphi f = f \circ \varphi$ for $f \in H(\Omega)$. Let $u \in H(\Omega)$. The multiplication operator M_u is defined by $M_u f = u \cdot f$ for $f \in H(\Omega)$.

If $n = 1$, the open unit ball $\mathbb{B}$ becomes the open unit disk $\mathbb{D}$. Let $m \in \mathbb{N}_0$. The well-known mth differentiation operator D^m on $H(\mathbb{D})$ is defined by

$$D^m f(z) = f^{(m)}(z),$$

where $f^{(0)} = f$. If $m = 1$, it is reduced to the classical differentiation operator D. As expected, there has been some considerable interest in investigating products of differentiation and other related operators. For example, the most common products

$$M_u C_\varphi D, \ C_\varphi M_u D, \ C_\varphi D M_u, \ M_u D C_\varphi, \ D M_u C_\varphi, \ D C_\varphi M_u \qquad (1)$$

were extensively studied (see, for example, [1–4]). One of the reasons why people are interested in the six product-type operators is that people need to obtain further methods and techniques for studying their properties. Some other products containing differentiation operators can also be found in [5–8] and the related references therein. However, it is easy to see that if one studies the operators in (1) one by one, it will require a commitment of time and energy. In order to surmount this malpractice, the authors in [9] therefore introduced and investigated the following sum operator (for some later and continuous studies, see, for example, [10–12])

$$T_{u_0,u_1,\varphi} = M_{u_0}C_\varphi + M_{u_1}C_\varphi D, \tag{2}$$

where $u_0, u_1 \in H(\mathbb{D})$ and $\varphi \in S(\mathbb{D})$. Sure enough, the operator $T_{u_0,u_1,\varphi}$ allows unified research for the operators in (1). More precisely, it follows that

$$M_u C_\varphi D = T_{0,u,\varphi}, \qquad C_\varphi M_u D = T_{0,u\circ\varphi,\varphi}, \qquad M_u D C_\varphi = T_{0,u\cdot\varphi',\varphi},$$
$$C_\varphi D M_u = T_{u'\circ\varphi,u\circ\varphi,\varphi}, \qquad D M_u C_\varphi = T_{u',u\cdot\varphi',\varphi}, \qquad D C_\varphi M_u = T_{(u'\circ\varphi)\cdot\varphi',(u\circ\varphi)\cdot\varphi'}.$$

A very natural way of extending the operators in (1) can be achieved in terms of replacing D by D^m. That is,

$$M_u C_\varphi D^m, \quad C_\varphi M_u D^m, \quad C_\varphi D^m M_u, \quad M_u D^m C_\varphi, \quad D^m M_u C_\varphi, \quad D^m C_\varphi M_u. \tag{3}$$

The significance of this extension is that in overcoming some difficulties such as those caused by $(f \circ \varphi)^{(m)}$, some methods and techniques have been excavated. For example, the following famous Faà di Bruno's formula (see [13]) was used:

$$(f \circ \varphi)^{(m)}(z) = \sum_{k=0}^{m} f^{(k)}(\varphi(z)) B_{m,k}(\varphi'(z), \ldots, \varphi^{(m-k+1)}(z)), \tag{4}$$

where

$$B_{m,k} := B_{m,k}(x_1, x_2, \ldots, x_{m-k+1}) = \sum \frac{m!}{\prod_{i=1}^{m-k+1} j_i!} \prod_{i=1}^{m-k+1} \left(\frac{x_i}{i!}\right)^{j_i} \tag{5}$$

is the Bell polynomial, the sum is taken over all non-negative integer sequences $j_1, j_2, \ldots, j_{m-k+1}$ satisfying $\sum_{i=1}^{m-k+1} j_i = k$ and $\sum_{i=1}^{m-k+1} i j_i = m$. In particular, if $k = 0$, we have $B_{0,0} = 1$ and $B_{m,0} = 0$ for $m \in \mathbb{N}$. If $k = 1$, then $B_{i,1} = x_i$. If $m = k = i$, then $B_{i,i} = x_1^i$. By using the Faà di Bruno's formula, the operators in (3) were studied (see, for example, [14–17]). Motivated by the above-mentioned discussions, one should naturally consider defining an operator such that the operators in (3) can be studied in a unified manner. There may be many people who have the same idea as us. Actually, the authors in [18] introduced the following operator, which achieved the expectations

$$T^m_{u_0,\ldots,u_m,\varphi} = \sum_{i=0}^{m} M_{u_i} C_\varphi D^i, \tag{6}$$

where $u_0, u_1, \ldots, u_m \in H(\mathbb{D})$ and $\varphi \in S(\mathbb{D})$. It is clear that if $m = 1$, the operator in (6) is reduced to the operator in (2). We first see that the operators $M_u C_\varphi D^m$ and $C_\varphi M_u D^m$ can be easily expressed into forms of the operator $T^m_{u_0,\ldots,u_m,\varphi}$, where functions $u_0, u_1, \ldots,$ and u_m equal what is very simple and clear. Moreover, it seems to be difficult to express other operators in (3). However, we can still do it in terms of replacing x_j with $\varphi^{(j)}$ in the Bell polynomial as follows

$$M_u D^m C_\varphi = T^m_{u_0 = u \cdot B^\varphi_{m,0}, u_1 = u \cdot B^\varphi_{m,1}, \ldots, u_m = u \cdot B^\varphi_{m,m}, \varphi'}$$

$$C_\varphi D^m M_u = T^m_{u_0 = C^0_m u^{(m)} \circ \varphi, u_1 = C^1_m u^{(m-1)} \circ \varphi, \ldots, u_m = C^m_m u \circ \varphi, \varphi'}$$

$$D^m M_u C_\varphi = T^m_{u_0 = \sum_{i=0}^m C^i_m u^{(m-i)} \cdot B^\varphi_{i,0}, u_1 = \sum_{i=1}^m C^i_m u^{(m-i)} \cdot B^\varphi_{i,1}, \ldots, u_m = C^m_m u \cdot B^\varphi_{m,m}, \varphi'}$$

$$D^m C_\varphi M_u = T^m_{u_0 = \sum_{i=0}^m C^i_m (u \circ \varphi)^{(m-i)} \cdot B^\varphi_{i,0}, u_1 = \sum_{i=1}^m C^i_m (u \circ \varphi)^{(m-i)} \cdot B^\varphi_{i,1}, \ldots, u_m = C^m_m (u \circ \varphi) \cdot B^\varphi_{m,m}, \varphi'}$$

where

$$B^\varphi_{i,j} = B_{i,j}(\varphi', \varphi'', \ldots, \varphi^{i-j+1}).$$

One of the natural ways to extend the differentiation operator on domains in $\mathbb{C}^n$ is the radial derivative operator defined by

$$\Re f(z) = \sum_{j=1}^n z_j \frac{\partial f}{\partial z_j}(z). \tag{7}$$

As expected, the products of the composition, multiplication, and radial derivative operators

$$M_u C_\varphi \Re, \quad C_\varphi M_u \Re, \quad C_\varphi \Re M_u, \quad M_u \Re C_\varphi, \quad \Re M_u C_\varphi, \quad \Re C_\varphi M_u \tag{8}$$

were studied (see, for example, [19–21]). Correspondingly, the operator in (2) was extended into the following operator in [22], which completed the unified studies of the operators in (8)

$$T_{u_0, u_1, u_2, \varphi} = M_{u_0} C_\varphi + M_{u_1} C_\varphi \Re + M_{u_2} \Re C_\varphi, \tag{9}$$

where $u_0, u_1, u_2 \in H(\mathbb{B})$ and $\varphi \in S(\mathbb{B})$. Recently, it has been continuously investigated in [23–25].

Interestingly, the radial derivative operator can be employed iteratively, that is, if $\Re^{m-1} f$ is defined for some $m \in \mathbb{N} \setminus \{1\}$, then $\Re^m f$ is naturally defined by $\Re^m f = \Re(\Re^{m-1} f)$. If $m = 0$, then we regard that $\Re^0 f = f$. By using the mth iterated radial derivative operator, we obtain the related product-type operators

$$M_u C_\varphi \Re^m, \quad C_\varphi M_u \Re^m, \quad C_\varphi \Re^m M_u, \quad M_u \Re^m C_\varphi, \quad \Re^m M_u C_\varphi, \quad \Re^m C_\varphi M_u. \tag{10}$$

The operator $M_u C_\varphi \Re^m$ at first written as $\Re^m_{u,\varphi}$ was introduced and studied in [26]. We still reconsidered the operator in [27,28]. One of the reasons why we reconsider the operator is that we need to obtain more methods and techniques to study its properties. If people consider the fact that $C_\varphi M_u \Re^m = M_{u \circ \varphi} C_\varphi \Re^m$, then the operator $M_u C_\varphi \Re^m$ can be regarded as the simplest one in (10). The relatively more simple one in (10) is the operator $C_\varphi \Re^m M_u$. From a direct calculation, we obtain that

$$C_\varphi \Re^m M_u = \sum_{i=0}^m C^i_m M_{(\Re^{m-i} u) \circ \varphi} C_\varphi \Re^i. \tag{11}$$

Motivated by (11), we then in [29] directly introduced and characterized the boundedness and compactness of the sum operator

$$\mathfrak{S}^m_{\vec{u},\varphi} = \sum_{i=0}^m M_{u_i} C_\varphi \Re^i. \tag{12}$$

The boundedness and compactness of the operator were characterized again in [30], and as an application, the same properties of the operator $C_\varphi \Re^m M_u$ were also characterized.

Here, what we want to emphasize is that the most complicated one in (10) is the operator $\Re^m M_u C_\varphi$, if you notice that $\Re^m C_\varphi M_u = \Re^m M_{u \circ \varphi} C_\varphi$, which has been investigated very recently in [31].

1.2. Motivations of the Paper

When we examine the operator $\mathfrak{S}^m_{\vec{u},\varphi}$, we find that it is defined by the operator $M_{u_i} C_\varphi \Re^i$, which can be regarded as the simplest operator in (10). Naturally, we can try to extend the definition by using other operators in (10). To this end, in this paper, we introduce the sum operator

$$S^{k,l}_{\vec{u},\vec{v},\varphi} = M_{u_0} C_\varphi + \sum_{i=1}^{k} M_{u_i} C_\varphi \Re^i + \sum_{j=1}^{l} M_{v_j} \Re^j C_\varphi, \tag{13}$$

where $u_0, u_1, \ldots, u_k, v_1, \ldots, v_l \in H(\mathbb{B})$, $\varphi \in S(\mathbb{B})$, and $k, l \in \mathbb{N}$. By using the operator, the operators in (10) can be easily expressed into the following forms

$$\begin{aligned}
M_u C_\varphi \Re^m &= S^{m,l}_{u_0 \equiv \cdots \equiv u_{m-1} \equiv 0, u_m = u, v_1 \equiv \cdots \equiv v_l \equiv 0, \varphi} \\
C_\varphi M_u \Re^m &= S^{m,l}_{u_0 \equiv \cdots \equiv u_{m-1} \equiv 0, u_m = u \circ \varphi, v_1 \equiv \cdots \equiv v_l \equiv 0, \varphi} \\
C_\varphi \Re^m M_u &= S^{m,l}_{u_0 = C^0_m(\Re^m u) \circ \varphi, u_1 = C^1_m(\Re^{m-1} u) \circ \varphi, \ldots, u_m = C^m_m u \circ \varphi, v_1 \equiv \cdots \equiv v_l \equiv 0, \varphi} \\
M_u \Re^m C_\varphi &= S^{k,m}_{u_0 \equiv \cdots \equiv u_k \equiv 0, v_1 \equiv \cdots \equiv v_{m-1} \equiv 0, v_m = u, \varphi} \\
\Re^m M_u C_\varphi &= S^{k,m}_{u_1 \equiv \cdots \equiv u_k \equiv 0, u_0 = C^0_m \Re^m u, v_1 = C^1_m \Re^{m-1} u, \ldots, v_m = C^m_m u, \varphi} \\
\Re^m C_\varphi M_u &= S^{k,m}_{u_1 \equiv \cdots \equiv u_k \equiv 0, u_0 = C^0_m \Re^m (u \circ \varphi), v_1 = C^1_m \Re^{m-1}(u \circ \varphi), \ldots, v_m = C^m_m u \circ \varphi, \varphi}
\end{aligned} \tag{14}$$

One very obvious major difference between the operators $\mathfrak{S}^m_{\vec{u},\varphi}$ and $S^{k,l}_{\vec{u},\vec{v},\varphi}$ is that there are some terms $M_{v_j} \Re^j C_\varphi$ in the expression of $S^{k,l}_{\vec{u},\vec{v},\varphi}$. When the jth iterated radial derivative operator $\Re^j$ lies between the operators M_u and C_φ in the product $M_u \Re^j C_\varphi$, we find that there exist some insurmountable difficulties caused by $\Re^j(f \circ \varphi)$ (see [31]). We, therefore, guess that there also exist some difficulties in the study of the operator $S^{k,l}_{\vec{u},\vec{v},\varphi}$. Motivated by this, we study this operator from Bloch-type space to weighted-type space in this paper. On the other hand, as far as we know, the operator $S^{k,l}_{\vec{u},\vec{v},\varphi}$ has not been studied so far. This study is considerably interesting to a large number of readers. For example, we will prove that in some sense, the operator $S^{k,l}_{\vec{u},\vec{v},\varphi}$ is bounded or compact from Bloch-type space to weighted-type space if and only if each operator defined in (13) is bounded or compact. This is a very exciting phenomenon, but it may be not right for the general case, that is, from the boundedness of the operator $T = T_1 + T_2 + \cdots + T_m$, where T_i is a linear operator from Banach spaces X to Y, it cannot deduce the boundedness of the operator $T_i : X \to Y$.

1.3. Bloch-Type and Weighted-Type Spaces

A positive continuous function ϕ on the interval $[0, 1)$ is called normal (see [32]), if there are $\lambda \in [0, 1)$, a and b ($0 < a < b$) such that

$$\frac{\phi(r)}{(1-r)^a} \text{ is decreasing on } [\lambda, 1), \quad \lim_{r \to 1} \frac{\phi(r)}{(1-r)^a} = 0;$$

$$\frac{\phi(r)}{(1-r)^b} \text{ is increasing on } [\lambda, 1), \quad \lim_{r \to 1} \frac{\phi(r)}{(1-r)^b} = +\infty.$$

The functions $\{\phi, \psi\}$ will be called a normal pair, if ϕ is normal and for b in above definition of normal function there exists $\beta > b$ such that

$$\phi(r)\psi(r) = (1-r^2)^\beta.$$

If ϕ is normal, then there exists ψ such that $\{\phi, \psi\}$ is a normal pair (see [32]). Note that if $\{\phi, \psi\}$ is a normal pair, then ψ is also normal. The purpose of introducing normal pair is to characterize the duality of spaces defined by the normal functions (see, for example, [33,34]). For such a function, the following examples were given in [6]:

$$\mu(r) = (1-r^2)^\alpha, \quad \alpha \in (0, +\infty),$$

$$\mu(r) = (1-r^2)^\alpha \{\log 2(1-r^2)^{-1}\}^\beta, \quad \alpha \in (0,1), \quad \beta \in [\frac{\alpha-1}{2}\log 2, 0],$$

and

$$\mu(r) = (1-r^2)^\alpha \{\log\log e^2(1-r^2)^{-1}\}^\gamma, \quad \alpha \in (0,1), \quad \gamma \in [\frac{\alpha-1}{2}\log 2, 0].$$

The following fact can be used to prove that there exist a lot of non-normal functions. It follows from [35] that if μ is normal, then for each $s \in (0,1)$ there exists a positive constant $C = C(s)$ such that

$$C^{-1}\mu(t) \leq \mu(r) \leq C\mu(t) \tag{15}$$

for $0 \leq r \leq t \leq r + s(1-r)$. From (15), it is easy to check that the following functions are non-normal

$$\mu(r) = |\sin(\log \frac{1}{1-r})|v_\alpha(r) + 1$$

and

$$\mu(r) = |\sin(\log \frac{1}{1-r})|v_\alpha(r) + \frac{1}{e^{e^{\frac{1}{1-r}}}},$$

where

$$v_\alpha(r) = [(1-r)(\log \frac{e}{1-r})^\alpha]^{-1}.$$

From the definition of the normal function, we have that there exists a positive constant $\delta \in (0,1)$ such that for $r \in (\delta, 1)$ it follows that $\phi(r) \leq (1-r)^a$, which shows that $\sup_{r \in (\delta,1)} \phi(r) \leq (1-\delta)^a$. Since ϕ is continuous and positive on $[0, \delta]$, it follows that $\max_{r \in [0,\delta]} \phi(r) < +\infty$. Therefore, the normal function is bounded on $[0,1)$.

Let ϕ be a normal function. The Bloch-type space $\mathcal{B}_\phi(\mathbb{B})$ consists of all $f \in H(\mathbb{B})$ such that

$$\|f\|_{\beta_\phi(\mathbb{B})} = \sup_{z \in \mathbb{B}} \phi(|z|)|\Re f(z)| < +\infty.$$

$\mathcal{B}_\phi(\mathbb{B})$ is a Banach space with the norm

$$\|f\|_{\mathcal{B}_\phi(\mathbb{B})} = |f(0)| + \|f\|_{\beta_\phi(\mathbb{B})}.$$

In particular, if $\phi(r) = (1-r^2)\log \frac{e}{1-r^2}$, then the space $\mathcal{B}_\phi(\mathbb{B})$ is the logarithmic Bloch space $\mathcal{B}_{\log}(\mathbb{B})$. If $\phi(r) = (1-r^2)^\alpha$ ($\alpha > 0$), then the space $\mathcal{B}_\phi(\mathbb{B})$ is simplified to the classical weighted Bloch space $\mathcal{B}_\odot(\mathbb{B})$. One can see [36] for some results on the Bloch-type spaces. The operators involved Bloch-type spaces, including Toeplitz operators, composition operators, weighted composition operators, products of composition, multiplication and mth differentiation operators, and so on (see, for example, [37–41]).

A positive and continuous function μ on $\mathbb{B}$ is said to be weight. Then, the weighted-type space $H_\mu^\infty(\mathbb{B})$ consists all $f \in H(\mathbb{B})$ such that

$$\|f\|_{H_\mu^\infty(\mathbb{B})} = \sup_{z \in \mathbb{B}} \mu(z)|f(z)| < +\infty.$$

$H_\mu^\infty(\mathbb{B})$ is a Banach space with the norm $\|\cdot\|_{H_\mu^\infty(\mathbb{B})}$. In particular, if $\mu(z) = (1 - |z|^2)^\sigma$, where $\sigma > 0$, then the space $H_\mu^\infty(\mathbb{B})$ is the classical weighted-type space $H_\sigma^\infty(\mathbb{B})$. If $\mu \equiv 1$, then the $H_\mu^\infty(\mathbb{B})$ becomes the well-known bounded holomorphic function space $H^\infty(\mathbb{B})$. Many operators acting from or to the weighted-type spaces have been investigated (see, for example, [3,7,17,42] and the related references therein). It can be seen that the Bloch-type space and weighted-type space are metric spaces. One can see [43] and the related references therein for getting some profound results of metric spaces.

Let X and Y be two Banach spaces. A linear operator $T : X \to Y$ is bounded if there exists a positive constant K such that $\|Tf\|_Y \leq K\|f\|_X$ for all $f \in X$. The operator $T : X \to Y$ is compact if it maps bounded sets into relatively compact sets. The norm $\|T\|_{X \to Y}$ of the operator $T : X \to Y$ is defined by

$$\|T\|_{X \to Y} = \sup_{\|f\|_X \leq 1} \|Tf\|_Y.$$

As usual, we use the notation $j = \overline{k, l}$ instead of writing $j = k, \ldots, l$, where $k, l \in \mathbb{N}_0$ and $k \leq l$. Some positive numbers are denoted by C, and they may vary in different situations. The notation $a \lesssim b$ (resp. $a \gtrsim b$) means that there is a normal number C such that $a \leq Cb$ (resp. $a \geq Cb$). When $a \lesssim b$ and $b \gtrsim a$, we write $a \asymp b$.

2. Preliminary Results

In this section, we need several elementary results for proving the main results. We first have the following result (see [44]).

Lemma 1. *Let X, Y be Banach spaces of holomorphic functions on $\mathbb{B}$. Suppose that:*

(a) *The point evaluation functionals on X are continuous;*
(b) *The closed unit ball of X is a compact subset of X in the topology of uniform convergence on compact sets;*
(c) *$T : X \to Y$ is continuous when X and Y are given the topology of uniform convergence on compact sets.*

Then, the bounded operator $T : X \to Y$ is compact if and only if for every bounded sequence $\{f_m\}$ in X such that $f_m \to 0$ uniformly on compact sets such as $m \to \infty$, it follows that $\{Tf_m\}$ converges to zero in the norm of Y as $m \to \infty$.

We obtain the following characterization of the compactness, which can be proved similar to that in [45], and can also be proved according to Lemma 1. Therefore, we omit the proof.

Lemma 2. *Let ϕ be normal on $[0, 1)$, $u_i \in H(\mathbb{B})$, $i = \overline{0, k}$, $v_j \in H(\mathbb{B})$, $\overline{j = 1, l}$, and $\varphi \in S(\mathbb{B})$, and μ a weight function on $\mathbb{B}$. Then, the bounded operator $S_{\vec{u}, \vec{v}, \varphi}^{k,l} : \mathcal{B}_\phi(\mathbb{B}) \to H_\mu^\infty(\mathbb{B})$ is compact if and only if for any bounded sequence $\{f_m\}$ in $\mathcal{B}_\phi(\mathbb{B})$ such that $f_m \to 0$ uniformly on any compact subset of $\mathbb{B}$ as $m \to \infty$, it follows that*

$$\lim_{m \to \infty} \|S_{\vec{u}, \vec{v}, \varphi}^{k,l} f_m\|_{H_\mu^\infty(\mathbb{B})} = 0.$$

The next Lemmas 3–5 are needed and obtained from [31].

Lemma 8. *Let $N \in \mathbb{N}$, $\varphi \in S(\mathbb{B})$ and ϕ be normal on $[0,1)$. Then, there exists a positive constant C independent of $f \in \mathcal{B}_\phi(\mathbb{B})$ and $z \in \mathbb{B}$ such that*

$$|\mathfrak{R}^N(f \circ \varphi)(z)| \leq C \sum_{j=1}^{N} \frac{B_{N,j}(|\mathfrak{R}\varphi(z)|)}{\phi(|z|)(1-|\varphi(z)|^2)^{j-1}} \|f\|_{\mathcal{B}_\phi(\mathbb{B})}.$$

Proof. From Remark 1 (i), it is obvious that

$$\sum_{k_1,\ldots,k_j} C^{(N)}_{k_1,\ldots,k_j} \prod_{t=1}^{j} |\mathfrak{R}^{k_t}\varphi(z)| = B_{N,j}(|\mathfrak{R}\varphi(z)|), \tag{30}$$

where $k_1 + k_2 + \cdots + k_j = N$ and $j = \overline{1,N}$. Hence, by applying Cauchy–Schwarz inequality, and using Lemmas 3 and 7, we have

$$\begin{aligned}|\mathfrak{R}^N(f \circ \varphi)(z)| &\leq \sum_{l_1=1}^{n}\sum_{l_2=1}^{n}\cdots\sum_{l_N=1}^{n}\left|\frac{\partial^N f}{\partial z_{l_1}\partial z_{l_2}\cdots\partial z_{l_N}}(\varphi(z))\right|\sum_{k_1,\ldots,k_N}C^{(N)}_{k_1,\ldots,k_N}\prod_{t=1}^{N}|\mathfrak{R}^{k_t}\varphi_{l_t}(z)|\\ &+ \sum_{l_1=1}^{n}\sum_{l_2=1}^{n}\cdots\sum_{l_{N-1}=1}^{n}\left|\frac{\partial^{N-1} f}{\partial z_{l_1}\partial z_{l_2}\cdots\partial z_{l_{N-1}}}(\varphi(z))\right|\sum_{k_1,\ldots,k_{N-1}}C^{(N)}_{k_1,\ldots,k_{N-1}}\prod_{t=1}^{N-1}|\mathfrak{R}^{k_t}\varphi_{l_t}(z)|\\ &+ \cdots + \sum_{l=1}^{n}\left|\frac{\partial f}{\partial z_l}(\varphi(z))\right|\sum_{k_1}C^{(N)}_{k_1}\left|\mathfrak{R}^{k_1}\varphi_l(z)\right|\\ &\leq C\left(\frac{B_{N,N}(|\mathfrak{R}\varphi(z)|)}{\phi(|z|)(1-|\varphi(z)|^2)^{N-1}}\|f\|_{\mathcal{B}_\phi(\mathbb{B})} + \frac{B_{N,N-1}(|\mathfrak{R}\varphi(z)|)}{\phi(|z|)(1-|\varphi(z)|^2)^{N-2}}\|f\|_{\mathcal{B}_\phi(\mathbb{B})}\right.\\ &\left.+ \cdots + \frac{B_{N,1}(|\mathfrak{R}\varphi(z)|)}{\phi(|z|)}\|f\|_{\mathcal{B}_\phi(\mathbb{B})}\right).\end{aligned} \tag{31}$$

From (31), the desired result follows. □

Remark 2. *If $\varphi = z$, then from Lemma 8, we have that there exists a positive constant C independent of $f \in \mathcal{B}_\phi(\mathbb{B})$ and $z \in \mathbb{B}$ such that*

$$|\mathfrak{R}^N f(z)| \leq C \sum_{j=1}^{N} \frac{B_{N,j}(|z|)}{\phi(|z|)(1-|z|^2)^{j-1}}\|f\|_{\mathcal{B}_\phi(\mathbb{B})} \asymp \frac{|z|}{\phi(|z|)(1-|z|^2)^{N-1}}\|f\|_{\mathcal{B}_\phi(\mathbb{B})},$$

where $B_{N,j}(|z|) = B_{N,j}(|z|,|z|,\ldots,|z|)$.

The next lemma offers an important test function used in the proofs of the main results.

Lemma 9. *Let ϕ be normal on $[0,1)$. Then, for each $t \geq b-1$ and fixed $w \in \mathbb{B}$, the following function is in $\mathcal{B}_\phi(\mathbb{B})$*

$$f_{w,t}(z) = \frac{1-|w|^2}{\phi(|w|)}\left(\frac{1-|w|^2}{1-\langle z,w\rangle}\right)^{t+1}. \tag{32}$$

Moreover,

$$\sup_{w \in \mathbb{B}} \|f_{w,t}\|_{\mathcal{B}_\phi(\mathbb{B})} \lesssim 1. \tag{33}$$

Proof. Since the definition of function ϕ, we have

$$\phi(|z|)|\Re f_{w,t}(z)| = (t+1)\frac{\phi(|z|)}{\phi(|w|)}\frac{(1-|w|^2)^{t+1}|\langle z,w\rangle|}{|1-\langle z,w\rangle|^{t+2}}$$
$$\leq (t+1)\frac{\phi(|z|)}{(1-|z|)^{t+1}}\frac{(1-|w|^2)^{t+1}}{\phi(|w|)} \leq C < +\infty. \tag{34}$$

Therefore, we have that (33) holds. □

Remark 3. *It is obvious that the function defined in (32) satisfies the following estimate*

$$|f_{w,t}(z)| \leq \frac{(1-|w|^2)(1+|w|)^t}{\phi(|w|)} \leq C\frac{(1-|w|^2)}{\phi(|w|)}.$$

This shows that $f_{w,t}$ uniformly converges to zero on any compact subset of $\mathbb{B}$ as $|w| \to 1$.

Finally, we need the following lemma (see [26]).

Lemma 10. *If $a > 0$, then*

$$D_n(a) = \begin{vmatrix} 1 & 1 & \cdots & 1 \\ a & a+1 & \cdots & a+n-1 \\ a(a+1) & (a+1)(a+2) & \cdots & (a+n-1)(a+n) \\ \vdots & \vdots & & \vdots \\ \prod_{k=0}^{n-2}(a+k) & \prod_{k=0}^{n-2}(a+k+1) & \cdots & \prod_{k=0}^{n-2}(a+k+n-1) \end{vmatrix} = \prod_{k=1}^{n-1} k!.$$

3. The Condition on the Symbols

Let $\varphi(z) = (\varphi_1(z), \ldots, \varphi_n(z)) \in S(\mathbb{B})$ and $\Re^m\varphi(z) = (\Re^m\varphi_1(z), \ldots, \Re^m\varphi_n(z))$. To characterize the boundedness and compactness of the operator $\Re M_u C_\varphi$, the authors in [19] proposed the condition: there exists a $\lambda \in (0,1)$ such that if $|\varphi(z)| > \lambda$, then

$$|\Re\varphi(z)| \leq \frac{1}{\lambda}|\langle\Re\varphi(z), \varphi(z)\rangle|. \tag{35}$$

In the characterization of the boundedness and compactness of the operator $T_{u_0,u_1,u_2,\varphi}$, the authors in [25] introduced the condition on symbols u_1, u_2 and φ: there are $\rho \in (0,1)$ and a positive constant C such that if $|\varphi(z)| > \rho$, then

$$|u_1(z)\varphi(z) + u_2(z)\Re\varphi(z)| \leq C|\langle u_1(z)\varphi(z) + u_2(z)\Re\varphi(z), \varphi(z)\rangle|. \tag{36}$$

The authors in [22] also gave a special relationship such that the symbols u_1, u_2, and φ satisfied the condition.

Conditions (35) and (36) hold for all symbols if $n = 1$, which shows that it is more complicated for $n > 1$. Since $\Re M_u C_\varphi$ can be regarded as the operator $T_{\Re u,0,u,\varphi}$, we deduce that condition (36) is reduced to condition (35).

Motivated by previous studies mentioned such as [19,22,25], here we introduce the condition concerning all symbols φ, u_i and v_j, $i,j = \overline{1,l}$: there exist $\delta \in (0,1)$ and a positive constant C such that if $z \in K = \{z \in \mathbb{B} : |\varphi(z)| > \delta\}$, then for every $j = \overline{1,l}$

$$\left|\sum_{i=j}^{l}(u_i(z)B_{i,j}(\varphi(z)) + v_i(z)B_{i,j}(\Re\varphi(z)))\right|$$
$$\leq C\left|\sum_{i=j}^{l}(u_i(z)B_{i,j}(|\varphi(z)|^2) + v_i(z)B_{i,j}(\langle\Re\varphi(z),\varphi(z)\rangle))\right|, \tag{37}$$

where
$$B_{i,j}(\varphi(z)) := B_{i,j}(\varphi(z), \varphi(z), \ldots, \varphi(z))$$

and
$$B_{i,j}(\Re\varphi(z)) := B_{i,j}(\Re\varphi(z), \Re^2\varphi(z), \ldots, \Re^{i-j+1}\varphi(z)).$$

Since $B_{1,1}(x) = x$, the condition (37) is reduced to condition (36) if $l = 1$.

Remark 4. *The case of $k = l$ is assumed in the condition (37). If $k \neq l$, for example $k > l$, then by setting $v_{l+1} \equiv v_{l+2} \equiv \cdots \equiv v_k = 0$, we see that the condition (37) is equivalent to the following conditions*

$$\left|\sum_{i=j}^{l}(u_i(z)B_{i,j}(\varphi(z)) + v_i(z)B_{i,j}(\Re\varphi(z)))\right| \leq C\left|\sum_{i=j}^{l}(u_i(z)B_{i,j}(|\varphi(z)|^2) + v_i(z)B_{i,j}(\langle\Re\varphi(z),\varphi(z)\rangle))\right|$$

for $j = \overline{1,l}$, and

$$\left|\sum_{i=j}^{k}u_i(z)B_{i,j}(\varphi(z))\right| \leq C\left|\sum_{i=j}^{k}u_i(z)B_{i,j}(|\varphi(z)|^2)\right|$$

for $j = \overline{l,k}$.

If $l > k$, then by setting $u_{k+1} \equiv u_{k+2} \equiv \cdots \equiv u_l = 0$, we also see that the condition (37) is equivalent to the following conditions

$$\left|\sum_{i=j}^{k}(u_i(z)B_{i,j}(\varphi(z)) + v_i(z)B_{i,j}(\Re\varphi(z)))\right| \leq C\left|\sum_{i=j}^{k}(u_i(z)B_{i,j}(|\varphi(z)|^2) + v_i(z)B_{i,j}(\langle\Re\varphi(z),\varphi(z)\rangle))\right|$$

for $j = \overline{1,k}$, and

$$\left|\sum_{i=j}^{l}v_i(z)B_{i,j}(\Re\varphi(z))\right| \leq C\left|\sum_{i=j}^{l}v_i(z)B_{i,j}(\langle\Re\varphi(z),\varphi(z)\rangle)\right|$$

for $j = \overline{k,l}$.

We need to discuss what kind of symbols can satisfy the condition. Assume $n > 1$, then we see that the following example satisfies the condition (37).

Example 1. *Let $\varphi(z) = (z_1, z_2/2, \ldots, z_n/n)$, $u_i(z) = a_i z_1$, and $v_i(z) = b_i z_1$, $i = \overline{1,l}$, where constants a_i and b_i are positive. Then, these symbols satisfy the condition (37).*

Proof. It is easy to see that $\Re^i\varphi(z) = \varphi(z)$ for each $i = \overline{1,l}$. Hence, we obtain that

$$\left|\sum_{i=j}^{l}(u_i(z)B_{i,j}(|\varphi(z)|^2) + v_i(z)B_{i,j}(\langle\Re\varphi(z),\varphi(z)\rangle))\right| = \sum_{i=j}^{l}|z_1||\langle(a_i+b_i)B_{i,j}(\varphi(z)),\varphi(z)\rangle|$$

$$= \sum_{i=j}^{l}|z_1||(a_i+b_i)B_{i,j}(\varphi(z))||\varphi(z)|^j \geq \delta^j \sum_{i=j}^{l}|z_1||(a_i+b_i)B_{i,j}(\varphi(z))|$$

$$= \delta^j \left|\sum_{i=j}^{l}(u_i(z)B_{i,j}(\varphi(z)) + v_i(z)B_{i,j}(\Re\varphi(z)))\right|,$$

which implies that (37) holds. □

Except for the above example, we also see that if $n = 1$, all symbols satisfy the condition.

Proposition 1. *If $n = 1$, all symbols φ, u_i and v_i, $i = \overline{1,l}$ satisfy the condition (37).*

Proof. Since

$$\left|\sum_{i=j}^{l}(u_i(z)B_{i,j}(|\varphi(z)|^2) + v_i(z)B_{i,j}(\langle \Re\varphi(z), \varphi(z)\rangle))\right|$$

$$= \left|\left\langle \sum_{i=j}^{l}(u_i(z)B_{i,j}(\varphi(z)) + v_i(z)B_{i,j}(\Re\varphi(z))), \varphi(z)^j \right\rangle\right|,$$

we have

$$\left|\sum_{i=j}^{l}(u_i(z)B_{i,j}(|\varphi(z)|^2) + v_i(z)B_{i,j}(\langle \Re\varphi(z), \varphi(z)\rangle))\right|$$

$$= \left|\sum_{i=j}^{l}(u_i(z)B_{i,j}(\varphi(z)) + v_i(z)B_{i,j}(\Re\varphi(z)))\right| |\varphi(z)|^j$$

$$\geq \delta^j \left|\sum_{i=j}^{l}(u_i(z)B_{i,j}(\varphi(z)) + v_i(z)B_{i,j}(\Re\varphi(z)))\right|,$$

which implies that (37) holds for all symbols φ, u_i and v_i, $i = \overline{1,l}$. □

For $n > 1$, it is difficult, but we still give the following result.

Proposition 2. *Let $\varphi \in S(\mathbb{B})$ and $u_i, v_i \in H(\mathbb{B})$ for each $i = \overline{1,l}$. Then, the following statements hold.*

(i) If $\sum_{i=j}^{l}(u_i(z)B_{i,j}(\varphi(z)) + v_i(z)B_{i,j}(\Re\varphi(z))$ and $\varphi(z)^j$ are linearly dependent for each $z \in K$, $j = \overline{1,l}$, then the condition (37) holds;

(ii) If $v_i \equiv 0$ for $i = \overline{1,l}$, then the condition (37) holds.

Proof. (i) If $\sum_{i=j}^{l}(u_i(z)B_{i,j}(\varphi(z)) + v_i(z)B_{i,j}(\Re\varphi(z))$ and $\varphi(z)^j$ are linearly dependent for each $z \in K$, $j = \overline{1,l}$, we have

$$\left|\sum_{i=j}^{l}(u_i(z)B_{i,j}(|\varphi(z)|^2) + v_i(z)B_{i,j}(\langle \Re\varphi(z), \varphi(z)\rangle))\right|$$

$$= \left|\left\langle \sum_{i=j}^{l}(u_i(z)B_{i,j}(\varphi(z)) + v_i(z)B_{i,j}(\Re\varphi(z))), \varphi(z)^j \right\rangle\right|$$

$$= \left|\sum_{i=j}^{l}(u_i(z)B_{i,j}(\varphi(z)) + v_i(z)B_{i,j}(\Re\varphi(z)))\right| |\varphi(z)|^j$$

$$\geq \delta^j \left|\sum_{i=j}^{l}(u_i(z)B_{i,j}(\varphi(z)) + v_i(z)B_{i,j}(\Re\varphi(z)))\right|,$$

which implies that (37) holds.

(ii) If $v_i \equiv 0$ for $i = \overline{1,l}$, we have

$$\left|\sum_{i=j}^{l}u_i(z)B_{i,j}(|\varphi(z)|^2)\right| = \left|\sum_{i=j}^{l}u_i(z)B_{i,j}(\varphi(z))\right| |\varphi(z)|^j \geq \delta^j \left|\sum_{i=j}^{l}u_i(z)B_{i,j}(\varphi(z))\right|,$$

which implies that (37) holds. □

4. Boundedness and Compactness of the Operator $S_{\vec{u},\vec{v},\varphi}^{k,l} : \mathcal{B}_\phi(\mathbb{B}) \to H_\mu^\infty(\mathbb{B})$

We now begin to characterize the boundedness of the operator $S_{\vec{u},\vec{v},\varphi}^{k,l} : \mathcal{B}_\phi(\mathbb{B}) \to H_\mu^\infty(\mathbb{B})$. We first consider the case of $k = l$.

Theorem 1. *Assume that (37) is satisfied, $k, l \in \mathbb{N}$, $k = l$, $u_0 \in H(\mathbb{B})$, $u_i, v_i \in H(\mathbb{B})$, $i = \overline{1,l}$, ϕ normal on $[0,1)$, $\varphi \in S(\mathbb{B})$ and μ a weight function on $\mathbb{B}$. Then, the operator $S_{\vec{u},\vec{v},\varphi}^{k,l} : \mathcal{B}_\phi(\mathbb{B}) \to H_\mu^\infty(\mathbb{B})$ is bounded if and only if*

$$I_0 := \sup_{z \in \mathbb{B}} \frac{\mu(z)|u_0(z)|(1-|\varphi(z)|^2)}{\phi(|\varphi(z)|)} < +\infty \tag{38}$$

and

$$I_j := \sup_{z \in \mathbb{B}} \frac{\mu(z)|\sum_{i=j}^l (u_i(z) B_{i,j}(\varphi(z)) + v_i(z) B_{i,j}(\Re\varphi(z)))|}{\phi(|\varphi(z)|)(1-|\varphi(z)|^2)^{j-1}} < +\infty \tag{39}$$

for $j = \overline{1,l}$.

Moreover, if the operator $S_{\vec{u},\vec{v},\varphi}^{k,l} : \mathcal{B}_\phi(\mathbb{B}) \to H_\mu^\infty(\mathbb{B})$ is bounded, then the following asymptotic relationship holds

$$\|S_{\vec{u},\vec{v},\varphi}^{k,l}\|_{\mathcal{B}_\phi(\mathbb{B}) \to H_\mu^\infty(\mathbb{B})} \asymp \sum_{j=0}^l I_j. \tag{40}$$

Proof. Suppose that (38) and (39) hold. From Lemma 6, Lemma 7 and Remark 1 (i), we have

$$\mu(z)\Big|u_0(z)f(\varphi(z)) + \sum_{i=1}^l u_i(z)\Re^i f(\varphi(z)) + \sum_{j=1}^l u_j(z)\Re^j(f \circ \varphi)(z)\Big|$$

$$\leq \mu(z)|u_0(z)f(\varphi(z))| + \mu(z)\Big|\sum_{i=1}^l \big(u_i(z)\Re^i f(\varphi(z)) + v_i(z)\Re^i(f \circ \varphi)(z)\big)\Big|$$

$$= \mu(z)|u_0(z)f(\varphi(z))| + \mu(z)\Big|\sum_{i=1}^l \sum_{j=1}^i \Big(u_i(z) \sum_{l_1=1}^n \cdots \sum_{l_j=1}^n \Big(\frac{\partial^j f}{\partial z_{l_1} \partial z_{l_2} \cdots \partial z_{l_j}}(\varphi(z)) \sum_{k_1,\ldots,k_j} C_{k_1,\ldots,k_j}^{(i)} \prod_{t=1}^j \varphi_{l_t}(z)\Big)$$

$$+ v_i(z) \sum_{l_1=1}^n \cdots \sum_{l_j=1}^n \Big(\frac{\partial^j f}{\partial z_{l_1} \partial z_{l_2} \cdots \partial z_{l_j}}(\varphi(z)) \sum_{k_1,\ldots,k_j} C_{k_1,\ldots,k_j}^{(i)} \prod_{t=1}^j \Re^{k_t}\varphi_{l_t}(z)\Big)\Big)\Big|$$

$$= \mu(z)|u_0(z)f(\varphi(z))| + \mu(z)\Big|\sum_{j=1}^l \sum_{i=j}^l \Big(u_i(z) \sum_{l_1=1}^n \cdots \sum_{l_j=1}^n \Big(\frac{\partial^j f}{\partial z_{l_1} \partial z_{l_2} \cdots \partial z_{l_j}}(\varphi(z)) \sum_{k_1,\ldots,k_j} C_{k_1,\ldots,k_j}^{(i)} \prod_{t=1}^j \varphi_{l_t}(z)\Big)$$

$$+ v_i(z) \sum_{l_1=1}^n \cdots \sum_{l_j=1}^n \Big(\frac{\partial^j f}{\partial z_{l_1} \partial z_{l_2} \cdots \partial z_{l_j}}(\varphi(z)) \sum_{k_1,\ldots,k_j} C_{k_1,\ldots,k_j}^{(i)} \prod_{t=1}^j \Re^{k_t}\varphi_{l_t}(z)\Big)\Big)\Big|$$

$$\lesssim \mu(z)|u_0(z)f(\varphi(z))| + \mu(z) \sum_{j=1}^l \sum_{l_1=1}^n \cdots \sum_{l_j=1}^n \Big|\frac{\partial^j f}{\partial z_{l_1} \partial z_{l_2} \cdots \partial z_{l_j}}(\varphi(z))\Big|\Big|\sum_{i=j}^l \sum_{k_1,\ldots,k_j} C_{k_1,\ldots,k_j}^{(i)} \Big(u_i(z) \prod_{t=1}^j \varphi_{l_t}(z)$$

$$+ v_i(z) \prod_{t=1}^j \Re^{k_t}\varphi_{l_t}(z)\Big)\Big|$$

$$\lesssim \frac{\mu(z)|u_0(z)|(1-|\varphi(z)|^2)}{\phi(|\varphi(z)|)}\|f\|_{\mathcal{B}_\phi(\mathbb{B})} + \sum_{j=1}^{l} \frac{\mu(z)\left|\sum_{i=j}^{l}\sum_{k_1,\ldots,k_j} C_{k_1,\ldots,k_j}^{(i)}\left(u_i(z)\varphi(z)^j + v_i(z)\prod_{t=1}^{j}\Re^{k_t}\varphi(z)\right)\right|}{\phi(|\varphi(z)|)(1-|\varphi(z)|^2)^{j-1}}\|f\|_{\mathcal{B}_\phi(\mathbb{B})}$$

$$= \frac{\mu(z)|u_0(z)|(1-|\varphi(z)|^2)}{\phi(|\varphi(z)|)}\|f\|_{\mathcal{B}_\phi(\mathbb{B})} + \sum_{j=1}^{l} \frac{\mu(z)\left|\sum_{i=j}^{l}\left(u_i(z)B_{i,j}(\varphi(z)) + v_i(z)B_{i,j}(\Re\varphi(z))\right)\right|}{\phi(|\varphi(z)|)(1-|\varphi(z)|^2)^{j-1}}\|f\|_{\mathcal{B}_\phi(\mathbb{B})}$$

$$= \left(I_0 + \sum_{j=1}^{l} I_j\right)\|f\|_{\mathcal{B}_\phi(\mathbb{B})} = \sum_{j=0}^{l} I_j\|f\|_{\mathcal{B}_\phi(\mathbb{B})}.$$

From this, it follows that

$$\|S_{\vec{u},\vec{v},\varphi}^{k,l}f\|_{H_\mu^\infty(\mathbb{B})} \leq \left(C\sum_{j=0}^{l} I_j\right)\|f\|_{\mathcal{B}_\phi(\mathbb{B})}. \tag{41}$$

By taking the supremum in inequality (41) over the unit ball in the space $\mathcal{B}_\phi(\mathbb{B})$, using conditions (38) and (39), we have that the operator $S_{\vec{u},\vec{v},\varphi}^{k,l} : \mathcal{B}_\phi(\mathbb{B}) \to H_\mu^\infty(\mathbb{B})$ is bounded. Moreover, from (41) and the definition of operator norm, we have

$$\|S_{\vec{u},\vec{v},\varphi}^{k,l}\|_{\mathcal{B}_\phi(\mathbb{B}) \to H_\mu^\infty(\mathbb{B})} \leq C\sum_{j=0}^{l} I_j. \tag{42}$$

Now, suppose that $S_{\vec{u},\vec{v},\varphi}^{k,l} : \mathcal{B}_\phi(\mathbb{B}) \to H_\mu^\infty(\mathbb{B})$ is bounded. Then, there exists a positive constant C independent of $f \in \mathcal{B}_\phi(\mathbb{B})$ such that

$$\|S_{\vec{u},\vec{v},\varphi}^{k,l}f\|_{H_\mu^\infty(\mathbb{B})} \leq C\|f\|_{\mathcal{B}_\phi(\mathbb{B})}. \tag{43}$$

By using test function $f(z) = 1 \in \mathcal{B}_\phi(\mathbb{B})$, we have

$$K := \sup_{z \in \mathbb{B}} \mu(z)|u_0(z)| < +\infty. \tag{44}$$

By using test function $f_k(z) = z_k^j \in \mathcal{B}_\phi(\mathbb{B})$, $k = \overline{1,n}$ and $j = \overline{1,l}$, from (44) and the boundedness of $S_{\vec{u},\vec{v},\varphi}^{k,l} : \mathcal{B}_\phi(\mathbb{B}) \to H_\mu^\infty(\mathbb{B})$, we have

$$\mu(z)\left|u_0(z)\varphi_k(z)^j + \sum_{i=j}^{l}\left(u_i(z)B_{i,j}(\varphi(z)) + v_i(z)B_{i,j}(\Re\varphi_k(z))\right)\right| < +\infty \tag{45}$$

for each $j \in \{1,2,\ldots,l\}$. Using (44), (45) and the triangle inequality and the fact $|\varphi(z)| \leq 1$, we have

$$\sup_{z \in \mathbb{B}} \mu(z)\left|\sum_{i=j}^{l}(u_i(z)B_{i,j}(\varphi(z)) + v_i(z)B_{i,j}(\Re\varphi(z)))\right|$$

$$= \sup_{z \in \mathbb{B}} \mu(z)\sqrt{\sum_{k=1}^{n}\left|\sum_{i=j}^{l}(u_i(z)B_{i,j}(\varphi_k(z)) + v_i(z)B_{i,j}(\Re\varphi_k(z)))\right|^2}$$

$$\leq C + \sup_{z \in \mathbb{B}} \mu(z)\sqrt{\sum_{k=1}^{n}\left|u_0(z)\varphi_k(z)^j\right|^2} \tag{46}$$

$$\leq C + \sup_{z \in \mathbb{B}} \mu(z)|u_0(z)||\varphi(z)|^j$$

$$\leq C + K < +\infty.$$

- The second one is where $t_1 = s_u$. In this case, we have

$$|Cov(Y_{s_1}\ldots Y_{s_u}, Y_{t_1}\ldots Y_{t_v})| \leq \left(\frac{C\|K\|_\infty}{n\mu_n \mathbb{E}[K_1(x)]}\right)^{u+v} \mathbb{E}\left[|K_1^2(x)|\right]$$

$$\leq \phi_x(h_n)\left(\frac{C}{n\mu_n\phi_x(h_n)}\right)^{u+v}. \quad (A11)$$

So, we are in a position for Kallabis and Newmann's inequality for the variable Y_i, $i = 1, \ldots, n$, where

$$K_n = \frac{C}{n\mu_n\sqrt{\phi_x(h_n)}}, \quad M_n = \frac{C}{\mu_n n\phi_x(h_n)} \quad \text{and} \quad Var\left(\sum_{i=1}^n Y_i\right) = O\left(\frac{1}{n\phi_x(h_n)}\right).$$

It allows us to have

$$\mathbb{P}\left(\left|\widetilde{R}_N^*(x) - \mathbb{E}\left[\widetilde{R}_N^*(x)\right]\right| > \eta\sqrt{\frac{\log n}{n^{1-\xi}\phi_x(h_n)}}\right)$$

$$\leq \mathbb{P}\left(\left|\sum_{i=1}^n Y_i\right| > \eta\sqrt{\frac{\log n}{n^{1-\xi}\phi_x(h_n)}}\right)$$

$$\leq \exp\left\{-\frac{\eta^2 \log n/(2n^{1-\xi}\phi_x(h_n))}{\left(Var(\sum_{i=1}^n Y_i) + C\mu_n^{-1}(n\phi_x(h_n))^{-\frac{1}{3}}\left(\frac{\log n}{n^{1-\xi}\phi_x(h_n)}\right)^{\frac{5}{6}}\right)}\right\}$$

$$\leq \exp\left\{-\frac{\eta^2 \log n}{Cn^{-\xi} + \mu_n^{-1}n^{-\xi/6}\left(\frac{\log^5 n}{n\phi_x(h_n)}\right)^{\frac{1}{6}}}\right\}$$

$$\leq C'\exp\left\{-C\eta^2 \log n\right\}. \quad (A12)$$

Choosing the η adequately leads to achieving the proof of (A3).
Next, to prove (A1), use Holder's inequality to write that

$$\left|\mathbb{E}\left[\widetilde{R}_N(x)\right] - \mathbb{E}\left[\widetilde{R}_N^*(x)\right]\right| \leq \frac{1}{n\mathbb{E}[K_1(x)]}\left|\mathbb{E}\left[\sum_{i=1}^n Y_i^{-1}\mathbb{1}_{\{|Y_i|<\mu_n\}}K_i(x)\right]\right|$$

$$\leq \frac{1}{\mathbb{E}[K_1(x)]}\mathbb{E}\left[|Y_i|^{-1}\mathbb{1}_{\{|Y_i|<\mu_n\}}K_1(x)\right]$$

$$\leq C\phi_x^{-1/2}(h_n)\exp\left(-\mu_n^{-1}/4\right).$$

Since $\mu_n = n^{-\xi/6}$, which allows us to obtain

$$\left|\mathbb{E}\left[\widetilde{R}_N(x)\right] - \mathbb{E}\left[\widetilde{R}_N^*(x)\right]\right| = o\left(\left(\frac{\log n}{n^{1-\xi}\phi_x(h_n)}\right)^{1/2}\right).$$

We use Markov's inequality to obtain the last claimed result (A2). Hence, for all $\epsilon > 0$

$$\mathbb{P}\left[\left|\widetilde{R}_N(x) - \widetilde{R}_N^*(x)\right| > \epsilon\right] = \mathbb{P}\left[\left|\frac{1}{n\phi_x(h_n)}\sum_{i=1}^n Y_i^{-1}\mathbb{1}_{|Y_i|^{-1}>\mu_n}K_i(x)\right| > \epsilon\right]$$

$$\leq n\mathbb{P}\left[|Y_1|^{-1} > \mu_n\right]$$

$$\leq Cn\exp\left(-\mu_n^{-1}\right).$$

Then,

$$\sum_{n\geq 1} \mathbb{P}\left(\left|\widetilde{R}_N(x) - \widetilde{R}_N^*(x)\right| > \epsilon_0\left(\sqrt{\frac{\log n}{n^{1-\xi}\phi_x(h_n)}}\right)\right) \leq C \sum_{n\geq 1} n\exp\left(-\mu_n^{-1}\right). \quad (A13)$$

Use the definition of μ_n to achieve the proof of the lemma. □

Proof of Lemma 2. Once again, the focus is on the first statement's proof; the second statement is obtained in the same way. In fact, the proof of both results uses the stationarity of the couples (X_i, Y_i). Therefore, we write

$$|\mathbb{E}\widetilde{R}_N(x) - R_1(x)| = \frac{1}{\mathbb{E}[K_1(x)]} \mathbb{E}\left[(K_1(x))\left(R_1(x) - \mathbb{E}\left[Y_1^{-1}|X_1\right]\right)\right]. \quad (A14)$$

The conditions (D2) and (D4) imply

$$|R_1(X_1) - R_1(x)| \leq Ch^{k_1}.$$

Hence,

$$|\mathbb{E}\widetilde{R}_N(x) - R_1(x)| \leq Ch^{k_1}.$$

□

Proof of Corollary 1. Clearly, we can obtain that

$$|\widetilde{R}_D(x)| \leq \frac{R_2(x)}{2} \Rightarrow |\widetilde{R}_D(x) - R_2(x)| \geq \frac{R_2(x)}{2}.$$

So,

$$\mathbb{P}\left(|\widetilde{R}_D(x)| \leq \frac{R_2(x)}{2}\right) \leq \mathbb{P}\left(|\widetilde{R}_D(x) - R_2(x)| > \frac{R_2(x)}{2}\right).$$

Consequently,

$$\sum_{n=1}^{\infty} \mathbb{P}\left(|\widetilde{R}_D(x)| < \frac{R_2(x)}{2}\right) < \infty.$$

□

References

1. Narula, S.C.; Wellington, J.F. Prediction, linear regression and the minimum sum of relative errors. *Technometrics* **1977**, *19*, 185–190. [CrossRef]
2. Chatfield, C. The joys of consulting. *Significance* **2007**, *4*, 33–36. [CrossRef]
3. Chen, K.; Guo, S.; Lin, Y.; Ying, Z. Least absolute relative error estimation. *J. Am. Statist. Assoc.* **2010**, *105*, 1104–1112. [CrossRef]
4. Yang, Y.; Ye, F. General relative error criterion and M-estimation. *Front. Math. China* **2013**, *8*, 695–715. [CrossRef]
5. Jones, M.C.; Park, H.; Shin, K.-I.; Vines, S.K.; Jeong, S.-O. Relative error prediction via kernel regression smoothers. *J. Stat. Plan. Inference* **2008**, *138*, 2887–2898. [CrossRef]
6. Mechab, W.; Laksaci, A. Nonparametric relative regression for associated random variables. *Metron* **2016**, *74*, 75–97. [CrossRef]
7. Attouch, M.; Laksaci, A.; Messabihi, N. Nonparametric RE-regression for spatial random variables. *Stat. Pap.* **2017**, *58*, 987–1008. [CrossRef]
8. Demongeot, J.; Hamie, A.; Laksaci, A.; Rachdi, M. Relative-error prediction in nonparametric functional statistics: Theory and practice. *J. Multivar. Anal.* **2016**, *146*, 261–268. [CrossRef]
9. Cuevas, A. A partial overview of the theory of statistics with functional data. *J. Stat. Plan. Inference* **2014**, *147*, 1–23. [CrossRef]
10. Goia, A.; Vieu, P. An introduction to recent advances in high/infinite dimensional statistics. *J. Multivar. Anal.* **2016**, *146*, 1–6. [CrossRef]
11. Ling, N.; Vieu, P. Nonparametric modelling for functional data: Selected survey and tracks for future. *Statistics* **2018**, *52*, 934–949. [CrossRef]
12. Aneiros, G.; Cao, R.; Fraiman, R.; Genest, C.; Vieu, P. Recent advances in functional data analysis and high-dimensional statistics. *J. Multivar. Anal.* **2019**, *170*, 3–9. [CrossRef]
13. Aneiros, G.; Horova, I.; Hušková, M.; Vieu, P. On functional data analysis and related topics. *J. Multivar. Anal.* **2022**, *189*, 3–9. [CrossRef]

14. Chowdhury, J.; Chaudhuri, P. Convergence rates for kernel regression in infinite-dimensional spaces. *Ann. Inst. Stat. Math.* **2020**, *72*, 471–509. [CrossRef]
15. Li, B.; Song, J. Dimension reduction for functional data based on weak conditional moments. *Ann. Stat.* **2022**, *50*, 107–128. [CrossRef]
16. Douge, L. Théorèmes limites pour des variables quasi-associées hilbertiennes. *Ann. L'Isup* **2010**, *54*, 51–60.
17. Bouzebda, S.; Laksaci, A.; Mohammedi, M. The k-nearest neighbors method in single index regression model for functional quasi-associated time series data. *Rev. Mat. Complut.* **2023**, *36*, 361–391. [CrossRef]
18. Ferraty, F.; Vieu, P. *Nonparametric Functional Data Analysis*; Springer Series in Statistics; Theory and Practice; Springer: New York, NY, USA, 2006.
19. Hardle, W.; Marron, J.S. Bootstrap simultaneous error bars for nonparametric regression. *Ann. Stat.* **1991**, *16*, 1696–1708. [CrossRef]
20. Wilcox, R. *Introduction to Robust Estimation and Hypothesis Testing*; Elsevier Academic Press: Burlington, MA, USA, 2005.
21. Kallabis, R.S.; Neumann, M.H. An exponential inequality under weak dependence. *Bernoulli* **2006**, *12*, 333–335. [CrossRef]

Disclaimer/Publisher's Note: The statements, opinions and data contained in all publications are solely those of the individual author(s) and contributor(s) and not of MDPI and/or the editor(s). MDPI and/or the editor(s) disclaim responsibility for any injury to people or property resulting from any ideas, methods, instructions or products referred to in the content.

Lemma 3. Let $N \in \mathbb{N}$ and $\varphi = (\varphi_1, \ldots, \varphi_n) \in S(\mathbb{B})$. Then, for any $z \in \mathbb{B}$ and $f \in H(\mathbb{B})$

$$\mathfrak{R}^N(f \circ \varphi)(z) = \sum_{j=1}^{N} \sum_{l_1=1}^{n} \cdots \sum_{l_j=1}^{n} \left(\frac{\partial^j f}{\partial z_{l_1} \partial z_{l_2} \cdots \partial z_{l_j}}(\varphi(z)) \sum_{k_1,\ldots,k_j} C_{k_1,\ldots,k_j}^{(N)} \prod_{t=1}^{j} \mathfrak{R}^{k_t} \varphi_{l_t}(z) \right), \quad (16)$$

where $k_1 + k_2 + \cdots + k_j = N$, $j = \overline{1,N}$, and $C_{k_1,k_2,\ldots,k_j}^{(N)}$ are some positive integers with respect to the positive integers $k_1, k_2, \ldots, k_j$.

Lemma 4. Let $w \in \mathbb{B}$, $N \in \mathbb{N}$, $s > 0$, $\varphi \in S(\mathbb{B})$ and

$$g_{w,s}(z) = \frac{1}{(1 - \langle z, w \rangle)^s}, \quad z \in \mathbb{B}.$$

Then

$$\mathfrak{R}^N(g_{w,s} \circ \varphi)(z) = \sum_{j=1}^{N} \left(\prod_{k=0}^{j-1}(s+k) \right) \sum_{k_1,\ldots,k_j} C_{k_1,\ldots,k_j}^{(N)} \frac{\prod_{t=1}^{j} \langle \mathfrak{R}^{k_t} \varphi(z), w \rangle}{(1 - \langle \varphi(z), w \rangle)^{s+j}}, \quad (17)$$

where constants $C_{k_1,k_2,\ldots,k_j}^{(N)}$ are defined in Lemma 3.

Let

$$B_{i,j}(\langle \mathfrak{R}\varphi(z), w \rangle) := B_{i,j}\Big(\langle \mathfrak{R}\varphi(z), w \rangle, \langle \mathfrak{R}^2 \varphi(z), w \rangle, \ldots, \langle \mathfrak{R}^{i-j+1} \varphi(z), w \rangle \Big).$$

We also have the following version of Lemma 4.

Lemma 5. Let $N \in \mathbb{N}$ and $\{g_{w,s}\}$ be the family of functions defined in Lemma 4. Then

$$\mathfrak{R}^N(g_{w,s} \circ \varphi)(z) = \sum_{j=1}^{N} \left(\prod_{k=0}^{j-1}(s+k) \right) \frac{B_{N,j}(\langle \mathfrak{R}\varphi(z), w \rangle)}{(1 - \langle \varphi(z), w \rangle)^{s+j}}. \quad (18)$$

Remark 1. (i) From Lemmas 4 and 5, we obtain

$$\sum_{k_1,\ldots,k_j} C_{k_1,\ldots,k_j}^{(N)} \prod_{t=1}^{j} \langle \mathfrak{R}^{k_t} \varphi(z), w \rangle = B_{N,j}(\langle \mathfrak{R}\varphi(z), w \rangle),$$

where $k_1 + k_2 + \cdots + k_j = N$ and $j = \overline{1,N}$.

(ii) If $\varphi = z$, then from [20] we have

$$\mathfrak{R}^N g_{w,s}(z) = \sum_{j=1}^{N} a_j^{(N)} \left(\prod_{k=0}^{j-1}(s+k) \right) \frac{\langle z, w \rangle^j}{(1 - \langle z, w \rangle)^{s+j}}, \quad (19)$$

where the sequences $\{a_j^{(N)}\}_{j \in \overline{1,N}}$, $N \in \mathbb{N}$, are defined by the relations $a_N^{(N)} = a_1^{(N)} = 1$ for $N \in \mathbb{N}$ and $a_j^{(N)} = j a_j^{(N-1)} + a_{j-1}^{(N-1)}$ for $2 \leq j \leq N-1$, $N \geq 3$. Moreover, it is easy to obtain that constants $C_{k_1,\ldots,k_j}^{(N)}$ satisfy the following conclusion

$$\sum_{k_1,\ldots,k_j} C_{k_1,\ldots,k_j}^{(N)} = a_j^{(N)} = B_{N,j}(1,1,\ldots,1), \quad (20)$$

where $k_1 + k_2 + \cdots + k_j = N$ and $j = \overline{1,N}$.

(iii) Let

$$B_{N,j}(\langle z, w \rangle) := B_{N,j}(\langle z, w \rangle, \langle z, w \rangle, \ldots, \langle z, w \rangle).$$

From (19) and (20), we obtain the following version of the Formula (19)

$$\Re^N g_{w,s}(z) = \sum_{j=1}^{N} \Big(\prod_{k=0}^{j-1}(s+k)\Big) \frac{B_{N,j}(\langle z,w\rangle)}{(1-\langle z,w\rangle)^{s+j}}. \tag{21}$$

The following result is the point-evaluation estimate for the space $\mathcal{B}_\phi(\mathbb{B})$.

Lemma 6. *Let ϕ be normal on $[0,1)$. Then, there is a positive constant C independent of $f \in \mathcal{B}_\phi(\mathbb{B})$ and $z \in \mathbb{B}$ such that*

$$|f(z)| \leq C \frac{1-|z|^2}{\phi(|z|)} \|f\|_{\mathcal{B}_\phi(\mathbb{B})}. \tag{22}$$

Proof. Theorem 3.1 in [36] shows that $f \in \mathcal{B}_\phi(\mathbb{B})$ if and only if there is a function $g \in L^\infty(\mathbb{B})$ such that

$$f(z) = \int_{\mathbb{B}} \frac{g(w)}{\phi(|w|)(1-\langle z,w\rangle)^{n+t}} dv_t(w), \tag{23}$$

where $t > \max\{b-1, 0\}$ and $z \in \mathbb{B}$. Moreover, $\|f\|_{\mathcal{B}_\phi(\mathbb{B})} \asymp \|g\|_\infty$. From Lemma 2.2 in [46], it follows that

$$\frac{\phi(|z|)}{\phi(|w|)} \leq \Big(\frac{1-|z|^2}{1-|w|^2}\Big)^a + \Big(\frac{1-|z|^2}{1-|w|^2}\Big)^b \tag{24}$$

for $z, w \in \mathbb{B}$, where a and b are the parameters in the definition of the normal function. By (24), we have

$$\begin{aligned}
\phi(|z|)|f(z)| &\leq C\phi(|z|) \int_{\mathbb{B}} \frac{|g(w)|}{\phi(|w|)|1-\langle z,w\rangle|^{n+t}} dv_t(w) \\
&\leq C \int_{\mathbb{B}} \frac{\phi(|z|)}{\phi(|w|)} \frac{|g(w)|}{|1-\langle z,w\rangle|^{n+t}} dv_t(w) \\
&\leq C\|g\|_\infty \int_{\mathbb{B}} \frac{(1-|z|^2)^a(1-|w|^2)^{t-a}}{|1-\langle z,w\rangle|^{n+t}} dv(w) \\
&\quad + C\|g\|_\infty \int_{\mathbb{B}} \frac{(1-|z|^2)^b(1-|w|^2)^{t-b}}{|1-\langle z,w\rangle|^{n+t}} dv(w).
\end{aligned} \tag{25}$$

If $a < 1$ and $b < 1$, from Theorem 1.12 in [47] and (25), then we have

$$\phi(|z|)|f(z)| \leq C((1-|z|^2)^a + (1-|z|^2)^b)\|g\|_\infty \leq C(1-|z|^2)\|f\|_{\mathcal{B}_\phi(\mathbb{B})}.$$

If $a < 1$ and $b = 1$, since

$$\lim_{|z|\to 1}(1-|z|^2)\ln\frac{1}{1-|z|^2} = 0, \tag{26}$$

from Theorem 1.12 in [47] and (25), we have

$$\phi(|z|)|f(z)| \leq C\Big((1-|z|^2)^a + (1-|z|^2)\ln\frac{1}{1-|z|^2}\Big)\|g\|_\infty \leq C(1-|z|^2)\|f\|_{\mathcal{B}_\phi(\mathbb{B})}.$$

If $a < 1$ and $b > 1$, from Theorem 1.12 in [47] and (25), then we have

$$\phi(|z|)|f(z)| \leq C((1-|z|^2)^a + (1-|z|^2))\|g\|_\infty \leq C(1-|z|^2)\|f\|_{\mathcal{B}_\phi(\mathbb{B})}.$$

If $a = 1$ and $b > 1$, from Theorem 1.12 in [47], (25) and (26), then we have

$$\phi(|z|)|f(z)| \leq C\Big((1-|z|^2)\ln\frac{1}{1-|z|^2} + (1-|z|^2)\Big)\|g\|_\infty \leq C(1-|z|^2)\|f\|_{\mathcal{B}_\phi(\mathbb{B})}.$$

If $a > 1$ and $b > 1$, from Theorem 1.12 in [47] and (25), then we have

$$\phi(|z|)|f(z)| \leq C((1-|z|^2) + (1-|z|^2))\|g\|_\infty \leq C(1-|z|^2)\|f\|_{\mathcal{B}_\phi(\mathbb{B})}.$$

Combining the above discussions, we obtain

$$\phi(|z|)|f(z)| \leq C(1-|z|^2)\|f\|_{\mathcal{B}_\phi(\mathbb{B})}.$$

The proof is finished. □

The following result is an estimate for the higher-order partial derivative of functions in the space $\mathcal{B}_\phi(\mathbb{B})$.

Lemma 7. *Let $N \in \mathbb{N}$ and ϕ be normal on $[0,1)$. Then, for every multi-index $k = (l_1, \ldots, l_j)$ such that $|k| = N$, there is a positive constant C independent of $f \in \mathcal{B}_\phi(\mathbb{B})$ and $z \in \mathbb{B}$ such that*

$$\left|\frac{\partial^N f(z)}{\partial z_{k_1}^{l_1} \partial z_{k_2}^{l_2} \cdots \partial z_{k_j}^{l_j}}\right| \leq \frac{C}{\phi(|z|)(1-|z|^2)^{N-1}}\|f\|_{\mathcal{B}_\phi(\mathbb{B})}. \tag{27}$$

Proof. From (23), we have

$$\frac{\partial^N f(z)}{\partial z_{k_1}^{l_1} \partial z_{k_2}^{l_2} \cdots \partial z_{k_j}^{l_j}} = C\int_\mathbb{B} \frac{\overline{w}_{k_1}^{l_1}\overline{w}_{k_2}^{l_2}\cdots\overline{w}_{k_j}^{l_j}g(w)}{\phi(|w|)(1-\langle z,w\rangle)^{n+N+t}}dv_t(w) \tag{28}$$

for some $C = C(n, N, t)$ independent of f and z.

Moreover, from Lemma 2.2 in [46], we have that for all $z, w \in \mathbb{B}$

$$\frac{\phi(|z|)}{\phi(|w|)} \leq \Big(\frac{1-|z|^2}{1-|w|^2}\Big)^a + \Big(\frac{1-|z|^2}{1-|w|^2}\Big)^b.$$

From this, (28) and Theorem 1.12 in [47], we have

$$\phi(|z|)(1-|z|^2)^{N-1}\left|\frac{\partial^N f(z)}{\partial z_{k_1}^{l_1} \partial z_{k_2}^{l_2} \cdots \partial z_{k_j}^{l_j}}\right| \leq C\phi(|z|)\int_\mathbb{B}\frac{|g(w)|(1-|z|^2)^{N-1}}{\phi(|w|)|1-\langle z,w\rangle|^{n+N+t}}dv_t(w)$$

$$\leq C\int_\mathbb{B}\frac{\phi(|z|)}{\phi(|w|)}\frac{|g(w)|(1-|z|^2)^{N-1}}{|1-\langle z,w\rangle|^{n+N+t}}dv_t(w)$$

$$\leq C\|g\|_\infty(1-|z|^2)^{N-1}\int_\mathbb{B}\frac{(1-|z|^2)^a(1-|w|^2)^{t-a}}{|1-\langle z,w\rangle|^{n+N+t}}dv(w) \tag{29}$$

$$+C\|g\|_\infty(1-|z|^2)^{N-1}\int_\mathbb{B}\frac{(1-|z|^2)^b(1-|w|^2)^{t-b}}{|1-\langle z,w\rangle|^{n+N+t}}dv(w)$$

$$\leq C\|g\|_\infty \lesssim \|f\|_{\mathcal{B}_\phi(\mathbb{B})}.$$

The proof is finished. □

Let

$$B_{i,j}(|\Re\varphi(z)|) := B_{i,j}\Big(|\Re\varphi(z)|, |\Re^2\varphi(z)|, \ldots, |\Re^{i-j+1}\varphi(z)|\Big).$$

Let $w \in \mathbb{B}$ and $d_k = k+1$. For each $j \in \{1, 2, \ldots, l\}$ and constants $c_k = c_k^{(j)}$, $k = \overline{0, l}$, let

$$h_w^{(j)}(z) = \sum_{k=0}^{l} c_k^{(j)} f_{w,k}(z), \tag{47}$$

where $f_{w,k}$ is defined in Lemma 9. By Lemma 9, we have

$$L_j = \sup_{w \in \mathbb{B}} \|h_w^{(j)}\|_{\mathcal{B}_\phi(\mathbb{B})} < +\infty. \tag{48}$$

From (43), (48), Lemma 5 and Remark 1 (iii), we have

$$L_j \|S_{\vec{u},\vec{v},\varphi}^{k,l}\|_{\mathcal{B}_\phi(\mathbb{B}) \to H_\mu^\infty(\mathbb{B})} \geq \|S_{\vec{u},\vec{v},\varphi}^{k,l} h_{\varphi(w)}^{(j)}\|_{H_\mu^\infty(\mathbb{B})}$$

$$= \sup_{z \in \mathbb{B}} \mu(z) \left| u_0(z) h_{\varphi(w)}^{(j)}(\varphi(z)) + \sum_{i=1}^{l} \left(u_i(z) \Re^i h_{\varphi(w)}^{(j)}(\varphi(z)) + v_i(z) \Re^i (h_{\varphi(w)}^{(j)} \circ \varphi)(z) \right) \right|$$

$$\geq \mu(w) \left| u_0(w) h_{\varphi(w)}^{(j)}(\varphi(w)) + \sum_{i=1}^{l} \left(u_i(w) \Re^i h_{\varphi(w)}^{(j)}(\varphi(w)) + v_i(w) \Re^i (h_{\varphi(w)}^{(j)} \circ \varphi)(w) \right) \right|$$

$$= \mu(w) \left| u_0(w) h_{\varphi(w)}^{(j)}(\varphi(w)) + \sum_{i=1}^{l} \left(u_i(w) \sum_{k=0}^{l} c_k \Re^i f_{\varphi(w),k}(\varphi(w)) + v_i(w) \sum_{k=0}^{l} c_k \Re^i (f_{\varphi(w),k} \circ \varphi)(w) \right) \right|$$

$$= \mu(w) \left| u_0(w)(1 - |\varphi(w)|^2) \frac{c_0 + c_1 + \cdots + c_l}{\phi(|\varphi(w)|)} \right.$$

$$+ \sum_{i=1}^{l} \left(u_i(w) B_{i,1}(|\varphi(w)|^2) + v_i(w) B_{i,1}(\langle \Re \varphi(w), \varphi(w) \rangle) \right) \frac{(d_0 c_0 + \cdots + d_l c_l)}{\phi(|\varphi(w)|)}$$

$$+ \cdots$$

$$+ \sum_{i=j}^{l} \left(u_i(w) B_{i,j}(|\varphi(w)|^2) + v_i(w) B_{i,j}(\langle \Re \varphi(w), \varphi(w) \rangle) \right) \frac{(d_0 \cdots d_{j-1} c_0 + \cdots + d_l \cdots d_{l+j-1} c_l)}{\phi(|\varphi(w)|)(1 - |\varphi(w)|^2)^{j-1}}$$

$$+ \cdots$$

$$+ \left. \left(u_l(w) B_{l,l}(\varphi(w)) + v_l(w) B_{l,l}(\langle \Re \varphi(w), \varphi(w) \rangle) \right) \frac{(d_0 \cdots d_{l-1} c_0 + \cdots + d_l \cdots d_{2l-1} c_l)}{\phi(|\varphi(w)|)(1 - |\varphi(w)|^2)^{l-1}} \right|. \tag{49}$$

Since $d_k > 0$, $k = \overline{0, l}$, by Lemma 10, we have the following linear equations

$$\begin{pmatrix} 1 & 1 & \cdots & 1 \\ d_0 & d_1 & \cdots & d_l \\ \vdots & \vdots & \ddots & \vdots \\ \prod_{k=0}^{j-1} d_k & \prod_{k=0}^{j-1} d_{k+1} & \cdots & \prod_{k=0}^{j-1} d_{k+l} \\ \vdots & \vdots & \ddots & \vdots \\ \prod_{k=0}^{l-1} d_k & \prod_{k=0}^{l-1} d_{k+1} & \cdots & \prod_{k=0}^{l-1} d_{k+l} \end{pmatrix} \begin{pmatrix} c_0 \\ c_1 \\ \vdots \\ c_j \\ \vdots \\ c_l \end{pmatrix} = \begin{pmatrix} 0 \\ 0 \\ \vdots \\ 1 \\ \vdots \\ 0 \end{pmatrix}. \tag{50}$$

From (49), (50) and (37), we have

$$L_j \| S^{k,l}_{\vec{u},\vec{v},\varphi} \|_{\mathcal{B}_\phi(\mathbb{B}) \to H^\infty_\mu(\mathbb{B})} \geq \sup_{z \in K} \frac{\mu(z) |\sum_{i=j}^{l}(u_i(z)B_{i,j}(|\varphi(z)|^2)+v_i(z)B_{i,j}(\langle\Re\varphi(z),\varphi(z)\rangle))|}{\phi(|\varphi(z)|)(1-|\varphi(z)|^2)^{j-1}}$$

$$= \sup_{z \in K} \frac{\mu(z) \left|\left\langle \sum_{i=j}^{l}\left(u_i(z)B_{i,j}(\varphi(z)) + v_i(z)B_{i,j}(\Re\varphi(z))\right), \varphi(z)^j \right\rangle\right|}{\phi(|\varphi(z)|)(1-|\varphi(z)|^2)^{j-1}} \qquad (51)$$

$$\gtrsim \sup_{z \in K} \frac{\mu(z) |\sum_{i=j}^{l}\left(u_i(z)B_{i,j}(\varphi(z)) + v_i(z)B_{i,j}(\Re\varphi(z))\right)|}{\phi(|\varphi(z)|)(1-|\varphi(z)|^2)^{j-1}}.$$

On the other hand, from (46), we have

$$\sup_{z \in \mathbb{B} \setminus K} \frac{\mu(z) |\sum_{i=j}^{l}\left(u_i(z)B_{i,j}(\varphi(z)) + v_i(z)B_{i,j}(\Re\varphi(z))\right)|}{\phi(|\varphi(z)|)(1-|\varphi(z)|^2)^{j-1}}$$

$$\leq \sup_{z \in \mathbb{B}} \frac{\mu(z) |\sum_{i=j}^{l}\left(u_i(z)B_{i,j}(\varphi(z)) + v_i(z)B_{i,j}(\Re\varphi(z))\right)|}{\max_{|z| \leq \delta} \phi(z)(1-\delta^2)^{j-1}} < +\infty. \qquad (52)$$

From (51) and (52), we find that (39) holds for $j = \overline{1,l}$.

For constants $c_k = c_k^{(0)}$, $k = \overline{0,l}$, let

$$h_w^{(0)}(z) = \sum_{k=0}^{l} c_k^{(0)} f_{w,k}(z). \qquad (53)$$

By Lemma 9, we know that $L_0 = \sup_{w \in \mathbb{B}} \|h_w^{(0)}\|_{\mathcal{B}_\phi(\mathbb{B})} < +\infty$. From this, (49), (50) and Lemma 10, we obtain

$$L_0 \| S^{k,l}_{\vec{u},\vec{v},\varphi} \|_{\mathcal{B}_\phi(\mathbb{B}) \to H^\infty_\mu(\mathbb{B})} \geq \frac{\mu(z)|u_0(z)|(1-|\varphi(z)|^2)}{\phi(|\varphi(z)|)}. \qquad (54)$$

Hence, we have that $I_0 < +\infty$. Moreover, we have

$$C \| S^{k,l}_{\vec{u},\vec{v},\varphi} \|_{\mathcal{B}_\phi(\mathbb{B}) \to H^\infty_\mu(\mathbb{B})} \geq \sum_{j=0}^{l} I_j. \qquad (55)$$

From (42) and (55), we obtain (40). The proof is completed. □

The following result gives a sufficient condition for the boundedness of the operator $S^{k,l}_{\vec{u},\vec{v},\varphi} : \mathcal{B}_\phi(\mathbb{B}) \to H^\infty_\mu(\mathbb{B})$ for $k = l$. It does not need to satisfy the condition (37).

Corollary 1. Let $k, l \in \mathbb{N}$, $k = l$, $u_0 \in H(\mathbb{B})$, $u_i, v_i \in H(\mathbb{B})$, $i = \overline{1,l}$, ϕ normal on $[0,1)$, $\varphi \in S(\mathbb{B})$ and μ a weight function on $\mathbb{B}$. If

$$\sup_{z \in \mathbb{B}} \frac{\mu(z)|u_0(z)|(1-|\varphi(z)|^2)}{\phi(|\varphi(z)|)} < +\infty$$

and

$$\sup_{z \in \mathbb{B}} \frac{\mu(z)|\sum_{i=j}^{l}(u_i(z)B_{i,j}(\varphi(z)) + v_i(z)B_{i,j}(\Re\varphi(z)))|}{(1-|\varphi(z)|^2)^{j-1}} < +\infty$$

for $j = \overline{1,l}$, then the operator $S^{k,l}_{\vec{u},\vec{v},\varphi} : \mathcal{B}_\phi(\mathbb{B}) \to H^\infty_\mu(\mathbb{B})$ is bounded.

If we consider some special symbols, we can obtain the following interesting results. For example, if we let $v_j \equiv 0$, $j = \overline{1,l}$, then the operator $S_{\vec{u},\vec{v},\varphi}^{k,l}$ is reduced to the operator $\mathfrak{S}_{\vec{u},\varphi}^k$, that is,

$$\mathfrak{S}_{\vec{u},\varphi}^k = \sum_{i=0}^{k} M_{u_i} C_\varphi \mathfrak{R}^i.$$

Then, from Theorem 3.2 in [30], we can obtain similarly the following result, which is right without any additional conditions on the symbols.

Theorem 2. *The operators $M_{u_i} C_\varphi \mathfrak{R}^i : \mathcal{B}_\phi(\mathbb{B}) \to H_\mu^\infty(\mathbb{B})$, $i = \overline{0,k}$, are bounded operator if and only if $\mathfrak{S}_{\vec{u},\varphi}^k : \mathcal{B}_\phi(\mathbb{B}) \to H_\mu^\infty(\mathbb{B})$ is bounded and*

$$\mu(z)|u_i(z)||\varphi(z)| < +\infty \tag{56}$$

for each $i = \overline{1,k}$.

Moreover, if we consider $u_i \equiv 0$, $i = \overline{1,k}$, then the operator $S_{\vec{u},\vec{v},\varphi}^{k,l}$ becomes the following operator, denoted by $S_{\vec{v},\varphi}^l$. Namely,

$$S_{\vec{v},\varphi}^l = \sum_{j=0}^{l} M_{v_j} \mathfrak{R}^j C_\varphi.$$

For this special case, the condition (37) becomes: there exist $\delta \in (0,1)$ and two positive constants C_1 and C_2 such that if $z \in K = \{z \in \mathbb{B} : |\varphi(z)| > \delta\}$, then

$$|\mathfrak{R}^j \varphi(z)| \leq C_1 |\langle \mathfrak{R}^j \varphi(z), \varphi(z) \rangle| \leq C_2 |\langle \mathfrak{R}\varphi(z), \varphi(z) \rangle|^j \tag{57}$$

for every $j = \overline{1,l}$.

Then, from Remark 4.1 in [31], we have the following interesting result.

Theorem 3. *Assume that (57) is satisfied. Then, the operator $S_{\vec{v},\varphi}^l : \mathcal{B}_\phi(\mathbb{B}) \to H_\mu^\infty(\mathbb{B})$ is bounded if and only if the operators $M_{v_j} \mathfrak{R}^j C_\varphi : \mathcal{B}_\phi(\mathbb{B}) \to H_\mu^\infty(\mathbb{B})$, $j = \overline{0,l}$, are bounded.*

Remark 5. *The boundedness can be discussed similarly for two cases of $k > l$ and $k < l$. Here, we omit.*

We next begin to consider the compactness of the operator $S_{\vec{u},\vec{v},\varphi}^{k,l} : \mathcal{B}_\phi(\mathbb{B}) \to H_\mu^\infty(\mathbb{B})$ only for $k = l$.

Theorem 4. *Assume that (37) is satisfied, $k, l \in \mathbb{N}$, $k = l$, $u_0 \in H(\mathbb{B})$, $u_i, v_i \in H(\mathbb{B})$, $i = \overline{1,l}$, ϕ normal on $[0,1)$, $\varphi \in S(\mathbb{B})$ and μ a weight function on $\mathbb{B}$. Then, the operator $S_{\vec{u},\vec{v},\varphi}^{k,l} : \mathcal{B}_\phi(\mathbb{B}) \to H_\mu^\infty(\mathbb{B})$ is compact if and only if the operator $S_{\vec{u},\vec{v},\varphi}^{k,l} : \mathcal{B}_\phi(\mathbb{B}) \to H_\mu^\infty(\mathbb{B})$ is bounded,*

$$\lim_{|\varphi(z)| \to 1} \frac{\mu(z)|u_0(z)|(1 - |\varphi(z)|^2)}{\phi(|\varphi(z)|)} = 0 \tag{58}$$

and

$$\lim_{|\varphi(z)| \to 1} \frac{\mu(z)|\sum_{i=j}^{l}(u_i(z) B_{i,j}(\varphi(z)) + v_i(z) B_{i,j}(\mathfrak{R}\varphi(z)))|}{\phi(|\varphi(z)|)(1 - |\varphi(z)|^2)^{j-1}} = 0 \tag{59}$$

for $j = \overline{1,l}$.

Proof. Assume that $S_{\vec{u},\vec{v},\varphi}^{k,l} : \mathcal{B}_\phi(\mathbb{B}) \to H_\mu^\infty(\mathbb{B})$ is compact. It is obvious that $S_{\vec{u},\vec{v},\varphi}^{k,l} : \mathcal{B}_\phi(\mathbb{B}) \to H_\mu^\infty(\mathbb{B})$ is bounded. If $\|\varphi\|_\infty < 1$, then it is clear that (58) and (59) are true. Therefore, we suppose that $\|\varphi\|_\infty = 1$. Let $\{z_m\}$ be a sequence in $\mathbb{B}$ such that $|\varphi(z_m)| \to 1$ as $m \to \infty$ and $h_m^{(j)} = h_{\varphi(z_m)}^{(j)}$, where $h_w^{(j)}$ are defined in (47) for a fixed $j \in \{1, 2, \ldots, l\}$. Then, we have that $\sup_{m \in \mathbb{N}} \|h_m^{(j)}\|_{\mathcal{B}_\phi(\mathbb{B})} < +\infty$. By Remark 3, we have that $h_m^{(j)} \to 0$ uniformly on any compact subset of $\mathbb{B}$ as $m \to \infty$. Hence, by Lemma 2 we obtain

$$\lim_{m \to \infty} \|S_{\vec{u},\vec{v},\varphi}^{k,l} h_m^{(j)}\|_{H_\mu^\infty(\mathbb{B})} = 0. \tag{60}$$

From (51), for sufficiently large m, we have that

$$\frac{\mu(z_m) |\sum_{i=j}^l (u_i(z_m) B_{i,j}(\varphi(z_m)) + v_i(z_m) B_{i,j}(\Re\varphi(z_m)))|}{\phi(|\varphi(z_m)|)(1 - |\varphi(z_m)|^2)^{j-1}} \leq \|S_{\vec{u},\vec{v},\varphi}^{k,l} h_m^{(j)}\|_{H_\mu^\infty(\mathbb{B})}. \tag{61}$$

Taking $m \to \infty$ in (61), by using (60), we have that (59) holds for $j = \overline{1,l}$.

Furthermore, let $h_m^{(0)} = h_{\varphi(z_m)}^{(0)}$, where $h_w^{(0)}$ is defined in (53). Then, we also have that $\sup_{m \in \mathbb{N}} \|h_m^{(0)}\|_{\mathcal{B}_\phi(\mathbb{B})} < +\infty$ and $h_m^{(0)} \to 0$ uniformly on any compact subset of $\mathbb{B}$ as $m \to \infty$. Hence, by Lemma 2 we have

$$\lim_{m \to \infty} \|S_{\vec{u},\vec{v},\varphi}^{k,l} h_m^{(0)}\|_{H_\mu^\infty(\mathbb{B})} = 0. \tag{62}$$

From (54), we have

$$\frac{\mu(z_m) |u_0(z_m)| (1 - |\varphi(z_m)|^2)}{\phi(|\varphi(z_m)|)} \leq \|S_{\vec{u},\vec{v},\varphi}^{k,l} h_m^{(0)}\|_{H_\mu^\infty(\mathbb{B})}. \tag{63}$$

Letting $m \to \infty$ in (63) and using (62), we have that (58) holds.

Now, assume that $S_{\vec{u},\vec{v},\varphi}^{k,l} : \mathcal{B}_\phi(\mathbb{B}) \to H_\mu^\infty(\mathbb{B})$ is bounded. From (44) and (46), we have

$$\mu(z) |u_0(z)| \leq C < +\infty \tag{64}$$

and

$$\mu(z) \left| \sum_{i=j}^l (u_i(z) B_{i,j}(\varphi(z)) + v_i(z) B_{i,j}(\Re\varphi(z))) \right| \leq C < +\infty \tag{65}$$

for all $z \in \mathbb{B}$. On the other hand, from (58) and (59), we have that for arbitrary $\varepsilon > 0$, there is a $\delta \in (0,1)$ such that on K

$$\frac{\mu(z) |u_0(z)| (1 - |\varphi(z)|^2)}{\phi(|\varphi(z)|)} < \varepsilon. \tag{66}$$

and

$$\frac{\mu(z) |\sum_{i=j}^l (u_i(z) B_{i,j}(\varphi(z)) + v_i(z) B_{i,j}(\Re\varphi(z)))|}{\phi(|\varphi(z)|)(1 - |\varphi(z)|^2)^{j-1}} < \varepsilon. \tag{67}$$

Assume that $\{f_s\}$ is a sequence such that $\sup_{s \in \mathbb{N}} \|f_s\|_{\mathcal{B}_\phi(\mathbb{B})} \leq M$ and $f_s \to 0$ uniformly on any compact subset of $\mathbb{B}$ as $s \to \infty$. Then, by Lemmas 3, 6, and 7 and (64)–(67), we have

$$\|S_{\vec{u},\vec{v},\varphi}^{k,l} f_s\|_{H_\mu^\infty(\mathbb{B})}$$

$$= \sup_{z\in\mathbb{B}} \mu(z)\left|u_0(z)f(\varphi(z)) + \sum_{i=1}^{l}\left(u_i(z)\Re^i f(\varphi(z)) + v_i(z)\Re^i(f\circ\varphi)(z)\right)\right|$$

$$= \sup_{z\in K} \mu(z)\left|u_0(z)f(\varphi(z)) + \sum_{i=1}^{l}\left(u_i(z)\Re^i f(\varphi(z)) + v_i(z)\Re^i(f\circ\varphi)(z)\right)\right|$$

$$+ \sup_{z\in\mathbb{B}\setminus K} \mu(z)\left|u_0(z)f(\varphi(z)) + \sum_{i=1}^{l}\left(u_i(z)\Re^i f(\varphi(z)) + v_i(z)\Re^i(f\circ\varphi)(z)\right)\right|$$

$$\leq C \sup_{z\in K} \frac{\mu(z)|u_0(z)|(1-|\varphi(z)|^2)}{\phi(|\varphi(z)|)} \|f_s\|_{\mathcal{B}_\phi(\mathbb{B})} \qquad (68)$$

$$+ C \sup_{z\in K} \frac{\mu(z)|\sum_{i=j}^{l}\left(u_i(z)B_{i,j}(\varphi(z)) + v_i(z)B_{i,j}(\Re\varphi(z))\right)|}{\phi(|\varphi(z)|)(1-|\varphi(z)|^2)^{j-1}} \|f_s\|_{\mathcal{B}_\phi(\mathbb{B})}$$

$$+ \sup_{z\in\mathbb{B}\setminus K} \mu(z)|u_0(z)||f_s(\varphi(z))|$$

$$+ \sup_{z\in\mathbb{B}\setminus K} \sum_{j=1}^{l} \mu(z)\left|\sum_{i=j}^{l}\left(u_i(z)B_{i,j}(\varphi(z)) + v_i(z)B_{i,j}(\Re\varphi(z))\right)\right| \max_{\{l_1,l_2,\ldots,l_j\}} \left|\frac{\partial^j f_s}{\partial z_{l_1}\partial z_{l_2}\cdots\partial z_{l_j}}(\varphi(z))\right|$$

$$\leq CM\varepsilon + C \sup_{|w|\leq\delta} \sum_{j=0}^{l} \max_{\{l_1,l_2,\ldots,l_j\}} \left|\frac{\partial^j f_s}{\partial z_{l_1}\partial z_{l_2}\cdots\partial z_{l_j}}(w)\right|.$$

Since $f_s \to 0$ uniformly on any compact subset of $\mathbb{B}$ as $s \to \infty$, by Cauchy's estimates, we also have that $\frac{\partial^j f_s}{\partial z_{l_1}\partial z_{l_2}\cdots\partial z_{l_j}} \to 0$ uniformly on any compact subset of $\mathbb{B}$ as $s \to \infty$. From this and using the fact that $\{w \in \mathbb{B} : |w| \leq \delta\}$ is a compact subset of $\mathbb{B}$, by letting $s \to \infty$ in inequality (68), we obtain

$$\limsup_{s\to\infty} \|S_{\vec{u},\vec{v},\varphi}^{k,l} f_s\|_{H_\mu^\infty(\mathbb{B})} \leq CM\varepsilon.$$

Since ε is an arbitrary positive number, it follows that

$$\lim_{s\to\infty} \|S_{\vec{u},\vec{v},\varphi}^{k,l} f_s\|_{H_\mu^\infty(\mathbb{B})} = 0. \qquad (69)$$

From (69) and Lemma 2, the operator $S_{\vec{u},\vec{v},\varphi}^{k,l} : \mathcal{B}_\phi(\mathbb{B}) \to H_\mu^\infty(\mathbb{B})$ is compact. □

From Theorem 3.4 in [30] and Remark 4.2 in [31], we have the following interesting results.

Theorem 5. *The operator* $\mathfrak{S}_{\vec{u},\varphi}^{k} : \mathcal{B}_\phi(\mathbb{B}) \to H_\mu^\infty(\mathbb{B})$ *is compact and (56) holds if and only if the operators* $M_{u_i}C_\varphi\Re^i : \mathcal{B}_\phi(\mathbb{B}) \to H_\mu^\infty(\mathbb{B})$, $i = \overline{0,k}$ *are compact.*

Theorem 6. *Assume that (57) is satisfied. Then, the operator* $S_{\vec{v},\varphi}^{l} : \mathcal{B}_\phi(\mathbb{B}) \to H_\mu^\infty(\mathbb{B})$ *is compact if and only if the operators* $M_{v_j}\Re^j C_\varphi : \mathcal{B}_\phi(\mathbb{B}) \to H_\mu^\infty(\mathbb{B})$, $j = \overline{0,l}$ *are compact.*

5. Some Applications

As some applications of the results in Part 4, we can characterize the boundedness and compactness of the operators $M_u C_\varphi \Re^m$, $C_\varphi M_u \Re^m$, $C_\varphi \Re^m M_u$, $M_u \Re^m C_\varphi$, $\Re^m M_u C_\varphi$, and $\Re^m C_\varphi M_u : \mathcal{B}_\phi(\mathbb{B}) \to H_\mu^\infty(\mathbb{B})$. More specifically, all results of this section are obtained from the relationships in (14). Since

$$M_u C_\varphi \Re^m = S_{u_0\equiv\cdots\equiv u_{m-1}\equiv 0, u_m=u, v_1\equiv\cdots\equiv v_l\equiv 0, \varphi}^{m,l},$$

the following corollaries come from Proposition 2 (ii), Theorems 1 and 4.

Corollary 2. *Let $m \in \mathbb{N}$, $u \in H(\mathbb{B})$, ϕ normal on $[0,1)$, $\varphi \in S(\mathbb{B})$ and μ a weight on $\mathbb{B}$. Then, the operator $M_u C_\varphi \mathfrak{R}^m : \mathcal{B}_\phi(\mathbb{B}) \to H^\infty_\mu(\mathbb{B})$ is bounded if and only if*

$$L_j := \sup_{z \in \mathbb{B}} \frac{\mu(z)|u(z)||B_{m,j}(\varphi(z))|}{\phi(|\varphi(z)|)(1-|\varphi(z)|^2)^{j-1}} < +\infty.$$

for $j = \overline{1,m}$.

Moreover, if the operator $M_u C_\varphi \mathfrak{R}^m : \mathcal{B}_\phi(\mathbb{B}) \to H^\infty_\mu(\mathbb{B})$ is bounded, then the following asymptotic relationship holds

$$\|M_u C_\varphi \mathfrak{R}^m\|_{\mathcal{B}_\phi(\mathbb{B}) \to H^\infty_\mu(\mathbb{B})} \asymp \sum_{j=1}^m L_j.$$

Corollary 3. *Let $m \in \mathbb{N}$, $u \in H(\mathbb{B})$, ϕ normal on $[0,1)$, $\varphi \in S(\mathbb{B})$ and μ a weight on $\mathbb{B}$. Then, the operator $M_u C_\varphi \mathfrak{R}^m : \mathcal{B}_\phi(\mathbb{B}) \to H^\infty_\mu(\mathbb{B})$ is compact if and only if the operator $M_u C_\varphi \mathfrak{R}^m : \mathcal{B}_\phi(\mathbb{B}) \to H^\infty_\mu(\mathbb{B})$ is bounded and*

$$\lim_{|\varphi(z)| \to 1} \frac{\mu(z)|u(z)||B_{m,j}(\varphi(z))|}{\phi(|\varphi(z)|)(1-|\varphi(z)|^2)^{j-1}} = 0$$

for $j = \overline{1,m}$.

Since

$$C_\varphi M_u \mathfrak{R}^m = S^{m,l}_{u_0 \equiv \cdots \equiv u_{m-1} \equiv 0, u_m = u \circ \varphi, v_1 \equiv \cdots \equiv v_l \equiv 0, \varphi'}$$

the following corollaries come from Proposition 2 (ii), Theorems 1 and 4.

Corollary 4. *Let $m \in \mathbb{N}$, $u \in H(\mathbb{B})$, ϕ normal on $[0,1)$, $\varphi \in S(\mathbb{B})$ and μ a weight on $\mathbb{B}$. Then, the operator $C_\varphi M_u \mathfrak{R}^m : \mathcal{B}_\phi(\mathbb{B}) \to H^\infty_\mu(\mathbb{B})$ is bounded if and only if*

$$M_j := \sup_{z \in \mathbb{B}} \frac{\mu(z)|u(\varphi(z))||B_{m,j}(\varphi(z))|}{\phi(|\varphi(z)|)(1-|\varphi(z)|^2)^{j-1}} < +\infty$$

for $j = \overline{1,m}$.

Moreover, if the operator $C_\varphi M_u \mathfrak{R}^m : \mathcal{B}_\phi(\mathbb{B}) \to H^\infty_\mu(\mathbb{B})$ is bounded, then the following asymptotic relationship holds

$$\|C_\varphi M_u \mathfrak{R}^m\|_{\mathcal{B}_\phi(\mathbb{B}) \to H^\infty_\mu(\mathbb{B})} \asymp \sum_{j=1}^m M_j.$$

Corollary 5. *Let $m \in \mathbb{N}$, $u \in H(\mathbb{B})$, ϕ normal on $[0,1)$, $\varphi \in S(\mathbb{B})$ and μ a weight on $\mathbb{B}$. Then, the operator $C_\varphi M_u \mathfrak{R}^m : \mathcal{B}_\phi(\mathbb{B}) \to H^\infty_\mu(\mathbb{B})$ is compact if and only if the operator $C_\varphi M_u \mathfrak{R}^m : \mathcal{B}_\phi(\mathbb{B}) \to H^\infty_\mu(\mathbb{B})$ is bounded and*

$$\lim_{|\varphi(z)| \to 1} \frac{\mu(z)|u(\varphi(z))||B_{m,j}(\varphi(z))|}{\phi(|\varphi(z)|)(1-|\varphi(z)|^2)^{j-1}} = 0$$

for $j = \overline{1,m}$.

Since

$$C_\varphi \mathfrak{R}^m M_u = S^{m,l}_{u_0 = C_m^0(\mathfrak{R}^m u) \circ \varphi, u_1 = C_m^1(\mathfrak{R}^{m-1}u) \circ \varphi, \ldots, u_m = C_m^m u \circ \varphi, v_1 \equiv \cdots \equiv v_l \equiv 0, \varphi'}$$

the following results hold from Proposition 2 (ii), Theorems 1 and 4.

Corollary 6. Let $m \in \mathbb{N}$, $u \in H(\mathbb{B})$, ϕ normal on $[0,1)$, $\varphi \in S(\mathbb{B})$ and μ a weight on $\mathbb{B}$. Then, the operator $C_\varphi \mathfrak{R}^m M_u : \mathcal{B}_\phi(\mathbb{B}) \to H^\infty_\mu(\mathbb{B})$ is bounded if and only if

$$N_0 := \sup_{z \in \mathbb{B}} \frac{\mu(z)|(\mathfrak{R}^m u)(\varphi(z))|(1-|\varphi(z)|^2)}{\phi(|\varphi(z)|)} < +\infty$$

and

$$N_j := \sup_{z \in \mathbb{B}} \frac{\mu(z)|\sum_{i=j}^m (\mathfrak{R}^{m-i} u)(\varphi(z)) B_{i,j}(\varphi(z))|}{\phi(|\varphi(z)|)(1-|\varphi(z)|^2)^{j-1}} < +\infty$$

for $j = \overline{1,m}$.

Moreover, if the operator $C_\varphi \mathfrak{R}^m M_u : \mathcal{B}_\phi(\mathbb{B}) \to H^\infty_\mu(\mathbb{B})$ is bounded, then the following asymptotic relationship holds

$$\|C_\varphi \mathfrak{R}^m M_u\|_{\mathcal{B}_\phi(\mathbb{B}) \to H^\infty_\mu(\mathbb{B})} \asymp \sum_{j=0}^m N_j.$$

Corollary 7. Let $m \in \mathbb{N}$, $u \in H(\mathbb{B})$, ϕ normal on $[0,1)$, $\varphi \in S(\mathbb{B})$ and μ a weight on $\mathbb{B}$. Then, the operator $C_\varphi \mathfrak{R}^m M_u : \mathcal{B}_\phi(\mathbb{B}) \to H^\infty_\mu(\mathbb{B})$ is compact if and only if the operator $C_\varphi \mathfrak{R}^m M_u : \mathcal{B}_\phi(\mathbb{B}) \to H^\infty_\mu(\mathbb{B})$ is bounded,

$$\lim_{|\varphi(z)| \to 1} \frac{\mu(z)|(\mathfrak{R}^m u)(\varphi(z))|(1-|\varphi(z)|^2)}{\phi(|\varphi(z)|)} = 0$$

and

$$\lim_{|\varphi(z)| \to 1} \frac{\mu(z)|\sum_{i=j}^m (\mathfrak{R}^{m-i} u)(\varphi(z)) B_{i,j}(\varphi(z))|}{\phi(|\varphi(z)|)(1-|\varphi(z)|^2)^{j-1}} = 0$$

for $j = \overline{1,m}$.

Since

$$M_u \mathfrak{R}^m C_\varphi = S^{k,m}_{u_0 \equiv \cdots \equiv u_k \equiv 0, v_1 \equiv \cdots \equiv v_{m-1} \equiv 0, v_m = u, \varphi}$$

and the condition (37) is reduced to the following condition

$$\left| \sum_{j=1}^m B_{m,j}(\mathfrak{R}\varphi(z)) \right| \leq C \left| \sum_{j=1}^m B_{m,j}(\langle \mathfrak{R}\varphi(z), \varphi(z) \rangle) \right|, \tag{70}$$

we obtain the next results from Theorems 1 and 4.

Corollary 8. Assume that (70) is satisfied, $m \in \mathbb{N}$, $u \in H(\mathbb{B})$, ϕ normal on $[0,1)$, $\varphi \in S(\mathbb{B})$ and μ a weight on $\mathbb{B}$. Then, the operator $M_u \mathfrak{R}^m C_\varphi : \mathcal{B}_\phi(\mathbb{B}) \to H^\infty_\mu(\mathbb{B})$ is bounded if and only if

$$\widetilde{L}_j := \sup_{z \in \mathbb{B}} \frac{\mu(z)|u(z)||B_{m,j}(\mathfrak{R}\varphi(z))|}{\phi(|\varphi(z)|)(1-|\varphi(z)|^2)^{j-1}} < +\infty$$

for $j = \overline{1,m}$.

Moreover, if the operator $M_u \mathfrak{R}^m C_\varphi : \mathcal{B}_\phi(\mathbb{B}) \to H^\infty_\mu(\mathbb{B})$ is bounded, then the following asymptotic relationship holds

$$\|M_u \mathfrak{R}^m C_\varphi\|_{\mathcal{B}_\phi(\mathbb{B}) \to H^\infty_\mu(\mathbb{B})} \asymp \sum_{j=1}^m \widetilde{L}_j.$$

Corollary 9. Assume that (70) is satisfied, $m \in \mathbb{N}$, $u \in H(\mathbb{B})$, ϕ normal on $[0,1)$, $\varphi \in S(\mathbb{B})$ and μ a weight on $\mathbb{B}$. Then, the operator $M_u \Re^m C_\varphi : \mathcal{B}_\phi(\mathbb{B}) \to H_\mu^\infty(\mathbb{B})$ is compact if and only if the operator $M_u \Re^m C_\varphi : \mathcal{B}_\phi(\mathbb{B}) \to H_\mu^\infty(\mathbb{B})$ is bounded and

$$\lim_{|\varphi(z)| \to 1} \frac{\mu(z)|u(z)||B_{m,j}(\Re \varphi(z))|}{\phi(|\varphi(z)|)(1-|\varphi(z)|^2)^{j-1}} = 0$$

for $j = \overline{1,m}$.

Since

$$\Re^m M_u C_\varphi = S_{u_1 \equiv \cdots \equiv u_k \equiv 0, u_0 = C_m^0 \Re^m u, v_1 = C_m^1 \Re^{m-1} u, \ldots, v_m = C_m^m u, \varphi}^{k,m}$$

and the condition (37) is reduced to the following condition

$$\left|\sum_{i=j}^m C_m^i (\Re^{m-i} u)(z) B_{i,j}(\Re \varphi(z))\right| \leq C \left|\sum_{i=j}^m C_m^i (\Re^{m-i} u)(z) B_{i,j}(\langle \Re \varphi(z), \varphi(z)\rangle)\right| \quad (71)$$

for $j = \overline{1,m}$. We have the following corollaries from Theorems 1 and 4.

Corollary 10. Assume that (71) is satisfied, $m \in \mathbb{N}$, $u \in H(\mathbb{B})$, ϕ normal on $[0,1)$, $\varphi \in S(\mathbb{B})$ and μ a weight on $\mathbb{B}$. Then, the operator $\Re^m M_u C_\varphi : \mathcal{B}_\phi(\mathbb{B}) \to H_\mu^\infty(\mathbb{B})$ is bounded if and only if

$$\widetilde{M}_0 := \sup_{z \in \mathbb{B}} \frac{\mu(z)|(\Re^m u)(z)|(1-|\varphi(z)|^2)}{\phi(|\varphi(z)|)} < +\infty$$

and

$$\widetilde{M}_j := \sup_{z \in \mathbb{B}} \frac{\mu(z)|\sum_{i=j}^m C_m^i (\Re^{m-i} u)(z) B_{i,j}(\Re \varphi(z))|}{\phi(|\varphi(z)|)(1-|\varphi(z)|^2)^{j-1}} < +\infty$$

for $j = \overline{1,m}$.

Moreover, if the operator $\Re^m M_u C_\varphi : \mathcal{B}_\phi(\mathbb{B}) \to H_\mu^\infty(\mathbb{B})$ is bounded, then the following asymptotic relationship holds

$$\|\Re^m M_u C_\varphi\|_{\mathcal{B}_\phi(\mathbb{B}) \to H_\mu^\infty(\mathbb{B})} \asymp \sum_{j=0}^m \widetilde{M}_j.$$

Corollary 11. Assume that (71) is satisfied, $m \in \mathbb{N}$, $u \in H(\mathbb{B})$, ϕ normal on $[0,1)$, $\varphi \in S(\mathbb{B})$ and μ a weight on $\mathbb{B}$. Then, the operator $\Re^m M_u C_\varphi : \mathcal{B}_\phi(\mathbb{B}) \to H_\mu^\infty(\mathbb{B})$ is compact if and only if the operator $\Re^m M_u C_\varphi : \mathcal{B}_\phi(\mathbb{B}) \to H_\mu^\infty(\mathbb{B})$ is bounded,

$$\lim_{|\varphi(z)| \to 1} \frac{\mu(z)|(\Re^m u)(z)|(1-|\varphi(z)|^2)}{\phi(|\varphi(z)|)} = 0$$

and

$$\lim_{|\varphi(z)| \to 1} \frac{\mu(z)|\sum_{i=j}^m C_m^i (\Re^{m-i} u)(z) B_{i,j}(\Re \varphi(z))|}{\phi(|\varphi(z)|)(1-|\varphi(z)|^2)^{j-1}} = 0$$

for $j = \overline{1,m}$.

Since

$$\Re^m C_\varphi M_u = S_{u_1 \equiv \cdots \equiv u_k \equiv 0, u_0 = C_m^0 \Re^m (u \circ \varphi), v_1 = C_m^1 \Re^{m-1}(u \circ \varphi), \ldots, v_m = C_m^m u \circ \varphi, \varphi}^{k,m}$$

and the condition (37) is reduced to the following condition

$$\left|\sum_{i=j}^{m} C_m^i \Re^{m-i}(u \circ \varphi)(z) B_{i,j}(\Re\varphi(z))\right| \leq C \left|\sum_{i=j}^{m} C_m^i \Re^{m-i}(u \circ \varphi)(z) B_{i,j}(\langle \Re\varphi(z), \varphi(z)\rangle)\right| \quad (72)$$

for $j = \overline{1,m}$. we obtain the following corollaries from Theorems 1 and 4.

Corollary 12. *Assume that (72) is satisfied, $m \in \mathbb{N}$, $u \in H(\mathbb{B})$, ϕ normal on $[0,1)$, $\varphi \in S(\mathbb{B})$, and μ a weight on $\mathbb{B}$. Then, the operator $\Re^m C_\varphi M_u : \mathcal{B}_\phi(\mathbb{B}) \to H_\mu^\infty(\mathbb{B})$ is bounded if and only if*

$$\widetilde{N}_0 := \sup_{z \in \mathbb{B}} \frac{\mu(z)|\Re^m(u \circ \varphi)(z)|(1 - |\varphi(z)|^2)}{\phi(|\varphi(z)|)} < +\infty$$

and

$$\widetilde{N}_j := \sup_{z \in \mathbb{B}} \frac{\mu(z)|\sum_{i=j}^{m} C_m^i \Re^{m-i}(u \circ \varphi)(z) B_{i,j}(\Re\varphi(z))|}{\phi(|\varphi(z)|)(1 - |\varphi(z)|^2)^{j-1}} < +\infty$$

for $j = \overline{1,m}$.

Moreover, if the operator $\Re^m C_\varphi M_u : \mathcal{B}_\phi(\mathbb{B}) \to H_\mu^\infty(\mathbb{B})$ is bounded, then the following asymptotic relationship holds

$$\|\Re^m C_\varphi M_u\|_{\mathcal{B}_\phi(\mathbb{B}) \to H_\mu^\infty(\mathbb{B})} \asymp \sum_{j=0}^{m} \widetilde{N}_j.$$

Corollary 13. *Assume that (72) is satisfied, $m \in \mathbb{N}$, $u \in H(\mathbb{B})$, ϕ normal on $[0,1)$, $\varphi \in S(\mathbb{B})$ and μ a weight on $\mathbb{B}$. Then, the operator $\Re^m C_\varphi M_u : \mathcal{B}_\phi(\mathbb{B}) \to H_\mu^\infty(\mathbb{B})$ is compact if and only if the operator $\Re^m C_\varphi M_u : \mathcal{B}_\phi(\mathbb{B}) \to H_\mu^\infty(\mathbb{B})$ is bounded,*

$$\lim_{|\varphi(z)| \to 1} \frac{\mu(z)|\Re^m(u \circ \varphi)(z)|(1 - |\varphi(z)|^2)}{\phi(|\varphi(z)|)} = 0$$

and

$$\lim_{|\varphi(z)| \to 1} \frac{\mu(z)|\sum_{i=j}^{m} C_m^i \Re^{m-i}(u \circ \varphi)(z) B_{i,j}(\Re\varphi(z))|}{\phi(|\varphi(z)|)(1 - |\varphi(z)|^2)^{j-1}} = 0$$

for $j = \overline{1,m}$.

6. Conclusions

In this paper, we define the sum operator

$$S_{\vec{u},\vec{v},\varphi}^{k,l} = M_{u_0} C_\varphi + \sum_{i=1}^{k} M_{u_i} C_\varphi \Re^i + \sum_{j=1}^{l} M_{v_j} \Re^j C_\varphi$$

on some subspaces of $H(\mathbb{B})$, where $u_0, u_1, \ldots, u_k, v_1, \ldots, v_l \in H(\mathbb{B})$, $\varphi \in S(\mathbb{B})$, and $k, l \in \mathbb{N}$. We completely characterized the boundedness and compactness of the operator $S_{\vec{u},\vec{v},\varphi}^{k,l} : \mathcal{B}_\phi(\mathbb{B}) \to H_\mu^\infty(\mathbb{B})$ in terms of the behaviors of the symbols u_j, v_j, and φ. As an application, the corresponding results of the operators $M_u C_\varphi \Re^m$, $C_\varphi M_u \Re^m$, $C_\varphi \Re^m M_u$, $M_u \Re^m C_\varphi$, $\Re^m M_u C_\varphi$, $\Re^m C_\varphi M_u : \mathcal{B}_\phi(\mathbb{B}) \to H_\mu^\infty(\mathbb{B})$ are obtained. This paper can be viewed as a continuation and extension of the work of [30,31]. We hope that the study can attract more people's attention to such operators.

Author Contributions: Validation, Z.-J.J.; resources, C.-S.H. All authors have read and agreed to the published version of the manuscript.

Funding: This research received no external funding.

Data Availability Statement: Not applicable.

Acknowledgments: The authors would like to thank the anonymous referee for providing valuable comments for the improvement of this paper. Supported by the Sichuan Science and Technology Program (2022ZYD0010).

Conflicts of Interest: The authors declare no conflict of interest.

References

1. Sharma, A.K. Products of composition multiplication and differentiation between Bergman and Bloch type spaces. *Turk. J. Math.* **2011**, *35*, 275–291.
2. Jiang, Z.J. On a class of operators from weighted Bergman spaces to some spaces of analytic functions. *Taiwan J. Math.* **2011**, *15*, 2095–2121. [CrossRef]
3. Jiang, Z.J. On a product-type operator from weighted Bergman-Orlicz space to some weighted type spaces. *Appl. Math. Comput.* **2015**, *256*, 37–51. [CrossRef] [PubMed]
4. Jiang, Z.J. Generalized product-type operators from weighted Bergman-Orlicz spaces to Bloch-Orlicz spaces. *Appl. Math. Comput.* **2015**, *268*, 966–977. [CrossRef]
5. Hu, L.; Yang, R.; Li, S. Dirichlet-Morrey type spaces and Volterra integral operators. *J. Nonlinear Var. Anal.* **2021**, *5*, 477–491.
6. Jiang, Z.J. On Volterre composition operators from Bergman-type space to Bloch-type space. *Czechoslov. Math. J.* **2011**, *61*, 993–1005. [CrossRef]
7. Yang, W.; Yan, W. Generalized weighted composition operators from area Nevanlinna spaces to weighted-type spaces. *Bull. Korean Math. Soc.* **2011**, *48*, 1195–1205. [CrossRef]
8. Stević, S. Essential norm of some extensions of the generalized composition operators between kth weighted-type spaces. *J. Inequal. Appl.* **2017**, *2017*, 13. [CrossRef]
9. Stević, S.; Sharma, A.K.; Bhat, A. Products of multiplication composition and differentiation operators on weighted Bergman spaces. *Appl. Math. Comput.* **2011**, *217*, 8115–8125.
10. Guo, Z.; Shu, Y. On Stević-Sharma operators from Hardy spaces to Stević weighted spaces. *Math. Inequal. Appl.* **2020**, *23*, 217–229.
11. Guo, Z.; Liu, L.; Shu, Y. On Stević-Sharma operators from the mixed norm spaces to Zygmund-type spaces. *Math. Inequal. Appl.* **2021**, *24*, 445–461.
12. Stević, S.; Sharma, A.K.; Bhat, A. Essential norm of multiplication composition and differentiation operators on weighted Bergman spaces. *Appl. Math. Comput.* **2011**, *218*, 2386–2397. [CrossRef]
13. Johnson, W. The curious history of Faà di Bruno's formula. *Am. Math. Mon.* **2002**, *109*, 217–234.
14. Stević, S. Weighted differentiation composition operators from H^∞ and Bloch spaces to nth weighted-type spaces on the unit disk. *Appl. Math. Comput.* **2010**, *216*, 3634–3641. [CrossRef]
15. Jiang, Z.J. Product-type operators from Logarithmic Bergman-type spaces to Zygmund-Orlicz spaces. *Mediterr. J. Math.* **2016**, *13*, 4639–4659. [CrossRef]
16. Jiang, Z.J. Product-type operators from Zygmund spaces to Bloch-Orlicz spaces. *Complex Var. Elliptic Equ.* **2017**, *62*, 1645–1664. [CrossRef]
17. Li, S.; Stević, S. Weighted differentiation composition operators from the logarithmic Bloch space to the weighted-type space. *An. Stiintifice Univ. Ovidius Constanta* **2016**, *24*, 223–240. [CrossRef]
18. Wang, S.; Wang, M.F.; Guo, X. Products of composition, multiplication and iterated differentiation operators between Banach spaces of holomorphic functions. *Taiwan J. Math.* **2020**, *24*, 355–376. [CrossRef]
19. Jiang, Z.J.; Wang, X.F. Products of radial derivative and weighted composition operators from weighted Bergman-Orlicz spaces to weighted-type spaces. *Oper. Matrices* **2018**, *12*, 301–319. [CrossRef]
20. Stević, S. Weighted radial operator from the mixed-norm space to the nth weighted-type space on the unit ball. *Appl. Math. Comput.* **2012**, *218*, 9241–9247. [CrossRef]
21. Zhou, J.; Liu, Y.M. Products of radial derivative and multiplication operators from $F(p,q,s)$ to weighted-type spaces on the unit ball. *Taiwan J. Math.* **2013**, *17*, 161–178.
22. Liu, Y.M.; Yu, Y.Y. Products of composition, multiplication and radial derivative operators from logarithmic Bloch spaces to weighted-type spaces on the unit ball. *J. Math. Anal. Appl.* **2015**, *423*, 76–93. [CrossRef]
23. Liu, Y.M.; Liu, X.M.; Yu, Y.Y. On an extension of Stević-Sharma operator from the mixed-norm space to weighted-type spaces. *Complex Var. Elliptic Equ.* **2017**, *62*, 670–694. [CrossRef]
24. Liu, Y.M.; Yu, Y.Y. On an extension of Stević-Sharma operator from the general space to weighted-type spaces on the unit ball. *Complex Anal. Oper. Theory* **2017**, *11*, 261–288. [CrossRef]
25. Wang, S.; Wang, M.F.; Guo, X. Products of composition, multiplication and radial derivative operators between Banach spaces of holomorphic functions on the unit ball. *Complex Var. Elliptic Equ.* **2020**, *65*, 2026–2055. [CrossRef]

26. Stević, S. Weighted iterated radial composition operators between some spaces of holomorphic functions on the unit ball. *Abstr. Appl. Anal.* **2010**, *2010*, 801264. [CrossRef]
27. Stević, S.; Jiang, Z.J. Weighted iterated radial composition operators from weighted Bergman-Orlicz spaces to weighted-type spaces on the unit ball. *Math. Methods Appl. Sci.* **2021**, *44*, 8684–8696. [CrossRef]
28. Stević, S.; Jiang, Z.J. Weighted iterated radial composition operators from logarithmic Bloch spaces to weighted-type spaces on the unit ball. *Math. Methods Appl. Sci.* **2021**, *45*, 3083–3097. [CrossRef]
29. Stević, S.; Huang, C.S.; Jiang, Z.J. Sum of some product-type operators from Hardy spaces to weighted-type spaces on the unit ball. *Math. Methods Appl. Sci.* **2022**, *45*, 11581–11600. [CrossRef]
30. Huang, C.S.; Jiang, Z.J.; Xue, Y.F. Sum of some product-type operators from mixed-norm spaces to weighted-type spaces on the unit ball. *AIMS Math.* **2022**, *7*, 18194–18217. [CrossRef]
31. Huang, C.S.; Jiang, Z.J. Product-type operators from weighted Bergman-Orlicz spaces to weighted-type spaces on the unit ball. *J. Math. Anal. Appl.* **2023**, *519*, 126739. [CrossRef]
32. Shields, A.L.; Williams, D.L. Bounded projections, duality, and multipliers in spaces of analytic functions. *Trans. Am. Math. Soc.* **1971**, *162*, 287–302. [CrossRef]
33. Jevitć, M. Bounded projections and duality in mixed-norm spaces of analytic functions. *Complex Var. Elliptic Equ.* **1987**, *8*, 293–301. [CrossRef]
34. Shi, J.H. Duality and multipliers for mixed norm spaces in the ball (I). *Complex Var. Elliptic Equ.* **1994**, *25*, 119–130.
35. Peláez, J.; Rättyä, J. Weighted Bergman spaces induced by rapidly increasing weights. *Mem. Am. Math. Soc.* **2014**, *227*, 1–136. [CrossRef]
36. Zhang, X.J.; Li, M.; Guan, Y.; Li, J.F. Atomic decomposition for μ-Bloch space in $\mathbb{C}^n$. *Sci. Sin. Math.* **2015**, *45*, 1677–1688. (In Chinese)
37. Zhu, X.L. Generalized composition operators and Volterra composition operators on Bloch spaces in the unit ball. *Complex Var. Elliptic Equ.* **2009**, *54*, 95–102. [CrossRef]
38. Liang, Y.X.; Zhou, Z.H.; Chen, R.Y. Product of extended Cesàro operator and composition operator from the logarithmic Bloch-type space to $F(p,q,s)$ space on the unit ball. *J. Comput. Anal. Appl.* **2013**, *15*, 432–440.
39. Stević, S. On a new integral-type operator from the Bloch space to Bloch-type spaces on the unit ball. *J. Math. Anal. Appl.* **2009**, *354*, 426–434. [CrossRef]
40. Wu, Z.J.; Zhao, R.H.; Zorboska, N. Toeplitz operators on Bloch-type spaces. *Proc. Am. Math. Soc.* **2006**, *134*, 3531–3542. [CrossRef]
41. Wang, X.L.; Liu, T.S. Toeplitz operators on Bloch-type spaces in the unit ball of $\mathbb{C}^n$. *J. Math. Anal. Appl.* **2010**, *368*, 727–735. [CrossRef]
42. Zhu, X.L. Weighted composition operators from weighted-type spaces to Zygmund-type spaces. *Math. Inequal. Appl.* **2016**, *19*, 1067–1087. [CrossRef]
43. Zhu, J.M.; Wu, Y. Metric spaces with asymptotic property C and finite decomposition complexity. *J. Nonlinear Funct. Anal.* **2021**, *2021*, 15.
44. Tjani, M. Compact Composition Operators on Some Möbius Invariant Banach Space. Ph.D. Dissertation, Michigan State University, East Lansing, MI, USA, 1996.
45. Cowen, C.C.; Maccluer, B.D. *Composition Operators on Spaces of Analytic Functions*; CRC Press: Boca Raton, FL, USA, 1995.
46. Zhang, X.J.; Xi, L.H.; Fan, H.X.; Li, J.F. Atomic decomposition of μ-Bergman space in $\mathbb{C}^n$. *Acta Math. Sci.* **2014**, *34*, 779–789. [CrossRef]
47. Zhu, K.H. *Spaces of Holomorphic Functions in the Unit Ball*; Springer: New York, NY, USA, 2005.

Disclaimer/Publisher's Note: The statements, opinions and data contained in all publications are solely those of the individual author(s) and contributor(s) and not of MDPI and/or the editor(s). MDPI and/or the editor(s) disclaim responsibility for any injury to people or property resulting from any ideas, methods, instructions or products referred to in the content.

Article

Matrix Representations for a Class of Eigenparameter Dependent Sturm–Liouville Problems with Discontinuity

Shuang Li, Jinming Cai * and Kun Li

School of Mathematical Sciences, Qufu Normal University, Qufu 273165, China; qslikun@qfnu.edu.cn (K.L.)
* Correspondence: caijinming@qfnu.edu.cn

Abstract: Matrix representations for a class of Sturm–Liouville problems with eigenparameters contained in the boundary and interface conditions were studied. Given any matrix eigenvalue problem of a certain type and an eigenparameter-dependent condition, a class of Sturm–Liouville problems with this specified condition was constructed. It has been proven that each Sturm–Liouville problem is equivalent to the given matrix eigenvalue problem.

Keywords: Atkinson type; finite spectrum; eigenparameter-dependent interface condition; matrix representation

Citation: Li, S.; Cai, J.; Li, K. Matrix Representations for a Class of Eigenparameter Dependent Sturm–Liouville Problems with Discontinuity. *Axioms* **2023**, *12*, 479. https://doi.org/10.3390/axioms12050479

Academic Editor: Inna Kalchuk

Received: 18 April 2023
Revised: 9 May 2023
Accepted: 12 May 2023
Published: 15 May 2023

Copyright: © 2023 by the authors. Licensee MDPI, Basel, Switzerland. This article is an open access article distributed under the terms and conditions of the Creative Commons Attribution (CC BY) license (https://creativecommons.org/licenses/by/4.0/).

1. Introduction

Recently, Sturm–Liouville problems (SLPs) with discontinuity inside intervals have attracted significant attention from scholars due to their wide application in various fields. For example, one application involves a string loaded with point masses [1–5]. Generally speaking, the eigenparameter only appears in the equation, but in many actual phenomena, it is necessary for the eigenparameter to appear in the boundary conditions, such as heat conduction at the liquid–solid interface [6], and so on. Due to its physical significance, many scholars have studied the problem of boundary conditions containing a spectral parameter [7–14]. In recent decades, more researchers have studied eigenparameter-dependent SLPs with discontinuity, including the asymptotic behavior of eigenvalues, the inverse spectral theory, the finite spectrum, the oscillation of eigenfunctions, etc., see [9,10,15–19].

Regular SLPs have an infinite countable number of eigenvalues that are bounded below and unbounded above. However, Atkinson, in his well-celebrated book [20], stated that finite eigenvalues may exist under certain conditions. Kong and Zettl [18] solved this problem by constructing a class of regular SLPs, which has exactly $\mathfrak{N}$ eigenvalues for every positive integer $\mathfrak{N}$; they obtained the corresponding matrix representations in [19]. This special problem is called Atkinson-type SLPs (ASLPs). Ao et al. generalized this problem to various differential operators, for example, ASLPs with interface conditions, ASLPs with eigenparameters contained in boundary conditions, higher-order differential operators, etc. [21–26]. They discussed the existence of a finite spectrum and gave the corresponding matrix representation. In particular, Ao et al. proved that ASLPs with interface conditions have, at most, $\mathfrak{M} + \mathfrak{N} + 2$ eigenvalues and gave the corresponding matrix representation in [23]. Moreover, the authors generalized the problem to eigenparameter-dependent ASLPs [24].

In recent years, SLPs with interface conditions dependent on parameters have also captured the attention of researchers, see [2–4] and references therein. In reference [2], the author obtained the operator–theoretic formulation. The asymptotic properties of eigenvalues were given for SLPs with interface conditions that were rationally dependent on the parameters in [3]. In work by Mukhtarov et al. [4], Green's function was provided for eigenparameter-dependent SLPs with interface conditions.

In a recent paper, Ao et al. proved that SLPs with interface conditions dependent on the eigenparameter still have a finite spectrum [27]. Here, the following question arises:

When the eigenparameter appears in both the boundary and interface conditions, does it affect the number in the spectrum? In this paper, we will solve this problem. We study an SLP in which an eigenparameter is contained in both the boundary and interface conditions, regardless of whether it is self-adjoint or non-self-adjoint. We prove that the problem has, at most, $\mathfrak{M} + \mathfrak{N} + 5$ eigenvalues, which is different from the results in [27], where the number of eigenvalues is, at most, $\mathfrak{M} + \mathfrak{N} + 4$. Moreover, we provide an example to illustrate our conclusion (as it turns out, it affects the number of eigenvalues). The basic method we used in this paper is a factorization of the characteristic function.

The rest of this paper is organized as follows: Some preliminaries are given in Section 2. In Section 3, we show that the number of eigenvalues of the considered problem is finite. In Section 4, the corresponding matrix representation is given, and for a given specific type of matrix eigenvalue problem, we construct a class of SLPs with the same boundary and interface conditions, ensuring that they have the same eigenvalues.

2. Preliminaries

In this work, we investigate the SL equation

$$-(q(t)f'(t))' + p(t)f(t) = \mu w(t)f(t), \ t \in \mathfrak{I} = [c, \eta) \cup (\eta, d], \ -\infty < c < d < \infty \quad (1)$$

with boundary conditions at the endpoints c and d, as follows

$$\xi_1 f(c) + \xi_2 (qf')(c) + \xi_3 f(d) + \xi_4 (qf')(d) = \mu[\xi'_1 f(c) + \xi'_2 (qf')(c) + \xi'_3 f(d) + \xi'_4 (qf')(d)], \quad (2)$$

$$\tau_1 f(c) + \tau_2 (qf')(c) + \tau_3 f(d) + \tau_4 (qf')(d) = \mu[\tau'_1 f(c) + \tau'_2 (qf')(c) + \tau'_3 f(d) + \tau'_4 (qf')(d)], \quad (3)$$

and interface conditions

$$f(\eta + 0) = (\mathfrak{e}_1 \mu + \mathfrak{e}'_1) f(\eta - 0) + (\mathfrak{e}_2 \mu + \mathfrak{e}'_2)(qf')(\eta - 0), \quad (4)$$

$$(qf')(\eta + 0) = (\mathfrak{e}_3 \mu + \mathfrak{e}'_3) f(\eta - 0) + (\mathfrak{e}_4 \mu + \mathfrak{e}'_4)(qf')(\eta - 0), \quad (5)$$

where $f(\eta + 0)$ and $f(\eta - 0)$ denote the right and left limits of $f(t)$ at η, respectively. $\mu \in \mathbb{C}$ is a spectral parameter; $\xi_i, \tau_i, \mathfrak{e}_i, \xi'_i, \tau'_i, \mathfrak{e}'_i \in \mathbb{R}$ ($i = \overline{1,4}$), and

$$\text{rank}\begin{pmatrix} \xi_1 & \xi_2 & \xi_3 & \xi_4 \\ \xi'_1 & \xi'_2 & \xi'_3 & \xi'_4 \end{pmatrix} = 2, \ \text{rank}\begin{pmatrix} \tau_1 & \tau_2 & \tau_3 & \tau_4 \\ \tau'_1 & \tau'_2 & \tau'_3 & \tau'_4 \end{pmatrix} = 2,$$

$$\text{rank}\begin{pmatrix} \xi_1 & \xi_2 & \xi_3 & \xi_4 \\ \tau_1 & \tau_2 & \tau_3 & \tau_4 \end{pmatrix} = 2, \ \text{rank}\begin{pmatrix} \xi'_1 & \xi'_2 & \xi'_3 & \xi'_4 \\ \tau'_1 & \tau'_2 & \tau'_3 & \tau'_4 \end{pmatrix} = 2. \quad (6)$$

We assume that the coefficients satisfy the following conditions

$$\frac{1}{q(t)}, \ p(t), \ w(t) \in L^1(\mathfrak{I}, \mathbb{R}), \quad (7)$$

where $L^1(\mathfrak{I}, \mathbb{R}) = \{f : \mathfrak{I} \mapsto \mathbb{R} | \int_I |f(t)| dt < \infty\}$.

We suppose that $Rank[A_\mu | B_\mu] = 2$ and $\det(\Gamma_\mu) \neq 0$, where

$$A_\mu = \begin{pmatrix} \xi_1 - \mu \xi'_1 & \xi_2 - \mu \xi'_2 \\ \tau_1 - \mu \tau'_1 & \tau_2 - \mu \tau'_2 \end{pmatrix}, \ B_\mu = \begin{pmatrix} \xi_3 - \mu \xi'_3 & \xi_4 - \mu \xi'_4 \\ \tau_3 - \mu \tau'_3 & \tau_4 - \mu \tau'_4 \end{pmatrix}, \quad (8)$$

$$\Gamma_\mu = \begin{pmatrix} \mathfrak{e}_1 \mu + \mathfrak{e}'_1 & \mathfrak{e}_2 \mu + \mathfrak{e}'_2 \\ \mathfrak{e}_3 \mu + \mathfrak{e}'_3 & \mathfrak{e}_4 \mu + \mathfrak{e}'_4 \end{pmatrix}, \quad (9)$$

then (2)–(5) turn into

$$A_\mu F(c) + B_\mu F(d) = 0, \quad F(\eta + 0) = \Gamma_\mu F(\eta - 0), \quad F = \begin{pmatrix} f \\ qf' \end{pmatrix}.$$

Equation (1) can be represented as

$$\begin{cases} u' = sv, \\ v' = (p - \mu w)u. \end{cases} \tag{10}$$

by using $\begin{cases} u = f, \\ v = qf'. \end{cases}$

Definition 1. *(Reference [18])* $f(t)$ *is called a trivial solution of (1) if* $f(t) \equiv q(t)f'(t) \equiv 0$, $t \in \mathfrak{J}$.

Let $\Phi(t, \mu) = [\varrho_{kl}(t, \mu)]$ $(k, l = 1, 2)$ be the fundamental solution matrix of system (10), satisfying (4) and (5) as follows

$$\Phi(t, \mu) = \begin{cases} \Phi_1(t, \mu), & t \in [c, \eta), \\ \Phi_2(t, \mu), & t \in (\eta, d], \end{cases} \tag{11}$$

with the initial condition $\Phi_1(c, \mu) = I$.

Define $\Lambda(\mu) := \det[A_\mu + B_\mu \Phi_2(d, \mu)]$. Let

$$H(\mu) = \begin{pmatrix} \mathfrak{h}_{11}(\mu) & \mathfrak{h}_{12}(\mu) \\ \mathfrak{h}_{21}(\mu) & \mathfrak{h}_{22}(\mu) \end{pmatrix},$$

where

$$\mathfrak{h}_{11}(\mu) = (\xi_3 - \mu \xi_3')(\tau_2 - \mu \tau_2') - (\xi_2 - \mu \xi_2')(\tau_3 - \mu \tau_3'),$$
$$\mathfrak{h}_{12}(\mu) = (\xi_1 - \mu \xi_1')(\tau_3 - \mu \tau_3') - (\xi_3 - \mu \xi_3')(\tau_1 - \mu \tau_1'),$$
$$\mathfrak{h}_{21}(\mu) = (\xi_4 - \mu \xi_4')(\tau_2 - \mu \tau_2') - (\xi_2 - \mu \xi_2')(\tau_4 - \mu \tau_4'),$$
$$\mathfrak{h}_{22}(\mu) = (\xi_1 - \mu \xi_1')(\tau_4 - \mu \tau_4') - (\xi_4 - \mu \xi_4')(\tau_1 - \mu \tau_1').$$

By a direct calculation, we know

$$\Lambda(\mu) = \det[A_\mu + B_\mu \Phi_2(d, \mu)]$$
$$= \left| \begin{pmatrix} \xi_1 - \mu \xi_1' & \xi_2 - \mu \xi_2' \\ \tau_1 - \mu \tau_1' & \tau_2 - \mu \tau_2' \end{pmatrix} + \begin{pmatrix} \xi_3 - \mu \xi_3' & \xi_4 - \mu \xi_4' \\ \tau_3 - \mu \tau_3' & \tau_4 - \mu \tau_4' \end{pmatrix} \begin{pmatrix} \varrho_{11}(d, \mu) & \varrho_{12}(d, \mu) \\ \varrho_{21}(d, \mu) & \varrho_{22}(d, \mu) \end{pmatrix} \right|$$
$$= \det(A_\mu) + \det(B_\mu) - \det(B_\mu)$$
$$+ [(\xi_3 - \mu \xi_3')(\tau_2 - \mu \tau_2') - (\xi_2 - \mu \xi_2')(\tau_3 - \mu \tau_3')]\varrho_{11}(d, \mu)$$
$$+ [(\xi_1 - \mu \xi_1')(\tau_3 - \mu \tau_3') - (\xi_3 - \mu \xi_3')(\tau_1 - \mu \tau_1')]\varrho_{12}(d, \mu)$$
$$+ [(\xi_4 - \mu \xi_4')(\tau_2 - \mu \tau_2') - (\xi_2 - \mu \xi_2')(\tau_4 - \mu \tau_4')]\varrho_{21}(d, \mu)$$
$$+ [(\xi_1 - \mu \xi_1')(\tau_4 - \mu \tau_4') - (\xi_4 - \mu \xi_4')(\tau_1 - \mu \tau_1')]\varrho_{22}(d, \mu)$$
$$+ (\xi_3 - \mu \xi_3')(\tau_4 - \mu \tau_4')\varrho_{22}(d, \mu)\varrho_{11}(d, \mu) + (\xi_4 - \mu \xi_4')(\tau_3 - \mu \tau_3')\varrho_{21}(d, \mu)\varrho_{12}(d, \mu)$$
$$- (\xi_4 - \mu \xi_4')(\tau_3 - \mu \tau_3')\varrho_{22}(d, \mu)\varrho_{11}(d, \mu) + (\xi_3 - \mu \xi_3')(\tau_4 - \mu \tau_4')\varrho_{21}(d, \mu)\varrho_{12}(d, \mu)$$
$$= \det(A_\mu) + \det(B_\mu) + \mathfrak{h}_{11}(\mu)\varrho_{11}(d, \mu) + \mathfrak{h}_{12}(\mu)\varrho_{12}(d, \mu) + \mathfrak{h}_{21}(\mu)\varrho_{21}(d, \mu)$$
$$+ \mathfrak{h}_{22}(\mu)\varrho_{22}(d, \mu) + [(\xi_3 - \mu \xi_3')(\tau_4 - \mu \tau_4') - (\xi_4 - \mu \xi_4')(\tau_3 - \mu \tau_3')] \times$$
$$[\varrho_{11}(d, \mu)\varrho_{22}(d, \mu) - \varrho_{12}(d, \mu)\varrho_{21}(d, \mu) - 1],$$

since $\det(\Phi_2(d,\mu)) = \det(\Phi_1(d,\mu)) = 1$, so $\varrho_{11}(d,\mu)\varrho_{22}(d,\mu) - \varrho_{12}(d,\mu)\varrho_{21}(d,\mu) - 1 = 0$, we have

$$\Lambda(\mu) = \det(A_\mu) + \det(B_\mu) + \mathfrak{h}_{11}(\mu)\varrho_{11}(d,\mu) + \mathfrak{h}_{12}(\mu)\varrho_{12}(d,\mu) \\ + \mathfrak{h}_{21}(\mu)\varrho_{21}(d,\mu) + \mathfrak{h}_{22}(\mu)\varrho_{22}(d,\mu). \tag{12}$$

Proposition 1. $\Lambda(\mu) = 0 \iff \mu$ *is an eigenvalue of (1)–(5).*

Proof. We suppose $\Lambda(\mu) = 0$, then the equation $[A_\mu + B_\mu \Phi_2(d,\mu)]C = 0$ has non-zero solutions. We solve the initial value problem

$$F' = \begin{pmatrix} 0 & s \\ p - \mu w & 0 \end{pmatrix} F, \ F = \begin{pmatrix} f \\ pf' \end{pmatrix} \text{on } J, \ F(c) = C,$$

then we have $F(d) = \Phi_2(d,\mu)F(c)$ and $[A_\mu + B_\mu \Phi_2(d,\mu)]F(c) = 0$, we can obtain $A_\mu F(c) + B_\mu F(d) = 0$, so μ is an eigenvalue.

On the contrary, if μ is an eigenvalue and f is an eigenfunction, then $F = \begin{pmatrix} f \\ pf' \end{pmatrix}$ satisfies $F(d) = \Phi_2(d,\mu)F(c)$; thus, $[A_\mu + B_\mu \Phi_2(d,\mu)]F(c) = 0$. If $F(c) = 0$, then it is a trivial solution. This contradicts f being an eigenfunction, so we have $\det[A_\mu + B_\mu \Phi_2(d,\mu)] = 0$. □

3. The Finite Spectrum Problem of (1)–(5)

Problems (1)–(5) have finite eigenvalues in this section. In the sequel, we always suppose that (7) holds, and there is a partition of $\mathfrak{J}$

$$c = c_0 < c_1 < c_2 < \cdots < c_{2\mathfrak{M}} < \eta < d_1 < d_2 < \cdots < d_{2\mathfrak{N}+1} = d, \tag{13}$$

for $\mathfrak{M}, \mathfrak{N} \in \mathbb{Z}_+$, such that

$$\frac{1}{q(t)} = 0, t \in \cup_{i=0}^{\mathfrak{M}-1}[c_{2i}, c_{2i+1}] \cup [c_{2\mathfrak{M}}, \eta) \cup (\eta, d_1] \cup_{j=1}^{\mathfrak{N}}[d_{2j}, d_{2j+1}]; \\ p(t) = w(t) = 0, t \in \cup_{i=0}^{\mathfrak{M}-1}[c_{2i+1}, c_{2i+2}] \cup_{j=0}^{\mathfrak{N}-1}[d_{2j+1}, d_{2j+2}]; \tag{14}$$

$$\int_{c_{2i+1}}^{c_{2i+2}} \frac{1}{q(t)} dt \neq 0, i = \overline{0, \mathfrak{M}-1}; \int_{d_{2j+1}}^{d_{2j+2}} \frac{1}{q(t)} dt \neq 0, j = \overline{0, \mathfrak{N}-1}; \\ \int_{c_{2i}}^{c_{2i+1}} w(t) dt \neq 0, i = \overline{0, \mathfrak{M}-1}; \int_{d_{2j}}^{d_{2j+1}} w(t) dt \neq 0, j = \overline{1, \mathfrak{N}}; \tag{15} \\ \int_{\eta}^{d_1} w(t) dt \neq 0, \int_{2\mathfrak{M}}^{\eta} w(t) dt \neq 0.$$

Definition 2. *(Reference [1]) If an SL Equation (1) satisfies (13)–(15), then Equation (1) is called an Atkinson type.*

Definition 3. *(Reference [1]) If there exists an Equation (1) of the Atkinson type, then (1)–(5) is called an Atkinson type.*

Definition 4. Let (13)–(15) hold. We define the following notations.

$$
\begin{aligned}
s_i &:= \int_{c_{2i-1}}^{c_{2i}} \frac{1}{q(t)} dt, \quad i = 1, 2, \ldots, \mathfrak{M}; \\
p_i &:= \int_{c_{2i}}^{c_{2i+1}} p(t) dt, \quad w_i := \int_{c_{2i}}^{c_{2i+1}} w(t) dt, \quad i = \overline{0, \mathfrak{M}-1}; \\
p_{\mathfrak{M}} &:= \int_{c_{2\mathfrak{M}}}^{\eta} p(t) dt, \quad w_{\mathfrak{M}} := \int_{c_{2\mathfrak{M}}}^{\eta} w(t) dt; \\
\tilde{s}_j &:= \int_{d_{2j-1}}^{d_{2j}} \frac{1}{q(t)} dt, \quad j = 1, 2, \ldots, \mathfrak{N}; \\
\tilde{p}_0 &:= \int_{\eta}^{d_1} p(t) dt, \quad \tilde{p}_j := \int_{d_{2j}}^{d_{2j+1}} p(t) dt, \quad j = \overline{1, \mathfrak{N}}; \\
\tilde{w}_0 &:= \int_{\eta}^{d_1} w(t) dt, \quad \tilde{w}_j := \int_{d_{2j}}^{d_{2j+1}} w(t) dt, \quad j = \overline{1, \mathfrak{N}}.
\end{aligned}
\quad (16)
$$

Next, we give two fundamental solution matrices of system (10).

Lemma 1. $\Phi(t, \mu)$ defined as (11), we have

$$\Phi_1(c_1, \mu) = \begin{pmatrix} 1 & 0 \\ p_0 - \mu w_0 & 1 \end{pmatrix},$$

$$\Phi_1(c_3, \mu) = \begin{pmatrix} 1 + (p_0 - \mu w_0) s_1 & s_1 \\ \varrho_{21}(c_3, \mu) & 1 + (p_1 - \mu w_1) s_1 \end{pmatrix},$$

where $\varrho_{21}(c_3, \mu) = (p_0 - \mu w_0) + (p_1 - \mu w_1) + (p_0 - \mu w_0)(p_1 - \mu w_1) s_1$.
In general, for $1 \leq i \leq \mathfrak{M} - 1$, we have

$$\Phi_1(c_{2i+1}, \mu) = \begin{pmatrix} 1 & s_i \\ p_i - \mu w_i & 1 + (p_i - \mu w_i) s_i \end{pmatrix} \Phi_1(c_{2i-1}, \mu),$$

particularly,

$$\Phi_1(\eta - 0, \mu) = \begin{pmatrix} 1 & s_{\mathfrak{M}} \\ p_{\mathfrak{M}} - \mu w_{\mathfrak{M}} & 1 + (p_{\mathfrak{M}} - \mu w_{\mathfrak{M}}) s_{\mathfrak{M}} \end{pmatrix} \Phi_1(c_{2\mathfrak{M}-1}, \mu).$$

Proof. From (14), we know that u is constant on $\cup_{i=0}^{\mathfrak{M}-1}[c_{2i}, c_{2i+1}] \cup [c_{2\mathfrak{M}}, \eta)$ by $\frac{1}{q(t)} = 0$ and v is constant on $\cup_{i=0}^{\mathfrak{M}-1}[c_{2i+1}, c_{2i+2}]$ by $p(t) = w(t) = 0$. Thus, we can obtain the result by using the iterative method. □

Using similar methods in Lemma 1, we have

Lemma 2. For each $\mu \in \mathbb{C}$, we denote

$$\Theta(t, \mu) = [\psi_{kl}(t, \mu)] (k, l = 1, 2) \quad (17)$$

a fundamental solution matrix of the system (10) with interface conditions (4) and (5), and satisfy the initial condition $\Theta(\eta + 0, \mu) = I$. Then we have

$$\Theta(d_1, \mu) = \begin{pmatrix} 1 & 0 \\ \tilde{p}_0 - \mu \tilde{w}_0 & 1 \end{pmatrix}.$$

Generally, for $1 \leq j \leq \mathfrak{N}$,

$$\Theta(d_{2j+1},\mu) = \begin{pmatrix} 1 & \tilde{s}_j \\ \tilde{p}_j - \mu\tilde{w}_j & 1 + (\tilde{p}_j - \mu\tilde{w}_j)\tilde{s}_j \end{pmatrix} \Theta(d_{2j-1},\mu).$$

Lemma 3. *Let $\Phi(t,\mu)$ and $\Theta(t,\mu)$ be defined in (11) and (17), respectively. Then we have*

$$\Phi_2(d,\mu) = \Theta(d,\mu)\Gamma_\mu \Phi_1(\eta - 0, \mu), \quad t \in (\eta, d],$$

where Γ_μ is defined in (9).

Proof. From the two fundamental solutions, $\Theta(t,\mu)$ and $\Phi(t,\mu)$ of system (10), and the given initial value, we can obtain

$$\Theta(t,\mu) = \Phi_2(t,\mu)\Phi_2^{-1}(\eta + 0, \mu),$$

from (4) and (5), we have

$$\Phi_2(\eta + 0, \mu) = \Gamma_\mu \Phi_1(\eta - 0, \mu).$$

Particularly, let $t = d$, we obtain

$$\Phi_2(d,\mu) = \Theta(d,\mu)\Gamma_\mu \Phi_1(\eta - 0, \mu).$$

□

In light of Lemmas 1–3, we can obtain the following theorem, and problems (1)–(5) have finite eigenvalues:

Theorem 1. *Let (14)-(16) hold, $H(\mu)$ is defined as above. Assume $\mathfrak{e}_2 \neq 0$; thus,*

Conditions	The number of eigenvalues
If $\xi'_4\tau'_2 - \xi'_2\tau'_4 \neq 0$;	$\mathfrak{M} + \mathfrak{N} + 5$
If $\xi'_4\tau'_2 - \xi'_2\tau'_4 = 0$; $w_0\tilde{w}_\mathfrak{N}(\tau_4\xi'_2 + \xi_2\tau'_4 - \xi_4\tau'_2 - \tau_2\xi'_4)$ $-\tilde{w}_\mathfrak{N}(\xi'_1\tau'_4 - \xi'_4\tau'_1) - w_0(\tau'_2\xi'_3 - \xi'_2\tau'_3) \neq 0$;	$\mathfrak{M} + \mathfrak{N} + 4$
If $\xi'_4\tau'_2 - \xi'_2\tau'_4 = \xi'_3\tau'_2 - \xi'_2\tau'_3 = \xi'_1\tau'_4 - \xi'_4\tau'_1$ $= \tau_4\xi'_2 + \xi_2\tau'_4 - \xi_4\tau'_2 - \tau_2\xi'_4 = 0$; $\xi'_1\tau'_3 - \xi'_3\tau'_1 + w_0\tilde{w}_\mathfrak{N}(\xi_4\tau_2 - \xi_2\tau_4)$ $-w_0(\xi_2\tau'_3 + \xi'_2\tau_3 - \xi_3\tau'_2 - \xi'_3\tau_2)$ $-\tilde{w}_\mathfrak{N}(\xi_4\tau'_1 + \xi'_4\tau_1 - \xi_1\tau'_4 - \xi'_1\tau_4) \neq 0$;	$\mathfrak{M} + \mathfrak{N} + 3$
If $\xi'_4\tau'_2 - \xi'_2\tau'_4 = \xi'_3\tau'_2 - \xi'_2\tau'_3 = \xi'_1\tau'_4 - \xi'_4\tau'_1$ $= \xi_4\tau_2 - \xi_2\tau_4 = \xi'_1\tau'_3 - \xi'_3\tau'_1 = \tau_4\xi'_2 + \xi_2\tau'_4 - \xi_4\tau'_2 - \tau_2\xi'_4$ $= \xi_2\tau'_3 + \xi'_2\tau_3 - \xi_3\tau'_2 - \xi'_3\tau_2 = \xi_4\tau'_1 + \xi'_4\tau_1 - \xi_1\tau'_4 - \xi'_1\tau_4 = 0$; $\xi_3\tau'_1 + \xi'_3\tau_1 - \xi_1\tau'_3 - \xi'_1\tau_3$ $-\tilde{w}_\mathfrak{N}(\xi_1\tau_4 - \xi_4\tau_1) - w_0(\xi_3\tau_2 - \xi_2\tau_3) \neq 0$;	$\mathfrak{M} + \mathfrak{N} + 2$
If $\xi'_4\tau'_2 - \xi'_2\tau'_4 = \xi'_3\tau'_2 - \xi'_2\tau'_3 = \xi'_1\tau'_4 - \xi'_4\tau'_1 = \xi_4\tau_2 - \xi_2\tau_4$ $= \xi'_1\tau'_3 - \xi'_3\tau'_1 = \xi_3\tau_2 - \xi_2\tau_3 = \xi_1\tau_4 - \xi_4\tau_1$ $= \tau_4\xi'_2 + \xi_2\tau'_4 - \xi_4\tau'_2 - \tau_2\xi'_4 = \xi_2\tau'_3 + \xi'_2\tau_3 - \xi_3\tau'_2 - \xi'_3\tau_2$ $= \xi_4\tau'_1 + \xi'_4\tau_1 - \xi_1\tau'_4 - \xi'_1\tau_4 = \xi_3\tau'_1 + \xi'_3\tau_1 - \xi_1\tau'_3 - \xi'_1\tau_3 = 0$; $\xi_1\tau_3 - \xi_3\tau_1 \neq 0$;	$\mathfrak{M} + \mathfrak{N} + 1$

If none of the conditions in the table above are met, then (1)–(5) have ι eigenvalues for $\iota \in \{1, 2, \cdots, \mathfrak{M} + \mathfrak{N}\}$ or the system can be degenerate.

Proof. Firstly, by Lemma 3, we know that $\Phi_2(d,\mu) = \Theta(d,\mu)\Gamma_\mu \Phi_1(\eta - 0, \mu)$; next, we can obtain the structure of $\Phi_2(d, \mu)$ by a direct calculation.

If $\mathfrak{e}_2 \neq 0$, we can obtain the structure of $\Phi_2(d, \mu)$, as follows:

$$\varrho_{11}(d,\mu) = Y\tilde{Y}\big[(\mathfrak{e}_2\mu + \mathfrak{e}_2')(p_\mathfrak{M} - \mu w_\mathfrak{M})(\tilde{p}_0 - \mu \tilde{w}_0) + (\mathfrak{e}_1\mu + \mathfrak{e}_1')(\tilde{p}_0 - \mu \tilde{w}_0) + \mathfrak{e}_3\mu + \mathfrak{e}_3'$$
$$+(\mathfrak{e}_4\mu + \mathfrak{e}_4')(p_\mathfrak{M} - \mu w_\mathfrak{M})\big] \times \prod_{i=0}^{\mathfrak{M}-1}(p_i - \mu w_i)\prod_{j=1}^{\mathfrak{N}-1}(\tilde{p}_j - \mu \tilde{w}_j) + \tilde{\varrho}_{11}(\mu),$$

$$\varrho_{12}(d,\mu) = Y\tilde{Y}\big[(\mathfrak{e}_2\mu + \mathfrak{e}_2')(p_\mathfrak{M} - \mu w_\mathfrak{M})(\tilde{p}_0 - \mu \tilde{w}_0) + (\mathfrak{e}_1\mu + \mathfrak{e}_1')(\tilde{p}_0 - \mu \tilde{w}_0) + \mathfrak{e}_3\mu + \mathfrak{e}_3'$$
$$+(\mathfrak{e}_4\mu + \mathfrak{e}_4')(p_\mathfrak{M} - \mu w_\mathfrak{M})\big] \times \prod_{i=1}^{\mathfrak{M}-1}(p_i - \mu w_i)\prod_{j=1}^{\mathfrak{N}-1}(\tilde{p}_j - \mu \tilde{w}_j) + \tilde{\varrho}_{12}(\mu),$$

$$\varrho_{21}(d,\mu) = Y\tilde{Y}\big[(\mathfrak{e}_2\mu + \mathfrak{e}_2')(p_\mathfrak{M} - \mu w_\mathfrak{M})(\tilde{p}_0 - \mu \tilde{w}_0) + (\mathfrak{e}_1\mu + \mathfrak{e}_1')(\tilde{p}_0 - \mu \tilde{w}_0) + \mathfrak{e}_3\mu + \mathfrak{e}_3'$$
$$+(\mathfrak{e}_4\mu + \mathfrak{e}_4')(p_\mathfrak{M} - \mu w_\mathfrak{M})\big] \times \prod_{i=0}^{\mathfrak{M}-1}(p_i - \mu w_i)\prod_{j=1}^{\mathfrak{N}}(\tilde{p}_j - \mu \tilde{w}_j) + \tilde{\varrho}_{21}(\mu),$$

$$\varrho_{22}(d,\mu) = Y\tilde{Y}\big[(\mathfrak{e}_2\mu + \mathfrak{e}_2')(p_\mathfrak{M} - \mu w_\mathfrak{M})(\tilde{p}_0 - \mu \tilde{w}_0) + (\mathfrak{e}_1\mu + \mathfrak{e}_1')(\tilde{p}_0 - \mu \tilde{w}_0) + +\mathfrak{e}_3\mu + \mathfrak{e}_3'$$
$$(\mathfrak{e}_4\mu + \mathfrak{e}_4')(p_\mathfrak{M} - \mu w_\mathfrak{M})\big] \times \prod_{i=1}^{\mathfrak{M}-1}(p_i - \mu w_i)\prod_{j=1}^{\mathfrak{N}}(\tilde{p}_j - \mu \tilde{w}_j) + \tilde{\varrho}_{22}(\mu),$$

where $Y = \prod_{i=1}^{\mathfrak{M}} s_i$, $\tilde{Y} = \prod_{j=1}^{\mathfrak{N}} \tilde{s}_j$, $\tilde{\varrho}_{kl}(\mu) = o(Y\tilde{Y})$ when $\min\{s_i, \tilde{s}_j : i = \overline{1,\mathfrak{M}}, j = \overline{1,\mathfrak{N}}\} \to \infty, k, l = 1, 2$.

So if $\mathfrak{e}_2 \neq 0$, it follows that the degrees of $\varrho_{11}(d,\mu), \varrho_{12}(d,\mu), \varrho_{21}(d,\mu)$ and $\varrho_{22}(d,\mu)$ in μ are $\mathfrak{M} + \mathfrak{N} + 2$, $\mathfrak{M} + \mathfrak{N} + 1$, $\mathfrak{M} + \mathfrak{N} + 3$, and $\mathfrak{M} + \mathfrak{N} + 2$, respectively. According to (12) and Proposition 1, if $\xi_4' \tau_2' - \xi_2' \tau_4' \neq 0$ in $\mathfrak{h}_{21}(\mu)$, we can obtain the highest degree of μ in $\Lambda(\mu)$ is $\mathfrak{M} + \mathfrak{N} + 5$; hence, $\Lambda(\mu)$ has $\mathfrak{M} + \mathfrak{N} + 5$ roots. Moreover, other cases can be obtained by using similar methods. □

Remark 1. *In Theorem 1, if $\mathfrak{e}_2 = 0$, but $\mathfrak{e}_2' \neq 0$, we can obtain the same conclusions. In fact, the highest degree of μ in $\Lambda(\mu)$ is $\mathfrak{M} + \mathfrak{N} + 4$. Thus, it has $\mathfrak{M} + \mathfrak{N} + 4$, $\mathfrak{M} + \mathfrak{N} + 3$, $\mathfrak{M} + \mathfrak{N} + 2$, $\mathfrak{M} + \mathfrak{N} + 1$, $\mathfrak{M} + \mathfrak{N}$ eigenvalues, respectively.*

Example 1. *We study a specific SLP:*

$$\begin{cases} -(q(t)f'(t))' + p(t)f(t) = \mu w(t)f(t), & t \in \mathfrak{I} = (-1, 0) \cup (0, 2). \\ A_\mu F(-1) + B_\mu F(2) = 0, \\ F(0+) - \Gamma_\mu F(0-) = 0, \end{cases}$$

where

$$A_\mu = \begin{pmatrix} 1 & \mu \\ 0 & 2\mu \end{pmatrix}, \quad B_\mu = \begin{pmatrix} 1 & 2\mu + 1 \\ 0 & \mu \end{pmatrix}, \quad \Gamma_\mu = \begin{pmatrix} \mu & 2\mu \\ 1 & 0 \end{pmatrix}.$$

We choose $\mathfrak{M} = \mathfrak{N} = 1$, and $q(t), p(t), w(t)$ are piece-wise constant functions:

$$q(t) = \begin{cases} \infty, & (-1, -\frac{2}{3}) \\ \frac{1}{3}, & (-\frac{2}{3}, -\frac{1}{3}) \\ \infty, & (-\frac{1}{3}, 0) \\ \infty, & (0, \frac{1}{2}) \\ \frac{1}{2}, & (\frac{1}{2}, 1) \\ \infty, & (1, 2) \end{cases}, \quad p(t) = \begin{cases} 3, & (-1, -\frac{2}{3}) \\ 0, & (-\frac{2}{3}, -\frac{1}{3}) \\ 6, & (-\frac{1}{3}, 0) \\ 2, & (0, \frac{1}{2}) \\ 0, & (\frac{1}{2}, 1) \\ 1, & (1, 2) \end{cases}, \quad w(t) = \begin{cases} 3, & (-1, -\frac{2}{3}) \\ 0, & (-\frac{2}{3}, -\frac{1}{3}) \\ 3, & (-\frac{1}{3}, 0) \\ 2, & (0, \frac{1}{2}) \\ 0, & (\frac{1}{2}, 1) \\ 1, & (1, 2) \end{cases}.$$

From the conditions, we know $\mathfrak{e}_2 = 2 \neq 0$. By a direct calculation, we have

$$\Lambda(\mu) = 6\mu^7 - 53\mu^6 + 142\mu^5 - 71\mu^4 - 166\mu^3 + 142\mu^2 + 17\mu.$$

Then the number of eigenvalues of this problem is 7.

$$\mu_1 \approx -1.0291, \ \mu_2 \approx -0.1071, \ \mu_3 = 0, \ \mu_4 \approx 1.4317 + 0.1083i,$$

$$\mu_5 \approx 1.4317 - 0.1083i, \ \mu_6 \approx 3.1662, \ \mu_7 \approx 3.9400.$$

Figure 1 shows the trace of $\Lambda(\mu)$. For clarity, we use a logarithmic scale for the vertical axis. We label trajectories above the horizontal axis in red and trajectories below the horizontal axis in blue. The alternating red and blue pattern represents the zero of the $\Lambda(\mu)$. By doing so, we can observe that the function has five real roots, meeting our desired outcome.

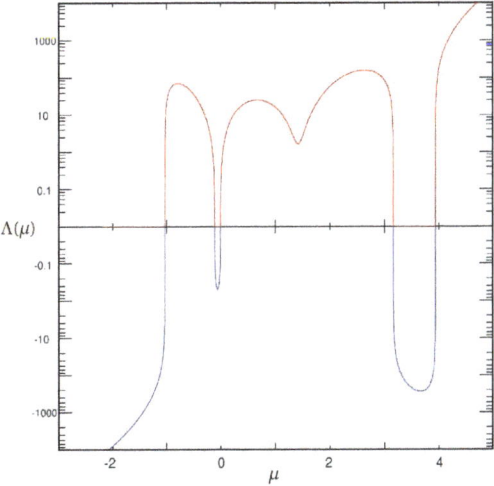

Figure 1. Characteristic function in Example 1.

4. Matrix Presentations of (1)–(5)

In this section, we discuss the matrix representations of problems (1)–(5) with finite spectra.

Definition 5. *If the eigenvalues of SLPs of the Atkinson type coincide with matrix eigenvalue problems, then we call them equivalent.*

For (1)–(5), we rebuild the matrix eigenvalue problems, which have the following form

$$BT = \mu FT,$$

whose eigenvalues coincide with the corresponding SLPs of the Atkinson type. Assume (16) holds, we have

$$q_i = \left(\int_{c_{2i-1}}^{c_{2i}} s \right)^{-1}, \ i = 1, 2, \cdots, \mathfrak{M};$$

$$\tilde{q}_j = \left(\int_{d_{2j-1}}^{d_{2j}} s \right)^{-1}, \ j = 1, 2, \cdots, \mathfrak{N}. \qquad (18)$$

In accordance with (14)–(15), we know $q_i, w_i, \tilde{q}_j, \tilde{w}_j \in \mathbb{R} \setminus \{0\}$. In addition, by (14) and (15), for each solution (u,v) of system (10), on the sub-intervals where $s \equiv 0$, we know that u is constant; regarding the sub-intervals where $p \equiv w \equiv 0$, we know that v is constant.

Let

$$u(t) = \begin{cases} u_i, & t \in [c_{2i}, c_{2i+1}], i = 0, \ldots, \mathfrak{M}-1, \\ u_{\mathfrak{M}}, & t \in [c_{2\mathfrak{M}}, \eta), \\ \tilde{u}_0, & t \in (\eta, d_1], \\ \tilde{u}_j, & t \in [d_{2j}, d_{2j+1}], j = 1, \ldots, \mathfrak{N}; \end{cases} \qquad (19)$$

$$v(t) = \begin{cases} v_i, & t \in [c_{2i}, c_{2i+1}], i = 0, \ldots, \mathfrak{M}-1, \\ \tilde{v}_j, & t \in [d_{2j}, d_{2j+1}], j = 1, \ldots, \mathfrak{N}; \end{cases}$$

and

$$v_0 = v(c_0) = v(c), \tilde{v}_{\mathfrak{N}+1} = v(d_{2\mathfrak{N}+1}) = v(d), v_{\mathfrak{M}+1} = v(\eta-0), \tilde{v}_0 = v(\eta+0). \qquad (20)$$

Lemma 4. *([23]) Suppose that Equation (1) is of the Atkinson type. Then for each solution (u,v) of (10), we have*

$$q_i(u_i - u_{i-1}) = v_i, \quad i = 1, 2, \cdots, \mathfrak{M}, \qquad (21)$$

$$v_{i+1} - v_i = u_i(p_i - \mu w_i), \quad i = 0, 1, \cdots, \mathfrak{M}, \qquad (22)$$

$$\tilde{q}_j(\tilde{u}_j - \tilde{u}_{j-1}) = \tilde{v}_j, \quad j = 1, 2, \cdots, \mathfrak{N}, \qquad (23)$$

$$\tilde{v}_{j+1} - \tilde{v}_j = \tilde{u}_j(\tilde{p}_j - \mu \tilde{w}_j), \quad j = 0, 1, \cdots, \mathfrak{N}. \qquad (24)$$

On the contrary, for any solution, u_i ($i = \overline{0, \mathfrak{M}}$), v_i ($i = \overline{0, \mathfrak{M}+1}$), $\tilde{u}_j$ ($j = \overline{0, \mathfrak{N}}$), and $\tilde{v}_j$ ($j = \overline{0, \mathfrak{N}+1}$) of systems (21)–(24), there exists a unique solution (u,v) of system (10), such that (19) and (20) holds.

Theorem 2. *Suppose $\xi_i, \tau_i, \mathfrak{e}_i, \xi'_i, \tau'_i, \mathfrak{e}'_i \in \mathbb{R}$ ($i = \overline{1,4}$) satisfy (6)–(9) and $\mathfrak{e}_2 \neq 0$. Define an $(\mathfrak{M}+\mathfrak{N}+5) \times (\mathfrak{M}+\mathfrak{N}+5)$ matrix $\mathfrak{Q}$ as follows:*

$$\begin{pmatrix}
\xi_2 & \xi_1 & & & & & & & & & & & \xi_3 & \xi_4 \\
1 & q_1 & -q_1 & & & & & & & & & & & \\
-q_1 & q_1+q_2 & -q_2 & & & & & & & & & & & \\
& \ddots & \ddots & \ddots & & & & & & & & & & \\
& & -q_{\mathfrak{M}-1} & q_{\mathfrak{M}-1}+q_{\mathfrak{M}} & -q_{\mathfrak{M}} & & & & & & & & & \\
& & & -q_{\mathfrak{M}} & q_{\mathfrak{M}} & -1 & & & & & & & & \\
& & & & -\mathfrak{e}'_1 & -\mathfrak{e}'_2 & 1 & & & & & & & \\
& & & & \mathfrak{e}'_3 & \mathfrak{e}'_4 & \tilde{q}_1 & -\tilde{q}_1 & & & & & & \\
& & & & & & -\tilde{q}_1 & \tilde{q}_1+\tilde{q}_2 & -\tilde{q}_2 & & & & & \\
& & & & & & & \ddots & \ddots & \ddots & & & & \\
& & & & & & & & -\tilde{q}_{\mathfrak{N}-1} & \tilde{q}_{\mathfrak{N}-1}+\tilde{q}_{\mathfrak{N}} & -\tilde{q}_{\mathfrak{N}} & & & \\
& & & & & & & & & -\tilde{q}_{\mathfrak{N}} & \tilde{q}_{\mathfrak{N}} & -1 & & \\
\tau_2 & \tau_1 & & & & & & & & & & & \tau_3 & \tau_4
\end{pmatrix}.$$

Let $\mathfrak{P} = \text{diag}\,(0, p_0, p_1, p_2, \ldots, p_\mathfrak{M}, 0, \tilde{p}_0, \tilde{p}_1, \tilde{p}_2, \ldots, \tilde{p}_{\mathfrak{N}-1}, \tilde{p}_\mathfrak{N}, 0)$ and

$$\mathfrak{W} = \begin{pmatrix} \zeta'_2 & \zeta'_1 & & & & & & & & & & & \zeta'_3 & \zeta'_4 \\ & w_0 & & & & & & & & & & & & \\ & & w_1 & & & & & & & & & & & \\ & & & \ddots & & & & & & & & & & \\ & & & & w_{\mathfrak{M}-1} & & & & & & & & & \\ & & & & & w_\mathfrak{M} & & & & & & & & \\ & & & & & & e_1 & e_2 & & & & & & \\ & & & & & & -e_3 & -e_4 & \tilde{w}_0 & & & & & \\ & & & & & & & & & \tilde{w}_1 & & & & \\ & & & & & & & & & & \ddots & & & \\ & & & & & & & & & & & \tilde{w}_{\mathfrak{N}-1} & & \\ & & & & & & & & & & & & \tilde{w}_\mathfrak{N} & \\ \tau'_2 & \tau'_1 & & & & & & & & & & & \tau'_3 & \tau'_4 \end{pmatrix}.$$

Then SLPs (1)–(5) are equivalent to matrix eigenvalue problems

$$(\mathfrak{Q} + \mathfrak{P})U = \mu \mathfrak{W} U, \tag{25}$$

where $U = (v_0, u_0, u_1, \cdots, u_\mathfrak{M}, v_{\mathfrak{M}+1}, \tilde{u}_0, \tilde{u}_1, \cdots, \tilde{u}_\mathfrak{N}, \tilde{v}_{\mathfrak{N}+1})^T$. Furthermore, (19) shows the relationship between the eigenfunction $u(x)$ of problems (1)–(5) and eigenvector U of (25), in terms of sharing the same eigenvalues.

Proof. Between the solutions of the following system:

$$q_1(u_1 - u_0) - v_0 = u_0(p_0 - \mu w_0), \tag{26}$$

$$q_{i+1}(u_{i+1} - u_i) - q_i(u_i - u_{i-1}) = u_i(p_i - \mu w_i), \quad i = 1, 2, \ldots, \mathfrak{M} - 1, \tag{27}$$

$$v_{\mathfrak{M}+1} - q_\mathfrak{M}(u_\mathfrak{M} - u_{\mathfrak{M}-1}) = u_\mathfrak{M}(p_\mathfrak{M} - \mu w_\mathfrak{M}), \tag{28}$$

$$\tilde{q}_1(\tilde{u}_1 - \tilde{u}_0) - \tilde{v}_0 = \tilde{u}_0(\tilde{p}_0 - \mu \tilde{w}_0), \tag{29}$$

$$\tilde{q}_{j+1}(\tilde{u}_{j+1} - \tilde{u}_j) - \tilde{q}_j(\tilde{u}_j - \tilde{u}_{j-1}) = \tilde{u}_j(\tilde{p}_j - \mu \tilde{w}_j), \quad j = 1, 2, \ldots, \mathfrak{N} - 1, \tag{30}$$

$$\tilde{v}_{\mathfrak{N}+1} - \tilde{q}_\mathfrak{N}(\tilde{u}_\mathfrak{N} - \tilde{u}_{\mathfrak{N}-1}) = \tilde{u}_\mathfrak{N}(\tilde{p}_\mathfrak{N} - \mu \tilde{w}_\mathfrak{N}). \tag{31}$$

and those of (21)–(24), a one-to-one correspondence exists by the assumption.

Now, we suppose u_i ($i = \overline{0, \mathfrak{M}}$) and v_i ($i = \overline{0, \mathfrak{M}+1}$) are solutions of systems (21) and (22). Then (26)–(28) follow from (21) to (22). Similarly, (29)–(31) follow from (23) to (24) by assuming that $\tilde{u}_j$ ($j = \overline{0, \mathfrak{N}}$) and $\tilde{v}_j$ ($j = \overline{0, \mathfrak{N}}$) are solutions of systems (23) and (24).

In other words, let u_i ($i = \overline{0, \mathfrak{M}}$) be a solution of (26)–(28); thus, v_0 and $v_{\mathfrak{M}+1}$ can be calculated by (26) and (28). Assume that v_i ($i = \overline{1, \mathfrak{M}}$) is defined in (21). Then, using (26), and utilizing induction on (27), (22) holds. Moreover, (23) and (24) can be similarly obtained.

Hence, according to Theorem 2, any solution of (10) is uniquely determined by solutions of (26)–(31). Note the first row of matrix (25)

$$\zeta'_2 v_0 + \zeta'_1 u_0 + \zeta'_3 \tilde{u}_\mathfrak{N} + \zeta'_4 \tilde{v}_{\mathfrak{N}+1} = \mu(\zeta'_2 v_0 + \zeta'_1 u_0 + \zeta'_3 \tilde{u}_\mathfrak{N} + \zeta'_4 \tilde{v}_{\mathfrak{N}+1}), \tag{32}$$

and the last row of matrix (25)

$$\tau_2 v_0 + \tau_1 u_0 + \tau_3 \tilde{u}_\mathfrak{M} + \tau_4 \tilde{v}_{\mathfrak{N}+1} = \mu(\tau_2' v_0 + \tau_1' u_0 + \tau_3' \tilde{u}_\mathfrak{M} + \tau_4' \tilde{v}_{\mathfrak{N}+1}), \tag{33}$$

substituting

$$u_0 = u(c) = f(c), \tilde{u}_\mathfrak{M} = u(d) = f(d), v_0 = v(c) = (qf')(c), \tilde{v}_{\mathfrak{N}+1} = v(d) = (qf')(d),$$

into (32) and (33), we obtain (2) and (3). From (4) to (5), we obtain

$$\tilde{u}_0 = (\mathfrak{e}_1 \mu + \mathfrak{e}_1') u_\mathfrak{M} + (\mathfrak{e}_2 \mu + \mathfrak{e}_2') v_{\mathfrak{M}+1}, \ \tilde{v}_0 = (\mathfrak{e}_3 \mu + \mathfrak{e}_3') u_\mathfrak{M} + (\mathfrak{e}_4 \mu + \mathfrak{e}_4') v_{\mathfrak{M}+1}, \tag{34}$$

and let $U = (v_0, u_0, u_1, \cdots, u_\mathfrak{M}, v_{\mathfrak{M}+1}, \tilde{u}_0, \tilde{u}_1, \cdots, \tilde{u}_\mathfrak{N}, \tilde{v}_{\mathfrak{N}+1})^T$. Then the equivalence follows from (26) to (34). □

The following result shows that the SLP of the Atkinson type is equivalent to the SLP with piecewise constant coefficients in the sense that they have similar eigenvalues.

Theorem 3. *Suppose that (1) is of the Atkinson type and q_i ($i = \overline{1, \mathfrak{M}}$), $\tilde{q}_j$ ($j = \overline{1, \mathfrak{N}}$), p_i, w_i ($i = \overline{0, \mathfrak{M}}$), $\tilde{p}_j, \tilde{w}_j$ ($j = \overline{0, \mathfrak{N}}$) are defined in (16) and (18). Denote piecewise constant functions $\bar{q}, \bar{p}, \bar{w}$ on $\mathfrak{J}$ by*

$$\bar{q}(t) = \begin{cases} q_i(c_{2i} - c_{2i-1}), & t \in [c_{2i-1}, c_{2i}], i = 1, \ldots, \mathfrak{M}, \\ \infty, & t \in \cup_{i=1}^{\mathfrak{M}} [c_{2i-2}, c_{2i-1}] \cup [c_{2\mathfrak{M}}, \eta), \\ \tilde{q}_j(d_{2j} - d_{2j-1}), & t \in [d_{2j-1}, d_{2j}], j = 1, \ldots, \mathfrak{N}, \\ \infty, & t \in \cup_{j=1}^{\mathfrak{N}} [d_{2j}, d_{2j+1}] \cup (\eta, d_1]; \end{cases} \tag{35}$$

$$\bar{p}(t) = \begin{cases} \frac{p_i}{c_{2i+1} - c_{2i}}, & t \in [c_{2i}, c_{2i+1}], i = 0, \ldots, \mathfrak{M} - 1, \\ \frac{p_\mathfrak{M}}{\eta - c_{2\mathfrak{M}}}, & t \in [c_{2\mathfrak{M}}, \eta), \\ 0, & t \in \cup_{i=1}^{\mathfrak{M}} [c_{2i-1}, c_{2i}], \\ \frac{\tilde{p}_j}{d_{2j+1} - d_{2j}}, & t \in [d_{2j}, d_{2j+1}], j = 1, \ldots, \mathfrak{N}, \\ \frac{\tilde{p}_0}{d_1 - \eta}, & t \in (\eta, d_1], \\ 0, & t \in \cup_{j=1}^{\mathfrak{N}} [d_{2j-1}, d_{2j}]; \end{cases} \tag{36}$$

$$\bar{w}(t) = \begin{cases} \frac{w_i}{c_{2i+1} - c_{2i}}, & t \in [c_{2i}, c_{2i+1}], i = 0, \ldots, \mathfrak{M} - 1, \\ \frac{w_\mathfrak{M}}{\eta - c_{2\mathfrak{M}}}, & t \in [c_{2\mathfrak{M}}, \eta), \\ 0, & t \in \cup_{i=1}^{\mathfrak{M}} [c_{2i-1}, c_{2i}], \\ \frac{\tilde{w}_j}{d_{2j+1} - d_{2j}}, & t \in [d_{2j}, d_{2j+1}], j = 1, \ldots, \mathfrak{N}, \\ \frac{\tilde{w}_0}{d_1 - \eta}, & t \in (\eta, d_1], \\ 0, & t \in \cup_{j=1}^{\mathfrak{N}} [d_{2j-1}, d_{2j}]; \end{cases} \tag{37}$$

Suppose that (2)–(5) hold. Then the eigenvalues of SLPs (1)–(5) coincide with the eigenvalues of the SLP

$$-(\bar{q}(t) f'(t))' + \bar{p}(t) f(t) = \mu \bar{w}(t) f(t), t \in \mathfrak{J} \tag{38}$$

with (2)–(5).

Proof. It is observed that SLPs (1)–(5) and (29), (2)–(5) determine the same

$$q_i, i = 1, 2, \ldots, \mathfrak{M}, \quad p_i, w_i, i = 0, 1, \ldots, \mathfrak{M};$$

$$\tilde{q}_j, j = 1, 2, \ldots, \mathfrak{N}, \quad \tilde{p}_j, \tilde{w}_j, j = 0, 1, \ldots, \mathfrak{N}.$$

Thus, they are equivalent to the same matrix eigenvalue problem, based on Theorem 2. The results follow. □

In light of Theorem 3, we know that for a fixed set of Equations (2)–(5) on a given interval, there exists a family of SLPs of the Atkinson type, which have the same eigenvalues as SLPs (38), (2)–(5). We refer to this family as the equivalent family of SLPs (38), (2)–(5).

Next, we will illustrate that matrix eigenvalue problems in the following form:

$$AT = \mu FT \tag{39}$$

have representations as Atkinson-type SLPs.

Theorem 4. *Let $n \geq 7$, $\mathfrak{e}_i, \mathfrak{e}'_i$ ($i = 1, 2, 3, 4$) in (4) and (5) satisfy $\det(\Gamma_\mu) \neq 0$ (where Γ_μ is defined in (9)), assume $\mathfrak{e}_2 \neq 0$. Assume that A is an $n \times n$ matrix as follows:*

$$\begin{pmatrix}
a_{11} & a_{12} & & & & & & & & & & a_{1,n-1} & a_{1n} \\
1 & a_{22} & a_{23} & & & & & & & & & & \\
& a_{23} & a_{33} & a_{34} & & & & & & & & & \\
& & \ddots & \ddots & \ddots & & & & & & & & \\
& & & a_{m,m+1} & a_{m+1,m+1} & a_{m+1,m+2} & & & & & & & \\
& & & & a_{m+1,m+2} & a_{m+2,m+2} & -1 & & & & & & \\
& & & & & a_{m+3,m+2} & a_{m+3,m+3} & 1 & & & & & \\
& & & & & a_{m+4,m+2} & a_{m+4,m+3} & a_{m+4,m+4} & a_{m+4,m+5} & & & & \\
& & & & & & & a_{m+4,m+5} & a_{m+5,m+5} & a_{m+5,m+6} & & & \\
& & & & & & & & \ddots & \ddots & \ddots & & \\
& & & & & & & & & a_{n-2,n-3} & a_{n-2,n-2} & a_{n-2,n-1} & \\
& & & & & & & & & & a_{n-2,n-1} & a_{n-1,n-1} & -1 \\
a_{n1} & a_{n2} & & & & & & & & & & a_{n,n-1} & a_{nn}
\end{pmatrix},$$

where $a_{j,j+1} \neq 0$ ($j = 2, 3, \ldots, n-2$), $2 \leq m \leq n-5$, $a_{ij} \in \mathbb{R}$ ($1 \leq i, j \leq n$), $a_{21} = a_{m+3,m+4} = 1$, $a_{m+2,m+3} = a_{n-1,n} = -1$. Let F be an $n \times n$ matrix of the following form:

$$\begin{pmatrix}
f_{11} & f_{12} & & & & & & & & & f_{1,n-1} & f_{1n} \\
& f_{22} & & & & & & & & & & \\
& & f_{33} & & & & & & & & & \\
& & & \ddots & & & & & & & & \\
& & & & f_{m+1,m+1} & & & & & & & \\
& & & & & f_{m+2,m+2} & & & & & & \\
& & & & & f_{m+3,m+2} & f_{m+3,m+3} & & & & & \\
& & & & & f_{m+4,m+2} & f_{m+4,m+3} & f_{m+4,m+4} & & & & \\
& & & & & & & & f_{m+5,m+5} & & & \\
& & & & & & & & & \ddots & & \\
& & & & & & & & & & f_{n-2,n-2} & \\
& & & & & & & & & & & f_{n-1,n-1} \\
f_{n1} & f_{n2} & & & & & & & & & f_{n,n-1} & f_{nn}
\end{pmatrix},$$

where $f_{jj} \neq 0$, $f_{jj} \in \mathbb{R}$ ($j = 2, 3, \ldots, n-1$), and

$$\operatorname{rank}\begin{pmatrix} a_{11} & a_{12} & a_{1,n-1} & a_{1n} \\ a_{n1} & a_{n2} & a_{n,n-1} & a_{nn} \end{pmatrix} = 2, \quad \operatorname{rank}\begin{pmatrix} f_{11} & f_{12} & f_{1,n-1} & f_{1n} \\ f_{n1} & f_{n2} & f_{n,n-1} & f_{nn} \end{pmatrix} = 2,$$

$$\operatorname{rank}\begin{pmatrix} a_{11} & a_{12} & a_{1,n-1} & a_{1n} \\ f_{11} & f_{12} & f_{1,n-1} & f_{1n} \end{pmatrix} = 2, \quad \operatorname{rank}\begin{pmatrix} a_{n1} & a_{n2} & a_{n,n-1} & a_{nn} \\ f_{n1} & f_{n2} & f_{n,n-1} & f_{nn} \end{pmatrix} = 2.$$

Then (39) represents an Atkinson-type SLP in the form of (1)–(5). Furthermore, SLPs (38), (2)–(5) have unique representations when a fixed partition (13) of $\mathfrak{J}$ is given, using the notations in (16) and (18). All SL representations of (39) are given by the corresponding equivalent families of SLPs (38), (2)–(5).

Proof. Let $\mathfrak{M} = m$, $\mathfrak{N} = n - m - 5$, $\mathfrak{J} = [c, \eta) \cup (\eta, d]$, $-\infty < c < d < \infty$. Firstly, one defines the parameters in (2) and (3), let

$$\xi_2 = a_{11}, \quad \xi_1 = a_{12}, \quad \xi_3 = a_{1,n-1}, \quad \xi_4 = a_{1n};$$
$$\tau_2 = a_{n1}, \quad \tau_1 = a_{n2}, \quad \tau_3 = a_{n,n-1}, \quad \tau_4 = a_{nn};$$
$$\xi'_2 = f_{11}, \quad \xi'_1 = f_{12}, \quad \xi'_3 = af_{1,n-1}, \quad \xi'_4 = f_{1n};$$
$$\tau'_2 = f_{n1}, \quad \tau'_1 = f_{n2}, \quad \tau'_3 = f_{n,n-1}, \quad \tau'_4 = f_{nn};$$

and

$$-\mathfrak{e}'_1 = a_{m+3,m+2}, \quad -\mathfrak{e}'_2 = a_{m+3,m+3}, \quad \mathfrak{e}'_3 = a_{m+4,m+2}, \quad \mathfrak{e}'_4 = a_{m+4,m+3};$$
$$\mathfrak{e}_1 = f_{m+3,m+2}, \quad \mathfrak{e}_2 = f_{m+3,m+3}, \quad -\mathfrak{e}_3 = f_{m+4,m+2}, \quad -\mathfrak{e}_4 = f_{m+4,m+3}.$$

For a given partition of $\mathfrak{J}$ by (13), one can define piecewise constant functions $\tilde{q}$, $\tilde{p}$ and $\tilde{w}$ on the interval $\mathfrak{J}$ that satisfies (7), (14) and (15), as follows:

$$q_i = -a_{i+1,i+2}, \quad i = \overline{1, \mathfrak{M}}, \qquad \tilde{q}_j = -a_{\mathfrak{M}+j+3,\mathfrak{M}+j+4}, \quad j = \overline{1, \mathfrak{N}};$$
$$w_i = f_{i+2,i+2}, \quad i = \overline{0, \mathfrak{M}}, \qquad \tilde{w}_j = f_{\mathfrak{M}+j+4,\mathfrak{M}+j+4}, \quad j = \overline{0, \mathfrak{N}};$$

and

$$p_0 = a_{22} - q_1, \quad p_i = a_{i+2,i+2} - q_i - q_{i+1}, \quad i = \overline{1, \mathfrak{M}-1},$$
$$p_{\mathfrak{M}} = a_{\mathfrak{M}+2,\mathfrak{M}+2} - q_{\mathfrak{M}};$$
$$\tilde{p}_0 = a_{\mathfrak{M}+4,\mathfrak{M}+4} - \tilde{q}_1, \quad \tilde{p}_j = a_{\mathfrak{M}+j+4,\mathfrak{M}+j+4} - \tilde{q}_j - \tilde{q}_{j+1}, \quad j = \overline{1, \mathfrak{N}-1},$$
$$\tilde{p}_n = a_{\mathfrak{M}+\mathfrak{N}+4,\mathfrak{M}+\mathfrak{N}+4} - \tilde{q}_{\mathfrak{N}}.$$

Next, we define $\tilde{q}$, $\tilde{p}$ and $\tilde{w}$ by (35)–(37), respectively. Such piecewise constant functions, $\tilde{q}$, $\tilde{p}$, and $\tilde{w}$ on interval $\mathfrak{J}$, satisfying (7) and (14) and (15), are found; Equation (38) is of the Atkinson type, and (16) and (18) satisfy with q, p, and w replaced by $\tilde{q}$, $\tilde{p}$, and $\tilde{w}$, respectively. Obviously, Equation (39) is of the same form as Equation (25). Therefore, the problem (39) is equivalent to the SLPs (1)–(5) by Theorem 2. The last part is yielded by Theorem 3. □

Remark 2. *If $\xi'_i = \tau'_i = \mathfrak{e}_i = 0$ ($i = \overline{1,4}$) in (2)–(5), then the problem under consideration degenerates to the case discussed in [22].*

If $\mathfrak{e}_i = 0$ ($i = \overline{1,4}$) in (4) and (5), then the problem under consideration degenerates to the case discussed in [26].

Author Contributions: Writing-original draft preparation, S.L.; writing-review and supervision, J.C.; review and editing, K.L. All authors have read and agreed to the published version of the manuscript.

Funding: This research is supported by the Natural Science Foundation of Shandong Province (nos. ZR2020QA010, ZR2020QA009), Postdoctoral Foundation of China (2020M682139), and the Natural Science Foundation of China (61973183).

Data Availability Statement: Data sharing is not applicable to this article as no datasets were generated or analyzed during the current study.

Acknowledgments: The authors thank the reviewers for their comments and detailed suggestions. They significantly improved the presentation of this paper.

Conflicts of Interest: The authors declare no conflict of interest.

References

1. Likov, A.V. *The Theory of Heat and Mass Transfer*, 2nd ed.; Springer: Berlin/Heidelberg, Germany, 1963. (In Russian)
2. Şen, E. A class of second-order differential operators with eigenparameter-dependent boundary and transmission conditions. *Math. Methods Appl. Sci.* **2014**, *37*, 2952–2961. [CrossRef]
3. Bartels, C.; Currie, S.; Watson, B.A. Sturm-Liouville problems with transfer condition Herglotz-dependent on the eigenparameter: Eigenvalue asymptotics. *Complex Anal. Oper. Theory* **2021**, *71*, 1–29. [CrossRef]
4. Akdoğan, Z.; Demirci, M.; Mukhtarov, O.S. Green function of discontinuous boundary value problem with transmission conditions. *Math. Methods Appl. Sci.* **2007**, *30*, 1719–173. [CrossRef]
5. Mukhtarov, O.S.; Aydemir, K. Spectral analysis of alpha-semi periodic 2-interval Sturm-Liouville problems. *Qual. Theory Dyn. Syst.* **2022**, *21*, 1–14. [CrossRef]
6. Fulton, C. Two-point boundary value problems with eigenvalue parameter contained in the boundary conditions. *Proc. R. Soc. Edinb. Sect. Math.* **1977**, *77*, 293–308. [CrossRef]
7. Guo, Y.; Wei, G. Inverse nodal problem for Dirac equations with boundary conditions polynomially dependent on the spectral parameter. *Results Math.* **2015**, *67*, 95–110. [CrossRef]
8. Kerimov, N.B.; Maris, E.A. On the uniform convergence of Fourier series expansions for Sturm-Liouville problems with a spectral parameter in the boundary conditions. *Results Math.* **2018**, *102*, 1–16. [CrossRef]
9. Sat, M. Interior inverse problem for Sturm-Liouville operator with eigenparameter dependent boundary conditions. In *Bulletin of the Transilvania*; Series III: Mathematics, Informatics, Physics; University of Brasov: Brasov, Romania, 2017; Volume 10, pp. 129–141.
10. Yang, C.; Pivovarchik, V.N. Inverse nodal problem for Dirac system with spectral parameter in boundary conditions. *Complex Anal. Oper. Theory* **2013**, *7*, 1211–1230. [CrossRef]
11. Li, K.; Zhang, M.; Zheng, Z. Dependence of eigenvalues of Dirac system on the parameters. *Stud. Appl. Math.* **2023**, *150*, 1201–1216. [CrossRef]
12. Guliyev, N.J. Schrödinger operators with distributional potentials and boundary conditions dependent on the eigenvalue parameter. *J. Math. Phys.* **2019**, *60*, 063501. [CrossRef]
13. Guliyev, N.J. A Riesz basis criterion for Schrödinger operators with boundary conditions dependent on the eigenvalue parameter. *Anal. Math. Phys.* **2020**, *60*, 1–8. [CrossRef]
14. Guliyev, N.J. On two-spectra inverse problems. *Proc. Amer. Math. Soc.* **2020**, *10*, 4491–4502. [CrossRef]
15. Yang, C.; Yang, X. An interior inverse problem for the Sturm-Liouville operator with discontinuous conditions. *Appl. Math. Lett.* **2009**, *22*, 1315–1319. [CrossRef]
16. Prather, C.L.; Shaw, J.K. On the oscillation of differential transforms of eigenfunction expansions. *Trans. Am. Math. Soc.* **1983**, *280*, 187–206. [CrossRef]
17. Zhang, L.; Ao, J. Inverse spectral problem for Sturm-Liouville operator with coupled eigenparameter dependent boundary conditions of the Atkinson type. *Inverse Probl. Sci. Eng.* **2019**, *27*, 1689–1702. [CrossRef]
18. Kong, Q.; Wu, H.; Zettl, A. Sturm-Liouville problems with finite spectrum. *J. Math. Anal. Appl.* **2001**, *263*, 748–762. [CrossRef]
19. Kong, Q.; Volkmer, H.; Zettl, A. Matrix representations of Sturm-Liouville problems with finite spectrum. *Results Math.* **2009**, *54*, 103–116. [CrossRef]
20. Atkinson, F.V. *Discrete and Continuous Boundary Value Problems*, 2nd ed.; Academic Press: New York, NY, USA; London, UK, 1964.
21. Ao, J.; Sun, J. Matrix representations of fourth-order boundary value problems with coupled or mixed boundary conditions. *Linear Multilinear Algebra* **2015**, *63*, 1590–1598. [CrossRef]
22. Ao, J.; Sun, J.; Zhang, M. The finite spectrum of Sturm-Liouville problems with transmission conditions. *Appl. Math. Comput.* **2011**, *218*, 1166–1173. [CrossRef]
23. Ao, J.; Sun, J.; Zhang, M. Matrix representations of Sturm-Liouville problems with transmission conditions. *Comput. Math. Appl.* **2012**, *63*, 1335–1348. [CrossRef]
24. Ao, J.; Sun, J.; Zhang, M. The finite spectrum of Sturm-Liouville problems with transmission conditions and eigenparameter dependent boundary conditions. *Results Math.* **2013**, *63*, 1057–1070. [CrossRef]
25. Ge, S.; Wang, W.; Ao, J. Matrix representations of fourth order boundary value problems with periodic boundary conditions. *Appl. Math. Comput.* **2014**, *227*, 601–609. [CrossRef]
26. Cai, J.; Zheng, Z. Matrix representations of Sturm-Liouville problems with coupled eigenparameter dependent boundary conditions and transmission conditions. *Math. Methods Appl. Sci.* **2018**, *41*, 3495–3508. [CrossRef]
27. Zhang, N.; Ao, J.-J. Finite spectrum of Sturm-Liouville problems with transmission conditions dependent on the spectral parameter. *Numer. Funct. Anal. Optim.* **2023**, *44*, 21–35. [CrossRef]

Disclaimer/Publisher's Note: The statements, opinions and data contained in all publications are solely those of the individual author(s) and contributor(s) and not of MDPI and/or the editor(s). MDPI and/or the editor(s) disclaim responsibility for any injury to people or property resulting from any ideas, methods, instructions or products referred to in the content.

Article

Initial Coefficients Upper Bounds for Certain Subclasses of Bi-Prestarlike Functions

Tareq Hamadneh [1,†,‡], Ibraheem Abu Falahah [2,†,‡], Yazan Alaya AL-Khassawneh [3,†,‡], Abdallah Al-Husban [4,†,‡], Abbas Kareem Wanas [5,*,†,‡] and Teodor Bulboacă [6,†,‡]

1. Department of Mathematics, Al Zaytoonah University of Jordan, Amman 11733, Jordan; t.hamadneh@zuj.edu.jo
2. Department of Mathematics, Faculty of Science, The Hashemite University, P.O. Box 330127, Zarqa 13133, Jordan; iabufalahah@hu.edu.jo
3. Data Science and Artificial Intelligence Department, Zarqa University, Zarqa 13110, Jordan; ykhassawneh@zu.edu.jo
4. Department of Mathematics, Faculty of Science and Technology, Irbid National University, P.O. Box 2600, Irbid 21110, Jordan; dralhosban@inu.edu.jo
5. Department of Mathematics, College of Science, University of Al-Qadisiyah, Al Diwaniyah 58001, Iraq
6. Faculty of Mathematics and Computer Science, Babeş-Bolyai University, 400084 Cluj-Napoca, Romania; bulboaca@math.ubbcluj.ro
* Correspondence: abbas.kareem.w@qu.edu.iq
† These authors contributed equally to this work.
‡ Dedicated to the memory of Professor Walter K. Hayman (1926–2000).

Abstract: In this article, we introduce and study the behavior of the modules of the first two coefficients for the classes $\mathcal{N}_\Sigma(\gamma, \lambda, \delta, \mu; \alpha)$ and $\mathcal{N}_{\Sigma^*}(\gamma, \lambda, \delta, \mu; \beta)$ of normalized holomorphic and bi-univalent functions that are connected with the prestarlike functions. We determine the upper bounds for the initial Taylor–Maclaurin coefficients $|a_2|$ and $|a_3|$ for the functions of each of these families, and we also point out some special cases and consequences of our main results. The study of these classes is closely connected with those of Ruscheweyh who in 1977 introduced the classes of prestarlike functions of order μ using a convolution operator and the proofs of our results are based on the well-known Carathéodory's inequality for the functions with real positive part in the open unit disk. Our results generalize a few of the earlier ones obtained by Li and Wang, Murugusundaramoorthy et al., Brannan and Taha, and could be useful for those that work with the geometric function theory of one-variable functions.

Keywords: holomorphic functions; univalent functions; bi-univalent functions; convolution (Hadamard) product; prestarlike functions; coefficient estimates; Taylor–Maclaurin coefficients

MSC: 30C45; 30C50

1. Introduction

We denote by $\mathcal{A}$ the family of functions which are analytic in the open unit disk $\mathbb{U} := \{z \in \mathbb{C} : |z| < 1\}$ and with the following normalized form:

$$f(z) = z + \sum_{k=2}^{\infty} a_k z^k, \ z \in \mathbb{U}. \quad (1)$$

Let $\mathcal{S}$ denote the subclass of $\mathcal{A}$ of the functions that are univalent in $\mathbb{U}$. From the *Koebe one-quarter theorem* [1], all the functions $f \in \mathcal{S}$ have an inverse f^{-1} defined by

$$f^{-1}(f(z)) = z \ (z \in \mathbb{U})$$

and
$$f\left(f^{-1}(w)\right) = w \quad \left(|w| < r_0(f),\ r_0(f) \geq \frac{1}{4}\right).$$

In addition, for every function $f \in \mathcal{S}$, there exists an inverse function $f^{-1}: f(\mathbb{U}) \to \mathbb{U}$ analytic in the domain $f(\mathbb{U})$, but it is not sure that $f(\mathbb{U}) \subseteq \mathbb{U}$. Therefore, if we denote by g the analytic continuation of f^{-1} to the unit disk $\mathbb{U}$, assuming that it exists, then

$$g(w) := f^{-1}(w) = w - a_2 w^2 + \left(2a_2^2 - a_3\right)w^3 - \left(5a_2^3 - 5a_2 a_3 + a_4\right)w^4 + \dots,\ w \in \mathbb{U}. \quad (2)$$

A function $f \in \mathcal{A}$ is called to be *bi-univalent* in $\mathbb{U}$ if both f and $g = f^{-1}$ are univalent in $\mathbb{U}$ and Σ denotes the class of normalized bi-univalent functions in $\mathbb{U}$. For the historical account and for many relevant examples of functions belonging to the class Σ, see the pioneering work connected with this subject of Srivastava et al. [2], which has actually been of crucial importance for studies of bi-univalent functions in recent years. According to this article of Srivastava et al. [2], we would like to recall here some examples of functions belonging to the class Σ, such as

$$\frac{z}{1-z},\quad -\log(1-z)\quad \text{and}\quad \frac{1}{2}\log\left(\frac{1+z}{1-z}\right).$$

Thus, the class Σ is not empty, while the Koebe function does not belongs to Σ.

In a large number of papers which appeared after the work of Srivastava et al. [2], the authors defined and studied the different families of the bi-univalent function class Σ (as can be seen, for example, in [3–22]), but only non-sharp estimates on the initial coefficients $|a_2|$ and $|a_3|$ in the Taylor–Maclaurin expansion (1) were obtained in many of these recent papers. The problem of finding the upper bounds for the general coefficient of the power series expansion coefficients

$$|a_n|\quad (n \in \mathbb{N} \setminus \{1,2\},\ \mathbb{N} := \{1,2,3,\dots\})$$

for functions $f \in \Sigma$ is still not completely solved for many subclasses of the bi-univalent function class Σ (as can be seen, for example, in [11,14,15]).

For two analytic functions in $\mathbb{U}$, namely $F(z) = \sum_{k=0}^{\infty} \alpha_k z^k$ and $G(z) = \sum_{k=0}^{\infty} \beta_k z^k$, "$*$" usually denotes the *convolution* (or *Hadamard*) *product* of these functions by

$$(F * G)(z) := \sum_{k=0}^{\infty} \alpha_k \beta_k z^k,\ z \in \mathbb{U}.$$

In [23], Ruscheweyh defined and investigated the family of *prestarlike functions of order* μ, that are the functions f with the property that $f * I_\mu$ is a starlike function of order μ in $\mathbb{U}$, where

$$I_\mu(z) := \frac{z}{(1-z)^{2(1-\mu)}},\ z \in \mathbb{U}\quad (0 \leq \mu < 1).$$

Remark that the function I_μ could be written in the form

$$I_\mu(z) = z + \sum_{k=2}^{\infty} \varphi_k(\mu) z^k,\ z \in \mathbb{U},$$

where

$$\varphi_k(\mu) = \frac{\prod_{j=2}^{k}(j - 2\mu)}{(k-1)!},\ k \geq 2.$$

In addition, we note that φ_k is a decreasing function and satisfies the limit property

$$\lim_{k\to\infty} \varphi_k(\mu) = \begin{cases} \infty, & \text{if } \mu < \frac{1}{2}, \\ 1, & \text{if } \mu = \frac{1}{2}, \\ 0, & \text{if } \mu > \frac{1}{2}. \end{cases}$$

Next, we recall the following lemma that will be used as a main tool in the proofs of our two main results.

Lemma 1 ([1,24]). *(Carathéodory's inequality) If $h \in \mathcal{P}$, then*

$$|c_k| \leq 2 \quad (k \in \mathbb{N}),$$

where $\mathcal{P}$ is the class of all functions h analytic in $\mathbb{U}$, for which

$$\operatorname{Re} h(z) > 0, \ z \in \mathbb{U},$$

with

$$h(z) = 1 + c_1 z + c_2 z^2 + \ldots, \ z \in \mathbb{U}.$$

2. Initial Coefficient Estimates for the Bi-Univalent Function Subclass $\mathcal{N}_\Sigma(\gamma, \lambda, \delta, \mu; \alpha)$

First, we will first define the new subclass $\mathcal{N}_\Sigma(\gamma, \lambda, \delta, \mu; \alpha)$ of the bi-univalent function as follows:

Definition 1. *A function $f \in \Sigma$ of the form (1) belongs to the bi-univalent function class $\mathcal{N}_\Sigma(\gamma, \lambda, \delta, \mu; \alpha)$ if it satisfies the conditions*

$$\left| \arg\left(\left(\frac{z(f * I_\mu)'(z)}{(f * I_\mu)(z)} \right)^\gamma \left[(1-\delta) \frac{z(f * I_\mu)'(z)}{(f * I_\mu)(z)} + \delta \left(1 + \frac{z(f * I_\mu)''(z)}{(f * I_\mu)'(z)} \right) \right]^\lambda \right) \right| < \frac{\alpha\pi}{2}, z \in \mathbb{U}, \quad (3)$$

and

$$\left| \arg\left(\left(\frac{w(g * I_\mu)'(w)}{(g * I_\mu)(w)} \right)^\gamma \left[(1-\delta) \frac{w(g * I_\mu)'(w)}{(g * I_\mu)(w)} + \delta \left(1 + \frac{w(g * I_\mu)''(w)}{(g * I_\mu)'(w)} \right) \right]^\lambda \right) \right| < \frac{\alpha\pi}{2}, w \in \mathbb{U}, \quad (4)$$

where

$$0 < \alpha \leq 1, \ 0 \leq \gamma \leq 1, \ 0 \leq \lambda \leq 1, \ 0 \leq \delta \leq 1,$$

and $g = f^{-1}$ is given by (2).

Remark 1. *The subclass $\mathcal{N}_\Sigma(\gamma, \lambda, \delta, \mu; \alpha)$ generalizes some well-known families considered in earlier studies and which will be recalled below:*

(i) *For $\gamma = 0, \lambda = 1$ and $\mu = \frac{1}{2}$, the class $\mathcal{N}_\Sigma(\gamma, \lambda, \delta, \mu; \alpha)$ reduces to the class $M_\Sigma(\alpha, \delta)$, which was investigated by Li and Wang [25], that is*

$$M_\Sigma(\alpha, \delta) := \left\{ f \in \Sigma : \left| \arg\left[(1-\delta)\frac{zf'(z)}{f(z)} + \delta\left(1 + \frac{zf''(z)}{f'(z)}\right) \right] \right| < \frac{\alpha\pi}{2}, \ z \in \mathbb{U}, \text{ and} \right.$$

$$\left. \left| \arg\left[(1-\delta)\frac{wg'(w)}{g(w)} + \delta\left(1 + \frac{wg''(w)}{g'(w)}\right) \right] \right| < \frac{\alpha\pi}{2}, \ w \in \mathbb{U} \right\},$$

where $g = f^{-1}$ is defined like in (2).

(ii) For $\gamma = 1$, $\lambda = 0$ and $\mu = \frac{1}{2}$, the class $\mathcal{N}_\Sigma(\gamma, \lambda, \delta, \mu; \alpha)$ reduces to the class $S_{\Sigma^*}(\alpha)$ that was defined and studied by Brannan and Taha [26] by

$$S_{\Sigma^*}(\alpha, \delta) := \left\{ f \in \Sigma : \left|\arg \frac{zf'(z)}{f(z)}\right| < \frac{\alpha\pi}{2}, z \in \mathbb{U}, \text{ and } \left|\arg \frac{wg'(w)}{g(w)}\right| < \frac{\alpha\pi}{2}, w \in \mathbb{U} \right\},$$

where $g = f^{-1}$ is defined as in (2).

Remark 2. *We would like to emphasize that, for appropriate parameter choices, the classes $\mathcal{N}_\Sigma(\gamma, \lambda, \delta, \mu; \alpha)$ are not empty. Thus, if we consider $\mu = \frac{1}{2}$, then* $\mathrm{I}_{\frac{1}{2}}(z) = \frac{z}{1-z} = \sum_{k=1}^{\infty} z^k$, *and letting* $f_*(z) = \frac{z}{1-z}$, *it is easy to check that* $f_* \in \mathcal{S}$, *and moreover,* $f_* \in \Sigma$ *with* $g(w) = f_*^{-1}(w) = \frac{w}{1+w}$.
A simple computation shows that the conditions (3) and (4) become

$$\left|\arg\left(\left(\frac{1}{1-z}\right)^\gamma \left(\frac{1+\delta z}{1-z}\right)^\lambda\right)\right| < \frac{\alpha\pi}{2}, \quad (5)$$

and

$$\left|\arg\left(\left(\frac{1}{1+w}\right)^\gamma \left(\frac{1-\delta w}{1+w}\right)^\lambda\right)\right| < \frac{\alpha\pi}{2}, \quad (6)$$

respectively. For the particular case $\gamma = \frac{1}{3}$, $\delta = \frac{1}{2}$ and $\lambda = \frac{1}{5}$, using the 2D plot of the MAPLE™ computer software, we obtain the image of the open unit disk $\mathbb{U}$ by the function

$$\Phi(z) := \left(\frac{1}{1-z}\right)^\gamma \left(\frac{1+\delta z}{1-z}\right)^\lambda$$

which is the same with those by

$$\Psi(w) := \left(\frac{1}{1+w}\right)^\gamma \left(\frac{1-\delta w}{1+w}\right)^\lambda$$

and it is shown in Figure 1:

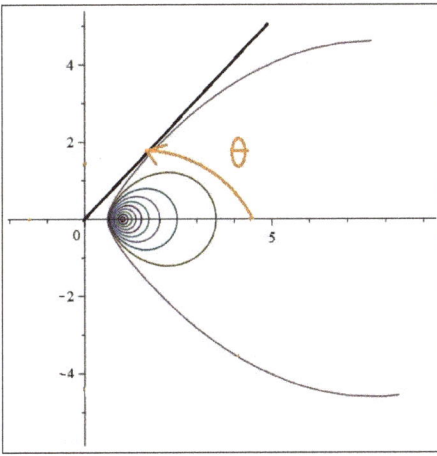

Figure 1. The image of $\Phi(\mathbb{U}) = \Psi(\mathbb{U})$.

Since $\overline{\Phi(z)} = \Phi(\overline{z})$ and similarly for Ψ, it follows that the domains $\Phi(\mathbb{U}) = \Psi(\mathbb{U})$ are symmetric with respect to the real axe. Therefore, if θ is the positive argument of the tangent starting from the origin to the boundary of the domain $\Phi(\mathbb{U})$ that is $\Phi(\partial\mathbb{U})$, for $\alpha \geq \tan\theta$ (see also Figure 1), we obtain that the inequalities (5) and (6) are satisfied, and hence $f_*(z) = \frac{z}{1-z} \in \mathcal{N}_\Sigma\left(\frac{1}{3}, \frac{1}{5}, \frac{1}{2}, \frac{1}{2}; \alpha\right)$.

Concluding, for appropriate choices of the parameters γ, λ, δ, μ and α, the subclasses $\mathcal{N}_\Sigma(\gamma, \lambda, \delta, \mu; \alpha)$ are not empty.

Our first main result is presented in the below theorem where we found upper bounds for the first two coefficients $|a_2|$ and $|a_3|$ of the power series expansion of the functions belonging to these classes.

Theorem 1. *Let the function $f \in \mathcal{N}_\Sigma(\gamma, \lambda, \delta, \mu; \alpha)$, with $0 < \alpha \leq 1, 0 \leq \gamma \leq 1, 0 \leq \lambda \leq 1, 0 \leq \delta \leq 1$ be given by (1). Then,*

$$|a_2| \leq \frac{\alpha}{\sqrt{\left|\alpha(1-\mu)\Phi(\mu, \gamma, \lambda, \delta) + (1-\alpha)(1-\mu)^2(\gamma + \lambda(\delta+1))^2\right|}}$$

and

$$|a_3| \leq \frac{\alpha^2}{8(1-\mu)^2(\gamma + \lambda(\delta+1))^2} + \frac{\alpha}{(1-\mu)(3-2\mu)(\gamma + \lambda(2\delta+1))},$$

where

$$\Phi(\mu, \gamma, \lambda, \delta) = (1-\mu)\left[\gamma(\gamma-1) + \lambda(\delta+1)(2\gamma + (\lambda-1)(\delta+1)) - 2(\gamma + \lambda(3\delta+1))\right] \\ + (3-2\mu)(\gamma + \lambda(2\delta+1)). \quad (7)$$

Proof. According to the conditions (3) and (4), we have

$$\left(\frac{z(f*I_\mu)'(z)}{(f*I_\mu)(z)}\right)^\gamma \left[(1-\delta)\frac{z(f*I_\mu)'(z)}{(f*I_\mu)(z)} + \delta\left(1 + \frac{z(f*I_\mu)''(z)}{(f*I_\mu)'(z)}\right)\right]^\lambda = [p(z)]^\alpha, \quad (8)$$

and

$$\left(\frac{w(g*I_\mu)'(w)}{(g*I_\mu)(w)}\right)^\gamma \left[(1-\delta)\frac{w(g*I_\mu)'(w)}{(g*I_\mu)(w)} + \delta\left(1 + \frac{w(g*I_\mu)''(w)}{(g*I_\mu)'(w)}\right)\right]^\lambda = [q(w)]^\alpha, \quad (9)$$

where $g = f^{-1}$, with the functions $p, q \in \mathcal{P}$ having the power series representations

$$p(z) = 1 + p_1 z + p_2 z^2 + p_3 z^3 + \dots, \ z \in \mathbb{U}, \quad (10)$$

and

$$q(w) = 1 + q_1 w + q_2 w^2 + q_3 w^3 + \dots, \ w \in \mathbb{U}. \quad (11)$$

Equating the corresponding coefficients of (8) and (9), we obtain that

$$2(1-\mu)(\gamma + \lambda(\delta+1))a_2 = \alpha p_1, \quad (12)$$

$$2(1-\mu)(3-2\mu)(\gamma + \lambda(2\delta+1))a_3 \\ + 2(1-\mu)^2\left[\gamma(\gamma-1) + \lambda(\delta+1)(2\gamma + (\lambda-1)(\delta+1)) - 2(\gamma + \lambda(3\delta+1))\right]a_2^2 \\ = \alpha p_2 + \frac{\alpha(\alpha-1)}{2}p_1^2, \quad (13)$$

$$-2(1-\mu)(\gamma + \lambda(\delta+1))a_2 = \alpha q_1, \quad (14)$$

and
$$2(1-\mu)(3-2\mu)(\gamma+\lambda(2\delta+1))(2a_2^2-a_3)$$
$$+2(1-\mu)^2\left[\gamma(\gamma-1)+\lambda(\delta+1)(2\gamma+(\lambda-1)(\delta+1))-2(\gamma+\lambda(3\delta+1))\right]a_2^2 \quad (15)$$
$$=\alpha q_2+\frac{\alpha(\alpha-1)}{2}q_1^2.$$

Using (12) and (14), it follows that
$$p_1=-q_1, \quad (16)$$
and
$$8(1-\mu)^2(\gamma+\lambda(\delta+1))^2 a_2^2=\alpha^2(p_1^2+q_1^2), \quad (17)$$
and if we add (13) to (15), we obtain
$$4(1-\mu)\Phi(\mu,\gamma,\lambda,\delta)a_2^2=\alpha(p_2+q_2)+\frac{\alpha(\alpha-1)}{2}\left(p_1^2+q_1^2\right), \quad (18)$$
where $\Phi(\mu,\gamma,\lambda,\delta)$ is given by (7).

Substituting the value of $p_1^2+q_1^2$ from (17) into the right-hand side of (18), a simple computation leads to
$$a_2^2=\frac{\alpha^2(p_2+q_2)}{4\alpha(1-\mu)\Phi(\mu,\gamma,\lambda,\delta)+4(1-\alpha)(1-\mu)^2(\gamma+\lambda(\delta+1))^2}. \quad (19)$$

Taking the modules of both sides of (19) and using the Lemma 1 for the coefficients p_2 and q_2, we obtain
$$|a_2|\leq \frac{\alpha}{\sqrt{\left|\alpha(1-\mu)\Phi(\mu,\gamma,\lambda,\delta)+(1-\alpha)(1-\mu)^2(\gamma+\lambda(\delta+1))^2\right|}}.$$

In order to determine the upper bound of $|a_3|$, subtracting (15) from (13), we have
$$4(1-\mu)(3-2\mu)(\gamma+\lambda(2\delta+1))\left(a_3-a_2^2\right)=\alpha(p_2-q_2)+\frac{\alpha(\alpha-1)}{2}\left(p_1^2-q_1^2\right). \quad (20)$$

Substituting the value of a_2^2 from (17) into (20) and using (16), we obtain
$$a_3=\frac{\alpha^2\left(p_1^2+q_1^2\right)}{8(1-\mu)^2(\gamma+\lambda(\delta+1))^2}+\frac{\alpha(p_2-q_2)}{4(1-\mu)(3-2\mu)(\gamma+\lambda(2\delta+1))}. \quad (21)$$

Taking the modules for both sides of (21) and once again using Lemma 1 for the coefficients p_1, p_2, q_1 and q_2, it follows that
$$|a_3|\leq \frac{\alpha^2}{8(1-\mu)^2(\gamma+\lambda(\delta+1))^2}+\frac{\alpha}{(1-\mu)(3-2\mu)(\gamma+\lambda(2\delta+1))},$$
and the proof of our theorem is complete. □

Remark 3. *Note that Theorem 1 generalizes some earlier results obtained by different authors:*

(i) *If, in this theorem, we choose $\gamma=0$, $\lambda=1$, and $\mu=\frac{1}{2}$, then we have the following result of Li and Wang ([25] Theorem 2.2):*

Let f be given by (1) in the class $M_\Sigma(\alpha,\delta):=\mathcal{N}_\Sigma\left(0,1,\delta,\frac{1}{2};\alpha\right)$, $0\leq\alpha<1$, $\delta\geq 0$. Then,
$$|a_2|\leq\frac{2\alpha}{(1+\delta)(\alpha+1+\delta-\alpha\delta)}$$

and
$$|a_3| \le \frac{4\alpha^2}{(1+\delta)^2} + \frac{\alpha}{1+2\delta}.$$

(ii) For the special case $\gamma = 1$, $\lambda = 0$ and $\mu = \frac{1}{2}$, we obtain the result of Murugusundaramoorthy et al. ([27] Corollary 6), that is:

Let f be given by (1) be in the class $\mathcal{S}_\Sigma^\alpha := \mathcal{N}_\Sigma\left(1, 0, \delta, \frac{1}{2}; \alpha\right)$, $0 < \alpha \le 1$. Then,

$$|a_2| \le \frac{2\alpha}{\alpha+1}, \quad |a_3| \le 4\alpha^2 + \alpha.$$

3. Initial Coefficient Estimates for the Bi-Univalent Function Subclass $\mathcal{N}_{\Sigma^*}(\gamma, \lambda, \delta, \mu; \beta)$

In the next main result of the paper, we also found the upper bounds of the two initial coefficients of the power series. Thus, we define the subclass $\mathcal{N}_{\Sigma^*}(\gamma, \lambda, \delta, \mu; \beta)$ of the class of bi-univalent functions.

Definition 2. *A function $f \in \Sigma$ of the form (1) is called to be in subclass $\mathcal{N}_{\Sigma^*}(\gamma, \lambda, \delta, \mu; \beta)$ of the class of bi-univalent functions if it satisfies the conditions*

$$\mathrm{Re}\left\{\left(\frac{z(f * I_\mu)'(z)}{(f * I_\mu)(z)}\right)^\gamma \left[(1-\delta)\frac{z(f * I_\mu)'(z)}{(f * I_\mu)(z)} + \delta\left(1 + \frac{z(f * I_\mu)''(z)}{(f * I_\mu)'(z)}\right)\right]^\lambda\right\} > \beta, z \in \mathbb{U}, \quad (22)$$

and

$$\mathrm{Re}\left\{\left(\frac{w(g * I_\mu)'(w)}{(g * I_\mu)(w)}\right)^\gamma \left[(1-\delta)\frac{w(g * I_\mu)'(w)}{(g * I_\mu)(w)} + \delta\left(1 + \frac{w(g * I_\mu)''(w)}{(g * I_\mu)'(w)}\right)\right]^\lambda\right\} > \beta, w \in \mathbb{U}, \quad (23)$$

where

$$0 \le \beta < 1, \ 0 \le \gamma \le 1, \ 0 \le \lambda \le 1, \ 0 \le \delta \le 1,$$

and $g = f^{-1}$ is given by (2).

Remark 4. *The subclass $\mathcal{N}_{\Sigma^*}(\gamma, \lambda, \delta, \mu; \beta)$ is a generalization of some well-known classes investigated previously, which we recall below:*

1. *For $\gamma = 0$, $\lambda = 1$ and $\mu = \frac{1}{2}$, the class $\mathcal{N}_{\Sigma^*}(\gamma, \lambda, \delta, \mu; \beta)$ is reduced to the subclass $B_\Sigma(\beta, \delta)$ introduced by Li and Wang [25], as follows*

$$B_\Sigma(\beta, \delta) := \left\{f \in \Sigma : \mathrm{Re}\left[(1-\delta)\frac{zf'(z)}{f(z)} + \delta\left(1 + \frac{zf''(z)}{f'(z)}\right)\right] > \beta, \ z \in \mathbb{U}, \ \text{and}\right.$$

$$\left.\mathrm{Re}\left[(1-\delta)\frac{wg'(w)}{g(w)} + \delta\left(1 + \frac{wg''(w)}{g'(w)}\right)\right] > \beta, \ w \in \mathbb{U}\right\},$$

where $g = f^{-1}$ is defined as in (2).

2. *For $\gamma = 1$, $\lambda = 0$, and $\mu = \frac{1}{2}$, the class $\mathcal{N}_{\Sigma^*}(\gamma, \lambda, \delta, \mu; \beta)$ is reduced to the subclass $S_{\Sigma^*}(\beta)$ that was already investigated by Brannan and Taha [26], and was defined by*

$$S_{\Sigma^*}(\beta) := \left\{f \in \Sigma : \mathrm{Re}\,\frac{zf'(z)}{f(z)} > \beta, \ z \in \mathbb{U}, \ \text{and} \ \mathrm{Re}\,\frac{wg'(w)}{g(w)} > \beta, \ w \in \mathbb{U}\right\},$$

where $g = f^{-1}$ is defined as in (2).

Remark 5. *Considering the same values of the parameters γ, λ, δ, μ, and α as in the Remark 2, for the function $f_*(z) = \frac{z}{1-z}$, we obtain that the inequalities (22) and (23) become*

$$\operatorname{Re}\Phi(z) > \beta,\ z \in \mathbb{U}, \quad \operatorname{Re}\Psi(w) > \beta,\ w \in \mathbb{U},$$

respectively. As can be seen in Figure 1, there exists a positive value of $\beta < 1$ such that the above two inequalities hold, hence $f_*(z) = \frac{z}{1-z} \in \mathcal{N}_{\Sigma^*}\left(\frac{1}{3}, \frac{1}{5}, \frac{1}{2}, \frac{1}{2}; \beta\right)$

Consequently, for appropriate choices of the parameters γ, λ, δ, μ, and β, the subclasses $\mathcal{N}_{\Sigma^*}(\gamma, \lambda, \delta, \mu; \beta)$ are not empty.

Our second main result presented in the next theorem gives upper bounds for the two initial coefficients of the functions belonging to the class $\mathcal{N}_{\Sigma^*}(\gamma, \lambda, \delta, \mu; \beta)$.

Theorem 2. *If the function $f \in \mathcal{N}_{\Sigma^*}(\gamma, \lambda, \delta, \mu; \beta)$, with $0 \leq \beta < 1$, $0 \leq \gamma \leq 1$, $0 \leq \lambda \leq 1$, $0 \leq \delta \leq 1$, is given by (1), then*

$$|a_2| \leq 2\sqrt{\frac{1-\beta}{(1-\mu)(\gamma+2)(\gamma+1)+2\mu\lambda(2\lambda-1)}}$$

and

$$|a_3| \leq \frac{4(1-\beta)^2}{[(1-\mu)(\gamma+1)+\mu(2\lambda-1)]^2} + \frac{2(1-\beta)}{(1-\mu)(\gamma+2)+\mu(3\lambda-1)}.$$

Proof. From the relations (22) and (23), it follows that the functions $p, q \in \mathcal{P}$ exist such that

$$\left(\frac{z(f*I_\mu)'(z)}{(f*I_\mu)(z)}\right)^\gamma \left[(1-\delta)\frac{z(f*I_\mu)'(z)}{(f*I_\mu)(z)} + \delta\left(1 + \frac{z(f*I_\mu)''(z)}{(f*I_\mu)'(z)}\right)\right]^\lambda = \beta + (1-\beta)p(z), \quad (24)$$

and

$$\left(\frac{w(g*I_\mu)'(w)}{(g*I_\mu)(w)}\right)^\gamma \left[(1-\delta)\frac{w(g*I_\mu)'(w)}{(g*I_\mu)(w)} + \delta\left(1 + \frac{w(g*I_\mu)''(w)}{(g*I_\mu)'(w)}\right)\right]^\lambda = \beta + (1-\beta)q(w), \quad (25)$$

where $g = f^{-1}$, and the functions $p, q \in \mathcal{P}$ have the series expansions given by (10) and (11), respectively. Equating the corresponding coefficients of (24) and (25), we deduce

$$2(1-\mu)(\gamma + \lambda(\delta+1))a_2 = (1-\beta)p_1, \tag{26}$$

$$2(1-\mu)(3-2\mu)(\gamma + \lambda(2\delta+1))a_3$$
$$+ 2(1-\mu)^2\left[\gamma(\gamma-1) + \lambda(\delta+1)(2\gamma + (\lambda-1)(\delta+1)) - 2(\gamma + \lambda(3\delta+1))\right]a_2^2$$
$$= (1-\beta)p_2, \tag{27}$$

$$-2(1-\mu)(\gamma + \lambda(\delta+1))a_2 = (1-\beta)q_1, \tag{28}$$

and

$$2(1-\mu)(3-2\mu)(\gamma + \lambda(2\delta+1))(2a_2^2 - a_3)$$
$$+ 2(1-\mu)^2\left[\gamma(\gamma-1) + \lambda(\delta+1)(2\gamma + (\lambda-1)(\delta+1)) - 2(\gamma + \lambda(3\delta+1))\right]a_2^2 \tag{29}$$
$$= (1-\beta)q_2.$$

From (26) and (28), we find that

$$p_1 = -q_1, \tag{30}$$

and
$$8(1-\mu)^2(\gamma+\lambda(\delta+1))^2 a_2^2 = (1-\beta)^2(p_1^2+q_1^2). \tag{31}$$

By adding (27) and (29), we obtain
$$4(1-\mu)\Phi(\mu,\gamma,\lambda,\delta)a_2^2 = (1-\beta)(p_2+q_2), \tag{32}$$

where $\Phi(\mu,\gamma,\lambda,\delta)$ is given by (7). Consequently, we have
$$a_2^2 = \frac{(1-\beta)(p_2+q_2)}{4(1-\mu)\Phi(\mu,\gamma,\lambda,\delta)}.$$

Applying the Lemma 1 for the coefficients p_2 and q_2, it follows that
$$|a_2| \leq \sqrt{\frac{1-\beta}{(1-\mu)\Phi(\mu,\gamma,\lambda,\delta)}}.$$

To obtain the upper bound of $|a_3|$, by subtracting (29) from (27), we obtain
$$4(1-\mu)(3-2\mu)(\gamma+\lambda(2\delta+1))\left(a_3-a_2^2\right) = (1-\beta)(p_2-q_2)$$

or equivalently,
$$a_3 = a_2^2 + \frac{(1-\beta)(p_2-q_2)}{4(1-\mu)(3-2\mu)(\gamma+\lambda(2\delta+1))}. \tag{33}$$

Substituting the value of a_2^2 from (31) into (33), it follows that
$$a_3 = \frac{(1-\beta)^2(p_1^2+q_1^2)}{8(1-\mu)^2(\gamma+\lambda(\delta+1))^2} + \frac{(1-\beta)(p_2-q_2)}{4(1-\mu)(3-2\mu)(\gamma+\lambda(2\delta+1))}.$$

Finally, applying once again the Lemma 1 for the coefficients p_1, p_2, q_1, and q_2, we obtain
$$|a_3| \leq \frac{(1-\beta)^2}{(1-\mu)^2(\gamma+\lambda(\delta+1))^2} + \frac{(1-\beta)}{(1-\mu)(3-2\mu)(\gamma+\lambda(2\delta+1))}.$$

Thus, we completed the proof of Theorem 2. □

Remark 6. *Theorem 2 also generalizes some previous results as follows:*

(i) If we choose, in this theorem, that $\gamma = 0$, $\lambda = 1$, and $\mu = \frac{1}{2}$, then we obtain the result of Li and Wang ([25] Theorem 3.2) as follows:
Let f be given by (1) in the class $B_\Sigma(\beta,\delta) := \mathcal{N}_{\Sigma^*}\left(0,1,\delta,\frac{1}{2};\beta\right)$, $0 \leq \beta < 1$, $0 \leq \delta \leq 1$. Then
$$|a_2| \leq \sqrt{\frac{2(1-\beta)}{1+\delta}}.$$

(ii) For $\gamma = 1$, $\lambda = 0$ and $\mu = \frac{1}{2}$, we obtain the next result of Murugusundaramoorthy et al. ([27] Corollary 7):
Let f be given by (1) in the class $\mathcal{S}_\Sigma(\beta) := \mathcal{N}_{\Sigma^*}\left(1,0,\delta,\frac{1}{2};\beta\right)$, $0 \leq \beta < 1$, $0 \leq \delta \leq 1$. Then
$$|a_2| \leq \sqrt{2-2\beta}, \quad |a_3| \leq 4(1-\beta)^2+(1-\beta).$$

4. Conclusions

In this article, we defined two new subclasses of bi-univalent functions, that are $\mathcal{N}_\Sigma(\gamma,\lambda,\delta,\mu;\alpha)$ and $\mathcal{N}_{\Sigma^*}(\gamma,\lambda,\delta,\mu;\beta)$, with the aid of the arguments and real parts' upper bounds, respectively. In these definitions, we used the convolution product with the function I_μ first defined in [23]. For some particular cases of parameters, the classes $\mathcal{N}_\Sigma(\gamma, \lambda, \delta, \mu; \alpha)$ generalize those introduced by Li and Wang [25] and Brannan and Taha [26], while $\mathcal{N}_{\Sigma^*}(\gamma, \lambda, \delta, \mu; \beta)$ extends the classes $B_\Sigma(\beta, \delta)$ of Li and Wang [25], and $S_{\Sigma^*}(\beta)$ is defined as studied by Brannan and Taha [26].

The two main results give upper bounds for the first two coefficients of the power series for the functions that belong to these families. Our main results extend those of Li and Wang ([25] Theorem 2.2), Li and Wang ([25] Theorem 3.2), Murugusundaramoorthy et al. ([27] Corollary 6) and Murugusundaramoorthy et al. ([27] Corollary 7).

We would like to mention that neither of the main theorems give the best (i.e., the lowest) upper bounds for $|a_2|$ and $|a_3|$ for the functions that belong to the subclasses $\mathcal{N}_\Sigma(\gamma, \lambda, \delta, \mu; \alpha)$ and $\mathcal{N}_{\Sigma^*}(\gamma, \lambda, \delta, \mu; \beta)$. To find the best (that is the lowest, or so-called the sharp) upper bounds of these coefficients remains an interesting open question, and could motivate researchers to find other methods for this type of study.

Moreover, another open question is to find upper bounds for the general coefficients $|a_n|$, $n \geq 4$ for the functions of these new classes. Our attempts for the coefficient $|a_4|$ fail because of the very complicated expression of this coefficient, but still remains a challenging problem; maybe another approach could give a satisfactory result in this sense.

Author Contributions: Conceptualization, T.H., I.A.F., Y.A.A.-K., A.A.-H., A.K.W. and T.B.; methodology, T.H., I.A.F., Y.A.A.-K., A.A.-H., A.K.W. and T.B.; software, A.K.W. and T.B.; validation, T.H., I.A.F., Y.A.A.-K., A.A.-H., A.K.W. and T.B.; formal analysis, T.H., I.A.F., Y.A.A.-K., A.A.-H., A.K.W. and T.B.; investigation, T.H., I.A.F., Y.A.A.-K., A.A.-H., A.K.W. and T.B.; resources, T.H., I.A.F., Y.A.A.-K., A.A.-H., A.K.W. and T.B.; data curation, T.H., I.A.F., Y.A.A.-K., A.A.-H., A.K.W. and T.B.; writing—original draft preparation, A.K.W. and T.B.; writing—review and editing, A.K.W. and T.B.; visualization, A.K.W. and T.B.; supervision, T.H., I.A.F., Y.A.A.-K., A.A.-H., A.K.W. and T.B.; project administration, T.H., I.A.F., Y.A.A.-K., A.A.-H., A.K.W. and T.B. All authors have read and agreed to the published version of the manuscript.

Funding: This research received no external funding.

Data Availability Statement: Our manuscript has no associated data.

Acknowledgments: The authors are grateful to the reviewers of this article for providing valuable remarks, comments, and advice in order to improve the quality of the paper.

Conflicts of Interest: The authors declare no conflict of interest.

References

1. Duren, P.L. *Univalent Functions*; Grundlehren der Mathematischen Wissenschaften, Band 259; Springer: New York, NY, USA; Berlin/Heidelberg, Germany; Tokyo, Japan, 1983.
2. Srivastava, H.M.; Mishra, A.K.; Gochhayat, P. Certain subclasses of analytic and bi-univalent functions. *Appl. Math. Lett.* **2010**, *23*, 1188–1192. [CrossRef]
3. Abirami, C.; Magesh, N.; Yamini, J. Initial bounds for certain classes of bi-univalent functions defined by Horadam polynomials. *Abstr. Appl. Anal.* **2020**, *2020*, 7391058. [CrossRef]
4. Adegani, E.A.; Bulut, S.; Zireh, A.A. Coefficient estimates for a subclass of analytic bi-univalent functions. *Bull. Korean Math. Soc.* **2018**, *55*, 405–413.
5. Güney, H.Ö.; Murugusundaramoorthy, G.; Sokół, J. Subclasses of bi-univalent functions related to shell-like curves connected with Fibonacci numbers. *Acta Univ. Sapientiae Math.* **2018**, *10*, 70–84. [CrossRef]
6. Magesh, N.; Bulut, S. Chebyshev polynomial coefficient estimates for a class of analytic bi-univalent functions related to pseudo-starlike functions. *Afr. Mat.* **2018**, *29*, 203–209. [CrossRef]
7. Páll-Szabó, Á.O.; Wanas, A.K. Coefficient estimates for some new classes of bi-Bazilevič functions of Ma-Minda type involving the Sălăgean integro-differential operator. *Quaest. Math.* **2021**, *44*, 495–502.
8. Şeker, B. On a new subclass of bi-univalent functions defined by using Sălăgean operator. *Turk. J. Math.* **2018**, *42*, 2891–2896. [CrossRef]
9. Srivastava, H.M. Operators of basic (or q-) calculus and fractional q-calculus and their applications in geometric function theory of complex analysis. *Iran. J. Sci. Technol. Trans. A Sci.* **2020**, *44*, 327–344. [CrossRef]
10. Srivastava, H.M.; Altınkaya, Ş.; Yalçin, S. Certain subclasses of bi-univalent functions associated with the Horadam polynomials. *Iran. J. Sci. Technol. Trans. A Sci.* **2019**, *43*, 1873–1879. [CrossRef]

11. Srivastava, H.M.; Eker, S.S.; Hamidi, S.G.; Jahangiri, J.M. Faber polynomial coefficient estimates for bi-univalent functions defined by the Tremblay fractional derivative operator. *Bull. Iran. Math. Soc.* **2018**, *44*, 149–157. [CrossRef]
12. Srivastava, H.M.; Gaboury, S.; Ghanim, F. Coefficient estimates for some general subclasses of analytic and bi-univalent functions. *Afr. Mat.* **2017**, *28*, 693–706. [CrossRef]
13. Srivastava, H.M.; Gaboury, S.; Ghanim, F. Coefficient estimates for a general subclass of analytic and bi-univalent functions of the Ma-Minda type. *Rev. Real Acad. Cienc. Exactas Fís. Nat. Ser. A Mat. (RACSAM)* **2018**, *112*, 1157–1168. [CrossRef]
14. Srivastava, H.M.; Motamednezhad, A.; Adegani, E.A. Faber polynomial coefficient estimates for bi-univalent functions defined by using differential subordination and a certain fractional derivative operator. *Mathematics* **2020**, *8*, 172. [CrossRef]
15. Srivastava, H.M.; Sakar, F.M.; Güney, H.Ö. Some general coefficient estimates for a new class of analytic and bi-univalent functions defined by a linear combination. *Filomat* **2018**, *32*, 1313–1322. [CrossRef]
16. Srivastava, H.M.; Wanas, A.K.; Srivastava, R. Applications of the q-Srivastava-Attiya operator involving a certain family of bi-univalent functions associated with the Horadam polynomials. *Symmetry* **2021**, *13*, 1230. [CrossRef]
17. Alshanti, W.G.; Alshanty, A.; Zraiqat, A.; Jebril, I.H.; Hammad, M.A.; Batiha, I.M. Cubature formula for double integrals based on Ostrowski type inequality. *Int. J. Differ. Equ.* **2022**, *17*, 379–387.
18. Saadeh, R.; Al-Smadi, M.; Gumah, G.; Khalil, H.; Khan, R.A. Numerical investigation for solving two-point fuzzy boundary value problems by reproducing kernel approach. *Appl. Math. Inf. Sci.* **2016**, *10*, 2117–2129. [CrossRef]
19. Wanas, A.K.; Cotîrlă, L.-I. Applications of $(M-N)$-Lucas polynomials on a certain family of bi-univalent functions. *Mathematics* **2022**, *10*, 595. [CrossRef]
20. Juma, A.R.S.; Al-Fayadh, A.; Vijayalakshmi, S.P.; Sudharsan, T.V. Upper bound on the third hnkel determinant of the class of univalent functions using an operator. *Afr. Mat.* **2022**, *33*, 56. [CrossRef]
21. Shahab, N.H.; Juma, A.R.S. Coefficient bounds for certain subclasses for meromorphic functions involving quasi subordination. *AIP Conf. Proc.* **2022**, *2400*, 030001.
22. Amourah, A.; Alsoboh, A.; Ogilat, O.; Gharib, G.M.; Saadeh, R.; Al Soudi, M. A generalization of Gegenbauer polynomials and bi-univalent functions. *Axioms* **2023**, *12*, 128. [CrossRef]
23. Ruscheweyh, S. Linear operators between classes of prestarlike functions. *Comment. Math. Helv.* **1977**, *52*, 497–509. [CrossRef]
24. Carathéodory, C. Über den Variabilitätsbereich der Fourier'schen Konstanten von positiven harmonischen Funktionen. *Rend. Circ. Mat. Palermo Ser. 2* **1911**, *32*, 193–217. [CrossRef]
25. Li, X.-F.; Wang, A.-P. Two new subclasses of bi-univalent functions. *Int. Math. Forum* **2012**, *7*, 1495–1504.
26. Brannan, D.A.; Taha, T.S. On some classes of bi-univalent functions. *Stud. Univ. Babeş-Bolyai Math.* **1986**, *31*, 70–77.
27. Murugusundaramoorthy, G.; Magesh, N.; Prameela, V. Coefficient bounds for certain subclasses of bi-univalent function. *Abstr. Appl. Anal.* **2013**, *2013*, 573017. [CrossRef]

Disclaimer/Publisher's Note: The statements, opinions and data contained in all publications are solely those of the individual author(s) and contributor(s) and not of MDPI and/or the editor(s). MDPI and/or the editor(s) disclaim responsibility for any injury to people or property resulting from any ideas, methods, instructions or products referred to in the content.

Article

On Hermite–Hadamard-Type Inequalities for Functions Satisfying Second-Order Differential Inequalities

Ibtisam Aldawish [1], Mohamed Jleli [2] and Bessem Samet [2,*]

[1] Department of Mathematics and Statistics, College of Science, Imam Mohammad Ibn Saud Islamic University (IMSIU), Riyadh 11566, Saudi Arabia
[2] Department of Mathematics, College of Science, King Saud University, Riyadh 11451, Saudi Arabia; jleli@ksu.edu.sa
* Correspondence: bsamet@ksu.edu.sa

Abstract: Hermite–Hadamard inequality is a double inequality that provides an upper and lower bounds of the mean (integral) of a convex function over a certain interval. Moreover, the convexity of a function can be characterized by each of the two sides of this inequality. On the other hand, it is well known that a twice differentiable function is convex, if and only if it admits a nonnegative second-order derivative. In this paper, we obtain a characterization of a class of twice differentiable functions (including the class of convex functions) satisfying second-order differential inequalities. Some special cases are also discussed.

Keywords: convex functions; Hermite–Hadamard inequality; second-order differential inequalities

MSC: 26A51; 26D15; 26D10

1. Introduction

Inequalities involving convex functions are very useful in many branches of mathematics. The Hermite–Hadamard inequality is the one of the most important inequality for convex functions. This inequality provides an upper and lower bounds of the mean of a convex function over a certain interval. It is mostly used in mathematics to study the properties of convex functions and their applications in optimization and approximation theory, see, e.g., [1–3].

A real-valued function f defined in an interval I is convex if:

$$f(\iota y + (1-\iota)z) \leq \iota f(y) + (1-\iota) f(z)$$

for every $\iota \in [0,1]$ and $y, z \in I$. If f is twice differentiable, then f is convex, if and only if its second derivative is nonnegative. The Hermite–Hadamard inequality can be stated as follows: Let f be a real-valued convex function in an interval I. Then, for all $x, y \in I$ with $x < y$, we have:

$$f\left(\frac{x+y}{2}\right) \leq \frac{1}{y-x} \int_x^y f(\tau)\,d\tau \leq \frac{f(x)+f(y)}{2}. \tag{1}$$

Many generalizations and extensions of (1) can be found in the literature. For instance, Dragomir and Agarwal [2] studied the following class of functions:

$$\mathcal{F} = \{f : [a,b] \to \mathbb{R} : f \text{ is differentiable}, |f'| \text{ is convex}\}.$$

They proved that, if $f \in \mathcal{F}$, then:

$$\left| \frac{1}{b-a} \int_a^b f(x)\,dx - \frac{f(a)+f(b)}{2} \right| \leq \frac{b-a}{8}\left(|f'(a)| + |f'(b)|\right).$$

Some improvements and extensions of the above result have been obtained by some authors, see, e.g., [4–7]. Other extensions of (1) to various classes of functions have been obtained: s-convex functions [8–11], log-convex functions [12–14], h-convex functions [15,16], and m-convex functions [17–20]. For other classes of functions, we refer to [21–24] and the references therein. Some extensions of Hermite–Hadamard inequality to a higher dimension can be found in [25–29].

It is interesting to notice that each of the two sides of (1) provides a characterization of convex functions. Namely, if f is a real valued continuous function in an interval I, then the following statements are equivalent:

(i) f is convex;
(ii) For all $x, y \in I$ with $x < y$:

$$\frac{1}{y-x}\int_x^y f(\tau)\,d\tau \geq f\left(\frac{x+y}{2}\right);$$

(iii) For all $x, y \in I$ with $x < y$:

$$\frac{1}{y-x}\int_x^y f(\tau)\,d\tau \leq \frac{f(x)+f(y)}{2}. \qquad (2)$$

The proof of the implication (ii) $\Longrightarrow$ (i) can be found in ([30], p. 98). For the proof of the implication (iii) $\Longrightarrow$ (i), we refer to (Problem Q, [31], p. 15). On the other hand, one can check easily that (iii) is equivalent to:

$$\int_x^y f(\tau)\,d\tau \leq H'(x)f(x) - H'(y)f(y) \qquad (3)$$

for all $x, y \in I$ with $x < y$, where:

$$H(z) = \frac{1}{2}(z-x)(y-z), \quad x \leq z \leq y.$$

Observe that H is the unique (nonnegative) solution to the boundary value problem:

$$\begin{cases} H''(z) = -1, & x < z < y, \\ H(x) = H(y) = 0. \end{cases}$$

From the above remarks, we deduce that, if f is twice differentiable in I, then $f'' \geq 0$ (i.e., f is convex), if and only if (3) holds for all $x, y \in I$ with $x < y$. Thus, (3) provides a characterization of twice differentiable functions in I, having a nonnegative second derivative.

Motivated by the above discussion, our aim in this paper is to obtain a characterization of the class of twice continuously differentiable functions f in I, satisfying second-order differential inequalities of the form:

$$(\alpha f')' + \beta f + \gamma \geq 0, \qquad (4)$$

where α is twice continuously differentiable in I and β, γ are continuous in I. We shall assume that for all $x, y \in I$ with $x < y$, there exists a unique nonnegative solution H to the boundary value problem:

$$\begin{cases} (\alpha(z)H'(z))' + \beta(z)H(z) = -1, & x < z < y, \\ H(x) = H(y) = 0. \end{cases}$$

The rest of the paper is organized as follows. Section 2 is devoted to the main results and their proofs. Namely, we establish a characterization of the class of functions f

satisfying differential inequalities of the form (4). In Section 3, we discuss some special cases of (4).

2. Main Results

For any interval J of $\mathbb{R}$, by $C^n(J)$, where $n \geq 0$ is a natural number, we mean the space of n-continuously differentiable functions in J.

Let I be an open interval of $\mathbb{R}$. Let $\alpha \in C^1(I)$ and $\beta, \gamma \in C(I)$. Throughout this section, it is assumed that for all $x, y \in I$ with $x < y$, there exists a unique nonnegative solution $H \in C^2(]x,y[) \cap C([x,y])$ to the Dirichlet boundary value problem:

$$\begin{cases} (\alpha(z)H'(z))' + \beta(z)H(z) = -1, & x < z < y, \\ H(x) = H(y) = 0. \end{cases} \quad (5)$$

We are concerned with the class of functions $f \in C^2(I)$ satisfying the second-order differential inequality:

$$(\alpha(z)f'(z))' + \beta(z)f(z) + \gamma(z) \geq 0, \quad z \in I. \quad (6)$$

Our main result, which is stated below, provides a characterization of this class of functions.

Theorem 1. *Let $\alpha \in C^1(I)$, $\beta, \gamma \in C(I)$ and $f \in C^2(I)$. The following statements are equivalent:*
(i) *(6) holds;*
(ii) *For all $x, y \in I$ with $x < y$, it holds that:*

$$\int_x^y f(\tau) \, d\tau \leq H'(x)\alpha(x)f(x) - H'(y)\alpha(y)f(y) + \int_x^y \gamma(\tau)H(\tau) \, d\tau. \quad (7)$$

Proof. Assume that (6) holds. Let $x, y \in I$ with $x < y$. Multiplying (6) by H (notice that $H \geq 0$) and integrating over $]x, y[$, we obtain:

$$\int_x^y (\alpha(\tau)f'(\tau))'H(\tau) \, d\tau + \int_x^y \beta(\tau)f(\tau)H(\tau) \, d\tau \geq -\int_x^y \gamma(\tau)H(\tau) \, d\tau. \quad (8)$$

An integration by parts gives us that:

$$\int_x^y (\alpha(\tau)f'(\tau))'H(\tau) \, d\tau = [\alpha(\tau)f'(\tau)H(\tau)]_{\tau=x}^y - \int_x^y f'(\tau)(\alpha(\tau)H'(\tau)) \, d\tau.$$

On the other hand, by (5), we have $H(x) = H(y) = 0$, which yields:

$$[\alpha(\tau)f'(\tau)H(\tau)]_{\tau=x}^y = 0.$$

Then, it holds that:

$$\int_x^y (\alpha(\tau)f'(\tau))'H(\tau) \, d\tau = -\int_x^y f'(\tau)(\alpha(\tau)H'(\tau)) \, d\tau.$$

Integrating again by parts, we obtain:

$$\int_x^y (\alpha(\tau)f'(\tau))'H(\tau) \, d\tau$$
$$= -[f(\tau)\alpha(\tau)H'(\tau)]_{\tau=x}^y + \int_x^y f(\tau)(\alpha(\tau)H'(\tau))' \, d\tau$$
$$= -H'(y)\alpha(y)f(y) + H'(x)\alpha(x)f(x) + \int_x^y f(\tau)(\alpha(\tau)H'(\tau))' \, d\tau.$$

However, due to (5), we have $(\alpha(\tau)H'(\tau))' = -1 - \beta(\tau)H(\tau)$, which yields:

$$\int_x^y (\alpha(\tau)f'(\tau))'H(\tau)\,d\tau \qquad (9)$$
$$= -H'(y)\alpha(y)f(y) + H'(x)\alpha(x)f(x) - \int_x^y f(\tau)\,d\tau - \int_x^y \beta(\tau)f(\tau)H(\tau)\,d\tau.$$

Thus, (7) follows from (8) and (9). This shows that (i) $\Longrightarrow$ (ii). Assume now that (ii) holds. Let $x \in I$ be fixed. Then, for all $\varepsilon > 0$ (sufficiently small), we have:

$$\int_{x-\varepsilon}^{x+\varepsilon} f(\tau)\,d\tau \leq H'(x-\varepsilon)\alpha(x-\varepsilon)f(x-\varepsilon) - H'(x+\varepsilon)\alpha(x+\varepsilon)f(x+\varepsilon) + \int_{x-\varepsilon}^{x+\varepsilon} \gamma(\tau)H(\tau)\,d\tau, \qquad (10)$$

where H is the unique positive solution to the boundary value problem:

$$\begin{cases} (\alpha(z)H'(z))' + \beta(z)H(z) = -1, & x-\varepsilon < z < x+\varepsilon, \\ H(x-\varepsilon) = H(x+\varepsilon) = 0. \end{cases} \qquad (11)$$

Moreover, by (11), we have:

$$\int_{x-\varepsilon}^{x+\varepsilon} f(\tau)\,d\tau = -\int_{x-\varepsilon}^{x+\varepsilon} \big((\alpha(\tau)H'(\tau))' + \beta(\tau)H(\tau)\big)f(\tau)\,d\tau.$$

Integrating by parts, we obtain:

$$\int_{x-\varepsilon}^{x+\varepsilon} f(\tau)\,d\tau$$
$$= -\int_{x-\varepsilon}^{x+\varepsilon} (\alpha(\tau)H'(\tau))'f(\tau)\,d\tau - \int_{x-\varepsilon}^{x+\varepsilon} \beta(\tau)H(\tau)f(\tau)\,d\tau$$
$$= -\big[\alpha(\tau)H'(\tau)f(\tau)\big]_{\tau=x-\varepsilon}^{x+\varepsilon} + \int_{x-\varepsilon}^{x+\varepsilon} H'(\tau)\alpha(\tau)f'(\tau)\,d\tau - \int_{x-\varepsilon}^{x+\varepsilon} \beta(\tau)H(\tau)f(\tau)\,d\tau$$
$$= \alpha(x-\varepsilon)H'(x-\varepsilon)f(x-\varepsilon) - \alpha(x+\varepsilon)H'(x+\varepsilon)f(x+\varepsilon) + \big[H(\tau)\alpha(\tau)f'(\tau)\big]_{\tau=x-\varepsilon}^{x+\varepsilon}$$
$$- \int_{x-\varepsilon}^{x+\varepsilon} H(\tau)(\alpha(\tau)f'(\tau))'\,d\tau - \int_{x-\varepsilon}^{x+\varepsilon} \beta(\tau)H(\tau)f(\tau)\,d\tau.$$

Since $H(x-\varepsilon) = H(x+\varepsilon) = 0$, we obtain:

$$\int_{x-\varepsilon}^{x+\varepsilon} f(\tau)\,d\tau$$
$$= \alpha(x-\varepsilon)H'(x-\varepsilon)f(x-\varepsilon) - \alpha(x+\varepsilon)H'(x+\varepsilon)f(x+\varepsilon)$$
$$- \int_{x-\varepsilon}^{x+\varepsilon} H(\tau)\big((\alpha(\tau)f'(\tau))' + \beta(\tau)f(\tau)\big)\,d\tau.$$

Hence, by (10), it holds that:

$$\int_{x-\varepsilon}^{x+\varepsilon} H(\tau)\big((\alpha(\tau)f'(\tau))' + \beta(\tau)f(\tau) + \gamma(\tau)\big)\,d\tau \geq 0.$$

Since $H \geq 0$ and $(\alpha f')' + \beta f + \gamma \in C([x-\varepsilon, x+\varepsilon])$, then there exists $z_\varepsilon \in [x-\varepsilon, x+\varepsilon]$ such that:

$$(\alpha(z_\varepsilon)f'(z_\varepsilon))' + \beta(z_\varepsilon)f(z_\varepsilon) + \gamma(z_\varepsilon) \geq 0.$$

Passing to the limit as $\varepsilon \to 0^+$ in the above inequality, we obtain:

$$(\alpha(x)f'(x))' + \beta(x)f(x) + \gamma(x) \geq 0,$$

which proves that (6) holds. This shows that (ii) $\Longrightarrow$ (i). $\square$

Replacing f by $-f$ and γ by $-\gamma$ in Theorem 1, we obtain the following result.

Theorem 2. Let $\alpha \in C^1(I)$, $\beta, \gamma \in C(I)$ and $f \in C^2(I)$. The following statements are equivalent:
(i) $(\alpha(z)f'(z))' + \beta(z)f(z) + \gamma(z) \leq 0$, $z \in I$;
(ii) For all $x, y \in I$ with $x < y$, it holds that:

$$\int_x^y f(\tau)\,d\tau \geq H'(x)\alpha(x)f(x) - H'(y)\alpha(y)f(y) + \int_x^y \gamma(\tau)H(\tau)\,d\tau.$$

From Theorem 1, we deduce the following result.

Corollary 1. Let $\alpha \in C^1(I)$, $\beta, \gamma \in C(I)$ and $f \in C^2(I)$. If (6) holds, then for all $x, y \in I$ with $x < y$, we have:

$$\begin{aligned}\int_x^y f(\tau)\,d\tau &\leq H_1'(x)\alpha(x)f(x) - H_2'(y)\alpha(y)f(y) + \int_x^y \gamma(\tau)H(\tau)\,d\tau \\ &\quad - \left[H_1'\left(\frac{x+y}{2}\right) - H_2'\left(\frac{x+y}{2}\right)\right]\alpha\left(\frac{x+y}{2}\right)f\left(\frac{x+y}{2}\right),\end{aligned} \quad (12)$$

where H_1 and H_2 are the unique nonnegative solutions to the boundary value problems:

$$\begin{cases} (\alpha(z)H_1'(z))' + \beta(z)H_1(z) = -1, & x < z < \frac{x+y}{2} \\ H_1(x) = H_1\left(\frac{x+y}{2}\right) = 0 \end{cases}, \quad (13)$$

$$\begin{cases} (\alpha(z)H_2'(z))' + \beta(z)H_2(z) = -1, & \frac{x+y}{2} < z < y \\ H_2\left(\frac{x+y}{2}\right) = H_2(y) = 0 \end{cases}, \quad (14)$$

and

$$H(z) = \begin{cases} H_1(z) & \text{if } x < z < \frac{x+y}{2}, \\ H_2(z) & \text{if } \frac{x+y}{2} < z \leq y. \end{cases} \quad (15)$$

Proof. Writing (7) with $\frac{x+y}{2}$ instead of y, we obtain:

$$\begin{aligned}&\int_x^{\frac{x+y}{2}} f(\tau)\,d\tau \\ &\leq H_1'(x)\alpha(x)f(x) - H_1'\left(\frac{x+y}{2}\right)\alpha\left(\frac{x+y}{2}\right)f\left(\frac{x+y}{2}\right) + \int_x^{\frac{x+y}{2}} \gamma(\tau)H_1(\tau)\,d\tau.\end{aligned} \quad (16)$$

Similarly, writing (7) with $\frac{x+y}{2}$ instead of x, we obtain:

$$\begin{aligned}&\int_{\frac{x+y}{2}}^y f(\tau)\,d\tau \\ &\leq H_2'\left(\frac{x+y}{2}\right)\alpha\left(\frac{x+y}{2}\right)f\left(\frac{x+y}{2}\right) - H_2'(y)\alpha(y)f(y) + \int_{\frac{x+y}{2}}^y \gamma(\tau)H_2(\tau)\,d\tau.\end{aligned} \quad (17)$$

Adding (16) to (17), we obtain (12). □

Similarly, from Theorem 2, we deduce the following result.

Corollary 2. Let $\alpha \in C^1(I)$, $\beta, \gamma \in C(I)$ and $f \in C^2(I)$. If:

$$(\alpha(z)f'(z))' + \beta(z)f(z) + \gamma(z) \leq 0, \quad z \in I,$$

then for all $x, y \in I$ with $x < y$, we have:

$$\int_x^y f(\tau)\,d\tau \geq H_1'(x)\alpha(x)f(x) - H_2'(y)\alpha(y)f(y) + \int_x^y \gamma(\tau))H(\tau)\,d\tau$$
$$- \left[H_1'\left(\frac{x+y}{2}\right) - H_2'\left(\frac{x+y}{2}\right)\right]\alpha\left(\frac{x+y}{2}\right)f\left(\frac{x+y}{2}\right),$$

where H_1 (resp. H_2) is the unique nonnegative solution to (13) (resp. (14)) and H is defined by (15).

From Corollary 1, we deduce the following refinement of Hermite–Hadamard inequality (see [29]).

Corollary 3. *Let $f \in C^2(I)$ be a convex function. Then, for all $x, y \in I$ with $x < y$, we have:*

$$\frac{1}{y-x}\int_x^y f(\tau)\,d\tau \leq \frac{1}{2}\left(\frac{f(x)+f(y)}{2} + f\left(\frac{x+y}{2}\right)\right). \tag{18}$$

Proof. Taking:

$$\alpha = 1,\ \beta = \gamma = 0$$

in Corollary 1, we obtain:

$$H_1(z) = \frac{1}{4}(z-x)(x+y-2z),\quad x \leq z \leq \frac{x+y}{2}$$

and

$$H_2(z) = \frac{1}{4}(y-z)(2z-x-y),\quad \frac{x+y}{2} \leq z \leq y.$$

Then, by (12), we obtain (18). □

Similarly, from Corollary 2, we deduce the following result.

Corollary 4. *Let $f \in C^2(I)$ be a concave function. Then, for all $x, y \in I$ with $x < y$, we have*

$$\frac{1}{y-x}\int_x^y f(\tau)\,d\tau \geq \frac{1}{2}\left(\frac{f(x)+f(y)}{2} + f\left(\frac{x+y}{2}\right)\right).$$

3. Applications

In this section, some special cases of Theorems 1 and 2 are discussed. Namely, we provide characterizations of various classes of functions satisfying differential inequalities of type (6). We first consider the classes of functions:

$$\mathcal{F}_\ell^+ = \left\{f \in C^2(I) : f''(z) \geq \ell,\ z \in I\right\} \tag{19}$$

and

$$\mathcal{F}_\ell^- = \left\{f \in C^2(I) : f''(z) \leq \ell,\ z \in I\right\}, \tag{20}$$

where $\ell \in \mathbb{R}$ is a constant. Observe that for $\ell = 0$, $\mathcal{F}_0^+$ reduces to the class of twice continuously differentiable convex functions, while $\mathcal{F}_0^-$ reduces to the class of twice continuously differentiable concave functions. We recall that in [29], Niculescu and Persson proved that, if $f \in \mathcal{F}_\ell^+$, then for all $x, y \in I$ with $x < y$, it holds that:

$$\frac{f(x)+f(y)}{2} - \frac{1}{y-x}\int_x^y f(\tau)\,d\tau \geq \frac{\ell(y-x)^2}{12}. \tag{21}$$

Furthermore, if $f \in \mathcal{F}_\ell^-$, then for all $x, y \in I$ with $x < y$, it holds that:

$$\frac{f(x) + f(y)}{2} - \frac{1}{y-x}\int_x^y f(\tau)\, d\tau \leq \frac{\ell(y-x)^2}{12}. \tag{22}$$

In this section, we show that (21) (resp. (22)) provides a characterization of the class of functions $\mathcal{F}_\ell^+$ (resp. $\mathcal{F}_\ell^-$). We next consider the classes of functions

$$\mathcal{G}_\lambda^+ = \left\{ f \in C^2(I) : f''(z) - \lambda f(z) \geq 0,\ z \in I \right\} \tag{23}$$

and

$$\mathcal{G}_\lambda^- = \left\{ f \in C^2(I) : f''(z) - \lambda f(z) \leq 0,\ z \in I \right\}, \tag{24}$$

where $\lambda > 0$. Observe that when $\lambda = 0$, $\mathcal{G}_0^+$ reduces to the class of twice continuously differentiable convex functions, while $\mathcal{G}_0^-$ reduces to the class of twice continuously differentiable concave functions.

3.1. Characterizations of the Classes of Functions $\mathcal{F}_\ell^\pm$

Let I be an open interval of $\mathbb{R}$. Let $\ell \in \mathbb{R}$. The following result provides a characterization of the class of functions $\mathcal{F}_\ell^+$ defined by (19).

Corollary 5. *Let $f \in C^2(I)$. The following statements are equivalent:*

(i) $f \in \mathcal{F}_\ell^+$;
(ii) *For all $x, y \in I$ with $x < y$, (21) holds.*

Proof. Observe that:

$$\mathcal{F}_\ell^+ = \left\{ f \in C^2(I) : (\alpha(z) f'(z))' + \beta(z) f(z) + \gamma(z) \geq 0,\ z \in I \right\},$$

where

$$\alpha = 1,\ \beta = 0,\ \gamma = -\ell.$$

Hence, by Theorem 1, $f \in \mathcal{F}_\ell^+$, if and only if, for all $x, y \in I$ with $x < y$, it holds that:

$$\int_x^y f(\tau)\, d\tau \leq H'(x) f(x) - H'(y) f(y) - \ell \int_x^y H(\tau)\, d\tau, \tag{25}$$

where

$$H(z) = \frac{1}{2}(z-x)(y-z),\quad x \leq z \leq y$$

is the unique (nonnegative) solution to the boundary value problem:

$$\begin{cases} H''(z) = -1, & x < z < y, \\ H(x) = H(y) = 0. \end{cases}$$

On the other hand, for all $x, y \in I$ with $x < y$, we have:

$$H'(x)f(x) - H'(y)f(y) - \ell \int_x^y H(\tau) d\tau$$
$$= \frac{y-x}{2} f(x) - \frac{1}{2}(x-y)f(y) - \frac{\ell}{2} \int_x^y (-\tau^2 + (x+y)\tau - xy) d\tau$$
$$= (y-x)\frac{f(x)+f(y)}{2} - \frac{\ell}{2} \left[-\frac{\tau^3}{3} + \frac{x+y}{2}\tau^2 - xy\tau \right]_{\tau=x}^y$$
$$= (y-x)\frac{f(x)+f(y)}{2} - \frac{\ell}{12} \left(y^3 - x^3 - 3xy^2 + 3x^2y \right)$$
$$= (y-x)\frac{f(x)+f(y)}{2} - \frac{\ell}{12} (y-x)^3,$$

which shows that (25) is equivalent to (21). □

Similarly, using Theorem 2 (or replacing f by $-f$ and ℓ by $-\ell$ in Corollary 5), we obtain the following characterization of the class of functions $\mathcal{F}_\ell^-$ defined by (20).

Corollary 6. *Let $f \in C^2(I)$. The following statements are equivalent:*
(i) $f \in \mathcal{F}_\ell^-$;
(ii) *For all $x, y \in I$ with $x < y$, (22) holds.*

3.2. Characterizations of the Classes of Functions $\mathcal{G}_\lambda^\pm$

Let I be an open interval of $\mathbb{R}$ and $\lambda > 0$. We first need the following lemma. Its proof is elementary; we omit the details.

Lemma 1. *For all $x, y \in I$ with $x < y$, the following boundary value problem:*

$$\begin{cases} H''(z) - \lambda H(z) = -1, & x < z < y, \\ H(x) = H(y) = 0 \end{cases}$$

admits a unique nonnegative solution given by:

$$H(z) = \frac{e^{-\sqrt{\lambda}z} \left(e^{\sqrt{\lambda}x} - e^{\sqrt{\lambda}z} \right) \left(e^{\sqrt{\lambda}z} - e^{\sqrt{\lambda}y} \right)}{\lambda \left(e^{\sqrt{\lambda}x} + e^{\sqrt{\lambda}y} \right)}, \quad x \leq z \leq y. \tag{26}$$

The following result provides a characterization of the class of functions $\mathcal{G}_\lambda^+$ defined by (23).

Corollary 7. *Let $f \in C^2(I)$. The following statements are equivalent:*
(i) $f \in \mathcal{G}_\lambda^+$;
(ii) *For all $x, y \in I$ with $x < y$, it holds that:*

$$\int_x^y f(\tau) d\tau \leq \frac{e^{\sqrt{\lambda}y} - e^{\sqrt{\lambda}x}}{\sqrt{\lambda} \left(e^{\sqrt{\lambda}x} + e^{\sqrt{\lambda}y} \right)} (f(x) + f(y)). \tag{27}$$

Proof. Observe that:

$$\mathcal{G}_\lambda^+ = \left\{ f \in C^2(I) : (\alpha(z)f'(z))' + \beta(z)f(z) + \gamma(z) \geq 0, z \in I \right\},$$

where

$$\alpha = 1, \ \beta = -\lambda, \ \gamma = 0.$$

Hence, by Theorem 1, $f \in \mathcal{G}_\lambda^+$, if and only if, for all $x, y \in I$ with $x < y$, it holds that:

$$\int_x^y f(\tau)\, d\tau \leq H'(x)f(x) - H'(y)f(y), \tag{28}$$

where H is given by (26). On the other hand, for all $x, y \in I$ with $x < y$, we have:

$$H'(z) = \frac{e^{\sqrt{\lambda}(x-z+y)} - e^{\sqrt{\lambda}z}}{\sqrt{\lambda}\left(e^{\sqrt{\lambda}x} + e^{\sqrt{\lambda}y}\right)}, \quad x \leq z \leq y,$$

which yields:

$$H'(x) = \frac{e^{\sqrt{\lambda}y} - e^{\sqrt{\lambda}x}}{\sqrt{\lambda}\left(e^{\sqrt{\lambda}x} + e^{\sqrt{\lambda}y}\right)}$$

and

$$H'(y) = \frac{e^{\sqrt{\lambda}x} - e^{\sqrt{\lambda}y}}{\sqrt{\lambda}\left(e^{\sqrt{\lambda}x} + e^{\sqrt{\lambda}y}\right)} = -H'(x).$$

Hence, for all $x, y \in I$ with $x < y$, we have:

$$H'(x)f(x) - H'(y)f(y)$$
$$= H'(x)(f(x) + f(y))$$
$$= \frac{e^{\sqrt{\lambda}y} - e^{\sqrt{\lambda}x}}{\sqrt{\lambda}\left(e^{\sqrt{\lambda}x} + e^{\sqrt{\lambda}y}\right)}(f(x) + f(y)),$$

which shows that (28) is equivalent to (27). □

Remark 1. *Passing to the limit as* $\lambda \to 0^+$, *(27) reduces to the standard Hermite–Hadamard inequality (2).*

Similarly, using Theorem 2 (or replacing f by $-f$ in Corollary 7), we obtain the following characterization of the class of functions $\mathcal{G}_\lambda^-$ defined by (24).

Corollary 8. *Let* $f \in C^2(I)$. *The following statements are equivalent:*

(i) $f \in \mathcal{G}_\lambda^-$;
(ii) *For all* $x, y \in I$ *with* $x < y$, *it holds that:*

$$\int_x^y f(\tau)\, d\tau \geq \frac{e^{\sqrt{\lambda}y} - e^{\sqrt{\lambda}x}}{\sqrt{\lambda}\left(e^{\sqrt{\lambda}x} + e^{\sqrt{\lambda}y}\right)}(f(x) + f(y)).$$

4. Conclusions

The Hermite–Hadamard inequality (Inequality (1)) provides an upper and lower bounds of the (integral) mean of a convex function over a certain interval. Moreover, each of the two sides of (1) provides a characterization of convex functions. In the special case when a function f is twice differentiable in a certain interval I, the convexity of f is equivalent to the differential inequality $f'' \geq 0$ in I. Thus, it is natural to ask whether it is possible to obtain a characterization of twice differentiable functions satisfying more general differential inequalities. In this paper, we gave a positive answer to this question for the class of functions f satisfying differential inequalities of the form $(\alpha f')' + \beta f + \gamma \geq 0$ in I, where $\alpha \in C^1(I)$ and $\beta, \gamma \in C(I)$. Namely, assuming that for every $x, y \in I$ with $x < y$, the Dirichlet boundary value problem:

$$\begin{cases} (\alpha(z)H'(z))' + \beta(z)H(z) = -1, & x < z < y, \\ H(x) = H(y) = 0 \end{cases}$$

admits a unique nonnegative solution H. We show that the considered differential inequality is equivalent to:

$$\int_x^y f(\tau)\,d\tau \leq H'(x)\alpha(x)f(x) - H'(y)\alpha(y)f(y) + \int_x^y \gamma(\tau)H(\tau)\,d\tau$$

for every $x, y \in I$ with $x < y$. The above inequality is a generalization of the right side of Hermite–Hadamard inequality (1), which can be obtained by taking $\alpha = 1$ and $\beta = \gamma = 0$. We also discussed some special cases of α, β and γ, and provided some characterizations in those cases.

In this work, only second-order differential inequalities are investigated. It would be interesting to show whether it is possible to obtain a characterization of functions f satisfying higher-order differential inequalities. For instance, the class of functions f satisfying $f'''' \geq 0$ in I deserves to be studied.

Author Contributions: All authors contributed equally to this paper. All authors have read and agreed to the published version of the manuscript.

Funding: The authors extend their appreciation to the Deanship of Scientific Research at Imam Mohammad Ibn Saud Islamic University (IMSIU) for funding and supporting this work through Research Partnership Program no RP-21-09-03.

Data Availability Statement: Not applicable.

Conflicts of Interest: The authors declare no conflict of interest.

References

1. Dragomir, S.S.; Pearce, C.E.M. *Selected Topics on Hermite-Hadamard Inequalities and Applications*; RGMIA Monographs; Victoria University: Footscray, VIC, Australia, 2000.
2. Dragomir, S.S.; Agarwal, R.P. Two inequalities for differentiable mappings and applications to special means of real numbers and to trapezoidal formula. *Appl. Math. Lett.* **1998**, *11*, 91–95. [CrossRef]
3. Guessab, A.; Semisalov, B. Optimal general Hermite-Hadamard-type inequalities in a ball and their applications in multidimensional numerical integration. *Appl. Numer. Math.* **2021**, *170*, 83–108. [CrossRef]
4. Pearce, C.E.; Pecarić, J. Inequalities for differentiable mappings with application to special means and quadrature formulae. *Appl. Math. Lett.* **2000**, *13*, 51–55. [CrossRef]
5. Sarikaya, M.Z.; Saglam, A.; Yildirim, H. New inequalities of Hermite-Hadamard type for functions whose second derivatives absolute values are convex and quasi-convex. *Int. J. Open Probl. Comput. Sci. Math. (IJOPCM)* **2012**, *5*, 3. [CrossRef]
6. Latif, M.A. On some new inequalities of Hermite-Hadamard type for functions whose derivatives are s-convex in the second sense in the absolute value. *Ukr. Math. J.* **2016**, *67*, 1552–1571. [CrossRef]
7. Zhao, D.; Gulshan, G.; Ali, M.A.; Nonlaopon, K. Some new midpoint and trapezoidal-type inequalities for general convex functions in q-calculus. *Mathematics* **2022**, *10*, 444. [CrossRef]
8. Kórus, P. An extension of the Hermite-Hadamard inequality for convex and s-convex functions. *Aequ. Math.* **2019**, *93*, 527–534. [CrossRef]
9. Samraiz, M.; Perveen, Z.; Rahman, G.; Adil Khan, M.; Nisar, K.S. Hermite-Hadamard fractional inequalities for differentiable functions. *Fractal Fract.* **2022**, *6*, 60. [CrossRef]
10. Nasri, N.; Aissaoui, F.; Bouhali, K.; Frioui, A.; Meftah, B.; Zennir, K.; Radwan, T. Fractional weighted midpoint-type inequalities for s-convex functions. *Symmetry* **2023**, *15*, 612. [CrossRef]
11. Gulshan, G.; Budak, H.; Hussain, R.; Nonlaopon, K. Some new quantum Hermite-Hadamard type inequalities for s-convex functions. *Symmetry* **2022**, *14*, 870. [CrossRef]
12. Niculescu, P.C. The Hermite-Hadamard inequality for log convex functions. *Nonlinear Anal.* **2012**, *75*, 662–669. [CrossRef]
13. Dragomir, S. Refinements of the Hermite-Hadamard integral inequality for log-convex functions. *Aust. Math. Soc. Gaz.* **2000**, *28*, 129–134.
14. Dragomir, S. New inequalities of Hermite-Hadamard type for log-convex functions. *Khayyam J. Math.* **2017**, *3*, 98–115.
15. Dragomir, S.S. Inequalities of Hermite-Hadamard type for h-convex functions on linear spaces. *Proyecciones* **2015**, *34*, 323–341. [CrossRef]
16. Breaz, D.; Yildiz, C.; Cotirla, L.; Rahman, G. New Hadamard type inequalities for modified h-convex functions. *Fractal Fract.* **2023**, *7*, 216. [CrossRef]

17. Dragomir, S.S.; Toader, G. Some inequalities for m-convex functions. *Stud. Univ. Babes Bolyai Math.* **1993**, *38*, 21–28.
18. Dragomir, S.S. On some new inequalities of Hermite-Hadamard type for m-convex functions. *Tamkang J. Math.* **2002**, *33*, 1. [CrossRef]
19. Chen, D.; Anwar, M.; Farid, G.; Bibi, W. Inequalities for q-h-integrals via h-convex and m-convex functions. *Symmetry* **2023**, *15*, 666. [CrossRef]
20. Qi, Y.; Wen, Q.; Li, G.; Xiao, K.; Wang, S. Discrete Hermite-Hadamard-type inequalities for (s, m)-convex function. *Fractals* **2022**, *30*, 2250160. [CrossRef]
21. Zhao, D.F.; An, T.Q.; Ye, G.J.; Liu, W. New Jensen and Hermite-Hadamard type inequalities for h-convex interval-valued functions. *J. Inequal. Appl.* **2018**, *2018*, 302. [CrossRef]
22. Rashid, S.; Noor, M.A.; Noor, K.I.; Safdar, F.; Chu, Y.-M. Hermite-Hadamard inequalities for the class of convex functions on time scale. *Mathematics* **2019**, *7*, 956. [CrossRef]
23. Budak, H.; Ali, M.A.; Tarhanaci, M. Some new quantum Hermite-Hadamard-like inequalities for coordinated convex functions. *J. Optim. Theory Appl.* **2020**, *186*, 899–910. [CrossRef]
24. Samet, B. A convexity concept with respect to a pair of functions. *Numer. Funct. Anal. Optim.* **2022**, *43*, 522–540. [CrossRef]
25. Barani, A. Hermite-Hadamard and Ostrowski type inequalities on hemispheres. *Mediterr. J. Math.* **2016**, *13*, 4253–4263. [CrossRef]
26. Chen, Y. Hadamard's inequality on a triangle and on a polygon. *Tamkang J. Math.* **2004**, *35*, 247–254. [CrossRef]
27. De la Cal, J.; Cárcamo, J.; Escauriaza, L. A general multidimensional Hermite-Hadamard type inequality. *J. Math. Anal. Appl.* **2009**, *356*, 659–663. [CrossRef]
28. Mihailescu, M.; Niculescu, C. An extension of the Hermite-Hadamard inequality through subharmonic functions. *Glasg. Math. J.* **2007**, *49*, 509–514. [CrossRef]
29. Niculescu, C.P.; Persson, L.E. Old and new on the Hermite-Hadamard inequality. *Real Anal. Exch.* **2004**, *29*, 663–686. [CrossRef]
30. Hardy, G.H.; Littlewood, J.E.; Pólya, G. *Inequalities*; Cambridge University Press: Cambridge, UK, 1934.
31. Roberts, A.W.; Varberg, D.E. *Convex Functions*; Academic Press: Cambridge, MA, USA, 1973.

Disclaimer/Publisher's Note: The statements, opinions and data contained in all publications are solely those of the individual author(s) and contributor(s) and not of MDPI and/or the editor(s). MDPI and/or the editor(s) disclaim responsibility for any injury to people or property resulting from any ideas, methods, instructions or products referred to in the content.

Article

Measure-Based Extension of Continuous Functions and p-Average-Slope-Minimizing Regression

Roger Arnau, Jose M. Calabuig and Enrique A. Sánchez Pérez *

Instituto Universitario de Matemática Pura y Aplicada, Universitat Politècnica de València, Camino de Vera s/n, 46022 Valencia, Spain
* Correspondence: easancpe@mat.upv.es; Tel.: +34-963877660

Abstract: This work is inspired by some recent developments on the extension of Lipschitz real functions based on the minimization of the maximum value of the slopes of a reference set for this function. We propose a new method in which an integral p-average is optimized instead of its maximum value. We show that this is a particular case of a more general theoretical approach studied here, provided by measure-valued representations of the metric spaces involved, and a duality formula. For $p = 2$, explicit formulas are proved, which are also shown to be a particular case of a more general class of measure-based extensions, which we call ellipsoidal measure extensions. The Lipschitz-type boundedness properties of such extensions are shown. Examples and concrete applications are also given.

Keywords: Lipschitz; metric space; extension; measure

MSC: 26A16; 54C20

1. Introduction

The process of extending a real function $f: S \to \mathbb{R}$, where S is a subset of a metric space M, to the whole space M can be approached from different perspectives. For example, assuming a linear structure on M (i.e., M is a normed space), the Hahn–Banach theorem states that if S is a vector subspace of M and f is linear and continuous on S, f can be extended to a linear and continuous functional $F: M \to \mathbb{R}$. Moreover, the norm of the functional is preserved, such that $\|F\| = \|f\|$. On the other hand, the classical McShane–Whitney theorem gives the Lipschitz counterpart of this result. If M is just a metric space and $f: S \to \mathbb{R}$ is a Lipschitz map (no linearity involved), we can always find an extension of f to M preserving the Lipschitz constant [1,2].

There is a large class of variants of extension theorems for continuous and Lipschitz maps, which aim to cover different requirements on the results obtained. From the theoretical point of view, it is a first order problem to know under which requirements it is possible to find an extension of real-valued functions preserving some continuity property, e.g., continuity, uniform continuity, Lipschitz, etc. Let us expose some results in this direction. The classical Tietze theorem states that, given a normal topological space X, if S is a closed subset of X and $f: S \to \mathbb{R}$ is continuous, then there exists a continuous extension $\widehat{f}: X \to \mathbb{R}$ of f, and it can be chosen in such a way that $\inf_S f \leq \widehat{f} \leq \sup_S f$ on X [3]. In this case, continuity and point-wise bounds are preserved, but nothing is said about the extension procedure. In this direction, more recent results are known. For example, the next result is due to Matoušková (see [4] and also [5]). Let (X, τ) be a compact Hausdorff metric space, d a τ-lower semicontinuous metric on X, and $S \subset X$ a τ-closed set. Suppose that there is a real-valued continuous function g in S such that it is also Lipschitz with respect to d. Then there exists a continuous function f on X that extends g and $\min_S g \leq f \leq \max_S g$, and f is also Lipschitz with the same Lipschitz constant as g. Thus, continuity, the Lipschitz constant as well as point-wise bounds are preserved. When the analysis is restricted to

Citation: Arnau, R.; Calabuig, J.M.; Sánchez Pérez, E.A. Measure-Based Extension of Continuous Functions and p-Average-Slope-Minimizing Regression. *Axioms* **2023**, *12*, 359. https://doi.org/10.3390/axioms12040359

Academic Editors: Inna Kalchuk and Hari Mohan Srivastava

Received: 23 February 2023
Revised: 25 March 2023
Accepted: 6 April 2023
Published: 7 April 2023

Copyright: © 2023 by the authors. Licensee MDPI, Basel, Switzerland. This article is an open access article distributed under the terms and conditions of the Creative Commons Attribution (CC BY) license (https://creativecommons.org/licenses/by/4.0/).

subsets of Euclidean spaces, stronger results can be obtained. For example, for the case of non-expansive maps $N(S)$ in subsets S of Euclidean spaces (that is, functions $f: S \to X$ such that $\|f(x) - f(y)\| \le \|x - y\|$ for $x, y \in S$), we have the next result by Kopecká [6], [Th. 1.3]: let X be a Euclidean space and let $S \subset X$ be a compact subset. Then there exists a uniformly continuous function $F: N(S) \to N(X)$ such that, if $f \in N(S)$, then $F(f)|_S = f$, and if f is Lipschitz, then $F(f)$ is also Lipschitz with the same Lipschitz constant.

All these extension results have the common property of belonging to abstract existence. None of them provide effective computational procedures or explicit formulas. However, Lipschitz extensions have become a fundamental tool in many disciplines that are experiencing a strong growth in recent years, such as artificial intelligence (see, for example, [7–12]); thus, applied approaches are also needed.

In the present paper, we are interested in showing some explicit formulas to give concrete extensions satisfying certain Lipschitz-type inequalities. From this applied point of view, we have as a main reference the method of Oberman [13] and Milman [14]. This procedure minimizes for each $x \in M \setminus S$ the maximum slope of the segment from $f(x)$ to any $f(s)$ with $s \in S$ (see Figure 1). The slope is given by $|f(x) - f(s)|/d(x, s)$. For any possible value $y \in \mathbb{R}$ that we could assign to $F(x)$, the maximum value of the slope is given by

$$M_x(y) = \sup_{s \in S} \frac{|y - f(s)|}{d(x, s)} = \left\| \frac{y - f(\cdot)}{d(x, \cdot)} \right\|_\infty.$$

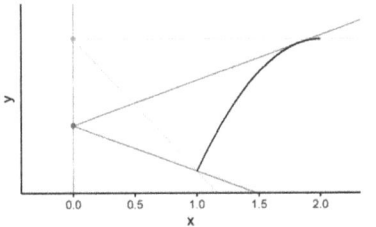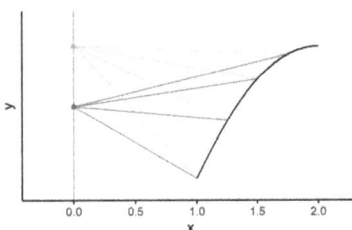

Figure 1. Geometric construction by Oberman and Milman (**left**) and the one that minimizes $M_x^p(y)$ for $p = 2$ (**right**). In black, the graph of $f(x) = -x^2 + 4x - 3$ for $1 \le x \le 2$, to be extended to the point $x = 0$. In blue, the point y that minimizes the problem, and in grey, an example point, $y = 1$.

The proposed extension is then given by $F(x) = \arg\min_{y \in \mathbb{R}} M_x(y)$. Since we want to define an extension of f, for each $s \in S$, we define $F(s) = f(s)$. In [13], it is shown that it can be explicitly computed, and important properties about the extension are also proven, such as that it preserves the Lipschitz constant (see also [14]).

Our idea in this paper is to study the extension of f defined as follows. For each $x \in M \setminus S$, we minimize, instead of the maximum, an "integral p-average" of the slopes of the segment from $f(x)$ to any of the values of $f(s)$ with $s \in S$. To compute this "p-average", we consider a probability Borel measure on S, $\mu \in \mathcal{P}(S)$, and fix $1 \le p < +\infty$. That is,

$$M_x^p(y) = \left(\int_S \left| \frac{y - f(s)}{d(x, s)} \right|^p d\mu(s) \right)^{\frac{1}{p}} = \left\| \frac{y - f(\cdot)}{d(x, \cdot)} \right\|_p.$$

This will be explained in Section 3. We intend to introduce some smoothing elements into the extensions in this way; this property has become an important feature in recent research on the subject, both from a theoretical and applied point of view (see, for example, [7,15]). In Section 3.1, we will see that the above minimization problem for $p = 2$ (when

S is compact and f is integrable) can be solved explicitly for $x \in M \setminus S$. The solution is given by the equation

$$F(x) = \left(\int_S \frac{f(s)}{d(x,s)^2} d\mu(s) \right) \cdot \left(\int_S \frac{1}{d(x,s)^2} d\mu(s) \right)^{-1}.$$

However, this article also has a more theoretical purpose. We show that the method explained above can be integrated into a more general framework for the extension of continuous maps defined on compact subsets of metric spaces. This is done in Section 2. In order to do so, if (M,d) is a metric space and $f : S \to \mathbb{R}$, we intend to find a suitable extension of f to M preserving some natural constant associated with Lipschitz-type inequalities. Let us first recall some basic concepts. If S is a compact set, we write $\mathcal{B}(S)$ for the associated Borel σ-algebra. As usual, we will denote by $\mathcal{M}(S)$ the Banach space of real-valued measures of bounded variation and by $\mathcal{C}(S)$ the Banach space of real-valued continuous functions. Recall that $\mathcal{M}(S)$ can be identified as the dual space of $\mathcal{C}(S)$ via the Riesz representation theorem; that is, $\mathcal{M}(S) = \mathcal{C}(S)^*$. If $\mu \in \mathcal{M}(S)$, $L^1(\mu)$ is the Lebesgue space of μ-integrable functions. Recall that a measure μ_0 is μ-continuous (or absolutely continuous with respect to μ) if $\mu(A) = 0$ implies $\mu_0(A) = 0$ for every $A \in \mathcal{B}(S)$. If $s \in S$, we write as usual $\delta_s \in \mathcal{M}(S)$ for the Dirac delta measure.

Our idea is to consider the function we want to extend $f \in \mathcal{C}(S)$ as a functional acting on the elements of a characteristic subset of its topological (linear) dual space: the space of regular Borel measures $\mathcal{M}(S)$. The subset $\mathcal{P}(S)$ of all the probability regular Borel measures on S will be used instead when the normalization is required.

Using the duality, we can write a Lipschitz-type inequality as a composition of two elements,

1. A map $x \mapsto \mu_x$, that relates each element x of M with a measure $\mu_x \in \mathcal{M}(S)$;
2. The function $f \in \mathcal{C}(S)$ being understood as an element of the pre-dual of $\mathcal{M}(S)$.

The inequality is $|\langle f, \mu_x - \mu_y \rangle| \leq K d(x,y)$, $x, y \in M$. It is easy to see that this definition makes sense for trivial cases; for instance, if we take $M = S$ and $x \mapsto \mu_x = \delta_x \in \mathcal{P}(S)$ as the representation map, we have that

$$|\langle f, \delta_x - \delta_y \rangle| = |f(x) - f(y)| \leq K d(x,y)$$

gives the standard Lipschitz inequality for $f : M \to \mathbb{R}$.

Finally, we analyze a particular class of average extensions in Section 4 as an application. We call them ellipsoidal measure extensions; we show some Lipschitz-type properties for this class and some examples. We refer to [16] for general issues on Lipschitz functions, ref. [17] for the definitions and results on functional analysis that are used, and [18] for the abstract concepts on topology.

2. Duality on $\mathcal{C}(S)$ and Measure-Based Extension of Continuous Functions

In this section, we present the main results and show some basic examples of our proposed extension of continuous maps from compact subsets of metric spaces. Then, we will show in later sections some particular types of extensions that conform to this abstract scheme, mainly the mean slope extension that we explained in the Introduction. We will demonstrate that duality over the space of continuous functions provides a useful setting for the analysis of an interesting class of Lipschitz maps.

Definition 1. *Let (M,d) be a metric space and consider a compact subset $S \subset M$. We say that a map $m : M \to \mathcal{M}(S)$ given by $m(x) = \mu_x$ is a measure representation.*

In most cases, we will also consider a measure μ controlling all the measures μ_x if such a μ exists. That is, we will take $\mu \in \mathcal{P}(S) \subset \mathcal{C}(S)^*$, which satisfies that the measures μ_x are μ-continuous for all $x \in M \setminus S$.

If $f \in \mathcal{C}(S)$, we can always consider the dual action on $m(M) \subset \mathcal{M}(S)$ as follows. Define the integral corresponding map for f provided by the function $\varphi_{m,f} : M \to \mathbb{R}$ given by the formula

$$\varphi_{m,f}(x) = \langle f, m(x) \rangle = \int_S f(s) \, d\mu_x(s), \quad x \in M.$$

Note that, once the subset S has been fixed and the representation by the measure m has been chosen, we have a linear mapping

$$\psi : \mathcal{C}(S) \to \mathbb{R}^M$$
$$f \mapsto \varphi_{m,f}.$$

We show in the next proposition that the continuity properties of $\varphi_{m,f}$ are inherited from m. Then, under some requirements on m, $\mathcal{C}(M)$ can be chosen to be the range of ψ.

Proposition 1. *Let $f : S \to \mathbb{R}$ be a continuous function and let $m : M \to \mathcal{M}(S)$ be a measure representation of M. Then,*

1. *If m is continuous on x, then $\varphi_{m,f}$ is continuous on x;*
2. *If m is uniformly continuous, then $\varphi_{m,f}$ is uniformly continuous;*
3. *If m is Lipschitz, then $\varphi_{m,f}$ is Lipschitz with $\mathrm{Lip}(\varphi_{m,f}) \leq \|f\|_{C(S)} \cdot \mathrm{Lip}(m)$.*

Proof. All statements follow from the fact that for any $x, y \in M$, we have

$$\left| \varphi_{m,f}(x) - \varphi_{m,f}(y) \right| = \left| \int_S f(s) \, d\mu_x(s) - \int_S f(s) \, d\mu_y(s) \right|$$
$$\leq \|f\|_{C(S)} \cdot \|\mu_x - \mu_y\|_{\mathcal{M}(S)};$$

thus, if m is Lipschitz, we have $\|\mu_x - \mu_y\|_{\mathcal{M}(S)} \leq \mathrm{Lip}(m) \cdot d(x,y)$. Therefore,

$$\left| \varphi_{m,f}(x) - \varphi_{m,f}(y) \right| \leq \|f\|_{C(S)} \cdot \mathrm{Lip}(m) \cdot d(x,y),$$

and so the result is proven. □

Recall that our main objective is to obtain a procedure that assigns to each $f : S \to \mathbb{R}$ a function $F : M \to \mathbb{R}$ that *extends* f, that is, $F|_S = f$. Let us give some formal definitions and results in this respect.

Definition 2. *Let S be a compact subspace of a metric space (M,d). An extension rule is a mapping $ER : \mathcal{C}(S) \to \mathbb{R}^M$ that extends the functions, that is, $ER(f)|_S = f$ for each $f \in \mathcal{C}(S)$.*

Proposition 2. *Let (M,d) be a metric space and let S be a compact subset of M. Let $\mu \in \mathcal{P}(S)$, and let m be a measure representation of M. Then, $f \mapsto \varphi_{m,f}$ is an extension rule if and only if $m(s) = \delta_s, s \in S$.*

In this case, we call the mapping $f \mapsto \varphi_{m,f}$ an integral extender map.

Proof. Fix $s \in S$ and observe that $f \mapsto \varphi_{m,f}$ preserves the value of the functions on s if and only if

$$\varphi_{m,f}(s) = \langle f, m(s) \rangle = f(s) = \langle f, \delta_s \rangle,$$

for any $f \in \mathcal{C}(S)$. Since $m(s) \in \mathcal{P}(S) \subset \mathcal{C}(S)^*$, this is only possible when $m(s)$ and δ_s are the same measure. □

The next theorem is a characterization of our extension procedure. We show in it that essentially, the linear extension rules, under some hypothesis, can be written in terms of an integral extender map introduced above.

Theorem 1. *Let S be a compact subset of a metric space M. An extension rule $ER: C(S) \to (\ell_\infty(M), \|\cdot\|_\infty)$ is a linear isometry that preserves the constant functions if and only if there exists a measure representation $m: M \to \mathcal{P}(S)$ with $m(s) = \delta_s$ for each $s \in S$ such that $ER(f) = \varphi_{m,f}$ for all $f \in C(S)$.*

Proof. Assume first that $ER(f) = \varphi_{m,f} = \langle m(\cdot), f \rangle$ with $m: M \to \mathcal{P}(S)$ as in the statement. Clearly, ER is linear, and for each f, $ER(f)$ extends f (Proposition 2). To see that ER is an isometry, let $f \in C(S)$. Then,

$$\|f\|_{C(S)} \leq \|ER(f)\|_\infty = \sup_{x \in M} |\langle f, m(x) \rangle| \leq \sup_{x \in M} \|f\|_{C(S)} \|m(x)\|_{\mathcal{P}(S)} \leq \|f\|_{C(S)}.$$

To see the converse, let us define m at each point of M. For $s \in S$, let $m(s) = \delta_s$, and for $x \in M \setminus S$, let $\xi_x : C(S) \to \mathbb{R}$ be defined as $\xi_x(f) = ER(f)(x)$. Since it is linear, so is ξ_x. For each $f \in C(S)$,

$$|\xi_x(f)| = |ER(f)(x)| \leq \|ER(f)\|_{C(S)} = \|f\|_{C(S)},$$

so $\xi_x \in C(S)^* = \mathcal{M}(S)$ and $\|\xi_x\| \leq 1$. Let us see that ξ_x is a positive functional. Let $\mathbf{1}$ denote the constant function on S such that $\mathbf{1}(s) = 1$. For $f \in C(S)$ such that $f \geq 0$, call $g = f - (\|f\|/2) \cdot \mathbf{1}$. Then,

$$\frac{\|f\|}{2} = \|g\|_{C(S)} = \|ER(g)\|_\infty = \left\|ER(f) - \frac{\|f\|}{2}\mathbf{1}\right\|_\infty \geq \frac{\|f\|}{2} - \xi_x(f),$$

so $\xi_x(f) \geq 0$. We conclude that $\xi_x \in \mathcal{P}(S)$, so it is the value we assign to $m(x)$. Thus, $\varphi_{m,f}(x) = \langle \xi_x, f \rangle = ER(f)(x)$. This finishes the proof. □

Note that in this result, we do not need any linear requirement of M, since the linearity of ER depends on the rank of the functions, which is $\mathbb{R}$.

Example 1. *Let S be a finite subset of a metric space M, so $C(S)$ coincides with the set of real Lipschitz functions on S. An example of extension rule $C(S) \to C(M)$ is the one provided by the mean of the McShane and the Whitney formulas [1,2]. For each $f \in C(S)$, this extension $\widehat{f}: M \to \mathbb{R}$ is defined on every $x \in M$ by*

$$\widehat{f}(x) = \frac{1}{2}\left(\sup_{s \in S}\{f(s) - \mathrm{Lip}(f)d(x,s)\} + \inf_{s \in S}\{f(s) + \mathrm{Lip}(f)d(x,s)\}\right).$$

It can be easily seen that it preserves the infima and suprema of the functions; see [12]. As a consequence, it preserves the norm ($\|f\|_{C(S)} = \|\widehat{f}\|_{C(M)}$) and the constant functions. However, it is not of the form $\widehat{f} = \varphi_{m,f}$ for any representation by a measure m, since it is non-linear. To see this, let, for example, $S = \{(0,0), (1,0), (0,1), (1,1)\} \subset \mathbb{R}^2$ with the Euclidean norm. Define for each $s \in S$ the function $f_s: S \to \mathbb{R}$ with values $f_s(s) = 1$, and let $f_s(t) = 0$ for every $t \neq s$. Clearly, $f = \sum_{s \in S} f_s$ is the constant function 1, so its extension on $x = (1/2, 1/2)$ is $\widehat{f}(x) = 1$. However, $\sum_{s \in S} \widehat{f_s}(x) = \sum_{s \in S} 1/2 = 2$, which is a contradiction.

Example 2. *Fix a measure $\mu \in \mathcal{P}(S)$. For every $x \in M$, the (sometimes called Kuratowski) function $s \mapsto d(x,s)$ is continuous, and hence, μ-integrable. Take the map $m: M \to \mathcal{M}(S)$ given by*

$$m(x)(A) = \mu_x(A) := \int_A d(x,s) \, d\mu(s), \quad A \in \mathcal{B}(S),$$

for each $x \in M$. Therefore, in this case, μ_x is always μ-continuous, and $d(x,\cdot)$ is the Radon–Nikodym derivative $d\mu_x/d\mu$.

For a function $f \in \mathcal{C}(S)$, consider

$$\varphi_{m,f}(x) = \int_S f(s)\, d\mu_x(s) = \int_S f(s)\, d(x,s)\, d\mu, \quad x \in M.$$

This formula can be used to compute a Lipschitz function $\varphi_{m,f} : M \to \mathbb{R}$. Indeed, for $x, y \in M$,

$$|\varphi_{m,f}(x) - \varphi_{m,f}(y)| = \left|\int_S f(s)\,(d(x,s) - d(y,s))\, d\mu(s)\right|$$
$$\leq \left(\int_S |f(s)|\, d\mu(s)\right) \cdot d(x,y)$$
$$= \|f\|_{L^1(\mu)} \cdot d(x,y),$$

and so the map $\varphi_{m,f}$ is Lipschitz and $\mathrm{Lip}(\varphi_{m,f}) \leq \|f\|_{L^1(\mu)} \leq \|f\|_{\mathcal{C}(S)}$. Then, the integral corresponding map $f \mapsto \varphi_{m,f}$ maps $\mathcal{C}(M)$ on $\mathrm{Lip}(M)$.

It is easy to see that this formula does not preserve the values of f when applied to the elements of S. To obtain an integral extender map, following Proposition 2, we can define $\overline{m}(s) = \delta_s$ for $s \in S$ and $\overline{m}(x) = m(x)$ for $x \in M \setminus S$. Then, $\varphi_{\overline{m},f}$ always extends f but may not preserve any continuity property. Since

$$|\mu_x - \delta_{s_0}| = \int_{S\setminus\{s_0\}} d(x,y)\, d\mu(s) + |1 - \mu(\{s_0\})\, d(x, s_0)|,$$

this quantity never converges to 0 when $x \to s_0$. For an explicit counterexample, let $S = \{0, 1\} \subset M = \mathbb{R}$ with $\mu = \frac{1}{2}(\delta_0 + \delta_1)$ and f as the identity map on S.

Example 3. Let us show a particular case of the example above. Let (M, d) be a discrete metric space, that is, $d(x, y) = 1$ if $x \neq y$. Then,

$$\varphi_{m,f}(x) = \int_S f(s)\, d\mu(s), \quad x \in M \setminus S.$$

Therefore, the extension of the function f on $M \setminus S$ is given by a constant, the μ−average of its values on S.

Example 4. Consider the fuzzy k-nearest neighbors algorithm presented in [11]. Let S be a finite subset of the metric space M. Assume that the points in S are "fuzzy" classified on a finite number of classes, $\mathscr{C}$. For each $s \in S$ and every class $c \in \mathscr{C}$, $u_c(s)$ denotes the "degree of membership" of the element s to the class c. The classification problem consists of assigning to a new point $x \in M \setminus S$ the class of $\mathscr{C}$ to which x is most likely to belong. Observe that this problem can be solved by extending the "degree of membership" functions $u_c : S \to [0, 1]$ to $S \cup \{x\}$ or the whole M.

The formula presented in [11] for a general parameter m can be computed using a measure representation in the following way. Let $\mu = \frac{1}{|S|}\sum_{s \in S} \delta_s \in \mathcal{P}(S)$ be the normalized counting measure on S, and for each $x \in M \setminus S$, define $m(x) = \mu_x$ as the measure given by the Radon–Nikodym derivative

$$\frac{d\mu_x}{d\mu}(s) = I_x^{-1} \cdot \frac{1}{d(s,x)^{2/(n-1)}} \chi_{N_k(x)}(s),$$

where $N_k(x)$ is the set of k nearest points to x in S, n is a size parameter, and

$$I_x = \int_{N_k(x)} \frac{1}{d(s,x)^{2/(n-1)}}\, d\mu(s)$$

is the normalization factor.

Then, the resulting formula to extend each u_c is

$$\varphi_{m,u_c}(x) = \langle u_c, m(x)\rangle$$
$$= I_x^{-1} \int_{N_k(x)} \frac{u_c(s)}{d(s,x)^{2/(n-1)}} d\mu(s)$$
$$= \frac{\sum_{s \in N_k(x)} u_c(s)/d(s,x)^{2/(n-1)}}{\sum_{s \in N_k(x)} 1/d(s,x)^{2/(n-1)}},$$

which is the original formula that can be found in [11].

3. The p–Average Slope Minimizing Extension

In this section, we explain a new method for extending functions in the context we have already fixed, which is based on the calculation of an average L^p–norm of the slopes defined by the point to which we intend to extend the function and the reference points. As we have explained in the Introduction, this is a mild version of the maximum slope minimization developed by Oberman [13] and Milman [14]. We will focus attention on the case $p = 2$, since the 2–average slope method gives a canonical example of measure-based extension, in which the measures μ_x can be computed explicitly and easily. As a generalization of this case, we will devote the last section of the article to what we call ellipsoidal measure extensions.

As before, (M, d) is a metric space, S is a compact subset, and f is a continuous function on S. The regression procedure that we propose is based on the minimization on each $x \in M \setminus S$ of the μ-average in $L^p(\mu)$ of the slopes of the line from $(x, F(x))$ to each $(s, f(s))$, computed as

$$M_x^p(y) = \left(\int_S \left|\frac{y - f(s)}{d(x,s)}\right|^p d\mu(s)\right)^{\frac{1}{p}} = \left\|\frac{y - f(\cdot)}{d(x,\cdot)}\right\|_{L^p(\mu)}, \quad (1)$$

for a fixed $1 < p < +\infty$.

First of all, observe that the condition that S is closed and $x \notin S$ ensures that $d(x,S) > 0$. As f is bounded, the slope function $|y - f(\cdot)|/d(x, \cdot)$ defined on S is continuous and bounded, so the integral is well-defined and finite for any $y \in \mathbb{R}$. Since the functions $y \mapsto |y - f(s)|^p$, $y \in \mathbb{R}$, are strictly convex for any s, $M_x^p(y)$ is also strictly convex and positive. This fact, together with the property that $M(y) \to \infty$ when y tends to $+\infty$ and $-\infty$, shows that M has a unique point in $\mathbb{R}$ where its minimum is attained.

Then, we define the extension on a point $x \in M \setminus S$ as

$$F(x) = \arg\min_{y \in \mathbb{R}} M_x^p(y) = \arg\min_{y \in \mathbb{R}} \int_S \left|\frac{y - f(s)}{d(x,s)}\right|^p d\mu(s). \quad (2)$$

For the values $s \in S$, we define $F(s) = f(s)$. We call this formula the p-average-slope-minimizing extension. We can see a geometric representation of this method compared with the one that minimizes the maximum slope at each point in Figure 1.

The minimization problem (2) for $x \in X \setminus S$ is equivalent to solving the equation

$$0 = \frac{\partial (M_x^p(y))^p}{\partial y} = p \int_S \left|\frac{y - f(s)}{d(x,s)}\right|^{p-1} \operatorname{sign}(y - f(s)) \, d\mu(s), \quad (3)$$

where $\operatorname{sign}(\cdot)$ denotes the sign function. This equation may not be solvable explicitly, but it can always be solved numerically using, for example, a Newton–Raphson method. Examples of the average slope minimizing extensions are shown in Figure 2, comparing different values of p.

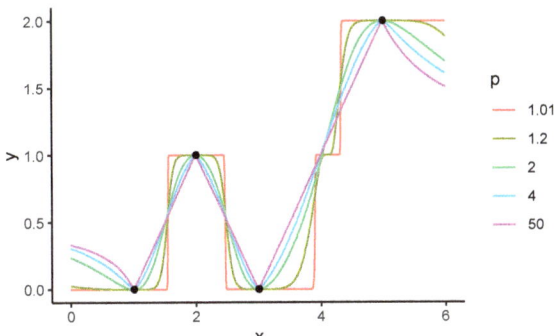

Figure 2. Interpolation of the points $(1,0), (2,1), (3,0)$, and $(5,2)$ using the formula of 2 for different values of p. The measure considered is the counting normalized measure $\mu = (\delta_1 + \delta_2 + \delta_3 + \delta_5)/4$.

3.1. Explicit Formula for $p = 2$

Let us explicitly calculate the extension on $x \in M \setminus S$ for $p = 2$. Equation (3) can be rewritten as

$$\frac{\partial (M_x^2(y))^2}{\partial y} = 2\left(y \int_S \frac{1}{d(x,s)^2} d\mu(s) - \int_S \frac{f(s)}{d(x,s)^2} d\mu(s)\right).$$

If we write I_x for the normalization constant $I_x = \int_S \frac{1}{d(x,s)^2} d\mu(s)$, the unique point where $\frac{\partial (M_x^2(y))^2}{\partial y} = 0$ is

$$y^* = I_x^{-1} \int_S \frac{f(s)}{d(x,s)^2} d\mu(s).$$

Clearly, $y^* = \arg\min_{y \in \mathbb{R}} M_x^2(y)$, so it is the searched value for $F(x)$. We can adapt the formula to understand it as an integral extender map. Let $\mu_x \in \mathcal{P}(S)$ be the Borel measure, defined as

$$\mu_x(A) = I_x^{-1} \int_A \frac{1}{d(s,x)^2} d\mu(s),$$

for each μ-measurable set A. For every $s \in S$, we define $\mu_s = \delta_s$ as the Dirac delta on s. Then, the extension F can be computed on x (using the notation explained in the previous section) as

$$F(x) = \int_S f(s) d\mu_x(s) = \langle \mu_x, f \rangle. \tag{4}$$

Observe that the "weight" function $s \mapsto I_x^{-1} \cdot \frac{1}{d(x,s)^2}$ acts as the Radon–Nikodym derivative $d\mu_x/d\mu$.

Remark 1. *Assume now that S is a finite set and $\mu \in \mathcal{P}(S)$ is the probability measure that assigns the same measure to each point,*

$$\mu = \frac{1}{|S|} \sum_{s \in S} \delta_s. \tag{5}$$

The function F is a (finite) convex combination of the values $\{f(s) : s \in S\}$ with weights inversely proportional to the square of the distance from x to s, that is

$$F(x) = \langle \mu_x, f \rangle = \sum_{s \in S} \mu_x(\{s\}) f(s) = \sum_{s \in S} \frac{\frac{1}{d(x,s)^2}}{\sum_{t \in S} \frac{1}{d(x,t)^2}} f(s). \tag{6}$$

We can see an example of the Radon–Nikodym derivatives of the measures μ_x in Figure 3.

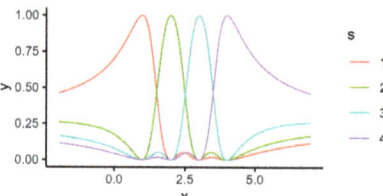

Figure 3. The values of $\frac{d\mu_x}{d\mu}(s)$ for $s \in S = \{1,2,3,4\}$ and $x \in [-2,7]$ on $(\mathbb{R}, |\cdot|)$.

Remark 2. *Note that the expression (6) is the same as that given in the fuzzy k-nearest neighbours algorithm presented in [11] and in Example (4) for $n = 2$ if we consider S defined only as the set of k nearest neighbours of x.*

We study in the rest of the section the continuity properties of the extension formula given in (4) for the finite set S. First of all, we show that it does not always preserve the Lipschitz continuity of f.

Example 5. *Consider $(\mathbb{R}, |\cdot|)$ and the subset $S = \{0,1\}$. Let $f : S \to \mathbb{R}$ be the identity map, $f(0) = 0, f(1) = 1$. Clearly, it is a Lipschitz map with constant 1.*

1. *We start with an example in which the measure $\mu \in \mathcal{P}(S)$ has non-trivial null sets. Let $\mu = \delta_0$. Then, following the previously explained extension procedure, we extend f to $F : \mathbb{R} \to \mathbb{R}$ by the given formula to obtain*

$$F(x) = \langle f, \mu_x \rangle = \frac{\int_S f(s)/d(s,x)^2 d\delta_0(s)}{\int_S 1/d(s,x)^2 d\delta_0(s)} = 0,$$

   for each $x \in \mathbb{R} \setminus S$ and $F|_S = f$. The result is the constant function 0 on $\mathbb{R} \setminus S$; see Figure 4 (left). However, the Lipschitz property of f has been lost. Indeed, observe that the inequality

$$|f(x) - f(1)| = 1 \leq K|x - 1|,$$

   does not hold for any $K > 0$ when x tends to 1.

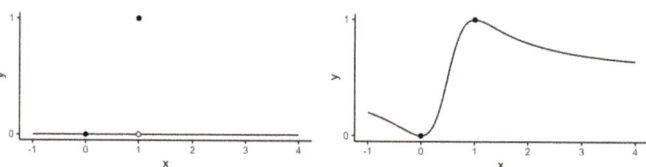

Figure 4. Minimizing average slope extension for $p = 2$ of the function $f(0) = 0, f(1) = 1$ for different measures. In the fist one, $\mu = \delta_0$, and in the second one, $\mu = \frac{1}{2}(\delta_0 + \delta_1)$.

2. *Let us show an example of a 1-Lipschitz map on a subset of the Euclidean space $(\mathbb{R}^2, \|\cdot\|_2)$ that does not extend to the whole space as a 1-Lipschitz map with the 2-average-slope minimization method. To avoid the pathological behaviour of the previous example, which is due to the existence of a point in S of measure 0, we can work with the measure given in (5), $\mu = \frac{1}{2}(\delta_0 + \delta_1)$.*

Then, for each $x \in \mathbb{R} \setminus S$, the 2-average slope minimization formula is given by (6), which is, in this case,

$$F(x) = \langle f, \mu_x \rangle = \frac{\frac{1}{(x-1)^2}}{\frac{1}{x^2} + \frac{1}{(x-1)^2}} = \frac{x^2}{2x^2 - 2x + 1};$$

see Figure 4 (right). A simple argument, using for example the mean value theorem, shows that F is Lipschitz ($\text{Lip}(F) \leq 2$). However, the Lipschitz constant is strictly bigger than 1 because

$$\left| f\left(\frac{1}{3}\right) - f\left(\frac{2}{3}\right) \right| = \left| \frac{1}{5} - \frac{4}{5} \right| = \frac{3}{5} > \frac{1}{3} = \left| \frac{1}{3} - \frac{2}{3} \right|.$$

In fact, it can be shown that the Lipschitz constant of F is exactly 2, and so the extension does not preserve the constant.

We have shown that the 2−average slope minimizing method does not preserve the Lipschitz constant; however, it satisfies other continuity properties that make this extension still interesting. We finish this section with some results on this. To avoid non-empty null subsets of S, we consider for the discrete case the measure given in Remark 1, $\mu = \frac{1}{|S|} \sum_{s \in S} \delta_s$. If $S = \{s\}$, it is obvious that the extension F will be a constant function $F(x) = f(s)$, so we assume in the rest of the work that $|S| \geq 2$.

Lemma 1. *Consider a finite subset $S \subset M$ that has at least two elements. For each $s \in S$, the function $x \mapsto \mu_x(\{s\})$ has the following properties:*

1. $\{\mu_{(\cdot)}(\{s\}) : M \to [0,1]\}_{s \in S}$ *form a partition of the unity.*
2. $\mu_{(\cdot)}(\{s\})$ *are Lipschitz functions with a Lipschitz constant less than or equal to*

$$K_s = (2 + 2\sqrt{2}) \sum_{t \neq s} \frac{1}{d(s,t)}.$$

3. *If $(M, d) = (\mathbb{R}, |\cdot|)$, $\mu_{(\cdot)}(\{s\})$ are differentiable functions with $\frac{\partial \mu_x(\{s\})}{\partial x}\big|_{x=t} = 0$ for each $t \in S$.*

Proof. By fixing $s \in S$, we study the properties of $x \mapsto \mu_x(\{s\}) = \frac{d\mu_x}{d\mu}(s)$.

1. The first statement is obvious.
2. Let $s \in S$. We can see that $\mu_{(\cdot)}(\{s\})$ is continuous at any point of M using the continuity of the functions $d(t, \cdot)$ and some elementary calculations. However, we are going to see a stronger property of these functions.
   Let $\lambda = 2 + 2\sqrt{2}$ and $x, y \in M$. As $\mu_{(\cdot)}(\{s\})$ is bounded by 1, if $d(x, y) > \frac{1}{K_s}$, then $|\alpha_s(x) - \alpha_s(y)| \leq 1 \leq K_s d(x, y)$. Therefore, we can assume now that $d(x, y) \leq \frac{1}{K_s}$. We distinguish four cases.

   (a) We assume first that $x, y \notin S$. If we write $M(w) = \sum_{t \in S} \frac{1}{d(w,t)^2}$, for $w \in M$, then

$$|\mu_x(\{s\}) - \mu_y(\{s\})| = \frac{\left| \sum_{t \in S} \frac{d(y,s)^2}{d(y,t)^2} - \sum_{t \in S} \frac{d(x,s)^2}{d(x,t)^2} \right|}{M(x)M(y)d(x,s)^2 d(y,s)^2}$$

$$\leq \sum_{t \neq s} \frac{|d(y,s)^2 d(x,t)^2 - d(x,s)^2 d(y,t)^2|}{M(x)M(y)d(x,s)^2 d(y,s)^2 d(x,t)^2 d(y,t)^2}.$$

Applying some elementary algebraic relations on the numerator, we obtain

$$|d(y,s)^2 d(x,t)^2 - d(x,s)^2 d(y,t)^2|$$
$$\leq |d(y,s)^2 d(x,t)^2 - d(y,s)^2 d(y,t)^2| + |d(y,s)^2 d(y,t)^2 - d(x,s)^2 d(y,t)^2|$$
$$= d(y,s)^2 |d(x,t)^2 - d(y,t)^2| + d(y,t)^2 |d(y,s)^2 - d(x,s)^2|$$
$$= d(y,s)^2 (d(x,t) + d(y,t))|d(x,t) - d(y,t)| + d(y,t)^2 (d(y,s) + d(x,s))|d(y,s) - d(x,s)|$$
$$\leq d(x,y)\big(d(y,s)^2 (d(x,t) + d(y,t)) + d(y,t)^2 (d(y,s) + d(x,s))\big).$$

Observe that $M(y)d(y,w)^2 \geq 1$ and $M(x)d(x,w)^2 d(x,w')^2 \geq d(x,w)^2 + d(x,w')^2$ for all $w, w' \in S$; thus,

$$\frac{|\mu_x(\{s\}) - \mu_y(\{s\})|}{d(x,y)} \leq \sum_{t \neq s} \frac{d(y,s)^2(d(x,t) + d(y,t)) + d(y,t)^2(d(y,s) + d(x,s))}{M(x)M(y)d(x,s)^2 d(x,t)^2 d(y,s)^2 d(y,t)^2}$$

$$\leq \sum_{t \neq s} \frac{d(x,t) + d(x,s) + d(y,t) + d(y,s)}{M(x)d(x,s)^2 d(x,t)^2}$$

$$\leq \sum_{t \neq s} \frac{2(d(x,t) + d(x,s)) + 2d(x,y)}{d(x,s)^2 + d(x,t)^2}.$$

Now, by applying the arithmetic-quadratic mean inequality, which states that $a^2 + b^2 \geq (a+b)^2/2$, we obtain

$$\frac{|\mu_x(\{s\}) - \mu_y(\{s\})|}{d(x,y)} \leq \sum_{t \neq s} \left(\frac{4(d(x,s) + d(x,t))}{(d(x,s) + d(x,t))^2} + \frac{2d(x,y)}{d(x,s)^2 + d(x,t)^2} \right)$$

$$\leq 4 \sum_{t \neq s} \left(\frac{1}{d(x,s) + d(x,t)} + \frac{d(x,y)}{(d(x,s) + d(x,t))^2} \right)$$

$$\leq 4 \sum_{t \neq s} \frac{1}{d(s,t)} + 4d(x,y) \sum_{t \neq s} \frac{1}{d(s,t)^2}.$$

Then, by the previous bound and taking into account that $d(x,y) \leq \frac{1}{K_s}$, we obtain

$$\frac{|\mu_x(\{s\}) - \mu_y(\{s\})|}{d(x,y)} \leq 4 \sum_{t \neq s} \frac{1}{d(s,t)} + 4d(x,y) \sum_{t \neq s} \frac{1}{d(s,t)^2}$$

$$\leq 4 \sum_{t \neq s} \frac{1}{d(s,t)} + 4 \frac{1}{K_s} \left(\sum_{t \neq s} \frac{1}{d(s,t)} \right)^2$$

$$\leq 4 \left(1 + \frac{1}{\lambda} \right) \sum_{t \neq s} \frac{1}{d(s,t)} = K_s.$$

(b) If $x \in M \setminus S$ and $y = s$,

$$|\mu_x(\{s\}) - \mu_y(\{s\})| = 1 - \mu_x(\{s\}) \leq \frac{\sum_{t \neq s} \frac{1}{d(x,t)^2}}{\frac{1}{d(x,y)^2}} = d(x,y) \cdot \sum_{t \neq s} \frac{d(x,y)}{d(x,t)^2}.$$

Reasoning as before, as we assume that $d(x,y) < \frac{1}{K_s}$, for each $t \neq s$, $\lambda d(x,y) \leq \frac{\lambda}{K_s} \leq d(s,t) \leq d(y,x) + d(x,t)$, so $d(x,y) \leq (\lambda - 1)d(x,y) \leq d(x,t)$. Moreover, $d(s,t) \leq d(y,x) + d(x,t) \leq \frac{1}{K_s} + d(x,t) \leq \frac{1}{\lambda} d(s,t)$, which implies that $d(x,t) \geq (1 - \frac{1}{\lambda})d(s,t) \geq \frac{1}{\lambda}d(s,t)$. Thus,

$$|\mu_x(\{s\}) - \mu_y(\{s\})| \leq d(x,y) \cdot \sum_{t \neq s} \frac{1}{d(x,t)} \leq d(x,y) \cdot \sum_{t \neq s} \frac{\lambda}{d(s,t)} \leq K_s d(x,y).$$

(c) Let $x \in M \setminus S$ and $y \in S$ different from s, using the case 2b,

$$|\mu_x(\{s\}) - \mu_y(\{s\})| = \mu_x(\{s\}) = 1 - \sum_{t \neq s} \mu_x(\{t\}) \leq 1 - \mu_x(\{y\})$$

$$= |\mu_y(\{s\}) - \mu_x(\{y\})| \leq K_s d(x,y).$$

(d) In the last case, we suppose that $x, y \in S$. If $x \neq s \neq y$, $\alpha_s(x) = 0 = \alpha_s(y)$, so we can assume that, for example, $x = s$ and $y \neq s$. Then,

$$|\mu_x(\{s\}) - \mu_y(\{s\})| = 1 = \frac{1}{d(x,y)} \cdot d(x,y) \leq K_s d(x,y).$$

Summing up the four cases, we have proved the desired inequality.

3. We assume now that $M = \mathbb{R}$. Let $x \in \mathbb{R}$. We are going to calculate the limit

$$\lim_{y \to x} \frac{\mu_y(\{s\}) - \mu_x(\{s\})}{y - x}.$$

We distinguish now three cases.

(a) If $x \notin S = \overline{S}$, consider the same neighborhood V of x in which $d(y,s) > 0$ for all $s \in S$ and $y \in V$. Then, as the function $d(\cdot, s) = |(\cdot) - s|$ does not vanish on V, it is differentiable and also $\mu_{(\cdot)}(\{s\})$, in particular on x.

(b) If $x = s$,

$$\lim_{y \to s} \frac{\mu_y(\{s\}) - \mu_x(\{s\})}{y - x} = \lim_{y \to s} \frac{-\sum_{t \neq s} \frac{1}{(y-t)^2}}{\frac{y-s}{(y-s)^2} + \sum_{t \neq s} \frac{y-s}{(y-t)^2}} = 0.$$

(c) If $s \neq x = s_0 \in S$, we have

$$\lim_{y \to s_0} \frac{\mu_y(\{s\}) - \mu_x(\{s\})}{y - x} = \lim_{y \to s} \frac{\frac{1}{(y-s)^2}}{\frac{y-s_0}{(y-s_0)^2} + \sum_{t \neq s_0} \frac{y-s_0}{(y-t)^2}} = 0.$$

□

Although the bound provided in part 2 of Lemma 1 seems to be accurate, we do not know if it can be improved by using other arguments.

Question: Is the bound for the Lipschitz constant provided in Lemma 1 the best possible?

As a consequence of the previous result, we obtain the following:

Proposition 3. Let (M, d) be a metric space, and let S be a finite subset of M. Consider a function $f : S \to \mathbb{R}$ and let $F : M \to \mathbb{R}$ be the extension of f given by (6). Then,

1. $\inf_{x \in M} F(x) = \inf_{s \in S} f(s)$ and $\sup_{x \in M} F(x) = \sup_{s \in S} f(s)$.
2. $F : M \to \mathbb{R}$ is a Lipschitz function.
3. If $(M, d) = (\mathbb{R}, |\cdot|)$, $F : M \to \mathbb{R}$ is a differentiable function with $F'(s) = 0$ for all $s \in S$.

Proof. The proofs are a direct consequence of Lemma 1. Observe that $m : M \to \mathcal{P}(S)$, so $m(x) = \mu_x$ is a Lipschitz function, since

$$\|m(x) - m(y)\|_{\mathcal{M}(S)} = \sum_{s \in S} |\mu_x(\{s\}) - \mu_y(\{s\})| \leq \sum_{s \in S} K_s d(x,y),$$

Therefore, according to Proposition 1, $\text{Lip}(F) \leq \|f\|_{\mathcal{C}(S)} \sum_{s \in S} K_s$. We give here some better bounds for the Lipschitz constant of F in terms of $\text{Lip}(f)$:

$$\operatorname{Lip}(F) \leq (2+2\sqrt{2}) \sum_{s\in S}\sum_{t\neq s} \frac{1}{d(s,t)} \min_{\xi\in\mathbb{R}} \max_{s\in S} |f(s)-\xi|$$

$$= (1+\sqrt{2}) \sum_{s\in S}\sum_{t\neq s} \frac{1}{d(s,t)} \left(\max f(S) - \min f(S) \right)$$

$$\leq (1+\sqrt{2}) \sum_{s\in S}\sum_{t\neq s} \frac{1}{d(s,t)} \operatorname{Diam}(S) \operatorname{Lip}(f).$$

$$\operatorname{Lip}(F) \leq (2+2\sqrt{2}) \max_{s\in S} \sum_{t\neq s} \frac{1}{d(s,t)} \min_{\xi\in\mathbb{R}} \sum_{s\in S} |f(s)-\xi|$$

$$\leq (2+2\sqrt{2}) \max_{s\in S} \sum_{t\neq s} \frac{1}{d(s,t)} \sum_{s\in S}\sum_{t\neq s} d(s,t) \frac{1}{|S|} \operatorname{Lip}(f).$$

□

Corollary 1. *If we fix a finite subset S of M, the extension rule $f \mapsto F$ from $\mathcal{C}(S)$ to $\mathcal{C}(M)$ provided by (6) is a linear isometric mapping. Moreover, it preserves constant functions and the infima and suprema of the involved functions.*

3.2. More Examples for $p = 2$

To conclude this section, we show in the following more visual examples of the formulas provided for the 2-average-slope-minimizing extension. Our goal is to show that, under certain geometric conditions, we can expect better smoothness properties for the extended functions, although the Lipschitz constants are not preserved in general.

Example 6. *Let us consider the example studied by Oberman in [13] [Example 1], where $S = \{-1,1\}$ in $\mathbb{R}$ with the absolute value norm and $f(-1) = -1$, $f(1) = 1$.*

We can extend f to $\mathbb{R}$ by applying the mean of the McShane and Whitney extension. We write F_1 for it. On the other hand, following the explicit formula given in [13], the extension studied by Oberman and Milmam can be computed as

$$F_2(x) = \frac{d(-1,x)\cdot 1 + d(1,x)\cdot(-1)}{d(-1,x)+d(1,x)} = \frac{|x+1|-|x-1|}{|x+1|+|x-1|},$$

for $x \in \mathbb{R}\setminus\{-1,1\}$. To calculate the 2-average-slope-minimizing extension, we consider the measure on $\mu = \frac{1}{2}(\delta_{-1}+\delta_1)$ on S. The resulting extension for $x \in \mathbb{R}\setminus\{-1,1\}$ is then given by

$$F_3(x) = \frac{-1/(x+1)^2 + 1/(x-1)^2}{1/(x+1)^2 + 1/(x-1)^2} = \frac{2x}{x^2+1}.$$

We can see the representation of both extension functions in Figure 5. As proved in Lemma 1 (3), F_3 is differentiable, unlike the extensions F_1 and F_2.

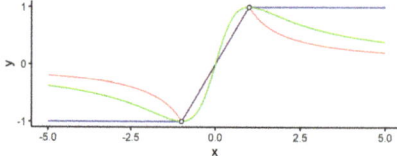

Figure 5. Extension of the function $f(-1) = -1$, $f(1) = 1$ using three different methods. In blue, F_1, the mean of the McShane and Whitney formulas; in red F_2, the one proposed by Oberman and Milman; and in green, F_3, our proposal, the 2−average slope minimizing extension.

Example 7. We set now an example similar to the previous one shown in Example 6. Let $S = [-1,1] \subset \mathbb{R}$ and let $f : S \to \mathbb{R}$, $f(s) = s$. We compute the same extensions F_1, F_2 and F_3. For the cases F_1 and F_2, we obtain the same result. For the case of F_3, we consider on S the Lebesgue measure, which we again call μ. We obtain that the value for $x \in \mathbb{R} \setminus S$ is, by applying the second fundamental theorem of calculus,

$$F_3(x) = \frac{\int_S f(s)/(x-s)^2 d\mu(s)}{\int_S 1/(x-s)^2 d\mu(s)} = x + \frac{x^2-1}{2}\log\left(\left|\frac{x-1}{x+1}\right|\right).$$

The results can be seen in Figure 6. Contrary to what happens in the previous example, we can observe that, in this case, our formula does not provide a smoother approximation due to the weight of the rest of the points of the interval that, as it is computing an average value, has a relevant role in this approximation.

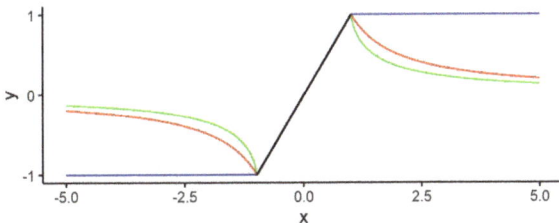

Figure 6. Extension the function $f(s) = s$ for $s \in [-1,1]$ using three different methods. In black, the original function, f; in blue F_1, the mean of the McShane and Whitney formulas; in red F_2, the one by Oberman and Milman; and in green F_3, the 2−average slope minimizing extension.

Example 8. We finish with another example on $\mathbb{R}^2$. Let $D = \{(x,y) \in \mathbb{R}^2 : 2 \leq \|(x,y)\| \leq 3\}$ be an annulus inside the ball $M = \{(x,y) \in \mathbb{R}^2 : \|(x,y)\| \leq 3\}$. Consider on D a sample S of $81,000$ points and let $\mu = \frac{1}{|S|}\sum_{s \in S} \delta_s$ as an approximation of the Lebesgue measure on C. Let $f : S \to \mathbb{R}$ be the function

$$f(x,y) = x^3 - 3xy^2;$$

that is, $z = f(x,y)$ is the monkey saddle surface on the region $(x,y) \in S$. We extend f to $M \setminus D$ using the same 2-average-slope-minimizing extension formula. The resulting function $F : M \setminus D \to \mathbb{R}$ can be seen in Figure 7.

The result is very similar to the monkey saddle surface in $M \setminus D$. In fact, the maximum error committed in the approximation $\max\{F(x,y) - (x^3 - 3xy^2) : (x,y) \in M \setminus D\}$ is less than 3×10^{-7}.

 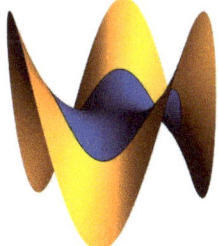

Figure 7. Extension of the function $f(x,y) = x^3 - 3xy^2$ defined on $D = \{(x,y) \in \mathbb{R}^2 : 2 \leq \|(x,y)\| \leq 3\}$ using the 2-average-slope-minimizing extension.

Moreover, that surface can also be reconstructed using only the information of f on the circumference $C = \{(x,y) \in \mathbb{R}^2 : \|(x,y)\| = 2\}$. Now, we consider on C a sample S of 1000 points and let $\mu = \frac{1}{|S|}\sum_{s \in S} \delta_s$ as an approximation of the line integral measure on C. We extend the function to $B = \{(x,y) \in \mathbb{R}^2 : \|(x,y)\| < 2\}$ using the same method. This example can be seen in Figure 8. The maximum error committed by the extension compared to the original function $f(x,y) = x^3 - 3xy^2$ on B is now less than 3×10^{-6}.

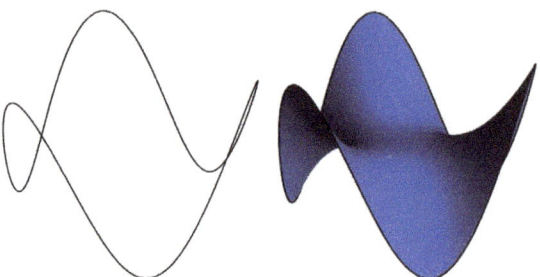

Figure 8. Extension of the function $f(x,y) = x^3 - 3xy^2$ defined on $D = \{(x,y) \in R^2 : \|(x,y)\| = 2\}$ using the 2-average-slope-minimizing extension.

The explicit formula calculated for the case $p = 2$ makes it easy to find the best extension of the Lipschitz function. However, we have found no equivalent (or even approximate) formula for any case with $p \neq 2$. This suggests the following open question for the interested reader.

Question: Is it possible to provide an explicit formula for the best extension for the case $p \neq 2$?

4. Application: Ellipsoidal Measure Extensions

Motivated by the extension formulas based on integral averages that we have shown, in this section, we introduce a particular class of measure representation of the metric space by considering a normalization requirement. We will treat representations such as $m : M \to \mathcal{P}(S)$, i.e., $m(x)$ are probability measures. This requirement provides a different way of considering the Lipschitz property of the integral extenders. We need to fix a radial function, and the Lipschitz inequality will hold for elements of M that have the same value of the average of this radial function. The simplest way to define this property is in terms of the Radon–Nikodym derivatives of the measures $m(x) = \mu_x$ with respect to μ, as we do below.

Definition 3. *Let (M,d) be a metric space and let S be a compact subspace. Let $\mu \in \mathcal{P}(S)$ and consider a measure representation of M, $m : M \to \mathcal{P}(S)$. We say that m is an ellipsoidal measure representation if there exists a measurable function $\psi : \mathbb{R}^+ \to \mathbb{R}^+$ such that for all $x \in M \setminus S$ and $A \in \mathcal{B}(S)$,*

$$m(x)(A) = \mu_x(A) = \int_A \psi(d(x,s))d\mu(s).$$

In other words, the Radon–Nikodym derivative $\frac{d\mu_x}{d\mu} : S \to \mathbb{R}^+$ only depends on the distance from x to s.

Since $m(x)$ is a probability measure, in most cases, we will compute it as the normalization of a finite measure,

$$m(x)(A) = \mu_x(A) = \frac{\int_A \psi(d(x,s))d\mu(s)}{\int_S \psi(d(x,s))d\mu(s)}. \qquad (7)$$

Let us illustrate this notion with some examples.

Example 9. *Let us start with a negative example. Let*
$$M = \{(0,0), (0,1), (1,0), (1,1)\}$$
with the Euclidean distance and let $S = \{(0,0), (1,1)\}$ with the measure $\mu = \frac{1}{2}(\delta_{(0,0)} + \delta_{(1,1)})$. Let $m : \to \mathcal{P}(S)$ be defined as
$$m\big((0,0)\big) = \delta_{(0,0)}, \ m\big((0,1)\big) = \delta_{(0,0)}, \ m\big((1,0)\big) = \delta_{(1,1)}, \ m\big((1,1)\big) = \delta_{(1,1)}.$$
Then, m is not an ellipsoidal measure representation, since the points in $M \setminus S$ satisfy
$$d\big((0,1), s\big) = d\big((1,0), s\big),$$
but $m\big((0,1)\big)$ and $m\big((1,0)\big)$ are different measures.

Example 10. *Let us consider the normalization of the measure representation given by Example 2. It is a typical case of ellipsoidal measure representation. Fix $\mu \in \mathcal{P}(S)$ and consider the map $m : M \to \mathcal{P}(S)$ given by*
$$x \mapsto m(x)(A) = \mu_x(A) := \frac{\int_A d(x,s)\,d\mu(s)}{\int_S d(x,s)\,d\mu(s)}, \quad x \in M \setminus S, \quad A \in \mathcal{B}(S),$$
and $m(s) = \delta_s$ for $s \in S$. Then, we have the integral corresponding map
$$\varphi_{m,f}(x) = \langle f, \mu_x \rangle = \frac{\int_S f(s)\,d(x,s)\,d\mu(s)}{\int_S d(x,s)\,d\mu(s)}, \quad x \in M,$$
for each $f \in \mathcal{C}(S)$. Simple computations show that for any $x, y \in M$,
$$\|\mu_x - \mu_y\| \leq d(x,y) \cdot \frac{2}{\int_S d(x,s)\,d\mu(s)}.$$
Assuming that $I = \inf_{x \in M} \int_S d(x,s)\,d\mu(s) > 0$, we obtain that m is Lipschitz. Thus, by Proposition 1, for any $f \in \mathcal{C}(S)$, we have that $\varphi_{m,f} \in \mathcal{C}(M)$, and moreover, it is a Lipschitz function with $\mathrm{Lip}(\varphi_{m,f}) \leq 2I^{-1} \cdot \|f\|_{\mathcal{C}(S)}$. Recall that $\varphi_{m,f}$ is not necessarily an extension of f.

In the above example, the Lipschitz inequality is preserved in the comparison between any pair of elements for which the extension is defined. However, this need not be true in general for ellipsoidal measure representations. Instead, we will prove below the most interesting property of these representations: the Lipschitz inequality is always preserved when involving elements with the same "average radial distance" to the set S. This is the reason for using the term ellipsoidal measure representation.

Let m be such a representation, and take a fixed ψ as in (7). For any $r > 0$, consider the "ellipsoidal set"
$$M_r = \left\{ x \in M \setminus S : \int_S \psi(d(x,s))\,d\mu(s) = r \right\}.$$

If $M_r \neq \emptyset$, we can study the Lipschitz condition of $\varphi_{m,f}$ on M_r. Therefore, by fixing the continuous function $\psi : \mathbb{R}^+ \to \mathbb{R}^+$, we say that a function $f : M \to \mathbb{R}$ is radial-Lipschitz

if for any $r > 0$ such that for $M_r \neq \emptyset$, there exists a constant L_r such that $\text{Lip}(f|_{M_r}) \leq L_r$; that is,
$$|f(x) - f(y)| \leq L_r \cdot d(x,y),$$
for all $x, y \in M_r$.

Example 11. *Continuing with Example 2, the characteristic bound for ellipsoidal measures is provided by the following computations. Fix $r \in \mathbb{R}^+$ such that the ellipsoidal set $M_r = \{x \in M : \int_S d(x,y) d\mu(s) = r\}$ is non-empty. For $x, y \in M_r$,*

$$\left|\varphi_{m,f}(x) - \varphi_{m,f}(y)\right| = \frac{1}{r}\left|\int_S f(s)\left(d(x,s) - d(y,s)\right) d\mu(s)\right|$$
$$\leq \frac{1}{r}\left(\int_S |f(s)| d\mu(s)\right) \cdot d(x,y) = \frac{\|f\|_{L^1(\mu)}}{r} \cdot d(x,y),$$

and so the map $\varphi_{m,f}$ is radial-Lipschitz and

$$\text{Lip}(\varphi_{m,f}|_{M_r}) \leq \frac{\|f\|_{L^1(\mu)}}{r}.$$

Observe that on each ellipsoidal set M_r, the Lipschitz constant of $\varphi_{m,f}$ has been improved compared to that of Example 10,

$$\text{Lip}(\varphi_{m,f}) \leq \frac{2}{\inf\{r > 0 : M_r \neq \emptyset\}} \|f\|_{\mathcal{C}(S)}. \tag{8}$$

The next result provides a bound for the Lipschitz constant restricted to the ellipsoidal set M_r for the integral expression that is given by the optimization explained in Section 3.1, in which the norm in $L^2(\mu)$ is considered. We need to define the following class of sets. For $r \in \mathbb{R}^+$, M_r is the set

$$M_r := \left\{x \in M \setminus S : r = \int_S \frac{1}{d(x,s)^2} d\mu(s)\right\},$$

that is well-defined since S is closed, so the function $s \mapsto \frac{1}{d(x,s)}$ belongs to $L^2(\mu)$ for every $x \in M \setminus S$.

Proposition 4. *Fix $\mu \in \mathcal{P}(S)$. Consider the function $m : M \to \mathcal{P}(S)$ and the ellipsoidal measure representation given by the function $\psi(t) = \frac{1}{t^2}$ on $M \setminus S$; that is,*

$$m(x)(A) = \mu_x(A) = \frac{\int_A 1/d(x,s)^2 d\mu(s)}{\int_S 1/d(x,s)^2 d\mu(s)}, \quad x \in M \setminus S, \quad A \in \mathcal{B}(S),$$

and $m_s = \delta_s$ for $s \in S$.

Let $r > 0$ such that $M_r \neq \emptyset$ and suppose that $Q_r = \sup_{x \in M_r} \|1/d(x,\cdot)^2\|_{L^2(\mu)}$ is finite. Then, $m|_{M_r} : M_r \to \mathcal{P}(S)$ is Lipschitz with

$$\text{Lip}(m|_{M_r}) \leq \frac{2Q_r}{r^{\frac{1}{2}}}.$$

Moreover, for every $f \in \mathcal{C}(S)$, $\varphi_{m,f}(x) = \int_S f(s) d\mu_x$, $x \in M$, defines a Lipschitz function when restricted to M_r, and

$$\text{Lip}(\varphi_{m,f}|_{M_r}) \leq \frac{2Q_r}{r^{\frac{1}{2}}} \|f\|_{\mathcal{C}(S)}.$$

Proof. Let r be as in the statement and $x, y \in M_r$. Then,

$$\|\mu_x - \mu_y\|_{\mathcal{M}(S)} = \frac{1}{r} \int_S \left| \frac{1}{d(x,s)^2} - \frac{1}{d(y,s)^2} \right| d\mu(s)$$

$$= \frac{1}{r} \int_S \frac{|d(x,s) - d(y,s)|(d(x,s) + d(y,s))}{d(x,s)^2 d(y,s)^2} d\mu(s)$$

$$\leq \frac{d(x,y)}{r} \left(\int_S \frac{1}{d(x,s)d(y,s)^2} d\mu(s) + \int_S \frac{1}{d(x,s)^2 d(y,s)} d\mu(s) \right).$$

Now, using the Cauchy–Schwarz inequality, we obtain

$$\|\mu_x - \mu_y\|_{\mathcal{M}(S)} \leq \frac{d(x,y)}{r} \left(\left(\int_S \frac{1}{d(x,s)^2} \right)^{\frac{1}{2}} \left(\int_S \frac{1}{d(y,s)^4} \right)^{\frac{1}{2}} + \left(\int_S \frac{1}{d(y,s)^2} \right)^{\frac{1}{2}} \left(\int_S \frac{1}{d(x,s)^4} \right)^{\frac{1}{2}} \right)$$

$$\leq \frac{d(x,y)}{r} 2r^{\frac{1}{2}} Q_r = d(x,y) \frac{2 Q_r}{r^{\frac{1}{2}}}.$$

The last statement is a consequence of reasoning as in Proposition 1. □

Example 12. *Let $M = [-2, 2] \times [-2, 2] \subset \mathbb{R}^2$ with the Euclidean distance and let S be a mesh of the set $C = \{(x, y) \in \mathbb{R}^2 : \frac{1}{2} \leq \max(|x|, |y|) \leq 1\}$ with $121,200$ points and a spacing of 0.005. We consider on S the counting normalized measure $\mu = \frac{1}{|S|} \sum_{s \in S} \delta_s$ as in Remark 1.*

We can see in Figure 9 a representation of the value of $\int_S 1/d(x,s)^2 d\mu$ for each $x \in M \setminus C$ and some relevant sets M_r.

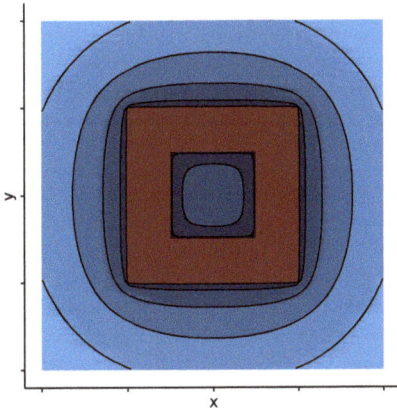

Figure 9. In red, the set C. In different shades of blue, the value of $\int_S 1/d(x,s)^2 d\mu(s)$ for each $x \in M \setminus C$. We have fixed some bands of constant value to facilitate the understanding of the graphic. Some sets M_r are plotted in black for $r \in \{\frac{1}{4}, \frac{1}{2}, 1, 2, 4\}$.

Finally, consider on S the function $f : S \to \mathbb{R}$, defined as

$$f(x, y) = x \cdot \cos(10y); \tag{9}$$

see Figure 10. We extend f to the whole M using the 2-average-slope-minimizing extension, $\varphi_{m,f} : M \to \mathbb{R}$, with $m(x) = \mu_x$ defined as in (6). The result is shown in Figure 10.

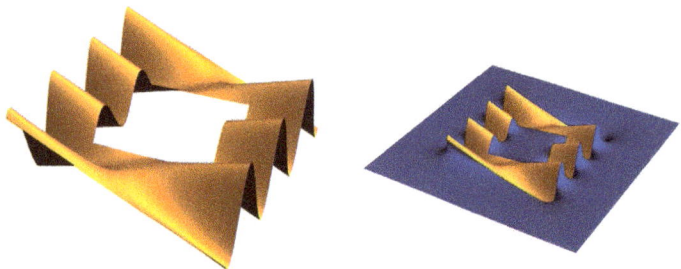

Figure 10. Extension of the function $f(x,y) = x \cdot \cos(10y)$ defined on $C = \{(x,y) \in \mathbb{R}^2 : \frac{1}{2} \leq \max(|x|,|y|) \leq 1\}$ using the 2-average-slope-minimizing method.

5. Conclusions

Given a compact subset S of a metric space M, we define the notion of measure representation of the whole metric space by assigning a measure μ_x on S to each element $x \in M$. This representation is shown to be useful for generating extension formulas for functions defined on S to all M via what we call integral extensor maps. Although these ideas seem very abstract, we show that the new Lipschitz function extension techniques we introduce (the p−slope-minimizing extensions) can be understood as particular cases of this general setting for $p = 2$. These new extension formulas are based on the calculation of an integral average of the slopes of the lines given by the points of S and the point to which we want to extend the function. They prove to be useful for modulating the smoothness of the produced functions, which is not at all given in the case of the classical McShane and Whitney formulas. However, they do not, in general, preserve the Lipschitz constant, but we show some bounds for the resulting Lipschitz norms. For example, we show that in some special cases (such as the ellipsoidal measure extensions we present in the last section), good control of the Lipschitz norms is possible on certain subsets of the metric space with a natural geometric description.

Author Contributions: Conceptualization, R.A., J.M.C. and E.A.S.P.; formal analysis, R.A. and E.A.S.P.; investigation, R.A., J.M.C. and E.A.S.P.; methodology, E.A.S.P.; supervision, J.M.C.; writing—original draft, R.A. and E.A.S.P.; writing—review and editing, R.A. and J.M.C. All authors have read and agreed to the present version of the manuscript.

Funding: The first author was supported by a contract of the Programa de Ayudas de Investigación y Desarrollo (PAID-01-21), Universitat Politècnica de València. The third author was supported by Grant PID2020-112759GB-I00 funded by MCIN/AEI /10.13039/501100011033.

Institutional Review Board Statement: Not applicable.

Informed Consent Statement: Not applicable.

Data Availability Statement: Not applicable.

Conflicts of Interest: The authors declare that they have no conflict of interest.

References

1. McShane, E.J. Extension of range of functions. *Bull. Amer. Math. Soc.* **1934**, *40*, 837–842. [CrossRef]
2. Whitney, H. Analytic extensions of differentiable functions defined in closed sets. *Trans. Amer. Math. Soc.* **1934**, *36*, 63–89. [CrossRef]
3. Tietze, H. Uber Funktionen, die auf einer abgeschlossenen Menge stetig sind. *J. für die Reine und Angew. Math.* **1915**, *145*, 9–14. [CrossRef]
4. Matoušková, E. Extensions of continuous and Lipschitz functions. *Can. Math. Bull.* **2000**, *43*, 208–217. [CrossRef]
5. Oberhammer, L. Extension of Lipschitz Functions. Ph.D. Thesis, University of Innsbruck, Innsbruck, Austria, 2016.
6. Kopecká, E. Extending Lipschitz mappings continuously. *J. Appl. Anal.* **2012**, *18*, 167–177. [CrossRef]
7. Asadi, K.; Misra, D.; Littman, M. Lipschitz continuity in model-based reinforcement learning. In Proceedings of the International Conference on Machine Learning, Stockholm, Sweden, 10–15 July 2018; pp. 264–273

8. Ashlagi, Y.; Gottlieb; L.A.; Kontorovich, A. Functions with average smoothness: Structure, algorithms, and learning. In Proceedings of the Conference on Learning Theory, Budapest, Hungary, 9–11 June 2011; pp. 186–236.
9. Calabuig, J.M.; Falciani, H.; Sánchez-Pérez, E.A. Dreaming machine learning: Lipschitz extensions for reinforcement learning on financial markets. *Neurocomputing* **2020**, *398*, 172–184. [CrossRef]
10. Falciani, H.; Sánchez-Pérez, E.A. Semi-Lipschitz functions and machine learning for discrete dynamical systems on graphs. *Mach. Learn.* **2022**, *111*, 1765–1797. [CrossRef]
11. Keller, J.M.; Gray, M.R.; Givens, J.A. A fuzzy k-nearest neighbor algorithm. *IEEE Trans. Syst. Man Cybern. Syst.* **1985**, *4*, 580–585. [CrossRef]
12. von Luxburg, U.; Bousquet, O. Distance-Based Classification with Lipschitz Functions. *J. Mach. Learn. Res.* **2004**, *5*, 669–695.
13. Oberman, A. An explicit solution of the Lipschitz extension problem. *Proc. Am. Math. Soc.* **2008**, *136*, 4329–4338. [CrossRef]
14. Milman, V.A. Lipschitz continuations of linearly bounded functions. *Sb. Math.* **1998**, *189*, 1179. [CrossRef]
15. Shvartsman, P. Whitney-type extension theorems for jets generated by Sobolev functions. *Adv. Math.* **2017**, *313*, 379–469. [CrossRef]
16. Cobzaş, Ş; Miculescu, R; Nicolae, A. *Lipschitz Functions*; Springer: Cham, Switzerland, 2019.
17. Aliprantis, C.D.; Border, K.C. *Infinite Dimensional Analysis: A Hitchhiker's Guide*, 3rd ed.; Springer: Heidelberg/Berlin, Germany, 2006.
18. Kelley, J.L. *General Topology, Vol. 27 of Graduate Texts in Mathematics*; Springer: Berlin/Heidelberg, Germany, 1975.

Disclaimer/Publisher's Note: The statements, opinions and data contained in all publications are solely those of the individual author(s) and contributor(s) and not of MDPI and/or the editor(s). MDPI and/or the editor(s) disclaim responsibility for any injury to people or property resulting from any ideas, methods, instructions or products referred to in the content.

Article

Coinciding Mean of the Two Symmetries on the Set of Mean Functions

Lenka Mihoković

Faculty of Electrical Engineering and Computing, University of Zagreb, Unska 3, 10000 Zagreb, Croatia; lenka.mihokovic@fer.hr

Abstract: On the set $\mathcal{M}$ of mean functions, the symmetric mean of M with respect to mean M_0 can be defined in several ways. The first one is related to the group structure on $\mathcal{M}$, and the second one is defined trough Gauss' functional equation. In this paper, we provide an answer to the open question formulated by B. Farhi about the matching of these two different mappings called symmetries on the set of mean functions. Using techniques of asymptotic expansions developed by T. Burić, N. Elezović, and L. Mihoković (Vukšić), we discuss some properties of such symmetries trough connection with asymptotic expansions of means involved. As a result of coefficient comparison, a new class of means was discovered, which interpolates between harmonic, geometric, and arithmetic mean.

Keywords: mean; asymptotic expansion; symmetry; Catalan numbers

MSC: 26E60; 41A60; 26E40; 39B22

Citation: Mihoković, L. Coinciding Mean of the Two Symmetries on the Set of Mean Functions. *Axioms* 2023, 12, 238. https://doi.org/10.3390/axioms12030238

Academic Editor: Inna Kalchuk

Received: 1 February 2023
Revised: 21 February 2023
Accepted: 23 February 2023
Published: 25 February 2023

Copyright: © 2023 by the author. Licensee MDPI, Basel, Switzerland. This article is an open access article distributed under the terms and conditions of the Creative Commons Attribution (CC BY) license (https://creativecommons.org/licenses/by/4.0/).

1. Introduction

Function $M: \mathbf{R}^+ \times \mathbf{R}^+ \to \mathbf{R}$ is called a mean if for all $s, t \in \mathbf{R}^+$

$$\min(s,t) \leq M(s,t) \leq \max(s,t). \tag{1}$$

Mean M is symmetric if for all $s, t \in \mathbf{R}^+$

$$M(s,t) = M(t,s)$$

and homogeneous (of degree 1) if for all $\lambda, s, t \in \mathbf{R}^+$

$$M(\lambda s, \lambda t) = \lambda M(s,t).$$

This paper was motivated by the problem of matching two different mappings on the set of mean functions formulated in paper [1] in which author introduced algebraic and topological structures on the set $\mathcal{M}_\mathcal{D}$ of symmetric means on a symmetric domain $\mathcal{D}$ with additional property

$$M(s,t) = s \Rightarrow s = t, \quad \forall (s,t) \in \mathcal{D}.$$

The first mapping is related to the group structure and the second one is defined trough Gauss' functional equation. It was found that those mappings coincide for arithmetic, geometric, and harmonic mean, but the question of the existence of other solutions remained open. We shall take $\mathcal{D} = \mathbf{R}^+ \times \mathbf{R}^+$.

First, let $\mathcal{A}_\mathcal{D}$ be set of all functions $f: \mathcal{D} \to \mathbf{R}$ such that

$$(\forall (x,y) \in \mathcal{D}) \ f(x,y) = -f(y,x).$$

$(\mathcal{A}_\mathcal{D}, +)$ is an abelian group with the neutral element 0. Function $\varphi: \mathcal{M}_\mathcal{D} \to \mathcal{A}^\mathcal{D}$ defined by

$$\varphi(M)(x,y) := \begin{cases} \log\left(-\frac{M(x,y)-x}{M(x,y)-y}\right), & x \neq y, \\ 0, & x = y, \end{cases}$$

is a bijection. The composition law $*: \mathcal{M}_\mathcal{D} \times \mathcal{M}_\mathcal{D} \to \mathcal{M}_\mathcal{D}$ is defined by

$$M_1 * M_2 = \varphi^{-1}(\varphi(M_1) + \varphi(M_2)).$$

Thus $(\mathcal{M}_\mathcal{D}, *)$ is an abelian group with the neutral element $\varphi^{-1}(0) = A$. It can also easily be shown that the explicit formula for the composition law $*$ holds:

$$(M_1 * M_2)(x,y) = \begin{cases} \frac{x(M_1-y)(M_2-y)+y(M_1-x)(M_2-x)}{(M_1-x)(M_2-x)+(M_1-y)(M_2-y)}, & x \neq y, \\ x, & x = y. \end{cases} \quad (2)$$

For the sake of simplicity, variables (x,y) were omitted. By sum and difference of means, we assume usual pointwise addition and subtraction. More on the topological structures on set of bivariate means can also be found in [2].

Based on the operation $*$ defined in (2), the first type of the symmetry was defined.

Definition 1 ([1]). *The symmetric mean M_2 to a mean M_1 with respect to mean M_0 via the group structure $(\mathcal{M}_\mathcal{D}, *)$ is defined with the expression*

$$S_{M_0}(M_1) = M_2 \Leftrightarrow M_1 * M_2 = M_0 * M_0. \quad (3)$$

Combining (3) with (2), the explicit formula for symmetric mean of mean M_1 with respect to M_0 can easily be calculated:

$$S_{M_0}(M_1) = \frac{x(M_1-x)(M_0-y)^2 - y(M_0-x)^2(M_1-y)}{(M_1-x)(M_0-y)^2 - (M_0-x)^2(M_1-y)}. \quad (4)$$

We shall see the behavior of S_{M_0} for some basic well known means M_0. For $(s,t) \in \mathcal{D} = \mathbf{R}^+ \times \mathbf{R}^+$ let

$$A(s,t) = \frac{s+t}{2}, \quad G(s,t) = \sqrt{st}, \quad H(s,t) = \frac{2st}{s+t},$$

be the arithmetic, geometric, and harmonic means, respectively.

Example 1 ([1]). *For any mean $M \in \mathcal{M}_\mathcal{D}$, we have:*
1. $S_A(M) = 2A - M$,
2. $S_G(M) = \frac{G^2}{M}$,
3. $S_H(M) = \frac{HM}{2M-H}$.

Notice that the denominator in $S_H(M)$ from Example 1 cannot be equal to 0, since $M = \frac{1}{2}H$ does not satisfy the left hand side inequality in (1) and, hence, it is not a mean.

Another type of symmetry, independent of the group structure $(\mathcal{M}_\mathcal{D}, *)$, can also be defined.

Definition 2 ([1]). *Mean M_2 is said to be functional symmetric mean of M_1 with respect to M_0 if the following functional equation is satisfied:*

$$\sigma_{M_0}(M_1) = M_2 \Leftrightarrow M_0(M_1, M_2) = M_0. \quad (5)$$

We can also say that mean M_0 is the functional middle of M_1 and M_2. Defining equation on the right side of the equivalence relation (5) is known as the Gauss functional equation. Some authors refer to means M_1 and M_2 as a pair of M_0-complementary means.

Mean M_0 is also said to be (M_1, M_2)-invariant. For recent related results, see [3–6] and also survey article on invariance of means [7] and references therein. Furthermore, if functional symmetric mean exists, then it is unique.

With respect to the same means as in the latter exmple, we may calculate the symmetric means. For instance, when $M_0 = H$, we have

$$H(M, \sigma_H(M)) = H \Leftrightarrow \frac{2M\sigma_H(M)}{M+\sigma_H(M)} = H \Leftrightarrow 2M\sigma_H(M) = H(M + \sigma_H(M)) \Leftrightarrow \sigma_H(M) = \frac{HM}{2M-H}.$$

Other symmetric pairs, with respect to A and G, are obtained in similar manner.

Example 2 ([1]). *For any mean $M \in \mathcal{M}_\mathcal{D}$, we have:*

1. $\sigma_A(M) = 2A - M$,
2. $\sigma_G(M) = \frac{G^2}{M}$,
3. $\sigma_H(M) = \frac{HM}{2M-H}$.

Taking into account Examples 1 and 2, in which the same mappings appear with respect to arithmetic, geometric, and harmonic mean appear, the author in [1] states the following.

Open question. For which mean functions M_0 on $\mathcal{D} = \mathbf{R}^+ \times \mathbf{R}^+$ do the two symmetries, S and σ, with respect to M_0, coincide?

The goal of this paper is to analyze the open question and offer the answer in the setting of symmetric homogeneous means, which possess the asymptotic expansion. Techniques of asymptotic expansions were developed in [8–10] and appeared to be very useful in comparison and finding inequalities for bivariate means ([11,12]), comparison of bivariate parameter means ([10]), finding optimal parameters in convex combinations of means ([12,13]), and solving the functional equations of the form $B(A(x)) = C(x)$, where asymptotic expansions of B and C are known ([14]). In the latter example, A, B, and C are functions of a real variable, which possess asymptotic expansion as $x \to \infty$ with respect to asymptotic sequences $(x^{w-n})_{n \in \mathbf{N}_0}$, $(x^{u-n})_{n \in \mathbf{N}_0}$, and $(x^{v-n})_{n \in \mathbf{N}_0}$, respectively, where w, u, and v are real numbers. When used with $B(x) = f(x)$ and $C(x) = \frac{1}{t-s} \int_s^t f(x+u)\,du$, finding $A(x)$ is then equivalent to determining integral f-mean $I_f(x+s, x+t) = f^{-1}\left(\frac{1}{t-s}\int_{x+s}^{x+t} f(u)\,du\right)$ for a given function f as it was described in detail in above mentioned paper. We may perceive the significance of this approach when explicit formula for the inverse function is not known, which is case for the digamma function.

Techniques and results applyed in this paper were described in Section 2. In the next step, we obtained the algorithm for calculating the coefficients in the asymptotic expansions of means $M_2^S = S_{M_0}(M_1)$ and $M_2^\sigma = \sigma_{M_0}(M_1)$. Comparing the first few obtained coefficents, we anticipated the general form of the coefficients in the asymptotic expansion of mean M_0 for which symmetries S_{M_0} and σ_{M_0} coincide, i.e., such that $M_2^S = M_2^\sigma$.

At the beginning of Section 3, we found closed formula and explored some properties, such as limit behavior and monotonocity with respect to the parameter. We proved that proposed function represents the well defined one parameter class of means. We have shown that it also covers, as the special cases, means from Examples 1 and 2.

Lastly, in Section 4, we have proved that this class of means answered the open question and stated the hypothesis that there were not any other solutions in the context of homogeneous symmetric means, which possess asymptotic power series expansions.

In addition, methods presented in this paper may be useful with similar problems regarding functional equations, especially in case when the explicit formula for included function was not known.

2. Asymptotic Expansions

Recall the definition of an asymptotic power series expansion as $x \to \infty$.

Definition 3. *The series $\sum_{n=0}^{\infty} c_n x^{-n}$ is said to be an asymptotic expansion of a function $f(x)$ as $x \to \infty$ if for each $N \in \mathbf{N}$*

$$f(x) = \sum_{n=0}^{N} c_n x^{-n} + o(x^{-N}).$$

Main properties of asymptotic series and asymptotic expansions can be found in [15]. Taylor series expansion can also be seen as an asymptotic expansion, but the converse is not generally true, and the asymptotic series may also be divergent. The main characteristic of asymptotic expansion is that it provides good approximation using a finite number of terms while letting $x \to \infty$.

Beacause of the intrinsity (1), mean M would possess the asymptotic power series as $x \to \infty$ of the form

$$M(x+s, x+t) = \sum_{n=0}^{\infty} c_n(s,t) x^{-n+1}$$

with $c_0(s,t) = 1$. For a homogeneous symmetric mean, the coefficients $c_n(s,t)$ are also homogeneous symmetric polynomials of degree n in variables s and t, and for $s = -t$, they have a simpler form. Let the means included possess the asymptotic expansions as $x \to \infty$ of the form

$$M_0(x-t, x+t) = \sum_{n=0}^{\infty} c_n t^{2n} x^{-2n+1}, \qquad (6)$$

$$M_1(x-t, x+t) = \sum_{n=0}^{\infty} a_n t^{2n} x^{-2n+1},$$

$$M_2(x-t, x+t) = \sum_{n=0}^{\infty} b_n t^{2n} x^{-2n+1}.$$

Conversely, it can also be shown that the expansion in variables $(x-t, x+t)$ is sufficent to obtain the so-called two variable expansion, i.e., the expansion in variables $(x+s, x+t)$. Furthermore, note that

$$a_0 = b_0 = c_0 = 1. \qquad (7)$$

In this section, we will find the asymptotic expansions of means $M_2^S = S_{M_0}(M_1)$ and $M_2^\sigma = \sigma_{M_0}(M_1)$.

2.1. Symmetry S_{M_0}

Recall the recently developed results for tansformations of asymptotic series, i.e., the complete asymptotic expansions of the quotient and the power of asymptotic series.

Lemma 1 ([10], Lemma 1.1.). *Let function $f(x)$ and $g(x)$ have the following asymptotic expansions ($a_0 \neq 0, b_0 \neq 0$) as $x \to \infty$:*

$$f(x) \sim \sum_{n=0}^{\infty} a_n x^{-n}, \qquad g(x) \sim \sum_{n=0}^{\infty} b_n x^{-n}.$$

Then, asymptotic expansion of their quotient $f(x)/g(x)$ reads as

$$\frac{f(x)}{g(x)} \sim \sum_{n=0}^{\infty} c_n x^{-n},$$

where coefficients c_n are defined by

$$c_n = \frac{1}{b_0}\left(a_n - \sum_{k=0}^{n-1} b_{n-k} c_k\right).$$

Lemma 2 ([8,16]). *Let $m(x)$ be a function with asymptotic expansion ($c_0 \neq 0$):*

$$m(x) \sim \sum_{n=0}^{\infty} c_n x^{-n}, \quad (x \to \infty).$$

Then, for all real r, it holds

$$[m(x)]^r \sim \sum_{n=0}^{\infty} P[n, r, (c_j)_{j \in \mathbf{N}_0}] x^{-n}$$

where

$$P[0, r, (c_j)_{j \in \mathbf{N}_0}] = c_0^r,$$
$$P[n, r, (c_j)_{j \in \mathbf{N}_0}] = \frac{1}{nc_0} \sum_{k=1}^{n} [k(1+r) - n] c_k P[n-k, r, (c_j)_{j \in \mathbf{N}_0}]. \tag{8}$$

Symmetric mean with respect to mean M_0 of mean M_1 via the group structure $(\mathcal{M}_\mathcal{D}, *)$ as a consequence of (4) can be expressed as:

$$\begin{aligned}
M_2^S(x-t, x+t) &= S_{M_0}(M_1)(x-t, x+t) \\
&= \frac{(x-t)(M_1 - x + t)(M_0 - x - t)^2 - (x+t)(M_0 - x + t)^2(M_1 - x - t)}{(M_1 - x + t)(M_0 - x - t)^2 - (M_0 - x + t)^2(M_1 - x - t)} \\
&= \frac{(x-t)(\overline{M}_1 + t)(\overline{M}_0 - t)^2 - (x+t)(\overline{M}_0 + t)^2(\overline{M}_1 - t)}{(\overline{M}_1 + t)(\overline{M}_0 - t)^2 - (\overline{M}_0 + t)^2(\overline{M}_1 - t)} \\
&= x + \frac{2t^2 \overline{M}_0 - t^2 \overline{M}_1 - \overline{M}_0^2 \overline{M}_1}{t^2 + \overline{M}_0^2 - 2\overline{M}_0 \overline{M}_1},
\end{aligned}$$

where $\overline{M}_i$, $i = 1, 2, 3$, stands for $M_i - x$. The variables $(x - t, x + t)$ were omitted for the sake of symplicity. Further calculations reveal that:

$$M_2^S(x-t, x+t) = x + t^2 x^{-1} \Big[(2c_1 - a_1) +$$
$$+ \sum_{n=0}^{\infty} \Big(2c_{n+2} - a_{n+2} + \sum_{k=0}^{n} \Big(\sum_{j=0}^{k} (c_{j+1} c_{k-j+1}) a_{n+1-k} \Big) \Big) t^{2n+2} x^{-2n-2} \Big] \times$$
$$\times \Big[1 + \sum_{n=0}^{\infty} \sum_{k=0}^{n} c_{k+1}(c_{n-k+1} - 2a_{n-k+1}) t^{2n+2} x^{-2n-2} \Big]^{-1}.$$

Coefficients b_n^S for $n \geq 1$ are obtained using Lemma 1 for the division of asymptotic series. Hence, we have the following:

$$b_0^S = 1,$$
$$b_n^S = \text{num}_n - \sum_{k=0}^{n-2} \text{den}_{n-1-k} b_{k+1}^S, \quad n \geq 1,$$

where $(\text{num}_n)_{n \in \mathbf{N}_0}$ and $(\text{den}_n)_{n \in \mathbf{N}_0}$ dentote auxiliary sequences, which appear in the numerator and the denominator:

$$\text{num}_0 = 2c_1 - a_1,$$
$$\text{num}_n = 2c_{n+1} - a_{n+1} + \sum_{k=0}^{n-1} \Big(\sum_{j=0}^{k} (c_{j+1} c_{k-j+1}) a_{n-k} \Big), \quad n \geq 1,$$

and
$$den_0 = 1,$$
$$den_n = \sum_{k=0}^{n-1} c_{k+1}(c_{n-k} - 2a_{n-k}), \quad n \geq 1.$$

We shall calculate the first few coefficients:

$b_0^S = 1,$

$b_1^S = 2c_1 - a_1,$

$b_2^S = 2c_2 - a_2 - 2c_1(a_1 - c_1)^2,$

$b_3^S = 2c_3 - a_3 - 2(a_1 - c_1)(2a_2c_1 + c_1^2(2a_1^2 - 3a_1c_1 + c_1^2) + (a_1 - 3c_1)c_2),$

$b_4^S = 2c_4 - a_4 - 2(a_2^2 c_1 + 4a_1^4 c_1^3 + 4a_1^3 c_1(-3c_1^3 + c_2)$
$\quad + 2a_2((3a_1 - 2c_1)(a_1 - c_1)c_1^2 + (a_1 - 2c_1)c_2)$
$\quad + a_1^2(13c_1^5 - 15c_1^2 c_2 + c_3) + 2a_1(a_3 c_1 - 3c_1^6 + 8c_1^3 c_2 - c_2^2 - 2c_1 c_3)$
$\quad + c_1(-2a_3 c_1 + c_1^6 - 5c_1^3 c_2 + 3c_2^2 + 3c_1 c_3)),$

$b_5^S = 2c_5 - a_5 - 2(-2a_4 c_1^2 + 8a_1^5 c_1^4 + 4a_3 c_1^4 - c_1^9 - 4a_3 c_1 c_2 + 7c_1^6 c_2 - 10c_1^3 c_2^2$
$\quad + c_2^3 + a_2^2(6a_1 c_1^2 - 5c_1^3 + c_2) + 4a_1^4 c_1^2(-7c_1^3 + 3c_2) - 5c_1^4 c_3 + 6c_1 c_2 c_3$
$\quad + 2a_1^3(19c_1^6 - 24c_1^3 c_2 + c_2^2 + 2c_1 c_3) + 2a_2(a_3 c_1 + 8a_1^3 c_1^3 - 3c_1^6 + 8c_1^3 c_2$
$\quad - c_2^2 + 6a_1^2 c_1(-3c_1^3 + c_2) - 2c_1 c_3 + a_1(13c_1^5 - 15c_1^2 c_2 + c_3)) + 3c_1^2 c_4$
$\quad + a_1^2(6a_3 c_1^2 - 5c_1(5c_1^6 - 13c_1^3 c_2 + 3c_2^2 + 3c_1 c_3) + c_4) + 2a_1(a_4 c_1$
$\quad + a_3(-5c_1^3 + c_2) + 2(2c_1^8 - 9c_1^5 c_2 + 6c_1^2 c_2^2 + 4c_1^3 c_3 - c_2 c_3 - c_1 c_4))).$

2.2. Symmetry σ_{M_0}

The problem of functional symmetic mean corresponds the functional equation
$$M_0(x - t, x + t) = M_0(M_1(x - t, x + t), M_2(x - t, x + t))$$

which we will solve in terms of asymptotic series. To this end, we shall use the following result from Burić and Elezović about the asymptotic expansion of the composition of means.

Theorem 1 ([17], Theorem 2.2.). *Let M and N be given homogeneous symmetric means with asymptotic expansions*
$$M(x - t, x + t) = \sum_{k=0}^{\infty} a_k t^{2k} x^{-2k+1}, \quad N(x - t, x + t) = \sum_{k=0}^{\infty} b_k t^{2k} x^{-2k+1},$$

and let F be homogeneous symmetric mean with expansion
$$F(x - t, x + t) = \sum_{k=0}^{\infty} \gamma_k t^{2k} x^{-2k+1}.$$

Then, the composition $H = F(M, N)$ has asymptotic expansion
$$H(x - t, x + t) = \sum_{k=0}^{\infty} h_n t^{2n} x^{-2n+1},$$

where coefficients (h_n) are calculated by
$$h_n = \sum_{k=0}^{\lfloor \frac{n}{2z} \rfloor} \gamma_k \sum_{j=0}^{n-2zk} P[j, 2k, (d_m)_{m \in \mathbf{N}_0}] P[n - 2zk - j, -2k + 1, (c_m)_{m \in \mathbf{N}_0}].$$

Sequences (c_n) and (d_n) are defined by

$$c_n = \frac{1}{2}(a_n + b_n), \quad d_n = \frac{1}{2}(a_{n+z} - b_{n+z}), \quad n \geq 0,$$

where z is the smallest number such that $d_n \neq 0$.

Applying Theorem 1 on $M = M_1$, $N = M_2$ (or equivalently $M = M_2$, $N = M_1$) and $F = M_0$, we obtain the asymptotic expansion of the composition $M_0(M_1, M_2)$. Since the equation $M_0 = M_0(M_1, M_2)$ holds, on the other side, in Theorem 1, we also have $H = M_0$. The coeficients in the asymptotic expansion of the composition $M_0(M_1, M_2)$ equal the coefficients c_n in the asymptotic expansion of mean M_0. In the end, we obtain the recursive algorithm for coefficients c_n:

$c_0 = 1$;

$$c_n = \sum_{k=0}^{\lfloor \frac{n}{2z} \rfloor} c_k \sum_{j=0}^{n-2zk} P[j, 2k, (\tfrac{1}{2}(a_m - b_m^\sigma))_{m \geq z}] P[n - 2zk - j, -2k+1, (\tfrac{1}{2}(a_m + b_m^\sigma))_{m \in \mathbf{N}_0}], \quad (9)$$

where $P[n, r, (c_m)_{m \in \mathbf{N}_0}]$, $n \in \mathbf{N}_0$ denotes the n-th coefficient in the asymptotic expansion of r-th power of the asymptotic seires with coefficients $(c_m)_{m \in \mathbf{N}_0}$, as it was defined in (8). Because of (7), z is always greater or equal to 1.

For $z = 1$ we calculate the first few coefficients:

$c_0 = 1,$

$c_1 = \dfrac{1}{2}(a_1 + b_1^\sigma),$

$c_2 = \dfrac{1}{2}(a_2 + b_2^\sigma) + \dfrac{1}{4}(a_1 - b_1^\sigma)^2 c_1,$

$c_3 = \dfrac{1}{2}(a_3 + b_3^\sigma) - \dfrac{1}{8}(a_1 - b_1^\sigma)(a_1^2 - 4a_2 - (b_1^\sigma)^2 + 4b_2^\sigma) c_1,$

$c_4 = \dfrac{1}{2}(a_4 + b_4^\sigma) + \dfrac{1}{16}((a_1^4 + 4a_2^2 - 8a_3 b_1^\sigma + (b_1^\sigma)^4 + 2a_2((b_1^\sigma)^2 - 4b_2^\sigma)$
$\quad - 2a_1^2(3a_2 + (b_1^\sigma)^2 - b_2^\sigma) - 6(b_1^\sigma)^2 b_2^\sigma + 4(b_2^\sigma)^2$
$\quad + 4a_1(2a_3 + b_1^\sigma(a_2 + b_2^\sigma) - 2b_3^\sigma) + 8b_1^\sigma b_3^\sigma)c_1 + (a_1 - b_1^\sigma)^4 c_2),$

$c_5 = \dfrac{1}{2}(a_5 + b_5^\sigma) - \dfrac{1}{32}((a_1^5 + a_1^4 b_1^\sigma - 4a_2^2 b_1^\sigma + 16a_4 b_1^\sigma - 4a_3(b_1^\sigma)^2 + (b_1^\sigma)^5$
$\quad - 2a_1^3(4a_2 + (b_1^\sigma)^2) + 16a_3 b_2^\sigma - 8(b_1^\sigma)^3 b_2^\sigma + 12 b_1^\sigma (b_2^\sigma)^2$
$\quad - 8a_2(2a_3 + b_1^\sigma b_2^\sigma - 2b_3^\sigma) + 2a_1^2(6a_3 - (b_1^\sigma)^3 + 4b_1^\sigma b_2^\sigma - 2b_3^\sigma) + 12(b_1^\sigma)^2 b_3^\sigma$
$\quad - 16 b_2^\sigma b_3^\sigma - 16 b_1^\sigma b_4^\sigma + a_1(12a_2^2 - 16a_4 - 8a_3 b_1^\sigma + (b_1^\sigma)^4 + 8a_2((b_1^\sigma)^2 - b_2^\sigma)$
$\quad - 4(b_2^\sigma)^2 - 8 b_1^\sigma b_3^\sigma + 16 b_4^\sigma))c_1 - (a_1 - b_1^\sigma)^3(3a_1^2 - 8a_2 - 3(b_1^\sigma)^2 + 8b_2^\sigma)c_2).$

The connetcion between b_n^σ and c_n with the highest index n in each equation is linear. In the expression (9), b_n^σ appears ony in the second part

$$P[n - 2zk - j, -2k+1, (\tfrac{1}{2}(a_m + b_m^\sigma))_{m \in \mathbf{N}_0}], \quad (10)$$

when $k = j = 0$. Then, (10) becomes $P[n, 1, (\tfrac{1}{2}(a_m + b_m^\sigma))_{m \in \mathbf{N}_0}]$, which represents the n-th coefficient in the $\sum_{n=0}^{\infty} \tfrac{1}{2}(a_n + b_n^\sigma) t^{2n} x^{-2n+1}$ to the power of 1, which equals $\tfrac{1}{2}(a_n + b_n^\sigma)$. So, we can easily extract b_n^σ. The first few coefficients b_n^σ are:

$b_0^\sigma = 1,$

$b_1^\sigma = 2c_1 - a_1,$

$$b_2^\sigma = 2c_2 - a_2 - \frac{1}{2}c_1(a_1 - b_1^\sigma),$$

$$b_3^\sigma = 2c_3 - a_3 + \frac{1}{4}(a_1 - b_1^\sigma)(a_1^2 - 4a_2 - (b_1^\sigma)^2 + 4b_2^\sigma)c_1,$$

$$b_4^\sigma = 2c_4 - a_4 - \frac{1}{8}((a_1^4 + 4a_2^2 - 8a_3 b_1^\sigma + (b_1^\sigma)^4 + 2a_2((b_1^\sigma)^2 - 4b_2^\sigma)$$
$$- 2a_1^2(3a_2 + (b_1^\sigma)^2 - b_2^\sigma) - 6(b_1^\sigma)^2 b_2^\sigma + 4(b_2^\sigma)^2$$
$$+ 4a_1(2a_3 + b_1^\sigma(a_2 + b_2^\sigma) - 2b_3^\sigma) + 8b_1^\sigma b_3^\sigma)c_1 + (a_1 - b_1^\sigma)^4 c_2),$$

$$b_5^\sigma = 2c_5 - a_5 + \frac{1}{16}((a_1^5 + a_1^4 b_1^\sigma - 4a_2^2 b_1^\sigma + 16a_4 b_1^\sigma - 4a_3(b_1^\sigma)^2 + (b_1^\sigma)^5$$
$$- 2a_1^3(4a_2 + (b_1^\sigma)^2) + 16a_3 b_2^\sigma - 8(b_1^\sigma)^3 b_2^\sigma + 12 b_1^\sigma (b_2^\sigma)^2$$
$$- 8a_2(2a_3 + b_1^\sigma b_2^\sigma - 2b_3^\sigma) + 2a_1^2(6a_3 - (b_1^\sigma)^3 + 4b_1^\sigma b_2^\sigma - 2b_3^\sigma) + 12(b_1^\sigma)^2 b_3^\sigma$$
$$- 16 b_2^\sigma b_3^\sigma - 16 b_1^\sigma b_4^\sigma + a_1(12a_2^2 - 16a_4 - 8a_3 b_1^\sigma + (b_1^\sigma)^4 + 8a_2((b_1^\sigma)^2 - b_2^\sigma)$$
$$- 4(b_2^\sigma)^2 - 8b_1^\sigma b_3^\sigma + 16 b_4^\sigma))c_1 - (a_1 - b_1^\sigma)^3(3a_1^2 - 8a_2 - 3(b_1^\sigma)^2 + 8b_2^\sigma)c_2).$$

For beter understanding the role of the parameter z, we shall recall the idea behind the proof of Theorem 1. The composition $F(M, N)$ has the asymptotic expansion

$$F(M(x - t, x + t), N(x - t, x + t)) =$$
$$= F\left(\frac{M+N}{2} - \frac{N-M}{2}, \frac{M+N}{2} + \frac{N-M}{2}\right)$$
$$= \sum_{k=0}^{\infty} \gamma_k \left(\frac{N-M}{2}\right)^{2k} \left(\frac{M+N}{2}\right)^{-2k+1}.$$

Larger z corresponds with the equating a_i and b_i^σ and some parts of the coefficients c_n reduce. Observation of the cases with $z > 1$ in sequel did not provide any new information about the ceofficients c_n.

2.3. Comparison of Coefficients

Sequences $(b_n^S)_{n \in \mathbb{N}_0}$ and $(b_n^\sigma)_{n \in \mathbb{N}_0}$ represent the coefficients in asymptotic expansions of means, which are results of mappings $S_{M_0}(M_1)$ and $\sigma_{M_0}(M_1)$, respectively. Since we are looking for a mean M_0 such those mappings coincide, b_n^S and b_n^σ need to be equal. Since the equality must hold for any mean M_1, we may suppose that $z = 1$, which is equivalent with $a_1 \neq c_1$. Equating b_0^S with b_0^σ and b_1^S with b_1^σ does not provide any new information, except

$$b_0 = b_0^S = b_0^\sigma = 1 \text{ and } b_1 = b_1^S = b_1^\sigma = 2c_1 - a_1.$$

With such b_1^σ we may express b_2^σ as

$$b_2^\sigma = 2c_2 - a_2 - 2c_1(a_1 - c_1)^2,$$

which is already equal to b_2^S. Now, we can substitute

$$b_2 = b_2^S = b_2^\sigma = 2c_2 - a_2 - 2c_1(a_1 - c_1)^2,$$

in b_3^σ to obtain

$$b_3^\sigma = 2c_3 - a_3 - 2c_1(a_1 - c_1)(2a_2 + 2c_1(a_1 - c_1)^2 + c_1^2 - a_1 c_1 - 2c_2),$$

which, after equating with b_3^S, gives the following condition

$$(a_1 - c_1)^2(c_1^2 + c_1^3 + c_2) = 0.$$

Since we assumed that a_1 and c_1 are not equal, it is necessarily
$$c_2 = -c_1^2(1+c_1).$$

Now, we have
$$b_3 = b_3^S = b_3^g = 2c_3 - a_3 - 2c_1(a_1-c_1)\Big((3-4a_1)c_1^2 + a_1(2a_1-1)c_1 + 2a_2 + 4c_1^3\Big).$$

After substitutions, we observe the next coefficient
$$\begin{aligned}b_4^g &= 2c_4 - a_4 - 2c_1\big(2a_2c_1(-a_1(6c_1+1) + 3a_1^2 + 2c_1(2c_1+1))\\ &\quad + c_1\big(c_1(-4a_1^3(4c_1+1) + a_1^2(2c_1+1)(15c_1+2) - 2a_1c_1(14c_1(c_1+1)+3)\\ &\quad + 4a_1^4 + c_1^2(c_1(11c_1+15)+5)\big) - 2a_3\big) + 2c_3(c_1-a_1) + a_2^2 + 2a_1a_3\end{aligned}$$

which, after equating with b_4^S, gives the following condition:
$$(a_1-c_1)^2\Big(2c_1^3(c_1+1)^2 - c_3\Big) = 0,$$

and we conclude that it must be
$$c_3 = 2c_1^3(1+c_1)^2.$$

We continue with this procedure as it was described above. Further calculations reveal that the first few coefficients c_n have the following form:
$$\begin{aligned}c_0 &= 1,\\ c_1 &= c,\\ c_2 &= -c^2(1+c),\\ c_3 &= 2c^3(1+c)^2,\\ c_4 &= -5c^4(1+c)^3,\\ c_5 &= 14c^5(1+c)^4,\\ c_6 &= -42c^6(1+c)^5.\end{aligned}$$

After these first steps, it is natural to state the following hypothesis about the general formula for the coefficients in the asymptotic expansion of mean M_0:
$$\begin{aligned}c_0 &= 1,\\ c_n &= (-1)^{n-1}C_{n-1}c^n(1+c)^{n-1},\ n \geq 1,\end{aligned} \tag{11}$$

where C_n denotes the n-th Catalan number. Catalan numbers appear in many occasions, and their behavior has been widely explored. Here, we mention only a few properties, which we will use in sequel. Catalan numbers are defined by
$$C_n = \frac{1}{n+1}\binom{2n}{n},\quad n \in \mathbf{N}_0$$

and they satisfy the recursive relation
$$C_{n+1} = \sum_{k=0}^{n} C_k C_{n-k},\quad n \in \mathbf{N}_0.$$

Based on this recursive relation, the generating function for Catalan numbers can be obtained ([18]):

$$\sum_{n=0}^{\infty} C_n y^n = \frac{1 - \sqrt{1-4y}}{2y}, \qquad (12)$$

which is convergent for $|y| < \frac{1}{4}$.

3. New Mean Function

In this section, we shall find closed a form for a mean whose coefficients are given in (11). We start from asymptotic expansion (6):

$$\begin{aligned} M_0(x-t, x+t) &= x + \sum_{n=1}^{\infty} (-1)^{n-1} C_{n-1} c^n (1+c)^{n-1} t^{2n} x^{-2n+1} \\ &= x + \sum_{n=0}^{\infty} (-1)^n C_n c^{n+1} (1+c)^n t^{2n+2} x^{-2n-1} \\ &= x + c t^2 x^{-1} \sum_{n=0}^{\infty} C_n \left[-\frac{c(1+c)t^2}{x^2} \right]^n. \end{aligned} \qquad (13)$$

Introducing the substitution $y = -\frac{c(1+c)t^2}{x^2}$, as $x \to \infty$ and thereby $y \to 0$, yields

$$M_0(x-t, x+t) = x + c t^2 x^{-1} \sum_{n=0}^{\infty} C_n y^n,$$

and, then, according to the formula (12), for $c + 1 \neq 0$, we obtain

$$\begin{aligned} M_0(x-t, x+t) &= x + c t^2 x^{-1} \frac{1 - \sqrt{1-4y}}{2y} \\ &= \frac{1+2c}{2(1+c)} x + \frac{1}{2(1+c)} \sqrt{x^2 + 4c(1+c)t^2}. \end{aligned} \qquad (14)$$

Abandoning series expansion in this moment, from the Equation (14) with substitution

$$x = \frac{a+b}{2}, \quad t = \frac{b-a}{2},$$

we obtain the expression for M_0 in terms of variables a and b. For $c \in \mathbf{R} \setminus \{-1\}$ and $a, b > 0$ we define function $L_c \colon \mathbf{R}^+ \times \mathbf{R}^+ \to \mathbf{R}^+$

$$L_c(a,b) = \frac{a+b}{2} \frac{1+2c}{2(1+c)} + \frac{1}{2(1+c)} \sqrt{\left(\frac{a+b}{2}\right)^2 + 4c(1+c)\left(\frac{b-a}{2}\right)^2}. \qquad (15)$$

Remark 1. *Function L_c is well defined for all $(a,b) \in \mathbf{R}^+ \times \mathbf{R}^+$ as we can rearrange terms under the square root:*

$$\begin{aligned} \left(\frac{a+b}{2}\right)^2 + 4c(1+c)\left(\frac{b-a}{2}\right)^2 &= \frac{1}{4}\left((a+b)^2 + 4c(1+c)(b-a)^2\right) \\ &= \frac{1}{4}\left((1+2c)^2(a-b)^2 + 4ab\right) > 0. \end{aligned}$$

Remark 2. *For $c = -1$ function L_c corresponds to the harmonic mean which will be proved in sequel. Therefore, definition (15) can be considered for all $c \in \mathbf{R}$.*

Remark 3. *Formula for L_c can also be written in a following way:*

$$L_c(a,b) = A(a,b) \frac{1+2c}{2(1+c)} + \frac{1}{2(1+c)} \sqrt{A(a,b)^2 + 4c(1+c)(A(a,b)^2 - G(a,b)^2)}. \qquad (16)$$

3.1. Limit Cases and Monotonicity

In this subsection, we study properties of L_c with respect to parameter c. First, we state the following proposition, which can be proved using basic methods of mathematical analysis.

Proposition 1. *For a fixed pair* $(a,b) \in \mathbf{R}^+ \times \mathbf{R}^+$, *function* L_c *holds*

1. $\lim\limits_{c \to -\infty} L_c(a,b) = \min(a,b)$,
2. $\lim\limits_{c \to -1-} L_c(a,b) = \lim\limits_{c \to -1+} L_c(a,b) = \dfrac{2ab}{a+b} = H(a,b)$
3. $\lim\limits_{c \to +\infty} L_c(a,b) = \max(a,b)$,

It is well known that the following double inequality holds

$$H < A < G.$$

Also, $H = L_c$ for $c \to -1$, $G = L_c$ for $c = -\tfrac{1}{2}$, and $A = L_c$ for $c = 0$. In the next Theorem, we explore the ordering of means L_c with respect to parameter c.

Theorem 2. *For a fixed pair* $(a,b) \in \mathbf{R}^+ \times \mathbf{R}^+$, $a \neq b$, *function* $f \colon \mathbf{R} \setminus \{-1\} \to \mathbf{R}$,

$$f(c) = L_c(a,b)$$

is strictly increasing.

Proof. Starting form the (16), with $A = A(a,b)$ and $G = G(a,b)$, we have

$$f(c) = A\frac{1+2c}{2(1+c)} + \frac{1}{2(1+c)}\sqrt{g(c)},$$

where

$$g(c) = A^2 + 4c(1+c)\left(A^2 - G^2\right) > 0$$

according to Remarks 1 and 3. The first derivative of function f equals

$$\begin{aligned}
f'(c) &= \frac{1}{2(1+c)^2}\left(A + 2(1+2c)(1+c)(A^2 - G^2)g(c)^{-\tfrac{1}{2}} - g(c)^{\tfrac{1}{2}}\right) \\
&= \frac{1}{2(1+c)^2 g(c)^{\tfrac{1}{2}}}\left(Ag(c)^{\tfrac{1}{2}} + 2(1+2c)(1+c)(A^2 - G^2) - g(c)\right) \\
&= \frac{1}{2(1+c)^2 g(c)^{\tfrac{1}{2}}}\left(Ag(c)^{\tfrac{1}{2}} + 2(1+c)(A^2 - G^2) - A^2\right).
\end{aligned}$$

So, the condition $f'(c) > 0$ is equivalent to

$$Ag(c)^{\tfrac{1}{2}} > A^2 - 2(1+c)(A^2 - G^2).$$

If the right-hand side is negative, than the inequality obviusly holds. If it is positive, then we may observe the squared inequality:

$$A^2 g(c) > A^4 - 4(1+c)(A^2 - G^2)A^2 + 4(1+c)^2(A^2 - G^2)$$

which is equivalent to

$$4c(1+c)A^2(A^2 - G^2) > -4(1+c)(A^2 - G^2)A^2 + 4(1+c)^2(A^2 - G^2)$$

and
$$(A^2 - G^2)(1+c)^2 G^2 > 0$$
which is true for $a \neq b$ and $c \neq 1$. □

Since L_c assumes values between minimum and maximum of a and b, we may conclude the following.

Corollary 1. *For $c \in \mathbf{R}$ funcion L_c is a mean.*

Remark 4. *Notice that we proved that L_c is a strict mean, i.e., for $a \neq b$, strict inequalities hold:*
$$\min(a,b) < M(a,b) < \max(a,b).$$

3.2. Special Cases

Before we continue further, let us see what happens with some of the special cases of parameter c. We shall also connect results form this paper with the previously obtained asymptotic expansions of classical means.

Example 3. (a) $\quad c = -1$. Then mean has two non-zero coefficients:
$$c_0 = 1, \quad c_1 = c, \quad c_n = 0, \; n \geq 2.$$

Corresponding asymptotic expansion is finite. From (13), we obtain
$$L_c(x-t, x+t) = x - t^2 x^{-1},$$
which, after substitution $x = \frac{a+b}{2}$, $t = \frac{b-a}{2}$ becomes
$$L_c(a,b) = \frac{a+b}{2} - \frac{(b-a)^2}{4} \cdot \frac{2}{a+b} = \frac{2ab}{a+b} = H(a,b).$$

(b) $\quad c = 0$. All coefficients except c_0 equal zero. Then, either from the (13) or (14), we obtain
$$L_c(x-t, x+t) = x,$$
and after the substitution
$$L_c(a,b) = \frac{a+b}{2} = A(a,b).$$

(c) $\quad c = -\frac{1}{2}$. The coefficients are
$$c_0 = 1, \quad c_n = -\frac{1}{2^{2n-1}} C_{n-1}, \; n \geq 1. \tag{17}$$

Coefficients (17) correspond to the coefficients in asymptotic expansion of geometric mean obtained in [9] for $\alpha = 0$ and $\beta = t$, and also to coefficients of power mean M_p with $p = 0$ obtained in [10]. On the other side, from the formula (14), we obtain
$$L_c(x-t, x+t) = \sqrt{x^2 - t^2},$$
and, after substitution
$$L_c(a,b) = \sqrt{ab} = G(a,b).$$

From the example above, we see that we covered the cases of means for which in [1] was stated that symmetries S and σ coincide.

4. Answer to the Open Question

Theorem 3. *For mean L_c, $c \in \mathbf{R}$, defined in* (15), *symmetries S_{L_c} and σ_{L_c} coincide.*

Proof. Let us rewrite mean L_c in the following manner:

$$L_c(a,b) = \frac{1}{4(1+c)}\left[(1+2c)(a+b) + \sqrt{(a+b)^2 + 4c(1+c)(b-a)^2}\right].$$

For $M_0 = L_c$ and variable mean $M_1 = M$, there exists symmetric mean $\sigma = \sigma_{L_c}(M)$, i.e., the condition $L_c(M, \sigma) = L_c$ holds, which yields (for the sake of brevity, the variables will be ommited):

$$\frac{1}{4(1+c)}\left[(1+2c)(M+\sigma) + \sqrt{(M+\sigma)^2 + 4c(1+c)(M-\sigma)^2}\right] = L_c,$$

or equivalently

$$\sqrt{(M+\sigma)^2 + 4c(1+c)(M-\sigma)^2} = 4(1+c)L_c - (1+2c)(M+\sigma).$$

We rearrange the terms and, because of the existence of mean $\sigma = \sigma_{L_c}(M)$, we may square the latter expression:

$$M^2(1+2c)^2 + 2M\sigma(1-4c-4c^2) + \sigma^2(1+2c)^2$$
$$= [4(1+c)L_c - (1+2c)M]^2 - 2[4(1+c)L_c - (1+2c)M]^2 + \sigma^2(1-2c)^2.$$

The terms $\sigma^2(1-2c)^2$ cancel from both sides. Further calculation gives

$$2M(1-4c-4c^2)\sigma + 2\big(4(1+c)L_c - (1+2c)M\big)(1+2c)\sigma$$
$$= -M^2(1+2c)^2 + \big(4(1+c)L_c - (1+2c)M\big)^2,$$

and finally

$$\sigma = \frac{L_c\big((1+2c)M - 2(1+c)L_c\big)}{2cM - (1+2c)L_c}. \tag{18}$$

Thus, we obtained the explicit expression for mean $\sigma = \sigma_{L_c}(M)$ in terms of M and L_c.

On the other side, from (4), we know that

$$S_{L_c}(M) = \frac{a(M-a)(L_c-b)^2 - b(L_c-a)^2(M-b)}{(M-a)(L_c-b)^2 - (L_c-a)^2(M-b)},$$

which may be written as

$$S_{L_c}(M) = \frac{K_1 M - K_2}{K_0 M - K_1}, \tag{19}$$

where

$$K_0 = (L_c - b)^2 - (L_c - a)^2,$$
$$K_1 = a(L_c - b)^2 - b(L_c - a)^2,$$
$$K_2 = a^2(L_c - b)^2 - b^2(L_c - a)^2.$$

By equating the results of mappings σ and S with respect to mean L_c of a mean M and employing Formulas (18) and (19), we obtain

$$\frac{L_c\big((1+2c)M - 2(1+c)L_c\big)}{2cM - (1+2c)L_c} = \frac{K_1 M - K_2}{K_0 M - K_1}.$$

which needs to be proved. We calculate

$$L_c[2(1+c)L_c - (1+2c)M](K_0M - K_1) = [(1+2c)L_c - 2cM](K_1M - K_2).$$

Grouping by the powers of M yields

$$[M_0(1+2c)K_0 - 2cK_1]M^2 + 2\left[K_2c - (1+c)L_c^2 K_0\right]M$$
$$+ L_c[2(1+c)L_c K_1 - (1+2c)K_2] = 0. \qquad (20)$$

Now, we simplify each coefficient by the powers of M. First,

$$M_0(1+2c)K_0 - 2cK_1 =$$
$$= M_0(1+2c)\left[(L_c - b)^2 - (L_c - a)^2\right] - 2c\left[a(L_c - b)^2 - b(L_c - a)^2\right]$$
$$= (a - b)\left[2(1+c)L_c^2 - (a+b)(1+2c)L_c + 2abc\right],$$

second,

$$cK_2 - (1+c)L_c^2 K_0 =$$
$$= c\left[a^2(L_c - b)^2 - b^2(L_c - a)^2\right] - (1+c)L_c^2\left[(L_c - b)^2 - (L_c - a)^2\right]$$
$$= -(a - b)L_c\left[2(1+c)L_c^2 - (a+b)(1+2c)L_c + 2abc\right],$$

and third

$$2(1+c)L_c K_1 - (1+2c)K_2 =$$
$$= 2(1+c)L_c\left[a(L_c - b)^2 - b(L_c - a)^2\right] - (1+2c)\left[a^2(L_c - b)^2 - b^2(L_c - a)^2\right]$$
$$= (a - b)L_c\left[2(1+c)L_c^2 - (a+b)(1+2c)L_c + 2abc\right].$$

Hence, the equation (20) factorizes as

$$(a - b)\left[2(1+c)L_c^2 - (a+b)(1+2c)L_c + 2abc\right]\left(M^2 - 2L_c M + L_c^2\right) = 0. \qquad (21)$$

Notice that the mean L_c defined in (15) is one of the solutions of quadratic equation

$$2(1+c)L_c^2 - (a+b)(1+2c)L_c + 2abc,$$

and the condition (21) is fulfilled, which proves the theorem. □

We will close this section with a conjecture. Based on the analysis in this paper, we may conclude the following.

Hypothesis 1. *Symmetric homogeneous mean, which has the asymptotic power series expansion and fulfills the requirements of the open question from [1] necessarily has the same coefficients as mean L_c, $c \in \mathbf{R}$.*

5. Concluding Remarks

Using techniques of asymptotic expansions, we were able to compare two symmetries of different origins on the set of mean functions. Finding asymptotic series expansion for both of them, in terms of recursive algorithm for their coefficients, enabled us to carry out the coefficient comparison, which resulted in obtaining a class of means, which interpolates between harmonic, geometric, and arithmetic mean.

Methods presented in this paper may be useful with various problems regarding bivariate means and further. For example, in case of dual means, generalized inverses of means and similar problems where some functional connection is given, and especially when the explicit formula for some of the means involved, was not known.

Funding: This research received no external funding.

Institutional Review Board Statement: Not applicable.

Informed Consent Statement: Not applicable.

Data Availability Statement: Not applicable.

Conflicts of Interest: The authors declare no conflict of interest.

References

1. Farhi, B. Algebraic and topological structures on the set of mean functions and generalization of the AGM mean. *Colloq. Math.* **2013**, *132*, 139–149. [CrossRef]
2. Raissouli, M.; Chergui, M. On a metric topology on the set of bivariate means. *Acta Univ. Sapientiae Math.* **2022**, *14*, 147–159. [CrossRef]
3. Głazowska, D.; Matkowski, J. Generalized Classical Weighted Means, the Invariance, Complementarity and Convergence of Iterates of the Mean-Type Mappings. *Results Math.* **2022**, *77*, 72. [CrossRef]
4. Matkowski, J.; Nowicka, M.; Witkowski, A. Explicit Solutions of the Invariance Equation for Means. *Results Math.* **2017**, *71*, 397–410. [CrossRef]
5. Toader, G.; Costin, I.; Toader, S. Invariance in Some Families of Means. In *Functional Equations in Mathematical Analysis*; Springer: New York, NY, USA,
6. Toader, S.; Rassias, T.M.; Toader, G. A Gauss type functional equation. *Int. J. Math. Math. Sci.* **2001**, *25*, 856942. [CrossRef]
7. Jarczyk, J.; Jarczyk, W. Invariance of means. *Aequat. Math.* **2018**, *92*, 801–872. [CrossRef]
8. Chen, C.-P.; Elezović, N.; Vukšić, L. Asymptotic formulae associated with the Wallis power function and digamma function. *J. Class. Anal.* **2013**, *2*, 151–166. [CrossRef]
9. Elezović, N.; Vukšić, L. Asymptotic expansions of bivariate classical means and related inequalities. *J. Math. Inequal.* **2014**, *8*, 707–724. [CrossRef]
10. Elezović, N.; Vukšić, L. Asymptotic expansions and comparison of bivariate parameter means. *Math. Inequal. Appl.* **2014** *17*, 1225–1244. [CrossRef]
11. Elezović, N. Asymptotic inequalities and comparison of classical means. *J. Math. Inequal.* **2015**, *9*, 177–196. [CrossRef]
12. Elezović, N.; Mihoković, L. Inequalities between reciprocals of means. *Sarajevo J. Math.* **2015**, *11*, 171–180.
13. Vukšić, L. Seiffert means, asymptotic expansions and inequalities. *Rad Hrvat. Akad. Znan. Umjet. Mat. Znan.* **2015**, *19*, 129–142.
14. Elezović, N.; Vukšić, L. Asymptotic expansions of integral means and applications to the ratio of gamma functions. *Appl. Math. Comput.* **2014**, *235*, 187–200. [CrossRef]
15. Erdélyi, A. *Asymptotic Expansions*; Dover Publications: Mineola, NY, USA, 1956.
16. Gould, H.W. Coefficient identities for powers of Taylor and Dirichlet series. *Am. Math. Monthly* **1974**, *81*, 3–14. [CrossRef]
17. Burić, T.; Elezović, N. Computation and analysis of the asymptotic expansions of the compound means. *Appl. Math. Comput.* **2017**, *303*, 48–54. [CrossRef]
18. Graham, R.L.; Knuth, D.B.; Patashnik, O. *Concrete Mathematics*; Addison-Wesley: New York, NY, USA, 1989.

Disclaimer/Publisher's Note: The statements, opinions and data contained in all publications are solely those of the individual author(s) and contributor(s) and not of MDPI and/or the editor(s). MDPI and/or the editor(s) disclaim responsibility for any injury to people or property resulting from any ideas, methods, instructions or products referred to in the content.

Article
From Symmetric Functions to Partition Identities

Mircea Merca

Department of Mathematical Methods and Models, Fundamental Sciences Applied in Engineering Research Center, University Politehnica of Bucharest, 060042 Bucharest, Romania; mircea.merca@profinfo.edu.ro

Abstract: In this paper, we show that some classical results from q-analysis and partition theory are specializations of the fundamental relationships between complete and elementary symmetric functions.

Keywords: symmetric functions; q-binomial coefficients; partitions

MSC: 11P81; 11P82; 05A19; 05A20

1. Introduction

A partition $\lambda = (\lambda_1, \lambda_2, \ldots, \lambda_k)$ of a positive integer n is a weakly decreasing sequence of positive integers whose sum is n. The positive integers in the sequence are called parts [1]. To indicate that $\lambda = (\lambda_1, \lambda_2, \ldots, \lambda_k)$ is a partition of n, we consider the notation $\lambda \vdash n$.

In the following, we recall some essential facts about monomial symmetric functions. Proofs and more details can be found in Macdonald's book [2]. If $\lambda = (\lambda_1, \lambda_2, \ldots, \lambda_k)$ is an integer partition with $k \leqslant n$ then, the monomial symmetric function

$$m_\lambda(x_1, x_2, \ldots, x_n) = m_{(\lambda_1, \lambda_2, \ldots, \lambda_k)}(x_1, x_2, \ldots, x_n)$$

is the sum of the monomial $x_1^{\lambda_1} x_2^{\lambda_2} \cdots x_k^{\lambda_k}$ and all distinct monomials obtained from this by a permutation of variables. For instance, with $\lambda = (2,1,1)$ and $n = 4$, we have:

$$\begin{aligned} m_{(2,1,1)}(x_1, x_2, x_3, x_4) = {}& x_1^2 x_2 x_3 + x_1 x_2^2 x_3 + x_1 x_2 x_3^2 + x_1^2 x_2 x_4 + x_1 x_2^2 x_4 + x_1 x_2 x_4^2 \\ & + x_1^2 x_3 x_4 + x_1 x_3^2 x_4 + x_1 x_3 x_4^2 + x_2^2 x_3 x_4 + x_2 x_3^2 x_4 + x_2 x_3 x_4^2. \end{aligned}$$

If every monomial in a symmetric function has total degree k, then we say that this symmetric function is homogeneous of degree k.

The kth complete homogeneous symmetric function h_k is the sum of all monomials of total degree k in these variables, i.e.,

$$h_k(x_1, x_2, \ldots, x_n) = \sum_{\lambda \vdash k} m_\lambda(x_1, x_2, \ldots, x_n) = \sum_{1 \leqslant i_1 \leqslant i_2 \leqslant \cdots \leqslant i_k \leqslant n} x_{i_1} x_{i_2} \cdots x_{i_k},$$

and the kth elementary symmetric function is defined by

$$e_k(x_1, x_2, \ldots, x_n) = m_{(1^k)}(x_1, x_2, \ldots, x_n) = \sum_{1 \leqslant i_1 < i_2 < \cdots < i_k \leqslant n} x_{i_1} x_{i_2} \cdots x_{i_k},$$

where $e_0(x_1, x_2, \ldots, x_n) = h_0(x_1, x_2, \ldots, x_n) = 1$. In particular, the case $\lambda = (k)$ provides the kth power sum symmetric function

$$p_k(x_1, x_2, \ldots, x_n) = m_{(k)}(x_1, x_2, \ldots, x_n) = \sum_{i=1}^n x_i^k,$$

with $p_0(x_1, x_2, \ldots, x_n) = n$.

In this paper, we aim to show that some results from q-analysis and partition theory can easily be derived as specializations of the fundamental relationships between complete and elementary symmetric functions. To do this, we consider the q-binomial coefficients

$$\begin{bmatrix} n \\ k \end{bmatrix} = \begin{bmatrix} n \\ k \end{bmatrix}_q = \begin{cases} \frac{(q;q)_n}{(q;q)_k (q;q)_{n-k}}, & n, k \text{ integers}, 0 \leq k \leq n, \\ 0, & \text{otherwise}, \end{cases}$$

as specializations of symmetric functions, namely

$$h_k(1, q, \ldots, q^n) = \begin{bmatrix} n+k \\ k \end{bmatrix} \tag{1}$$

and

$$e_k(1, q, \ldots, q^{n-1}) = q^{\binom{k}{2}} \begin{bmatrix} n \\ k \end{bmatrix}. \tag{2}$$

Here, and in the following, we use the customary q-series notation:

$$(a;q)_n = \begin{cases} 1, & \text{for } n = 0, \\ (1-a)(1-aq)\cdots(1-aq^{n-1}), & \text{for } n > 0; \end{cases}$$
$$(a;q)_\infty = \lim_{n \to \infty} (a;q)_n.$$

Because $(a;q)_\infty$ diverges when $a \neq 0$ and $|q| \geq 1$, whenever $(a;q)_\infty$ appears in a formula, we shall assume $|q| < 1$. All identities may be understood in the sense of formal power series in q.

The content of this paper is structured as follows. In the next section, we consider the generating function of the complete homogeneous symmetric functions and derive the q-identities obtained by Cauchy and Euler. In Section 3, we note that Rothe's q-binomial theorem is a specialization of the generating function of the elementary symmetric functions. In Section 4, we consider the derivates of the generating functions of the complete and elementary symmetric functions and obtain Uchimura's identity, which provides connections between partitions and divisors. In Section 5, Newton's identities allow for us to obtain a curios q-identity of Euler. Combinatorial interpretations involving well-known functions in partition theory accompany these results in each section.

2. Complete Homogeneous Symmetric Functions

It is well-known that the complete homogeneous symmetric functions are characterized by the following formal power series identity in t:

$$H(t) = \sum_{k=0}^{\infty} h_k(x_1, x_2, \ldots, x_n) t^k = \prod_{i=1}^{n} (1 - x_i t)^{-1}. \tag{3}$$

From (3), with x_j replaced by q^{j-1} for each $j \in \{1, 2, \ldots, n\}$, we obtain a well-known identity, which was proved by Cauchy ([3], Theorem 26).

Theorem 1 (Cauchy). *If n is any nonnegative integer and $|q|$ and $|t|$ are both less than 1, then*

$$\sum_{k=0}^{\infty} \begin{bmatrix} n+k \\ k \end{bmatrix} t^k = \frac{1}{(t;q)_{n+1}}.$$

Some combinatorial interpretations of this theorem can easily be derived if we consider the following partition functions.

Definition 1. *Let n, i and j be non-negative integers. We define $p(n; i, j)$ as the number of partitions of n into at most i parts, with each being, at most, j.*

For example, $p(5;3,4) = 4$, and the partitions in question are

$$(4,1),\ (3,2),\ (3,1,1),\ (2,2,1).$$

The generating function of the $p(n;i,j)$ is given by the following Cayley's theorem ([3], Theorem 24) often attributed to Sylvester.

Theorem 2 (Cayley). *Let i and j be positive integers. Then,*

$$\sum_{n=0}^{\infty} p(n;i,j)\, q^n = \begin{bmatrix} i+j \\ i \end{bmatrix}.$$

Definition 2. *Let n and i be a non-negative integers. We define:*
(i) $p_e(n;i)$ *as the number of partitions of n divided into an even number of parts, with most being i parts;*
(ii) $p_o(n;i)$ *as the number of partitions of n divided into an odd number of parts, with most being i parts;*
(iii) $p(n;i)$ *as the number of partitions of n divided into, at most, i parts.*

It is clear that $p(n;i) = p_e(n;i) + p_o(n;i)$. For example, the partitions of 5 into at most 3 parts are:

$$(5),\ (4,1),\ (3,2),\ (3,1,1),\ (2,2,1).$$

We see that $p(5;3) = 5$, $p_e(5;3) = 2$ and $p_o(5;3) = 3$. On the other hand, it is well-known that

$$\sum_{n=0}^{\infty} \left(p_e(n;i) \pm p_o(n;i)\right) q^n = \frac{1}{(\pm q;q)_i}.$$

We have the following result.

Corollary 1. *Let n and i be nonnegative integers. Then,*

$$p_e(n;i+1) \pm p_o(n;i+1) = \sum_{j=0}^{n} (\pm 1)^j\, p(n-j;i,j).$$

Proof. The case $t = \pm q$ of Theorem 1 reads as follows

$$\sum_{j=0}^{\infty} \begin{bmatrix} i+j \\ j \end{bmatrix} (\pm q)^j = \frac{1}{(\pm q;q)_{i+1}}.$$

We can write

$$\sum_{j=0}^{\infty}\sum_{n=0}^{\infty} (\pm 1)^j p(n;i,j)\, q^{n+j} = \sum_{n=0}^{\infty} \left(p_e(n;i+1) \pm p_o(n;i+1)\right) q^n.$$

The identity follows by comparing coefficients of q^n on both sides of this equation. □

Take into account that $p(n;i,j)$ is symmetric in i and j, i.e., $p(n;i,j) = p(n;j,i)$, the identity given by Corollary 1 can be rewritten as

$$p_e(n;i+1) \pm p_o(n;i+1) = \sum_{j=0}^{n} (\pm 1)^j p(n-j;j,i).$$

Definition 3. *Let n, and i be a non-negative integer. We define:*
(i) $p_O(n;i)$ *as the number of partitions of n into odd parts, each, at most, $2i-1$;*
(ii) $p_O(n)$ *as the number of partitions of n into odd parts.*

For example, the partitions of 5 into odd parts are:

$$(5), (3,1,1), (1,1,1,1,1).$$

We can see that $p_\mathcal{O}(5) = 3$, $p_\mathcal{O}(5;1) = 1$ and $p_\mathcal{O}(5;2) = 2$. It is well-known that

$$\sum_{n=0}^{\infty} p_\mathcal{O}(n;i)\, q^n = \frac{1}{(q;q^2)_i}$$

and

$$\sum_{n=0}^{\infty} p_\mathcal{O}(n)\, q^n = \frac{1}{(q;q^2)_\infty}.$$

By replacing q by q^2 and t by q in Theorem 1, we deduce the following partition identity.

Corollary 2. *Let n and j be nonnegative integers. Then,*

$$p_\mathcal{O}(n;j+1) = \sum_{i=0}^{\lfloor n/2 \rfloor} p(\lfloor n/2 \rfloor - i; 2i, j).$$

The limiting case $n \to \infty$ of Theorem 1 is given by the following theorem of Euler ([3]: Theorem 25).

Theorem 3 (Euler). *If $|q| < 1$ and $|t| < 1$, then*

$$\sum_{k=0}^{\infty} \frac{t^k}{(q;q)_k} = \frac{1}{(t;q)_\infty}.$$

We consider the following partition functions.

Definition 4. *Let n, i and j be a non-negative integer. We define:*
(i) $p_e(n)$ *as the number of partitions of n into an even number of parts;*
(ii) $p_o(n)$ *as the number of partitions of n into an odd number of parts;*
(iii) $p(n)$ *as the number of partitions of n.*

It is clear that $p(n) = p_e(n) + p_o(n)$. For example, the partitions of 5 are:

$$(5), (4,1), (3,2), (3,1,1), (2,2,1), (2,1,1,1), (1,1,1,1,1).$$

We see that $p_e(5) = 3$, $p_o(5) = 4$ and $p(5) = 7$. In addition, we know that

$$\sum_{n=0}^{\infty} (p_e(n) \pm p_o(n))\, q^n = \frac{1}{(\pm q; q)_\infty}.$$

Thus, the case $t = \pm q$ of Theorem 3 allows for us to derive the following partition identities.

Corollary 3. *Let n be a nonnegative integer. Then,*

$$p_e(n) \pm p_o(n) = \sum_{j=0}^{n} (\pm 1)^j\, p(n-j;j).$$

Using Theorem 3, with q replaced by q^2 and t replaced by q, we can derive the limiting case $j \to \infty$ of Corollary 2.

Corollary 4. *Let n be a nonnegative integer. Then,*

$$p_O(n) = \sum_{i=0}^{\lfloor n/2 \rfloor} p(\lfloor n/2 \rfloor - i; 2i).$$

3. Elementary Symmetric Functions

Recall that the elementary symmetric functions are characterized by the following identity of the formal power series in t:

$$E(t) = \sum_{k=0}^{\infty} e_k(x_1, x_2, \ldots, x_n) t^k = \prod_{i=1}^{n}(1 + x_i t). \tag{4}$$

The following result is known as Rothe's q-binomial theorem ([3], Theorem 12). This can be obtained by (4), replacing x_j with q^{j-1} for each $j \in \{1, 2, \ldots, n\}$.

Theorem 4 (Rothe's q-binomial theorem). *If n is any nonnegative integer and $|q|$ and $|t|$ are both less than 1, then*

$$\sum_{k=0}^{n} \begin{bmatrix} n \\ k \end{bmatrix} q^{\binom{k}{2}} t^k = (-t; q)_n.$$

In analogy with Definition 2, we consider the following functions, involving partitions into distinct parts.

Definition 5. *Let n, i and j be a non-negative integer. We define:*
(i) *$p_{De}(n; i)$ as the number of partitions of n into an even number of distinct parts, with each, at most, i;*
(ii) *$p_{Do}(n; i)$ as the number of partitions of n into an odd number of distinct parts, with each, at most, i;*
(iii) *$p_D(n; i)$ as the number of partitions of n into distinct parts, each, at most, i.*

It is clear that $p_D(n; i) = p_{De}(n; i) + p_{Do}(n; i)$. For example, the partitions of 9 into distinct parts, with each, at most, 6 are:

$$(6,3),\ (6,2,1),\ (5,4),\ (5,3,1),\ (4,3,2).$$

We see that $p_{De}(9; 6) = 2$, $p_{Do}(9; 6) = 3$ and $p_D(9; 6) = 5$. Moreover, we know that

$$\sum_{n=0}^{\infty} \left(p_{De}(n; i) \pm p_{Do}(n; i)\right) q^n = (\mp q; q)_i.$$

Thus, the case $t = \pm q$ of Theorem 4 allows for us to derive the following partition identities.

Corollary 5. *Let n, j be nonnegative integers. Then*

$$p_{De}(n; j) \pm p_{Do}(n; j) = \sum_{i=0}^{j} (\pm 1)^i p(n - i(i+1)/2; i, j - i).$$

Proof. The case $t = \pm q$ of Theorem 4 reads as follows

$$\sum_{i=0}^{j} (\pm 1)^i \begin{bmatrix} j \\ i \end{bmatrix} q^{\binom{i+1}{2}} = (\mp q; q)_j.$$

Theorem 2 implies that $\begin{bmatrix} j \\ i \end{bmatrix}$ is the generating function for partitions into at most i parts, with each, at most, $j - i$. Thus, we can write

$$\sum_{i=0}^{j} \sum_{n=0}^{\infty} (\pm 1)^i p(n;i,j-i) q^{n+i(i+1)/2} = \sum_{n=0}^{\infty} (p_{De}(n;j) \pm p_{Do}(n;j)) q^n.$$

The identity can be derived by comparing coefficients of q^n on both sides of this equation. □

Definition 6. *Let n, and i be a non-negative integer. We define:*

(i) $p_{OD}(n;i)$ as the number of partitions of n into distinct odd parts, with each, at most, $2i - 1$;
(ii) $p_{OD}(n)$ as the number of partitions of n into distinct odd parts.

For example, the partitions of 18 into distinct odd parts are:

$$(17,1), (15,3), (13,5), (11,7), (9,5,3,1).$$

We see that $p_{OD}(18) = 5$, $p_{OD}(18;5) = 1$, $p_{OD}(18;6) = 2$, $p_{OD}(18;7) = 3$, $p_{OD}(18;8) = 4$. It is well-known that

$$\sum_{n=0}^{\infty} p_{OD}(n;i) q^n = (-q;q^2)_i$$

and

$$\sum_{n=0}^{\infty} p_{OD}(n) q^n = (-q;q^2)_\infty.$$

By replacing q by q^2 and t with q in Theorem 4, we deduce the following partition identities.

Corollary 6. *Let n and j be nonnegative integers. Then,*

(i) $p_{OD}(2n;j) = \sum_{i=0}^{\infty} p(n - 2i^2; 2i, j - 2i)$;

(ii) $p_{OD}(2n+1;j) = \sum_{i=0}^{\infty} p(n - 2i(i+1); 2i+1, j - (2i+1))$.

The limiting case $n \to \infty$ of Theorem 4 offers another theorem of Euler ([3], Theorem 27).

Theorem 5 (Euler). *If $|q| < 1$, then*

$$\sum_{k=0}^{\infty} \frac{q^{\binom{k}{2}} t^k}{(q;q)_k} = (-t;q)_\infty.$$

We consider the following partition functions.

Definition 7. *Let n be a non-negative integer. We define:*

(i) $p_{De}(n)$ as the number of partitions of n into an even number of distinct parts;
(ii) $p_{Do}(n)$ as the number of partitions of n into an odd number of distinct parts;
(iii) $p_D(n)$ as the number of partitions of n into distinct parts.

It is clear that $p_D(n) = p_{De}(n) + p_{Do}(n)$. For example, the partitions of 9 into distinct parts are:

$$(9), (8,1), (7,2), (6,3), (6,2,1), (5,4), (5,3,1), (4,3,2).$$

We see that $p_{De}(9) = 4$, $p_{Do}(9) = 4$ and $p_D(9) = 8$. In addition, we know that

$$\sum_{n=0}^{\infty} (p_{De}(n) \pm p_{Do}(n))q^n = (\mp q; q)_{\infty}.$$

Thus, the case $t = \pm q$ of Theorem 5 allows for us to derive the following partition identities.

Corollary 7. *Let n be a nonnegative integer. Then,*

$$p_{De}(n) \pm p_{Do}(n) = \sum_{j=0}^{n} (\pm 1)^j p(n - j(j+1)/2; j).$$

Using Theorem 5, with q replaced by q^2 and t replaced by q, we can derive the limiting case $j \to \infty$ of Corollary 6.

Corollary 8. *Let n be a nonnegative integer. Then,*

(i) $p_{OD}(2n) = \sum_{i=0}^{\infty} p(n - 2i^2; 2i);$

(ii) $p_{OD}(2n+1) = \sum_{i=0}^{\infty} p(n - 2i(i+1); 2i+1).$

4. Partitions and Divisors

Some interesting connections between partitions and divisors can easily be derived if we consider the derivatives of the generating functions of the complete and elementary symmetric functions.

Theorem 6. *Let n be a non-negative integer. Then,*

(i) $\sum_{k=1}^{n+1} \dfrac{q^{k-1} t}{1 - q^{k-1} t} = \dfrac{1}{(t;q)_{n+1}} \sum_{k=1}^{n+1} (-1)^{k-1} \begin{bmatrix} n+1 \\ k \end{bmatrix} q^{\binom{k}{2}} k\, t^k;$

(ii) $\sum_{k=1}^{\infty} \begin{bmatrix} n+k \\ k \end{bmatrix} k\, t^k = \dfrac{1}{(t;q)_{n+1}^2} \sum_{k=1}^{n+1} (-1)^{k-1} \begin{bmatrix} n+1 \\ k \end{bmatrix} q^{\binom{k}{2}} k\, t^k.$

Proof. (i) We have

$$\frac{d}{dt} \ln(E(t)) = \sum_{k=1}^{n+1} \frac{d}{dt} \ln(1 + x_k t) = \sum_{k=1}^{n+1} \frac{x_k}{1 + x_k t}$$

On the other hand, we can write

$$\frac{d}{dt} \ln(E(t)) = \left(\prod_{k=1}^{n+1} \frac{1}{1 + x_k t}\right) \left(\sum_{k=1}^{n+1} k\, e_k(x_1, x_2, \ldots, x_{n+1}) t^{k-1}\right).$$

Thus, we deduce that

$$\sum_{k=1}^{n+1} \frac{x_k t}{1 + x_k t} = \left(\prod_{k=1}^{n+1} \frac{1}{1 + x_k t}\right) \left(\sum_{k=1}^{n+1} k\, e_k(x_1, x_2, \ldots, x_{n+1}) t^k\right).$$

The first identity easily follows by replacing t by $-t$ and x_k by q^{k-1} for each $k \in \{1, 2, \ldots, n+1\}$.

(ii) We can write

$$\sum_{k=1}^{\infty} k h_k(x_1, x_2, \ldots, x_{n+1}) t^{k-1} = \frac{d}{dt} \prod_{i=1}^{n+1} (1 - x_i t)^{-1}$$

$$= \left(\prod_{i=1}^{n+1} (1 - x_i t)^{-2} \right) \left(\sum_{k=1}^{n+1} (-1)^k k e_k(x_1, x_2, \ldots, x_{n+1}) t^{k-1} \right).$$

The proof easily follows by replacing x_k by q^{k-1} for each $k \in \{1, 2, \ldots, n+1\}$. □

The first identity of Theorem 6 is known and can be seen in ([4], Equation (7)). The following identity can be derived as a consequence of Theorem 6.

Corollary 9. *Let n be a non-negative integer. Then,*

$$\sum_{k=1}^{\infty} \begin{bmatrix} n+k \\ k \end{bmatrix} k t^k = \frac{1}{(t;q)_{n+1}} \sum_{k=1}^{n+1} \frac{q^{k-1} t}{1 - q^{k-1} t}.$$

We consider the following divisor functions.

Definition 8. *Let n and k be positive integers. We define:*
(i) $\tau(n;k)$ *as the number of divisors of n less than or equal to k;*
(ii) $\tau(n)$ *as the number of divisors of n.*

We known that

$$\sum_{n=0}^{\infty} \tau(n;k) q^n = \sum_{n=1}^{k} \frac{q^n}{1 - q^n}$$

and

$$\sum_{n=0}^{\infty} \tau(n) q^n = \sum_{n=1}^{\infty} \frac{q^n}{1 - q^n}.$$

By replacing t with q in Corollary 9, we easily deduce the following identity involving partitions and divisors.

Corollary 10. *Let n and j be positive integers. Then,*

$$\sum_{i=1}^{n} i \, p(n-i; i, j) = \sum_{i=0}^{n} p(n-i; j+1) \tau(i; j+1).$$

The limiting case $n \to \infty$ of Theorem 6 and Corollary 9 reads as follows.

Theorem 7. *For $|q| < 1$, we have*

(i) $\displaystyle\sum_{k=1}^{\infty} \frac{q^{k-1} t}{1 - q^{k-1} t} = \frac{1}{(t;q)_{\infty}} \sum_{k=1}^{\infty} (-1)^{k-1} \frac{k t^k}{(q;q)_k} q^{\binom{k}{2}};$

(ii) $\displaystyle\sum_{k=1}^{\infty} \frac{k t^k}{(q;q)_k} = \frac{1}{(t;q)_{\infty}^2} \sum_{k=1}^{\infty} (-1)^{k-1} \frac{k t^k}{(q;q)_k} q^{\binom{k}{2}};$

(iii) $\displaystyle\sum_{k=1}^{\infty} \frac{k t^k}{(q;q)_k} = \frac{1}{(t;q)_{\infty}} \sum_{k=1}^{\infty} \frac{q^{k-1} t}{1 - q^{k-1} t}.$

We note that the case $t = q$ of the first identity of Theorem 7 can be seen in ([4], Theorem 1):

$$\sum_{k=1}^{\infty} \frac{q^k}{1 - q^k} = \frac{1}{(q;q)_{\infty}} \sum_{k=1}^{\infty} (-1)^{k-1} \frac{k q^{\binom{k+1}{2}}}{(q;q)_k}.$$

This identity was stated without proof by Eisenstein ([3], Theorem 39). We have the following combinatorial interpretation of this identity.

Corollary 11. *Let n be a positive integer. Then,*

$$\sum_{k=-\infty}^{\infty} (-1)^k \tau(n - k(3k-1)/2) = \sum_{k=1}^{\infty} (-1)^{k-1} k \, p(n - k(k+1)/2; k).$$

The case $t = q$ of the third identity of Theorem 7 is known as Uchimura's theorem ([3], Theorem 38).

Theorem 8 (Uchimura). *For $|q| < 1$,*

$$\sum_{n=1}^{\infty} \tau(n) \, q^n = (q;q)_\infty \sum_{n=1}^{\infty} \frac{n \, q^n}{(q;q)_n}.$$

We consider the following counting function.

Definition 9. *Let n be a non-negative integer. We define $s(n)$ as the number of parts in all the partitions of n.*

The partitions of 4 are:

$$(4), \ (3,1), \ (2,2), \ (2,1,1), \ (1,1,1,1).$$

We have $s(4) = 1 + 2 + 2 + 3 + 4 = 12$. It is known that

$$\sum_{n=1}^{\infty} s(n) \, q^n = \frac{1}{(q;q)_\infty} \sum_{n=1}^{\infty} \frac{q^n}{1-q^n}.$$

This generating function allows for us to derive two identities:

$$\tau(n) = \sum_{k=-\infty}^{\infty} (-1)^k s(n - k(3k-1)/2)$$

and

$$s(n) = \sum_{k=1}^{n} \tau(k) \, p(n-k).$$

The case $t = q$ of the third identity of Theorem 7 allows for us to deduce a new decomposition for $s(n)$.

Corollary 12. *Let n be a non-negative integer. Then,*

$$s(n) = \sum_{k=1}^{n} k \, p(n-k; k).$$

5. Newton's Identities

There is a fundamental relationship between the elementary symmetric functions and the complete homogeneous ones:

$$\sum_{j=0}^{k} (-1)^k e_k(x_1, x_2, \ldots, x_n) \, h_{n-k}(x_1, x_2, \ldots, x_n) = 0,$$

which is valid for all $k > 0$, and any number of variables n. By replacing x_i with q^{i-1}, we derive the following identity.

Theorem 9. *Let n and k be positive integers. Then,*

$$\sum_{j=0}^{k}(-1)^j q^{\binom{j}{2}}\begin{bmatrix}n+1\\j\end{bmatrix}\begin{bmatrix}n+k-j\\k-j\end{bmatrix} = 0.$$

The limiting case $n \to \infty$ of this theorem reads as follows

$$\sum_{j=0}^{k}(-1)^j \frac{q^{\binom{j}{2}}}{(q;q)_j (q;q)_{k-j}} = 0.$$

By multiplying this identity by $(q;q)_k$, we obtain the following result which, is the case $t = 1$ of Theorem 4:

$$\sum_{j=0}^{k}(-1)^j q^{\binom{j}{2}}\begin{bmatrix}k\\j\end{bmatrix} = 0.$$

The limiting case $k \to \infty$ of this identity is the case $t = 1$ of Theorem 5:

$$\sum_{j=0}^{\infty}(-1)^j \frac{q^{\binom{j}{2}}}{(q;q)_j} = 0.$$

We have the following combinatorial interpretations of the last two identities.

Corollary 13. *Let n and k be positive integers. Then,*

(i) $\sum_{j=0}^{k}(-1)^j p(n - j(j-1)/2; j, k-j) = 0;$

(ii) $\sum_{j=0}^{\infty}(-1)^j p(n - j(j-1)/2; j) = 0.$

The problem of expressing power sum symmetric polynomials in terms of elementary symmetric polynomials and vice versa was solved a long time ago. This was also the case for the problem of expressing power sum symmetric polynomials in terms of complete symmetric polynomials and vice versa. The relations are given as Newton's identities

$$k h_k(x_1, x_2, \ldots, x_n) = \sum_{j=1}^{k} h_{k-j}(x_1, x_2, \ldots, x_n) p_j(x_1, x_2, \ldots, x_n)$$

and

$$k e_k(x_1, x_2, \ldots, x_n) = \sum_{j=1}^{k} (-1)^{j-1} e_{k-j}(x_1, x_2, \ldots, x_n) p_j(x_1, x_2, \ldots, x_n)$$

and are well known. Using these identities, with x_i replaced by q^{i-1}, we can obtain the following identities.

Theorem 10. *Let n and k be positive integers. Then,*

(i) $k \begin{bmatrix}n+k\\k\end{bmatrix} = \sum_{j=1}^{k} \begin{bmatrix}n+k-j\\k-j\end{bmatrix} \frac{1-q^{j(n+1)}}{1-q^j};$

(ii) $k q^{\binom{k}{2}} \begin{bmatrix}n\\k\end{bmatrix} = \sum_{j=1}^{k}(-1)^{j-1} q^{\binom{k-j}{2}} \begin{bmatrix}n\\k-j\end{bmatrix} \frac{1-q^{j(n+1)}}{1-q^j}.$

The limiting case $n \to \infty$ of this theorem reads as follows.

Theorem 11. Let n and k be positive integers. Then,

(i) $\quad \dfrac{k}{(q;q)_k} = \sum_{j=1}^{k} \dfrac{1}{(1-q^j)(q;q)_{k-j}};$

(ii) $\quad \dfrac{k q^{\binom{k}{2}}}{(q;q)_k} = \sum_{j=1}^{k} (-1)^{j-1} \dfrac{q^{\binom{k-j}{2}}}{(1-q^j)(q;q)_{k-j}}.$

We have the following combinatorial interpretations of these identities.

Corollary 14. Let n and k be positive integers. Then,

(i) $\quad k\, p(n;k) = \sum_{i=0}^{n} \sum_{\substack{j=1 \\ j|i}}^{k} p(n-i; k-j);$

(ii) $\quad k\, p(n;k) = \sum_{i=0}^{n} \sum_{\substack{j=1 \\ j|i}}^{k} (-1)^{j-1} p\left(n - i + \binom{k}{2} - \binom{k-j}{2}; k-j\right).$

By multiplying both sides of the firs identity of Theorem 11 by $(q;q)_k$, we obtain a curious q-identity of Euler ([3], Theorem 17).

Theorem 12 (Euler). Let k be a positive integer. Then,

$$k = \sum_{j=1}^{k} (q;q)_{j-1} \begin{bmatrix} k \\ j \end{bmatrix}.$$

Recently, Merca [4] proved that the complete, elementary and power sum symmetric functions are related by

$$p_k(x_1, x_2, \ldots, x_n) = \sum_{j=1}^{k} (-1)^{j-1} j\, e_j(x_1, x_2, \ldots, x_n)\, h_{k-j}(x_1, x_2, \ldots, x_n).$$

Using this relation, with x_i replaced by q^{i-1}, we can derive the following identity.

Theorem 13. Let n and k be positive integers. Then,

$$\sum_{j=1}^{k} (-1)^{j-1} j\, q^{\binom{j}{2}} \begin{bmatrix} n+1 \\ j \end{bmatrix} \begin{bmatrix} n+k-j \\ k-j \end{bmatrix} = \dfrac{1 - q^{k(n+1)}}{1 - q^k}.$$

The limiting case $n \to \infty$ of this theorem reads as follows:

$$\sum_{j=1}^{k} (-1)^{j-1} j\, q^{\binom{j}{2}} \dfrac{1}{(q;q)_j (q;q)_{k-j}} = \dfrac{1}{1 - q^k}.$$

By multiplying both sides of this identity by $(q;q)_k$, we can obtain the following result.

Theorem 14. Let k be a positive integer. Then,

$$\sum_{j=1}^{k} (-1)^{j-1} j\, q^{\binom{j}{2}} \begin{bmatrix} k \\ j \end{bmatrix} = (q;q)_{k-1}.$$

We note the following combinatorial interpretation of this theorem.

Corollary 15. *Let n and k be positive integers. Then,*

$$p_{De}(n;k-1) - p_{Do}(n;k-1) = \sum_{j=1}^{k}(-1)^{j-1}j\,p(n-j(j-1)/2;j,k-j).$$

The case $t = -q$ of Theorem 5 is given by

$$(q;q)_\infty = \sum_{j=0}^{\infty}(-1)^j \frac{q^{\binom{j}{2}}}{(q;q)_j}.$$

The limiting case $k \to \infty$ of Theorem 14 provides another representation of Euler's function $(q;q)_\infty$.

Theorem 15. *For $|q| < 1$,*

$$(q;q)_\infty = \sum_{j=1}^{\infty}(-1)^{j-1} \frac{j\,q^{\binom{j}{2}}}{(q;q)_j}.$$

As a consequences of this result, we can derive the following recurrence relation for $p(n;k)$.

Corollary 16. *Let n be a positive integer. Then,*

$$\sum_{j=1}^{\infty}(-1)^{j-1}j\,p(n-j(j-1)/2;j) = \begin{cases} (-1)^n, & \text{if } n = m(3m-1)/2,\, m \in \mathbb{Z}, \\ 0, & \text{otherwise.} \end{cases}$$

6. Concluding Remarks

The partition identities obtained in this paper are specializations of the fundamental relations between complete and elementary symmetric functions. There are other relations between complete and elementary symmetric functions, which can be used to derive partitions identities. For example, the following relations between complete and elementary symmetric functions

$$\sum_{k=0}^{\lfloor n/2 \rfloor} h_k(x_1^2, x_2^2, \ldots, x_m^2)\, e_{n-2k}(x_1, x_2, \ldots, x_m) = h_n(x_1, x_2, \ldots, x_m)$$

and

$$\sum_{k=0}^{\lfloor n/4 \rfloor} h_k(x_1^4, \ldots, x_m^4)\, e_{n-4k}(x_1, \ldots, x_m) = \sum_{k=0}^{\lfloor n/2 \rfloor} (-1)^k h_k(x_1^2, \ldots, x_m^2)\, h_{n-2k}(x_1, \ldots, x_m)$$

was introduced by Merca [5] to obtain generalizations of two identities of Guo and Yang for the q-binomial coefficients. The partition identities that can be derived by considering these relations can be seen in [5,6].

Motivated by the relations obtained in [5], Merca introduced an infinite family of relations between complete and elementary symmetric functions ([7], Theorem 1.1). It would be interesting to see what partition identities can be obtained as combinatorial interpretations of ([7], Theorem 1.1).

Funding: This research received no external funding.

Institutional Review Board Statement: Not applicable.

Informed Consent Statement: Not applicable.

Data Availability Statement: Not applicable.

Conflicts of Interest: The author declares no conflict of interest.

References

1. Andrews, G.E. *The Theory of Partitions*; Cambridge Mathematical Library, Cambridge University Press: Cambridge, UK, 1998; Reprint of the 1976 original.
2. Macdonald, I. *Symmetric Functions and Hall Polynomials*; Oxford Univ. Press: Oxford, UK, 1979
3. Johnson, W.P. *An Introduction to q-Analysis*; American Mathematical Society: Providence, RI, USA, 2020.
4. Merca, M. A new look on the generating function for the number of divisors. *J. Number Theory* **2015**, *149*, 57–69. [CrossRef]
5. Merca, M. Generalizations of two identities of Guo and Yang. *Quaest. Math.* **2018**, *41*, 643–652. [CrossRef]
6. Merca, M. Combinatorial interpretations of two identities of Guo and Yang. *Contrib. Discret. Math.* **2021**, *16*, 20–27.
7. Merca, M. Bernoulli numbers and symmetric functions. *Rev. R. Acad. Cienc. Exactas Fís. Nat. Ser. A Math. RACSAM* **2020**, *114*, 20. [CrossRef]

Disclaimer/Publisher's Note: The statements, opinions and data contained in all publications are solely those of the individual author(s) and contributor(s) and not of MDPI and/or the editor(s). MDPI and/or the editor(s) disclaim responsibility for any injury to people or property resulting from any ideas, methods, instructions or products referred to in the content.

Article

New Formulas and Connections Involving Euler Polynomials

Waleed Mohamed Abd-Elhameed [1,*] and Amr Kamel Amin [2,3]

[1] Department of Mathematics, Faculty of Science, Cairo University, Giza 12613, Egypt
[2] Department of Basic Sciences, Adham University College, Umm AL-Qura University, Makkah 21955, Saudi Arabia
[3] Department of Mathematics and Computer Science, Faculty of Science, Beni-Suef University, Beni-Suef 62514, Egypt
* Correspondence: waleed@cu.edu.eg

Abstract: The major goal of the current article is to create new formulas and connections between several well-known polynomials and the Euler polynomials. These formulas are developed using some of these polynomials' well-known fundamental characteristics as well as those of the Euler polynomials. In terms of the Euler polynomials, new formulas for the derivatives of various symmetric and non-symmetric polynomials, including the well-known classical orthogonal polynomials, are given. This leads to the deduction of several new connection formulas between various polynomials and the Euler polynomials. As an important application, new closed forms for the definite integrals for the product of various symmetric and non-symmetric polynomials with the Euler polynomials are established based on the newly derived connection formulas.

Keywords: Euler polynomials; special polynomials; hypergeometric functions; definite integrals; connection formulas

1. Introduction

Numerous problems in various fields, such as approximation theory and theoretical physics, depend on special functions. Considerable research has been conducted on several well-known polynomial sequences and the numbers that they are associated with. Therefore, from both theoretical and practical aspects, it is interesting to investigate various special functions. Among the essential special functions are the well-known Hermite, Laguerre, and Jacobi polynomials. These classical orthogonal polynomials were extensively studied by many authors, both theoretically and practically; see, for example, [1–4]. The Jacobi polynomials include six special polynomials. Four of these polynomials are symmetric: the ultraspherical, Legendre, and the first and second kinds of Chebyshev polynomials. The polynomials, namely, the third- and fourth-kind Chebyshev polynomials, are two celebrated non-symmetric classes of Jacobi polynomials. All six classes of Jacobi polynomials have their parts in approximation theory and numerical analysis; see, for example, [5–7]. Other types of polynomials were also studied by many authors. For example, the Lucas and Fibonacci sequences, as well as their extensions and modified polynomials, were investigated by many authors. The authors in [8,9] studied certain kinds of generalized Fibonacci and generalized Lucas polynomials and their corresponding numbers. Furthermore, they employed them to find reduction formulas for some even and odd radicals. New identities of Horadam sequences of integers with four parameters were introduced by the authors in [10]. In [11], certain Appel polynomials are treated using a matrix technique. To handle bivariate Appell polynomials, matrix calculus was used in [12]. Classical and quantum orthogonal polynomials are extensively studied in [13].

Euler polynomials and Euler numbers have been the subject of numerous contemporary and older investigations. For example, the author in [14] developed some relations between the Bernoulli and Euler polynomials. Some properties on the integral of the product of several Euler polynomials are presented in [15]. In [16], the authors discussed the

Citation: Abd-Elhameed, W.M.; Amin, A.K. New Formulas and Connections Involving Euler Polynomials. *Axioms* **2022**, *11*, 743. https://doi.org/10.3390/axioms11120743

Academic Editor: Inna Kalchuk

Received: 13 November 2022
Accepted: 12 December 2022
Published: 18 December 2022

Publisher's Note: MDPI stays neutral with regard to jurisdictional claims in published maps and institutional affiliations.

Copyright: © 2022 by the authors. Licensee MDPI, Basel, Switzerland. This article is an open access article distributed under the terms and conditions of the Creative Commons Attribution (CC BY) license (https://creativecommons.org/licenses/by/4.0/).

decomposition of the linear combinations of Euler polynomials with odd degrees. In [17], the authors found some identities for Euler and Bernoulli polynomials and their zeros. Other identities for the product of two Bernoulli and Euler polynomials were obtained in [18]. New types of Euler polynomials and numbers are developed in [19]. For some other classes relating to Euler polynomials, one can refer, for example, to [20,21]. From a practical point of view, Euler polynomials were utilized to treat different types of differential and integral equations. For example, in [22], certain fractional-order delay integro-differential equations were numerically treated using an operational matrix of derivatives based on the utilization of fractional-order Euler polynomials. In [23], a numerical scheme utilizing Euler wavelets was derived to handle the fractional order pantograph Volterra delay-integro-differential equation. Two-dimensional Volterra integral equations of the fractional-order were treated using two-dimensional Euler polynomials in [24].

The various formulas of special functions are important from both theoretical and practical perspectives. For example, the expressions for the high-order derivatives of different polynomials in terms of their original ones can be used to obtain some spectral solutions to different differential equations. For example, in [25], new expressions for the third- and fourth-kinds of Chebyshev polynomials were established and utilized for solving specific even-order BVPs. Some other expressions for the high-order derivatives were utilized in [26] for treating linear and non-linear BVPs of even order. The author in [27] found new derivative formulas for the sixth-kind Chebyshev polynomials and used them to provide a numerical solution to the non-linear Burgers' equation in one dimension. Additionally, among the important formulas concerned with special functions are the connection and linearization formulas. These formulas are useful in some applications (see, for example, [28]).

This paper aims to find some new formulas concerning the Euler polynomials. To be more precise, the objectives of the current paper can be listed in the following items:

- Developing new expressions for the high-order derivatives of different symmetric and non-symmetric polynomials in terms of Euler polynomials.
- Deducing connection formulas between different polynomials and Euler polynomials.
- Presenting an application to the derived connection formulas. Several new definite integral formulas of the product of different symmetric and non-symmetric polynomials with the Euler polynomials in closed forms.

The paper is organized as follows. Section 2 introduces an overview of Euler polynomials. In addition, some properties of some celebrated symmetric and non-symmetric polynomials are presented in this section. Section 3 develops new expressions for the derivatives of symmetric and non-symmetric polynomials as combinations of Euler polynomials. Section 4 is interested in deducing connection formulas between symmetric and non-symmetric polynomials with the Euler polynomials. In Section 5, an application to the connection formulas presented in Section 4 is displayed. More precisely, some new definite integral formulas of the product of different symmetric and non-symmetric polynomials with the Euler polynomials are given. Finally, Section 6 reports some conclusions.

2. Preliminaries and Some Essential Formulas

This section is interested in presenting an overview of the Euler polynomials and their related numbers. Furthermore, we introduce some properties of symmetric and non-symmetric polynomials. In addition, an account of some classes of polynomials that will be connected with Euler polynomials is given.

2.1. An Account of Euler Polynomials

The classical Euler polynomials $E_m(x)$ can be defined with the aid of the generating function [29]

$$\frac{2 e^{xz}}{e^z + 1} = \sum_{m=0}^{\infty} E_m(x) \frac{z^m}{m!}, \quad |z| < \pi.$$

The corresponding Euler number is given by

$$E_m = 2^m E_m\left(\tfrac{1}{2}\right).$$

This is the inversion formula of Euler polynomials:

$$x^m = \frac{1}{2}\sum_{k=0}^{m} c_k \binom{m}{m-k} E_{m-k}(x), \quad m \geq 0, \qquad (1)$$

where c_k is defined as

$$c_k = \begin{cases} 2, & k = 0, \\ 1, & k > 0. \end{cases}$$

Additionally, among the famous identities of the polynomials $E_m(x)$ are the following identities [29]:

$$\frac{d}{dx} E_m(x) = m\, E_{m-1}(x),$$

$$\int_a^b E_m(x)\,dx = \frac{E_{m+1}(b) - E_{m+1}(a)}{m+1}.$$

2.2. An Overview on Symmetric and Non-Symmetric Polynomials

Let us consider, respectively, the two classes of symmetric and non-symmetric polynomials, $\{P_i(x)\}_{i\geq 0}$ and $\{Q_i(x)\}_{i\geq 0}$. We can express these polynomials as:

$$P_i(x) = \sum_{m=0}^{\lfloor \frac{i}{2} \rfloor} A_{m,i}\, x^{i-2m}, \qquad (2)$$

$$Q_i(x) = \sum_{m=0}^{i} B_{m,i}\, x^{i-m}, \qquad (3)$$

where the symbol $\lfloor z \rfloor$ denotes the well-known floor function.

We give some of the celebrated symmetric and non-symmetric polynomials. We first refer to the classical normalized Jacobi polynomials $V_m^{(\lambda,\delta)}(x)$. These polynomials can be written in a hypergeometric form as [30]

$$V_m^{(\lambda,\delta)}(x) = {}_2F_1\left(\begin{matrix} -m, m+\lambda+\delta+1 \\ \lambda+1 \end{matrix} \;\Big|\; \frac{1-x}{2} \right).$$

Jacobi polynomials include six important classes of polynomials. The ultraspherical, Legendre, and first-and second-kind Chebyshev polynomials are symmetric Jacobi polynomials, so they can be expressed as in (2), while the two celebrated third- and fourth-kind Chebyshev polynomials are particular polynomials of the non-symmetric Jacobi polynomials, so they can be expressed as in (3). In addition, we have the following identities [31]:

$$T_m(x) = V_m^{(-\frac{1}{2},-\frac{1}{2})}(x), \qquad U_m(x) = (m+1)\, V_m^{(\frac{1}{2},\frac{1}{2})}(x),$$
$$V_m(x) = V_m^{(-\frac{1}{2},\frac{1}{2})}(x), \qquad W_m(x) = (2m+1)\, V_m^{(\frac{1}{2},-\frac{1}{2})}(x),$$
$$P_m(x) = V_m^{(0,0)}(x), \qquad G_m^{(\delta)}(x) = V_m^{(\delta-\frac{1}{2},\delta-\frac{1}{2})}(x),$$

where the first-, second-, third-, and fourth kinds of Chebyshev polynomials are, respectively, denoted by the symbols $T_m(x), U_m(x), V_m(x),$ and $W_m(x)$. Additionally, the polynomials $P_n(x)$ and $G_n^{(\delta)}(x)$ denote the Legendre and ultraspherical polynomials, respectively.

The helpful books by Andrews et al. [32] and Mason and Handscomb [33] are both excellent resources for in-depth surveys of Jacobi polynomials and their celebrated classes.

Additionally, among the non-symmetric Jacobi polynomials are the shifted Jacobi polynomials on $[0,1]$. These polynomials are defined as

$$\tilde{V}_m^{(\lambda,\delta)}(x) = V_m^{(\lambda,\delta)}(2x-1).$$

We comment here that all six shifted special polynomials of the shifted Jacobi polynomials are non-symmetric. The power form representation of $\tilde{V}_m^{(\lambda,\delta)}(x)$ is given by [34]:

$$\tilde{V}_m^{(\lambda,\delta)}(x) = \frac{m!\,\Gamma(1+\lambda)}{\Gamma(1+m+\lambda)} \sum_{r=0}^{m} \frac{(-1)^r\,(1+\delta)_m\,(1+\lambda+\delta)_{2m-r}}{(m-r)!\,r!\,(1+\delta)_{m-r}\,(1+\lambda+\delta)_m} x^{m-r}. \quad (4)$$

Note that the symbol $(z)_\ell$ in Formula (4) represents the Pochhammer function defined as:
$(z)_\ell = \dfrac{\Gamma(z+\ell)}{\Gamma(z)}$.

Among the important symmetric polynomials are the Fibonacci and Lucas polynomials and their generalizations and modifications (see, [35]). Recently, Abd-Elhameed et al. in [9] studied two polynomials generalizing Fibonacci and Lucas polynomials. These polynomials may be constructed with the aid of the following two recursive formulas:

$$F_k^{A,B}(x) = A\,x\,F_{k-1}^{A,B}(x) + B\,F_{k-2}^{A,B}(x), \quad F_0^{A,B}(x) = 1,\ F_1^{A,B}(x) = A\,x,\quad k \geq 2, \quad (5)$$

and

$$L_k^{R,S}(x) = R\,x\,L_{k-1}^{R,S}(x) + S\,L_{k-2}^{R,S}(x), \quad L_0^{R,S}(x) = 2,\ L_1^{R,S}(x) = R\,x,\quad k \geq 2. \quad (6)$$

It is to be noted that several celebrated classes of polynomials can be obtained as special cases of the two generalized classes of $F_k^{A,B}(x)$ and $L_k^{R,S}(x)$ (see, [9]). For example, the Fibonacci polynomials $F_{k+1}(x)$ and Lucas polynomials $L_k(x)$ can be considered as special cases of $F_k^{A,B}(x)$ and $L_k^{R,S}(x)$. In fact, we have:

$$F_{k+1}(x) = F_k^{1,1}(x), \quad L_k(x) = L_k^{1,1}(x).$$

Furthermore, the power form representations of the generalized polynomials $F_i^{A,B}(x)$ and $L_i^{R,S}(x)$ are, respectively, given as follows [9]:

$$F_i^{A,B}(x) = \sum_{m=0}^{\lfloor \frac{i}{2} \rfloor} \binom{i-m}{m} B^m\,A^{i-2m}\,x^{i-2m}, \quad i \geq 0, \quad (7)$$

$$L_i^{R,S}(x) = i \sum_{m=0}^{\lfloor \frac{i}{2} \rfloor} \frac{S^m\,R^{i-2m}\,\binom{i-m}{m}}{i-m} x^{i-2m}, \quad i \geq 1.$$

3. New Expressions for the Derivatives of Some Celebrated Polynomials in Terms of Euler Polynomials

This section is devoted to developing new expressions for the high-order derivatives of some symmetric and non-symmetric polynomials in terms of Euler polynomials.

3.1. Derivative Expressions for Some Symmetric Polynomials

In this section, we give the derivatives of some symmetric polynomials in terms of the Euler polynomials. To be more precise, the derivatives of the generalized Fibonacci polynomials that are defined in (5), the generalized Lucas polynomials that are defined in (6), the ultraspherical polynomials, and the Hermite polynomials will be expressed in terms of the Euler polynomials.

Theorem 1. *Let n and ℓ be two non-negative integers with $n \geq \ell$. The derivatives of the generalized Fibonacci polynomials $F_n^{A,B}$ defined in (5) have the following expansion in terms of Euler polynomials:*

$$D^\ell F_n^{A,B}(x) = A^n \left(\sum_{r=0}^{\lfloor \frac{n-\ell}{2} \rfloor} \frac{A^{-2r} B^r (n-r)!(2r)! + n!r!}{2r!(2r)!(-\ell+n-2r)!} \, {}_2F_1\left(\begin{array}{c} -r, -r + \frac{1}{2} \\ -n \end{array} \bigg| -\frac{4B}{A^2} \right) E_{n-\ell-2r}(x) \right.$$

$$\left. + n! \sum_{r=0}^{\lfloor \frac{1}{2}(n-\ell-1) \rfloor} \frac{{}_2F_1\left(\begin{array}{c} -r, -r - \frac{1}{2} \\ -n \end{array} \bigg| -\frac{4B}{A^2} \right)}{2(2r+1)!(-\ell+n-2r-1)!} E_{n-\ell-2r-1}(x) \right). \qquad (8)$$

Proof. The power-form representation of the polynomials $F_n^{A,B}(x)$ in (7) allows one to write

$$D^\ell F_n^{A,B}(x) = \sum_{m=0}^{\lfloor \frac{n-\ell}{2} \rfloor} \frac{A^{n-2m} B^m (1-2m+n)_m (1-\ell-2m+n)_\ell}{m!} x^{n-2m-\ell}.$$

Inserting the inversion formula of the Euler polynomials (1) yields the following relation:

$$D^\ell F_n^{A,B}(x) = \sum_{m=0}^{\lfloor \frac{n-\ell}{2} \rfloor} \frac{A^{n-2m} B^m (1-2m+n)_m (1-\ell-2m+n)_\ell}{2m!} \times$$

$$\sum_{s=0}^{n-2m-\ell} c_s \binom{-\ell-2m+n}{-\ell-2m+n-s} E_{n-2m-s-\ell}(x).$$

After some algebraic computations, the last formula can be rewritten in the form

$$D^\ell F_n^{A,B}(x) = \sum_{r=0}^{\lfloor \frac{n-\ell}{2} \rfloor} \frac{1}{2(n-2r-\ell)!} \sum_{s=0}^{r} \frac{c_{2r-2s} A^{n-2s} B^s (n-s)!}{s!(2r-2s)!} E_{n-\ell-2r}(x)$$

$$+ \sum_{r=0}^{\lfloor \frac{1}{2}(n-\ell-1) \rfloor} \frac{1}{2(-\ell+n-2r-1)!} \sum_{s=0}^{r} \frac{c_{2r-2s-1} A^{n-2s} B^s (n-s)!}{s!(2r-2s+1)!} E_{n-\ell-2r-1}(x).$$

Based on the following two identities:

$$\sum_{s=0}^{r} \frac{c_{2r-2s} A^{n-2s} B^s (n-s)!}{s!(2r-2s)!} = \frac{A^n \left(A^{-2r} B^r (n-r)!(2r)! + n!r! \, {}_2F_1\left(\begin{array}{c} -r, -r+\frac{1}{2} \\ -n \end{array} \bigg| -\frac{4B}{A^2} \right) \right)}{r!(2r)!},$$

$$\sum_{s=0}^{r} \frac{c_{2r-2s-1} A^{n-2s} B^s (n-s)!}{s!(2r-2s+1)!} = \frac{A^n n! \, {}_2F_1\left(\begin{array}{c} -r, -r-\frac{1}{2} \\ -n \end{array} \bigg| -\frac{4B}{A^2} \right)}{(2r+1)!},$$

Formula (8) can be obtained. This proves Theorem 1. □

Remark 1. *It is to be noted that, for the case corresponding to the choice $B = -\frac{A^2}{4}$, Formula (8) can be simplified due to the Chu–Vandermond identity. The following corollary exhibits this result.*

Corollary 1. *For the case* $B = -\frac{A^2}{4}$, *Formula (8) reduces to the following one:*

$$D^\ell F_n^{A,-\frac{A^2}{4}}(x) = \frac{1}{2} A^n \sum_{r=0}^{\lfloor \frac{n-\ell}{2} \rfloor} \frac{\frac{(-\frac{1}{4})^r (n-r)!}{r!} + \frac{n!\left(n-2r+\frac{3}{2}\right)_r}{(2r)!(n-r+1)_r}}{(-\ell+n-2r)!} E_{n-\ell-2r}(x) \qquad (9)$$
$$+ \frac{1}{2} A^n n! \sum_{r=0}^{\lfloor \frac{1}{2}(n-\ell-1) \rfloor} \frac{\left(n-2r+\frac{1}{2}\right)_r}{(2r+1)!\,(-\ell+n-2r-1)!\,(n-r+1)_r} E_{n-\ell-2r-1}(x).$$

Proof. The substitution by $B = -\frac{A^2}{4}$ into Formula (8) yields

$$D^\ell F_n^{A,-\frac{A^2}{4}}(x) = = \frac{1}{2} A^n \sum_{r=0}^{\lfloor \frac{n-\ell}{2} \rfloor} \frac{\left(-\frac{1}{4}\right)^r (n-r)!(2r)! + n!r!\,{}_2F_1\!\left(\begin{array}{c}-r,-r+\frac{1}{2}\\-n\end{array}\Big|1\right)}{r!\,(2r)!\,(-\ell+n-2r)!} E_{n-\ell-2r}(x)$$
$$+ \frac{1}{2} A^n n! \sum_{r=0}^{\lfloor \frac{1}{2}(n-\ell-1) \rfloor} \frac{{}_2F_1\!\left(\begin{array}{c}-r,-r-\frac{1}{2}\\-n\end{array}\Big|1\right)}{(2r+1)!\,(-\ell+n-2r-1)!} E_{n-\ell-2r-1}(x).$$

Chu–Vandermonde identity implies the following two identities:

$${}_2F_1\!\left(\begin{array}{c}-r,-r+\frac{1}{2}\\-n\end{array}\Big|1\right) = \frac{\left(n-2r+\frac{3}{2}\right)_r}{(n-r+1)_r},$$

$${}_2F_1\!\left(\begin{array}{c}-r,-r-\frac{1}{2}\\-n\end{array}\Big|1\right) = \frac{\left(n-2r+\frac{1}{2}\right)_r}{(n-r+1)_r},$$

therefore, the following formula can be obtained:

$$D^\ell F_n^{A,-\frac{A^2}{4}}(x) = \frac{1}{2} A^n \sum_{r=0}^{\lfloor \frac{n-\ell}{2} \rfloor} \frac{\frac{(-\frac{1}{4})^r (n-r)!}{r!} + \frac{n!\left(n-2r+\frac{3}{2}\right)_r}{(2r)!(n-r+1)_r}}{(-\ell+n-2r)!} E_{n-\ell-2r}(x)$$
$$+ \frac{1}{2} A^n n! \sum_{r=0}^{\lfloor \frac{1}{2}(n-\ell-1) \rfloor} \frac{\left(n-2r+\frac{1}{2}\right)_r}{(2r+1)!\,(-\ell+n-2r-1)!\,(n-r+1)_r} E_{n-\ell-2r-1}(x).$$

□

Remark 2. *An expression for the derivatives of Chebyshev polynomials of the first kind can be obtained as a direct special case of Formula (9). The following corollary displays this important specific result.*

Corollary 2. *Let n and ℓ be two non-negative integers with $n \geq \ell$. The derivatives of the Chebyshev polynomials of the second kind can be represented in terms of Euler polynomials as*

$$D^\ell U_n(x) = 2^{n-1} \sum_{r=0}^{\lfloor \frac{n-\ell}{2} \rfloor} \frac{\frac{(-\frac{1}{4})^r (n-r)!}{r!} + \frac{n!\left(n-2r+\frac{3}{2}\right)_r}{(2r)!(n-r+1)_r}}{(-\ell+n-2r)!} E_{n-\ell-2r}(x)$$
$$+ 2^{n-1} n! \sum_{r=0}^{\lfloor \frac{1}{2}(n-\ell-1) \rfloor} \frac{\left(n-2r+\frac{1}{2}\right)_r}{(2r+1)!\,(-\ell+n-2r-1)!\,(n-r+1)_r} E_{n-\ell-2r-1}(x).$$

Theorem 2. *Let n and ℓ be two non-negative integers with $n \geq \ell$. The derivatives of the ultraspherical polynomials $G_n^{(\delta)}(x)$ can be expanded in terms of Euler polynomials as in the following form:*

$$D^\ell G_n^{(\delta)}(x) = \frac{n!\,\Gamma\left(\delta+\frac{1}{2}\right)}{\sqrt{\pi}\,\Gamma(n+2\delta)} \times$$

$$\sum_{r=0}^{\lfloor\frac{n-\ell}{2}\rfloor} \frac{2^{n-2r+2\delta-2}\left((-1)^r (2r)!\,\Gamma(n-r+\delta) + \frac{4^r r!\,\Gamma(n+\delta)(n-2r+\delta+\frac{1}{2})_r}{(n-r+\delta)_r}\right)}{r!\,(2r)!\,(-\ell+n-2r)!} E_{n-\ell-2r}(x) \tag{10}$$

$$+ \frac{n!\,2^{n+2\delta-2}\,\Gamma\left(\delta+\frac{1}{2}\right)\Gamma(n+\delta)}{\sqrt{\pi}\,\Gamma(n+2\delta)} \sum_{r=0}^{\lfloor\frac{1}{2}(n-\ell-1)\rfloor} \frac{\left(n-2r+\delta-\frac{1}{2}\right)_r}{(2r+1)!\,(-\ell+n-2r-1)!(n-r+\delta)_r} E_{n-\ell-2r-1}(x).$$

Proof. The power form representation of the ultraspherical polynomials given by

$$G_n^{(\delta)}(x) = \frac{n!\,\Gamma(2\delta+1)}{2\Gamma(\delta+1)\,\Gamma(n+2\delta)} \sum_{m=0}^{\lfloor\frac{n}{2}\rfloor} \frac{(-1)^m\,2^{n-2m}\,\Gamma(n-m+\delta)}{m!\,(n-2m)!} x^{n-2m},$$

enables one to write:

$$D^\ell G_n^{(\delta)}(x) = \frac{n!\,\Gamma\left(\delta+\frac{1}{2}\right)}{\sqrt{\pi}\,\Gamma(n+2\delta)} \sum_{m=0}^{\lfloor\frac{n-\ell}{2}\rfloor} \frac{(-1)^m\,2^{-2m+n+2\delta-1}\,\Gamma(-m+n+\delta)}{m!\,(-\ell-2m+n)!} x^{n-2m-\ell},$$

which can be written again with the aid of the inversion Formula (1) into the form

$$D^\ell G_n^{(\delta)}(x) = \frac{n!\,\Gamma\left(\delta+\frac{1}{2}\right)}{2\sqrt{\pi}\,\Gamma(n+2\delta)} \times$$

$$\sum_{m=0}^{\lfloor\frac{n-\ell}{2}\rfloor} \frac{(-1)^m\,2^{-2m+n+2\delta-1}\,\Gamma(-m+n+\delta)}{m!\,(-\ell-2m+n)!} \sum_{s=0}^{n-2m-\ell} c_s \binom{-\ell-2m+n}{-\ell-2m+n-s} E_{n-2m-s-\ell}(x).$$

Some lengthy algebraic computations lead to

$$D^\ell G_n^{(\delta)}(x) = \frac{n!\,\Gamma\left(\delta+\frac{1}{2}\right)}{\sqrt{\pi}\,\Gamma(n+2\delta)} \left(\sum_{r=0}^{\lfloor\frac{n-\ell}{2}\rfloor} \frac{1}{(-\ell+n-2r)!} \sum_{s=0}^{r} \frac{(-1)^s c_{2r-2s}\,2^{n-2s+2\delta-2}\,\Gamma(n-s+\delta)}{s!\,(2r-2s)!} E_{n-\ell-2r}(x) \right.$$

$$\left. + \sum_{r=0}^{\lfloor\frac{1}{2}(n-\ell-1)\rfloor} \frac{1}{(-\ell+n-2r-1)!} \sum_{s=0}^{r} \frac{(-1)^s c_{2r-2s+1}\,2^{n-2s+2\delta-2}\,\Gamma(n-s+\delta)}{s!\,(2r-2s+1)!} E_{n-\ell-2r-1}(x) \right). \tag{11}$$

To transform (11) into a simplified formula, we will find closed forms for the two interior sums that appear in it. Regarding the first sum, we can write

$$\sum_{s=0}^{r} \frac{(-1)^s c_{2r-2s}\,2^{n-2s+2\delta-2}\,\Gamma(n-s+\delta)}{s!(2r-2s)!}$$

$$= 2^{n+2\delta-2}\left(\frac{\left(-\frac{1}{4}\right)^r \Gamma(n-r+\delta)}{r!} + \frac{\Gamma(n+\delta)\,{}_2F_1\left(\begin{array}{c}-r+\frac{1}{2},-r\\1-n-\delta\end{array}\bigg|1\right)}{(2r)!} \right), \tag{12}$$

and accordingly, the Chu–Vandermonde identity implies the following identity:

$$\sum_{s=0}^{r} \frac{c_{2r-2s}(-1)^s 2^{n-2s+2\delta-2}\Gamma(n-s+\delta)}{s!(2r-2s)!} =$$

$$\frac{2^{n+2\delta-2}}{r!}\left(\left(-\frac{1}{4}\right)^r \Gamma(n-r+\delta) + \frac{r!\Gamma(n+\delta)\left(n-2r+\delta+\frac{1}{2}\right)_r}{(2r)!(n-r+\delta)_r}\right).$$

Regarding the second sum, set

$$M_{r,n} = \sum_{s=0}^{r} \frac{c_{2r-2s+1}(-1)^s 2^{n-2s+2\delta-2}\Gamma(n-s+\delta)}{s!(2r-2s+1)!},$$

and employ the important algorithm of Zeilberger [36] to show that the following recurrence relation of order one is satisfied by $M_{r,n}$:

$$M_{r+1,n} - \frac{(3-2n+4r-2\delta)(5-2n+4r-2\delta)}{4(r+1)(2r+3)(3-2n+2r-2\delta)(1-n+r-\delta)} M_{r,n} = 0, \quad M_{0,n} = 1,$$

which can be immediately solved to give

$$\sum_{s=0}^{r} \frac{(-1)^s c_{2r-2s+1} 2^{n-2s+2\delta-2}\Gamma(n-s+\delta)}{s!(2r-2s+1)!} = \frac{2^{n+2\delta-2}\Gamma(n+\delta)\left(n-2r+\delta-\frac{1}{2}\right)_r}{(2r+1)!(n-r+\delta)_r}. \quad (13)$$

In virtue of the two Identities (12) and (13), Formula (11) can be put into the simpler formula:

$$D^\ell G_n^{(\delta)}(x) = \frac{n!\Gamma\left(\delta+\frac{1}{2}\right)}{\sqrt{\pi}\,\Gamma(n+2\delta)} \times$$

$$\sum_{r=0}^{\lfloor\frac{n-\ell}{2}\rfloor} \frac{2^{n-2r+2\delta-2}\left((-1)^r (2r)!\Gamma(n-r+\delta) + \frac{4^r r!\Gamma(n+\delta)\left(n-2r+\delta+\frac{1}{2}\right)_r}{(n-r+\delta)_r}\right)}{r!(2r)!(-\ell+n-2r)!} E_{n-\ell-2r}(x)$$

$$+ \frac{n!\,2^{n+2\delta-2}\,\Gamma\left(\delta+\frac{1}{2}\right)\Gamma(n+\delta)}{\sqrt{\pi}\,\Gamma(n+2\delta)} \sum_{r=0}^{\lfloor\frac{1}{2}(n-\ell-1)\rfloor} \frac{\left(n-2r+\delta-\frac{1}{2}\right)_r}{(2r+1)!(-\ell+n-2r-1)!(n-r+\delta)_r} E_{n-\ell-2r-1}(x).$$

This proves Theorem 2. □

Remark 3. *Since the Legendre and Chebyshev polynomials of the first and second kinds are included in the ultraspherical polynomials, $G_n^{(\delta)}$, three specific expressions for the derivatives of these polynomials can be inferred as direct special cases of Formula (10). These expressions can be seen in the subsequent corollary.*

Corollary 3. *Let n and ℓ be two non-negative integers with $n \geq \ell$. The formulas that express the derivatives of Legendre and Chebyshev polynomials of the first and second kinds in terms of Euler polynomials are given as follows:*

$$D^\ell P_n(x) = \frac{1}{\sqrt{\pi}} \sum_{r=0}^{\lfloor \frac{n-\ell}{2} \rfloor} \frac{2^{n-2r-1} \left((-1)^r (2r)! \, \Gamma\left(n-r+\frac{1}{2}\right) + \frac{4^r r! \, \Gamma\left(n+\frac{1}{2}\right)(n-2r+1)_r}{(n-r+\frac{1}{2})_r} \right)}{r! \, (2r)! \, (-\ell+n-2r)!} E_{n-\ell-2r}(x)$$
$$+ \frac{2^{n-1} \Gamma\left(\frac{1}{2}+n\right)}{\sqrt{\pi}} \sum_{r=0}^{\lfloor \frac{1}{2}(n-\ell-1) \rfloor} \frac{(n-2r)_r}{(2r+1)! \, (-\ell+n-2r-1)! \left(n-r+\frac{1}{2}\right)_r} E_{n-\ell-2r-1}(x), \tag{14}$$

$$D^\ell T_n(x) = n! \sum_{r=0}^{\lfloor \frac{n-\ell}{2} \rfloor} \frac{2^{n-2r-2} \left((-1)^r (2r)! + 4^r r! \left(n-2r+\frac{1}{2}\right)_r \right)}{r! \, (2r)! \, (-\ell+n-2r)! \, (n-r)_r} E_{n-\ell-2r}(x)$$
$$+ 2^{n-2} n! \sum_{r=0}^{\lfloor \frac{1}{2}(n-\ell-1) \rfloor} \frac{\left(n-2r-\frac{1}{2}\right)_r}{(2r+1)! \, (-\ell+n-2r-1)! \, (n-r)_r} E_{n-\ell-2r-1}(x), \tag{15}$$

$$D^\ell U_n(x) = \frac{1}{2} \sum_{r=0}^{\lfloor \frac{n-\ell}{2} \rfloor} \frac{2^{n-2r} \left(2^{2r} n! \, r! \left(n-2r+\frac{3}{2}\right)_r + (-1)^r (2r)! (n-r)! (n-r+1)_r \right)}{r! \, (2r)! \, (-\ell+n-2r)! \, (n-r+1)_r} E_{n-\ell-2r}(x)$$
$$+ 2^{n-1} n! \sum_{r=0}^{\lfloor \frac{1}{2}(n-\ell-1) \rfloor} \frac{\left(n-2r+\frac{1}{2}\right)_r}{(2r+1)! \, (-\ell+n-2r-1)! \, (n-r+1)_r} E_{n-\ell-2r-1}(x). \tag{16}$$

Proof. Formulas (14), (15) and (16) can be obtained as special cases of Formula (10) by setting $\delta = \frac{1}{2}, 0, 1$, respectively. □

Remark 4. *Expressions for the derivatives of other symmetric polynomials can be derived using similar techniques to those used in the proofs of Theorems 1 and 2. Some outcomes in this regard are shown by the following two theorems:*

Theorem 3. *Let n and ℓ be two non-negative integers with $n \geq \ell$. The derivatives of the Hermite polynomials H_n can be expanded in terms of Euler polynomials as*

$$D^\ell H_n(x) = n! \sum_{r=0}^{\lfloor \frac{n-\ell}{2} \rfloor} \frac{(-1)^r 2^{n-2r-1} \left(1 + {}_1F_1\left(-r; \frac{1}{2}; 1\right)\right)}{r! \, (-\ell+n-2r)!} E_{n-\ell-2r}(x)$$
$$+ \sum_{r=0}^{\lfloor \frac{1}{2}(n-\ell-1) \rfloor} \frac{U\left(-r, \frac{3}{2}, 1\right)}{(-\ell+n-2r-1)! \, (2r+1)!} E_{n-\ell-2r-1}(x), \tag{17}$$

where $U(a, b; z)$ is the well-known confluent hypergeometric [37].

Proof. Based on the power form representation of Hermite polynomials given by [37]

$$H_n(x) = n! \sum_{m=0}^{\lfloor \frac{n}{2} \rfloor} \frac{(-1)^m 2^{n-2m}}{m! (n-2m)!} x^{n-2m},$$

along with the inversion formula of Euler polynomials (1), and performing similar steps that followed in the proof of Theorem 1, Formula (17) can be obtained. □

Theorem 4. *Let n and ℓ be two non-negative integers with $n \geq \ell$. The derivatives of the generalized Lucas polynomials that are constructed by (6) can be expanded in terms of Euler polynomials as*

$$D^\ell L_n^{R,S}(x) = \frac{1}{2} R^n \sum_{r=0}^{\lfloor \frac{n-\ell}{2} \rfloor} \frac{R^{-2r} S^r n(n-r-1)!(2r)! + n!r! \, _2F_1\left(\begin{array}{c}-r,-r+\frac{1}{2}\\1-n\end{array}\Big| -\frac{4S}{R^2}\right)}{r!(2r)!(-\ell+n-2r)!} E_{n-\ell-2r}(x)$$

$$+ \frac{1}{2} R^n n! \sum_{r=0}^{\lfloor \frac{1}{2}(n-\ell-1) \rfloor} \frac{_2F_1\left(\begin{array}{c}-r,-r-\frac{1}{2}\\1-n\end{array}\Big| -\frac{4S}{R^2}\right)}{(2r+1)!(-\ell+n-2r-1)!} E_{n-\ell-2r-1}(x).$$
(18)

Proof. Similar to the proof of Theorem 1. □

3.2. Derivative Expressions for Some Non-Symmetric Polynomials

This section is confined to developing new expressions for the derivatives of some non-symmetric polynomials in terms of Euler polynomials. To be more precise, the expressions for the derivatives of the shifted Jacobi, Laguerre, and Schröder polynomials will be presented.

Theorem 5. *Let n and ℓ be two non-negative integers with $n \geq \ell$. The derivatives of the shifted Jacobi polynomials can be written in terms of the Euler polynomials as*

$$D^\ell \tilde{V}_n^{(\lambda,\delta)}(x) = \frac{n!\,\Gamma(\lambda+1)}{2\,\Gamma(n+\lambda+1)\,\Gamma(n+\lambda+1+\delta)} \times$$

$$\sum_{m=0}^{n-\ell} \frac{\Gamma(2n-m+\lambda+\delta+1)}{m!\,(n-m-\ell)!\,\Gamma(n-m+\lambda+1)\,\Gamma(n-m+\delta+1)} \times \qquad (19)$$

$$((-1)^m \Gamma(n-m+\lambda+1)\,\Gamma(n+\delta+1) + \Gamma(n+\lambda+1)\,\Gamma(n-m+\delta+1))\, E_{n-\ell-m}(x).$$

Proof. The representation of the shifted Jacobi polynomials in (4) serves to obtain the following formula:

$$D^\ell \tilde{V}_n^{(\lambda,\delta)}(x) = \frac{n!\,\Gamma(n+\delta+1)\,\Gamma(\lambda+1)}{\Gamma(n+\lambda+1)\,\Gamma(n+\delta+1+\lambda)} \sum_{r=0}^{n+m-\ell} \frac{(-1)^r \Gamma(2n-r+\delta+\lambda+1)}{r!\,(-\ell+n-r)!\,\Gamma(n-r+\delta+1)} x^{n-r-\ell},$$

hence, when the inversion Formula (1) is applied, it yields the following formula:

$$D^\ell \tilde{V}_n^{(\lambda,\delta)}(x) = \frac{n!\,\Gamma(n+\delta+1)\,\Gamma(\lambda+1)}{2\,\Gamma(n+\lambda+1)\,\Gamma(n+\delta+1+\lambda)} \times$$

$$\sum_{r=0}^{n+m-\ell} \frac{(-1)^r \Gamma(2n-r+\delta+\lambda+1)}{r!\,(-\ell+n-r)!\,\Gamma(n-r+\delta+1)} \sum_{t=0}^{n-\ell-r} c_t \binom{-\ell+n-r}{-\ell+n-r-t} E_{n-r-\ell-t}(x).$$

Rearranging the terms in the last formula turns it into the following form:

$$D^\ell \tilde{V}_n^{(\lambda,\delta)}(x) = \frac{n!\,\Gamma(n+\delta+1)\,\Gamma(\lambda+1)}{2\,\Gamma(n+\lambda+1)\,\Gamma(n+\delta+1+\lambda)} \sum_{m=0}^{n-\ell} \frac{1}{(-\ell+n-m)!} \times \qquad (20)$$

$$\sum_{r=0}^m \frac{(-1)^r c_{m-r} \Gamma(2n-r+\delta+\lambda+1)}{(m-r)!\,r!\,\Gamma(n-r+\delta+1)} E_{n-\ell-m}(x).$$

The second sum that appears on the right-hand side of (20) can be rewritten in the following form:

$$\sum_{r=0}^m \frac{(-1)^r c_{m-r} \Gamma(2n-r+\delta+\lambda+1)}{r!\,(m-r)!\,\Gamma(n-r+\delta+1)} =$$

$$\frac{(-1)^m \Gamma(n+\delta+1)\,\Gamma(2n-m+\delta+\lambda+1) + \Gamma(n-m+\delta+1)\,\Gamma(2n+\delta+\lambda+1)\,H_{m,n}}{m!\,\Gamma(n+\delta+1)\,\Gamma(n-m+\delta+1)},$$

where $H_{m,n}$ is given by

$$H_{m,n} = {}_2F_1\left(\begin{array}{c}-m,-n-\delta\\-2n-\delta-\lambda\end{array}\Big|1\right).$$

Chu-Vandermond identity implies that

$${}_2F_1\left(\begin{array}{c}-m,-n-\delta\\-2n-\delta-\lambda\end{array}\Big|1\right) = \frac{(n-m+\lambda+1)_m}{(2n-m+\delta+\lambda+1)_m},$$

thus, the following identity can be obtained:

$$\sum_{r=0}^{m}\frac{(-1)^r c_{m-r}\Gamma(2n-r+\delta+\lambda+1)}{(m-r)!\,r!\,\Gamma(n-r+\delta+1)} = \frac{\left(\frac{(-1)^m}{\Gamma(n-m+\delta+1)}+\frac{\Gamma(n+\lambda+1)}{\Gamma(n+\delta+1)\,\Gamma(n-m+\lambda+1)}\right)\Gamma(2n-m+\delta+\lambda+1)}{m!}.$$

The reduction of the last sum enables one to reduce Formula (20) in the following simpler form:

$$D^\ell \tilde{V}_n^{(\lambda,\delta)}(x) = \frac{n!\,\Gamma(\lambda+1)}{2\,\Gamma(n+\lambda+1)\,\Gamma(n+\lambda+1+\delta)} \times$$

$$\sum_{m=0}^{n-\ell} \frac{\Gamma(2n-m+\lambda+\delta+1)}{m!\,(n-m-\ell)!\,\Gamma(n-m+\lambda+1)\,\Gamma(n-m+\delta+1)} \times$$

$$((-1)^m\,\Gamma(n-m+\lambda+1)\,\Gamma(n+\delta+1) + \Gamma(n+\lambda+1)\,\Gamma(n-m+\delta+1))\,E_{n-\ell-m}(x).$$

This finalizes the proof of Theorem 5. □

Taking into consideration the six special polynomials of the shifted Jacobi polynomials, six special formulas of Formula (19) can be obtained. The following two corollaries present these formulas.

Corollary 4. *Let n and ℓ be two non-negative integers with $n \geq \ell$. The following expressions give the derivatives of the shifted ultraspherical, shifted Legendre, and shifted Chebyshev polynomials of the first and second kinds:*

$$D^\ell \tilde{G}_n^{(\delta)}(x) = \frac{n!\,\Gamma\left(\delta+\frac{1}{2}\right)}{\Gamma(n+2\delta)}\sum_{m=0}^{\lfloor\frac{n-\ell}{2}\rfloor}\frac{\Gamma(2(n-m+\delta))}{(2m)!\,(-\ell+n-2m)!\,\Gamma\left(\frac{1}{2}+n-2m+\delta\right)}E_{n-\ell-2m}(x),$$

$$D^\ell \tilde{P}_n(x) = \sum_{m=0}^{\lfloor\frac{n-\ell}{2}\rfloor}\frac{(2n-2m)!}{(2m)!\,(n-2m)!\,(-\ell+n-2m)!}E_{n-\ell-2m}(x),$$

$$D^\ell \tilde{T}_n(x) = n\sqrt{\pi}\sum_{m=0}^{\lfloor\frac{n-\ell}{2}\rfloor}\frac{(2n-2m+1)!}{(2m)!\,(-\ell+n-2m)!\,\Gamma\left(n-2m+\frac{1}{2}\right)}E_{n-\ell-2m}(x),$$

$$D^\ell \tilde{U}_n(x) = \frac{1}{2}\sqrt{\pi}\sum_{m=0}^{\lfloor\frac{n-\ell}{2}\rfloor}\frac{(2n-2m+1)!}{(2m)!\,(-\ell+n-2m)!\,\Gamma\left(n-2m+\frac{3}{2}\right)}E_{n-\ell-2m}(x).$$

Corollary 5. Let n and ℓ be two non-negative integers with $n \geq \ell$. The derivatives of the shifted third- and fourth-kind Chebyshev polynomials are, respectively, given by the following expressions:

$$D^\ell \tilde{V}_n(x) = \frac{1}{2}\sqrt{\pi} \left(\sum_{m=0}^{\lfloor \frac{n-\ell}{2} \rfloor} \frac{(2n-2m+1)!}{(2m)!(-\ell+n-2m)!\Gamma\left(n-2m+\frac{3}{2}\right)} E_{n-\ell-2m}(x) \right.$$
$$\left. - \sum_{m=0}^{\lfloor \frac{1}{2}(n-\ell-1) \rfloor} \frac{(2n-2m-1)!}{(2m)!(-\ell+n-2m-1)!\Gamma\left(n-2m+\frac{1}{2}\right)} E_{n-\ell-2m-1}(x) \right), \quad (21)$$

$$D^\ell \tilde{W}_n(x) = \frac{1}{2}\sqrt{\pi} \left(\sum_{m=0}^{\lfloor \frac{n-\ell}{2} \rfloor} \frac{(2n-2m+1)!}{(2m)!(-\ell+n-2m)!\Gamma\left(n-2m+\frac{3}{2}\right)} E_{n-\ell-2m}(x) \right.$$
$$\left. + \sum_{m=0}^{\lfloor \frac{1}{2}(n-\ell-1) \rfloor} \frac{(2n-2m-1)!}{(2m)!(-\ell+n-2m-1)!\Gamma\left(n-2m+\frac{1}{2}\right)} E_{n-\ell-2m-1}(x) \right). \quad (22)$$

Theorem 6. For non-negative integers n and q with $n \geq q$, the derivatives of the generalized Laguerre polynomials $L_n^{(\lambda)}(x)$ can be expanded in terms of the Euler polynomials as

$$D^\ell L_n^{(\lambda)}(x) = \frac{1}{2}\Gamma(n+\lambda+1) \sum_{m=0}^{n-\ell} \frac{(-1)^{n+m}\left(1 + {}_1F_1(-m; n-m+\lambda+1; 1)\right)}{m!(-\ell+n-m)!\Gamma(n-m+\lambda+1)} E_{n-\ell-m}(x). \quad (23)$$

Proof. The proof can be done with the aid of the following formula [37]:

$$L_n^{(\lambda)}(x) = \frac{\Gamma(n+\lambda+1)}{n!} \sum_{k=0}^{n} \frac{(-1)^{n-k}\binom{n}{k}}{\Gamma(n+\lambda-k+1)} x^{n-k},$$

along with Formula (1). □

Theorem 7. For non-negative integers n and q with $n \geq q$, the derivatives of the Schröder polynomials can be expanded in terms of Euler polynomials as

$$D^\ell S_n(x) = \frac{1}{2(n+1)!} \sum_{m=0}^{n-\ell} \frac{(n+1)!(2n-m)! + (2n)!(n-m+1)! \, {}_2F_1\left(\begin{array}{c}-m,-n-1\\-2n\end{array}\middle|-1\right)}{m!(n-m+1)!(-\ell+n-m)!} \times \quad (24)$$
$$E_{n-\ell-m}(x).$$

Proof. The proof can be done with the aid of the following representation of Schröder polynomials [38]

$$S_n(x) = \sum_{r=0}^{n} \frac{\binom{2r}{r}\binom{n+r}{n-r}}{j+1} x^r,$$

along with Formula (1). □

4. Connection Formulas of Different Polynomials with Euler Polynomials

In this section, the connection formulas between some symmetric and non-symmetric polynomials and the Euler polynomials are given. In fact, since all the derivative formulas developed in Section 3 are valid for $\ell = 0$, it is an easy matter to deduce the connection formulas as special cases of these formulas.

4.1. Connection Formulas between Some Symmetric Polynomials and Euler Polynomials

In this section, we present new connection formulas between some symmetric polynomials and Euler polynomials. More precisely, the connection formulas between the ultraspherical, generalized Fibonacci, generalized Lucas, and Hermite polynomials and Euler polynomials will be presented.

Corollary 6. *For every non-negative integer n, the following connection formulas hold:*

$$U_n^{(\delta)}(x) = \frac{n!\,\Gamma\left(\delta + \frac{1}{2}\right)}{\sqrt{\pi}\,\Gamma(n+2\delta)} \times$$

$$\left(\sum_{r=0}^{\lfloor \frac{n}{2} \rfloor} \frac{2^{n-2r+2\delta-2}\left((-1)^r(2r)!\,\Gamma(n-r+\delta) + \frac{4^r r!\,\Gamma(n+\delta)\left(-n+r-\delta+\frac{1}{2}\right)_r}{(1-n-\delta)_r}\right)}{r!\,(2r)!\,(n-2r)!} E_{n-2r}(x) \right. \tag{25}$$

$$\left. + \Gamma(n+\delta) \sum_{r=0}^{\lfloor \frac{n-1}{2} \rfloor} \frac{2^{n+2\delta-2}\left(-n+r-\delta+\frac{3}{2}\right)_r}{(2r+1)!\,(n-2r-1)!\,(1-n-\delta)_r} E_{n-2r-1}(x) \right),$$

$$P_n(x) = \frac{1}{\sqrt{\pi}} \sum_{r=0}^{\lfloor \frac{n}{2} \rfloor} \frac{2^{n-1}\left(\frac{\left(-\frac{1}{4}\right)^r \Gamma\left(n-r+\frac{1}{2}\right)}{r!} + \frac{\Gamma\left(n+\frac{1}{2}\right)(n-2r+1)_r}{(2r)!\left(n-r+\frac{1}{2}\right)_r}\right)}{(n-2r)!} E_{n-2r}(x)$$

$$+ \frac{2^{n-1}\Gamma\left(n+\frac{1}{2}\right)}{\sqrt{\pi}} \sum_{r=0}^{\lfloor \frac{n-1}{2} \rfloor} \frac{(n-2r)_r}{(2r+1)!\,(n-2r-1)!\left(n-r+\frac{1}{2}\right)_r} E_{n-2r-1}(x),$$

$$T_n(x) = n! \sum_{r=0}^{\lfloor \frac{n}{2} \rfloor} \frac{2^{n-2r-2}\left((-1)^r(2r)! + 4^r r!\left(n-2r+\frac{1}{2}\right)_r\right)}{r!\,(2r)!\,(n-2r)!\,(n-r)_r} E_{n-2r}(x)$$

$$+ 2^{n-2} n! \sum_{r=0}^{\lfloor \frac{n-1}{2} \rfloor} \frac{\left(n-2r-\frac{1}{2}\right)_r}{(2r+1)!\,(n-2r-1)!\,(n-r)_r} E_{n-2r-1}(x),$$

$$U_n(x) = \frac{1}{2} n! \sum_{r=0}^{\lfloor \frac{n}{2} \rfloor} \frac{2^n\left(\left(-\frac{1}{4}\right)^r(2r)! + r!\left(n-2r+\frac{3}{2}\right)_r\right)}{r!\,(2r)!\,(n-2r)!\,(n-r+1)_r} E_{n-2r}(x)$$

$$+ 2^{n-1} n! \sum_{r=0}^{\lfloor \frac{n-1}{2} \rfloor} \frac{\left(n-2r+\frac{1}{2}\right)_r}{(2r+1)!\,(n-2r-1)!\,(n-r+1)_r} E_{n-2r-1}(x).$$

Proof. All formulas listed in Corollary 6 are direct consequences of Theorem 2 and Corollary 3 with the same arrangement of their equations. They can be deduced by setting $\ell = 0$. □

Corollary 7. *Let n be any positive integer. The following are the generalized Fibonacci–Euler, the generalized Lucas–Euler, and the Hermite–Euler connection formulas.*

$$F_n^{A,B}(x) = A^n \left(\sum_{r=0}^{\lfloor \frac{n}{2} \rfloor} \frac{A^{-2r} B^r (n-r)!\,(2r)! + n!\,r!\,{}_2F_1\left(\begin{matrix}-r, -r+\frac{1}{2}\\-n\end{matrix}\bigg| -\frac{4B}{A^2}\right)}{2\,r!\,(2r)!\,(n-2r)!} E_{n-2r}(x) \right.$$

$$\left. + n! \sum_{r=0}^{\lfloor \frac{n-1}{2} \rfloor} \frac{{}_2F_1\left(\begin{matrix}-r, -r-\frac{1}{2}\\-n\end{matrix}\bigg| -\frac{4B}{A^2}\right)}{2\,(2r+1)!\,(n-2r-1)!} E_{n-2r-1}(x) \right), \tag{26}$$

$$L_n^{R,S}(x) = \frac{1}{2} R^n n! \left(\sum_{r=0}^{\lfloor \frac{n}{2} \rfloor} \frac{R^{-2r} S^r n(n-r-1)!(2r)! + n! \, r! \, _2F_1\left(\begin{array}{c} -r, -r+\frac{1}{2} \\ 1-n \end{array} \middle| -\frac{4S}{R^2}\right)}{r!(2r)!(n-2r)!} E_{n-2r}(x) \right.$$

$$\left. + n! \sum_{r=0}^{\lfloor \frac{n-1}{2} \rfloor} \frac{_2F_1\left(\begin{array}{c} -r, -r-\frac{1}{2} \\ 1-n \end{array} \middle| -\frac{4S}{R^2}\right)}{(2r+1)!(n-2r-1)!} E_{n-2r-1}(x) \right), \tag{27}$$

$$H_n(x) = n! \sum_{r=0}^{\lfloor \frac{n}{2} \rfloor} \frac{(-1)^r 2^{n-2r-1} \left(1 + {}_1F_1\left(-r; \frac{1}{2}; 1\right)\right)}{r!(n-2r)!} E_{n-2r}(x)$$

$$+ 2^{n-1} n! \sum_{r=0}^{\lfloor \frac{n-1}{2} \rfloor} \frac{1}{(2r+1)!(n-2r-1)!} U\left(-r, \frac{3}{2}, 1\right) E_{n-2r-1}(x). \tag{28}$$

Proof. Formulas (26), (27) and (28) are, respectively, special cases of Formulas (8), (18) and (17) for the case $\ell = 0$. □

4.2. Connection Formulas between Some Non-Symmetric Polynomials with Euler Polynomials

In this section, we introduce new connection formulas between some non-symmetric polynomials and Euler polynomials. The shifted Jacobi–Euler, generalized Laguerre–Euler, and Schröder–Euler connection formulas will be displayed.

Corollary 8. *Let n be a non-negative integer. The shifted Jacobi–Euler connection formula is*

$$\tilde{V}_n^{(\lambda,\delta)}(x) = \frac{n!\,\Gamma(\lambda+1)}{2\Gamma(n+\lambda+1)\,\Gamma(n+\lambda+1+\delta)} \times$$
$$\sum_{m=0}^n \frac{(\Gamma(-m+n+\delta+1)\,\Gamma(n+\lambda+1) + (-1)^m\,\Gamma(n+\delta+1)\,\Gamma(1-m+n+\lambda))}{m!\,(n-m)!\,\Gamma(-m+n+\delta+1)\Gamma(1-m+n+\lambda)} \times \tag{29}$$
$$\Gamma(-m+2n+\delta+\lambda+1)\,E_{n-m}(x).$$

Proof. Formula (29) can be immediately deduced for Formula (19) by setting $q = 0$. □

Corollary 9. *Let n be a non-negative integer. The following are the ultraspherical-Euler, Legendre-Euler, first-kind-Euler, and second-kind-Euler connection formulas*

$$\tilde{G}_n^{(\delta)}(x) = \frac{n!\,\Gamma\left(\delta+\frac{1}{2}\right)}{\Gamma(n+2\delta)} \sum_{m=0}^{\lfloor \frac{n}{2} \rfloor} \frac{\Gamma(2(n-m+\delta))}{(2m)!\,(n-2m)!\,\Gamma\left(\frac{1}{2}+n-2m+\delta\right)} E_{n-2m}(x),$$

$$\tilde{P}_n(x) = \sum_{m=0}^{\lfloor \frac{n}{2} \rfloor} \frac{(2n-2m)!}{(2m)!\,((n-2m)!)^2} E_{n-2m}(x),$$

$$\tilde{T}_n(x) = n\sqrt{\pi} \sum_{m=0}^{\lfloor \frac{n}{2} \rfloor} \frac{(2n-2m-1)!}{(2m)!\,(n-2m)!\,\Gamma\left(n-2m+\frac{1}{2}\right)} E_{n-2m}(x),$$

$$\tilde{U}_n(x) = \frac{1}{2}\sqrt{\pi} \sum_{m=0}^{\lfloor \frac{n}{2} \rfloor} \frac{(2n-2m+1)!}{(2m)!\,(n-2m)!\,\Gamma\left(n-2m+\frac{3}{2}\right)} E_{n-2j}(x).$$

Proof. Corollary 9 is a special case of Corollary 4 for $\ell = 0$. □

Corollary 10. *The following are the shifted third-kind Chebyshev–Euler and shifted fourth-kind Chebyshev–Euler connection formulas.*

$$\tilde{V}_n(x) = \frac{1}{2}\sqrt{\pi}\left(\sum_{m=0}^{\lfloor\frac{n}{2}\rfloor}\frac{(2n-2m+1)!}{(2m)!\,(n-2m)!\,\Gamma\left(n-2m+\frac{3}{2}\right)}E_{n-2m}(x)\right.\tag{30}$$
$$\left.-\sum_{m=0}^{\lfloor\frac{n-1}{2}\rfloor}\frac{(2n-2m-1)!}{(2m)!\,(n-2m-1)!\,\Gamma\left(n-2m+\frac{1}{2}\right)}E_{n-2m-1}(x)\right),$$

$$\tilde{W}_n(x) = \frac{1}{2}\sqrt{\pi}\left(\sum_{m=0}^{\lfloor\frac{n}{2}\rfloor}\frac{(2n-2m+1)!}{(2m)!\,(n-2m)!\,\Gamma\left(n-2m+\frac{3}{2}\right)}E_{n-2m}(x)\right.\tag{31}$$
$$\left.+\sum_{m=0}^{\lfloor\frac{n-1}{2}\rfloor}\frac{(2n-2m-1)!}{(2m)!\,(n-2m-1)!\,\Gamma\left(n-2m+\frac{1}{2}\right)}E_{n-2m-1}(x)\right).$$

Proof. Formulas (30) and (31) are, respectively, special ones of Formulas (21) and (22) only by setting $\ell = 0$. □

Corollary 11. *The following are the generalized Laguerre–Euler and Schröder–Euler connection formulas:*

$$L_n^{(\lambda)}(x) = \frac{1}{2}\Gamma(n+\lambda+1)\sum_{m=0}^{n}\frac{(-1)^{n+m}(1+{_1F_1}(-m;n-m+\lambda+1;1))}{m!\,(n-m)!\,\Gamma(n-m+\lambda+1)}E_{n-m}(x),\tag{32}$$

$$S_n(x) = \frac{1}{2(n+1)!}\sum_{m=0}^{n}\frac{(n+1)!\,(2n-m)!+(2n)!\,(n-m+1)!\,{_2F_1}\left(\begin{matrix}-m,-n-1\\-2n\end{matrix}\middle|-1\right)}{m!\,(n-m)!\,(n-m+1)!}E_{n-m}(x).\tag{33}$$

Proof. Formulas (32) and (33) are, respectively, special ones of Formula (23) and (24) only by setting $\ell = 0$. □

5. Application to Compute Some New Integrals

This section is confined to developing an application to the connection formulas between different polynomials and the Euler polynomials. In this regard, new formulas are developed for computing some definite integrals of the products of different symmetric and non-symmetric polynomials with Euler polynomials. In fact, the connection coefficients aid in the evaluation of the desired definite integrals.

5.1. Definite Integrals for the Product of Euler Polynomials with Symmetric Polynomials

This section is interested in introducing a new explicit formula for evaluating a definite integral for the product of the Euler polynomial of any degree with a symmetric polynomial of any degree. After that, we apply this general formula to evaluate the definite integral for the product of Euler polynomials with some celebrated symmetric polynomials.

Theorem 8. *Let $\phi_n(x)$ be any symmetric polynomial that can be expressed as in (2), and let it have the following connection formula with Euler polynomials:*

$$\phi_n(x) = \sum_{r=0}^{\lfloor\frac{n}{2}\rfloor} R_{r,n}\,E_{n-2r}(x) + \sum_{r=0}^{\lfloor\frac{n-1}{2}\rfloor} \tilde{R}_{r,n}\,E_{n-2r-1}(x).\tag{34}$$

The following integral formula is valid:

$$\int_0^1 \phi_n(x)\, E_m(x)\, dx = 4m! \left(\sum_{r=0}^{\lfloor \frac{n}{2} \rfloor} \frac{(-1)^n (2^{m+n-2r+2}-1)(n-2r)!}{(m+n-2r+2)!} B_{m+n-2r+2}\, R_{r,n} \right.$$
$$\left. + \sum_{r=0}^{\lfloor \frac{n-1}{2} \rfloor} \frac{(-1)^{n+1}(2^{m+n-2r+1}-1)(n-2r-1)!}{(m+n-2r+1)!} B_{m+n-2r+1}\, \tilde{R}_{r,n} \right), \quad (35)$$

and B_n are the well-known Bernoulli numbers.

Proof. The connection Formula (34) immediately yields

$$\int_0^1 \phi_n(x)\, E_m(x)\, dx = \sum_{r=0}^{\lfloor \frac{n}{2} \rfloor} R_{r,n} \int_0^1 E_m(x) E_{n-2r}(x)\, dx + \sum_{r=0}^{\lfloor \frac{n-1}{2} \rfloor} \tilde{R}_{r,n} \int_0^1 E_m(x) E_{n-2r-1}(x)\, dx. \quad (36)$$

In virtue of the well-known formula [29]:

$$\int_0^1 E_m(x) E_n(x)\, dx = F_{m,n} = \frac{4(-1)^n (2^{m+n+2}-1)\, n!\, m!}{(m+n+2)!} B_{m+n+2}. \quad (37)$$

Formula (36) can be transformed into the following formula:

$$\int_0^1 \phi_n(x)\, E_m(x)\, dx = \sum_{r=0}^{\lfloor \frac{n}{2} \rfloor} R_{r,n}\, F_{m,n-2r} + \sum_{r=0}^{\lfloor \frac{n-1}{2} \rfloor} \tilde{R}_{r,n}\, F_{m,n-2r-1},$$

and this leads to the following integral formula:

$$\int_0^1 \phi_n(x)\, E_m(x)\, dx = 4m! \left(\sum_{r=0}^{\lfloor \frac{n}{2} \rfloor} \frac{(-1)^n (2^{m+n-2r+2}-1)(n-2r)!}{(m+n-2r+2)!} B_{m+n-2r+2}\, R_{r,n} \right.$$
$$\left. + \sum_{r=0}^{\lfloor \frac{n-1}{2} \rfloor} \frac{(-1)^{n+1}(2^{m+n-2r+1}-1)(n-2r-1)!}{(m+n-2r+1)!} B_{m+n-2r+1}\, \tilde{R}_{r,n} \right).$$

This proves Theorem 8. □

Remark 5. *As a consequence of Theorem 8 along with the connection formulas stated in Section 4, several new definite integral formulas of the product of some symmetric polynomials with the Euler polynomials can be obtained. The following corollaries exhibit these formulas.*

Corollary 12. *For all non-negative integers m and n, the following definite integral formula holds:*

$$\int_0^1 G_n^{(\delta)}(x)\, E_m(x)\, dx = \frac{(-1)^n m!\, n!\, \Gamma\left(\delta + \frac{1}{2}\right)}{\sqrt{\pi}\, \Gamma(n+2\delta)} \sum_{r=0}^{\lfloor \frac{n}{2} \rfloor} \frac{2^{n-2r+2\delta}\left(2^{m+n-2r+2}-1\right)}{r!\, (2r)!\, (m+n-2r+2)!} \times$$
$$\left((-1)^r (2r)!\, \Gamma(n-r+\delta) + \frac{4^r r!\, \Gamma(n+\delta)\left(-n+r-\delta+\frac{1}{2}\right)_r}{(1-n-\delta)_r} \right) B_{m+n-2r+2} \quad (38)$$
$$+ \frac{2^{n+2\delta} m!\, n!\, \Gamma\left(\delta+\frac{1}{2}\right)\Gamma(n+\delta)}{\sqrt{\pi}\, \Gamma(n+2\delta)} \sum_{r=0}^{\lfloor \frac{n-1}{2} \rfloor} \frac{(-1)^{n+1}\left(2^{m+n-2r+1}-1\right)\left(-n+r-\delta+\frac{3}{2}\right)_r}{(2r+1)!\, (m+n-2r+1)!\, (1-n-\delta)_r} B_{m+n-2r+1}.$$

Proof. This result is a direct consequence of the connection Formula (25) along with the integral Formula (35). □

The following three specific formulas of Formula (38) are concerned with the definite integral formulas for the products of Legendre and Chebyshev polynomials of the first and second kinds with Euler polynomials.

Corollary 13. *Let m and n be any non-negative integers. The following definite integral formulas apply:*

$$\int_0^1 P_n(x) E_m(x)\, dx =$$

$$\frac{(-1)^n 2^{n+1} m!}{\sqrt{\pi}} \sum_{r=0}^{\lfloor \frac{n}{2} \rfloor} \frac{\left(2^{m+n-2r+2} - 1\right) \left(\frac{\left(-\frac{1}{4}\right)^r \Gamma\left(n-r+\frac{1}{2}\right)}{r!} + \frac{\Gamma\left(n+\frac{1}{2}\right)(n-2r+1)_r}{(2r)!\,(n-r+\frac{1}{2})_r} \right)}{(m+n-2r+2)!} B_{m+n-2r+2} \quad (39)$$

$$+ (-1)^{n+1} 2^{2-n} m! \sum_{r=0}^{\lfloor \frac{n-1}{2} \rfloor} \frac{\left(2^{m+n+1} - 4^r\right)(2n-2r-1)!}{(2r+1)!\,(n-2r-1)!\,(m+n-2r+1)!} B_{m+n-2r+1},$$

$$\int_0^1 T_n(x) E_m(x)\, dx =$$

$$m!\, n! \left(\sum_{r=0}^{\lfloor \frac{n}{2} \rfloor} \frac{(-2)^{n-2r} \left(2^{m+n-2r+2} - 1\right)\left((-1)^r (2r)! + 4^r r! \left(\frac{1}{2}+n-2r\right)_r\right)}{r!\,(2r)!\,(m+n-2r+2)!\,(n-r)_r} B_{m+n-2r+2} \right. \quad (40)$$

$$\left. + \sum_{r=0}^{\lfloor \frac{n-1}{2} \rfloor} \frac{(-2)^{n-2r}\left(-2^{m+n+1} + 4^r\right)\left(-\frac{1}{2}+n-2r\right)_r}{(2r+1)!\,(m+n+1-2r)!\,(n-r)_r} B_{m+n-2r+1} \right), \quad n \geq 1,$$

$$\int_0^1 U_n(x) E_m(x)\, dx =$$

$$m! \left(\sum_{r=0}^{\lfloor \frac{n}{2} \rfloor} \frac{(-2)^{n-2r+1}\left(-2^{m+n+2} + 4^r\right) n! \left(\left(-\frac{1}{4}\right)^r (2r)! + r!\left(n-2r+\frac{3}{2}\right)_r\right)}{r!\,(2r)!\,(m+n-2r+2)!\,(n-r+1)_r} B_{m+n-2r+2} \right. \quad (41)$$

$$\left. + n! \sum_{r=0}^{\lfloor \frac{n-1}{2} \rfloor} \frac{(-2)^{n-2r+1}\left(2^{m+n+1} - 4^r\right)\left(\frac{1}{2}+n-2r\right)_r}{(2r+1)!\,(m+n+1-2r)!\,(n-r+1)_r} B_{m+n-2r+1} \right).$$

Proof. Formulas (39), (40) and (41) can be obtained as special cases of Formula (38) by setting $\delta = \frac{1}{2}, 0, 1$, respectively. □

The following corollary is concerned with the definite integrals of the two generalized Fibonacci and generalized Lucas polynomials with the Euler polynomials.

Corollary 14. *For all non-negative integers m and n, the following definite integral formulas apply:*

$$\int_0^1 F_n^{A,B}(x)\, E_m(x)\, dx = 2\, A^n\, m! \times$$

$$\sum_{r=0}^{\lfloor \frac{n}{2} \rfloor} \frac{(-1)^n \left(2^{m+n-2r+2} - 1\right) \left(A^{-2r} B^r (n-r)!\,(2r)! + n!\, r!\, {}_2F_1\!\left(\begin{array}{c} -r, -r+\frac{1}{2} \\ -n \end{array} \bigg| -\frac{4B}{A^2} \right) \right)}{r!\,(2r)!\,(m+n-2r+2)!} \times \quad (42)$$

$$B_{m+n-2r+2} + 2A^n m!\, n! \sum_{r=0}^{\lfloor \frac{n-1}{2} \rfloor} \frac{(-1)^{n+1}\left(2^{m+n-2r+1} - 1\right) {}_2F_1\!\left(\begin{array}{c} -r, -r-\frac{1}{2} \\ -n \end{array} \bigg| -\frac{4B}{A^2} \right)}{(2r+1)!\,(m+n-2r+1)!} B_{m+n-2r+1},$$

$$\int_0^1 L_n^{R,S}(x) E_m(x)\, dx = 2(-1)^n m! \sum_{r=0}^{\lfloor \frac{n}{2} \rfloor} \frac{(2^{m+n-2r+2}-1) R^n}{r!\,(2r)!\,(m+n-2r+2)!} \times$$

$$\left(n R^{-2r} S^r (n-r-1)!\,(2r)! + n!\,r!\, {}_2F_1\left(\begin{array}{c}-r, -r+\frac{1}{2} \\ 1-n\end{array}\bigg| -\frac{4S}{R^2}\right)\right) B_{m+n-2r+2} \tag{43}$$

$$+ 2(-1)^{n+1} m!\, n!\, R^n \sum_{r=0}^{\lfloor \frac{n-1}{2} \rfloor} \frac{(2^{m+n-2r+1}-1)\, {}_2F_1\left(\begin{array}{c}-r, -r-\frac{1}{2} \\ 1-n\end{array}\bigg| -\frac{4S}{R^2}\right)}{(2r+1)!\,(m+n-2r+1)!} B_{m+n-2r+1}, \quad n \geq 1.$$

Proof. Formulas (42) and (43) can be obtained, respectively, as by the application to Theorem 8 along with the two connection Formulas (26) and (27). □

Corollary 15. *For all non-negative integers m and n, the following definite integral formula applies:*

$$\int_0^1 H_n(x) E_m(x)\, dx = m!\, n! \times$$

$$\left(\sum_{r=0}^{\lfloor \frac{n}{2} \rfloor} \frac{(-1)^{n-r} 2^{n-2r+1} (2^{m+n-2r+2}-1)\left(1 + {}_1F_1\left(-r; \frac{1}{2}; 1\right)\right)}{r!\,(m+n-2r+2)!} B_{m+n-2r+2} \right.$$

$$\left. + \sum_{r=0}^{\lfloor \frac{n-1}{2} \rfloor} \frac{(-2)^{n-2r+1}(2^{m+n+1}-4^r)}{(2r+1)!\,(m+n-2r+1)!} U\left(-r, \frac{3}{2}, 1\right) B_{m+n-2r+1} \right).$$

Proof. Direct application to Theorem 8 making use of the connection formula (28) yields the desired result. □

5.2. Definite Integrals for the Product of Euler Polynomials with Non-Symmetric Polynomials

This section focuses on developing a new closed expression for a definite integral for the product of the Euler polynomial of any degree with any non-symmetric polynomial of any degree. Furthermore, it focuses on some specific definite integrals for the product of Euler polynomials with some celebrated non-symmetric polynomials. In this regard, the following theorem will be stated and proved.

Theorem 9. *Let $\phi_n(x)$ by any non-symmetric polynomial that is connected with Euler polynomials by the following formula:*

$$\phi_n(x) = \sum_{r=0}^n S_{r,n}\, E_{n-r}(x). \tag{44}$$

The following integral formula applies:

$$\int_0^1 \phi_n(x)\, E_m(x)\, dx = 4 m! \sum_{r=0}^n \frac{(-1)^{n-r}(2^{m+n-r+2}-1)(n-r)!}{(m+n-r+2)!} B_{m+n-r+2} S_{r,n}.$$

Proof. Based on the connection Formula (44), one has the following integral formula:

$$\int_0^1 \phi_n(x)\, E_m(x)\, dx = \sum_{r=0}^n S_{r,n}\, F_{m,n-r},$$

where $F_{m,n}$ are given by (37). This leads to the formula

$$\int_0^1 \phi_n(x)\, E_m(x)\, dx = 4 m! \sum_{r=0}^n \frac{(-1)^{n-r}(2^{m+n-r+2}-1)(n-r)!}{(m+n-r+2)!} B_{m+n-r+2} S_{r,n}.$$

□

Remark 6. As a consequence of Theorem 9, along with the connection formulas in Section 4.2, several new definite integral formulas for the product of some non-symmetric polynomials with the Euler polynomials can be obtained. The following corollaries exhibit some of these integral formulas.

Corollary 16. For all positive integers m and n, the following integral formulas hold:

$$\int_0^1 \tilde{V}_n^{(\lambda,\delta)}(x) E_m(x)\, dx = \frac{2\, m!\, n!\, \Gamma(\lambda+1)}{\Gamma(n+\lambda+1)\Gamma(n+\delta+1+\lambda)} \times$$
$$\sum_{r=0}^n \frac{(-1)^{n-r} \left(2^{m+n-r+2}-1\right)\Gamma(2n-r+\delta+\lambda+1)}{r!\,(m+n+2-r)!\,\Gamma(n-r+\delta+1)\,\Gamma(n-r+\lambda+1)} \times \quad (45)$$
$$\left(\Gamma(n-r+\delta+1)\Gamma(n+\lambda+1) + (-1)^r \Gamma(n+\delta+1)\Gamma(n-r+\lambda+1)\right) B_{m+n-r+2}.$$

Proof. The proof is based on utilizing Theorem 9 along with the connection Formula (29). □

The following two corollaries give six special formulas of Formula (45).

Corollary 17. For all positive integers m and n, the following integral formulas hold:

$$\int_0^1 \tilde{G}_n^{(\delta)}(x) E_m(x)\, dx = \frac{4\,(-1)^n\, m!\, n!\, \Gamma\left(\delta+\tfrac{1}{2}\right)}{\Gamma(n+2\delta)} \sum_{r=0}^{\lfloor \tfrac{n}{2} \rfloor} \frac{\left(2^{m+n-2r+2}-1\right)\Gamma(2(n-r+\delta))}{(2r)!\,(m+n-2r+2)!\,\Gamma\left(n-2r+\delta+\tfrac{1}{2}\right)} \times \quad (46)$$
$$B_{m+n-2r+2},$$

$$\int_0^1 \tilde{P}_n(x) E_m(x)\, dx = 4\, m!\, (-1)^n \sum_{r=0}^{\lfloor \tfrac{n}{2} \rfloor} \frac{\left(2^{m+n-2r+2}-1\right)(2n-2r)!}{(2r)!\,(n-2r)!\,(m+n-2r+2)!} B_{m+n-2r+2}, \quad (47)$$

$$\int_0^1 \tilde{T}_n(x) E_m(x)\, dx = 4\,(-1)^n\, n\sqrt{\pi}\, m! \sum_{r=0}^{\lfloor \tfrac{n}{2} \rfloor} \frac{\left(2^{m+n-2r+2}-1\right)(2n-2r-1)!}{(2r)!\,\Gamma\!\left(n-2r+\tfrac{1}{2}\right)(m+n-2r+2)!} B_{m+n-2r+2}, \quad (48)$$

$$\int_0^1 \tilde{U}_n(x) E_m(x)\, dx = 2\,(-1)^n\, m!\, \sqrt{\pi} \sum_{r=0}^{\lfloor \tfrac{n}{2} \rfloor} \frac{\left(2^{m+n+2-2r}-1\right)(2n-2r+1)!}{(2r)!\,\Gamma\!\left(n-2r+\tfrac{3}{2}\right)(m+n-2r+2)!} B_{m+n-2r+2}. \quad (49)$$

Proof. Formula (46) can be obtained from the general Formula (45) if both λ and δ are replaced by $\left(\delta-\tfrac{1}{2}\right)$. Formulas (47), (48) and (49) are special ones of Formula (46) for the cases $\delta = \tfrac{1}{2}, 0, 1$, respectively. □

Corollary 18. For all positive integers m and n, the following integral formulas hold:

$$\int_0^1 \tilde{V}_n(x) E_m(x)\, dx = \sqrt{\pi}\, m! \times$$
$$\sum_{r=0}^n \frac{(-1)^{n-r}\left(2^{m+n-r+2}-1\right)(1+(-1)^r+2(1+(-1)^r)n-2r)(2n-r)!}{r!\,\Gamma\!\left(n-r+\tfrac{3}{2}\right)(m+n+2-r)!} B_{m+n-r+2}, \quad (50)$$

$$\int_0^1 \tilde{W}_n(x) E_m(x)\, dx = \sqrt{\pi}\, m! \times$$
$$\sum_{r=0}^n \frac{(-1)^{n-r}\left(2^{m+n-r+2}-1\right)(1+2n+(-1)^r(2n-2r+1))(2n-r)!}{r!\,\Gamma\!\left(n-r+\tfrac{3}{2}\right)(m+n+2-r)!} B_{m+n-r+2}. \quad (51)$$

Proof. Formulas (50) and (51) can be obtained as direct special cases of Formula (45) for the three cases $\lambda = -\tfrac{1}{2}, \delta = \tfrac{1}{2}$, and $\lambda = \tfrac{1}{2}, \delta = -\tfrac{1}{2}$, respectively. □

Corollary 19. For all positive integers m and n, the following integral formula holds:

$$\int_0^1 L_n^{(\lambda)}(x) E_m(x)\, dx = 2\, m!\, \Gamma(n+\lambda+1) \sum_{r=0}^n \frac{(2^{m+n-r+2}-1)(1+{}_1F_1(-r;n-r+\lambda+1;1))}{r!\,(m+n-r+2)!\,\Gamma(n-r+\lambda+1)} \times$$
$$B_{m+n-r+2}.$$

Proof. Direct application to Theorem 9, taking into consideration the connection Formula (32), will yield the desired result. □

Corollary 20. *For all positive integers m and n, the following integral formula holds:*

$$\int_0^1 S_n(x)\, E_m(x)\, dx = 2m! \times$$
$$\sum_{r=0}^n \frac{(-1)^{n-r}\left(2^{m+n-r+2}-1\right)\left((n+1)!\,(2n-r)! + (2n)!\,(n-r+1)!\ {}_2F_1\!\left(\begin{array}{c}-r,-n-1\\-2n\end{array}\bigg|-1\right)\right)}{(n+1)!\,r!\,(n-r+1)!\,(m+n+2-r)!} \times$$
$$B_{m+n-r+2}.$$

Proof. Direct application to Theorem 9 taking into consideration the connection Formula (33) will yield the desired result. □

6. Concluding Remarks

In this article, we developed new identities involving the Euler polynomials. We established new derivative expressions for different polynomials in terms of Euler polynomials. Connection formulas between various polynomials and the Euler polynomials. We proved that the connection coefficients are in many cases simple and free of any hypergeometric functions, but in other cases, they involve certain hypergeometric functions. An interesting application is provided where various definite integrals involving Euler polynomials are computed exactly in closed forms to highlight the significance of the derived connection formulas. We intend to derive further identities and integrals involving Euler polynomials in the near future based on other formulas between different polynomials and Euler polynomials. We think that the majority of the findings in this work are novel, and they might be applicable to other areas of mathematics.

Author Contributions: W.M.A.-E. contributed to conceptualization, methodology, software, validation, formal analysis, investigation, Writing—Original draft, Writing—review & editing. A.K.A. contributed to methodology, validation, investigation, original draft preparation, and funding Acquisition. All authors have read and agreed to the published version of the manuscript.

Funding: The second author: Amr Kamel Amin (akgadelrab@uqu.edu.sa) is funded by the Deanship for Research and Innovation, Ministry of Education in Saudi Arabia.

Data Availability Statement: Not applicable.

Acknowledgments: The authors extend their appreciation to the Deanship for Research and Innovation, Ministry of Education in Saudi Arabia for funding this research work through the project number: IFP22UQU4331287DSR038.

Conflicts of Interest: The authors declare no conflict of interest.

References

1. Singh, H. Jacobi collocation method for the fractional advection-dispersion equation arising in porous media. *Numer. Methods Partial. Differ. Equ.* **2022**, *38*, 636–653. [CrossRef]
2. Yalçinbaş, S.; Aynigül, M.; Sezer, M. A collocation method using Hermite polynomials for approximate solution of pantograph equations. *J. Frankl. Inst.* **2011**, *348*, 1128–1139. [CrossRef]
3. Gülsu, M.; Gürbüz, B.; Öztürk, Y.; Sezer, M. Laguerre polynomial approach for solving linear delay difference equations. *Appl. Math. Comput.* **2011**, *217*, 6765–6776. [CrossRef]

4. Doha, E.H.; Abd-Elhameed, W.M.; Bassuony, M.A. On using third and fourth kinds Chebyshev operational matrices for solving Lane-Emden type equations. *Rom. J. Phys.* **2015**, *60*, 281–292.
5. Mittal, A.K.; Balyan, L.K. Chebyshev pseudospectral approximation of two dimensional fractional Schrodinger equation on a convex and rectangular domain. *AIMS Math.* **2020**, *5*, 1642–1662. [CrossRef]
6. Ali, K.K.; Abd El Salam, M.A.; Mohamed, M.S. Chebyshev fifth-kind series approximation for generalized space fractional partial differential equations. *AIMS Math.* **2022**, *7*, 7759–7780. [CrossRef]
7. Abd-Elhameed, W.M.; Ahmed, H.M. Tau and Galerkin operational matrices of derivatives for treating singular and Emden–Fowler third-order-type equations. *Int. J. Mod. Phys.* **2022**, *33*, 2250061. [CrossRef]
8. Abd-Elhameed, W.M.; Zeyada, N.A. New formulas including convolution, connection and radicals formulas of k-Fibonacci and k-Lucas polynomials. *Indian J. Pure Appl. Math.* **2022**, *53*, 1006–1016. [CrossRef]
9. Abd-Elhameed, W.M.; Philippou, A.N.; Zeyada, N.A. Novel results for two generalized classes of Fibonacci and Lucas polynomials and their uses in the reduction of some radicals. *Mathematics* **2022**, *10*, 2342. [CrossRef]
10. Abd-Elhameed, W.M.; Amin, A.K.; Zeyada, N.A. Some new identities of a type of generalized numbers involving four parameters. *AIMS Math.* **2022**, *7*, 12962–12980. [CrossRef]
11. Aceto, L.; Malonek, H.R.; Tomaz, G. A unified matrix approach to the representation of Appell polynomials. *Integral Transform. Spec. Funct.* **2015**, *26*, 426–441. [CrossRef]
12. Costabile, F.A.; Gualtieri, M.I.; Napoli, A. General bivariate Appell polynomials via matrix calculus and related interpolation hints. *Mathematics* **2021**, *9*, 964. [CrossRef]
13. Ismail, M.E.H.; van Assche, W. *Classical and Quantum Orthogonal Polynomials in One Variable*; Cambridge University Press: Cambridge, UK, 2005; Volume 13.
14. Srivastava, H.M.; Pinter, A. Remarks on some relationships between the Bernoulli and Euler polynomials. *Appl. Math. Lett.* **2004**, *17*, 375–380. [CrossRef]
15. Kim, T. Some properties on the integral of the product of several Euler polynomials. *Quaest. Math.* **2015**, *38*, 553–562. [CrossRef]
16. Pintér, A.; Rakaczki, C. On the decomposability of the linear combinations of Euler polynomials with odd degrees. *Symmetry* **2019**, *11*, 739. [CrossRef]
17. Kim, T.; Ryoo, C.S. Some identities for Euler and Bernoulli polynomials and their zeros. *Axioms* **2018**, *7*, 56. [CrossRef]
18. Kim, D.S.; Kim, T.; Lee, S.S.; Kim, Y.H. Some identities for the product of two Bernoulli and Euler polynomials. *Adv. Differ. Equ.* **2012**, *2012*, 95. [CrossRef]
19. Masjed-Jamei, M.; Beyki, M.R.; Koepf, W. A new type of Euler polynomials and numbers. *Mediterr. J. Math.* **2018**, *15*, 1–17. [CrossRef]
20. Tabinda, N.; Mohd, S.; Serkan, A. A new class of Appell-type Changhee-Euler polynomials and related properties. *AIMS Math.* **2021**, *6*, 13566–13579.
21. Alam, N.; Khan, W.A.; Ryoo, C.S. A note on Bell-based Apostol-type Frobenius-Euler polynomials of complex variable with its certain applications. *Mathematics* **2022**, *10*, 2109. [CrossRef]
22. Rezabeyk, S.; Abbasbandy, S.; Shivanian, E. Solving fractional-order delay integro-differential equations using operational matrix based on fractional-order Euler polynomials. *Math. Sci.* **2020**, *14*, 97–107. [CrossRef]
23. Behera, S.; Ray, S.S. An efficient numerical method based on Euler wavelets for solving fractional order pantograph Volterra delay-integro-differential equations. *J. Comput. Appl. Math.* **2022**, *406*, 113825. [CrossRef]
24. Wang, Y.; Huang, J.; Wen, X. Two-dimensional Euler polynomials solutions of two-dimensional Volterra integral equations of fractional order. *Appl. Numer. Math.* **2021**, *163*, 77–95. [CrossRef]
25. Doha, E.H.; Abd-Elhameed, W.M.; Bassuony, M.A. On the coefficients of differentiated expansions and derivatives of Chebyshev polynomials of the third and fourth kinds. *Acta Math. Sci.* **2015**, *35*, 326–338. [CrossRef]
26. Abd-Elhameed, W.M.; Alkenedri, A.M. Spectral solutions of linear and nonlinear BVPs using certain Jacobi polynomials generalizing third-and fourth-kinds of Chebyshev polynomials. *CMES Comput. Model. Eng. Sci.* **2021**, *126*, 955–989. [CrossRef]
27. Abd-Elhameed, W.M. Novel expressions for the derivatives of sixth kind Chebyshev polynomials: Spectral solution of the non-linear one-dimensional Burgers' equation. *Fractal Fract.* **2021**, *5*, 53. [CrossRef]
28. Abd-Elhameed, W.M. New formulae between Jacobi polynomials and some fractional Jacobi functions generalizing some connection formulae. *Anal. Math. Phys.* **2019**, *9*, 73–98. [CrossRef]
29. Djordjevic, G.B.; Milovanovic, G.V. *Special Classes of Polynomials*; University of Nis, Faculty of Technology Leskovac, Leskovac, Serbia, 2014.
30. Abd-Elhameed, W.M. New product and linearization formulae of Jacobi polynomials of certain parameters. *Integral Transform. Spec. Funct.* **2015**, *26*, 586–599. [CrossRef]
31. Abd-Elhameed, W.M.; Ali, A. New specific and general linearization formulas of some classes of Jacobi polynomials. *Mathematics* **2020**, *9*, 74. [CrossRef]
32. Andrews, G.E.; Askey, R.; Roy, R. *Special Functions*; Cambridge University Press: Cambridge, UK, 1999; Volume 71.
33. Mason, J.C.; Handscomb, D.C. *Chebyshev Polynomials*; Chapman and Hall: New York, NY, USA; CRC: Boca Raton, FL, USA, 2003.
34. Abd-Elhameed, W.M.; Badah, B.M. New approaches to the general linearization problem of Jacobi polynomials based on moments and connection formulas. *Mathematics* **2021**, *9*, 1573. [CrossRef]
35. Koshy, T. *Fibonacci and Lucas Numbers with Applications*; John Wiley & Sons: Hoboken, NJ, USA, 2011; Volume 51.

36. Koepf, W. *Hypergeometric Summation*, 2nd ed.; Springer Universitext Series; Springer: Berlin/Heidelberg, Germany, 2014.
37. Rainville, E.D. *Special Functions*; The Maximalan Company: New York, NY, USA, 1960.
38. Liu, J.C. A supercongruence involving Delannoy numbers and Schröder numbers. *J. Number Theory* **2016**, *168*, 117–127. [CrossRef]

Article

Fractional Clique Collocation Technique for Numerical Simulations of Fractional-Order Brusselator Chemical Model

Mohammad Izadi [1] and Hari Mohan Srivastava [2,3,4,5,*]

[1] Department of Applied Mathematics, Faculty of Mathematics and Computer, Shahid Bahonar University of Kerman, Kerman 76169-14111, Iran
[2] Department of Mathematics and Statistics, University of Victoria, Victoria, BC V8W 3R4, Canada
[3] Department of Medical Research, China Medical University Hospital, China Medical University, Taichung 40402, Taiwan
[4] Department of Mathematics and Informatics, Azerbaijan University, 71 Jeyhun Hajibeyli Street, AZ1007 Baku, Azerbaijan
[5] Center for Converging Humanities, Kyung Hee University, 26 Kyungheedae-ro, Dongdaemun-gu, Seoul 02447, Republic of Korea
* Correspondence: harimsri@math.uvic.ca

Abstract: The primary focus of this research study is in the development of an effective hybrid matrix method to solve a class of nonlinear systems of equations of fractional order arising in the modeling of autocatalytic chemical reaction problems. The fractional operator is considered in the sense of Liouville–Caputo. The proposed approach relies on the combination of the quasi-linearization technique and the spectral collocation strategy based on generalized clique bases. The main feature of the hybrid approach is that it converts the governing nonlinear fractional-order systems into a linear algebraic system of equations, which is solved in each iteration. In a weighted L_2 norm, we prove the error and convergence analysis of the proposed algorithm. By using various model parameters in the numerical examples, we show the computational efficacy as well as the accuracy of our approach. Comparisons with existing available schemes show the high accuracy and robustness of the designed hybrid matrix collocation technique.

Keywords: clique functions; collocation points; convergent analysis; fractional Brusselator system; Liouville–Caputo derivative

1. Introduction

The Brusselator is a theoretical model for a type of autocatalytic reaction. In fact, this model is a common nonlinear reaction in which a reactant species interacts with other species to increase its production rate. The Brusselator model was proposed by Prigogine and Lefever [1] in 1968. It is also known that the Belousov–Zhabotinsky model and the chemical reactions of the Brusselator are the same [2–4]. By U, V, D, A, B, and E, we denote the chemical components in the chemical reaction. Generally, the reaction process can be described by the following four steps:

$$A \to U,$$
$$B + U \to V + D,$$
$$2U + V \to 3U,$$
$$U \to E.$$

We now assume that the species A and B are sufficiently available and can thus be modeled at a constant concentration. Further, note that the final products E and D are removed once they are produced from the reaction process. Under scaling the rate constant to unity, the rate equations become as follows

$$\begin{cases} \frac{d}{dt}\{U\} = \{A\} + \{U\}^2\{V\} - \{B\}\{U\} - \{U\}, \\ \frac{d}{dt}\{V\} = \{B\}\{U\} - \{U\}^2\{V\}. \end{cases} \quad (1)$$

Fractional integrals and derivatives have attracted considerable attention over the last decades. Due to a wide range of applications from theory to practice, they have gained increasing popularity in the modeling of various natural phenomena in engineering, physics, chemistry, economics, etc. It is found that the non-integer derivatives and integrals are more appropriate for describing the properties of several real processes and materials, see cf. [5,6]. However, the solutions to most fractional differential equations do not exist in terms of elementary functions. Therefore, it is essential to develop computational and approximate procedures for the numerical evaluation of fractional differential equations.

Our main goal is to study the fractional counterpart of the Brusselator model (1). To be precise, this research paper presents a power series solution based upon the (fractional) version of clique functions implemented in matrix formulation for the following nonlinear fractional-order Brusselator system of two equations

$$\begin{cases} {}^{LC}\mathcal{D}_\tau^\lambda u(\tau) = \theta - (\eta + 1)\, u(\tau) + u^2(\tau)\, v(\tau), \\ {}^{LC}\mathcal{D}_\tau^\lambda v(\tau) = \eta\, u(\tau) - u^2(\tau)\, v(\tau), \end{cases} \quad \tau \in [0,1], \quad (2)$$

where θ and η are two positive real numbers. Moreover, ${}^{LC}\mathcal{D}_\tau^\lambda$ presents the Liouville–Caputo fractional derivative of order $\lambda \in (0,1]$. The following initial conditions will accompany the above system, given as

$$u(0) = u_0, \quad v(0) = v_0. \quad (3)$$

If we set $\lambda = 1$, the classical system of the Brusselator system (1) will be obtained. The integer-order model of the Brusselator has been solved by three numerical approaches, including the Implicit Runge–Kutta method, the Adams method, and the Backward differential formula in [7].

1.1. Literature Review and Related Works

The fractional-order system (2) has been considered in the literature by many research scholars from different points of dynamic systems and numerical behaviors. The stability of the fractional Brusselator system was addressed in [8–10]. In [11], the existence of a limit cycle was proven numerically by the Adams–Bashforth–Moulton approach. The authors of [12,13] developed some nonstandard finite difference (NSFD) methods to solve (2) numerically. As a semi-analytical approach, the variational iteration method is devised in [14]. The polynomial least square technique was investigated in [15]. The operational matrix methods based on Bernstein and Legendre wavelet functions were studied in [16,17], respectively. The authors of [18] further developed three explicit and implicit techniques based on product integration, NFSD, and multi-step procedures. In all mentioned works above, the underlying fractional operator was taken as the Liouville–Caputo fractional derivative. However, let us mention that the Brusselator model with fractional derivatives in the sense of Liouville–Caputo, Caputo–Fabrizio, and Atangana–Baleanu was considered in [19] recently. In this paper, the dynamic characteristics of the model under three fractional derivatives have been investigated, and a three-stage iterative approach was also developed for the model under consideration. In addition, in [20], the fractal-fractional differential operators related to the power law, exponential decay, and the generalized Mittag–Leffler kernels were investigated. In the latter research work, the proposed numerical procedure is based on the Lagrange interpolating polynomial together with the theory of fractional calculus. Finally, let us mention that the PDE counterpart of the Brusselator model (2) has been investigated in the literature. Among others, we refer to the published papers [21–24]

1.2. Outline of This Paper

The primary purpose of the current research paper is to propose an effective hybrid technique. Our novel method is based on a combination of the quasi-linearization approach and matrix collocation method for an approximate treatment of the fractional Brusselator equations. The idea of a quasi-linearization method (QLM) is used to convert the nonlinear model into a family of linearized equations. Afterward, the spectral approach based on the (novel) generalized clique functions (GCFs) is employed to solve the quasi-linear equations in an iterative manner. Let us emphasize that the coefficients of all clique polynomials are all positive and integer-compared to the classical set of polynomials, such as Legendre, Chebyshev, Hermit, Laguerre, etc. Consequently, working with positive numbers yields more stable results during the computations. This would be the main motivation to employ the family of clique polynomials in the collocation matrix procedure over others. Another major advantage of the presented hybrid method, namely QLM-GCFs, is that it is not only effective in terms of required CPU time, but it provides high-order accuracy and better resolution characteristics compared to the existing numerical models in the literature. The accurateness and robustness of the spectral collocation strategies have been justified successfully by applying various model equations. Among others, let us mention the works [25–30].

The content of this research paper is organized as follows. Some basic facts on fractional calculus are reviewed in Section 2. Section 3 is devoted to the definition of clique basis functions. Moreover, a generalization of these functions is given. Then, the convergence analysis of this basis function is established in a weighted L_2 norm. A detailed description of the present QLM-GCFs technique is provided in Section 4. The results of the performed numerical simulations and experiments are given in Section 5. The concluding summary is given in Section 6.

2. Fractional Calculus: Basic Facts

Let us give some important facts about fractional calculus that will be used in the subsequent sections. For more detail, we refer the readers to the standard text [6] or some recent expository papers [31,32].

Let us first recall that the Riemann–Liouville fractional integral operator of order $\lambda > 0$ is given by

$$_0\mathcal{I}_\tau^\lambda[k](\tau) = \frac{1}{\Gamma(\lambda)} \int_0^\tau \frac{k(r)}{(\tau-r)^{1-\lambda}} dr,$$

where $\Gamma(\cdot)$ is the Gamma function and we assumed $k(\tau) \in C_\xi$, $\xi > -1$. We note that a real function $k(\tau)$, $\tau > 0$ belongs to the space C_ξ, $\xi \in \mathbb{R}$ if there exists a number $\mu \in \mathbb{R}$ and a function $l(\tau) \in C^\infty([0,\infty))$ such that $k(\tau) = \tau^\mu l(\tau)$. We also call that $k(\tau) \in C_\xi^n$ if and only if $k^{(n)}(\tau) \in C_\xi$ for a $n \in \mathbb{N}$.

We are now ready to define the fractional Liouville–Caputo derivative next.

Definition 1. *Assume that $k \in C_{-1}^n$ and $n-1 < \lambda < n$, $n \in \mathbb{N}$. The Liouville–Caputo fractional derivative of $k(\tau)$ of order λ is defined by*

$$^{LC}\mathcal{D}_\tau^\lambda k(\tau) = {_0\mathcal{I}_\tau^{n-\lambda}}[D^n k](\tau) = \frac{1}{\Gamma(n-\lambda)} \int_0^\tau (\tau-r)^{n-\lambda-1} k^{(n)}(r) dr, \quad \tau > 0,$$

where $D = \frac{d}{d\tau}$.

One should emphasize that the fractional operator $^{LC}\mathcal{D}_\tau^\lambda$ is a linear operator. If C is a constant number, we have

$$^{LC}\mathcal{D}_\tau^\lambda C = 0. \tag{4}$$

Our next goal is to compute the Liouville–Caputo fractional derivative of the function $k(\tau) = \tau^p$, where p is a constant. This can be performed through the following relations

$$^{LC}\mathcal{D}_\tau^\lambda \tau^p = \begin{cases} 0, & \text{for } \kappa \in \mathbb{N}_0 \text{ and } p < \lceil \lambda \rceil, \\ \dfrac{\Gamma(p+1)}{\Gamma(p+1-\lambda)} \tau^{p-\lambda}, & \text{for } p \in \mathbb{N}_0 \text{ and } p \geq \lceil \lambda \rceil \text{ or } p \notin \mathbb{N} \text{ and } p > \lfloor \lambda \rfloor. \end{cases} \tag{5}$$

Note that $\mathbb{N}_0 := \mathbb{N} \cup \{0\}$ and also we have utilized $\lceil \cdot \rceil$ and $\lfloor \cdot \rfloor$ as the ceil and floor functions respectively.

3. The Fractional-Order Clique Polynomial and Its Convergence Analysis

Here, we first consider the clique polynomials $\mathcal{C}_r(t)$ related to the cliques in a complete graph. We then introduce the fractional version of these polynomials. Hence, we establish the convergence analysis of these polynomials.

3.1. The Clique Functions: The Generalized Form

The clique polynomials were first introduced in [33] and associated with graph theory. However, they have been recently considered for numerical approximations of ordinary and fractional differential equations, see cf. [34–37]. Below, we first describe the main aspects of them.

Definition 2. *Over a bounded interval of the real line $[a, b]$, $(b > a \geq 0)$, we define the clique functions (CFs) as follows:*

$$\mathcal{C}_r(t) := \sum_{k=0}^{r} \binom{r}{k} t^k. \tag{6}$$

For $r = 0, 1$ in (6), we get $\mathcal{C}_0(t) = 1$ and $\mathcal{C}_1(t) = 1 + t$. One can easily observe that the following recursive formulation holds for this set of polynomials

$$\begin{cases} \mathcal{C}_{r+1}(t) = (1+t)\,\mathcal{C}_r(t), & r = 0, 1, \ldots, \\ \mathcal{C}_0(t) = 1. \end{cases} \tag{7}$$

By using recursion (7), we derive a few terms of CFs as

$$\mathcal{C}_2(t) = t^2 + 2t + 1,$$
$$\mathcal{C}_3(t) = t^3 + 3t^2 + 3t + 1,$$
$$\mathcal{C}_4(t) = t^4 + 4t^3 + 6t^2 + 4t + 1.$$

One can easily check that $\mathcal{C}_r(0) = 1$ and $\mathcal{C}_r(1) = 2^r$ for all values of $r \geq 0$. It is not a difficult task to check that these CFs satisfy a second-order differential equation in the form

$$\frac{d}{dt}\left[(t+1)^2 \frac{d}{dt} \mathcal{C}_r(t)\right] = r(r+1)\,\mathcal{C}_r(t), \quad r \in \mathbb{N}_0. \tag{8}$$

In what follows, we intend to use the CFs on an arbitrary interval $D_{a,b} := [a, b]$. We are also interested in using the generalized version of these polynomials of fractional order $0 < \alpha \leq 1$.

Definition 3. *Generalized CFs (GCFs) of degree r on $D_{a,b}$ are represented by $\mathcal{C}_r^\alpha(\tau)$ and defined by*

$$\mathcal{C}_r^\alpha(\tau) = \mathcal{C}_r(t), \quad t = \left(\frac{\tau}{L}\right)^\alpha, \tag{9}$$

where $L = b - a$.

With the help of this transformation, the explicit form in (6) will be given as follows:

$$C_r^\alpha(\tau) = \sum_{k=0}^{r} \frac{1}{L^{k\alpha}} \binom{r}{k} \tau^{k\alpha}, \quad r \in \mathbb{N}. \tag{10}$$

3.2. L_2-Convergent of GCFs

Let us investigate the convergence analysis of the GCFs in a weighted L_2 norm. In other words, we will investigate the behavior of the expansion series of a given function with respect to GCFs, especially when we increase the number of bases. We associate the following space to domain $D_{a,b}$ as [25]

$$L_{2,w}(D_{a,b}) = \{\ell : D_{a,b} \to \mathbb{R} \mid \ell \text{ is measurable and } \|\ell\|_w < \infty\}, \quad w(\tau) = 1/L,$$

Here, the related induced norm and inner product are given by

$$\langle \ell(\tau), k(\tau) \rangle_w = \int_a^b \ell(\tau) k(\tau) w(\tau) d\tau, \quad \|\ell\|_w^2 = \int_a^b |\ell(\tau)|^2 w(\tau) d\tau$$

Practically, a finite-dimensional subset, say $\mathcal{S}_R$, of the space $L_{2,w}(D_{a,b})$ is selected as

$$\mathcal{S}_R = \text{span}\langle \mathcal{C}_0^\alpha(\tau), \mathcal{C}_1^\alpha(\tau), \ldots, \mathcal{C}_R^\alpha(\tau) \rangle.$$

One observes that $\dim(\mathcal{S}_R) = R + 1$ and is also a closed subspace of $L_{2,w}(D_{a,b})$. It follows that $\mathcal{S}_R$ is a complete subspace of $L_{2,w}(D_{a,b})$. Thus, any given function $\ell \in L_{2,w}(D_{a,b})$ has a unique best (finest) approximation $\ell^\star \in \mathcal{S}_R$ in the following sense that

$$\|\ell(\tau) - \ell^\star(\tau)\|_w \leq \|\ell(\tau) - h(\tau)\|_w, \quad \forall h \in \mathcal{S}_R. \tag{11}$$

Generally, a given function $\ell(\tau) \in L_{2,w}(D_{a,b})$ can be expressed as a linear combination of GCFs. Thus, we have

$$\ell(\tau) = \sum_{r=0}^{\infty} \kappa_r \mathcal{C}_r^\alpha(\tau), \quad \tau \in D_{a,b}. \tag{12}$$

Here, the coefficients of κ_r are unknown for $r = 0, 1, \ldots$. By truncating the former series up to $(R+1)$ terms, we may approximate $\ell(\tau)$ in practice as

$$\ell(\tau) \approx \ell_R(\tau) = \sum_{r=0}^{R} \kappa_r \mathcal{C}_r^\alpha(\tau) = \boldsymbol{\mathcal{C}}_R^\alpha(\tau) \boldsymbol{K}_R, \tag{13}$$

where we have represented the involved finite series in a compact way by defining

$$\boldsymbol{\mathcal{C}}_R^\alpha(\tau) = [\mathcal{C}_0^\alpha(\tau) \quad \mathcal{C}_1^\alpha(\tau) \quad \ldots \quad \mathcal{C}_R^\alpha(\tau)], \quad \boldsymbol{K}_R = [\kappa_0 \quad \kappa_1 \quad \ldots \quad \kappa_R]^T. \tag{14}$$

Note that the first one is the vector of GCFs while $\boldsymbol{K}_R$ is the vector of unknowns. To derive an upper bound for the $E_R(\tau) = \ell(\tau) - \ell_R(\tau)$, we need the following result. A proof of the next theorem can be found in [38].

Theorem 1. *Let $\ell \in C^R(D_{a,b})$. If $l_R(\tau)$ represents the interpolating function of ℓ at R Chebyshev points on $D_{a,b}$, then we have*

$$|\ell(\tau) - l_R(\tau)| \leq \frac{2L^R \|\ell\|_{R,\infty}}{4^R R!}, \quad \|\ell\|_{R,\infty} := \max_{\tau \in D_{a,b}} |\ell^{(R)}(\tau)|.$$

Following [39], we establish the following error bound for the GCFs expansion series.

Theorem 2. *Suppose that $\ell \in C^R(D_{a,b}) \cap L_{w,2}(D_{a,b})$. If $\ell_R(\tau) = \mathbf{C}_R^\alpha(\tau) \mathbf{K}_R$ presents the best (finest) approximation of $\ell(\tau)$ out of $\mathcal{S}_{R,\alpha}$, then an error bound is given by*

$$\|E_R\|_w \leq \frac{2\|\ell\|_{R,\infty}}{4^R R!}.$$

Proof. Let us first define the new function $z(t) := \ell(t^{\frac{1}{\alpha}})$ on $D_{a,b}^\alpha := [a^\alpha, b^\alpha]$ and for any $\alpha > 0$. Applying Theorem 1 to function $z(t)$ with R Chebyshev nodes leads to the following error estimate

$$|z(t) - l_R(t)| \leq \frac{2\|z\|_{R,\infty}}{4^R R!}, \quad t \in D_{a,b}^\alpha.$$

We next substitute $t = \tau^\alpha$ in the preceding inequality. It follows that

$$|\ell(\tau) - l_R(\tau^\alpha)| \leq \frac{2\|\ell\|_{R,\infty}}{4^R R!}, \quad \tau \in D_{a,b}. \tag{15}$$

According to the theorem's assumption, we know that the approximate solution $\ell_R(\tau)$ is the finest approximation belonging to the space $\mathcal{S}_{R,\alpha}$. Thus, it holds that

$$\|\ell(\tau) - \ell_R(\tau)\|_w \leq \|\ell(\tau) - h(\tau)\|_w, \quad \forall h \in \mathcal{S}_R.$$

The former inequality is valid, particularly for $h = l_R(\tau^\alpha) \in \mathcal{S}_{R,\alpha}$. Employing this fact, as well as (15), we conclude that

$$\|\ell(\tau) - \ell_R(\tau)\|_w^2 \leq \|\ell(\tau) - l_R(\tau^\alpha)\|_w^2 = \int_a^b |\ell(\tau) - l_R(\tau^\alpha)|^2 w(\tau) d\tau$$

$$\leq \int_a^b \left|\frac{2\|\ell\|_{R,\infty}}{4^R R!}\right|^2 w(\tau) d\tau \leq \left[\frac{2\|\ell\|_{R,\infty}}{4^R R!}\right]^2 \int_a^b w(\tau) d\tau. \tag{16}$$

Using the fact that $\int_a^b w(\tau) d\tau = 1$, we only require the application of the square roots to the foregoing inequality. □

4. The Methodology of the QLM-GCFs Scheme

Instead of applying the direct collocation procedure to the underlying nonlinear model (2), our main aim is first to employ the quasi-linearization method (QLM) for (2) with initial conditions (3). Then, the generalized CFs (GCFs) collocation matrix technique is applied to the resultant family of linear subequations in an iterative manner.

4.1. The Basic Concept of QLM

By employing QLM, we can overcome the nonlinearity of a given model equation. The applicability of the QLM strategy has already been checked through tremendous research studies in the literature. For recent applications, we refer readers to [40–43].

By rewriting first the nonlinear coupled system (2) in a matrix representation form, we get

$$\mathbf{Z}^{(\lambda)}(\tau) = \mathbf{F}(\mathbf{Z}(\tau), \tau). \tag{17}$$

Here, we have utilized the following notations

$$\mathbf{Z}(\tau) := \begin{pmatrix} u(\tau) \\ v(\tau) \end{pmatrix}, \quad \mathbf{Z}^{(\lambda)}(\tau) := {}^{LC}\mathcal{D}_\tau^\lambda \begin{pmatrix} u(\tau) \\ v(\tau) \end{pmatrix}, \quad \mathbf{F}(\mathbf{Z}(\tau), \tau) := \begin{pmatrix} \theta - (\eta+1)u(\tau) + u^2(\tau)v(\tau) \\ \eta u(\tau) - u^2(\tau)v(\tau) \end{pmatrix}.$$

Suppose that $\mathbf{Z}_0(\tau)$ is a rough first approximation of $\mathbf{Z}(\tau)$. Thus, the QLM for (17) is written for $p = 0, 1, \ldots$ as

$$\mathbf{Z}_{p+1}^{(\lambda)}(\tau) \approx \mathbf{F}(\mathbf{Z}_p(\tau), \tau) + \mathbf{F}_\mathbf{Z}(\mathbf{Z}_p(\tau), \tau)\left(\mathbf{Z}_{p+1}(\tau) - \mathbf{Z}_p(\tau)\right).$$

Here, by $F_Z = \frac{d}{dZ}F$, we denote the corresponding Jacobian matrix. Let us note that the same initial conditions as (3) will be given to the last sequence of equations. After performing some straightforward calculations, we receive the following family of a linear system of equations as the result of QLM from model (17). Thus, we have

$$^{LC}\mathcal{D}_\tau^\lambda Z_{p+1}(\tau) + \xi_p(\tau) Z_{p+1}(\tau) = s_p(\tau), \qquad p = 0, 1, \ldots, \tag{18}$$

where

$$Z_{p+1}(\tau) = \begin{pmatrix} u_{p+1}(\tau) \\ v_{p+1}(\tau) \end{pmatrix}, \quad \xi_p(\tau) = \begin{pmatrix} \eta + 1 - 2u_p(\tau) v_p(\tau) & -u_p^2(\tau) \\ -\eta + 2u_p(\tau) v_p(\tau) & u_p^2(\tau) \end{pmatrix},$$

$$s_p(\tau) = \begin{pmatrix} \theta - 2u_p^2(\tau) v_p(\tau) \\ 2u_p^2(\tau) v_p(\tau) \end{pmatrix}.$$

Systemically, we can present the initial conditions (3) as

$$Z_{p+1}(0) = \begin{pmatrix} u_{p+1}(0) \\ v_{p+1}(0) \end{pmatrix} = \begin{pmatrix} u_0 \\ v_0 \end{pmatrix}. \tag{19}$$

To solve the quasi-linear systems (18)–(19) accurately, we will design a matrix collocation procedure based on the GCFs to receive an approximate solution.

4.2. The QLM-GCFs Technique

Supposedly, the unknown solutions of quasi-linear model (18) can be expanded as a combination of the cut series form (13) with $(R+1)$-terms. Further, assume that for a fixed $\alpha \in (0,1]$ the approximate solutions $\mathcal{U}_{R,\alpha}^{(p)}(\tau)$ and $\mathcal{V}_{R,\alpha}^{(p)}(\tau)$ to $u_p(\tau)$ and $v_p(\tau)$ in the iteration p for $p = 0, 1, \ldots$ are known. For $p = 0$, we utilize the initial guess $Z_0(\tau)$ as the starting point. In the next iteration, $p+1$, we seek the approximate solutions in the forms

$$u_{p+1}(\tau) \approx \mathcal{U}_{R,\alpha}^{(p+1)}(\tau) = \sum_{r=0}^{R} \kappa_{r,1}^{(p)} \mathcal{C}_r^\alpha(\tau), \quad v_{p+1}(\tau) \approx \mathcal{V}_{R,\alpha}^{(p+1)}(\tau) = \sum_{r=0}^{R} \kappa_{r,2}^{(p)} \mathcal{C}_r^\alpha(\tau), \tag{20}$$

for $\tau \in D_{a,b}$. Below, our primary job is to find the unknown coefficients $\{\kappa_{r,j}^{(p)}\}_{r=0}^R$ for $j = 1, 2$ and $p = 1, 2, \ldots$ by using a spectral matrix collocation approach relying on the GCFs. To this end, we first construct the matrix forms of the approximate solutions given in 20. Similar to (13), the finite series solutions in ((20)) for $j = 1, 2$ can be expressed as

$$\sum_{r=0}^{R} \kappa_{r,j}^{(p)} \mathcal{C}_r^\alpha(\tau) = \mathbf{C}_R^\alpha(\tau) \mathbf{K}_{R,j}^{(p)}, \tag{21}$$

where the unknown vectors $\mathbf{K}_{R,j}^{(p)}$ and the vector of GCFs are given by

$$\mathbf{K}_{R,j}^{(p)} = \begin{bmatrix} \kappa_{0,j}^{(p)} & \kappa_{1,j}^{(p)} & \cdots & \kappa_{R,j}^{(p)} \end{bmatrix}^T, \quad \mathbf{C}_R^\alpha(\tau) = [\mathcal{C}_0^\alpha(\tau) \; \mathcal{C}_1^\alpha(\tau) \; \cdots \; \mathcal{C}_R^\alpha(\tau)].$$

In the next Lemma, we further write the vector of basis functions in terms of monomials multiplied by a constant matrix.

Lemma 1. *The representation of the vector of GCFs is given by*

$$\mathbf{C}_R^\alpha(\tau) = \mathbf{\Pi}_R^\alpha(\tau) \mathbf{M}_R, \tag{22}$$

where $\mathbf{\Pi}_R^\alpha(\tau) = \begin{bmatrix} 1 & \tau^\alpha & \tau^{2\alpha} & \cdots & \tau^{R\alpha} \end{bmatrix}$ and $\mathbf{M}_R$ of size $(R+1) \times (R+1)$ is an upper triangular matrix whose components are obtained via (10). It reads

$$\mathbf{M}_R = \begin{pmatrix} \binom{0}{0} & \binom{1}{0} & \binom{2}{0} & \cdots & \binom{R-1}{0} & \binom{R}{0} \\ 0 & \mu_1\binom{1}{1} & \mu_1\binom{2}{1} & \cdots & \mu_1\binom{R-1}{1} & \mu_1\binom{R}{1} \\ 0 & 0 & \mu_2\binom{2}{2} & \cdots & \mu_2\binom{R-1}{2} & \mu_2\binom{R}{2} \\ \vdots & \vdots & \ddots & \ddots & & \vdots \\ 0 & & & \cdots & \mu_{R-1}\binom{R-1}{R-1} & \mu_{R-1}\binom{R}{R-1} \\ 0 & & & \cdots & & \mu_R\binom{R}{R} \end{pmatrix}, \quad \mu_j := L^{-j\alpha}, \ j = 1, 2, \ldots, R.$$

Proof. By virtue of relation (10), it is sufficient to multiply matrix $\mathbf{M}_R$ by $\mathbf{\Pi}_R^\alpha(\tau)$ from the left. □

Obviously, the diagonal elements of matrix $\mathbf{M}_R$ are all non-zero. Thus, this matrix is non-singular. In fact, we have $\det(\mathbf{M}_R) = L^{-R\alpha(R+1)/2}$.

If one combines two former relations (21) and (22), the approximate solutions are written as

$$\begin{cases} \mathcal{U}_{R,\alpha}^{(p+1)}(\tau) = \mathbf{C}_R^\alpha(\tau) \mathbf{K}_{R,1}^{(p)} = \mathbf{\Pi}_R^\alpha(\tau) \mathbf{M}_R \mathbf{K}_{R,1}^{(p)}, \\ \mathcal{V}_{R,\alpha}^{(p+1)}(\tau) = \mathbf{C}_R^\alpha(\tau) \mathbf{K}_{R,2}^{(p)} = \mathbf{\Pi}_R^\alpha(\tau) \mathbf{M}_R \mathbf{K}_{R,2}^{(p)}, \end{cases} \tau \in D_{a,b}. \tag{23}$$

Next, we need the λ-derivative of the approximate solutions. To do so, we apply the operator ${}^{LC}\mathcal{D}_\tau^\lambda$ to both sides of the relation (23). Thus, we get

$$\begin{cases} {}^{LC}\mathcal{D}_\tau^\lambda \mathcal{U}_{R,\alpha}^{(p+1)}(\tau) = \left({}^{LC}\mathcal{D}_\tau^\lambda \mathbf{\Pi}_R^\alpha(\tau)\right) \mathbf{M}_R \mathbf{K}_{R,1}^{(p)}, \\ {}^{LC}\mathcal{D}_\tau^\lambda \mathcal{V}_{R,\alpha}^{(p+1)}(\tau) = \left({}^{LC}\mathcal{D}_\tau^\lambda \mathbf{\Pi}_R^\alpha(\tau)\right) \mathbf{M}_R \mathbf{K}_{R,2}^{(p)}. \end{cases} \tag{24}$$

Consequently, we must only compute the λ-derivatives of the vector $\mathbf{\Pi}_R^\alpha(\tau)$. In this respect, we consider two properties (4) and (5) to calculate the fractional derivatives of $\mathbf{\Pi}_R^\alpha(\tau)$. As an example, we set $R = 3$ and $\lambda = \frac{3}{4}$. Now, using $\alpha = 1$ and $\alpha = \frac{1}{2}$ we get, respectively,

$${}^{LC}\mathcal{D}_\tau^{\frac{3}{4}} \mathbf{\Pi}_3^1(\tau) = \begin{bmatrix} 0 & \frac{1!}{\Gamma(\frac{5}{4})}\tau^{\frac{1}{4}} & \frac{2!}{\Gamma(\frac{9}{4})}\tau^{\frac{5}{4}} & \frac{3!}{\Gamma(\frac{13}{4})}\tau^{\frac{9}{4}} \end{bmatrix}, \quad {}^{LC}\mathcal{D}_\tau^{\frac{3}{4}} \mathbf{\Pi}_3^{\frac{1}{2}}(\tau) = \begin{bmatrix} 0 & 0 & \frac{1!}{\Gamma(\frac{5}{4})}\tau^{\frac{1}{4}} & \frac{\Gamma(\frac{5}{2})}{\Gamma(\frac{7}{4})}\tau^{\frac{3}{4}} \end{bmatrix}.$$

Practically, however, we can use the modified version of Algorithm 4.1 in [44] or [45] or Algorithm 3.1 in [46] with linear complexity $\mathcal{O}(R+1)$ to compute the λ-derivative of $\mathbf{\Pi}_R^\alpha(\tau)$. To continue, let us define the fractional derivative of the vector as

$$\mathbf{\Pi}_R^{(\lambda,\alpha)}(\tau) := {}^{LC}\mathcal{D}_\tau^\lambda \mathbf{\Pi}_R^\alpha(\tau). \tag{25}$$

We can now place this relation into (24) to arrive at

$${}^{LC}\mathcal{D}_\tau^\lambda \mathcal{U}_{R,\alpha}^{(p+1)}(\tau) = \mathbf{\Pi}_R^{(\lambda,\alpha)}(\tau) \mathbf{M}_R \mathbf{K}_{R,1}^{(p)}, \quad {}^{LC}\mathcal{D}_\tau^\lambda \mathcal{V}_{R,\alpha}^{(p+1)}(\tau) = \mathbf{\Pi}_R^{(\lambda,\alpha)}(\tau) \mathbf{M}_R \mathbf{K}_{R,2}^{(p)}. \tag{26}$$

We come back to the matrix differential equation (18). Vector $\mathbf{Z}_{p+1}(\tau)$ and its derivative $^{LC}\mathcal{D}_\tau^\lambda \mathbf{Z}_{p+1}(\tau)$ can be approximated as

$$\mathbf{Z}_{p+1} \approx \mathbf{Z}_R^{(p+1)}(\tau) := \begin{pmatrix} \mathcal{U}_{R,\alpha}^{(p+1)}(\tau) \\ \mathcal{V}_{R,\alpha}^{(p+1)}(\tau) \end{pmatrix},$$
$$^{LC}\mathcal{D}_\tau^\lambda \mathbf{Z}_{p+1}(\tau) \approx {}^{LC}\mathcal{D}_\tau^\lambda \mathbf{Z}_R^{(p+1)}(\tau) := \begin{pmatrix} {}^{LC}\mathcal{D}_\tau^\lambda \mathcal{U}_{R,\alpha}^{(p+1)}(\tau) \\ {}^{LC}\mathcal{D}_\tau^\lambda \mathcal{V}_{R,\alpha}^{(p+1)}(\tau) \end{pmatrix}. \tag{27}$$

Lemma 2. *In the matrix formats, the approximated solution $\mathbf{Z}_R^{(p+1)}(\tau)$, and its λ-derivative $^{LC}\mathcal{D}_\tau^\lambda \mathbf{Z}_R^{(p+1)}(\tau)$ in (27) can be stated as follows:*

$$\mathbf{Z}_R^{(p+1)}(\tau) = \widehat{\mathbf{\Pi}}(\tau)\,\widehat{\mathbf{M}}\,\widehat{\mathbf{K}}^{(p)}, \quad {}^{LC}\mathcal{D}_\tau^\alpha \mathbf{Z}_R^{(p+1)}(\tau) = \widehat{\mathbf{\Pi}}_\lambda(\tau)\,\widehat{\mathbf{M}}\,\widehat{\mathbf{K}}^{(p)}, \tag{28}$$

where the following notations are used: $\widehat{\mathbf{K}}^{(p)} = \begin{pmatrix} \mathbf{K}_{R,1}^{(p)} & \mathbf{K}_{R,2}^{(p)} \end{pmatrix}^T$ *and*

$$\widehat{\mathbf{\Pi}}(\tau) = \begin{pmatrix} \mathbf{\Pi}_R^\alpha(\tau) & 0 \\ 0 & \mathbf{\Pi}_R^\alpha(\tau) \end{pmatrix}, \quad \widehat{\mathbf{M}} = \begin{pmatrix} \mathbf{M}_R & 0 \\ 0 & \mathbf{M}_R \end{pmatrix}, \quad \widehat{\mathbf{\Pi}}_\lambda(\tau) = \begin{pmatrix} \mathbf{\Pi}_R^{(\lambda,\alpha)}(\tau) & 0 \\ 0 & \mathbf{\Pi}_R^{(\lambda,\alpha)}(\tau) \end{pmatrix}.$$

Proof. To conclude the results, we need to substitute two relations (23) and (26) into the corresponding vector forms in (27). □

We are then looking for a partitioning $D_{a,b}$ that will be used as a set of collocation points. To do so, we utilize $(R+1)$ equidistant points from interval $[a,b]$. Let us set

$$\tau_\rho := a + \frac{L}{R}\rho, \quad \rho = 0,1,\ldots,R. \tag{29}$$

Now, adding the aforementioned set of collocation points into the sequence of linear matrix differential equations (18) to get

$$^{LC}\mathcal{D}_\tau^\lambda \mathbf{Z}_{p+1}(\tau_\rho) + \boldsymbol{\xi}_p(\tau_\rho)\mathbf{Z}_{p+1}(\tau_\rho) = \mathbf{s}_p(\tau_\rho), \quad \rho = 0,1,\ldots,R, \tag{30}$$

for $p = 0,1,\ldots$. We next introduce the following matrix and vector notations

$$\boldsymbol{\Sigma}_p^\lambda = \begin{pmatrix} {}^{LC}\mathcal{D}_\tau^\lambda \mathbf{Z}_{p+1}(\tau_0) \\ {}^{LC}\mathcal{D}_\tau^\lambda \mathbf{Z}_{p+1}(\tau_1) \\ \vdots \\ {}^{LC}\mathcal{D}_\tau^\lambda \mathbf{Z}_{p+1}(\tau_R) \end{pmatrix}, \quad \boldsymbol{\Sigma}_p = \begin{pmatrix} \mathbf{Z}_{p+1}(\tau_0) \\ \mathbf{Z}_{p+1}(\tau_1) \\ \vdots \\ \mathbf{Z}_{p+1}(\tau_R) \end{pmatrix}, \quad \mathbf{S}_p = \begin{pmatrix} \mathbf{s}_p(\tau_0) \\ \mathbf{s}_p(\tau_1) \\ \vdots \\ \mathbf{s}_p(\tau_R) \end{pmatrix},$$

$$\boldsymbol{\Xi}_p = \begin{pmatrix} \boldsymbol{\xi}_p(\tau_0) & 0 & \cdots & 0 \\ 0 & \boldsymbol{\xi}_p(\tau_1) & \cdots & 0 \\ \vdots & \vdots & \ddots & \vdots \\ 0 & 0 & \cdots & \boldsymbol{\xi}_p(\tau_R) \end{pmatrix}.$$

In the vector representation, we are able to show relation (30) in a compact formulation as

$$\boldsymbol{\Sigma}_p^\lambda + \boldsymbol{\Xi}_p\boldsymbol{\Sigma}_p = \mathbf{S}_p, \quad p = 0,1,\ldots. \tag{31}$$

Our next aim is to derive the matrix expressions of $\boldsymbol{\Sigma}_p$ and $\boldsymbol{\Sigma}_p^\lambda$. By collocating two relations (28) at the collocations points, we render

Lemma 3. *The two relations (28) at the collocation point (29) can be written as follows:*

$$\boldsymbol{\Sigma}_p = \widetilde{\widehat{\boldsymbol{\Pi}}} \, \widehat{\boldsymbol{M}} \, \widehat{\boldsymbol{K}}^{(p)}, \qquad \boldsymbol{\Sigma}_p^{\lambda} = \widetilde{\widehat{\boldsymbol{\Pi}}}_{\lambda} \, \widehat{\boldsymbol{M}} \, \widehat{\boldsymbol{K}}^{(p)}, \qquad (32)$$

where the two matrices $\widetilde{\widehat{\boldsymbol{\Pi}}}$ and $\widetilde{\widehat{\boldsymbol{\Pi}}}_{\lambda}$ are given by

$$\widetilde{\widehat{\boldsymbol{\Pi}}} = [\widehat{\boldsymbol{\Pi}}(\tau_0) \quad \widehat{\boldsymbol{\Pi}}(\tau_1) \quad \ldots \quad \widehat{\boldsymbol{\Pi}}(\tau_R)]^T,$$

$$\widetilde{\widehat{\boldsymbol{\Pi}}}_{\lambda} = [\widehat{\boldsymbol{\Pi}}_{\lambda}(\tau_0) \quad \widehat{\boldsymbol{\Pi}}_{\lambda}(\tau_1) \quad \ldots \quad \widehat{\boldsymbol{\Pi}}_{\lambda}(\tau_R)]^T.$$

Here, the three matrices $\widehat{\boldsymbol{M}}, \widehat{\boldsymbol{\Pi}}$, and $\widehat{\boldsymbol{\Pi}}_{\lambda}$, as well as the vector $\widehat{\boldsymbol{K}}^{(p)}$, are defined in (28) previously.

Finally, we form the so-called fundamental matrix equation at each iteration p by placing the preceding relations (32) into (31). It follows that

$$\boldsymbol{A}_p \widehat{\boldsymbol{K}}^{(p)} = \boldsymbol{S}_p, \quad \text{or} \quad [\boldsymbol{A}_p; \boldsymbol{S}_p], \quad p = 0, 1, \ldots, \qquad (33)$$

where

$$\boldsymbol{A}_p := \left\{ \widetilde{\widehat{\boldsymbol{\Pi}}}_{\lambda} + \boldsymbol{\Xi}_p \widetilde{\widehat{\boldsymbol{\Pi}}} \right\} \widehat{\boldsymbol{M}}.$$

It should be noted that the last matrix equation (33) is a linear system with $2(R+1)$ unknowns $\kappa_{r,j}^{(p)}$ for $r = 0, 1, \ldots, R$ and $j = 1, 2$ to be specified as the coefficients of GCFs in the series solutions (20). However, the supplemented initial conditions (3) are not yet implemented and entered into the system (33). First, we consider the matrix representation forms (28) for the approximate solution $\boldsymbol{Z}_R^{(p+1)}(\tau)$. We then let $\tau \to 0$ arrive at

$$\widehat{\boldsymbol{A}_{0,p}} \widehat{\boldsymbol{K}}^{(p)} = \widehat{\boldsymbol{S}_0}, \quad \widehat{\boldsymbol{A}_{0,p}} := \widehat{\boldsymbol{\Pi}}(0) \, \widehat{\boldsymbol{M}}, \quad \widehat{\boldsymbol{S}_0} = \begin{pmatrix} u_0 \\ v_0 \end{pmatrix}, \quad \text{or} \quad \left[\widehat{\boldsymbol{A}_{0,p}}; \widehat{\boldsymbol{S}_0}\right].$$

Here, the two constants u_0 and v_0, are available from (3). The replacement of two rows of the matrix $[\boldsymbol{A}_p; \boldsymbol{S}_p]$ in (33) will be carried out next by the row matrix $\left[\widehat{\boldsymbol{A}_{0,p}}; \widehat{\boldsymbol{S}_0}\right]$. The modified fundamental matrix equation will be shown by

$$\widehat{\boldsymbol{A}_p} \widehat{\boldsymbol{K}}^{(p)} = \widehat{\boldsymbol{S}_p}, \quad \text{or} \quad \left[\widehat{\boldsymbol{A}_p}; \widehat{\boldsymbol{S}_p}\right]. \qquad (34)$$

To get the unknown coefficients of GCFs, it is sufficient to solve the modified algebraic linear system (34) in each iteration. Now, one requires a linear solver to be used to receive the solution of this system. After finding vector $\widehat{\boldsymbol{K}}^{(p)}$, all unknowns $\kappa_{r,j}^{(p)}$, for $j = 1, 2$, and $r = 0, 1, \ldots, R$ as the coefficients in the expansion series (20) will be found in iteration p. Thus, we get an approximate solution of model (2).

Algorithmically, we summarize all of the steps of the proposed QLM-GCs technique in Algorithm 1. Here, by $p_{\max}$ we denote the maximum number of iterations required to achieve the desired accuracy in the QLM method. It should be remarked that we have utilized the MATLAB notation $\boldsymbol{A}[i:j, s:k]$ to denote the submatrix of $\boldsymbol{A}$ formed by all entries in the intersection of rows $i, \ldots, j$ and columns $s, \ldots, k$.

Algorithm 1: An algorithmic description of the QLM-GCFs.

1: **procedure** QLM_GCFs($R, \lambda, \alpha, \theta, \eta, M_R, C_R^\alpha(\tau), u_0, v_0, p_{\max}$)
2: $p := 0; \quad m := R+1; \quad n := 2;$
3: $\Pi_R^\alpha(\tau) := \begin{bmatrix} 1 & \tau^\alpha & \tau^{2\alpha} & \cdots & \tau^{R\alpha} \end{bmatrix};$
4: $\Pi_R^{(\lambda,\alpha)}(\tau) := {}^{LC}\mathcal{D}_\tau^\lambda \Pi_R^\alpha(\tau);$ {Via calling to Algorithm 4.1 from [44]}
5: $\widehat{\Pi}(\tau) := \begin{pmatrix} \Pi_R^\alpha(\tau) & 0 \\ 0 & \Pi_R^\alpha(\tau) \end{pmatrix}; \quad \widehat{M} := \begin{pmatrix} M_R & 0 \\ 0 & M_R \end{pmatrix}; \quad \widehat{\Pi}_\lambda(\tau) = \begin{pmatrix} \Pi_R^{(\lambda,\alpha)}(\tau) & 0 \\ 0 & \Pi_R^{(\lambda,\alpha)}(\tau) \end{pmatrix};$
6: $Z_p(\tau) := 0; \quad u_p(\tau) := Z_p[1]; \quad v_p(\tau) := Z_p[2];$
7: $\boldsymbol{\zeta}_p(\tau) := \begin{pmatrix} \eta+1-2u_p(\tau)v_p(\tau) & -u_p^2(\tau) \\ -\eta+2u_p(\tau)v_p(\tau) & u_p^2(\tau) \end{pmatrix}; \quad \boldsymbol{s}_p(\tau) := \begin{pmatrix} \theta - 2u_p^2(\tau)v_p(\tau) \\ 2u_p^2(\tau)v_p(\tau) \end{pmatrix};$
{Using the collocation points (29)}
8: $\Xi_p := 0; \quad S_p := 0; \quad \{\Xi_p \in \mathbb{R}^{n*m \times n*m} \ \& \ S_p \in \mathbb{R}^{n*m \times 1}\}$
9: $\widetilde{\widehat{\Pi}} := 0; \quad \widetilde{\Pi}_\lambda := 0; \quad \{\widetilde{\widehat{\Pi}}, \widetilde{\Pi}_\lambda \in \mathbb{R}^{n*m \times n*m}\}$
10: **for** $j := 0, \ldots, R$
11: $\quad \Xi_p[n*j+1 : n*(j+1), n*j+1 : n*(j+1)] := \boldsymbol{\zeta}_p(\tau_j);$
12: $\quad S_p[n*j+1 : n*(j+1)] := \boldsymbol{s}_p(\tau_j);$
13: $\quad \widetilde{\widehat{\Pi}}[n*j+1 : n*(j+1), n*j+1 : n*(j+1), :] := \widehat{\Pi}(\tau_j);$
14: $\quad \widetilde{\Pi}_\lambda[n*j+1 : n*(j+1), n*j+1 : n*(j+1), :] := \widehat{\Pi}(\tau_j);$
15: **end for**
16: **for** $p := 1, \ldots, p_{\max}$
17: $\quad$ Fa_Sys := $\left(\widetilde{\widehat{\Pi}}_\lambda + \Xi_p \widetilde{\widehat{\Pi}}_\lambda\right)\widehat{M};$ rhs_Sys := $S_p;$
{Entering the I.C.}
18: $\quad$ Fa_Sys[1:2,:] := $\widehat{\Pi}(0)\widehat{M};$ rhs_Sys[1:2] := $[u_0, v_0]^T;$
19: $\quad \widehat{K}^{(p)} :=$ LinSolve(Fa_Sys, rhs_Sys);
20: $\quad \mathcal{U}_{R,\alpha}^{(p)}(\tau) := C_R^\alpha(\tau) K_{R,1}^{(p)}; \quad \mathcal{V}_{R,\alpha}^{(p)}(\tau) := C_R^\alpha(\tau) K_{R,2}^{(p)};$
21: $\quad$ Update $\boldsymbol{\zeta}_p(\tau)$ and $\boldsymbol{s}_p(\tau)$ in line 7 in terms of the former solutions;
22: $\quad$ Calculate two matrices Ξ_p and S_p in lines 11-12;
23: **end for**
24: **end;**

5. Numerical Results and Graphical Representations

In this part, a set of computational examples is provided to describe and support the theoretical findings. In this respect, we apply the QLM-GCFs to the fractional-order Brusselator of Equation (2) by solving the quasi-linear model Equation (17). For performing computational simulations, we use Matlab software version 2021a on a computer with 16 GB of RAM and a CPU with 2.2 GHz Intel® Core™ i7-10870H processor.

In the computational results, we utilize the QLM with parameter $p = 5$. Furthermore, in the QLM-GCFs, the initial approximation $Z_0(\tau)$ is selected as the zero function, or we take it as the initial condition (3). As previously mentioned, the exact solutions of this system are not available, especially when the order of the derivative is described in the fractional order. Therefore, we define the residual error functions (REFs) associated with the Brusselator model to measure the accuracy of the proposed spectral QLM-GCFs collocation technique. That is, in iteration $p = 1, 2, \ldots$, we define the error terms as

$$Res_{u,R,\alpha}^{(p)}(\tau) := \left| {}^{LC}\mathcal{D}_\tau^\lambda \mathcal{U}_{R,\alpha}^{(p)}(\tau) - \theta + (\eta+1)\mathcal{U}_{R,\alpha}^{(p)}(\tau) - \left(\mathcal{U}_{R,\alpha}^{(p)}(\tau)\right)^2 \mathcal{V}_{R,\alpha}^{(p)}(\tau) \right| \cong 0,$$

$$Res_{v,R,\alpha}^{(p)}(\tau) := \left| {}^{LC}\mathcal{D}_\tau^\lambda \mathcal{V}_{R,\alpha}^{(p)}(\tau) - \eta \mathcal{U}_{R,\alpha}^{(p)}(\tau) + \left(\mathcal{U}_{R,\alpha}^{(p)}(\tau)\right)^2 \mathcal{V}_{R,\alpha}^{(p)}(\tau) \right| \cong 0.$$

(35)

We also compute the L_∞ error norms (for a fixed p) via the relations

$$L_\infty^u \equiv L_\infty^u(R) := \max_{\tau \in D_{a,b}} \text{Res}_{u,R,\alpha}^{(p)}(\tau), \quad L_\infty^v \equiv L_\infty^v(R) := \max_{\tau \in D_{a,b}} \text{Res}_{v,R,\alpha}^{(p)}(\tau).$$

We further utilize the following relations to compute the obtained numerical order of convergence (Noc) related to the numerical technique applied to both solutions of the coupled system (2) given by

$$\text{Noc}_\infty^u := \log_2\left(\frac{L_\infty^u(R)}{L_\infty^u(2R)}\right), \quad \text{Noc}_\infty^v := \log_2\left(\frac{L_\infty^v(R)}{L_\infty^v(2R)}\right). \tag{36}$$

Note that these formulae are utilized to check the order of accuracy of our proposed technique in the L_∞ norm for both solutions.

Example 1. *As the first test case, let us consider the fractional Brusselator system by taking two parameters $\theta = 0$ and $\eta = 1$ to get*

$$\begin{cases} {}^{LC}\mathcal{D}_\tau^\lambda u(\tau) = -2u(\tau) + u^2(\tau)\,v(\tau), \\ {}^{LC}\mathcal{D}_\tau^\lambda v(\tau) = u(\tau) - u^2(\tau)\,v(\tau), \end{cases} \quad \lambda \in (0,1].$$

The given initial conditions are $u(0) = 1$, $v(0) = 1$. This example was considered in [14,16,17] previously.

Let us first set $a = 0, b = 1$ and take $R = 5$. We also consider $\lambda = 1$. Using $\alpha = 1$, the proposed QLM-GCFs with the collocation points $\{0, 2/10, 4/10, 6/10, 8/10, 1\}$, the following approximate solutions are obtained.

$$\mathcal{U}_{5,1}^{(5)}(\tau) = 0.044402695\,\tau^5 - 0.23533824\,\tau^4 + 0.4152989\,\tau^3 + 0.02746560\,\tau^2 - 1.0042497\,\tau + 1.0,$$
$$\mathcal{V}_{5,1}^{(5)}(\tau) = -0.02397666\,\tau^5 + 0.1692558\,\tau^4 - 0.4510957\,\tau^3 + 0.4843923\,\tau^2 + 0.002544616\,\tau + 1.0.$$

For $\lambda = 1$, let us compare our outcomes with those polynomial solutions obtained via the two (semi)analytical techniques. The first one is the polynomial least squares method (PLSM) [15] with the following approximations

$$x_{plsm}(t) = 0.0750974\,t^3 + 0.201028\,t^2 - 1.02827\,t + 1.0,$$
$$y_{plsm}(t) = -0.180088\,t^3 + 0.334087\,t^2 + 0.0271107\,t + 1.0.$$

The second method is the Legendre wavelet operational matrix method (LWOMM) [17], the solutions of which are reported as

$$y_1(t) = 1.0 - 1.0120\,t + 0.1211\,t^2 + 0.1517\,t^3,$$
$$y_2(t) = 1.0 + 0.0096\,t + 0.4069\,t^2 - 0.2461\,t^3.$$

In Figure 1, we show the above approximate solutions obtained by our method (black lines) and two other existing ones, i.e., the PLSM and LWOMM procedures. From this visualization, we conclude that the alignment between the results of QLM-GCFs and PLSM is more than the outcomes of our method and LWOMM. On the other hand, note that our solutions are obtained by using $R = 5$, which gives us the approximate polynomial solutions of five degrees compared to the three-degree polynomials reported by the LWOMM and PLSM. However, our proposed procedure can produce more accurate results just by increasing R. To be more precise, we plot the achieved REFs obtained via (35) when $R = 5, 10$, and 15. These experiments are shown in Figure 2.

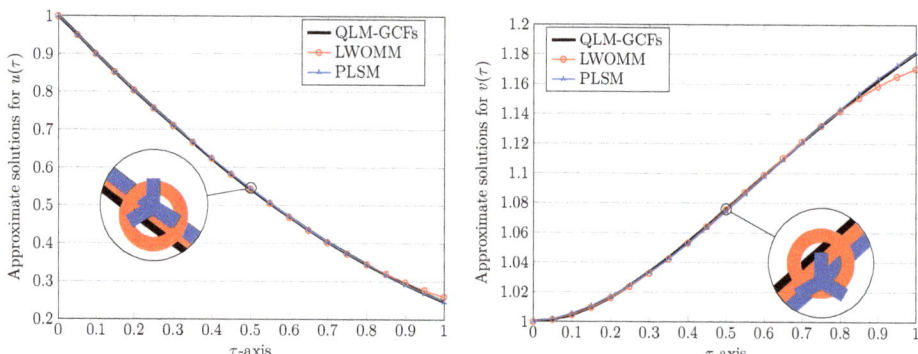

Figure 1. Comparisons of approximate solutions for $u(\tau)$ (**left**) and $v(\tau)$ (**right**) obtained via the QLM-GCFs technique in test case 1 with $R = 5$, $\lambda, \alpha = 1$, and $p = 5$.

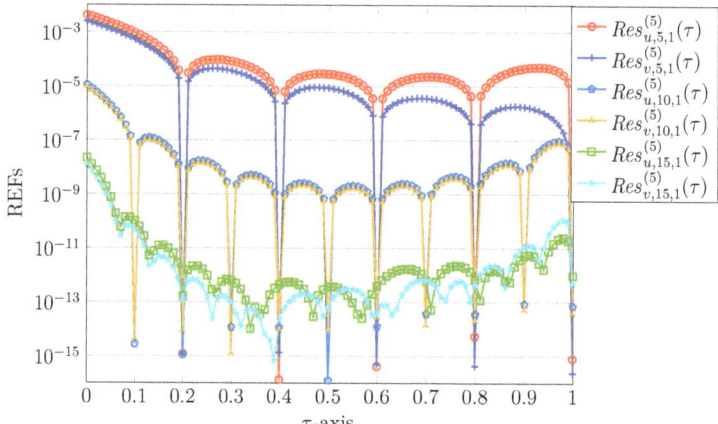

Figure 2. Comparisons of achieved REFs obtained via QLM-GCFs in test case 1 with $\lambda, \alpha = 1$, $R = 5, 10, 15$, and $p = 5$.

Finally, for the integer order $\lambda = 1$, we report the numerical results evaluated at some points $\tau \in [0, 1]$. For this purpose, we use $R = 10$ and show the outcomes of the proposed QLM-GCFs for both solutions in Table 1. Table 2 presents the maximum REF values achieved by using $R = 2^i$, $i = 1, 2, 3, 4, 5$. The corresponding Noc are also reported in this table related to both solutions $u(\tau)$ and $v(\tau)$. Higher order accuracy of the proposed method is visible from the results presented in Table 2. The required CPU times to solve modified system $\left[\widehat{A}_p; \widehat{S}_p\right]$ measured in seconds are shown in Table 2. The CPU's spent time clearly behaves linearly as the number of basis functions becomes two-fold.

Let us turn next to the fractional cases and set $\lambda = 0.75$. By employing the QLM-GCFs with $R = 10$, we obtain two approximate solutions for $0 \leq \tau \leq 1$ as given below. The obtained results for $\alpha = 1$ are given by

$$\mathcal{U}_{10,1}^{(5)}(\tau) = 11.965651\,\tau^{10} - 71.374363\,\tau^9 + 187.82167\,\tau^8 - 287.243\,\tau^7 + 283.18426\,\tau^6$$
$$- 188.87801\,\tau^5 + 87.324068\,\tau^4 - 28.680548\,\tau^3 + 7.4595572\,\tau^2 - 2.3034134\,\tau + 1.0,$$

$$\mathcal{V}_{10,1}^{(5)}(\tau) = 2.2725108\,\tau^{10} - 13.632576\,\tau^9 + 36.11913\,\tau^8 - 55.727909\,\tau^7 + 55.641481\,\tau^6$$
$$- 37.881744\,\tau^5 + 18.156988\,\tau^4 - 6.2694104\,\tau^3 + 1.4527369\,\tau^2 + 0.079421181\,\tau + 1.0.$$

Table 1. Numerical results and REFs for $u(\tau), v(\tau)$ obtained via the QLM-GCFs procedure using $R = 10$ and $p = 5$ in Example 1 with $\lambda, \alpha = 1$.

τ	$\mathcal{U}_{10,1}^{(5)}(\tau)$	$Res_{u,10,1}^{(5)}(\tau)$	$\mathcal{V}_{10,1}^{(5)}(\tau)$	$Res_{v,10,1}^{(5)}(\tau)$
0.1	0.900464302493772	2.7735×10^{-15}	1.004523943044246	4.6810×10^{-15}
0.2	0.803448542998189	1.1723×10^{-15}	1.016373836862601	8.9920×10^{-15}
0.3	0.710824317213952	1.2023×10^{-14}	1.033327205646229	1.3351×10^{-15}
0.4	0.623892736413153	1.1641×10^{-14}	1.053574529276645	1.0168×10^{-14}
0.5	0.543504717634733	1.3233×10^{-16}	1.075649740696301	1.0648×10^{-14}
0.6	0.470149961736370	1.2558×10^{-14}	1.098381593278497	2.8102×10^{-14}
0.7	0.404024163774677	3.7396×10^{-14}	1.120859071635027	1.4690×10^{-14}
0.8	0.345083563213368	3.6526×10^{-14}	1.142403440455486	2.1380×10^{-14}
0.9	0.293093303881749	8.6498×10^{-14}	1.162541379315871	5.4074×10^{-14}
1.0	0.247672792516836	7.3249×10^{-14}	1.180976444182846	4.0555×10^{-14}

Table 2. The results of L_∞ norms, the corresponding convergence rate, and CPU times in Example 1 with diverse R, $\lambda, \alpha = 1$, and $p = 5$.

R	L_∞^u	Noc_∞^u	L_∞^v	Noc_∞^v	CPU(s)
2	8.8464×10^{-2}	–	2.5585×10^{-1}	–	0.55877
4	2.3798×10^{-2}	1.8942	1.4707×10^{-2}	4.1207	0.83877
8	9.2239×10^{-5}	8.0113	1.1027×10^{-4}	7.0593	1.64742
16	1.0027×10^{-8}	13.167	1.0748×10^{-8}	13.325	3.67631
32	3.1173×10^{-11}	8.3294	6.7817×10^{-11}	7.3082	9.55585

The numerical results using $\alpha = 0.75$ are as follows

$$\mathcal{U}_{10,0.75}^{(5)}(\tau) = 1.0412945\,\tau^{\frac{9}{4}} - 0.0042152951\,\tau^{\frac{3}{2}} - 0.17590936\,\tau^6 - 1.087782\,\tau^{\frac{3}{4}} - 0.76166775\,\tau^{\frac{9}{2}}$$
$$- 1.273861\,\tau^3 - 0.0033094122\,\tau^{\frac{15}{2}} + 1.0551812\,\tau^{\frac{15}{4}} + 0.44543369\,\tau^{\frac{21}{4}} + 0.038673796\,\tau^{\frac{27}{4}} + 1.0,$$

$$\mathcal{V}_{10,0.75}^{(5)}(\tau) = 0.8351074\,\tau^3 + 0.7563994\,\tau^{\frac{3}{2}} + 0.084382784\,\tau^6 - 0.00029275212\,\tau^{\frac{3}{4}} + 0.44680831\,\tau^{\frac{9}{2}}$$
$$- 1.0399673\,\tau^{\frac{9}{4}} - 0.00064861533\,\tau^{\frac{15}{2}} - 0.60459347\,\tau^{\frac{15}{4}} - 0.2553921\,\tau^{\frac{21}{4}} - 0.01045752\,\tau^{\frac{27}{4}} + 1.0.$$

The former approximations for each solution of $u(\tau)$ and $v(\tau)$ related to two different values of $\alpha = 1$ and $\alpha = 0.75$ are depicted in Figures 3 and 4. In addition to the approximate solutions, we also visualize the associated REFs for each solution on the left plots. By looking at these figures, we infer that the approximate solutions related to both $\alpha = 1, 0.75$ are very close together. However, the achieved REFs for $\alpha = 0.75$ equal to the fractional order $\lambda = 0.75$ are smaller in magnitude than those obtained using $\alpha = 1$. Therefore, in the next experiments, we only consider the results obtained related to $\alpha = \lambda$.

Next, we consider $\lambda = 0.5$ and $R = 10$. Using $\alpha = 0.5$, the approximate solutions evaluated at some point $\tau \in [0, 1]$ are reported in Table 3. The corresponding absolute errors defined via relations (35) are also tabulated in Table 3.

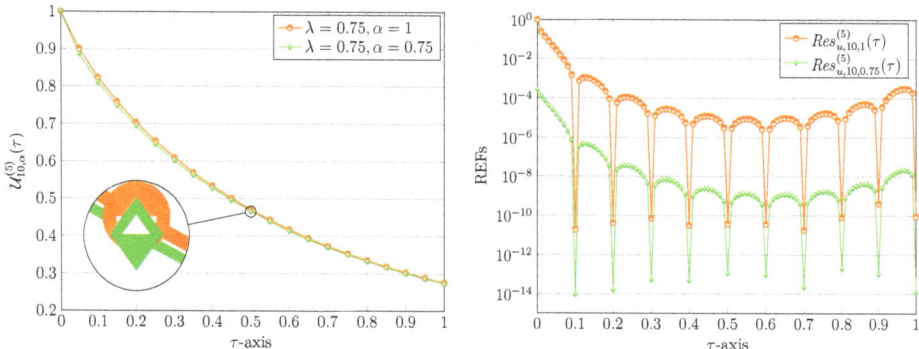

Figure 3. Comparisons of approximate solutions for $u(\tau)$ (**left**) and related REFs (**right**) obtained via the QLM-GCFs technique in Example 1 with $R = 10$, $\lambda = 0.75$, $\alpha = 1, 0.75$, and $p = 5$.

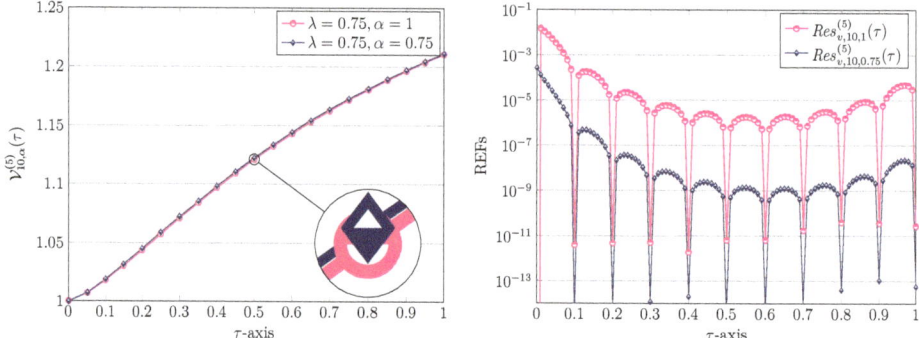

Figure 4. Comparisons of approximate solutions for $v(\tau)$ (**left**) and related REFs (**right**) obtained via the QLM-GCFs technique in Example 1 with $R = 10$, $\lambda = 0.75$, $\alpha = 1, 0.75$, and $p = 5$.

When $\lambda = 0.98$, different numerical methods, such as the variational iteration method (VIM) [14], the PLSM [15], the method based on an operational matrix of Bernstein polynomials [16], and LWOMM [17], reported the approximate solutions for this value. In all of these approaches, the solutions obtained are three-degree polynomials. However, here, we first consider the case $\alpha = 1$ and obtain the following approximate solutions

$$\mathcal{U}_{5,1}^{(5)}(\tau) = 0.038196735\,\tau^5 - 0.20054309\,\tau^4 + 0.32635768\,\tau^3 + 0.13961269\,\tau^2 - 1.054247\,\tau + 1.0,$$

$$\mathcal{V}_{5,1}^{(5)}(\tau) = -0.03637521\,\tau^5 + 0.2145241\,\tau^4 - 0.5073211\,\tau^3 + 0.5049069\,\tau^2 + 0.008199928\,\tau + 1.0.$$

Additionally, the maximum absolute values of REFs using $\alpha = 0.98$ are shown in Table 4 for various values of R as a power of 2. The related Nocs are also tabulated in this table. Moreover, we present the numerical results when $\lambda, \alpha = 0.75$ in Table 4. One can obviously observe a high order of accuracy for the proposed QLM-GCFs. Finally, for the first test case, we use various values of $\lambda = 0.25, 0.5, 0.75, 1$. Utilizing $R = 10$ and $\alpha = \lambda$, we plot the numerical solutions in Figure 5.

Table 3. Numerical results and REFs for $u(\tau), v(\tau)$ obtained via the QLM-GCFs procedure using $R = 10$, $p = 5$ in Example 1 with $\lambda, \alpha = 0.5$.

τ	$\mathcal{U}^{(5)}_{10,0.5}(\tau)$	$Res^{(5)}_{u,10,0.5}(\tau)$	$\mathcal{V}^{(5)}_{10,0.5}(\tau)$	$Res^{(5)}_{v,10,0.5}(\tau)$
0.1	0.676592310003481	2.8530×10^{-14}	1.059227208815533	1.4962×10^{-15}
0.2	0.573857423802071	1.1549×10^{-13}	1.096675293835927	1.0566×10^{-13}
0.3	0.507770381824183	1.3181×10^{-13}	1.124827045650820	1.3320×10^{-13}
0.4	0.459738270417381	6.8264×10^{-13}	1.147290159849651	2.6591×10^{-13}
0.5	0.422579704301791	1.0439×10^{-13}	1.165852096005718	1.5040×10^{-13}
0.6	0.392675915528585	4.1750×10^{-13}	1.181563743233397	4.5923×10^{-14}
0.7	0.367932268722878	9.3469×10^{-13}	1.195103916669479	4.5888×10^{-14}
0.8	0.347025860146580	7.5152×10^{-13}	1.206938751776391	1.2845×10^{-13}
0.9	0.329068932537851	3.1123×10^{-14}	1.217402627420391	7.1534×10^{-14}
1.0	0.313438314355603	1.2928×10^{-12}	1.226743490360364	1.1390×10^{-13}

Table 4. The results of L_∞ norms, the corresponding convergence rate in Example 1 with diverse R, $\lambda, \alpha = 0.75, 0.98$, and $p = 5$.

	$\lambda = 0.75$				$\lambda = 0.98$			
R	L^u_∞	Noc^u_∞	L^v_∞	Noc^v_∞	L^u_∞	Noc^u_∞	L^v_∞	Noc^v_∞
2	2.9301_{-02}	—	2.6438_{-01}	—	8.4327_{-02}	—	2.5731_{-01}	—
4	6.7159_{-02}	-1.1966	5.1045_{-02}	2.3727	2.6363_{-02}	1.6775	1.6514_{-02}	3.9617
8	5.9544_{-04}	6.8175	3.7342_{-04}	7.0948	9.6808_{-05}	8.0892	1.2087_{-04}	7.0941
16	8.0008_{-07}	9.5396	5.8560_{-07}	9.3167	1.5261_{-08}	12.631	1.5225_{-08}	12.955
32	2.3658_{-08}	5.0797	1.2673_{-08}	5.5301	4.7902_{-11}	8.3155	2.3028_{-11}	9.3689

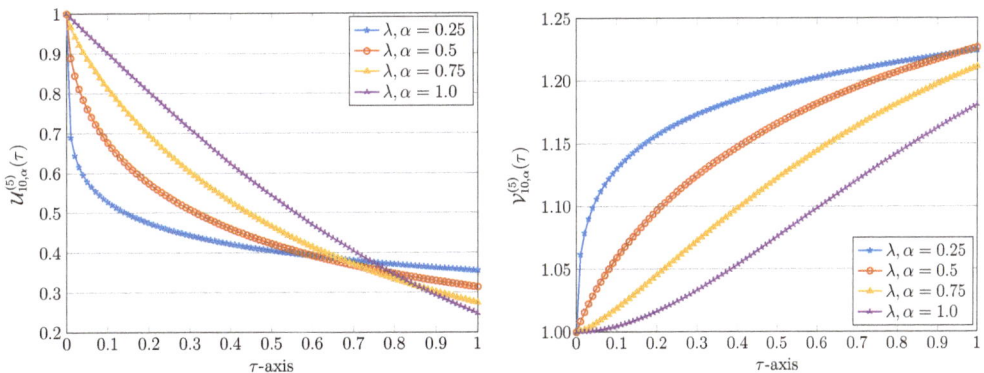

Figure 5. Comparisons of approximate solutions for $u(\tau)$ (**left**) and $v(\tau)$ (**right**) obtained via the QLM-GCFs technique in Example 1 with $R = 10$, $\lambda, \alpha = 0.25, 0.5, 0.75, 1$, and $p = 5$.

Example 2. *In the second model problem, we take $\theta = 0.5$ and $\eta = 0.1$. In this case, we consider the nonlinear coupled system*

$$\begin{cases} {}^{LC}\mathcal{D}^\lambda_\tau u(\tau) = 0.5 - 1.1\, u(\tau) + u^2(\tau)\, v(\tau), \\ {}^{LC}\mathcal{D}^\lambda_\tau v(\tau) = 0.1\, u(\tau) - u^2(\tau)\, v(\tau), \end{cases} \quad \lambda \in (0, 1].$$

Here, we use initial conditions $u(0) = 0.4, v(0) = 1.5$. This example was considered in [14,16,17] previously.

Let us first take $\lambda, \alpha = 1$. By using $R = 5$, the results of the approximations are as follows

$$\mathcal{U}_{5,1}^{(5)}(\tau) = -0.002595532\,\tau^5 - 0.01516870\,\tau^4 + 0.02354928\,\tau^3 - 0.002285779\,\tau^2 + 0.30026\,\tau + 0.4,$$

$$\mathcal{V}_{5,1}^{(5)}(\tau) = 0.007186591\,\tau^5 + 0.007075174\,\tau^4 - 0.02123004\,\tau^3 - 0.1484152\,\tau^2 - 0.2001643\,\tau + 1.5.$$

The REFs related to the above approximate solutions are shown in Figure 6. To show that the achieved REFs are decreasing as a function of R, we also plot the REFs related to $R = 10, 15$ in Figure 6. Clearly, the desired level of accuracy is achievable by increasing the number of basis functions.

We next tabulate the numerical results obtained by using $R = 10$ in Table 5. Here, we have used the midpoints $0.05, 0.15, \ldots, 0.95$ on the interval $[0, 1]$. Note that these midpoints are different from the points used in Table 1, which are exactly the same as the collocation points (29) when $R = 10$. In fact, the smallest magnitude of errors is achieved at the collocation points. Finally, for this test case and for $\lambda = 1$, we display the maximum absolute REFs achieved by utilizing various R numbers in Table 6. The associated Nocs are also visible in this table. The results show the exponential behavior in terms of the accuracy of the presented QLM-GCFs.

We now consider the fractional-order $0 < \lambda < 1$. By considering $\lambda = 0.5, 0.75$, we obtain the results of absolute values of REFs using various $R = 2, 4, \ldots, 32$, as shown in Table 7. The associated numerical order of convergence, i.e., Nocs, is also depicted in Table 7. Obviously, we can get a higher order accuracy by increasing R. Finally, we present numerical results computed at some points $\tau \in [0, 1]$ in Table 8. Here, we have used diverse values of $\lambda, \alpha = 0.25, 0.5, 0.75$.

Table 5. Numerical results and REFs for $u(\tau), v(\tau)$ obtained via the QLM-GCFs procedure using $R = 10, p = 5$ in Example 2 with $\lambda, \alpha = 1$.

τ	$\mathcal{U}_{10,1}^{(5)}(\tau)$	$Res_{u,10,1}^{(5)}(\tau)$	$\mathcal{V}_{10,1}^{(5)}(\tau)$	$Res_{v,10,1}^{(5)}(\tau)$
0.05	0.420364987163538	5.4281×10^{-08}	1.464193736210683	6.9171×10^{-08}
0.15	0.458172247718453	2.8803×10^{-09}	1.395407097431014	3.6639×10^{-09}
0.25	0.492300715744509	5.0979×10^{-10}	1.330238068232444	6.4809×10^{-10}
0.35	0.523000098574405	1.6945×10^{-10}	1.268512980921797	2.1555×10^{-10}
0.45	0.550506819287693	9.0387×10^{-11}	1.210065493419779	1.1521×10^{-10}
0.55	0.575044582788486	7.2710×10^{-11}	1.154736326110934	9.3018×10^{-11}
0.65	0.596824922738173	8.6618×10^{-11}	1.102373006480542	1.1144×10^{-10}
0.75	0.616047729841562	1.5522×10^{-10}	1.052829621356641	2.0132×10^{-10}
0.85	0.632901761975499	4.4405×10^{-10}	1.005966576578516	5.8234×10^{-10}
0.95	0.647565136639679	2.3660×10^{-09}	0.961650363916099	3.1497×10^{-09}

Table 6. The results of L_∞ norms, the corresponding convergence rate, and CPU times in Example 2 with diverse R, $\lambda, \alpha = 1$, and $p = 5$.

R	L_∞^u	Noc_∞^u	L_∞^v	Noc_∞^v
2	2.3453×10^{-2}	—	3.1850×10^{-2}	—
4	1.5211×10^{-3}	3.9466	3.7107×10^{-3}	3.1015
8	1.5652×10^{-6}	9.9245	3.1978×10^{-7}	13.502
16	3.8244×10^{-11}	15.321	5.1169×10^{-11}	12.610
32	4.0160×10^{-13}	6.5733	5.1238×10^{-14}	9.9638

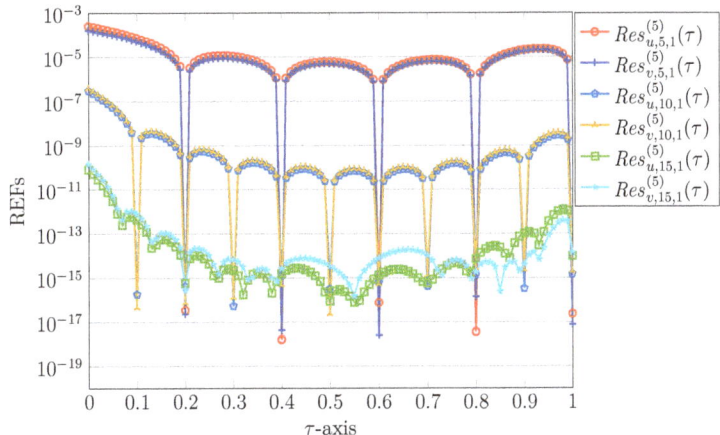

Figure 6. Comparisons of achieved REFs obtained via QLM-GCFs in Example 2 with $\lambda, \alpha = 1$, $R = 5, 10, 15$, and $p = 5$.

Table 7. The results of L_∞ norms and the corresponding convergence rate in Example 2 with diverse R, $\lambda, \alpha = 0.5, 0.75$, and $p = 5$.

	$\lambda = 0.5$				$\lambda = 0.75$			
R	L_∞^u	Noc_∞^u	L_∞^v	Noc_∞^v	L_∞^u	Noc_∞^u	L_∞^v	Noc_∞^v
2	8.3797_{-02}	–	1.7867_{-01}	–	6.2299_{-02}	–	1.0729_{-01}	–
4	5.0780_{-02}	0.7226	6.4041_{-02}	1.4802	4.2712_{-02}	3.8665	3.0414_{-03}	5.1406
8	5.6280_{-03}	3.1736	3.8246_{-03}	4.0656	4.1380_{-04}	3.3676	5.3709_{-04}	2.5015
16	1.2860_{-04}	5.4516	4.9033_{-05}	6.2854	6.9800_{-08}	12.533	6.5807_{-08}	12.995
32	1.8406_{-07}	9.4485	3.9839_{-07}	6.9434	1.1363_{-11}	12.585	4.3433_{-11}	10.565

Table 8. Numerical results and REFs for $u(\tau), v(\tau)$ obtained via the QLM-GCFs procedure using $R = 10$, $p = 5$ in Example 2 with $\lambda, \alpha = 0.25, 0.5, 0.75$.

	$\lambda = \alpha = 0.25$		$\lambda = \alpha = 0.5$		$\lambda = \alpha = 0.75$	
τ	$\mathcal{U}_{10,\alpha}^{(5)}(\tau)$	$\mathcal{V}_{10,\alpha}^{(5)}(\tau)$	$\mathcal{U}_{10,\alpha}^{(5)}(\tau)$	$\mathcal{V}_{10,\alpha}^{(5)}(\tau)$	$\mathcal{U}_{10,\alpha}^{(5)}(\tau)$	$\mathcal{V}_{10,\alpha}^{(5)}(\tau)$
0.05	0.53635357	1.36264701	0.54865158	1.35823553	0.47111143	1.40197516
0.15	0.59116199	1.26326681	0.62140849	1.25622929	0.54574688	1.28946276
0.25	0.61628002	1.20991192	0.65785082	1.18993711	0.59572321	1.20586462
0.35	0.63187140	1.17308734	0.68077488	1.13917346	0.63266615	1.13749235
0.45	0.64277275	1.14501830	0.69648157	1.09776992	0.66096850	1.07937071
0.55	0.65091723	1.12240609	0.70772186	1.06280079	0.68300039	1.02887191
0.65	0.65726824	1.10352709	0.71595859	1.03259028	0.70025234	0.98436225
0.75	0.66237220	1.08736331	0.72206423	1.00606805	0.71374714	0.94472572
0.85	0.66656700	1.07326219	0.72660021	0.98249967	0.72422723	0.90915154
0.95	0.67007499	1.06078003	0.72994787	0.96135501	0.73225308	0.87702453

6. Conclusions

Generalized (fractional-order) clique basis functions (GCFs) have been used to devise not only an effective but also an accurate spectral matrix collocation approach for finding approximate solutions of the nonlinear Brusselator system of equations of fractional order arising in chemical modeling. The fractional derivative is described in the Liouville–Caputo sense. To overcome the underlying nonlinearity of the model, the method of quasi-linearization (QLM) is first employed to receive a family of linearized equations. Afterward, the spectral clique collocation procedure is used to solve this sequence of equations iteratively. The convergence analysis of the proposed combined QLM-GCFs is established. To support the theoretical findings and in order to show the applicability of the QLM-GCFs, a set of numerical test examples is carried out. The results presented in the tables and figures indicate the accuracy of the proposed approach over the existing numerical models and the gain in computational efficiency in terms of CPU time. The presented technique is straightforward, easy to implement, and computationally less demanding.

Author Contributions: Conceptualization, M.I. and H.M.S.; methodology, M.I. and H.M.S.; software, M.I.; validation, M.I. and H.M.S.; formal analysis, M.I. and H.M.S.; funding acquisition, H.M.S.; investigation, M.I. and H.M.S.; writing—original draft preparation, M.I.; writing—review and editing, M.I. and H.M.S. All authors have read and agreed to the published version of the manuscript.

Funding: This research received no external funding.

Institutional Review Board Statement: Not applicable

Informed Consent Statement: Not applicable.

Data Availability Statement: Not applicable.

Conflicts of Interest: The authors declare no conflict of interest.

References

1. Prigogine, I.; Lefever, R. Symmetry breaking instabilities in dissipative systems II. *J. Chem. Phys.* **1968**, *48*, 1695–1700. [CrossRef]
2. Epstein, I.R.; Pojman, J.K. *An Introduction to Nonlinear Chemical Dynamics: Oscillations, Waves, Patterns, and Chaos*; Oxford University Press: New York, NY, USA, 1998.
3. Gray, P.; Scott, S.K.; Merkin J.H. The Brusselator model of oscillatory reactions: relationships between two-variable and four-variable models with rigorous application of mass conservation and detailed balance. *J. Chem. Soc. Faraday Trans.* **1988**, *84*, 993–1011. [CrossRef]
4. Field, R.J.; Györgyi L. *Chaos in Chemistry and Biochemistry*; World Scientific: Singapore, 1993.
5. Hilfer, R. (Ed.) *Applications of Fractional Calculus in Physics*; World Scientific: River Edge, NJ, USA, 2000.
6. Kilbas, A.A.; Srivastava, H.M.; Trujillo, J.J. *Theory and Application of Fractional Differential Equations*; North-Holland Mathematics Studies: Amsterdam, The Netherllands, 2006; Volume 204.
7. Tong, T.O.; Kekana, M.C.; Shatalov, M.Y.; Moshokoa, S.P. Numerical investigation of Brusselator chemical model by residual function using Mathematica software. *J. Comput. Theoret. Nanosci.* **2020**, *17*, 2947–2954. [CrossRef]
8. Gafiychuk, V.; Datsko, B.; Stability analysis and limit cycle in fractional system with Brusselator nonlinearities. *Phys. Lett. A* **2008**, *372*, 4902–4904. [CrossRef]
9. Sun, M.; Tan, Y.; Chen, L. Dynamical behaviors of the Brusselator system with impulsive input. *J. Math. Chem.* **2008**, *44*, 637–649. [CrossRef]
10. Yuan, L.G.; Kuang, J.H. Stability and a numerical solution of fractional-order Brusselator chemical reaction system. *J. Fract. Calc. Appl.* **2017**, *8*, 38–47.
11. Wang, Y.; Li, C. Does the fractional Brusselator with efficient dimension less than 1 have a limit cycle? *Phys. Lett. A* **2007**, *363*, 414–419. [CrossRef]
12. Ongun, M.Y.; Arslan, D.; Garrappa, R. Nonstandard finite difference schemes for a fractional-order Brusselator system. *Adv. Differ. Equ.* **2013**, *2013*, 102. [CrossRef]
13. Zafar, Z.U.A.; Rehan, K.; Mushtaq, M.; Rafiq, M. Numerical treatment for nonlinear Brusselator chemical model. *J. Differ. Equ. Appl.* **2017**, *23*, 521–538. [CrossRef]
14. Jafari, H.; Kadem, A.; Baleanu, D. Variational iteration method for a fractional-order Brusselator system. *Abstr. Appl. Anal.* **2014**, *2014*, 496323. [CrossRef]
15. Bota, C.; Caruntu, B. Approximate analytical solutions of the fractional-order Brusselator system using the polynomial least squares method. *Adv. Math. Phys.* **2015**, *2015*, 450235. [CrossRef]
16. Khan, H.; Jafari, H.; Khan, R.A.; Tajadodi, H.; Johnston, S.J. Numerical solutions of the nonlinear fractional-order Brusselator system by Bernstein polynomials. *Sci. World J.* **2014**, *2014*, 257484. [CrossRef] [PubMed]
17. Chang, P.; Isah, A. Legendre wavelet operational matrix of fractional derivative through wavelet-polynomial transformation and its applications in solving fractional order Brusselator system. *J. Phys. Conf. Ser.* **2016**, *693*, 012001. [CrossRef]

18. Ongun, M.Y.; Arslan, D.; Farzi, J. Numerical solutions of fractional order autocatalytic chemical reaction model. *Süleyman Demirel Ünivers. Fen Bilim. Enstitüsü Dergisi* **2017**, *21*, 165–172. [CrossRef]
19. Asv, R.K.; Devi, S. A novel three-step iterative approach for oscillatory chemical reactions of fractional Brusselator model. *Int. J. Model. Simul.* **2022**, *204*, 1–20. [CrossRef]
20. Saad, K.M. Fractal-fractional Brusselator chemical reaction. *Chaos Solit. Fract.* **2021**, *150*, 11187. [CrossRef]
21. Mohammadi, M.; Mokhtari, R.; Schaback, R. A meshless method for solving the 2D Brusselator reaction-diffusion system. *Comput. Model. Eng. Sci.* **2014**, *101*, 113–138.
22. Tlidi, M.; Gandica, Y.; Sonnino, G.; Averlant, E.; Panajotov, K. Self-Replicating spots in the Brusselator model and extreme events in the one-dimensional case with delay. *Entropy* **2016**, *18*, 64. [CrossRef]
23. Alfifi, H.Y. Feedback control for a diffusive and delayed Brusselator model: Semi-analytical solutions. *Symmetry* **2021**, *13*, 725. [CrossRef]
24. Mittal, A.K.; Balyan, L.K. A highly accurate time–space pseudospectral approximation and stability analysis of two dimensional Brusselator model for chemical systems. *Int. J. Appl. Comput. Math.* **2019**, *5*, 140. [CrossRef]
25. Izadi, M.; Samei, M.E. Time accurate solution to Benjamin-Bona-Mahony Burgers equation via Taylor-Boubaker series scheme. *Bound. Value Probl.* **2022**, *2022*, 17. [CrossRef]
26. Razavi, M.; Hosseini, M.M.; Salemi, A. Error analysis and Kronecker implementation of Chebyshev spectral collocation method for solving linear PDEs. *Comput. Methods Differ. Equ.* **2022**, *10*, 914–927.
27. Izadi, M.; Srivastava, H.M.; Adel, W. An effective approximation algorithm for second-order singular functional differential equations. *Axioms* **2022**, *11*, 133. [CrossRef]
28. Chouhan, D.; Mishra, V.; Srivastava, H.M. Bernoulli wavelet method for numerical solution of anomalous infiltration and diffusion modeling by nonlinear fractional differential equations of variable order. *Results Appl. Math.* **2021**, *10*, 100146. [CrossRef]
29. Izadi, M.; Srivastava, H.M. An efficient approximation technique applied to a non-linear Lane-Emden pantograph delay differential model. *Appl. Math. Comput.* **2021**, *401*, 126123. [CrossRef]
30. Yüzbaşı, Ş.; Izadi, M. Bessel-quasilinearization technique to solve the fractional-order HIV-1 infection of CD4+ T-cells considering the impact of antiviral drug treatment. *Appl. Math. Comput.* **2022**, *431*, 127319. [CrossRef]
31. Srivastava, H.M. Some parametric and argument variations of the operators of fractional calculus and related special functions and integral transformations. *J. Nonlinear Convex Anal.* **2021**, *22*, 1501–1520.
32. Srivastava, H.M. An introductory overview of fractional-calculus operators based upon the Fox-Wright and related higher transcendental functions. *J. Adv. Eng. Comput.* **2021**, *5*, 135–166. [CrossRef]
33. Hoede, C.; Li, X. Clique polynomials and independent set polynomials of graphs. *Discrete Math.* **1994**, *125*, 219–228. [CrossRef]
34. Kumbinarasaiah, S. A new approach for the numerical solution for the non-linear Klein–Gordon equation. *SeMA J.* **2020**, *77*, 435–456. [CrossRef]
35. Ganji, R.M.; Jafari, H.; Kgarose, M.; Mohammadi, A. Numerical solutions of time-fractional Klein-Gordon equations by clique polynomials. *Alexandria Eng. J.* **2021**, *60*, 4563-4571. [CrossRef]
36. Adel, W.; Kumbinarasaiah, S. A new clique polynomial approach for fractional partial differential equations. *Int. J. Nonlinear Sci. Numer. Simul.* **2022**. [CrossRef]
37. Heydari, M.H.; Razzaghi, M. Highly accurate solutions for space-time fractional Schrödinger equations with non-smooth continuous solution using the hybrid clique functions. *Math. Sci.* **2021**. [CrossRef]
38. Stewart, G.W. *Afternotes on Numerical Analysis*; SIAM: Philadephia, PA, USA, 1996; Volume 49.
39. Yuttanan, B.; Razzaghi, M.; Vo T.N. A fractional-order generalized Taylor wavelet method for nonlinear fractional delay and nonlinear fractional pantograph differential equations. *Math. Methods Appl. Sci.* **2021**, *44*, 4156–4175. [CrossRef]
40. Izadi, M. An approximation technique for first Painlevé equation. *TWMS J. Appl. Eng. Math.* **2021**, *11*, 739–750.
41. Izadi, M.; Yüzbaşı, Ş.; Noeiaghdam, S. Approximating solutions of non-linear Troesch's problem via an efficient quasi-linearization Bessel approach. *Mathematics* **2021**, *9*, 1841. [CrossRef]
42. Srivastava, H.M.; Shah, F.A.; Irfan, Md. Generalized wavelet quasi-linearization method for solving population growth model of fractional order. *Math. Methods Appl. Sci.* **2020**, *43*, 8753–8762. [CrossRef]
43. Izadi, M.; Srivastava, H.M. Generalized Bessel quasilinearlization technique applied to Bratu and Lane-Emden type equations of arbitrary order. *Fractal Fract.* **2021**, *5*, 179. [CrossRef]
44. Izadi, M.; Yüzbaşı, Ş.; Adel, W. A new Chelyshkov matrix method to solve linear and nonlinear fractional delay differential equations with error analysis. *Math. Sci.* **2022**. [CrossRef]
45. Izadi, M.; Srivastava, H.M. A novel matrix technique for multi-order pantograph differential equations of fractional order. *Proc. R. Soc. Lond. Ser. A Math. Phys. Eng. Sci.* **2021**, *477*, 2021031. [CrossRef]
46. Izadi, M.; Yüzbaşı, Ş.; Cattani, C. Approximating solutions to fractional-order Bagley-Torvik equation via generalized Bessel polynomial on large domains. *Ricerche Mat.* **2021**. [CrossRef]

Article

Non-Canonical Functional Differential Equation of Fourth-Order: New Monotonic Properties and Their Applications in Oscillation Theory

Amany Nabih [1,2], Clemente Cesarano [3,*], Osama Moaaz [4,5,*], Mona Anis [5] and Elmetwally M. Elabbasy [5]

[1] Faculty of Science, Mansoura University, Mansoura 35516, Egypt
[2] Department of Basic Sciences, Higher Future Institute of Engineering and Technology in Mansoura, Mansoura 35516, Egypt
[3] Section of Mathematics, International Telematic University Uninettuno, Corso Vittorio Emanuele II 39, 00186 Rome, Italy
[4] Department of Mathematics, College of Science, Qassim University, P.O. Box 6644, Buraydah 51452, Saudi Arabia
[5] Department of Mathematics, Faculty of Science, Mansoura University, Mansoura 35516, Egypt
* Correspondence: c.cesarano@uninettunouniversity.net (C.C.); o_moaaz@mans.edu.eg (O.M.)

Abstract: In the present article, we iteratively deduce new monotonic properties of a class from the positive solutions of fourth-order delay differential equations. We discuss the non-canonical case in which there are possible decreasing positive solutions. Then, we find iterative criteria that exclude the existence of these positive decreasing solutions. Using these new criteria and based on the comparison and Riccati substitution methods, we create sufficient conditions to ensure that all solutions of the studied equation oscillate. In addition to having many applications in various scientific domains, the study of the oscillatory and non-oscillatory features of differential equation solutions is a theoretically rich field with many intriguing issues. Finally, we show the importance of the results by applying them to special cases of the studied equation.

Keywords: delay differential equation; higher-order; oscillatory; nonoscillatory; non-canonical case

1. Introduction

In this work, we study the asymptotic behavior of solutions to the fourth-order delay differential equation of the form

$$(h(\mathfrak{r})(\Phi'''(\mathfrak{r}))^\alpha)' + q(\mathfrak{r})\Phi^\alpha(\tau(\mathfrak{r})) = 0, \tag{1}$$

where $\mathfrak{r} \geq \mathfrak{r}_0$. Through the paper, the next conditions are satisfied:

(V1) $\alpha > 0$ is a quotient of odd positive integers;
(V2) $h, q, \tau \in C([\mathfrak{r}_0, \infty), (0, \infty))$, $\tau(\mathfrak{r}) < \mathfrak{r}$, $\lim_{\mathfrak{r}\to\infty} \tau(\mathfrak{r}) = \infty$, and

$$\eta(\mathfrak{r}_0) = \int_{\mathfrak{r}_0}^\infty h^{-1/\alpha}(v)dv < \infty. \tag{2}$$

By a solution of (1), we mean a function $\Phi \in C([\mathfrak{r}_*, \infty), \mathbb{R})$, $\mathfrak{r}_* \geq \mathfrak{r}_0$ such that $\Phi(\mathfrak{r})$ satisfies (1) on $[\mathfrak{r}_*, \infty)$. In what follows, we suppose that solutions of (1) exist and can be continued indefinitely to the right. Furthermore, we consider only solutions $\Phi(\mathfrak{r})$ of (1) that satisfy $\sup\{|\Phi(\mathfrak{r})| : \mathfrak{r}_* \leq \mathfrak{r}\} > 0$ for all $\mathfrak{r} \geq \mathfrak{r}_*$, and we tacitly assume that (1) possesses such solutions.

Definition 1. *A solution Φ of (1) is said to be non-oscillatory if, essentially, it is positive or negative; otherwise, it is said to be oscillatory. If all of its solutions oscillate, the equation itself is called oscillatory.*

The delay differential equations are a subclass of functional differential equations. The concept of delay in systems is proposed as a key role in modeling when representing the time taken to complete some hidden operations. Examples of the delay in the predator–prey model occur when the predator birth rate is affected by previous levels of predator or prey rather than only current levels. With the rapid development of communication technologies, sending measured signals to the remote-control center has become increasingly simple. However, the main problem facing engineers is the inevitable time delay between the measurement and the signal received by the controller, and this time delay must be taken into account at the design stage to avoid risks of experimental instability and potential damage, see [1,2].

Differential equations of the fourth-order delay can be found in the mathematical models of numerous biological, chemical, and physical phenomena. Examples of such applications include elastic problems and soil settlement. One model that can be represented by a fourth-order oscillatory equation with delay is the oscillatory traction of a muscle, which occurs when the muscle is under an inertial load [3].

One of two things is necessarily required to explain natural phenomena and problems that use differential equations in their modeling: either finding solutions to these equations or studying the properties of these solutions. However, the equations resulting from the modeling of natural phenomena are often non-linear differential equations that are difficult to find a closed-form solution to, and this has strongly stimulated the study of the qualitative behavior of these models. From here, strong interest has emerged in the study of the qualitative theory of differential equations, one of the most important branches of which is the theory of oscillation. Obtaining lower bounds for the separation between succeeding zeros, taking into account the number of zeros, studying the laws of distribution of the zeros, and establishing the conditions for the existence of oscillatory (non-oscillatory) solutions and/or convergence to zeroconstitute the essence of oscillation theory, see [4].

Finding sufficient conditions for the oscillatory and non-oscillatory properties of second and higher-order differential equations has been a persistent area of research over the last few years, see [5–7]. Among the numerous papers dealing with this subject, we refer in particular to the following.

Onose [8] focused on the oscillation of fourth-order functional differential equations

$$\left(h(\mathfrak{r})\Phi''(\mathfrak{r})\right)'' + f(\Phi(\tau(\mathfrak{r})), \mathfrak{r}) = 0$$

and

$$\left(h(\mathfrak{r})\Phi''(\mathfrak{r})\right)'' + q(\mathfrak{r})f(\Phi(\tau(\mathfrak{r}))) = \tau(\mathfrak{r}),$$

under the canonical case. The oscillation and non-oscillation of the fourth and higher-order differential equations have been the focus of the attention of numerous authors since this paper was first published.

Wu [9] and Kamo and Usami [10] studied the oscillatory of a fourth-order differential equation

$$\left(h(\mathfrak{r})|\Phi''(\mathfrak{r})|^{\alpha-1}\Phi''(\mathfrak{r})\right)'' + q|\Phi(\mathfrak{r})|^{\beta-1}\Phi(\mathfrak{r}) = 0,$$

when the noncanonical holds and the constants α and β are positive.

Grace et al. [11] focused on the oscillatory behavior of the fourth-order differential equation of the form

$$\left(h(\Phi')^{\alpha}\right)'''(\mathfrak{r}) + q(\mathfrak{r})f(\Phi(g(\mathfrak{r}))) = 0,$$

under the noncanonical case.

Zhang et al. [12] and Baculikova et al. [13] studied the oscillatory behavior of the higher-order differential equation

$$\left(h(\mathfrak{r})\left(\Phi^{n-1}(\mathfrak{r})\right)^{\alpha}\right)' + q(\mathfrak{r})f(\Phi(\tau(\mathfrak{r}))) = 0. \tag{3}$$

Ref. [12] provided some oscillation criteria for Equation (3), in which $f(\Phi) = \Phi^\beta$ and β is a quotient of odd positive integers. In [13], various techniques have been used in investigating higher-order differential equations. In the case where $n = 4$ and $f(\Phi) = \Phi^\alpha$, by the Riccatti technique, Zhang et al. [14] established some new criteria for the oscillation of all solutions of the fourth-order differential Equation (3).

Theorem 1. *Ref. [12] Let $n \geq 2$. Suppose that (2) holds. Further, assume that for some constant $\lambda_0 \in (0,1)$, the differential equation*

$$\Phi'(\mathfrak{r}) + q(\mathfrak{r})\left(\frac{\lambda_0 \tau^{n-1}(\mathfrak{r})}{(n-1)!h^{1/\alpha}(\tau(\mathfrak{r}))}\right)^\beta \Phi^{\beta/\alpha}(\tau(\mathfrak{r})) = 0, \tag{4}$$

is oscillatory. If

$$\limsup_{\mathfrak{r} \to \infty} \int_{\mathfrak{r}_0}^{\mathfrak{r}} \left(M^{\beta-\alpha} q(\jmath) \left(\frac{\lambda_1 \tau^{n-2}(\jmath)}{(n-2)!}\right)^\beta \eta^\alpha(\jmath) - \frac{\alpha^{\alpha+1}}{(\alpha+1)^{\alpha+1}} \frac{1}{\eta(\jmath) h^{1/\alpha}(\jmath)}\right) d\jmath = \infty, \tag{5}$$

for some constant $\lambda_1 \in (0,1)$ and for every constant $M > 0$, then every solution of (6) is oscillatory or tends to zero.

Zhang et al. [15] suggested some new oscillation criteria for an even-order delay differential equation

$$\left(h(\mathfrak{r})\left(\Phi^{n-1}(\mathfrak{r})\right)^\alpha\right)' + q(\mathfrak{r})\Phi^\beta(\tau(\mathfrak{r})) = 0, \tag{6}$$

in the noncanonical case with $n \geq 4$, where β is a quotient of odd positive integers.

Theorem 2. *Ref. [15] Let $n \geq 4$ be even, (V1), (V2), and (2). Suppose that differential Equation (4) is oscillatory for some constant $\lambda_0 \in (0,1)$. If (5) and*

$$\limsup_{\mathfrak{r} \to \infty} \int_{\mathfrak{r}_0}^{\mathfrak{r}} \left[M^{\beta-\alpha} q(\jmath) H^\alpha(\jmath) - \frac{\alpha^{\alpha+1}}{(\alpha+1)^{\alpha+1}} \frac{(H'(\jmath))^{\alpha+1}}{H(\jmath)\eta_1^\alpha(\jmath)}\right] d\jmath = \infty,$$

hold for some constants $\lambda_1 \in (0,1)$ and for every constant $M > 0$, then (6) is oscillatory, where

$$H(\mathfrak{r}) = \int_{\mathfrak{r}}^{\infty} (\jmath - \mathfrak{r})\eta(\jmath) d\jmath.$$

By using a generalized Riccatti substitution, in the case $f(\Phi) = q\Phi^\beta$ where q is a nonnegative function and β is a quotient of odd positive integers, Moaaz and Muhib [16] provided a new criterion for the oscillation of solutions of fourth-order quasi-linear differential equations

$$\left(h(\mathfrak{r})\left(\Phi'''(\mathfrak{r})\right)^\alpha\right)' + f(\mathfrak{r}, \Phi(\sigma(\mathfrak{r}))) = 0. \tag{7}$$

Theorem 3. *Ref. [16] Suppose that $\alpha \geq 1$ and the differential equation*

$$\Phi'(\mathfrak{r}) + q(\mathfrak{r})\left(\frac{\lambda_0 \tau^3(\mathfrak{r})}{3!h^{1/\alpha}(\tau(\mathfrak{r}))}\right)^\beta \Phi^{\beta/\alpha}(\tau(\mathfrak{r})) = 0, \tag{8}$$

oscillates where $\lambda_0 \in (0,1)$. If there is a positive function $\gamma \in C^1([\mathfrak{r}_0, \infty), (0, \infty))$ such that

$$\limsup_{\mathfrak{r} \to \infty} \int_{\mathfrak{r}_0}^{\mathfrak{r}} \left(\varphi(\jmath) - \frac{h(\jmath)\gamma(\jmath)}{(\alpha+1)^{\alpha+1}} \left(\frac{\gamma'(\jmath)}{\gamma(\jmath)} + \frac{(1+\alpha)}{h^{1/\alpha}(\jmath)\eta(\jmath)}\right)^{\alpha+1}\right) d\jmath = \infty, \tag{9}$$

holds for any positive constants c_1 and c_2 and for $\lambda_1 \in (0,1)$, where

$$\varphi(\mathfrak{r}) = \gamma(\mathfrak{r})q\left(\frac{\lambda_1}{2!}\tau^2\right)^\beta + (1-\alpha)\frac{\gamma(\mathfrak{r})}{h^{1/\alpha}(\mathfrak{r})\eta^{\alpha+1}(\mathfrak{r})}$$

then every solution of (6) is oscillatory or tends to zero.

Theorem 4. *Ref. [16] Suppose that Equation (8) oscillates where $\lambda_o \in (0,1)$. If there is a function $\gamma \in C^1([\mathfrak{r}_o, \infty), (0, \infty))$ such that*

$$\limsup_{\mathfrak{r}\to\infty} \frac{\eta^\alpha(\mathfrak{r})}{\gamma(\mathfrak{r})} \int_{\mathfrak{r}_o}^{\mathfrak{r}} \left(\gamma(\jmath)q(\jmath)\left(\frac{\lambda_1}{2!}\tau^2(\jmath)\right)^\alpha - \frac{h(\jmath)(\gamma'(\jmath))^{\alpha+1}}{(\alpha+1)^{\alpha+1}\gamma^\alpha(\jmath)}\right)d\jmath > 1, \qquad (10)$$

then every solution of (7) is oscillatory or converges to zero as $\mathfrak{r} \to \infty$ for $\lambda_1 \in (0,1)$.

Theorem 5. *Ref. [16] Suppose that $\alpha \geq 1$ and the differential Equation (8) is oscillatory or some constant $\lambda_o \in (0,1)$. If there is a function $\gamma \in C^1([\mathfrak{r}_o, \infty), (0, \infty))$ such that (9) and*

$$\limsup_{\mathfrak{r}\to\infty} \int_{\mathfrak{r}_o}^{\mathfrak{r}} \left[\psi(\jmath) - \frac{\gamma(\jmath)}{(\alpha+1)^{(\alpha+1)}\eta_1^\alpha(\mathfrak{r})}\left(\frac{\gamma'(\jmath)}{\gamma(\jmath)} + \frac{(1+\alpha)\eta_1(\jmath)}{\eta_2(\jmath)}\right)^{\alpha+1}\right] d\jmath = \infty, \qquad (11)$$

holds for $\lambda_1 \in (0,1)$, where

$$\psi(\mathfrak{r}) = q\gamma(\mathfrak{r}) + (1-\alpha)\gamma(\mathfrak{r})\eta_1(\mathfrak{r})/\eta_2^{\alpha+1}(\mathfrak{r}).$$

Then, (7) is oscillatory.

Elabbasy et al. [17] considered the even-order neutral differential equation with several delays

$$(h(\mathfrak{r})(z^{(n-1)}(\mathfrak{r}))^\alpha)' + \sum_{i=1}^k q_i(\mathfrak{r})f(\Phi(\tau_i(\mathfrak{r}))) = 0,$$

where $z(\mathfrak{r}) = \Phi(\mathfrak{r}) + p(\mathfrak{r})\Phi(\tau(\mathfrak{r}))$ and $n \geq 4$ with the noncanonical operator. Moaaz et al. [18] studied the fourth-order delay differential equation of the form

$$(h(\mathfrak{r})(\Phi'''(\mathfrak{r}))^\alpha)' + f(\mathfrak{r}, \Phi(\sigma(\mathfrak{r}))) = 0,$$

under the noncanonical case.

Lemma 1. *Ref. [19] Let $f \in C^n([\mathfrak{r}_o, \infty), (0, \infty))$. If the derivative $f^{(n)}(\mathfrak{r})$ is eventually of one sign for all large $\mathfrak{r}$, then there is a $\mathfrak{r}_\Phi$ such that $\mathfrak{r}_\Phi \geq \mathfrak{r}_o$ and an integer l, $0 \leq l \leq n$, with $n+l$ even for $f^{(n)}(\mathfrak{r}) \geq 0$, or $n+l$ odd for $f^{(n)}(\mathfrak{r}) \leq 0$ such that*

$$l > 0 \text{ implies } f^{(k)}(\mathfrak{r}) > 0 \text{ for } \mathfrak{r} \geq \mathfrak{r}_\Phi, \ k = 0, 1, \ldots, l-1,$$

and

$$l \leq n-1 \text{ implies } (-1)^{l+k} f^{(k)}(\mathfrak{r}) > 0 \text{ for } \mathfrak{r} \geq \mathfrak{r}_\Phi, \ k = l, l+1, \ldots, n-1.$$

Lemma 2. *Ref. [12] Let α be a ratio of two odd positive integers. Then,*

$$Lv^{(\alpha+1)/\alpha} - Kv \geq -\frac{\alpha^\alpha}{(\alpha+1)^{\alpha+1}} \frac{K^{\alpha+1}}{L^\alpha}, \quad L > 0 \qquad (12)$$

and

$$A^{(\alpha+1)/\alpha} - (A-B)^{(\alpha+1)/\alpha} \leq \frac{1}{\alpha} B^{1/\alpha}[(1+\alpha)A - B], \quad \alpha \geq 1, \ AB \geq 0. \qquad (13)$$

The main purpose of this work is to test the oscillation of solutions of a fourth-order delay differential Equation (1). This paper is organized as follows: In Section 2, we create new properties that help us achieve more effective terms in the oscillation of the studied equation. In Section 3, we apply the Riccati substitution in the general form and the comparison method to obtain criteria that excluded decreasing solutions. In Section 4, by combining the results known in the literature and the results we obtained, we set criteria that ensure the oscillation of the studied equation and offer an illustrative example to show our results. Finally, in Section 5, we conclude the article with a summary.

2. New Monotonic Properties

It is well known that positive solutions of delay differential equations must be categorized based on the sign of their derivatives when investigating their oscillatory behavior. Now, we assume that Φ is an eventually positive solution of (1). From the differential equation in (1) and taking into account that $q(\mathfrak{t}) > 0$, we have that $h(\mathfrak{t})(\Phi'''(\mathfrak{t}))^\alpha$ is a nonincreasing function. Furthermore, according to Lemma 1, we obtain the following three cases, eventually:

$$\begin{aligned}
\text{Case (1)}: &\quad \Phi'(\mathfrak{t}) > 0, \Phi'''(\mathfrak{t}) > 0 \text{ and } \Phi^{(4)}(\mathfrak{t}) < 0; \\
\text{Case (2)}: &\quad \Phi'(\mathfrak{t}) > 0, \Phi''(\mathfrak{t}) > 0 \text{ and } \Phi'''(\mathfrak{t}) < 0; \\
\text{Case (3)}: &\quad \Phi'(\mathfrak{t}) < 0, \Phi''(\mathfrak{t}) > 0 \text{ and } \Phi'''(\mathfrak{t}) < 0,
\end{aligned}$$

for $\mathfrak{t} \geq \mathfrak{t}_1$, where $\mathfrak{t}_1$ is sufficiently large. For convenience, we will symbolize the set of all eventually positive solutions of the Equation (1) by $^+$ and the set of all solutions with satisfying case (3) by $^+_3$.

In order to prove our main results, we define the following:

$$\eta_i(\mathfrak{t}) = \int_\mathfrak{t}^\infty \eta_{i-1}(\jmath) \mathrm{d}\jmath \text{ for } i = 1, 2.$$

and

$$\beta_* = \liminf_{\mathfrak{t} \to \infty} \frac{1}{\alpha} q(\mathfrak{t}) \eta_1^{-1}(\mathfrak{t}) \eta_2^{\alpha+1}(\mathfrak{t}).$$

In addition, we put

$$\mu_* = \liminf_{\mathfrak{t} \to \infty} \frac{\eta_2(\tau(\mathfrak{t}))}{\eta_2(\mathfrak{t})}.$$

It is useful to note that in view of (V2), $\mu_* \geq 1$. In the proofs, we will often use that there is $\mathfrak{t}_1 \geq \mathfrak{t}_o$ sufficiently large such that, for arbitrary $\beta \in (0, \beta_*)$ and $\mu \in [1, \mu_*)$, we have

$$q(\mathfrak{t}) \eta_1^{-1}(\mathfrak{t}) \eta_2^{\alpha+1}(\mathfrak{t}) \geq \alpha \beta, \tag{14}$$

and

$$\frac{\eta_2(\tau(\mathfrak{t}))}{\eta_2(\mathfrak{t})} \geq \mu.$$

on $[\mathfrak{t}_1, \infty)$.

Below, we define a sequence that is used to improve the monotonic properties of the positive solutions of (1).

Definition 2. *We define sequence* $\{\beta_n\}$ *as* $\beta_o = \sqrt[\alpha]{\beta_*}$ *and*

$$\beta_n = \frac{\beta_o \mu_*^{\beta_{n-1}}}{\sqrt[\alpha]{1 - \beta_{n-1}}}, \quad n \in \mathbb{N}. \tag{15}$$

Remark 1. By induction, it is easy to see that if, for any $n \in \mathbb{N}$, $\beta_i < 1$, for $i = 0,1,2,\ldots,n$. Then, β_{n+1} exists and
$$\beta_{n+1} = \ell_n \beta_n > \beta_n, \tag{16}$$
where ℓ_n is defined by
$$\ell_0 = \frac{\mu_*^{\beta_0}}{\sqrt[\alpha]{1-\beta_0}},$$
and
$$\ell_{n+1} = \mu_*^{\beta_0(\ell_n-1)}\sqrt[\alpha]{\frac{1-\beta_n}{1-\ell_n\beta_n}}, \quad n \in \mathbb{N}_0.$$

Lemma 3. *Assume that $\Phi \in C([\mathfrak{r}_0,\infty),(0,\infty))$ is a solution of (1) and Case (3) holds. If*
$$\int_{\mathfrak{r}_0}^{\infty}\left(\frac{1}{h(v)}\int_{\mathfrak{r}_1}^{v}q(\jmath)\mathrm{d}\jmath\right)^{1/\alpha}\mathrm{d}v = \infty, \tag{17}$$
then $\Phi(\mathfrak{r})$ converges to zero and $\Phi(\mathfrak{r})/\eta_2(\mathfrak{r})$ is eventually nondecreasing.

Proof. Assume that $\Phi \in {}^+$ and satisfies case (3). Then, we obtain that $\lim_{\mathfrak{r}\to\infty}\Phi(\mathfrak{r}) = \delta \geq 0$. We claim that $\lim_{\mathfrak{r}\to\infty}\Phi(\mathfrak{r}) = 0$. Assume the contrary that $\delta > 0$. Thus, there is $\mathfrak{r}_1 \geq \mathfrak{r}_0$ such that $\Phi(\tau(\mathfrak{r})) \geq \delta$ for $\mathfrak{r} \geq \mathfrak{r}_1$, and hence
$$\left(h(\mathfrak{r})\left(\Phi'''(\mathfrak{r})\right)^\alpha\right)' = -q(\mathfrak{r})\Phi^\alpha(\tau(\mathfrak{r})) \leq -\delta^\alpha q(\mathfrak{r}),$$
for $\mathfrak{r} \geq \mathfrak{r}_1$. Integrating the above inequality twice from $\mathfrak{r}_1$ to $\mathfrak{r}$, we have
$$\Phi'''(\mathfrak{r}) \leq -\delta\left(\frac{1}{h(\mathfrak{r})}\int_{\mathfrak{r}_1}^{\mathfrak{r}}q(\jmath)\mathrm{d}\jmath\right)^{1/\alpha}$$
and
$$\Phi''(\mathfrak{r}) \leq \Phi''(\mathfrak{r}_1) - \delta\int_{\mathfrak{r}_1}^{\mathfrak{r}}\left(\frac{1}{h(v)}\int_{\mathfrak{r}_1}^{v}q(\jmath)\mathrm{d}\jmath\right)^{1/\alpha}\mathrm{d}v.$$

Letting $\mathfrak{r} \to \infty$ and using (17), we obtain that $\lim_{\mathfrak{r}\to\infty}\Phi''(\mathfrak{r}) = -\infty$, which contradicts $\Phi''(\mathfrak{r}) > 0$. Thus, the proof is complete. Using the fact that $h^{1/\alpha}(\mathfrak{r})\Phi'''(\mathfrak{r})$ is nonincreasing, we see that
$$\Phi''(\mathfrak{r}) \geq -\int_{\mathfrak{r}}^{\infty}h^{-1/\alpha}(\jmath)h^{1/\alpha}(\jmath)\Phi'''(\jmath)\mathrm{d}\jmath \geq -h^{1/\alpha}(\mathfrak{r})\Phi'''(\mathfrak{r})\eta(\mathfrak{r}). \tag{18}$$

Now, we have
$$\begin{aligned}\left(\frac{\Phi''(\mathfrak{r})}{\eta(\mathfrak{r})}\right)' &= \frac{\eta(\mathfrak{r})\Phi'''(\mathfrak{r}) + h^{-1/\alpha}(\mathfrak{r})\Phi''(\mathfrak{r})}{\eta^2(\mathfrak{r})}\\ &= \frac{1}{h^{1/\alpha}(\mathfrak{r})\eta^2(\mathfrak{r})}\left[h^{1/\alpha}(\mathfrak{r})\Phi'''(\mathfrak{r})\eta(\mathfrak{r}) + \Phi''(\mathfrak{r})\right]\\ &\geq 0. \end{aligned}\tag{19}$$

Thus, we obtain
$$\Phi'(\mathfrak{r}) \leq -\int_{\mathfrak{r}}^{\infty}\eta(\jmath)\frac{\Phi''(\jmath)}{\eta(\jmath)}\mathrm{d}\jmath \leq -\frac{\Phi''(\mathfrak{r})}{\eta(\mathfrak{r})}\eta_1(\mathfrak{r}), \tag{20}$$

which implies

$$\left(\frac{\Phi'(\mathfrak{r})}{\eta_1(\mathfrak{r})}\right)' = \frac{\eta_1(\mathfrak{r})\Phi''(\mathfrak{r}) + \eta(\mathfrak{r})\Phi'(\mathfrak{r})}{\eta_1^2(\mathfrak{r})}$$

$$= \frac{1}{\eta_1^2(\mathfrak{r})}\left[\Phi''(\mathfrak{r})\eta_1(\mathfrak{r}) + \Phi'(\mathfrak{r})\eta(\mathfrak{r})\right]$$

$$\leq 0. \qquad (21)$$

This leads to

$$\Phi(\mathfrak{r}) \geq -\int_{\mathfrak{r}}^{\infty} \eta_1(\jmath)\frac{\Phi'(\jmath)}{\eta_1(\jmath)}d\jmath \geq -\frac{\Phi'(\mathfrak{r})}{\eta_1(\mathfrak{r})}\eta_2(\mathfrak{r}), \qquad (22)$$

hence

$$\left(\frac{\Phi(\mathfrak{r})}{\eta_2(\mathfrak{r})}\right)' = \frac{\eta_2(\mathfrak{r})\Phi'(\mathfrak{r}) + \eta_1(\mathfrak{r})\Phi(\mathfrak{r})}{\eta_2^2(\mathfrak{r})}$$

$$= \frac{1}{\eta_2^2(\mathfrak{r})}\left[\eta_2(\mathfrak{r})\Phi'(\mathfrak{r}) + \eta_1(\mathfrak{r})\Phi(\mathfrak{r})\right]$$

$$\geq 0. \qquad (23)$$

This completes the proof. □

Lemma 4. *Let $\beta_* > 0$ and $\mu_* < \infty$. If $\Phi \in C([\mathfrak{r}_0, \infty), (0, \infty))$ is a solution of (1) and Case (3) holds, then for any $n \in \mathbb{N}_o$*

$$\left(\frac{\Phi(\mathfrak{r})}{\eta_2^{\beta_n}(\mathfrak{r})}\right)' < 0.$$

Proof. Assume that $\Phi \in ^+$ and satisfies case (3) on $[\mathfrak{r}_1, \infty)$ where $\mathfrak{r}_1 \geq \mathfrak{r}_0$ such that $\Phi(\tau(\mathfrak{r})) > 0$ and (14) holds for $\mathfrak{r} \geq \mathfrak{r}_1$. Integrating (1) from $\mathfrak{r}_1$ to $\mathfrak{r}$, we have

$$h(\mathfrak{r})\left(\Phi'''(\mathfrak{r})\right)^\alpha = h(\mathfrak{r}_1)\left(\Phi'''(\mathfrak{r}_1)\right)^\alpha - \int_{\mathfrak{r}_1}^{\mathfrak{r}} q(\jmath)\Phi^\alpha(\tau(\jmath))d\jmath$$

$$\leq h(\mathfrak{r}_1)\left(\Phi'''(\mathfrak{r}_1)\right)^\alpha - \Phi^\alpha(\mathfrak{r})\int_{\mathfrak{r}_1}^{\mathfrak{r}} q(\jmath)d\jmath.$$

By using (14) in the above inequality, we obtain

$$h(\mathfrak{r})\left(\Phi'''(\mathfrak{r})\right)^\alpha \leq h(\mathfrak{r}_1)\left(\Phi'''(\mathfrak{r}_1)\right)^\alpha - \beta\Phi^\alpha(\mathfrak{r})\int_{\mathfrak{r}_1}^{\mathfrak{r}} \frac{\alpha}{\eta_1^{-1}(\jmath)\eta_2^{\alpha+1}(\jmath)}d\jmath$$

$$\leq h(\mathfrak{r}_1)\left(\Phi'''(\mathfrak{r}_1)\right)^\alpha - \beta\frac{\Phi^\alpha(\mathfrak{r})}{\eta_2^\alpha(\mathfrak{r})} + \beta\frac{\Phi^\alpha(\mathfrak{r})}{\eta_2^\alpha(\mathfrak{r}_1)}.$$

From Lemma 3, we have that $\lim_{\mathfrak{r}\to\infty} \Phi(\mathfrak{r}) = 0$. Hence, there is a $\mathfrak{r}_2 \in [\mathfrak{r}_1, \infty)$ such that

$$h(\mathfrak{r}_1)\left(\Phi'''(\mathfrak{r}_1)\right)^\alpha + \beta\frac{\Phi^\alpha(\mathfrak{r})}{\eta_2^\alpha(\mathfrak{r}_1)} < 0,$$

for $\mathfrak{r} \geq \mathfrak{r}_2$. Thus,

$$h(\mathfrak{r})\left(\Phi'''(\mathfrak{r})\right)^\alpha < -\beta\frac{\Phi^\alpha(\mathfrak{r})}{\eta_2^\alpha(\mathfrak{r})}$$

or

$$h^{1/\alpha}(\mathfrak{r})\Phi'''(\mathfrak{r})\eta_2(\mathfrak{r}) < -\sqrt[\alpha]{\beta}\Phi(\mathfrak{r}) = -\varepsilon_o\beta_o\Phi(\mathfrak{r}), \qquad (24)$$

where $\varepsilon_0 = \sqrt[\alpha]{\beta}/\beta_o$ is an arbitrary constant from $(0,1)$. Note that,

$$h^{1/\alpha}(\mathfrak{r})\Phi'''(\mathfrak{r})\eta(\mathfrak{r}) \geq \int_{\mathfrak{r}}^{\infty} h^{-1/\alpha}(\jmath)h^{1/\alpha}(\jmath)\Phi'''(\jmath)\mathrm{d}\jmath \geq -\Phi''(\mathfrak{r}),$$

then,

$$\Phi''(\mathfrak{r}) \geq -h^{1/\alpha}(\mathfrak{r})\eta(\mathfrak{r})\Phi'''(\mathfrak{r}).$$

By repeating this step twice over $[\mathfrak{r}, \infty)$, we obtain

$$\Phi'(\mathfrak{r}) \leq h^{1/\alpha}(\mathfrak{r})\eta_1(\mathfrak{r})\Phi'''(\mathfrak{r}) \tag{25}$$

and

$$\Phi(\mathfrak{r}) \geq -h^{1/\alpha}(\mathfrak{r})\eta_2(\mathfrak{r})\Phi'''(\mathfrak{r}).$$

From (24) and (25), we obtain

$$\frac{\Phi'(\mathfrak{r})}{\eta_1(\mathfrak{r})} \leq h^{1/\alpha}(\mathfrak{r})\Phi'''(\mathfrak{r})$$

and

$$\frac{\Phi'(\mathfrak{r})}{\eta_1(\mathfrak{r})} \leq -\sqrt[\alpha]{\beta}\frac{\Phi(\mathfrak{r})}{\eta_2(\mathfrak{r})},$$

hence,

$$\eta_2(\mathfrak{r})\Phi'(\mathfrak{r}) + \sqrt[\alpha]{\beta}\eta_1(\mathfrak{r})\Phi(\mathfrak{r}) \leq 0.$$

Therefore,

$$\left(\frac{\Phi(\mathfrak{r})}{\eta_2^{\sqrt[\alpha]{\beta}}(\mathfrak{r})}\right)' = \frac{\eta_2^{\sqrt[\alpha]{\beta}}(\mathfrak{r})\Phi'(\mathfrak{r}) + \sqrt[\alpha]{\beta}\eta_2^{\sqrt[\alpha]{\beta}-1}(\mathfrak{r})\eta_1(\mathfrak{r})\Phi(\mathfrak{r})}{\eta_2^{2\sqrt[\alpha]{\beta}}(\mathfrak{r})}$$

$$= \frac{\eta_2^{\sqrt[\alpha]{\beta}-1}[\sqrt[\alpha]{\beta}\eta_1(\mathfrak{r})\Phi(\mathfrak{r}) + \eta_2(\mathfrak{r})\Phi'(\mathfrak{r})]}{\eta_2^{2\sqrt[\alpha]{\beta}}(\mathfrak{r})}$$

$$= \frac{1}{\eta_2^{\sqrt[\alpha]{\beta}+1}(\mathfrak{r})}\left[\sqrt[\alpha]{\beta}\eta_1(\mathfrak{r})\Phi(\mathfrak{r}) + \eta_2(\mathfrak{r})\Phi'(\mathfrak{r})\right]$$

$$\leq 0.$$

Integrating (1) from $\mathfrak{r}_2$ to $\mathfrak{r}$ and using that $\Phi(\mathfrak{r})/\eta_2^{\sqrt[\alpha]{\beta}}(\mathfrak{r})$ is decreasing, we have

$$h(\mathfrak{r})(\Phi'''(\mathfrak{r}))^\alpha \leq h(\mathfrak{r}_2)(\Phi'''(\mathfrak{r}_2))^\alpha - \int_{\mathfrak{r}_2}^{\mathfrak{r}} q(\jmath)\eta_2^{\alpha\sqrt[\alpha]{\beta}}(\tau(\jmath))\frac{\Phi^\alpha(\tau(\jmath))}{\eta_2^{\alpha\sqrt[\alpha]{\beta}}(\tau(\jmath))}\mathrm{d}\jmath$$

$$\leq h(\mathfrak{r}_2)(\Phi'''(\mathfrak{r}_2))^\alpha - \left(\frac{\Phi(\tau(\mathfrak{r}))}{\eta_2^{\sqrt[\alpha]{\beta}}(\tau(\mathfrak{r}))}\right)^\alpha \int_{\mathfrak{r}_2}^{\mathfrak{r}} q(\jmath)\eta_2^{\alpha\sqrt[\alpha]{\beta}}(\tau(\jmath))\mathrm{d}\jmath,$$

hence,

$$h(\mathfrak{r})(\Phi'''(\mathfrak{r}))^\alpha \leq h(\mathfrak{r}_2)(\Phi'''(\mathfrak{r}_2))^\alpha - \left(\frac{\Phi(\mathfrak{r})}{\eta_2^{\sqrt[\alpha]{\beta}}(\mathfrak{r})}\right)^\alpha \int_{\mathfrak{r}_2}^{\mathfrak{r}} q(\jmath)\left(\frac{\eta_2(\tau(\jmath))}{\eta_2(\jmath)}\right)^{\alpha\sqrt[\alpha]{\beta}} \eta_2^{\alpha\sqrt[\alpha]{\beta}}(\jmath)\mathrm{d}\jmath.$$

It is clear that from (14), we have

$$h(\mathfrak{r})\left(\Phi'''(\mathfrak{r})\right)^\alpha \;\leq\; h(\mathfrak{r}_2)\left(\Phi'''(\mathfrak{r}_2)\right)^\alpha - \beta\left(\frac{\Phi(\mathfrak{r})}{\eta_2^{\sqrt[\alpha]{\beta}}(\mathfrak{r})}\right)^\alpha \int_{\mathfrak{r}_2}^{\mathfrak{r}} \frac{\alpha\left(\frac{\eta_2(\tau(j))}{\eta_2(j)}\right)^{\alpha\sqrt[\alpha]{\beta}}}{\eta_1(j)\eta_2^{\alpha+1-\alpha\sqrt[\alpha]{\beta}}(j)}\,dj$$

$$\leq\; h(\mathfrak{r}_2)\left(\Phi'''(\mathfrak{r}_2)\right)^\alpha - \frac{\beta}{1-\sqrt[\alpha]{\beta}}\mu^{\alpha\sqrt[\alpha]{\beta}}\left(\frac{\Phi(\mathfrak{r})}{\eta_2^{\sqrt[\alpha]{\beta}}(\mathfrak{r})}\right)^\alpha \int_{\mathfrak{r}_2}^{\mathfrak{r}} \frac{\alpha\left(1-\sqrt[\alpha]{\beta}\right)}{\eta_1(j)\eta_2^{\alpha+1-\alpha\sqrt[\alpha]{\beta}}(j)}\,dj,$$

which implies that,

$$h(\mathfrak{r})\left(\Phi'''(\mathfrak{r})\right)^\alpha \;\leq\; h(\mathfrak{r}_2)\left(\Phi'''(\mathfrak{r}_2)\right)^\alpha -$$
$$\frac{\beta}{1-\sqrt[\alpha]{\beta}}\mu^{\alpha\sqrt[\alpha]{\beta}}\left(\frac{\Phi(\mathfrak{r})}{\eta_2^{\sqrt[\alpha]{\beta}}(\mathfrak{r})}\right)^\alpha \left(\frac{1}{\eta_2^{\alpha\left(1-\sqrt[\alpha]{\beta}\right)}(\mathfrak{r})} - \frac{1}{\eta_2^{\alpha\left(1-\sqrt[\alpha]{\beta}\right)}(\mathfrak{r}_2)}\right). \tag{26}$$

Now, we claim that $\lim_{\mathfrak{r}\to\infty} \Phi(\mathfrak{r})/\eta_2^{\sqrt[\alpha]{\beta}}(\mathfrak{r}) = 0$. It is enough to show that there is $\epsilon > 0$ such that $\Phi(\mathfrak{r})/\eta_2^{\sqrt[\alpha]{\beta}+\epsilon}(\mathfrak{r})$ is eventually decreasing. Since $\eta_2(\mathfrak{r})$ tends to zero, there is a constant

$$\ell \in \left(\frac{\sqrt[\alpha]{1-\sqrt[\alpha]{\beta}}}{\mu\sqrt[\alpha]{\beta}}, 1\right)$$

and a $\mathfrak{r}_3 \geq \mathfrak{r}_2$ such that

$$\frac{1}{\eta_2^{\alpha\left(1-\sqrt[\alpha]{\beta}\right)}(\mathfrak{r})} - \frac{1}{\eta_2^{\alpha\left(1-\sqrt[\alpha]{\beta}\right)}(\mathfrak{r}_2)} > \ell^\alpha \frac{1}{\eta_2^{\alpha\left(1-\sqrt[\alpha]{\beta}\right)}(\mathfrak{r})}, \tag{27}$$

for $\mathfrak{r} \geq \mathfrak{r}_3$. By using (27) in (26), we obtain

$$h(\mathfrak{r})\left(\Phi'''(\mathfrak{r})\right)^\alpha \leq -\frac{\ell^\alpha \beta}{1-\sqrt[\alpha]{\beta}}\mu^{\alpha\sqrt[\alpha]{\beta}}\left(\frac{\Phi(\mathfrak{r})}{\eta_2(\mathfrak{r})}\right)^\alpha,$$

its mean,

$$h^{1/\alpha}(\mathfrak{r})\Phi'''(\mathfrak{r}) \leq -\left(\sqrt[\alpha]{\beta}+\epsilon\right)\frac{\Phi(\mathfrak{r})}{\eta_2(\mathfrak{r})}, \tag{28}$$

where

$$\epsilon = \sqrt[\alpha]{\beta}\left(\frac{\ell\mu\sqrt[\alpha]{\beta}}{\sqrt[\alpha]{1-\sqrt[\alpha]{\beta}}} - 1\right) > 0.$$

Thus, from (28),

$$\left(\frac{\Phi(\mathfrak{r})}{\eta_2^{\sqrt[\alpha]{\beta}+\epsilon}(\mathfrak{r})}\right)' \leq 0,$$

for $\mathfrak{r} \geq \mathfrak{r}_3$, and hence the claim is valid. Therefore, for $\mathfrak{r}_4 \in [\mathfrak{r}_3, \infty)$,

$$h(\mathfrak{r}_2)\left(\Phi'''(\mathfrak{r}_2)\right)^\alpha + \frac{\beta}{1-\sqrt[\alpha]{\beta}}\mu^{\alpha\sqrt[\alpha]{\beta}}\left(\frac{\Phi(\mathfrak{r})}{\eta_2^{\sqrt[\alpha]{\beta}}(\mathfrak{r})}\right)^\alpha \frac{1}{\eta_2^{\alpha\left(1-\sqrt[\alpha]{\beta}\right)}(\mathfrak{r}_2)} < 0,$$

for $\mathfrak{r} \geq \mathfrak{r}_4$. By using the above inequality in (26), we have

$$h(\mathfrak{r})(\Phi'''(\mathfrak{r}))^\alpha \leq h(\mathfrak{r}_2)(\Phi'''(\mathfrak{r}_2))^\alpha - \frac{\beta}{1-\sqrt[\alpha]{\beta}}\mu^\alpha \sqrt[\alpha]{\beta}\left(\frac{\Phi(\mathfrak{r})}{\eta_2^{\sqrt[\alpha]{\beta}}(\mathfrak{r})}\right)^\alpha \frac{1}{\eta_2^{\alpha(1-\sqrt[\alpha]{\beta})}(\mathfrak{r})}$$

$$+ \frac{\beta}{1-\sqrt[\alpha]{\beta}}\mu^\alpha \sqrt[\alpha]{\beta}\left(\frac{\Phi(\mathfrak{r})}{\eta_2^{\sqrt[\alpha]{\beta}}(\mathfrak{r})}\right)^\alpha \frac{1}{\eta_2^{\alpha(1-\sqrt[\alpha]{\beta})}(\mathfrak{r}_2)}$$

$$\leq h(\mathfrak{r}_2)(\Phi'''(\mathfrak{r}_2))^\alpha - \frac{\beta}{1-\sqrt[\alpha]{\beta}}\mu^\alpha \sqrt[\alpha]{\beta}\left(\frac{\Phi(\mathfrak{r})}{\eta_2(\mathfrak{r})}\right)^\alpha$$

$$+ \frac{\beta}{1-\sqrt[\alpha]{\beta}}\mu^\alpha \sqrt[\alpha]{\beta}\left(\frac{\Phi(\mathfrak{r})}{\eta_2^{\sqrt[\alpha]{\beta}}(\mathfrak{r})}\right)^\alpha \frac{1}{\eta_2^{\alpha(1-\sqrt[\alpha]{\beta})}(\mathfrak{r}_2)}$$

hence,

$$h(\mathfrak{r})(\Phi'''(\mathfrak{r}))^\alpha < -\frac{\beta}{1-\sqrt[\alpha]{\beta}}\mu^\alpha \sqrt[\alpha]{\beta}\Phi^\alpha(\mathfrak{r}),$$

or

$$h^{1/\alpha}(\mathfrak{r})\Phi'''(\mathfrak{r}) < -\frac{\sqrt[\alpha]{\beta}}{\sqrt[\alpha]{1-\sqrt[\alpha]{\beta}}}\mu\sqrt[\alpha]{\beta}\Phi(\mathfrak{r}) = -\epsilon_1\beta_1\Phi(\mathfrak{r}),$$

for $\mathfrak{r} \geq \mathfrak{r}_4$, where

$$\epsilon_1 = \sqrt[\alpha]{\frac{\beta(1-\sqrt[\alpha]{\beta_*})}{\beta_*(1-\sqrt[\alpha]{\beta})}}\frac{\mu\sqrt[\alpha]{\beta}}{\mu_*\sqrt[\alpha]{\beta_*}}$$

is an arbitrary constant from $(0,1)$ approaching 1 if $\beta \to \beta_*$ and $\mu \to \mu_*$. Hence,

$$\left(\frac{\Phi(\mathfrak{r})}{\eta_2^{\epsilon_1\beta_1}(\mathfrak{r})}\right) < 0,$$

for $\mathfrak{r} \geq \mathfrak{r}_4$. One can show that through induction, for any $n \in \mathbb{N}_o$ and $\mathfrak{r}$ large enough,

$$\left(\frac{\Phi(\mathfrak{r})}{\eta_2^{\epsilon_n\beta_n}(\mathfrak{r})}\right)' < 0,$$

where ϵ_n given by

$$\epsilon_o = \sqrt[\alpha]{\frac{\beta}{\beta_*}}$$

$$\epsilon_{n+1} = \epsilon_o \sqrt[\alpha]{\frac{1-\beta_n}{1-\epsilon_n\beta_n}}\frac{\mu^{\epsilon_n\beta_n}}{\mu_*^{\beta_n}}, \quad n \in \mathbb{N}_o$$

is an arbitrary constant from $(0,1)$ approaching 1 if $\beta \to \beta_*$ and $\mu \to \mu_*$. Finally, we claim that from any $n \in \mathbb{N}_o$

$$\left(\frac{\Phi(\mathfrak{r})}{\eta_2^{\epsilon_{n+1}\beta_{n+1}}(\mathfrak{r})}\right)' < 0$$

implies that from (16) and the fact that ϵ_{n+1} is arbitrary close to 1,

$$\epsilon_{n+1}\beta_{n+1} > \beta_n.$$

Hence, for $\mathfrak{r}$ large enough,

$$h^{1/\alpha}(\mathfrak{r})\Phi'''(\mathfrak{r})\eta_2(\mathfrak{r}) < -\epsilon_{n+1}\beta_{n+1}\Phi(\mathfrak{r}) < -\beta_n\Phi(\mathfrak{r}).$$

So, for any $n \in \mathbb{N}_0$ and $\mathfrak{r}$ large enough,

$$\left(\frac{\Phi(\mathfrak{r})}{\eta_2^{\beta_n}(\mathfrak{r})}\right)' < 0.$$

The proof is complete. □

3. Nonexistence of Solutions in the Class $\frac{+}{3}$

Theorem 6. *Suppose that (V1) and (V2) hold. If*

$$\limsup_{\mathfrak{r}\to\infty} \int_{\mathfrak{r}_0}^{\mathfrak{r}} \left[H^\alpha(\jmath)q(\jmath) \frac{\eta_2^{\alpha\beta_n}(\tau(\jmath))}{\eta_2^{\alpha\beta_n}(\jmath)} - \frac{\alpha^\alpha}{(\alpha+1)^{\alpha+1}} \frac{(H'(\jmath))^{\alpha+1}}{H(\jmath)\eta_1^\alpha(\jmath)} \right] d\jmath = \infty, \qquad (29)$$

then $\frac{+}{3} = \emptyset$. *Where*

$$H(\mathfrak{r}) = \int_{\mathfrak{r}}^{\infty} (\jmath - \mathfrak{r})\eta(\jmath)d\jmath.$$

Proof. Consider the case where (1) has a nonoscillatory solution. We can suppose that $\Phi \in {}^+$ eventually without losing generality. Assume that Φ satisfies case (3). Since $h(\mathfrak{r})(\Phi'''(\mathfrak{r}))^\alpha$ is nonincreasing, we obtain

$$h^{1/\alpha}(\jmath)\Phi'''(\jmath) \leq h^{1/\alpha}(\mathfrak{r})\Phi'''(\mathfrak{r}), \quad \jmath \geq \mathfrak{r} \geq \mathfrak{r}_1. \qquad (30)$$

By dividing (30) by $h^{1/\alpha}(\jmath)$ and integrating the resulting inequality from $\mathfrak{r}$ to ℓ, we obtain

$$\Phi''(\ell) \leq \Phi''(\mathfrak{r}) + h^{1/\alpha}(\mathfrak{r})\Phi'''(\mathfrak{r}) \int_{\mathfrak{r}}^{\ell} h^{1/\alpha}(\jmath)d\jmath.$$

Letting $\ell \to \infty$, we have

$$0 \leq \Phi''(\mathfrak{r}) + h^{1/\alpha}(\mathfrak{r})\Phi'''(\mathfrak{r})\eta(\mathfrak{r}),$$

which produces

$$\Phi''(\mathfrak{r}) \geq -\eta(\mathfrak{r})h^{1/\alpha}(\mathfrak{r})\Phi'''(\mathfrak{r}). \qquad (31)$$

Integrating (31) from $\mathfrak{r}$ to ∞, yields

$$-\Phi'(\mathfrak{r}) \geq -h^{1/\alpha}(\mathfrak{r})\Phi'''(\mathfrak{r}) \int_{\mathfrak{r}}^{\infty} \eta(\jmath)d\jmath. \qquad (32)$$

Again, integrating (32) from $\mathfrak{r}$ to ∞, we obtain

$$\Phi(\mathfrak{r}) \geq -h^{1/\alpha}(\mathfrak{r})\Phi'''(\mathfrak{r}) \int_{\mathfrak{r}}^{\infty} (\jmath - \mathfrak{r})\eta(\jmath)d\jmath.$$

Now, define the function ω by

$$\omega(\mathfrak{r}) := \frac{h(\mathfrak{r})(\Phi'''(\mathfrak{r}))^\alpha}{(\Phi(\mathfrak{r}))^\alpha}, \quad \mathfrak{r} \geq \mathfrak{r}_1. \qquad (33)$$

Then, we see that $\omega(\mathfrak{r}) < 0$ for $\mathfrak{r} \geq \mathfrak{r}_1$. Differentiating (33), we obtain

$$\omega'(\mathfrak{r}) = \frac{(h(\mathfrak{r})(\Phi'''(\mathfrak{r}))^\alpha)'}{(\Phi(\mathfrak{r}))^\alpha} - \alpha \frac{h(\mathfrak{r})(\Phi'''(\mathfrak{r}))^\alpha \Phi'(\mathfrak{r})}{(\Phi(\mathfrak{r}))^{\alpha+1}}.$$

It follows from (1) and (32) that

$$\omega'(\mathfrak{r}) \leq -q(\mathfrak{r}) \frac{\Phi^\alpha(\tau(\mathfrak{r}))}{(\Phi(\mathfrak{r}))^\alpha} - \alpha \omega^{1+1/\alpha}(\mathfrak{r}) \int_{\mathfrak{r}}^{\infty} \eta(\jmath)d\jmath.$$

$$\omega'(\mathfrak{r}) \leq -q(\mathfrak{r})\frac{\eta_2^{\alpha\beta_n}(\mathfrak{r})}{(\Phi(\mathfrak{r}))^\alpha}\frac{\Phi^\alpha(\tau(\mathfrak{r}))}{\eta_2^{\alpha\beta_n}(\mathfrak{r})} - \alpha\omega^{1+1/\alpha}(\mathfrak{r})\int_\mathfrak{r}^\infty \eta(j)dj.$$

Lemma 4 yields

$$-\frac{\eta_2^{\alpha\beta_n}(\tau(\mathfrak{r}))}{(\Phi(\tau(\mathfrak{r})))^\alpha} \geq -\frac{\eta_2^{\alpha\beta_n}(\mathfrak{r})}{(\Phi(\mathfrak{r}))^\alpha},$$

hence,

$$\omega'(\mathfrak{r}) \leq -q(\mathfrak{r})\frac{\eta_2^{\alpha\beta_n}(\tau(\mathfrak{r}))}{\eta_2^{\alpha\beta_n}(\mathfrak{r})} - \alpha\omega^{1+1/\alpha}(\mathfrak{r})\int_\mathfrak{r}^\infty \eta(j)dj. \tag{34}$$

Multiplying (34) by $H^\alpha(\mathfrak{r})$ and integrating the resulting inequality from $\mathfrak{r}_1$ to $\mathfrak{r}$, we have

$$H^\alpha(\mathfrak{r})\omega(\mathfrak{r}) - H^\alpha(\mathfrak{r}_1)\omega(\mathfrak{r}_1) - \alpha\int_{\mathfrak{r}_1}^\mathfrak{r} H'(j)H^{\alpha-1}(j)\omega(j)dj + \int_{\mathfrak{r}_1}^\mathfrak{r} q(j)\frac{\eta_2^{\alpha\beta_n}(\tau(j))}{\eta_2^{\alpha\beta_n}(j)}H^\alpha(j)dj$$
$$+\alpha\int_{\mathfrak{r}_1}^\mathfrak{r} \omega^{1+1/\alpha}(j)\eta_1(j)H^\alpha(j)dj \leq 0.$$

By using the inequality (12) with $K = -H'(j)H^{\alpha-1}(j)$, $L = \eta_1(j)H^\alpha(j)$, and $v = -\omega(j)$, we obtain

$$\int_{\mathfrak{r}_1}^\mathfrak{r}\left[q(j)\frac{\eta_2^{\alpha\beta_n}(\tau(j))}{\eta_2^{\alpha\beta_n}(j)}H^\alpha(j) - \frac{\alpha^\alpha}{(\alpha+1)^{\alpha+1}}\frac{(H'(j))^{\alpha+1}}{H(j)\eta_1^\alpha(j)}\right]dj \leq H^\alpha(\mathfrak{r}_1)\omega(\mathfrak{r}_1) + 1,$$

we obtain a contradiction with (29) by taking the lim sup on both sides of this inequality. The proof is now complete. □

Theorem 7. *Suppose that $\alpha \geq 1$. If there is a function $\gamma \in C^1([\mathfrak{r}_0, \infty), (0, \infty))$ such that*

$$\limsup_{\mathfrak{r}\to\infty}\int_{\mathfrak{r}_0}^\mathfrak{r}\left[\psi(j) - \frac{\gamma(j)}{(\alpha+1)^{(\alpha+1)}\eta_1^\alpha(\mathfrak{r})}\left(\frac{\gamma'(j)}{\gamma(j)} + \frac{(1+\alpha)\eta_1(j)}{\eta_2(j)}\right)^{\alpha+1}\right]dj = \infty, \tag{35}$$

where

$$\psi(\mathfrak{r}) = \gamma(\mathfrak{r})q(\mathfrak{r})\frac{\eta_2^{\alpha\beta_n}(\tau(\mathfrak{r}))}{\eta_2^{\alpha\beta_n}(\mathfrak{r})} + (1-\alpha)\gamma(\mathfrak{r})\eta_1(\mathfrak{r})/\eta_2^{\alpha+1}(\mathfrak{r}).$$

Then $\overset{+}{3} = \varnothing$.

Proof. Consider the case where (1) has a nonoscillatory solution. We can suppose that $\Phi \in {}^+$ eventually without losing generality. Assume that Φ satisfies case (3). Since $h(\mathfrak{r})(\Phi'''(\mathfrak{r}))^\alpha$ is non-increasing, we obtain

$$\Phi''(v) - \Phi''(\mathfrak{r}) = \int_\mathfrak{r}^v \frac{1}{h^{1/\alpha}(\zeta)}\left(h(\zeta)(\Phi'''(\zeta))^\alpha\right)^{1/\alpha}d\zeta$$
$$\leq h^{1/\alpha}(\mathfrak{r})\Phi'''(\mathfrak{r})\int_\mathfrak{r}^v \frac{1}{h^{1/\alpha}(\zeta)}d\zeta.$$

Letting $v \to \infty$, we have

$$\Phi''(\mathfrak{r}) \geq -h^{1/\alpha}(\mathfrak{r})\Phi'''(\mathfrak{r})\eta(\mathfrak{r}). \tag{36}$$

Integrating (36) from $\mathfrak{r}$ to ∞ yields

$$-\Phi'(\mathfrak{r}) \geq -h^{1/\alpha}(\mathfrak{r})\Phi'''(\mathfrak{r})\eta_1(\mathfrak{r}). \tag{37}$$

Again, integrating (37) from $\mathfrak{r}$ to ∞, we obtain

$$\Phi(\mathfrak{r}) \geq -h^{1/\alpha}(\mathfrak{r})\Phi'''(\mathfrak{r})\eta_2(\mathfrak{r}).$$

Now, define the function ω_1 by

$$\omega_1(\mathfrak{r}) = \gamma(\mathfrak{r})\left(\frac{h(\mathfrak{r})(\Phi'''(\mathfrak{r}))^\alpha}{(\Phi(\mathfrak{r}))^\alpha} + \frac{1}{\eta_2^\alpha(\mathfrak{r})}\right), \quad \mathfrak{r} \geq \mathfrak{r}_1. \tag{38}$$

Then, we see that $\omega_1(\mathfrak{r}) > 0$ for $\mathfrak{r} \geq \mathfrak{r}_1$. Therefore, we have

$$\omega_1'(\mathfrak{r}) = \frac{\gamma'(\mathfrak{r})}{\gamma(\mathfrak{r})}\omega_1(\mathfrak{r}) + \gamma(\mathfrak{r})\frac{\left(h(\mathfrak{r})(\Phi'''(\mathfrak{r}))^\alpha\right)'}{(\Phi(\mathfrak{r}))^\alpha} - \alpha\gamma(\mathfrak{r})\frac{h(\mathfrak{r})(\Phi'''(\mathfrak{r}))^\alpha\Phi'(\mathfrak{r})}{(\Phi(\mathfrak{r}))^{\alpha+1}} - \alpha\gamma(\mathfrak{r})\frac{\eta_2'(\mathfrak{r})}{\eta_2^{\alpha+1}(\mathfrak{r})}.$$

It follows from (1) that

$$\omega_1'(\mathfrak{r}) = \frac{\gamma'(\mathfrak{r})}{\gamma(\mathfrak{r})}\omega_1(\mathfrak{r}) - q(\mathfrak{r})\gamma(\mathfrak{r})\frac{\eta_2^{\alpha\beta_n}(\mathfrak{r})}{(\Phi(\mathfrak{r}))^\alpha}\frac{\Phi^\alpha(\tau(\mathfrak{r}))}{\eta_2^{\alpha\beta_n}(\mathfrak{r})} - \alpha\gamma(\mathfrak{r})\frac{h(\mathfrak{r})(\Phi'''(\mathfrak{r}))^\alpha\Phi'(\mathfrak{r})}{(\Phi(\mathfrak{r}))^{\alpha+1}} - \alpha\gamma(\mathfrak{r})\frac{\eta_2'(\mathfrak{r})}{\eta_2^{\alpha+1}(\mathfrak{r})}.$$

From (37) and (38), we find

$$\omega_1'(\mathfrak{r}) \leq \frac{\gamma'(\mathfrak{r})}{\gamma(\mathfrak{r})}\omega_1(\mathfrak{r}) - q(\mathfrak{r})\frac{\eta_2^{\alpha\beta_n}(\mathfrak{r})}{(\Phi(\mathfrak{r}))^\alpha}\frac{\Phi^\alpha(\tau(\mathfrak{r}))}{\eta_2^{\alpha\beta_n}(\mathfrak{r})} - \alpha\gamma(\mathfrak{r})\eta_1(\mathfrak{r})\left(\frac{\omega_1(\mathfrak{r})}{\gamma(\mathfrak{r})} - \frac{1}{\eta_2^\alpha(\mathfrak{r})}\right)^{1+1/\alpha}$$
$$+\alpha\gamma(\mathfrak{r})\frac{\eta_1(\mathfrak{r})}{\eta_2^{\alpha+1}(\mathfrak{r})}.$$

From Lemma 4, we obtain

$$-\frac{\eta_2^{\alpha\beta_n}(\tau(\mathfrak{r}))}{(\Phi(\tau(\mathfrak{r})))^\alpha} \geq -\frac{\eta_2^{\alpha\beta_n}(\mathfrak{r})}{(\Phi(\mathfrak{r}))^\alpha},$$

hence,

$$\omega_1'(\mathfrak{r}) \leq \frac{\gamma'(\mathfrak{r})}{\gamma(\mathfrak{r})}\omega_1(\mathfrak{r}) - \gamma(\mathfrak{r})q(\mathfrak{r})\frac{\eta_2^{\alpha\beta_n}(\tau(\mathfrak{r}))}{\eta_2^{\alpha\beta_n}(\mathfrak{r})} + \alpha\gamma(\mathfrak{r})\frac{\eta_1(\mathfrak{r})}{\eta_2^{\alpha+1}(\mathfrak{r})} - \alpha\gamma(\mathfrak{r})\eta_1(\mathfrak{r})\left(\frac{\omega_1(\mathfrak{r})}{\gamma(\mathfrak{r})} - \frac{1}{\eta_2^\alpha(\mathfrak{r})}\right)^{1+1/\alpha}.$$

By using the inequality (13) with $A = \omega_1(\mathfrak{r})/\gamma(\mathfrak{r})$ and $J = 1/\eta_2^\alpha(\mathfrak{r})$, we obtain

$$\omega_1'(\mathfrak{r}) \leq \frac{\gamma'(\mathfrak{r})}{\gamma(\mathfrak{r})}\omega_1(\mathfrak{r}) - \gamma(\mathfrak{r})q(\mathfrak{r})\frac{\eta_2^{\alpha\beta_n}(\tau(\mathfrak{r}))}{\eta_2^{\alpha\beta_n}(\mathfrak{r})} + \alpha\gamma(\mathfrak{r})\frac{\eta_1(\mathfrak{r})}{\eta_2^{\alpha+1}(\mathfrak{r})}$$
$$-\alpha\gamma(\mathfrak{r})\eta_1(\mathfrak{r})\left\{\left(\frac{\omega_1(\mathfrak{r})}{\gamma(\mathfrak{r})}\right)^{1+1/\alpha} - \frac{1}{\eta_2(\mathfrak{r})}\left((1+\alpha)\frac{\omega_1(\mathfrak{r})}{\gamma(\mathfrak{r})} - \frac{1}{\eta_2^\alpha(\mathfrak{r})}\right)\right\},$$

hence,

$$\omega_1'(\mathfrak{r}) \leq \left(\frac{\gamma'(\mathfrak{r})}{\gamma(\mathfrak{r})} + \frac{(1+\alpha)\eta_1(\mathfrak{r})}{\eta_2(\mathfrak{r})}\right)\omega_1(\mathfrak{r}) - \gamma(\mathfrak{r})q(\mathfrak{r})\frac{\eta_2^{\alpha\beta_n}(\tau(\mathfrak{r}))}{\eta_2^{\alpha\beta_n}(\mathfrak{r})} - \frac{\alpha\eta_1(\mathfrak{r})}{\gamma^{1/\alpha}(\mathfrak{r})}\omega_1^{1+1/\alpha}(\mathfrak{r})$$
$$-\frac{\gamma(\mathfrak{r})\eta_1(\mathfrak{r})}{\eta_2^{\alpha+1}(\mathfrak{r})} + \frac{\alpha\gamma(\mathfrak{r})\eta_1(\mathfrak{r})}{\eta_2^{\alpha+1}(\mathfrak{r})}.$$

Using the inequality (12) with $K = \gamma'(\mathfrak{r})/\gamma(\mathfrak{r}) + (1+\alpha)\eta_1(\mathfrak{r})/\eta_2(\mathfrak{r})$, $L = \alpha\eta_1(\mathfrak{r})/\gamma^{1/\alpha}(\mathfrak{r})$, and $v = \omega_1(\mathfrak{r})$, we obtain

$$\omega_1'(\mathfrak{r}) \leq -\gamma(\mathfrak{r})q(\mathfrak{r})\frac{\eta_2^{\alpha\beta_n}(\tau(\mathfrak{r}))}{\eta_2^{\alpha\beta_n}(\mathfrak{r})} + (\alpha-1)\frac{\gamma(\mathfrak{r})\eta_1(\mathfrak{r})}{\eta_2^{\alpha+1}(\mathfrak{r})}$$
$$+ \frac{\gamma(\mathfrak{r})}{(\alpha+1)^{(\alpha+1)}\eta_1^\alpha(\mathfrak{r})}\left(\frac{\gamma'(\mathfrak{r})}{\gamma(\mathfrak{r})} + \frac{(1+\alpha)\eta_1(\mathfrak{r})}{\eta_2(\mathfrak{r})}\right)^{\alpha+1}. \quad (39)$$

Integrating (39) from $\mathfrak{r}_1$ to $\mathfrak{r}$, we have

$$\int_{\mathfrak{r}_1}^{\mathfrak{r}} \left[\psi(\jmath) - \frac{\gamma(\jmath)}{(\alpha+1)^{(\alpha+1)}\eta_1^\alpha(\mathfrak{r})}\left(\frac{\gamma'(\jmath)}{\gamma(\jmath)} + \frac{(1+\alpha)\eta_1(\jmath)}{\eta_2(\jmath)}\right)^{\alpha+1}\right] d\jmath \leq \omega_1(\mathfrak{r}_1),$$

we obtain a contradiction with (35) by taking the lim sup on both sides of this inequality. The proof is now complete. □

Theorem 8. *Suppose that $\Phi \in C((\mathfrak{r}_0, \infty), (0, \infty))$ is a solution of (1). If the differential equation*

$$\Phi'(\mathfrak{r}) + \frac{1}{\eta_2(\tau(\mathfrak{r}))}\left(\int_{\mathfrak{r}}^{\infty}\int_{\zeta}^{\infty}\frac{\eta_2(\tau(v))}{h^{1/\alpha}(v)}\left(\int_{\mathfrak{r}_1}^{v} q(\jmath)d\jmath\right)^{1/\alpha} dv d\zeta\right)\Phi(\tau(\mathfrak{r})) = 0. \quad (40)$$

is oscillatory, then $\stackrel{+}{3} = \emptyset$.

Proof. Assume that $\Phi \in {}^+$ and satisfies case (3). From (1) and integrating from $\mathfrak{r}_1$ to $\mathfrak{r}$, we obtain

$$h(\mathfrak{r})(\Phi'''(\mathfrak{r}))^\alpha \leq -\Phi^\alpha(\tau(\mathfrak{r}))\int_{\mathfrak{r}_1}^{\mathfrak{r}} q(\jmath)d\jmath. \quad (41)$$

As in the proof of Lemma 3, we obtain that (19), (21), and (23) hold. Now, integrating (41) from $\mathfrak{r}$ to ∞ and using (23), we obtain

$$-\Phi''(\mathfrak{r}) \leq -\int_{\mathfrak{r}}^{\infty} \frac{\Phi(\tau(v))}{\eta_2(\tau(\mathfrak{r}))}\frac{\eta_2(\tau(\mathfrak{r}))}{h^{1/\alpha}(v)}\left(\int_{\mathfrak{r}_1}^{v} q(\jmath)d\jmath\right)^{1/\alpha} dv.$$

From Lemma 3, note that $\Phi(\mathfrak{r})/\eta_2(\mathfrak{r})$ is nondecreasing and yields

$$-\Phi''(\mathfrak{r}) \leq -\frac{\Phi(\tau(\mathfrak{r}))}{\eta_2(\tau(\mathfrak{r}))}\int_{\mathfrak{r}}^{\infty}\frac{\eta_2(\tau(\mathfrak{r}))}{h^{1/\alpha}(v)}\left(\int_{\mathfrak{r}_1}^{v} q(\jmath)d\jmath\right)^{1/\alpha} dv. \quad (42)$$

Integrating (42) from $\mathfrak{r}$ to ∞, we find

$$\Phi'(\mathfrak{r}) \leq -\int_{\mathfrak{r}}^{\infty}\frac{\Phi(\tau(\zeta))}{\eta_2(\tau(\zeta))}\int_{\zeta}^{\infty}\frac{\eta_2(\tau(\mathfrak{r}))}{h^{1/\alpha}(v)}\left(\int_{\mathfrak{r}_1}^{v} q(\jmath)d\jmath\right)^{1/\alpha} dv d\zeta$$
$$\leq -\frac{\Phi(\tau(\mathfrak{r}))}{\eta_2(\tau(\mathfrak{r}))}\int_{\mathfrak{r}}^{\infty}\int_{\zeta}^{\infty}\frac{\eta_2(\tau(v))}{h^{1/\alpha}(v)}\left(\int_{\mathfrak{r}_1}^{v} q(\jmath)d\jmath\right)^{1/\alpha} dv d\zeta.$$

As a result, it is clear that Φ is a positive solution to the first-order delay differential inequality

$$\Phi'(\mathfrak{r}) + \frac{1}{\eta_2(\tau(\mathfrak{r}))}\left(\int_{\mathfrak{r}}^{\infty}\int_{\zeta}^{\infty}\frac{\eta_2(\tau(v))}{h^{1/\alpha}(v)}\left(\int_{\mathfrak{r}_1}^{v} q(\jmath)d\jmath\right)^{1/\alpha} dv d\zeta\right)\Phi(\tau(\mathfrak{r})) \leq 0.$$

According to [20], Equation (40) also has a solution that is positive, creating a contradiction. The proof is now complete. □

Corollary 1. *Assume that* $\Phi \in C((\mathfrak{r}_0, \infty), (0, \infty))$ *is a solution of (1). If*

$$\liminf_{\mathfrak{r} \to \infty} \int_{\tau(\mathfrak{r})}^{\mathfrak{r}} \frac{1}{\eta_2(\tau(\xi))} \left(\int_{\xi}^{\infty} \int_{\zeta}^{\infty} \frac{\eta_2(\tau(v))}{h^{1/\alpha}(v)} \left(\int_{\mathfrak{r}_1}^{v} q(\jmath) d\jmath \right)^{1/\alpha} dv d\zeta \right) d\xi > \frac{1}{e}, \quad (43)$$

then $\overset{+}{3} = \varnothing$.

Proof. We remark that (43) ensures the oscillation of (40) using [20]. The proof is now complete. □

4. Application in Oscillation Theory

The criteria for oscillation depend on finding conditions that exclude each case of the derivatives of the solution separately. In many cases, we note that the most influential condition in the test of oscillation of the equation is the condition of excluding decreasing solutions. Therefore, improving the conditions for excluding decreasing solutions necessarily affects the improvement of oscillation criteria. In this section, we will set the criteria for testing oscillation for (1) to combine conditions known in the literature that exclude cases (1) and (2) of the derivatives of the solution with the new conditions in the previous section that exclude the existence of solutions that fulfill case (3).

In the next theorems, the proof of the case where (1) or (2) holds is the same as that of [16] (Theorem 2.1, Theorem 2.2). Moreover, either conditions (29) or (35), or (43), excludes case (3).

Theorem 9. *Assume that (29) holds. If (8) and (10) hold for some $\lambda_1 \in (0,1)$, then (1) oscillates.*

Theorem 10. *Assume that (35) holds. If (8) and (10) hold for some $\lambda_1 \in (0,1)$, then (1) oscillates.*

Theorem 11. *Assume that (43) holds. If (8) and (10) hold for some $\lambda_1 \in (0,1)$, then (1) oscillates.*

Example 1. *We consider*

$$\left(e^{\alpha \mathfrak{r}} (\Phi'''(\mathfrak{r}))^{\alpha} \right)' + q_0 e^{\alpha \mathfrak{r}} \Phi^{\alpha} \left(\mathfrak{r} - \arcsin\left(\sqrt{10}/10 \right) \right) = 0, \quad (44)$$

where $h(\mathfrak{r}) = e^{\alpha \mathfrak{r}}$, $q(\mathfrak{r}) = q_0 e^{\alpha \mathfrak{r}}$, $\tau(\mathfrak{r}) = \mathfrak{r} - \arcsin\left(\sqrt{10}/10 \right)$ *and* $\eta(\mathfrak{r}) = e^{-\mathfrak{r}}$. *Note that*

$$\begin{aligned} H(\mathfrak{r}) &= \int_{\mathfrak{r}}^{\infty} (\jmath - \mathfrak{r}) e^{-\jmath} d\jmath \\ &= e^{-\mathfrak{r}}. \end{aligned}$$

If we choose $\gamma(\mathfrak{r}) = e^{-\alpha \mathfrak{r}}$, *then we see that*

$$\eta_1(\mathfrak{r}) = e^{-\mathfrak{r}}, \eta_2(\mathfrak{r}) = e^{-\mathfrak{r}} \text{ and } \eta_2(\tau(\mathfrak{r})) = e^{-\left(\mathfrak{r} - \arcsin\left(\sqrt{10}/10 \right) \right)}.$$

It is easy to verify that

$$\ell_0 = \frac{e^{\sqrt{q_0/\alpha} \arcsin\left(\sqrt{10}/10 \right)}}{\sqrt{1 - \sqrt{\sqrt{q_0/\alpha}}}}, \quad \mu_* = \frac{e^{-\left(\mathfrak{r} - \arcsin\left(\sqrt{10}/10 \right) \right)}}{e^{-\mathfrak{r}}} = e^{\arcsin\left(\sqrt{10}/10 \right)},$$

$n = 0$, $\beta_* = q_0/\alpha$, *and* $\beta_0 = \sqrt{q_0/\alpha}$.

By using Theorem 9, we find conditions (8) and (10) are satisfied and the condition (29) holds if

$$q_0 > \frac{(\alpha)^{\alpha+1}}{(\alpha+1)^{\alpha+1} e^{\alpha \sqrt{q_0/\alpha} \arcsin\left(\sqrt{10}/10 \right)}}. \quad (45)$$

Therefore, Equation (44) is oscillatory if (45) holds. Additionally, by using Theorem 10, we find that condition (35) is satisfied if

$$q_0 > \frac{1}{e^{\alpha \sqrt{q_0/\alpha} \arcsin(\sqrt{10}/10)}} \left(\frac{1}{(\alpha+1)^{\alpha+1}} - (1-\alpha) \right). \tag{46}$$

Therefore, Equation (44) is oscillatory if (46) holds. Now, by using Theorem 2 and Theorem 5, Equation (44) is oscillatory if

$$q_0 > \frac{(\alpha)^{\alpha+1}}{(\alpha+1)^{\alpha+1}}. \tag{47}$$

Figure 1 illustrates the efficiency of conditions (45)–(47) in studying the oscillation of solutions of (44).

Remark 2. *To the best of our knowledge, the known related sharp criterion for (44) based on Example 1 gives*

$$q_0 > \left(\frac{\alpha}{\alpha+1} \right)^{\alpha+1}. \tag{48}$$

Note firstly that our criteria (45) and (46) essentially take into account the influence of the delay argument $\tau(\mathfrak{r})$, which has been neglected in all previous results of fourth-order equations.

Secondly, in the case where $\alpha = 1$, we get the results in Table 1. Therefore, we note that conditions (45) and (46) support the most efficient and sharp criterion for oscillation of Equation (44).

Table 1. Comparison of the different oscillation criteria of (44) with $\alpha = 1$.

Condition	(45)	(46)	(48)
Criterion	$q_0 > 0.215$	$q_0 > 0.215$	$q_0 > 0.250$

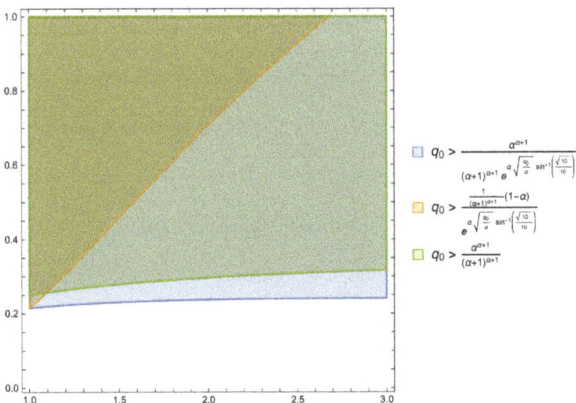

Figure 1. Regions for which conditions (45)–(47) are satisfied.

5. Conclusions

The study of oscillations for delay differential equations always begins with the classification of positive solutions based on the sign of their derivatives. The oscillation criteria depend on the conditions that exclude each case of the positive solutions. In many cases, the exclusion of decreasing solutions is the condition that has the most effect on the test for the oscillation of the equation. Therefore, improving the criteria for oscillation must obviously have an effect on improving the conditions for excluding decreasing solutions. In this work, we study the asymptotic properties of solutions to the fourth-order delay differential equation with the non-canonical operator. We have created new properties that help us have more effective terms in the oscillation of the Equation (1). We use the comparison theorem and more than one compensation for Riccatti to obtain criteria that guarantee the exclusion of decreasing solutions. After that, by combining well-known results with the results of Section 3, we set new criteria for the oscillation of the studied equation. Finally, we gave an example to illustrate the novelty and importance of our results. An open question is whether the neutral delay equation can be studied with the same technique used in this research.

Author Contributions: Conceptualization, A.N. and O.M.; methodology, A.N. and C.C.; software, M.A.; formal analysis, E.M.E.; investigation, O.M. and M.A.; writing—original draft preparation, A.N. and O.M.; writing—review and editing, C.C. and E.M.E. All authors have read and agreed to the published version of the manuscript.

Funding: This research received no external funding.

Data Availability Statement: Not applicable.

Conflicts of Interest: The authors declare no conflict of interest.

References

1. Hale, J.K. Functional differential equations. In *Analytic Theory of Differential Equations*; Springer: Berlin/Heidelberg, Germany, 1971; pp. 9–22.
2. Gopalsamy, K. *Stability and Oscillations in Delay Differential Equation in Delay Differential Equations of Population Dynamics*; Springer: Dordrecht, The Netherlands, 1992.
3. Oguztoreli, M.N.; Stein, R.B. An analysis of oscillations in neuro-muscular systems. *J. Math. Biol.* **1975**, *2*, 87–105.
4. Agarwal, R.P.; Bohner, M.; Li, W.T. *Nonoscillation and Oscillation Theory for Functional Differential Equations*; CRC Press: Boca Raton, FL, USA, 2004.
5. Santra, S.S.; Dassios, I.; Ghosh, T. On the asymptotic behavior of a class of second-order non-linear neutral differential Equations with multiple delays. *Axioms* **2020**, *9*, 134.
6. Wang, Y.; Meng, F. New Oscillation Results for Second-Order Neutral Differential Equations with Deviating Arguments. *Symmetry* **2020**, *12*, 1937. [CrossRef]
7. Muhib, A.; Moaaz, O.; Cesarano, C.; Askar, S.; Elabbasy, E.M. Neutral Differential Equations of Fourth-Order: New Asymptotic Properties of Solutions. *Axioms* **2022**, *11*, 52. [CrossRef]
8. Onose, H. Forced oscillation for functional differential equations of fourth order. *Bull. Fac. Sci. Ibaraki Univ. Ser. A* **1979**, *11*, 57–63.
9. Wu, F. Existence of eventually positive solutions of fourth order quasilinear differential equations. *J. Math. Anal. Appl.* **2012**, *389*, 632–646.
10. Kamo, K.I.; Usami, H. Oscillation theorems for fourth order quasilinear ordinary differential equations. *Stud. Sci. Math. Hung.* **2002**, *39*, 385–406.
11. Grace, S.R.; Agarwal, R.P.; Graef, J.R. Oscillation theorems for fourth order functional differential equations. *J. Appl. Math. Comput.* **2009**, *30*, 75–88. [CrossRef]
12. Zhang, C.; Li, T.; Sun, B.; Thandapani, E. On the oscillation of higher-order half-linear delay differential equations. *Appl. Math. Lett.* **2011**, *24*, 1618–1621. [CrossRef]
13. Baculikova, B.; Dzurina, J.; Graef, J.R. On the oscillation of higher-order delay differential equations. *J. Math. Sci.* **2012**, *187*, 12. [CrossRef]
14. Zhang, C.; Li, T.; Saker, S.H. Oscillation of fourth-order delay differential equations. *J. Math. Sci.* **2014**, *201*, 9. [CrossRef]
15. Zhang, C.; Agarwal, R.P.; Bohner, M.; Li, T. New results for oscillatory behavior of even-order half-linear delay differential equations. *Appl. Math. Lett.* **2013**, *26*, 179–183. [CrossRef]
16. Moaaz, O.; Muhib, A. New oscillation criteria for nonlinear delay differential equations of fourth-order. *Appl. Math. Comput.* **2020**, *377*, 125192.
17. Elabbasy, E.M.; Nabih, A.; Nofal, T.A.; Alharbi, W.R.; Moaaz, O. Neutral differential equations with noncanonical operator: Oscillation behavior of solutions. *AIMS Math.* **2021**, *6*, 3272–3287.
18. Moaaz, O.; Muhib, A.; Zakarya, M.; Abdel-Aty, A.H. Delay differential equation of fourth-order: Asymptotic analysis and oscillatory behavior. *Alex. Eng. J.* **2022**, *61*, 2919–2924. [CrossRef]
19. Philos, C.G. A new criterion for the oscillatory and asymptotic behavior of delay differential equations. *Bull. Acad. Pol. Sci. Ser. Sci. Math* **1981**, *29*, 367–370.
20. Philos, C.G. On the existence of nonoscillatory solutions tending to zero at ∞ for differential equations with positive delays. *Arch. Math.* **1981**, *36*, 168–178.

Article

A Novel Approach in Solving Improper Integrals

Mohammad Abu-Ghuwaleh, Rania Saadeh * and Ahmad Qazza

Department of Mathematics, Faculty of Science, Zarqa University, Zarqa 13110, Jordan
* Correspondence: rsaadeh@zu.edu.jo

Abstract: To resolve several challenging applications in many scientific domains, general formulas of improper integrals are provided and established for use in this article. The suggested theorems can be considered generators for new improper integrals with precise solutions, without requiring complex computations. New criteria for handling improper integrals are illustrated in tables to simplify the usage and the applications of the obtained outcomes. The results of this research are compared with those obtained by I.S. Gradshteyn and I.M. Ryzhik in the classical table of integrations. Some well-known theorems on improper integrals are considered to be simple cases in the context of our work. Some applications related to finding Green's function, one-dimensional vibrating string problems, wave motion in elastic solids, and computing Fourier transforms are presented.

Keywords: improper integrals; power series; analytic function; Cauchy residue theorem; Ramanujan's master theorem

MSC: 30E20; 33E20; 44A99

1. Introduction

Numerous studies on the topic of improper integrals have been published in recent years in a variety of scientific disciplines, including physics and engineering [1–7]. Due to this, mathematicians have been particularly interested in finding new theorems and methods to solve these integrals. Particularly in engineering, applied mathematical physics, electrical engineering, and other fields, it is sometimes necessary to handle erroneous integrals in computations or when describing models [8–16]. While some of these integrations can be handled easily, others require complex calculations. Many of these integrals require computer software to be solved as they cannot be calculated so manually. Additionally, numerical techniques may be employed to resolve some incorrect integrals that the aforementioned techniques are unable to resolve [17–23].

The process of evaluating improper integrals is not usually based on certain rules or techniques that can be applied directly. Many methods and techniques were established and introduced by mathematicians and physicists to present a closed form for indefinite integrals, the technique of double integrals, series methods, residue theorems, calculus under the integral sign, and other methods that are used to solve improper complex integrals exactly or approximately [24–31].

The residue theorem was first established by A.L. Cauchy in 1826, which is considered a powerful theorem in complex analysis. However, the applications that can be calculated using the residue theorem to compute integrals on real numbers require many precise constraints that should be satisfied in order to solve the integrals, including finding appropriate closed contours and also determining the poles. Another challenge in the process of applying the residue theorem is the difficulty and efforts in finding solutions for some integrations.

According to his published memoirs, Cauchy developed powerful formulas in mathematics using the residue theorem [4]. Researchers consider these formulas essential in treating and solving improper integrals. However, these results are considered simple cases when compared to the results that we present in this article. In addition, we show that the proposed theorems and results in this research are not based on the residue theorem.

One significant accomplishment in the sphere of definite and indefinite integrals is found in the master theorem of Ramanujan, which presents new expressions concerning the Milline transform of any continuous function in terms of the analytic Taylor series, and others [32–39]. It was implemented by Ramanujan and other researchers as a powerful tool in calculating definite and indefinite integrals and also in computing infinite series. The obtained results are as applicable and effective as Ramanujan's master theorem in handling and generating new formulas of integrals with direct solutions.

In this study, we introduce new theorems to simplify the procedure of computing improper integrals by presenting new theorems with proofs. Each theorem can generate many improper integral formulas that cannot be solved by usual techniques or would need a large amount of effort and time spent in order to be solved. The motivation of this work is to generate as many improper integrals and their values as possible to be used in different problems. The obtained results can be implemented to construct new tables of integrations so that researchers can use them in calculations and to check the accuracy of their answers while discovering new methods.

The main purpose of this work is to introduce simple new techniques to help researchers, mathematicians, engineers, physicists, etc., to solve some difficult improper integrals that cannot be treated or solved easily (and which require several theorems and a large amount of effort to solve). This goal is achieved by introducing some master theorems that can be implemented in order to solve difficult applications. The outcomes can be generalized and introduced in tables to obtain and to use the results of some improper integrals directly.

We organize this article as follows: In Section 2, we introduce some illustrative preliminaries; then, facts concerning analytic functions, master theorems, and results are presented in Section 3. Mathematical remarks and several applications are presented in Section 4. Finally, the conclusion of our research is presented in Section 5.

2. Preliminaries

In this section, some basic definitions and theorems related to our work are presented and illustrated for later use.

2.1. Basic Definitions and Lemmas

Definition 1 ([7])**.** *Suppose that a function f is analytic in a domain $\Omega \subseteq \mathbb{C}$, where $\mathbb{C}$ is the complex plane. Consider a disc $D \subseteq \Omega$ centered at z_0; then, the function f can be expressed in the following series expansion:*

$$f(z) = \sum_{n=0}^{\infty} a_n (z - z_0)^n,$$

where a_n is the coefficients of the series.

Definition 2 ([8])**.** *Assume that f is an analytic function; then, Taylor series expansion at any point x_0 of f in its domain is given by*

$$T(x) = \sum_{n=0}^{\infty} \frac{f^{(n)}(x_0)}{n!} (x - x_0)^n,$$

which converges to f in a neighborhood of x_0 point wisely.

2.2. Basic Formulas of Series and Improper Integrals

In this section, we introduce some series and improper integrals that are needed in our work.

Lemma 1. *The following factorization formula holds for* $n \in \mathbb{N}$, *as follows*

$$\frac{1}{(x^2+1^2)(x^2+3^2)...(x^2+(2n+1)^2)} = \frac{(-1)^n}{4^n(2n+1)!} \sum_{k=0}^{n} (-1)^k \binom{2n+1}{k} \frac{2n+1-2k}{(2n+1-2k)^2+x^2} \quad (1)$$

Proof. To prove Equation (1), we define an integral whose solution can be expressed by two different forms: the left side of Equation (1) and the right side of the equation.

Let

$$I = \int_0^\infty e^{-px}(\sin x)^{2a+1} dx, \quad (2)$$

where $p > 0$, $a \in \mathbb{N}$.

Taking the indefinite integral:

$$J = p^2 \int e^{-px}(\sin x)^{2a+1} dx \quad (3)$$

Applying integration by parts on Equation (3) twice, we obtain a reduction formula as follows:

$$J = -pe^{-px}(\sin x)^{2a+1} - (2a+1)e^{-px}\sin^{2a}x \cos x \\ +(2a+1)\int e^{-px}[2a((\sin x)^{2a-1} - (\sin x)^{2a+1}) - (\sin x)^{2a+1}] dx. \quad (4)$$

Taking the limit of the integrals in Equation (4) from 0 to ∞, we obtain:

$$\int_0^\infty e^{-px}(\sin x)^{2a+1} dx = \frac{(2a+1)(2a)}{p^2 + (2a+1)^2} \int_0^\infty e^{-px}(\sin x)^{2a-1} dx. \quad (5)$$

Applying Equation (5) $(a-1)$ times to the integral $\int_0^\infty e^{-px}(\sin x)^{2a-1} dx$, we obtain:

$$\int_0^\infty e^{-px}(\sin x)^{2a+1} dx \\ = \frac{(2a+1)(2a)(2a-1)(2a-2)...(3)(2)}{((2a+1)^2+p^2)((2a-1)^2+p^2)...(3+p^2)} \int_0^\infty e^{-px}\sin x \, dx. \quad (6)$$

The integral $\int_0^\infty e^{-px}\sin x \, dx$ can be calculated easily using twice integration by parts to obtain:

$$\int_0^\infty e^{-px}\sin x \, dx = \frac{1}{1+p^2}. \quad (7)$$

Substituting the fact in Equation (7) into Equation (6), we obtain:

$$\int_0^\infty e^{-px}(\sin x)^{2a+1} dx = \frac{(2a+1)!}{((2a+1)^2+p^2)((2a-1)^2+p^2)...(3+p^2)(1+p^2)}. \quad (8)$$

Therefore, the left side of Equation (1) is obtained.

Now, we express the solution of Equation (2) in another form, that is, to obtain the right side of Equation (1), as follows:

Using the power trigonometric formula deduced using De Moivre's formula, Euler's formula, and the binomial theorem [10] (p. 31)

$$(\sin(x))^{2a+1} = \frac{(-1)^a}{4^a} \sum_{k=0}^{a} (-1)^k \binom{2a+1}{k} \sin[(2a+1-2k)x]. \quad (9)$$

Substituting Equation (9) into Equation (2), we obtain:

$$\int_0^\infty e^{-px}(\sin x)^{2a+1}dx = \int_0^\infty e^{-px}\frac{(-1)^a}{4^a}\sum_{k=0}^{a}(-1)^k\binom{2a+1}{k}\sin[(2a+1-2k)x]dx \qquad (10)$$

Therefore, by changing the order of the integral and the sum in Equation (10), we obtain:

$$\int_0^\infty e^{-px}(\sin x)^{2a+1}dx = \frac{(-1)^a}{4^a}\sum_{k=0}^{a}(-1)^k\binom{2a+1}{k}\int_0^\infty e^{-px}\sin[(2a+1-2k)x]dx \qquad (11)$$

To evaluate the integral $\int_0^\infty e^{-px}\sin[(2a+1-2k)x]dx$, we apply twice integration by parts to obtain:

$$\int_0^\infty e^{-px}\sin[(2a+1-2k)x]dx = \frac{2a+1-2k}{(2a+1-2k)^2+p^2}. \qquad (12)$$

Substituting the result in Equation (12) into Equation (11), we obtain:

$$\int_0^\infty e^{-px}(\sin x)^{2a+1}dx = \frac{(-1)^a}{4^a}\sum_{k=0}^{a}(-1)^k\binom{2a+1}{k}\frac{2a+1-2k}{(2a+1-2k)^2+p^2}. \qquad (13)$$

Therefore, the right side of Equation (1) is obtained.

Then, equating Equation (13) with Equation (8); this, thus, completes the proof of Equation (21). □

Lemma 2. *The following factorization holds for* $n \in \mathbb{N}$ *as,*

$$\frac{1}{x(x^2+2^2)(x^2+4^2)\ldots(x^2+4n^2)} = \frac{1}{2^{2n}(2n)!}\left(\frac{1}{x}\binom{2n}{n} + 2\sum_{k=0}^{n-1}(-1)^{n+k}\binom{2n}{k}\frac{x}{(2n-2k)^2+x^2}\right). \qquad (14)$$

Proof. The proof is obtained by repeating the same process in proving Lemma (1), but by using the integral $\int_0^\infty e^{-px}(\sin x)^{2a}dx$, where $p > 0$ and $a \in \mathbb{N}$. □

Lemma 3. *The following factorization formula holds for* $n = 0, 1, \cdots,$ *and* $m = 1, 2, \cdots,$ *as follows:*

$$\frac{1}{[(x^2+1^2)(x^2+3^2)\ldots(x^2+(2n+1)^2)][x(x^2+2^2)(x^2+4^2)\ldots(x^2+4m^2)]}$$
$$= \frac{(-1)^n}{(2^{2m+2n})(m!)^2(2n+1)!}\sum_{s=0}^{n}(-1)^s\binom{2n+1}{s}\frac{2n+1-2s}{x((2n+1-2s)^2+x^2)} \qquad (15)$$
$$+ \frac{(-1)^n}{2^{2m+2n-1}(2m)!(2n+1)!}\left(\sum_{k=0}^{m-1}\sum_{s=0}^{n}(-1)^{m+k+s}\binom{2m}{k}\binom{2n+1}{s}\frac{x(2n+1-2s)}{((2m-2k)^2+x^2)((2n+1-2s)^2+x^2)}\right).$$

Proof. This is a direct result obtained by multiplying Equation (1) by Equation (14). □

Lemma 4. *The following formulas of improper integrals are created using Lemmas (1–3):*

$$\int_0^\infty \frac{\cos(\theta x)}{(x^2+1)(x^2+9)\ldots(x^2+(2n+1)^2)}dx$$
$$= \frac{(-1)^n}{(2n+1)!}\frac{\pi}{2^{2n+1}}\sum_{k=0}^{n}(-1)^k\binom{2n+1}{k}e^{\theta(2k-2n-1)}, \qquad (16)$$
$$\text{for } \theta \geq 0, n = 0, 1, \cdots$$

Proof. The formula is obtained by multiplying both sides of Equation (1) by $cos(\theta x)$, then integrating both sides from 0 to ∞, and using the well-known fact:

$$\int_0^\infty \frac{cos(\theta x)}{a^2+x^2}dx = \frac{\pi}{2a}e^{-a\theta},$$

where a and $\theta > 0$. □

$$\int_0^\infty \frac{x sin(\theta x)}{(x^2+1)(x^2+9)\cdots(x^2+(2n+1)^2)}dx$$
$$= \frac{(-1)^n}{(2n+1)!}\frac{\pi}{2^{2n+1}}\sum_{k=0}^n (-1)^k \binom{2n+1}{k}(2n-2k+1)e^{\theta(2k-2n-1)}, \quad (17)$$

for $\theta > 0$, $n = 0, 1, \cdots$.

Proof. The formula is obtained by differentiating both sides of Equation (16) with respect to θ. □

$$\int_0^\infty \frac{sin(\theta x)}{x(x^2+4)(x^2+16)\cdots(x^2+(2n)^2)}dx$$
$$= \frac{(-1)^n}{(2n)!}\frac{\pi}{2^{2n+1}}\left((-1)^n\binom{2n}{n}+2\sum_{k=0}^{n-1}(-1)^k\binom{2n}{k}e^{2\theta(k-n)}\right), \quad (18)$$

for $\theta > 0$, $n = 1, 2, \cdots$.

Proof. The formula is obtained by multiplying both sides of Equation (14) by $sin(\theta x)$, then integrating both sides from 0 to ∞, and using the well-known fact:

$$\int_0^\infty \frac{sin(\theta x)}{x(a^2+x^2)}dx = \frac{\pi}{2a^2}\left(1-e^{-a\theta}\right),$$

where θ and $a > 0$

$$\int_0^\infty \frac{cos(\theta x)}{(x^2+4)(x^2+16)\cdots(x^2+(2n)^2)}dx = \frac{(-1)^n \pi\, 2^{1-2n}}{(2n)!}\sum_{k=0}^{n-1}(-1)^k\binom{2n}{k}(k-n)e^{2\theta(k-n)}, \quad (19)$$

for $\theta \geq 0$, $n = 1, 2, \cdots$.

□

Proof. The formula is obtained by differentiating both sides of Equation (18) with respect to θ. □

Lemma 5. *Let $\theta > 0$ and $n = 0, 1, \cdots$, $m = 1, 2, \cdots$. Then, we have the following improper integrals:*

$$\int_0^\infty \frac{sin(\theta x)}{((x^2+1)(x^2+9)\cdots(x^2+(2n+1)^2))\,(x(x^2+4)(x^2+16)\cdots(x^2+4m^2))}dx$$
$$= \frac{(-1)^n \pi}{(2^{2m+2n+1})(m!)^2(2n+1)!}\sum_{s=0}^n (-1)^s \binom{2n+1}{s}\frac{1-e^{-\theta(2n+1-2s)}}{(2n+1-2s)} \quad (20)$$
$$+ \frac{(-1)^n \pi}{2^{2m+2n}(2m)!(2n+1)!}\sum_{k=0}^{m-1}\sum_{s=0}^n (-1)^{m+k+s}\binom{2m}{k}\binom{2n+1}{s}$$
$$\cdot \frac{(2n+1-2s)\left(e^{-\theta(2n+1-2s)}-e^{-\theta(2m-2k)}\right)}{(2m-2k)^2-(2n+1-2s)^2}.$$

Proof. The formula is obtained by multiplying both sides of Equation (15) by $sin(\theta x)$, then integrating both sides from 0 to ∞, and using the well-known facts:

$$\int_0^\infty \frac{\sin(\theta x)}{x(a^2+x^2)}dx = \frac{\pi}{2a^2}\left(1-e^{-a\theta}\right),$$

and

$$\int_0^\infty \frac{x\sin(\theta x)}{a^2+x^2}dx = \frac{\pi}{2}e^{-a\theta},$$

where θ and $a > 0$.

$$\int_0^\infty \frac{\cos(\theta x)}{((x^2+1)(x^2+9)\ldots(x^2+(2n+1)^2))((x^2+4)(x^2+16)\ldots(x^2+4m^2))}dx$$
$$= \frac{(-1)^n\pi}{(2^{2m+2n+1})(m!)^2(2n+1)!}\sum_{s=0}^n(-1)^s\binom{2n+1}{s}e^{-\theta(2n+1-2s)} + \frac{(-1)^n\pi}{2^{2m+2n}(2m)!(2n+1)!}$$
$$\sum_{k=0}^{m-1}\sum_{s=0}^n(-1)^{m+k+s}\binom{2m}{k}\binom{2n+1}{s}\frac{(2n+1-2s)\left((2m-2k)e^{-\theta(2m-2k)}-(2n+1-2s)e^{-\theta(2n+1-2s)}\right)}{(2m-2k)^2-(2n+1-2s)^2}$$

□

Proof. The formula can be obtained by differentiating both sides of Equation (20) with respect to θ. □

3. New Master Theorems

In this part, we present new theorems to help mathematicians, engineers, and physicists solve complicated improper integrals. To obtain our objective, we introduce some facts concerning analytic functions [7,9,12].

Assuming that f is an analytic function in a disc D centered at α, then using Taylor's expansion, where α, β and θ are real constants, we have

$$f(z) = \sum_{k=0}^\infty \frac{f^{(k)}(\alpha)}{k!}(z-\alpha)^k, \tag{21}$$

substituting $z = \alpha + \beta e^{i\theta x}$ into $f(z)$, where β is not completely arbitrary, since it must be smaller than the radius of D, we obtain

$$f\left(\alpha + \beta e^{i\theta x}\right) = \sum_{k=0}^\infty \frac{f^{(k)}(\alpha)}{k!}\beta^k e^{i\theta kx}, \ x \in \mathbb{R}. \tag{22}$$

Using the formulas

$$e^{i\theta x} + e^{-i\theta x} = 2\cos(\theta x), \ e^{i\theta x} - e^{-i\theta x} = 2i\sin(\theta x),$$

one can obtain

$$\frac{1}{2}\left(f\left(\alpha+\beta e^{i\theta x}\right)+f\left(\alpha+\beta e^{-i\theta x}\right)\right) = \frac{1}{2}\sum_{k=0}^\infty \frac{f^{(k)}(\alpha)}{k!}\beta^k\left(e^{i\theta kx}+e^{-i\theta kx}\right)$$
$$= \sum_{k=0}^\infty \frac{f^{(k)}(\alpha)}{k!}\beta^k\cos(k\theta x) \tag{23}$$
$$= f(\alpha) + f'(\alpha)\beta\cos(\theta x) + \frac{f''(\alpha)}{2!}\beta^2\cos(2\theta x) + \ldots.$$

Similarly,

$$\frac{1}{2i}\left(f\left(\alpha+\beta e^{i\theta x}\right)-f\left(\alpha+\beta e^{-i\theta x}\right)\right) = \frac{1}{2i}\sum_{k=0}^\infty \frac{f^{(k)}(\alpha)}{k!}\beta^k\left(e^{i\theta kx}-e^{-i\theta kx}\right)$$
$$= f'(\alpha)\beta\sin(\theta x) + \frac{f''(\alpha)}{2!}\beta^2\sin(2\theta x) + \ldots \tag{24}$$
$$= \sum_{k=1}^\infty \frac{f^{(k)}(\alpha)}{k!}\beta^k\sin(k\theta x).$$

Next, the parameters in Equations (23) and (24) can be modified in the following lemma.

Lemma 3. *Assume that $g(\alpha + z)$ is an analytic function that has the following series expansion:*

$$g(\alpha + z) = \sum_{k=0}^{\infty} M_k e^{-kz}, \qquad (25)$$

whether z be real or imaginary, and $\sum_{k=0}^{\infty} M_k$ is absolutely convergent. Then

$$\frac{1}{2}(g(\alpha - i\theta x) + g(\alpha + i\theta x)) = \frac{1}{2}\sum_{k=0}^{\infty} M_k \left(e^{ik\theta x} + e^{-ik\theta x}\right) = \sum_{k=0}^{\infty} M_k \cos(k\theta x), \qquad (26)$$

and,

$$\frac{1}{2i}(g(\alpha - i\theta x) - g(\alpha + i\theta x)) = \frac{1}{2i}\sum_{k=1}^{\infty} M_k \left(e^{ik\theta x} - e^{-ik\theta x}\right) = \sum_{k=1}^{\infty} M_k \sin(k\theta x), \qquad (27)$$

where $\theta > 0$, $\alpha \in \mathbb{R}$, and x is any real number.

The next part of this section includes the new master theorems that we establish. Moreover, we mention here that Cauchy's results in [3] are identical to our results with special choices of the parameters, as will be discussed later.

Theorem 1. *Let f be an analytic function in a disc D centered at α, where $\alpha \in \mathbb{R}$. Then, we have the following improper integral formula:*

$$\int_0^{\infty} \frac{f(\alpha + \beta e^{i\theta x}) + f(\alpha + \beta e^{-i\theta x})}{(x^2+1)(x^2+9)\cdots(x^2+(2n+1)^2)} dx \\ = \frac{(-1)^n}{(2n+1)!} \frac{\pi}{2^{2n}} \sum_{s=0}^{n} (-1)^s \binom{2n+1}{s} f\left(\alpha + \beta e^{\theta(2s-2n-1)}\right), \qquad (28)$$

where $\theta \geq 0$ and $n = 0, 1, 2, \cdots$.

Proof. Let

$$I = \int_0^{\infty} \frac{f(\alpha + \beta e^{i\theta x}) + f(\alpha + \beta e^{-i\theta x})}{(x^2+1)(x^2+9)\cdots(x^2+(2n+1)^2)} dx. \qquad (29)$$

Now, since f is an analytic function around α, substituting the fact in Equation (23) into Equation (29), we obtain

$$I = \int_0^{\infty} \frac{2\sum_{k=0}^{\infty} \frac{f^{(k)}(\alpha)\beta^k}{k!} \cos(k\theta x)}{(x^2+1)(x^2+9)\cdots(x^2+(2n+1)^2)} dx. \qquad (30)$$

Fubini's theorem implies changing the order of the summation and the improper integral to obtain

$$I = 2\sum_{k=0}^{\infty} \frac{f^{(k)}(\alpha)\beta^k}{k!} \int_0^{\infty} \frac{\cos(k\theta x)}{(x^2+1)(x^2+9)\cdots(x^2+(2n+1)^2)} dx. \qquad (31)$$

The fact in Equation (1) implies that Equation (31) becomes

$$I = 2\sum_{k=0}^{\infty} \frac{f^{(k)}(\alpha)\beta^k}{k!} \frac{(-1)^n}{(2n+1)!} \frac{\pi}{2^{2n+1}} \sum_{s=0}^{n} (-1)^s \binom{2n+1}{s} e^{k\theta(2s-2n-1)}. \qquad (32)$$

The result comes directly, by comparing the definition of the function g in Equation (25) with the definition of the function f in Equation (22), to obtain

$$I = \frac{(-1)^n}{(2n+1)!} \frac{\pi}{2^{2n}} \sum_{s=0}^{n} (-1)^s \binom{2n+1}{s} f\left(\alpha + \beta e^{\theta(2s-2n-1)}\right).$$

$\square$

Theorem 2. *Let f be an analytic function in a disc D centered at α, where $\alpha \in \mathbb{R}$. Then, we have the following improper integral formula:*

$$\int_0^\infty \frac{x\left(f(\alpha+\beta e^{i\theta x}) - f(\alpha+\beta e^{-i\theta x})\right)}{i(x^2+1)(x^2+9)\cdots(x^2+(2n+1)^2)} dx$$

$$= \frac{(-1)^n}{(2n+1)!} \frac{\pi}{2^{2n}} \sum_{s=0}^{n} (-1)^s \binom{2n+1}{s} (2n-2s+1)\left(f\left(\alpha+\beta e^{\theta(2s-2n-1)}\right) - f(\alpha)\right), \quad (33)$$

where $\theta > 0$ and $n = 0, 1, 2, \cdots$.

Proof. Let

$$I = \int_0^\infty \frac{x\left(f(\alpha+\beta e^{i\theta x}) - f(\alpha+\beta e^{-i\theta x})\right)}{i(x^2+1)(x^2+9)\cdots(x^2+(2n+1)^2)} dx. \quad (34)$$

Now, since f is an analytic function around α and substituting the fact in Equation (24) into Equation (34), we obtain

$$I = 2\sum_{k=1}^{\infty} \frac{f^{(k)}(\alpha)\beta^k}{k!} \int_0^\infty \frac{x(\sin(k\theta x))}{(x^2+1)(x^2+9)\cdots(x^2+(2n+1)^2)} dx. \quad (35)$$

Substituting the fact in Equation (2) into Equation (35), we obtain

$$I = 2\sum_{k=1}^{\infty} \frac{f^{(k)}(\alpha)\beta^k}{k!} \frac{(-1)^n}{(2n+1)!} \frac{\pi}{2^{2n+1}} \sum_{s=0}^{n}(-1)^s \binom{2n+1}{s}(2n-2s+1)e^{\theta k(2s-2n-1)}. \quad (36)$$

The fact in Equation (22) implies that Equation (36) becomes

$$I = \frac{(-1)^n}{(2n+1)!} \frac{\pi}{2^{2n}} \sum_{s=0}^{n}(-1)^s \binom{2n+1}{s}(2n-2s+1)\left(f\left(\alpha+\beta e^{\theta(2s-2n-1)}\right) - f(\alpha)\right).$$

Hence, this completes the proof. $\square$

We should point out that $f(\alpha)$ appears in Equation (33) because the lower index of the infinite summation started from $k = 1$ and not from $k = 0$, as is the case in Equation (29). Thus, when we want to express the answer in terms of the original function f, we add and subtract $f(\alpha)$ to obtain our result.

Theorem 3. *Let f be an analytic function in a disc D centered at α, where $\alpha \in \mathbb{R}$. Then, we have the following improper integral formula:*

$$\int_0^\infty \frac{f(\alpha+\beta e^{i\theta x}) - f(\alpha+\beta e^{-i\theta x})}{i\, x\, (x^2+4)(x^2+16)\cdots(x^2+(2n)^2)} dx = \frac{(-1)^n}{(2n)!} \frac{\pi}{2^{2n}} \left((-1)^n \binom{2n}{n} \psi + 2\sum_{s=0}^{n-1}(-1)^s \binom{2n}{s} \phi(s)\right), \quad (37)$$

where $\theta > 0$, $n = 1, 2, \cdots$, $\psi = f(\alpha+\beta) - f(\alpha)$ and $\phi(s) = f\left(\alpha+\beta e^{2\theta(s-n)}\right) - f(\alpha)$.

Proof. The proof of Theorem 3 can be obtained by similar arguments to Theorem 2 and using the fact (3) in Lemma 1. □

Theorem 4. *Let f be an analytic function in a disc D centered at $\alpha \in \mathbb{R}$. Then, we have the following improper integral formula:*

$$\int_0^\infty \frac{f(\alpha + \beta e^{i\theta x}) + f(\alpha + \beta e^{-i\theta x})}{(x^2+4)(x^2+16)\ldots(x^2+(2n)^2)} dx = \frac{(-1)^n \pi \, 2^{2-2n}}{(2n)!} \sum_{s=0}^{n-1}(-1)^s \binom{2n}{s}(s-n)f\left(\alpha + \beta e^{2\theta(s-n)}\right), \quad (38)$$

where $\theta \geq 0$, $n = 1, 2, \cdots$.

Proof. The proof of Theorem 4 can be obtained by similar arguments to Theorem 1 and using the fact (4) in Lemma 1. □

Theorem 5. *Let f be an analytic function in a disc D centered at α, where $\alpha \in \mathbb{R}$. Then, we have the following improper integral formula:*

$$\int_0^\infty \frac{f(\alpha+\beta e^{i\theta x}) - f(\alpha+\beta e^{-i\theta x})}{i\left((x^2+1)(x^2+9)\ldots(x^2+(2n+1)^2)\right)(x(x^2+4)(x^2+16)\cdots(x^2+4m^2))} dx$$
$$= \frac{(-1)^n \pi}{(2^{2m+2n})(m!)^2(2n+1)!} \sum_{s=0}^n (-1)^s \binom{2n+1}{s} \frac{(\varphi - \psi(s))}{(2n+1-2s)}$$
$$+ \frac{(-1)^n \pi}{2^{2m+2n-1}(2m)!(2n+1)!} \left(\sum_{k=0}^{m-1} \sum_{s=0}^n (-1)^{m+k+s} \binom{2m}{k}\binom{2n+1}{s}(2n+1 - 2s) \frac{(\psi(s) - \phi(k))}{\left((2m-2k)^2 - (2n+1-2s)^2\right)} \right), \quad (39)$$

where $\theta > 0$, $n = 0, 1, 2, \cdots$, $m = 1, 2, \cdots$, $\psi(s) = f\left(\alpha + \beta e^{-\theta(2n+1-2s)}\right)$, $\phi(k) = f\left(\alpha + \beta e^{-\theta(2m-2k)}\right)$, and $\varphi = f(\alpha + \beta)$.

Proof. Let

$$I = \int_0^\infty \frac{f(\alpha + \beta e^{i\theta x}) - f(\alpha + \beta e^{-i\theta x})}{i\left((x^2+1)(x^2+9)\ldots(x^2+(2n+1)^2)\right)(x(x^2+4)(x^2+16)\cdots(x^2+4m^2))} dx. \quad (40)$$

Now, since f is an analytic function around α and substituting the fact in Equation (24) into Equation (40), we obtain

$$I = 2\sum_{k=1}^\infty \frac{f^{(k)}(\alpha)\beta^k}{k!} \int_0^\infty \frac{\sin(\theta k x)}{\left((x^2+1)(x^2+9)\ldots(x^2+(2n+1)^2)\right)(x(x^2+4)(x^2+16)\cdots(x^2+4m^2))} dx. \quad (41)$$

Substituting the fact in Equation (9) into Equation (41), we obtain

$$I = 2\sum_{k=1}^\infty \frac{f^{(k)}(\alpha)\beta^k}{k!}(A+B), \quad (42)$$

where

$$A = \frac{(-1)^n \pi}{(2^{2m+2n+1})(m!)^2(2n+1)!} \sum_{s=0}^n (-1)^s \binom{2n+1}{s} \frac{1 - e^{-\theta k(2n+1-2s)}}{(2n+1-2s)},$$

$$B = \frac{(-1)^n \pi}{2^{2m+2n}(2m)!(2n+1)!} \left(\sum_{k=0}^{m-1}\sum_{s=0}^{n} (-1)^{m+k+s} \binom{2m}{k}\binom{2n+1}{s}(2n+1-2s) \frac{e^{-\theta k(2n+1-2s)} - e^{-\theta k(2m-2k)}}{(2m-2k)^2 - (2n+1-2s)^2} \right).$$

The fact in Equation (22) implies that Equation (42) becomes

$$\begin{aligned}I &= \frac{(-1)^n \pi}{(2^{2m+2n})(m!)^2(2n+1)!} \sum_{s=0}^{n}(-1)^s \binom{2n+1}{s} \frac{\varphi - \psi(s)}{2n+1-2s} \\ &+ \frac{(-1)^n \pi}{2^{2m+2n-1}(2m)!(2n+1)!} \left(\sum_{k=0}^{m-1}\sum_{s=0}^{n}(-1)^{m+k+s}\binom{2m}{k}\binom{2n+1}{s}(2n \\ &+1-2s) \frac{(\psi(s)-\phi(k))}{((2m-2k)^2-(2n+1-2s)^2)} \right),\end{aligned}$$

where $\psi(s) = f\left(\alpha + \beta e^{-\theta(2n+1-2s)}\right)$, $\phi(k) = f\left(\alpha + \beta e^{-\theta(2m-2k)}\right)$, and $\varphi = f(\alpha + \beta)$.
Hence, this completes the proof of Theorem 5. □

Theorem 6. *Let f be an analytic function in a disc D centered at α, where $\alpha \in \mathbb{R}$. Then, we have the following improper integral formula:*

$$\begin{aligned}\int_0^\infty &\frac{f\left(\alpha+\beta e^{i\theta x}\right)+f\left(\alpha+\beta e^{-i\theta x}\right)}{\left((x^2+1)(x^2+9)\ldots(x^2+(2n+1)^2)\right)\left((x^2+4)(x^2+16)\ldots(x^2+4m^2)\right)} dx \\ &= \frac{(-1)^n \pi}{(2^{2m+2n})(m!)^2(2n+1)!} \sum_{s=0}^{n}(-1)^s \binom{2n+1}{s} \psi(s) \\ &+ \frac{(-1)^n \pi}{2^{2m+2n-1}(2m)!(2n+1)!} \left(\sum_{k=0}^{m-1}\sum_{s=0}^{n}(-1)^{m+k+s}\binom{2m}{k}\binom{2n+1}{s} \right. \\ &\left. \frac{(2n+1-2s)((2m-2k)\phi(k)-(2n+1-2s)\psi(s))}{((2m-2k)^2-(2n+1-2s)^2)} \right),\end{aligned}$$
(43)

where $\theta \geq 0$, $n = 0,1,2,\cdots$, $m = 1,2,\cdots$, $\psi(s) = f\left(\alpha + \beta e^{-\theta(2n+1-2s)}\right)$, and $\phi(k) = f\left(\alpha + \beta e^{-\theta(2m-2k)}\right)$.

Proof The proof of Theorem 6 can be obtained by similar arguments to Theorem 5 and using the fact (6) in Lemma 2. □

The following table, Table 1 illustrates some corollaries of the theorems with special cases and presents some values of improper integrals under certain conditions.

Table 1. Improper integral formulas with the series representation as detailed in Equation (25).

	$f(x)$	$\int_0^\infty f(x)dx$	Conditions	No. of Theorem
1.	$\dfrac{g(\alpha-i\theta x)+g(\alpha+i\theta x)}{(x^2+1)(x^2+9)\cdots(x^2+(2n+1)^2)}$	$\dfrac{(-1)^n}{(2n+1)!}\dfrac{\pi}{2^{2n}}\sum_{s=0}^{n}(-1)^s\binom{2n+1}{s}g(\alpha-\theta(2s-2n-1))$,	$\theta \geq 0,$ $n=1,2,\ldots$	Theorem 1
2.	$\dfrac{x(g(\alpha-i\theta x)-g(\alpha+i\theta x))}{i(x^2+1)(x^2+9)\cdots(x^2+(2n+1)^2)}$	$\dfrac{(-1)^n}{(2n+1)!}\dfrac{\pi}{2^{2n}}\sum_{s=0}^{n}(-1)^s\binom{2n+1}{s}(2n-2s+1)(g(\alpha-\theta(2s-2n-1))-g(\alpha))$,	$\theta > 0,$ $n=1,2,\ldots$	Theorem 2
3.	$\dfrac{g(\alpha-i\theta x)+f(\alpha+i\theta x)}{(x^2+4)(x^2+16)\cdots(x^2+(2n)^2)}$	$\dfrac{(-1)^n\pi\, 2^{2-2n}}{(2n)!}\left(\sum_{s=0}^{n-1}(-1)^s\binom{2n}{s}(s-n)g(\alpha-2\theta(s-n))\right)$,	$\theta \geq 0,$ $n=1,2,\ldots$	Theorem 4
4.	$\dfrac{g(\alpha-i\theta x)+g(\alpha+i\theta x)}{((x^2+1)(x^2+9)\cdots(x^2+(2n+1)^2))} \cdot \dfrac{1}{((x^2+4)(x^2+16)\cdots(x^2+4m^2))}$	$\dfrac{(-1)^n \pi}{2^{2m-2n}(m!)^2(2n+1)!}\sum_{s=0}^{n}(-1)^s\binom{2n+1}{s}\psi(s) +$ $\dfrac{(-1)^n\pi}{2^{2m-2n-1}(2m)!(2n+1)!}\left(\sum_{k=0}^{m-1}\sum_{s=0}^{n}(-1)^{m+k+s}\binom{2m}{k}\binom{2n+1}{s}\right.$ $\left.\dfrac{(2n+1-2s)((2m-2k)^2\phi(k)-(2n+1-2s)\psi(s))}{(2m-2k)^2-(2n+1-2s)^2}\right)$, where $\psi(s)=g(\alpha+\theta(2n+1-2s))$ and $\phi(k)=g(\alpha+\theta(2m-2k))$	$\theta \geq 0,$ $n=0,1,2,\ldots$ $m=1,2,\ldots$	Theorem 6

4. Applications and Examples

In this section, we present the results, applications, and observations of the proposed theorems. We also show that the simple cases of the master theorems are identical to the results obtained by Cauchy, as detailed in his memoirs, using Residue Theorem 4. Additionally, some examples on difficult integrals that cannot be treated directly by usual methods are addressed. In this section, we show the applicability of our results in handling such problems.

4.1. Some Remarks on the Theorems

Remark 1. Letting $\alpha = 0$ and $n = 1$ in Theorem 3, we obtain

$$\int_0^\infty \frac{f(\beta e^{i\theta x}) - f(\beta e^{-i\theta x})}{i\,x(x^2+4)}\,dx = \frac{\pi}{4}\left(f(\beta) - f(\beta e^{-2\theta})\right), \tag{44}$$

where $\theta > 0$.

By letting $\frac{x}{2} = y$,

$$\frac{1}{4}\int_0^\infty \frac{f(\beta e^{2i\theta y}) - f(\beta e^{-2i\theta y})}{i\,y(y^2+1)}\,dy = \frac{\pi}{4}\left(f(\beta) - f(\beta e^{-2\theta})\right).$$

Letting $2\theta = \varphi$,

$$\int_0^\infty \frac{f(\beta e^{i\varphi y}) - f(\beta e^{-i\varphi y})}{i\,y(y^2+1)}\,dy = \pi\left(f(\beta) - f(\beta e^{-\varphi})\right).$$

This result appears in [10] (Theorem 4). Further, we show that Cauchy made a mistake in this result (see [4]) (P. 62 formula (10)).

The following table, Table 2 presents some remarks on improper integrals.

Table 2. Remarks on improper integrals, where $\theta > 0$.

	Conditions	Theo	$g(x)$	$\int_0^\infty g(x)\,dx$	Remarks
1	$\alpha = 0, \beta = 1$ and $n = 0$	1	$\dfrac{f(e^{i\theta x}) + f(e^{-i\theta x})}{(1+x^2)}$	$\pi f\left(e^{-\theta}\right)$	Cauchy's theorem [4] (p. 62 Formula (8)) and in [10] (3.037 Theorem 1) is identical.
2	$\alpha = 0, \beta = 1$ and $n = 0$	2	$\dfrac{x\left(f(e^{i\theta x}) - f(e^{-i\theta x})\right)}{i(1+x^2)}$	$\pi\left(f\left(e^{-\theta}\right) - f(0)\right)$	Cauchy made a mistake in this result see [4] (p. 62 Formula (8)). He corrected his result in his next memoir see [5,6].
3	$n = 1$	1	$\dfrac{f(\alpha + \beta e^{i\theta x}) + f(\alpha + \beta e^{-i\theta x})}{(x^2 + 1^2)(x^2 + 3^2)}$	$\dfrac{\pi}{4!}\left(3f(\alpha + \beta e^{-\theta}) - f(\alpha + \beta e^{-3\theta})\right)$	This result does not appear in [4,5,10].
4	$n = 1$	1	$\dfrac{x\left(f(\alpha + \beta e^{i\theta x}) - f(\alpha + \beta e^{-i\theta x})\right)}{i\,(x^2 + 1^2)(x^2 + 3^2)}$	$\dfrac{\pi}{8}\left(f(\alpha + \beta e^{-\theta}) - f(\alpha + \beta e^{-3\theta})\right)$	This result does not appear in [4,5,10].
5	$n = 2$	3	$\dfrac{f(\alpha + \beta e^{i\theta x}) - f(\alpha + \beta e^{-i\theta x})}{i\,x\,(x^2 + 2^2)(x^2 + 4^2)}$	$\dfrac{\pi}{192}\left(3(f(\alpha + \beta)) + f(\alpha + \beta e^{-4\theta}) - 4f(\alpha + \beta e^{-2\theta})\right)$	This result does not appear in [4,5,10].
6	$n = 1$	4	$\dfrac{f(\alpha + \beta e^{i\theta x}) + f(\alpha + \beta e^{-i\theta x})}{(x^2 + 2^2)(x^2 + 4^2)}$	$\dfrac{\pi}{48}\left(2f(\alpha + \beta e^{-2\theta}) - f(\alpha + \beta e^{-4\theta})\right)$	This result does not appear in [4,5,10].

4.2. Generating Improper Integrals

In this section, we show the mechanism of generating an infinite number of integrals by choosing the function $f(z)$ and finding the real or imaginary part. It is worth noting that some of these integrals with special cases appear in [40–43] when solving some applications related to finding Green's function, one-dimensional vibrating string problems, wave motion in elastic solids, and when using Fourier cosine and Fourier Sine transforms.

To illustrate the idea, we show some general examples that are applied on Theorems 1, 2, and 3, as follows:

1. Setting $f(z) = z^m$, $m \in \mathbb{R}^+$:

   - Using Theorem (1) and setting $\alpha = 0$ and $\beta = 1$ we have:

   $$f\left(e^{i\theta x}\right) + f\left(e^{-i\theta x}\right) = e^{i\theta mx} + e^{-i\theta mx} = 2\cos(\theta\, mx).$$

   Thus,

   $$\int_0^\infty \frac{2\cos(\theta\, mx)}{(x^2+1)(x^2+9)\cdots\left(x^2+(2n+1)^2\right)}\,dx = \frac{(-1)^n}{(2n+1)!}\frac{\pi}{2^{2n}}\sum_{s=0}^n (-1)^s \binom{2n+1}{s} e^{m\theta(2s-2n-1)}.$$

   where $\theta \geq 0$ and $n = 0, 1, 2, \cdots$

   Setting $m = 1$, the obtained integral is a Fourier cosine transform [40,41] of the function $f(t) = \frac{1}{(t^2+1)(t^2+9)\cdots(t^2+(2n+1)^2)}$.

   - Using Theorem (3), and setting $\alpha = 0$, $\beta = 1$ we have:

   $$\frac{1}{i}\left(f\left(e^{i\theta x}\right) - f\left(e^{-i\theta x}\right)\right) = \frac{1}{i}\left(e^{i\theta mx} + e^{-i\theta mx}\right) = 2\sin(\theta\, mx).$$

   Thus,

   $$\int_0^\infty \frac{2\sin(\theta\, mx)}{x\,(x^2+4)(x^2+16)\cdots\left(x^2+(2n)^2\right)}\,dx = \frac{(-1)^n}{(2n)!}\frac{\pi}{2^{2n}}\left((-1)^n\binom{2n}{n} + 2\sum_{s=0}^{n-1}(-1)^s\binom{2n}{s}e^{2\theta m(s-n)}\right).$$

   Setting $m = 1$, the obtained integral is a Fourier sine transform [40,41] of the function $f(t) = \frac{1}{t\,(t^2+4)(t^2+16)\cdots(t^2+(2n)^2)}$.

2. Setting $f(z) = e^z$.

   - Using Theorem (1), we have:

   $$f\left(\alpha + \beta e^{i\theta x}\right) + f\left(\alpha + \beta e^{-i\theta x}\right) = e^{\alpha + \beta e^{i\theta x}} + e^{\alpha + \beta e^{-i\theta x}} = 2e^{\alpha + \beta\cos(\theta x)}\cos(\beta\sin(\theta x)).$$

   $$\int_0^\infty \frac{2e^{\alpha + \beta\cos(\theta x)}\cos(\beta\sin(\theta x))}{(x^2+1)(x^2+9)\cdots\left(x^2+(2n+1)^2\right)}\,dx = \frac{(-1)^n}{(2n+1)!}\frac{\pi}{2^{2n}}\sum_{s=0}^n(-1)^s\binom{2n+1}{s}e^{\alpha + \beta e^{\theta(2s-2n-1)}},$$

   where $\theta \geq 0$ and $n = 0, 1, 2, \cdots$.

   - Using Theorem (2), we have:

   $$\frac{1}{i}\left(f\left(\alpha + \beta e^{i\theta x}\right) - f\left(\alpha + \beta e^{-i\theta x}\right)\right) = \frac{1}{i}\left(e^{\alpha + \beta e^{i\theta x}} - e^{\alpha + \beta e^{-i\theta x}}\right) = 2e^{\alpha + \beta\cos(\theta x)}\sin(\beta\sin(\theta x)).$$

Thus,
$$\int_0^\infty \frac{2xe^{\alpha+\beta\cos(\theta x)}\sin(\beta\sin(\theta x))}{i(x^2+1)(x^2+9)\cdots(x^2+(2n+1)^2)}dx$$
$$= \frac{(-1)^n}{(2n+1)!}\frac{\pi}{2^{2n}}\sum_{s=0}^{n}(-1)^s\binom{2n+1}{s}(2n-2s+1)\left(e^{\alpha+\beta e^{\theta(2s-2n-1)}} - e^\alpha\right).$$

3. Setting $f(z) = \sinh z$.
    - Using Theorem (1), we have:
    $$f(\alpha+\beta e^{i\theta x}) + f(\alpha+\beta e^{-i\theta x}) = \sinh(\alpha+\beta e^{i\theta x}) + \sinh(\alpha+\beta e^{-i\theta x})$$
    $$= 2\cos(\beta\sin(\theta x))\sinh(\alpha+\beta\cos(\theta x))$$

Thus,
$$\int_0^\infty \frac{2\cos(\beta\sin(\theta x))\sinh(\alpha+\beta\cos(\theta x))}{(x^2+1)(x^2+9)\cdots(x^2+(2n+1)^2)}dx$$
$$= \frac{(-1)^n}{(2n+1)!}\frac{\pi}{2^{2n}}\sum_{s=0}^{n}(-1)^s\binom{2n+1}{s}\sinh\left(\alpha+\beta e^{\theta(2s-2n-1)}\right)$$

   - Using Theorem (3), we have:

$$\frac{1}{i}\left(f(\alpha+\beta e^{i\theta x}) - f(\alpha+\beta e^{-i\theta x})\right) = \frac{1}{i}\left(\sinh(\alpha+\beta e^{i\theta x}) - \sinh(\alpha+\beta e^{-i\theta x})\right)$$
$$= 2\sin(\beta\sin(\theta x))\cosh(\alpha+\beta\cos(\theta x)).$$

Thus,
$$\int_0^\infty \frac{2\sin(\beta\sin(\theta x))\cosh(\alpha+\beta\cos(\theta x))}{x(x^2+4)(x^2+16)\cdots(x^2+(2n)^2)}dx$$
$$= \frac{(-1)^n}{(2n)!}\frac{\pi}{2^{2n}}\left((-1)^n\binom{2n}{n}(\sinh(\alpha+\beta)-\sinh(\alpha))\right.$$
$$\left.+2\sum_{s=0}^{n-1}(-1)^s\binom{2n}{s}\left(\sinh\left(\alpha+\beta e^{2\theta(s-n)}\right) - \sinh(\alpha)\right)\right),$$

where $\theta > 0$, $n = 1, 2, \cdots$.

4. Setting $f(z) = \cos(e^z)$
   - Using Theorem (1), we have:
   $$f(\alpha+\beta e^{i\theta x}) + f(\alpha+\beta e^{-i\theta x}) = \cos\left(e^{\alpha+\beta e^{i\theta x}}\right) + \cos\left(e^{\alpha+\beta e^{-i\theta x}}\right)$$
   $$= 2\cos\left(e^{\alpha+\beta\cos(\theta x)}\cos(\beta\sin(\theta x))\right)\cosh\left(\sin(\beta\sin(\theta x))e^{\alpha+\beta\cos(\theta x)}\right).$$

Thus,
$$\int_0^\infty \frac{2\cos\left(e^{\alpha+\beta\cos(\theta x)}\cos(\beta\sin(\theta x))\right)\cosh\left(\sin(\beta\sin(\theta x))e^{\alpha+\beta\cos(\theta x)}\right)}{(x^2+1)(x^2+9)\cdots(x^2+(2n+1)^2)}dx$$
$$= \frac{(-1)^n}{(2n+1)!}\frac{\pi}{2^{2n}}\sum_{s=0}^{n}(-1)^s\binom{2n+1}{s}\cos\left(\alpha+\beta e^{\theta(2s-2n-1)}\right).$$

5. Setting $f(z) = \ln(1+z)$,
   - Using Theorem (1), we have:
   $$f(1+\alpha+\beta e^{i\theta x}) + f(1+\alpha+\beta e^{-i\theta x}) = \ln(1+\alpha+\beta e^{i\theta x}) + \ln(1+\alpha+\beta e^{-i\theta x})$$
   $$= \ln((\alpha+1)^2 + \beta^2 + 2(\alpha+1)\beta\cos(\theta x)).$$

Thus,

$$\int_0^\infty \frac{\ln((\alpha+1)^2+\beta^2+2(\alpha+1)\beta\cos(\theta x))}{(x^2+1)(x^2+9)\cdots(x^2+(2n+1)^2)}dx$$
$$= \frac{(-1)^n}{(2n+1)!}\frac{\pi}{2^{2n}}\sum_{s=0}^n (-1)^s \binom{2n+1}{s}\ln\left(1+\alpha+\beta e^{\theta(2s-2n-1)}\right).$$

- Setting $\alpha = 0$ and $\beta = 1$, we have:

$$f(e^{i\theta x}) + f(e^{-i\theta x}) = \ln(1+e^{i\theta x}) + \ln(1+e^{-i\theta x})$$
$$= 2\ln\left|2\cos\left(\frac{\theta x}{2}\right)\right|.$$

Thus,

$$\int_0^\infty \frac{2\ln\left|2\cos\left(\frac{\theta x}{2}\right)\right|}{(x^2+1)(x^2+9)\cdots(x^2+(2n+1)^2)}dx$$
$$= \frac{(-1)^n}{(2n+1)!}\frac{\pi}{2^{2n}}\sum_{s=0}^n (-1)^s \binom{2n+1}{s}\ln\left(1+e^{\theta(2s-2n-1)}\right).$$

4.3. Solving Improper Integrals

In this section, some applications on complicated problems are introduced and solved directly depending on our new theorems. We note that the Mathematica and Maple software cannot solve such examples.

Example 1. Evaluate the following integral:

$$\int_0^\infty \frac{\ln^2\left|\tan\left(\frac{\theta x}{2}-\frac{\pi}{4}\right)\right|}{(x^2+4)(x^2+16)}dx,$$

where $\theta > 0$.

Solution: Using Theorem 1 and setting $\alpha = 0$, $\beta = 1$, and $n = 1$ or using Remark 6 Table 2 and setting $\alpha = 0$ and $\beta = 1$, we set

$$f(z) = \left(\tan^{-1}z\right)^2 = \frac{-1}{4}\ln^2\left(\frac{1-iz}{1+iz}\right).$$

Therefore, we have $f(e^{i\theta x}) = -\frac{1}{4}\ln^2\left(\frac{1-ie^{i\theta x}}{1+ie^{i\theta x}}\right)$, and $f(e^{i\theta x}) + f(e^{-i\theta x}) = 2\,Re f(e^{i\theta x})$. Thus, we obtain

$$\int_0^\infty \frac{f(e^{i\theta x})+f(e^{-i\theta x})}{(x^2+4)(x^2+16)}dx = \frac{-1}{4}\int_0^\infty \frac{\ln^2\left(\frac{1-ie^{i\theta x}}{1+ie^{i\theta x}}\right)+\ln^2\left(\frac{1-ie^{-i\theta x}}{1+ie^{-i\theta x}}\right)}{(x^2+4)(x^2+16)}dx$$
$$= \frac{-1}{4}\int_0^\infty \frac{2\,Re\left(\ln^2\left(\frac{1+\sin(\theta x)-i\cos(\theta x)}{1-\sin(\theta x)+i\cos(\theta x)}\right)\right)}{(x^2+4)(x^2+16)}dx$$
$$= \frac{-1}{2}\int_0^\infty \frac{Re(\ln(1+\sin(\theta x)-i\cos(\theta x))-\ln(1-\sin(\theta x)+i\cos(\theta x)))^2}{(x^2+4)(x^2+16)}dx$$
$$= \frac{-1}{2}\int_0^\infty \frac{Re\left(\pm i\frac{\pi}{2}-\ln\left|\tan\left(\frac{\theta x}{2}-\frac{\pi}{4}\right)\right|\right)^2}{(x^2+4)(x^2+16)}dx$$
$$= \frac{-1}{2}\int_0^\infty \frac{Re\left(-\frac{\pi^2}{4}+\ln^2\left|\tan\left(\frac{\theta x}{2}-\frac{\pi}{4}\right)\right|\pm i\pi\ln\left|\tan\left(\frac{\theta x}{2}-\frac{\pi}{4}\right)\right|\right)}{(x^2+4)(x^2+16)}dx$$
$$= \frac{-1}{2}\int_0^\infty \frac{-\frac{\pi^2}{4}+\ln^2\left|\tan\left(\frac{\theta x}{2}-\frac{\pi}{4}\right)\right|}{(x^2+4)(x^2+16)}dx = \frac{\pi}{24}\left(3\left(\tan^{-1}e^{-\theta}\right)^2-\left(\tan^{-1}e^{-3\theta}\right)^2\right).$$

$$\therefore \int_0^\infty \frac{\ln^2\left|\tan\left(\frac{\theta x}{2}-\frac{\pi}{4}\right)\right|}{(x^2+4)(x^2+16)}dx = \frac{\pi^3}{384}-\frac{\pi}{48}\left(3\left(\tan^{-1}e^{-\theta}\right)^2-\left(\tan^{-1}e^{-3\theta}\right)^2\right).$$

Example 2. Evaluate the following integral:

$$PV \int_0^\infty \frac{x \tan(\pi x)}{(x^2+2^2)(x^2+4^2)\cdots\left(x^2+(2n)^2\right)} dx, \qquad (45)$$

where $n = 1, 2, \cdots$.

Solution. Using Theorem 4, let $\alpha = 0$, $\beta = 1$ and $f(z) = \ln(1+z)$.

Therefore, we have

$$f(e^{i\theta x}) + f(e^{-i\theta x}) = \ln(1+e^{i\theta x}) + \ln(1+e^{-i\theta x}) = \ln(2\cos(\theta x) + 2)$$
$$= 2\ln\left|2\cos\left(\tfrac{\theta x}{2}\right)\right|.$$

Therefore, we have

$$I(\theta) = PV \int_0^\infty \frac{2\ln\left|2\cos\left(\tfrac{\theta x}{2}\right)\right|}{(x^2+2^2)(x^2+4^2)\cdots\left(x^2+(2n)^2\right)} dx = \frac{(-1)^n \pi\, 2^{2-2n}}{(2n)!} \left(\sum_{s=0}^{n-1} (-1)^s \binom{2n}{s}(s-n)\ln\left(1+e^{2\theta(s-n)}\right)\right).$$

Now, taking the derivative of $I(\theta)$ with respect to θ, we obtain

$$\frac{\partial I}{\partial \theta} = PV \int_0^\infty \frac{-x \tan\left(\tfrac{\theta x}{2}\right)}{(x^2+2^2)(x^2+4^2)\cdots(x^2+(2n)^2)} dx = \frac{(-1)^n \pi\, 2^{2-2n}}{(2n)!} \left(\sum_{s=0}^{n-1}(-1)^s \binom{2n}{s}(s-n)\frac{2(s-n)e^{2\theta(s-n)}}{e^{2\theta(s-n)}+1}\right).$$

Therefore,

$$PV \int_0^\infty \frac{x \tan(\pi x)}{(x^2+2^2)(x^2+4^2)\cdots(x^2+(2n)^2)} dx = \frac{(-1)^{n+1} \pi\, 2^{2-2n}}{(2n)!} \left(\sum_{s=0}^{n-1}(-1)^s \binom{2n}{s}(s-n)\frac{2(s-n)e^{4\pi(s-n)}}{e^{4\pi(s-n)}+1}\right).$$

Putting $n = 1$ in Equation (45), we obtain the following integral:

$$PV \int_0^\infty \frac{x \tan(\pi x)}{x^2+4} dx = \pi \frac{e^{-4\pi}}{e^{-4\pi}+1} = \frac{\pi}{(e^{4\pi}+1)}.$$

Example 3. Evaluate the following integral:

$$\int_0^\infty \frac{1+2\cos(\theta x)}{(x^2+1)(x^2+4)\,(1+4\cos(\theta x)+4)} dx,$$

where $\theta \geq 0$.

Solution. Using Theorem 5 and taking $\alpha = 0$ and $\beta = 1$, let $f(z) = \frac{1}{1+2e^z}$.

Thus, we have

$$f(e^{i\theta x}) + f(e^{-i\theta x}) = \left(\frac{1}{1+2e^{i\theta x}} + \frac{1}{1+2e^{-i\theta x}}\right) = \frac{2(1+2\cos(\theta x))}{1+4\cos(\theta x)+4}.$$

Therefore, setting $n = 0$ and $m = 1$, in Theorem 5, we obtain

$$\int_0^\infty \frac{1+2\cos(\theta x)}{(x^2+1)(x^2+4)\,(1+4\cos(\theta x)+4)} dx = \frac{\pi}{12}\left(\frac{2}{1+2e^{-\theta}} - \frac{1}{1+2e^{-\theta}}\right).$$

5. Conclusions

In this research, we introduce new theorems that simplify calculating improper integrals. These results can establish many instances of formulas of improper integrals and solve them directly without complicated calculations or computer software. We illustrate some remarks that analyze our work.

- The proposed theorems are considered powerful techniques for generating improper integrals and testing the results when using other methods to solve similar examples.
- These theorems can be illustrated in tables of integrations, with different values of functions and generate more results.
- The obtained improper integrals cannot be solved manually (simply) or by computer software such as Mathematica and Maple.

We intend to generalize the proposed theorems and make tables and algorithms to simplify their use during the applications. Additionally, these results can be used to solve differential equations by inverting the integrals into differential equations.

Author Contributions: Conceptualization, M.A.-G., R.S. and A.Q.; methodology, M.A.-G., R.S. and A.Q.; software, M.A.-G., R.S. and A.Q.; validation, M.A.-G., R.S. and A.Q.; formal analysis, M.A.-G., R.S. and A.Q.; investigation, M.A.-G., R.S. and A.Q.; resources, R.S. and A.Q.; data curation, M.A.-G., R.S. and A.Q.; writing—original draft preparation, M.A.-G., R.S. and A.Q.; writing—review and editing, M.A.-G., R.S. and A.Q.; visualization, M.A.-G., R.S. and A.Q.; supervision, M.A.-G., R.S. and A.Q.; project administration, R.S. and A.Q.; funding acquisition, M.A.-G., R.S. and A.Q. All authors have read and agreed to the published version of the manuscript.

Funding: This research received no external funding.

Data Availability Statement: Not applicable.

Conflicts of Interest: The authors declare no conflict of interest.

References

1. Arfken, G.B.; Weber, H.J. *Mathematical Methods for Physicists*, 5th ed.; Academic Press: Boston, MA, USA, 2000.
2. Nahin, P.J. *Inside Interesting Integrals*; Springer: New York, NY, USA, 2015.
3. Roussos, I. *Improper Riemann Integrals*; CRC, Taylor & Francis Group: Boca Raton, FL, USA, 2013.
4. Cauchy, A.L. *Memoire sur les Integrales Definies, Prises Entre des Limites Imaginaires*; Reprint of the 1825 Original; Oeuvres Completes d'Au914 Gustin Cauchy, Series II; Gauthier-Villars: Paris, France, 1974; Volume 15, pp. 41–89.
5. Cauchy, A.L. Sur diverses relations qui existent entre les résidus des fonctions et les intégrales définies. *Exerc. Mathématiques* **1826**, *1*, 95–113.
6. Harold, P.B. Cauchy's Residue Sore Thumb. *Am. Math. Mon.* **2018**, *125*, 16–28.
7. Stein, E.M.; Shakarchi, R. *Complex Analysis*; Princeton University Press: Princeton, NJ, USA, 2003.
8. Thomas, G.B.; Finney, R.L. *Calculus and Analytic Geometry*; Addison Wesley: Boston, MA, USA, 1996.
9. Henrici, P. *Applied and Computational Complex Analysis*; John Wiley & Sons: New York, NY, USA, 1988; Volume 1.
10. Zwillinger, D. *Table of Integrals, Series, and Products*; Academic Press: Cambridge, MA, USA, 2014.
11. Zwillinger, D. *CRC Standard Mathematical Tables and Formulas*; Chapman and Hall/CRC: London, UK, 2018.
12. Brown, J.W.; Churchill, R.V. *Complex Variables and Applications*; McGraw-Hill: New York, NY, USA, 1996.
13. Abu Ghuwaleh, M.; Saadeh, R.; Burqan, A. New Theorems in Solving Families of Improper Integrals. *Axioms* **2022**, *11*, 301. [CrossRef]
14. Abu-Ghuwaleh, M.; Saadeh, R.; Qazza, A. General Master Theorems of Integrals with Applications. *Mathematics* **2022**, *10*, 3547. [CrossRef]
15. Rasham, T.; Nazam, M.; Aydi, H.; Agarwal, R.P. Existence of Common Fixed Points of GeneralizedΔ-Implicit Locally Contractive Mappings on Closed Ball in Multiplicative G-metric Spaces with Applications. *Mathematics* **2022**, *10*, 3369. [CrossRef]
16. Rasham, T.; Nazam, M.; Aydi, H.; Shoaib, A.; Park, C.; Lee, J.R. Hybrid pair of multivalued mappings in modular-like metric spaces and applications. *AIMS Math.* **2022**, *7*, 10582–10595. [CrossRef]
17. Abu-Gdairi, R.; Al-Smadi, M.H. An Efficient Computational Method for 4th-order Boundary Value Problems of Fredholm IDEs. *Appl. Math. Sci.* **2013**, *7*, 4761–4774. [CrossRef]
18. Abu-Gdairi, R.; Al-Smadi, M.H.; Gumah, G. An Expansion Iterative Technique for Handling Fractional Differential Equations Using Fractional Power Series Scheme. *J. Math. Stat.* **2015**, *11*, 29–38. [CrossRef]
19. Li, L.; Liu, J.G.; Wang, L. Cauchy problems for Keller–Segel type time–space fractional diffusion equation. *J. Differ. Equ.* **2018**, *265*, 1044–1096. [CrossRef]

20. Yang, J.P.; Liao, Y.-S. Direct Collocation with Reproducing Kernel Approximation for Two-Phase Coupling System in a Porous Enclosure. *Mathematics* **2021**, *9*, 897. [CrossRef]
21. Li, Y.; Huang, M.; Li, B. Besicovitch Almost Periodic Solutions of Abstract Semi-Linear Differential Equations with Delay. *Mathematics* **2022**, *10*, 639. [CrossRef]
22. Laib, H.; Boulmerka, A.; Bellour, A.; Birem, F. Numerical solution of two-dimensional linear and nonlinear Volterra integral equations using Taylor collocation method. *J. Comput. Appl. Math.* **2022**, *417*, 114537. [CrossRef]
23. Finerman, A. (Ed.) *University Education in Computing Science: Proceedings of a Conference on Graduate Academic and Related Research Programs in Computing Science, Held at the State University of New York at Stony Brook, June 1967*; Academic Press: Cambridge, MA, USA, 2014.
24. Freihat, A.; Abu-Gdairi, R.; Khalil, H.; Abuteen, E.; Al-Smadi, M.; Khan, R.A. Fitted Reproducing Kernel Method for Solving a Class of third-Order Periodic Boundary Value Problems. *Am. J. Appl. Sci.* **2016**, *13*, 501–510. [CrossRef]
25. Saadeh, R.; Ghazal, B. A New Approach on Transforms: Formable Integral Transform and Its Applications. *Axioms* **2021**, *10*, 332. [CrossRef]
26. Saadeh, R.; Qazza, A.; Burqan, A. A New Integral Transform: ARA Transform and Its Properties and Applications. *Symmetry* **2020**, *12*, 925. [CrossRef]
27. Ahmed, S.A.; Qazza, A.; Saadeh, R. Exact Solutions of Nonlinear Partial Differential Equations via the New Double Integral Transform Combined with Iterative Method. *Axioms* **2022**, *11*, 247. [CrossRef]
28. Burqan, A.; Saadeh, R.; Qazza, A. A Novel Numerical Approach in Solving Fractional Neutral Pantograph Equations via the ARA Integral Transform. *Symmetry* **2022**, *14*, 50. [CrossRef]
29. Qazza, A.; Burqan, A.; Saadeh, R. A New Attractive Method in Solving Families of Fractional Differential Equations by a New Transform. *Mathematics* **2021**, *9*, 3039. [CrossRef]
30. Li, X.; Li, Y.; Liu, Z.; Li, J. Sensitivity analysis for optimal control problems described by nonlinear fractional evolution inclusions. *Fract. Calc. Appl. Anal.* **2018**, *21*, 1439–1470. [CrossRef]
31. Liu, Y.; Liu, Z.; Wen, C.-F. Existence of solutions for space-fractional parabolic hemivariational inequalities. *Discrete Contin. Dyn. Syst.-B* **2019**, *24*, 1297. [CrossRef]
32. Glaisher, J.W.L. A new formula in definite integrals. *Lond. Edinb. Dublin Philos. Mag. J. Sci.* **1874**, *48*, 53–55. [CrossRef]
33. Berndt, B. *Ramanujan's Notebooks, Part I*; Springer: New York, NY, USA, 1985.
34. Amdeberhan, T.; Espinosa, O.; Gonzalez, I.; Harrison, M.; Moll, V.H.; Straub, A. Ramanujan's Master Theorem. *Ramanujan J.* **2012**, *29*, 103–120. [CrossRef]
35. Glasser, M.L.; Milgram, M. Master theorems for a family of integrals. *Integral Transforms Spec. Funct.* **2014**, *25*, 805. [CrossRef]
36. Reynolds, R.; Stauffer, A. Derivation of Logarithmic and Logarithmic Hyperbolic Tangent Integrals Expressed in Terms of Special Functions. *Mathematics* **2020**, *8*, 687. [CrossRef]
37. Luchko, Y. General Fractional Integrals and Derivatives of Arbitrary Order. *Symmetry* **2021**, *13*, 755. [CrossRef]
38. Reynolds, R.; Stauffer, A. Table in Gradshteyn and Ryzhik: Derivation of Definite Integrals of a Hyperbolic Function. *Science* **2021**, *3*, 37. [CrossRef]
39. Prudnikov, A.P.; Brychkov, Y.A.; Marichev, O.I. *Integrals and Series: Direct Laplace Transforms*; Routledge: London, UK, 2018.
40. Boas, M.L. *Mathematical Methods in the Physical Sciences*; John Wiley & Sons: Hoboken, NJ, USA, 2006.
41. Bracewell, R.N. *The Fourier Transform and Its Applications*; McGraw-Hill: New York, NY, USA, 1986.
42. Duffy, D.G. *Green's Functions with Applications*; Chapman and Hall/CRC: Boca Raton, FL, USA, 2015.
43. Graff, K.F. *Wave Motion in Elastic Solids*; Courier Corporation: Chelmsford, MA, USA, 2012.

Article

On the Distribution of Kurepa's Function

Nicola Fabiano [1], Milanka Gardašević-Filipović [2], Nikola Mirkov [1,*], Vesna Todorčević [3] and Stojan Radenović [4]

[1] "Vinča" Institute of Nuclear Sciences—National Institute of the Republic of Serbia, University of Belgrade, Mike Petrovića Alasa 12–14, 11351 Belgrade, Serbia
[2] School of Computing, Union University, 11000 Belgrade, Serbia
[3] Department of Mathematics, Faculty of Organizational Sciences, University of Belgrade, Jove Ilića 154, 11000 Belgrade, Serbia
[4] Faculty of Mechanical Engineering, University of Belgrade, Kraljice Marije 16, 11120 Belgrade, Serbia
* Correspondence: nmirkov@vin.bg.ac.rs

Abstract: Kurepa's function and his hypothesis have been investigated by means of numerical simulation. Particular emphasis has been given to the conjecture on its distribution, that should be one of a random uniform distribution, which has been verified for large numbers. A convergence function for the two has been found.

Keywords: left factorial function; Kurepa's function; Kurepa's hypothesis

MSC: 05A10; 11A05; 11B65; 11B7

1. Introduction

It has been more than fifty years since the introduction of the simple arithmetic function and the hypothesis related to it, the former being the Kurepa's function and the latter known as the Kurepa's hypothesis. This hypothesis has defied the resolution ever since.

Namely, in [1], Kurepa defined the function,

$$K(n) = !n = \sum_{i=0}^{n-1} i!, \tag{1}$$

for $n \in \mathbb{N}$ following his earlier works [2–4]. Kurepa himself called the function the left factorial, at present the function is also called Kurepa's left factorial, or simply Kurepa's function. He subsequently extended this function to the complex plane [5]

$$K(z) = \int_0^{+\infty} e^{-t} \frac{t^z - 1}{t - 1} dt, \tag{2}$$

for $\Re(z) > 0$. An important property of this function is the following:

$$\lim_{x \to +\infty} \frac{K(x)}{\Gamma(x)} = 1, \tag{3}$$

where $\Gamma(x)$ represents the Gamma function. For more details, see [6], for Kurepa's selected papers with commentary on number theoretical problems, see [7], and regarding historical overview of the problem up to the fiftieth anniversary, see [8]. Some recent developments and further references could be found in [9,10].

In the same 1971 paper [1], Kurepa introduced his hypothesis on the function $K(n)$, which could be written in the following manner:

$$\mod(K(n), n) \not\equiv 0, \ n \in \mathbb{N}, \ n > 2, \tag{4}$$

where $\mod(K(n), n)$ signifies the remainder of the division of $K(n)$ by n. Up to today (2022), it has not been proved. In 2004, an attempt at a proof was presented in a paper that was later retracted by the authors [11,12]. In [13], the search for a counterexample of the hypothesis was performed, without success, for $n < 2^{34} \approx 1.718 \times 10^{10}$ by means of GPU computing.

The aim of this work is not to try to solve the original Kurepa's hypothesis, already discussed in great detail in [9,10], together with the properties of Kurepa's function and its extension on the complex plane. The scope is to investigate the conjecture first presented in [13] about the distribution of Kurepa's function as a function of $n \in \mathbb{N}$.

2. The Distribution Conjecture

While studying numerically the hypothesis, the authors of [13] made the following conjecture:
$$\mod(K(n), n)/n \tag{5}$$
is a random number in the range $[0, n]$ with uniform distribution in $(0, 1)$. In this paper, we will further numerically investigate this conjecture. Previously, in [9,10], we did an analysis of (5) on prime numbers distribution up to the value of $p = 116,447$, that is, the 11,000th prime number, where it is clearly shown how the difference with a uniform random distribution in $(0, 1)$ decreases with increasing number of prime numbers p considered.

Our new analysis is done with the software PARI/GP [14] for $n \in \mathbb{N}$ up to the value of $n = 4 \times 10^6$, for which $K(4 \times 10^6) > 10^{10^7}$. In the following figures, Figure 1a–d, we show the distribution of (5) for different ranges of n. As our largest n is 4×10^6, we have millions of points, so we could only present a small range for the distribution in order for the figure to be discernible from a black blob. The figures, for different ranges of n, visually do not appear to be different from a uniform random distribution in $(0, 1)$, the so-called white noise. A different choice of n ranges and starting points does not present substantial modifications to the figures. Additionally, compare those results to the one obtained in [9,10] for different ranges of the arguments, which are quite similar. We could also observe how Kurepa's hypothesis is satisfied, as there is no value of n in the investigated range for which $\mod(K(n), n) = 0$.

In Figure 2, we show the comparison of the results of $\mod(K(n), n)/n$ with respect to a random uniform distribution in $(0, 1)$ as a function of n, for the whole range of numbers considered, up to $n = 4 \times 10^6$. We observe that this fluctuation, naturally defined as the difference of (5) from the average of a random distribution in $(0,1)$, which is $1/2$, normalized to its average, that is

$$\text{fluctuation}(n) = \left(\frac{\frac{\mod(K(n),n)}{n} - \frac{1}{2}}{\frac{1}{2}} \right), \tag{6}$$

as a function of n, stabilizes above a certain number and then starts decreasing with increasing n, providing more support to the conjecture presented in Equation (5), for which the relation
$$\lim_{n \to +\infty} \text{fluctuation}(n) = 0, \tag{7}$$
holds true. Loosely speaking, it means that for large n, the average value of (5) is $1/2$. For n approximately larger than 10^6, the fluctuation in percentage is less than 0.2 and decreasing, being lower than 0.1 when n crosses the value of 3×10^6.

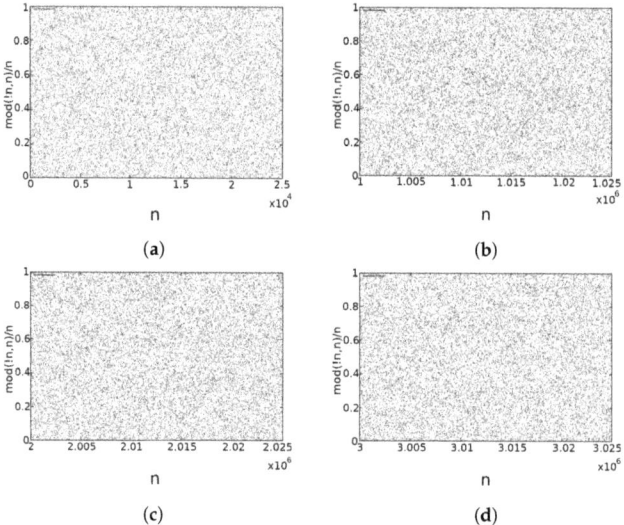

Figure 1. Distribution of mod $(K(n), n)/n$; (**a**) n in range $[0 \div 2.5] \times 10^4$, (**b**) n in range $[1.0 \div 1.025] \times 10^6$, (**c**) n in range $[2.0 \div 2.025] \times 10^6$, and (**d**) n in range $[3.0 \div 3.025] \times 10^6$.

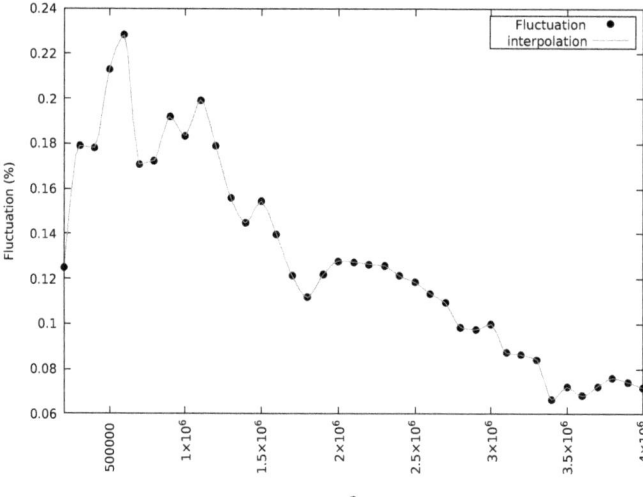

Figure 2. Difference of $\mod(K(n), n)/n$ from a random uniform distribution, in percentage.

To evaluate the speed at which the fluctuation decreases as a function of n, we have used a simple function:

$$A \exp(-n^\alpha), \qquad (8)$$

where the parameters A, α have been fitted to the data points for $n > 10^6$. The obtained results for the parameters in the range $n = [1 \times 10^6 \div 4 \times 10^6]$ are:

$$A = 37.8409, \ \alpha = 0.12034. \qquad (9)$$

This fit is compared to data points in Figure 3, and it is possible to observe a very good agreement with the function (8). The fluctuation goes to zero with increasing n as a negative exponential function of a small power of n. The simplicity of Equation (8) also allows us to estimate the limit value of n above which the fluctuation F should be lower than a fixed value by means of the equation

$$A \exp(-n^\alpha) = F \text{ implies } n = \sqrt[\alpha]{\ln\left(\frac{A}{F}\right)}. \tag{10}$$

For instance, n should be approximately larger than 2.7×10^6 in order to obtain a fluctuation F smaller than 0.1%; $n > 6.7 \times 10^6$ for $F < 0.05\%$, and $n > 40.7 \times 10^6$ for $F < 0.01\%$.

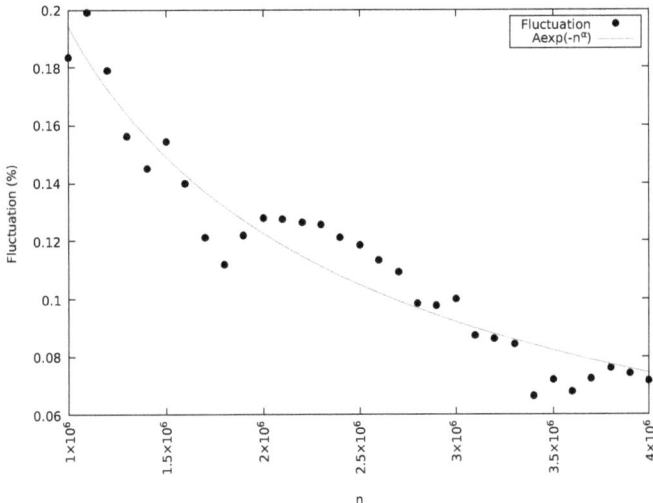

Figure 3. Fit of the function (8) to the data.

3. Conclusions and Outlook

After more than half a century from the introduction of Kurepa's hypothesis, there is still not even a hand-waving argument towards its possible solution. The best approach remains a numerical simulation that cannot provide a rigorous proof for its very nature. This fact also remains true for the distribution conjecture of Equation (5), which, curiously enough, is not due to Kurepa himself, but rather stemmed out from numerical simulations.

The present work did not solve the latter problem, but, for the first time, confirmed the conjecture, and as a byproduct Kurepa's hypothesis as well, for the values up to $n = 4 \times 10^6$. It also provides a convergence speed function given by an exponential of a mild power of n, Equation (8), a result not obtained previously. Moreover, this function shows convincingly that the behavior of Equation (7), the conjecture itself, should be true. Those results could help to indicate the path towards a formal and rigorous solution of Kurepa's hypothesis and the conjecture on its distribution, which are both lacking after all this time.

Author Contributions: Conceptualization N.F. and S.R.; methodology, N.F. and V.T.; formal analysis, N.M. and M.G.-F.; writing—original draft preparation, N.M. and M.G.-F.; supervision, S.R. and N.F. All authors have read and agreed to the published version of the manuscript.

Funding: This research received no external funding.

Data Availability Statement: Not applicable.

Acknowledgments: The research was partially funded by the Ministry of Education, Science and Technological Development of the Republic of Serbia.

Conflicts of Interest: The authors declare no conflict of interest.

References

1. Kurepa, Đ. On the left factorial function !N. *Math. Balk.* **1971**, *1*, 147–153.
2. Kurepa, Đ. O faktorijelima konačnih i beskonač nih brojeva. *Rad. Jugosl. Akad. Znan. Umjet.* **1953**, *296*, 105–112.
3. Kurepa, Đ. Uber die Faktoriellen der endlichen und unendlichen Zahlen. *Ac. Sci. Yougosl. Cl. Math.* **1954**, *4*, 51–64.
4. Kurepa, Đ. Factorials of cardinal numbers and trees. *Glasnik Mat. Fiz. Astr.* **1964**, *19*, 7–21.
5. Kurepa, Đ. Left factorial function in complex domain. *Math. Balk.* **1973**, *3*, 297–307.
6. Ivić, A.; Mijajlovixcx, Ž. On Kurepa's problems in number theory. *Publ. Inst. Math. Beogr.* **1995**, *57*, 19–28.
7. Kurepa, Đ. *Selected Papers of Đuro Kurepa*; Ivić, A., Mamuzić, Z., Mijajlović, Ž., Todorčević, S., Eds.; Matematički Institut SANU: Belgrade, Serbia, 1996; Section F, p. 555. Available online: http://www.mi.sanu.ac.rs/novi_sajt/publications/data/ZarkoMijajlovicSelectedPapersOfDjuroKurepa.pdf (accessed on 23 June 2022).
8. Mijajlović, Ž. *Fifty Years of Kurepa's !n Hypothesis*; Bulletin T.CLIV de l'Académie Serbe des Sciences et des Arts—2021, Classe des Sciences Mathématiques et Naturelles, Sciences Mathématiques, No. 46; Académie Serbe des Sciences et des Arts: Belgrade, Serbia, 2021; pp. 169–181. Available online: http://elib.mi.sanu.ac.rs/files/journals/bltn/46/bltnn46p169-181.pdf (accessed on 23 June 2022).
9. Fabiano, N.; Mirkov, N.; Mitrović, Z.D.; Radenović, S. On some new observations on Kurepa's left factorial. *Math. Anal. Contemp. Appl.* **2022**, *4*, 1–8. [CrossRef]
10. Fabiano, N.; Mirkov, N.; Mitrović, Z.D.; Radenović, S. A discussion on two old standing number theory problems: Collatz hypothesis, together with its relation to Planck's black body radiation, and Kurepa's conjecture on left factorial function. In *Advances in Applied Analysis and Number Theory*; Springer: Berlin/Heidelberg, Germany, 2022.
11. Barsky, D.; Benzaghou, B. Nombres de Bell et somme de factorielles. *J. Theor. Nr. Bordx.* 2004, *16*, 1–17. [CrossRef]
12. Barsky, D.; Benzaghou, B. Erratum a l'article Nombres de Bell et somme de factorielles. *J. Theor. Nr. Bordx.* **2011**, *23*, 527–527. [CrossRef]
13. Andrejić, V.; Tatarević, M. Searching for a counterexample to Kurepa's conjecture. *Math. Comput.* **2016**, *85*, 3061–3068. [CrossRef]
14. The PARI Group. PARI/GP Version 2.13.4 , Univ. Bordeaux. 2022. Available online: http://pari.math.u-bordeaux.fr/ (accessed on 23 June 2022).

MDPI
St. Alban-Anlage 66
4052 Basel
Switzerland
www.mdpi.com

Axioms Editorial Office
E-mail: axioms@mdpi.com
www.mdpi.com/journal/axioms

Disclaimer/Publisher's Note: The statements, opinions and data contained in all publications are solely those of the individual author(s) and contributor(s) and not of MDPI and/or the editor(s). MDPI and/or the editor(s) disclaim responsibility for any injury to people or property resulting from any ideas, methods, instructions or products referred to in the content.

www.ingramcontent.com/pod-product-compliance
Lightning Source LLC
LaVergne TN
LVHW070448100526
838202LV00014B/1684